TABLES OF HOUSES
TABLES DES MAISONS
HÄUSERTABELLEN
TABLAS DE CASAS

Placidus

Latitudes 1° — 66° North & South

1986 INTERNATIONAL EDITION

English — Français — Deutsch — Español

THE ROSICRUCIAN FELLOWSHIP
International Headquarters
2222 Mission Ave   P.O. Box 713
Oceanside, California 92054-0112
U.S.A.

Printed in France
by
Lienhart et Cie
07200 Aubenas

July 1986

CONTENTS – SOMMAIRE
INHALTSANGABE – INDICE

ENGLISH

FRANÇAIS

DEUTSCH

ESPAÑOL

INTRODUCTION

The Rosicrucian Fellowship is an International Association of Christian Mystics, founded in 1909 by Max Heindel, under the direction of the Elder Brothers of the Rosicrucian Order. It was created for the purpose of promulgating a definite, logical, and sequential teaching concerning the origin, evolution, and future development of the World and Man, showing both the spiritual and scientific aspects.

The Teachings of The Rosicrucian Fellowship do not regard the intellectual understanding of God and the Universe as an end in itself; far from it. The greater the intellect, the greater the danger of its misuse. Therefore this scientific Teaching is given in order that man may believe and start to live the spiritual life.

Astrology, as a spiritual science, explains the relationship between man and the Universe; it reveals the wonderful plan by which the whole of creation evolves towards perfection. It guides man and helps him to find his proper place in the Universe, to discover his own life's purpose, and to awaken his noblest aspirations and ideals. It also gives him a greater understanding of himself and others so that he may accept, serve, and love them more. The inner understanding gained through the study of spiritual Astrology opens the door to Universal Brotherhood.

In order fully to understand Astrology, it should be studied in the light of the Western Wisdom Teachings, specifically, the Law of Rebirth and the Law of Cause and Effect. Ultimately, perfect order will reign supreme in the universe as we create new destiny to balance and improve the old destiny brought from the past. By adding new and good destiny, we are able to change both our character and our environments in future lives.

ROSICRUCIAN FELLOWSHIP COURSES

The Rosicrucian Fellowship has been presenting the Western Wisdom Philosophy and Astrology for 75 years and publishes all the materials necessary for this study. The Western Wisdom Teachings make no statements not supported by reason and logic, satisfying the mind by giving clear explanations offering a reasonable solution to all mysteries.

There are no dues or tuition fees. All expenses of the organization are met by free-will offerings and the sale of books. Students have the opportunity to help in this great Work as the heart dictates and means permit. The Rosicrucian Fellowhip offers correspondence courses in several languages on a free-will offering basis.

WESTERN WISDOM PHILOSOPHY COURSES

The Preliminary Course of 12 lessons provides a basic understanding of the Western Wisdom Teachings. The Supplementary Course of 40 lessons is available after the student has completed the Preliminary lessons and requests further training.

COURSES IN SPIRITUAL ASTROLOGY

The Junior Astrology course of 26 lessons covers the basics of chart erection and the spiritual principles of delineation. The Senior Astrology Course of 12 lessons explains the higher spiritual aspects of the planets. The Senior Extension Astrology Course of 13 lessons covers an in-depth method of delineation, progressions, and transits.

Astrology is offered as an effective tool in the development of the higher faculty of the mind and intuition. This sacred science is taught with the stipulation that it will not be used to make money, but to help in the spiritual guidance and healing of suffering humanity.

COURSE IN BIBLE INTERPRETATION

A course of 28 lessons which makes clear some of the inner meanings of the Scriptures and gives the student a deeper understanding of the Holy Bible.

ROSICRUCIAN FELLOWSHIP PUBLICATIONS

The following textbooks written by Max Heindel, Christian Mystic and Initiate of the Rosicrucian Order, are also available:

THE ROSICRUCIAN COSMO-CONCEPTION — 705 pages

This book contains the basic principles of the Western Wisdom Philosophy and bridges the gap between science and religion by presenting the Teachings in a clear, easy-to-understand format. It contains a comprehensive outline of the evolutionary processes of man and the Universe, correlating science with religion. A scientific method of spiritual development is revealed that is in total harmony with the cosmic laws which promote soul growth.

SIMPLIFIED SCIENTIFIC ASTROLOGY — 198 pages

A complete textbook on the art of erecting a horoscope. This volume, which is written especially for beginners, makes it possible for the earnest student to instruct himself in the mathematics of Astrology necessary for chart erection. It also includes a section defining astrological terminology.

MESSAGE OF THE STARS — 733 pages

Written in collaboration with Augusta Foss-Heindel.

Contains a complete method of interpretation and delineation of the horoscope for character analysis and provides a simplified method of progressing the chart. It also includes an explanation of Medical Astrology which is illustrated with 36 example horoscopes.

ASTRO-DIAGNOSIS — 482 pages

Written in collaboration with Augusta Foss-Heindel

Astro-Diagnosis is the science and art of obtaining knowledge regarding the spiritual causes of man's infirmities as shown by the horoscope. Explanations in regard to reading the horoscope for the purpose of diagnosis are included. This book is unique in the field and includes 100 astrological charts which were selected from the many hundreds of case histories analyzed by the authors.

For more information and a free publications catalog, contact The Rosicrucian Fellowship, International Headquarters, 2222 Mission Avenue, P.O. Box 713, Oceanside, CA 92054-0112, USA

INTRODUCTION

Le Rosicrucian Fellowship est une Association Internationale de Mystiques Chrétiens, fondée en 1909 par Max Heindel, sous la direction des Frères Aînés de l'Orde de la Rose-Croix. Il a été créé dans le but de diffuser un enseignement précis, logique et structuré, sur l'origine, l'évolution et le développement futur de l'Homme et de l'Univers, sous leurs aspects spirituels et scientifiques.

Les Enseignements du Rosicrucian Fellowship ne considèrent pas la compréhension intellectuelle de Dieu et de l'Univers comme une fin en soi ; loin de là. Plus l'intellect est développé, plus il y a danger d'en faire mauvais usage. C'est pourquoi, ces Enseignements scienfitiques sont donnés à l'Homme afin que son coeur puisse croire ce que l'intellect a sanctionné et pour qu'il commence à vivre la vie mystique.

L'Astrologie, en tant que science spirituelle explique la relation entre l'Homme et l'Univers ; elle révèle le processus merveilleux par lequel toute la création évolue vers la perfection. Elle guide l'Homme et l'aide à trouver sa place dans l'Univers, à découvrir sa raison d'être ainsi qu'à éveiller ses aspirations et ses idéaux les plus nobles. De plus, elle donne à l'Homme une meilleure compréhension de lui-même et aussi des autres afin de les accepter, les servir et les aimer davantage. La compréhension intérieure acquise par l'étude de l'Astrologie spirituelle ouvre la porte à l'avénement de la Fraternité Universelle.

Afin de bien comprendre l'Astrologie, celle-ci doit être étudiée à la lumière des Enseignements de la Sagesse Occidentale et tout particulièrement en prenant en considération les Lois de la Réincarnation et de Cause à Effet. Un orde parfait régit l'Univers ; toute chose a une cause et rien n'arrive par hasard. Ce que nous sommes à présent est le résultat de ce que nous avons fait dans le passé, alors que nos actions présentes déterminent notre futur.

COURS DU ROSICRUCIAN FELLOWSHIP

Le Rosicrucian Fellowship enseigne la Philosophie et l'Astrologie de la Sagesse Occidentale depuis 75 ans et publie tout le matériel nécessaire pour leur étude. Les Enseignements de la Sagesse Occidentale ne font aucune affirmation qui ne soit supportée par la raison et la logique,ce qui satisfait l'intellect car il reçoit des réponses claires qui offrent une explication raisonnable de tous les mystères.

Il n'y a aucun tarif ou frais d'admission. Les dons volontaires et la vente des livres couvrent les dépenses encourues par l'Organisation. L'étudiant est laissé libre de contribuer à ce grand Oeuvre selon la voie de son coeur et les limites de ses moyens. Le Rosicrucian Fellowship offre aussi ses cours par correspondance en plusieurs langues, sur a lase du don volontaire.

COURS DE PHILOSOPHIE DE LA SAGESSE OCCIDENTALE

Le Cours Préliminaire en 12 leçons apporte une connaissance de base des Enseignements de la Sagesse Occidentale. Le Cours Supplémentaire, qui comporte 40 leçons, est disponible à l'étudiant qui a terminé le Cours Préliminaire et qui en fait la demande.

COURS D'ASTROLOGIE SPIRITUELLE

Le Cours Elémentaire d'Astrologie couvre en 26 leçons les notions de base du calcul du thème astrologique, ainsi que les principes spirituels de son interprétation. Le Cours Supplémentaire en 12 leçons explique plus à fond la nature spirituelle des planètes. Le Cours Supérieur en 13 leçons couvre en profondeur la méthode d'interprétation, les progressions et les transits.

L'Astrologie est offerte comme un instrument efficace pour le développement des facultés mentales supérieures et de l'intuition. Ceet science sacrée est enseignée à la condition qu'elle ne soit pas utilisée en échange de gain pécuniaire mais avec le seul dessein d'aider spirituellement et de soulager l'humanité souffrante.

COURS D'INTERPRETATION DE LA BIBLE

Ce Cours en 28 leçons amène lumière sur le sens profond des Ecritures Saintes et donne à l'étudiant une compréhension plus étendue de la Bible.

OUVRAGES PUBLIES PAR LE ROSICRUCIAN FELLOWSHIP

Les livres suivants sont également disponibles ; ils ont été écrits par Max Heindel, mystique chrétien et initié de l'Ordre de la Rose-Croix.

COSMOGONIE DES ROSE-CROIX - 705 pages

Ce livre contient les notions de base de la Philosopnhie de la Sagesse Occidentale, et comble le fossé existant entre la science et la religion car il présente les Enseignements d'une façon claire et facile à comprendre. Il présente de manière intelligible les bases du processus d'évolution de l'Homme et de l'Univers en mettant toujours en évidence le lien existant entre la science et la religion. Il révèle une méthode scientifique de développement spirituel qui est en harmonie complète avec les lois cosmiques qui régissent la croissance de l'âme.

ASTROLOGIE SCIENTIFIQUE SIMPLIFIEE -224 pages

Un livre complet sur l'art d'ériger un thème astrologique. Ce volume, spécialement destiné aux débutants, permet à l'étudiant sincère d'apprendre par lui-même les calculs nécessaires à l'élaboration d'un thème astrologique. Il comporte également une section qui définit les termes utilisés en Astrologie.

LE MESSAGE DES ASTRES - 733 pages

Ecrit en collaboration avec Augusta Foss-Heindel.

Ce livre contient une méthode complète d'interprétation du thème astrologique et d'analyse du caractère, et présente une méthode simple de progression du thème. Il comporte également une présentation de l'Astrologie Médicale illustrée de 36 exemples de thèmes astrologiques.

ASTRO-DIAGNOSTIC - 482 pages

Ecrit en collaboration avec Augusta Foss-Heindel.

L'Astro-Diagnostic est la science et l'art d'acquérir la connaissance des causes spirituelles des afflictions de l'Homme telles qu'elles figurent dans le thème astrologique. Des explications sur la manière de lire le thème dans le but de porter un diagnostic sont incluses. Ce livre est unique dans ce domaine et compte 100 thèmes astrologiques sélectionnés parmi plusieurs centaines de cas analysés par les auteurs.

Pour plus d'informations et pour obtenir le catalogue gratuit de nos ouvrages, veuillez vous adresser au Rosicrucian Fellowship, Siège International, 2222 Mission Avenue, P.O. Box 713, Oceanside, CA 92054-0112 U.S.A.

VORWORT

Die Rosenkreuzer-Gemeinschaft ist eine internationale Vereinigung christlicher Mystiker, die 1909 von Max Heindel gegründet wurde. Ihr internationaler Hauptsitz ist in Oceanside, Kalifornien, U.S.A. Ihr Ziel ist, eine verständliche, logische und lückenlose Lehre zu verkünden, die sich mit dem Ursprung, der Entstehung und der zukünftigen Entwicklung des Alls und des Menschen befaßt. Dabei zeigt sie sowohl die esoterische als auch die wissenschaftliche Seite dieses Problems auf und schafft damit eine harmonische Synthese zwischen Wissenschaft und Glaube.

Die Lehren der Rosenkreuzer-Gemeinschaft, für Menschen des Abendlandes bestimmt, stützen sich auf eigene, vernunftgemäße Erkenntnis. Sie bieten eine Antwort an für den, der sich nicht mit dem Glauben allein zufrieden geben kann, sondern auch verstehen will und nach vernunftgemässen Erklärungen fragt. Die Lehre vermittelt eine Botschaft des Friendens und läßt das Gefühl der Brüderlichkeit allen Menschen gegenüber gelten, die ernstlich die Wahrheit suchen, auch wenn sie auf verschiedenen Wegen gehen. Die Rosenkreuzerlehren zielen auf die Entwicklung hin des "rechten Denkens, rechten Fühlens und des rechten Handelns", die alle das Ergebnis der "Selbstdisziplin" sind. Der Wahlspruch der Rosenkreuzer-Philosophie lautet : Ein urteilsfähiger Intellekt, ein fühlendes Herz, ein gesunder Körper. Ihr höchstes Ideal ist : Dienen.

Die Astrologie, als esoterische Wissenschaft betrachtet, erklärt die Verbindung zwischen dem Menschen und dem Universum. Sie offenbart den wundervollen kosmischen Plan, nach dem die ganze Schöpfung sich zur Vollkommenheit weiterentwickelt. Sie führt den Menschen und hilft ihm seinen ordnungsgemäßen Platz im Kosmos zu finden, seine höchsten Beweggründe auszudrücken und seinen edelsten Idealen nachzustreben. Sie erlaubt es ihm auch seine Mitmenschen besser zu kennen, um sie besser anzunehmen, ihnen besser zu helfen und sie besser zu lieben. Das innere Wissen, das durch das Studium der spirituellen Astrologie entwickelt wird, ist die Tür, die zur universellen Bruderschaft führt.

Um die Astrologie wirklich zu verstehen, muß sie im Licht der esoterischen Weisheitslehren studiert werden, vor allem im Zusammenhang mit den Gesetzen von der Wiedergeburt und von Ursache und Wirkung. Im gesamten Weltall herrscht eine unübertreffliche Ordnung, alles hat eine Ursache und nichts geschieht rein zufällig. Was wir heute sind, ist das Ergebnis unserer Taten in der Vergangenheit und was wir heute tun, bestimmt unsere Zukunft.

KURSE UND VERÖFFENTLICHUNGEN
DER ROSENKREUZER-GEMEINSCHAFT

Die Rosenkreuzer-Gemeinschaft lehrt bereits seit mehr als 75 Jahren Philosophie und Astrologie der Rosenkreuzer und veröffentlicht alles notwendige Material für dieses Studium. Die Lehren der Rosenkreuzer werden nicht als letzte und ausschließliche Wahrheit auf diesem Gebiet verkündet. Sie machen keine Angaben, die von Verstand und Logik nicht erfaßt werden könnten. Sie lehren kein Dogma, sondern bieten eine solide Basis von Tatsachen und Grundsätzen an, über die der Studierende nachdenken muß. Mit dieser Weiterarbeit entwickelt der Wahrheitssuchende seine eigene Überzeugung und gelangt so zu eigenen Ansichten.

Diese Lehren werden auf der Grundlage freiwilliger Spenden verbreitet. Die esoterische Wissenschaft läuft Gefahr korrupt zu werden, wenn sie für Geld angeboten wird. Jeder esoterische Fortschritt ist das Ergebnis persönlicher Anstrengung. Die Initiation (= Einweihung) ist ein innerer Vorgang, der unabhängig von Riten und magischen Formeln ist. Sie kann für weltliche Schätze nicht erworben werden, sondern nur durch eigene Verdienste.

Die Rosenkreuzer-Gemeinschaft bietet kostenlos verschiedene Fernlehrgänge in verschiedenen Sprachen an.

Philosophie der Rosenkreuzer. Ein Fernlehrgang in 2 Teilen :

Einführungskursus. Er besteht aus 12 Lektionen und erlaubt ein tiefes Verstehen von : "Die Weltanschauung der Rosenkreuzer" von Max Heindel.

Ergänzungkursus. Er besteht aus 21 Lektionen, die sich mit der praktischen Anwendung der Rosenkreuzer-Philosophie beffassen. Sie haben zum Ziel den Studierenden auf fortgeschrittene Übungen vorzubereiten.

Esoterische Astrologie. Dieser Fernlehrgang gliedert sich in 3 Teile :

Grundkursus. Seine 26 Lektionen führen in die Berechnung eines Horoskopes und in die Prinzipien seiner esoterischen Deutung ein.

Fortgeschrittenenkursus. Seine 13 Lektionen bieten eine Methode für eine vertiefte Deutung des Horoskopes an.

Abschlußkursus. Seine 12 Lektionen lehren die Arbeit mit dem progressiven Horoskop, den Transiten und anderen Methoden astrologischer Vorausschau.

Die Astrologie stellt ein sehr wirkungsvolles Mittel dar, um eine hohe Geisteskraft zu entwickeln : die Intuition. Diese geheiligte Wissenschaft wird mit dem ausdrücklichen Vorbehalt gelehrt, daß sie nicht für Geld verkauft wird, sondern nur um der leidenden Menschheit zu helfen und um zu heilen.

Bibelkursus
Diese 28 Lektionen geben dem Studierenden die ersten Schlüssel einer esoterischen Bibelauslegung, die ihn zu einem tieferen Verständnis der Heiligen Schrift führen.

Folgende grundlegenden Veröffentlichungen Max Heindels sind verfügbar :

Die Weltanschauung der Rosenkreuzer. (705 S.)
Dieses esoterische Standardwerk enthält die Grundlagen der Rosenkreuzer-Philosophie. Es erklärt jedem Suchenden die großen Mysterien des Universums und des Menschen und bringt sie in Verbindung mit den Naturgesetzen. Dieses Buch erlaubt die Harmonie zwischen dem Intellekt (Wissenschaft) und dem Herz (Religion), eine Verbindung, die von fundamentaler Bedeutung ist.

Vereinfachte wissenschaftliche Astologie. (198 S.)
Ein Lehrbuch zur Berechnung eines Horoskopes, das auch ein philosophisches Astrologie-Lexikon und eine Tabelle der Planetenstunden enthält.

Die Botschaft der Sterne. (733 S.) - In Zusammenarbeit mit Augusta Foss-Heindel.
Hier werden fundamentale astrologische Deutungen in einer klaren, leicht verständlichen Sprache gegeben. 36 Horoskopbeispiele verschiedener Erkrankungen werden eingehend besprochen.

Astro-Diagnose. (482 S.) - In Zusammenarbeit mit Augusta Foss-Heindel.
Eine Abhandlung, die eine wissenschaftliche Methode erstellt, die eine astrologische Diagnose der geistigen Ursachen der Krankheiten erlaubt. Mehr als hundert Horoskope werden nach zwei Methoden besprochen : feste Sternzeichen und feste Häuser.

INTRODUCCION

La Fraternidad Rosacruz es una Asociación Internacional de Místicos Cristianos, fundada por Max Heindel en 1909, y bajo la dirección de los Hermanos Mayores de la Orden Rosacruz. Fue creada con el propósito de promulgar una enseñanza definida, lógica y progresiva, concerniente al origen, evolución, y futuro desarrollo del mundo y el hombre, demostrando su aspecto espiritual y científico.

Las Enseñanzas de la Fraternidad Rosacruz no consideran la comprensión intelectual de Dios y del Universo como un fin en sí mismo; lejos de ello. Cuanto mayor es el intelecto, tanto mayor es el peligro de su mal uso. Por lo tanto, esta Enseñanza científica es dada para que el hombre pueda creer y comenzar a vivir la vida espiritual.

La Astrología como una ciencia espiritual, explica la relación entre el hombre y el Universo y revela el maravilloso plan por medio del cual la creación entera evoluciona hacia la perfección. Ella guía al hombre y le ayuda a encontrar su lugar en el Universo, descubrir el propósito de su propia vida, y despertar sus más nobles aspiraciones e ideales. También le da un mayor entendimiento de sí mismo y de los demás, para que así pueda aceptarlos, servirlos y amarlos. El entendimiento interno adquirido a través del estudio de la Astrología espiritual abre la puerta para la Hermandad Universal.

A fin de entender completamente la Astrología, debería estudiarse a la luz de las Enseñanzas de la Sabiduría Occidental, y en especial la ley del Renacimiento y la de Causa y Efecto. Un orden perfecto y supremo, reina en el Universo: todo tiene su causa y nada sucede al azar. Lo que somos en este momento es el resultado de lo que hicimos en el pasado, y lo que hacemos ahora, construye nuestro futuro.

CURSOS DE LA FRATERNIDAD ROSACRUZ

La Fraternidad Rosacruz ha venido presentando la Filosofía de la Sabiduría Occidental y la Astrología durante sus 75 años de existencia y publica todos los materiales necesarios para su estudio. Las Enseñanzas de la Sabiduría Occidental no afirman nada que no sea respaldado por la lógica y la razón, satisfaciendo la mente mediante explicaciones claras que ofrecen una solución razonable a todos los misterios.

La Fraternidad Rosacruz ofrece cursos por correspondencia en varios idiomas sin costo alguno. No hay obligaciones o cuotas de dinero por la enseñanza impartida. Todos los gastos de la organización son cubiertos con las ofrendas voluntarias recibidas y la venta de nuestros libros. Los estudiantes tienen la oportunidad de ayudar en esta gran Obra de acuerdo a los dictados de su corazón y a como sus medios se lo permitan.

CURSOS DE FILOSOFIA DE LA SABIDURIA OCCIDENTAL

El Curso Preliminar de 12 lecciones da un entendimiento básico de las Enseñanzas de la Sabiduría Occidental. El Curso Suplementario de 40 lecciones está disponible después que el estudiante haya completado las lecciones del Preliminar y solicite una más amplia enseñanza.

CURSOS DE ASTROLOGIA ESPIRITUAL

El Curso Elemental de Astrología de 26 lecciones cubre los conceptos básicos para calcular un horóscopo y los principios espirituales aplicados en su interpretación. El Curso Superior de Astrología de 12 lecciones explica los aspectos espirituales más elevados con relación a los planetas. El Curso Superior Suplementario de Astrología de 13 lecciones enseña un método de interpretación más profundo, los tránsitos y las progresiones.

La Astrología se ofrece como una ayuda efectiva en el desarrollo de la facultad superior de la mente y la intuición. Esta sagrada ciencia es enseñada con la condición de no ser utilizada por dinero, sino para ayudar en la guía espiritual y la curación de la humanidad sufriente.

CURSO DE INTERPRETACION BIBLICA

Es un curso de 28 lecciones que clarifica los significados ocultos de las Escrituras y le da al estudiante un más profundo entendimiento de la Sagrada Biblia.

PUBLICACIONES DE LA FRATERNIDAD ROSACRUZ

Los siguientes libros escritos por Max Heindel, un Místico Cristiano e Iniciado de la Orden Rosacruz, están también disponibles:

EL CONCEPTO ROSACRUZ DEL COSMOS — 477 páginas

Este libro explica los principios básicos de la Filosofía de la Sabiduría Occidental y llena el vacío existente entre la ciencia y la religión, presentando las Enseñanzas en un formato fácil de entender. Contiene una delineación clara del proceso evolutivo del hombre y del Universo, correlacionando la ciencia con la religión. Enseña un método científico para el desarrollo espiritual, el cual está en armonía total con las leyes cósmicas que promueven el crecimiento anímico.

ASTROLOGIA CIENTIFICA SIMPLIFICADA — 220 páginas

Un libro completo de texto basado en el arte de calcular un horóscopo. Este volumen, escrito principalmente para los principiantes, le permite al fervoroso estudiante aprender por sí mismo las matemáticas de la Astrología, necesarias para el cálculo del horóscopo. También incluye una sección que define la terminología astrológica.

EL MENSAJE DE LAS ESTRELLAS — 588 páginas

Escrito con la colaboración de Augusta Foss Heindel.

Contiene un método completo de interpretación del horóscopo para el análisis del carácter y provee un método simplificado para su progresión. También incluye explicaciones sobre la Astrología Médica, ilustradas con 36 horóscopos como ejemplo.

ASTRODIAGNOSIS — 472 páginas

Escrito con la colaboración de Augusta Foss Heindel.

La Astrodiagnosis es una ciencia y un arte que se usa para conocer las causas espirituales de las enfermedades del hombre tal como se muestran en el horóscopo. Se incluyen explicaciones relativas a la lectura del horóscopo para efectos del diagnóstico. Este libro es único en su campo e incluye 100 horóscopos que fueron seleccionados entre los cientos de casos que los autores estudiaron.

Si desea más información, solicite nuestro catálogo de publicaciones a: The Rosicrucian Fellowship, Internacional Headquarters, 2222 Mission Avenue, P.O. Box 713, Oceanside, CA 92054-0112, U.S.A.

HOW TO COMPUTE FOR SOUTHERN LATITUDES

These Tables of Houses form an important link in our *Simplified Scientific* system of Astrology. By our original method they are readily usable for both North and South latitudes, even by beginners in Astrology.

To erect a chart for South latitude simply add twelve hours to the Sideral Time at Birth (see *Simplified Scientific Astrology* by Max Heindel, page 32) and enter the signs and degrees in the houses designated at the bottom of each Table.

Using the data for a birth on June 14, 1976, 11:30 A.M. (true local time), Melbourne, Australia, Lat. 38° S., Long. 145 E. (Melbourne uses the 150° Standard Meridian).

After finding the calculated Sideral Time at birth, add 12 hours for South Latitude:

Calculated Sidereal Time at birth....................	.5	01	00
Add 12 hours for South Latitude..................	..12		
South Sidereal Time...................	.17	01	00

With the South Sideral Time we turn to the *Table of Houses* and look for the Table listing latitude 38° (page 219) in the central column. From the small portion of the proper Table here printed for the convenience of the student we see that the nearest Sidereal Time is 16h. 59m. 11s. In line with that (in the column for 38°) we find the signs and degrees for our cusps:

♐ 16°, ♑ 8°, ♒ 2°, ♓5° 28', ♈ 21°, ♉ 22°

These we place in the 4th, 5th, 6th, 7th, 8th, and 9th houses as directed at the bottom of our Table as shown in the Chart on page 23.

When that is done it only remains to fill in the opposite degrees and signs in the opposite houses as usual to complete the Chart.

As latitude does not enter in the calculation of the planets' positions, they are calculated and placed in the same manner as if the Chart were for North Latitude.

COMMENT FAIRE LES CALCULS
POUR LES LATITUDES SUD

Ces Tables des Maisons constituent un élément important de notre système d'Astrologie Scientifique Simplifiée. Grâce à notre présentation originale elles peuvent être utilisées même par un débutant en Astrologie, aussi bien pour les latitudes Nord que pour les latitudes Sud.

Pour monter un thème pour les latitudes Sud, il suffit simplement d'ajouter douze heures à l'heure sidérale de la naissance (voir *Astrologie Scientifique Simplifié* par Max Heindel) et noter les signes et degrés dans les maisons inscrits au bas de chaque Table.

A titre d'exemple, nous utiliserons les coordonnées d'une naissance à Melbourne, le 14 juin 1976, 11h30 (heure locale vraie), lat. 38°S, long. 145°E (Melbourne utilise l'heure du 150 ème méridien).

Après avoir calculé l'heure sidérale à la naissance, ajoutez douze heures pour la latitude Sud :

Heure sidérale calculée de la naissance...............5   01   00
Ajoutez 12 heures (pour les latitudes Sud)........12
Heure sidérale du Sud................................17   01   00

Avec l'heure sidérale du Sud, nous nous reportons aux *Tables des Maisons* et cherchons la colonne de la Table pour la latitude 38° (au centre de la page 219). A partir de la section de la Table que nous avons reproduite (page 23) pour le bénéfice du lecteur, nous voyons que l'heure sidérale la plus proche est 16h 59m 11s. Sur la même ligne (dans la colonne de latitude 38°) nous trouvons les signes et degrés suivants pour les pointes des maisons :

✗ 16°, ♑ 18°, ♒ 2°, ♓ 5° 28', ♈ 21°, ♉ 22°

Ces coordonnées doivent être placées sur les 4ème, 5ème, 6ème, 7ème, 8ème et 9ème maisons comme indiqué au bas de notre Table et illustré par le thème de la page 23.

L'étape suivante consiste simplement à écrire sur les pointes des maisons opposées le signe opposé et le même degré, comme nous le faisons pour n'importe quel thème.

Comme la latitude n'entre pas en considération dans le calcul de la position des planètes, leur calcul est fait de la même façon que pour un thème de latitude Nord.

BERECHNUNGSANWEISUNG FÜR SÜDLICHE BREITE

Diese Häusertabellen bilden ein wichtiges Zwischenglied in unserem *Vereinfachten Wissenschaftlichen* System der Astrologie. Durch unsere Methode sind sie sowohl für nördliche als auch für südliche Breite leicht benutzbar, auch für Anfänger in der Astrologie.

Um eine Tafel für südliche Breite aufzustellen, braucht man nur 12 Stunden zur Sternzeit des Zeitpunkts der Geburt hinzuzufügen (siehe *Vereinfachte Wissenschaftliche Astrologie* von Max Heindel, Seite 32) und die Zeichen und Grade in die jeweils unten auf jeder Tafel angegebenen Häuser einzutragen.

Als Beispiel sollen gelten die Daten einer Geburt am 14.Juni 1976 um 11 Uhr 30 Ortszeit in Melbourne, Australien, 38° südliche Breite, 145° östliche Länge. (Melbourne benutzt den 150° Einheitsmeridian.)

Nachdem man die ausgerechnete Sternzeit des Zeitpunkts der Geburt gefunden hat, addiert man 12 Stunden für die südliche Breite.

Ausgerechnete Sternzeit des Zeitpunkts der Geburt 5   01   00
Plus 12 Stunden für die südliche Breite..............12
Südliche Sternzeit.......................................17   01   00

Mit der südlichen Sternzeit wenden wir uns zur Häusertafel und suchen die Tafel, die die 38° Breite in der mittleren Spalte aufführt (Seite 219). Aus dem Ausschnitt der zugehörigen Tafel, die hier für das bessere Verständnis des Studenten abgedruckt ist, wird erkennbar, daß die nahegelegenste Sternzeit 16 Stunden, 59 Minuten und 11 Sekunden ist. Damit übereinstimmend (in der Spalte für 38°) finden wir die Zeichen und Grade für unsere Positionen.

♐ 16°, ♑ 8°, ♒ 2°, ♓ 5° 28', ♈ 21°, ♉ 22°

Diese tragen wir in die 4ten, 5ten, 6ten, 7ten, 8ten und 9ten Häuser ein, wie es unten auf unserer Tafel angegeben und in der Liste auf Seite 23 gezeigt ist.

Danach sind nur noch die gegenüberliegenden Grade und Zeichen in die gegenüberliegenden Häuser wie gewöhnlich einzutragen, um die Liste zu vervollständigen.

Da die Breite nicht in die Berechnung der Position des Planeten einbezogen wird, wird sie ausgerechnet und genauso verwertet, als bestimme die Liste die nördliche Breite.

COMO CALCULAR LAS LATITUDES DEL SUR

Esta Tabla de Casas tiene un vínculo importante con nuestro sistema *Científico Simplificado* de Astrología. Con nuestro método original ésta puede usarse fácilmente, aún por los principiantes para hallar las latitudes tanto del Norte como del Sur.

Para calcular un horóscopo en la latitud Sur, agregue simplemente 12 horas a la Hora Sideral del Nacimiento (ver *Astrología Científica Simplificada* por Max Heindel, página 42) y anote los signos y grados de las casas que aparecen en la parte inferior de la Tabla.

Utilizando la información de un nacimiento ocurrido el 14 de junio de 1976, a las 11:30 AM (Hora Local Verdadera), en Melbourne, Australia, Lat. 38° S., Long. 145° E. (para Melbourne se usa el Meridiano 150°)

Después de hallar la Hora Sideral del nacimiento, agréguele 12 horas por ser una Latitud Sur:

Hora Sideral calculada al nacimiento.................5 01 00
más : 12 horas por ser Latitud Sur.................<u>12</u>
Hora Sideral Sur......................................17 01 00

Con la Hora Sideral Survamos a la *Tabla de Casas* y buscamos la tabla que corresponde a la latitud 38° (pag 219) en la columna del centro. Para conveniencia del estudiante transcribimos la información que aparece allí y vemos que la Hora Sideral más cercana es 16 h. 59m. 11s. En esta misma columna (38°) encontramos los signos y los grados que corresponden a las cúspides de las casas:

♐16°, ♑ 8°, ♒ 2°, ♓ 5° 28', ♈ 21°, ♉ 22°

Después escribimos estos signos y grados en la 4a, 5a, 6a, 7a, 8a, y 9a casas que aparecen en la parte inferior de nuestra Tabla y que se muestran en el horóscopo que aparece en la página 23.

Cuando se ha hecho lo anterior, solo queda escribir en las casas opuestas los signos opuestos con el mismo número de grados, tal como se hace ordinariamente al calcular un horóscopo.

Como la latitud no entra en el cálculo de las posiciones de los planetas, estos son calculados y colocados en la misma manera que si el horóscopo fuera para una Latitud del Norte.

LATITUDE 38° N.

SIDEREAL TIME	10 ♐	11 ♑	12 ♑	ASC ♒		2 ♈	3 ♉
H M S	°	°	°	°	'	°	°
16 33 27	10	2	25	25	46	12	15
16 37 43	11	3	26	27	20	13	16
16 41 59	12	4	27	28	55	15	18
16 46 17	13	5	28	0 ♓	32	16	19
16 50 34	14	6	29	2	9	18	20
16 54 53	15	7	♒	3	48	19	21
16 59 11	16	8	2	5	28	21	22
17 3 30	17	9	3	7	8	22	23
17 7 49	18	10	4	8	50	24	24
17 12 9	19	11	5	10	32	25	26
HOUSES	4	5	6	7		8	9

LATITUDE 38° S.

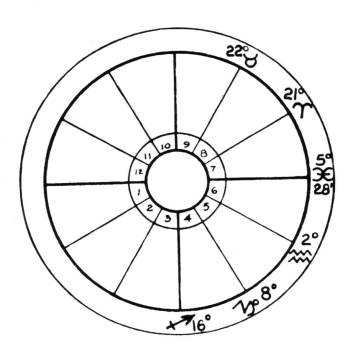

HOUSE CUSPS 4-9 (♐-♉)

– ATLAS –

COORDINATES
FOR PRINCIPAL CITIES OF THE WORLD

COORDONNÉES GÉOGRAPHIQUES
DES PRINCIPALES VILLES
DU MONDE

BEIORDNUNG FÜR
DIE WICHTIGSTEN
STÄDTE DER ERDE

COORDENADAS GEOGRAFICAS
DE LAS PRINCIPALES
CIUDADES DEL MUNDO

LATITUDES AND LONGITUDES
OF THE
PRINCIPAL CITIES
OF THE
WORLD

The following pages give the latitude and longitude of the principal cities of the world in alphabetical order. Each line contains the following information:

City, *Other name,* State, Country, Latitude, Longitude, Time.

Other name: When another city name is indicated in *italics,* refer to this one to obtain the latitude and longitude.

State: North American cities include the states or provinces to which they belong.

Country: Abbreviations for the names of the countries are given on pages 30-32.

Latitude: The latitude is given in degrees as *ddXmm: dd* represents the degrees, *X* a latitude situated to the North (N) or South (S) of the Equator, and *mm* the minutes of arc. For example, 46N12 represents a North latitude of 46° 12'.

Longitude: The longitude is directly given in degrees as *ddXmm: dd* represents the degrees, *X* a longitude situated to the East (E) or West (W) of Greenwich, and *mm* the minutes of arc. For example, 5W28 represents a West longitude of 5° 28'.

Time: Hours and minutes indicate the time difference East or West of Greenwich. For example, Washington, D.C. (77W00) equals 5h08W or 5 hours and 8 minutes West of Greenwich.

LATITUDES ET LONGITUDES
DES PRINCIPALES VILLES
DU MONDE

Les pages suivantes donnent la latitude et la longitude des principales villes du monde, citées par ordre alphabétique. Chaque ligne contient les informations suivantes :

Ville, Autre nom, Etat, Pays, Latitude, Longitude, Temps

Autre nom : Lorsqu'un autre nom de ville est donné en italiques, réferrez-vous à ce nom pour obtenir la latitude et la longitude.

Etat : Les villes d'Amérique du Nord sont suivies de l'état ou de la province où elles se trouvent.

Pays : Les abbréviations pour le nom des pays sont données aux pages 30 à 32.

Latitude : La latitude est donnée en degrés selon la formule *ddXmm. dd* represente les degrés, *X* la latitude Nord (N) ou Sud (S) et *mm* les minutes d'arc. Par exemple, 46N12 représente 46°12' de latitude Nord.

Longitude : La longitude est directement donnée en degrés selon la formule *ddXmm. dd* represente les degrés, *X* la longitude Est (E) ou Ouest (W) par rapport à Greenwich, et *mm* les minutes d'arc. Par exemple, 5W28 représente 5°38' de longitude Ouest.

Temps : Les heures et minutes indiquent la différence en temps, à l'Est ou à l'Ouest de Greenwich. Par exemple, Washington, D.C. (77WOO) équivaut à 5h08 W ou 5 heures et 8 minutes à l'Ouest de Greenwich.

BREITE UND LÄNGE
DER WELTHAUPTSTÄDTE

Die folgenden Seiten geben Breite und Länge für Welthauptstädte in alphabetischer Reihenfolge an. Jede Zeile enthält die folgenden Informationen:

Stadt, *Anderer Name,* Bundesstaat, Land, Breite, Länge, Zeit.

Anderer Name: Wenn ein anderer Name einer Stadt *kursiv* gedruckt ist, dann beziehe man sich auf diesen, um die Breite und Länge zu bestimmen.

Bundesstaat: Nordamerikanische Städte beinhalten die Bundesstaaten oder Provinzen, zu denen sie gehören.

Länder: Abkürzungen für Ländernamen sind auf den Seiten 30 bis 32 angegeben.

Breite: Die Breite ist in Grad angegeben, wie *ddXmm. dd* steht für Grad, *X* für eine Breite nördlich (n) oder südlich (s) des Äquators gelegen, und *mm* steht für die Bogenminuten. So stellt z.B. 46N12 die nördliche Breite von 46° 12' dar.

Länge: Die Länge ist direkt in Grad, wie *ddXmm,* angegeben. *dd* steht für Grad, *X* für die Länge östlich (o) oder westlich (w) von Greenwich gelegen, und *mm* sind Bogenminuten. So stellt z.B. 5W28 eine westliche Länge von 5° 28' dar.

Zeit: Studen und Minuten geben die Zeitunterschiede östlich und westlich von Greenwich an. So entspricht z.B. Washington D.C. (77W00) 5St08W oder 5 Stunden und 8 Minuten westlich von Greenwich.

LATITUDES Y LONGITUDES
DE LAS PRINCIPALES
CIUDADES DEL MUNDO

Las siguientes páginas dan las latitudes y longitudes de las principales ciudades del mundo en orden alfabético. Cada línea contiene la siguiente información:

Ciudad, *otro nombre,* Estado, País, Latitud, Longitud, Hora

Otro nombre: Cuando el nombre de otra ciudad es indicado en *itálicas,* refiérase a éste para obtener la latitud y la longitud.

Estado: Las ciudades de Norte América incluyen los estados o las provincias a las cuales pertenecen.

País: Las abreviaturas para los nombres de los países son dadas en las páginas 30-32.

Latitud: La latitud se da en grados como *ggXmm; gg* representa los grados, *X* una latitud situada al Norte (N) o al Sur (S) del Ecuador, y *mm* los minutos de arco. Por ejemplo, 46N12 representa una latitud del Norte de 46° 12'.

Longitud: La longitud es directamente dada en grados como *ggXmm; gg* representa los grados, *X* una longitud situada al Este (E) o al oeste (W) de Greenwich, y *mm* los minutos de arco. Por ejemplo, 5 W 28 representa una longitud Oeste de 5° 28'. (Oeste usa la abreviatura W en Inglés).

Hora: Las horas y minutos indican la diferencia de tiempo al Este u Oeste de Greenwich. Por ejemplo Washington, D.C. (77°W 00') es igual a 5 horas y 8 minutos al Oeste de Greenwich.

COUNTRY CODE TABLE
TABLE DES CODES DES PAYS
TABELLE DER LÄNDERABKÜRZUNGEN
TABLA DE LOS CÓDIGOS DE LOS PAÍSES

	ENGLISH	FRANÇAIS	DEUTSCH	ESPAÑOL
Afg.	Afghanistan	Afghanistan	Afghanistan	Afganistán
Alb.	Albania	Albanie	Albanien	Albania
Alg.	Algeria	Algérie	Algerien	Argelia
Andor.	Andorra	Andorre	Andorra	Andorra
Angola	Angola	Angola	Angola	Angola
Ant.P.	Lesser Antilles	Petites Antilles	Kleine Antillen	Pequeñas Antillas
Arg.	Argentina	Argentine	Argentinien	Argentina
Ar.S.	Saudi Arabia	Arabie Saoudite	Saudi-Arabien	Arabia Saudita
Atl.O.	Atlantic ocean	Océan Atlantique	Atlantischer Ozean	Océano Atlántico
Aust.	Australia	Australie	Australien	Australia
Aut.	Austria	Autriche	Österreich	Austria
Bahr.	Bahrein	Bahrein	Bahrain	Bahrein
Bal.I.	Balearic I.	Baléares I.	Balearen I.	Baleares I.
B.desh	Bangladesh	Bangladesh	Bangladesh	Bangladesh
Belg.	Belgium	Belgique	Belgien	Bélgica
Belize	Belize	Belize (Honduras brit.)	Belize	Belice
Benin	Benin	Bénin (Dahomey)	Benin	Benin
Bhutan	Bhutan	Bhoutan	Bhutan	Bután
Birm.	Burma	Birmanie	Birma	Birmania
Bol.	Bolivia	Bolivie	Bolivien	Bolivia
Bots.	Botswana	Botswana (Bechuanaland)	Botswana	Botswana
Brasil	Brazil	Brésil	Brasilien	Brasil
BRD	West Germany (GFR)	Allemagne de l'ouest (RFA)	Westdeutschland (BRD)	Alemania del oeste (RFA)
Brunei	Brunei	Brunei	Brunei	Brunei
Bulg.	Bulgaria	Bulgarie	Bulgarien	Bulgaria
Bur.	Burundi	Burundi	Burundi	Burundi
C.Afr.	Central African R.	Centrafricaine R.	Zentralafrikanische R.	Centroafricana R.
Cam.	Cameroon	Cameroun	Kamerun	Camerún
Can.	Canada	Canada	Kanada	Canadá
Can.I.	Canary I.	Canaries I.	Kanarische I.	Canarias I.
Chile	Chile	Chili	Chile	Chile
China	China	Chine	China	China
Chyp.	Cyprus	Chypre	Zypern	Chipre
C.Iv.	Ivory Coast	Côte d'Ivoire	Elfenbeinküste	Costa de Marfil
Col.	Columbia	Colombie	Kolumbien	Colombia
Congo	Congo	Congo	Kongo	Congo
Cor.N.	Korea, North	Corée du Nord	Nordkorea	Corea del Norte
Cor.S.	Korea, South	Corée du Sud	Südkorea	Corea del Sur
C.Rica	Costa Rica	Costa Rica	Kostarika	Costa Rica
Cuba	Cuba	Cuba	Kuba	Cuba
Dan.	Denmark	Danemark	Dänemark	Dinamarca
DDR	East Germany (GDR)	Allemagne de l'Est (RDA)	Ostdeutschland (DDR)	Alemania del este (RDA)
Djib.	Djibouti	Djibouti	Djibouti	Djibouti
Dom.	Dominican R.	Dominicaine R.	Dominikanische R.	Dominicana R.

	ENGLISH	*FRANÇAIS*	DEUTSCH	*ESPAÑOL*
E.A.U.	United Arab Emirates	*Emirats Arabes Unis*	Vereinigte Arab. Emiraten	*Emiratos Arabes Unidos*
Ecuad.	Ecuador	*Equateur*	Ecuador	*Ecuador*
Egy.	Egypt	*Egypte*	Ägypten	*Egipto*
Esp.	Spain	*Espagne*	Spanien	*España*
Eth.	Ethiopia	*Ethiopie*	Äthiopien	*Etiopia*
Finl.	Finland	*Finlande*	Finnland	*Finlandia*
Fr.	France	*France*	Frankreich	*Francia*
G.-B.	Great Britain	*Grande-Bretagne*	Grossbritannien	*Gran Bretaña*
Gabon	Gabon	*Gabon*	Gabun	*Gabón*
Gamb.	Gambia	*Gambie*	Gambia	*Gambia*
G.Bis.	Guinea-Bissau	*Guinée-Bissau*	Guinea-Bissau	*Guinea-Bissau*
G.eq.	Equatorial Guinea	*Guinée équatoriale*	Äquatorial Guinea	*Guinea ecuatorial*
Ghana	Ghana	*Ghana*	Ghana	*Ghana*
Grc.	Greece	*Grèce*	Griechenland	*Grecia*
Guat.	Guatemala	*Guatemala*	Guatemala	*Guatemala*
Gu.Fr.	French Guiana	*Guyane française*	Französisch-Guayana	*Guayana francesa*
Guin.	Guinea	*Guinée*	Guinea	*Guinea*
Guyana	Guyana	*Guyana*	Guayana	*Guyana*
Haiti	Haiti	*Haiti*	Haiti	*Haiti*
H.K.	Hong Kong	*Hongkong*	Hongkong	*Hong-Kong*
Hond.	Honduras	*Honduras*	Honduras	*Honduras*
Hong.	Hungary	*Hongrie*	Ungarn	*Hungria*
H.Vol.	Upper Volta	*Haute-Volta*	Obervolta	*Alto Volta*
Ind.	India	*Inde*	Indien	*India*
Ind.O.	Indian ocean	*Océan Indien*	Indischer Ozean	*Océano Indico*
Indon.	Indonesia	*Indonésie*	Indonesien	*Indonesia*
Iran	Iran	*Iran*	Iran	*Irán*
Iraq	Iraq	*Iraq*	Iraq	*Iraq*
Irl.	Ireland	*Irlande (Eire)*	Irland	*Irlanda*
Isl.	Iceland	*Islande*	Island	*Islandia*
Isr.	Israel	*Israël*	Israel	*Israel*
Ital.	Italy	*Italie*	Italien	*Italia*
Jama.	Jamaica	*Jamaïque*	Jamaika	*Jamaica*
Jap.	Japan	*Japon*	Japan	*Japón*
Jord.	Jordan	*Jordanie*	Jordanien	*Jordania*
Kamp.	Kampuchea (Cambodia)	*Kampuchea (Cambodge)*	Kampuchea (Kanbodscha)	*Kampuchea (Camboya)*
Kenya	Kenya	*Kenya*	Kenia	*Kenya*
Kuwait	Kuwait	*Koweit*	Kuwait	*Kuwait*
Laos	Laos	*Laos*	Laos	*Laos*
Lbn	Lebanon	*Liban*	Libanon	*Líbano*
Leso.	Lesotho	*Lesotho (Basutoland)*	Lesotho	*Lesotho*
Lib.	Libya	*Libye*	Libyen	*Libia*
Liber.	Liberia	*Liberia*	Liberia	*Liberia*
Liech.	Liechtenstein	*Liechtenstein*	Liechtenstein	*Liechtenstein*
Luxem.	Luxembourg	*Luxembourg*	Luxemburg	*Luxemburgo*
Madag.	Madagascar	*Madagascar*	Madagaskar	*Madagascar*
Malawi	Malawi	*Malawi (Nyasaland)*	Malawi	*Malawi*
Malay.	Malaysia	*Malaisie*	Malaysia	*Malasia*
Mali	Mali	*Mali*	Mali	*Mali*
Malta	Malta	*Malte*	Malta	*Malta*
Mar.	Morocco	*Maroc*	Marokko	*Marruecos*
Mau.I.	Mauritius I.	*Maurice I.*	Mauritius I.	*Mauricio I.*
Maur.	Mauritania	*Mauritanie*	Mauretanien	*Mauritania*
Mex.	Mexico	*Mexique*	Mexiko	*Méjico*
Monaco	Monaco	*Monaco*	Monaco	*Mónaco*
Mong.	Mongolia	*Mongolie*	Mongolei	*Mongolia*
Moz.	Mozambique	*Mozambique*	Mosambik	*Mozambique*
Namib.	Namibia	*Namibie*	Namibia	*Namibia*
N.Cal.	New Caledonia	*Nouvelle-Calédonie*	Neukaledonien	*Nueva Caledonia*
Nepal	Nepal	*Népal*	Nepal	*Nepal*

	ENGLISH	FRANÇAIS	DEUTSCH	ESPAÑOL
Nicar.	Nicaragua	Nicaragua	Nicaragua	Nicaragua
Nig.	Nigeria	Nigeria	Nigeria	Nigeria
Niger	Niger	Niger	Niger	Níger
Nor.	Norway	Norvège	Norwegen	Noruega
Nth.	Netherlands	Pays-Bas (Hollande)	Niederlande	Países Bajos (Holanda)
N.Zel.	New Zealand	Nouvelle-Zélande	Neuseeland	Nueva Zelanda
Oman	Oman	Oman	Oman	Omán
Pac.O.	Pacific ocean	Océan Pacifique	Pazifischer Ozean	Océano Pacífico
Pak.	Pakistan	Pakistan	Pakistan	Pakistan
Panama	Panama	Panama	Panama	Panamá
Pap.	Papua-New Guinea	Papouasie-Nouvelle-Guinée	Papua - Neuginea	Papuasia-Nueva Guinea
Parag.	Paraguay	Paraguay	Paraguay	Paraguay
Peru	Peru	Pérou	Peru	Perú
Phil.	Philippines	Philippines	Philippinen	Filipinas
Pol.	Poland	Pologne	Polen	Polonia
Port.	Portugal	Portugal	Portugal	Portugal
P.Rico	Puerto Rico	Porto Rico	Puerto Rico	Puerto Rico
Qatar	Qatar	Qatar	Katar	Qatar
Reu.I.	Reunion I.	Réunion I.	Reunion I.	Reunión I.
Roum.	Rumania	Roumanie	Rumänien	Rumania
Rwanda	Rwanda	Rwanda	Rwanda	Rwanda
S.Afr.	South Africa R.	Sud-Africaine R.	Südafrikanische R.	Sudafricana R.
Sal.I.	Solomon I.	Salomon I.	Salomonen I.	Salomón I.
Salv.	El Salvador	El Salvador	El Salvador	El Salvador
Seneg.	Senegal	Sénégal	Senegal	Senegal
S.Leo.	Sierra Leone	Sierra Leone	Sierra Leone	Sierra Leona
Somal.	Somalia	Somalie	Somalia	Somalia
Sr.Lka	Sri Lanka (Ceylon)	Sri Lanka (Ceylan)	Sri Lanka (Ceylon)	Sri Lanka (Ceilán)
Sudan	Sudan	Soudan	Sudan	Sudán
Sue.	Sweden	Suède	Schweden	Suecia
Sui.	Switzerland	Suisse	Schweiz	Suiza
Surin.	Surinam	Surinam	Surinam	Surinam
Swaz.	Swaziland	Swaziland (Ngwane)	Swasiland	Zwasilandia
Syr.	Syria	Syrie	Syrien	Siria
Taiwan	Taiwan	Taiwan (Formosa)	Taiwan	Taiwan
Tanz.	Tanzania	Tanzanie	Tansania	Tanzania
Tch.	Czechoslovakia	Tchécoslovaquie	Tschechoslowakei	Checoslovaquia
Tchad	Chad	Tchad	Tschad	Chad
Thai.	Thailand	Thailande (Siam)	Thailand	Tailandia
Togo	Togo	Togo	Togo	Togo
T.Tob.	Trinidad and Tobago	Trinité-et-Tobago	Trinidad und Tobago	Trinidad y Tobago
Tun.	Tunisia	Tunisie	Tunesien	Túnez
Tur.	Turkey	Turquie	Türkei	Turquía
Uganda	Uganda	Ouganda	Uganda	Uganda
URSS	USSR	URSS	UdSSr	URSS
Urug.	Uruguay	Uruguay	Uruguay	Uruguay
USA	United States	Etats-Unis	Vereinigte Staaten	Estados Unidos
Ven.	Venezuela	Venezuela	Venezuela	Venezuela
Viet.	Vietnam	Vietnam	Vietnam	Vietnam
Yem.d.	Yemen, dem. R.	Yémen, R. dém.	Jemen, dem. R.	Yemen, R. dem.
Yemen	Yemen	Yémen	Jemen	Yemen
Youg.	Yugoslavia	Yougoslavie	Jugoslawien	Yugoslavia
Zaire	Zaire	Zaïre	Zaïre	Zaira
Zamb.	Zambia	Zambie	Sambia	Zambia
Zimb.	Zimbabwe (Rhodesia)	Zimbabwe (Rhodésie)	Zimbabwe (Rhodesien)	Zimbabwe (Rodesia)

City	Lat.	Long.	Time	City	Lat.	Long.	Time
				Alburquerque, **Esp.**	39N13	6w59	0h28w
				Alcázar de San Juan, **Esp.**	39N24	3w12	0h13w
		*** A ***		Alcira, **Esp.**	39N10	0w27	0h02w
Aachen, **BRD**	50N46	6E06	0h24E	Alcoy, **Esp.**	38N42	0w29	0h02w
Aalst (Alost), **Belg.**	50N47	4E03	0h16E	Aleksandrovsk, → *Zaporozhye*,			
Aarau, **Sui.**	47N24	8E04	0h32E	**URSS**			
Aarschot, **Belg.**	50N59	4E50	0h19E	Alençon, **Fr.**	48N25	0E05	0h00E
Aba, **Nig.**	5N06	7E21	0h29E	Aleoutiennes I., **Pac.O.**	52N25	176w00	11h44w
Abadan, **Iran**	30N20	48E15	3h13E	Alep, → *Halab,* **Syr.**			
Abbeville, **Fr.**	50N06	1E51	0h07E	Alès, **Fr.**	44N08	4E05	0h16E
Abéché, **Tchad**	13N49	20E49	1h23E	Alessándria (Alexandrie), **Ital.**	44N55	8E37	0h34E
Abeokuta, **Nig.**	7N10	3E26	0h14E	Alesund, **Nor.**	62N28	6E11	0h25E
Aberdeen, **G.-B.**	57N10	2w04	0h08w	Alexandrette, → *Iskenderun,* **Tur.**			
Aberdeen, SD, **USA**	45N28	98w30	6h34w	Alexandria, **Roum.**	43N59	25E19	1h41E
Aberystwyth, **G.-B.**	52N25	4w05	0h16w	Alexandria, La., **USA**	31N19	92w29	6h10w
Abidjan, **C.Iv.**	5N19	4w01	0h16w	Alexandrie, → *Al Iskandereya,*			
Abo, → *Turku,* **Finl.**				**Egy.**			
Abomey, **Benin**	7N14	2E00	0h08E	Algeciras, **Esp.**	36N08	5w27	0h22w
Abu Dhabi, **E.A.U.**	24N28	54E25	3h38E	Alger (Algiers), **Alg.**	36N50	3E00	0h12E
Acapulco, **Mex.**	16N51	99w56	6h40w	Al Hillah, **Iraq**	32N28	44E29	2h58E
Acarigua, **Ven.**	9N35	69w12	4h37w	Al Hufuf (Hofouf), **Ar.S.**	25N20	49E34	3h18E
Accra, **Ghana**	5N33	0w15	0h01w	Alicante, **Esp.**	38N21	0w29	0h02w
Achacachi, **Bol.**	16s01	68w44	4h35w	Alice Springs, **Aust.**	23s42	133E52	8h55E
Acre, → *Akko, Isr.*				Aligarh, **Ind.**	27N54	78E04	5h12E
Adalya, → *Antalya,* **Tur.**				Al Iskandereya, **Egy.**	31N13	29E55	2h00E
Adana (Seyhan), **Tur.**	37N00	35E19	2h21E	Alkmaar, **Nth.**	52N38	4E44	0h19E
Adapazari, **Tur.**	40N45	30E23	2h02E	Allada, **Benin**	6N41	2E10	0h09E
Addis Ababa (Addis Abeba), **Eth.**	9N03	38E42	2h35E	Allahabad, **Ind.**	25N27	81E50	5h27E
Adelaide, **Aust.**	34s56	138E36	9h14E	Allenstein, → *Olsztyn,* **Pol.**			
Aden, **Yem.d.**	12N47	45E03	3h00E	Allentown, Pa., **USA**	40N37	75w30	5h02w
Adjohon, **Benin**	6N41	2E32	0h10E	Allepey, **Ind.**	9N30	76E22	5h05E
Adrar, **Alg.**	27N51	0w19	0h01w	Alma-Ata, **URSS**	43N19	76E55	5h08E
Afula, **Isr.**	32N36	35E17	2h21E	Almada, **Port.**	38N40	9w09	0h37w
Agadez, **Niger**	17N00	7E56	0h32E	Al Manamah, **Bahr.**	26N12	51E38	3h27E
Agadir, **Mar.**	30N30	9w40	0h39w	Al Mawsil, → *Mossoul,* **Iran**			
Agboville, **C.Iv.**	5N55	4w15	0h17w	Almelo, **Nth.**	52N21	6E40	0h27E
Agen, **Fr.**	44N12	0E38	0h03E	Almería, **Esp.**	36N50	2w26	0h10w
Agra, **Ind.**	27N09	78E00	5h12E	Al Qahira, **Egy.**	30N03	31E15	2h05E
Agram, → *Zagreb,* **Youg.**				Alsfeld, **BRD**	50N45	9E17	0h37E
Agrigento, **Ital.**	37N19	13E35	0h54E	Altdorf, **Sui.**	46N53	8E38	0h35E
Agrínio (Aghrinion), **Grc.**	38N38	21E25	1h26E	Altenburg, **DDR**	50N59	12E27	0h50E
Aguascalientes, **Mex.**	21N51	102w18	6h49w	Altoona, Pa., **USA**	40N32	78w23	5h14w
Ahmadabad (Ahmedabad), **Ind.**	23N03	72E40	4h51E	Amagasaki, → *Osaka,* **Jap.**			
Ahmadnagar, **Ind.**	19N08	74E48	4h59E	Amarillo, Tex., **USA**	35N14	101w50	6h47w
Ahvaz, **Iran**	31N17	48E43	3h15E	Ambala, **Ind.**	30N19	76E49	5h07E
Aix-en-Provence, **Fr.**	43N31	5E27	0h22E	Ambato, **Ecuad.**	1s18	78w39	5h15w
Aix-la-Chapelle, → *Aachen,* **BRD**				Ambatondrazaka, **Madag.**	17s49	48E28	3h14E
Ajaccio, Corse, **Fr.**	41N55	8E43	0h35E	Amberg in der Oberpfalz, **BRD**	49N26	11E52	0h47E
Ajmer, **Ind.**	26N29	74E40	4h59E	Ambon, **Indon.**	3s41	128E10	8h33E
Akita, **Jap.**	39N44	140E05	9h20E	Amersfoort, **Nth.**	52N09	5E23	0h22E
Akjoujt, **Maur.**	19N44	14w20	0h57w	Amiens, **Fr.**	49N54	2E18	0h09E
Akko, **Isr.**	32N55	35E04	2h20E	Amirauté I., **Pac.O.**	2s01	147E15	9h49E
Akola, **Ind.**	20N40	77E05	5h08E	Amman, **Jord.**	31N57	35E56	2h24E
Akron, Oh., **USA**	41N04	81w31	5h26w	Amoy, → *Hia-men,* **China**			
Aktyubinsk (Aktioubinsk), **URSS**	50N16	57E13	3h49E	Amravati (Amraoti), **Ind.**	20N58	77E50	5h11E
Akure, **Nig.**	7N14	5E08	0h21E	Amritsar, **Ind.**	31N35	74E56	5h00E
Albacete, **Esp.**	39N00	1w52	0h07w	Amsterdam, **Nth.**	52N21	4E54	0h20E
Albany, **Aust.**	34s57	117E54	7h52E	Amsterdam I., **Ind.O.**	37s50	77E30	5h10E
Albany, Ga., **USA**	31N37	84w10	5h37w	Amstetten, **Aut.**	48N08	14E52	0h59E
Albany, NY, **USA**	42N40	73w49	4h55w	An-chan (Anshan), **China**	41N05	122E58	8h12E
Albertville, **Fr.**	45N40	6E24	0h26E	Anchorage, Alas., **USA**	61N10	150w00	10h00w
Albi, **Fr.**	43N56	2E08	0h09E	Ancona, **Ital.**	43N37	13E31	0h54E
Alborg, **Dan.**	57N03	9E56	0h40E	Andaman I. (Port Blair), **Ind.O.**	11N40	92E44	6h11E
Albuquerque, NM, **USA**	35N05	106w38	7h07w				

City	Lat.	Long.	Time	City	Lat.	Long.	Time
Anderlecht, **Belg.**	50N50	4E19	0h17E	Ascoli Piceno, **Ital.**	42N52	13E35	0h54E
Andermatt, **Sui.**	46N38	8E36	0h34E	Ashdod, **Isr.**	31N48	34E38	2h19E
Andizhan (Andijan), **URSS**	40N48	72E23	4h50E	Asheville, NC, **USA**	35N35	82w35	5h30w
Andorra la Vella, **Andor.**	42N30	1E30	0h06E	Ashkhabad (Achkhabad), **URSS**	37N58	58E24	3h54E
Andria, **Ital.**	41N14	16E18	1h05E	Ashqelon, **Isr.**	31N40	34E35	2h18E
Anécho (Aneho), **Togo**	6N17	1E40	0h07E	Asmara (Asmera), **Eth.**	15N20	38E58	2h36E
Angermünde, **DDR**	53N01	14E01	0h56E	Assen, **Nth.**	53N00	6E34	0h26E
Angers, **Fr.**	47N29	0w32	0h02w	Assiout, → *Asyut,* **Egy.**			
Angoulême, **Fr.**	45N40	0E10	0h01E	Assisi, **Ital.**	43N04	12E37	0h50E
Anju, **Cor.N.**	39N36	125E42	8h23E	Assouan (Aswan), **Egy.**	24N05	32E56	2h12E
Ankara (Angora), **Tur.**	39N55	32E50	2h11E	Asti, **Ital.**	44N54	8E13	0h33E
Anklam, **DDR**	53N52	13E42	0h55E	Astrakhan (Astrakan), **URSS**	46N22	48E04	3h12E
Annaba, **Alg.**	36N55	7E47	0h31E	Asunción (Assomption), **Parag.**	25s15	57w40	3h51w
An Najaf (Nadjaf), **Iraq**	31N59	44E19	2h57E	Asyut, **Egy.**	27N14	31E07	2h04E
Annecy, **Fr.**	45N54	6E07	0h24E	Atakpamé, **Togo**	7N34	1E14	0h05E
An Nhon (Binh Dinh), **Viet.**	13N53	109E07	7h16E	Atar, **Maur.**	20N32	13w08	0h53w
Ansbach, **BRD**	49N18	10E36	0h42E	Atbara, **Sudan**	17N42	34E00	2h16E
Antakya, **Tur.**	36N12	36E10	2h25E	Ath (Aat), **Belg.**	50N38	3E47	0h15E
Antalya, **Tur.**	36N53	30E42	2h03E	Athènes (Athens), → *Athina,* **Grc.**			
Antananarivo, **Madag.**	18s52	47E30	3h10E	Athiémé, **Benin**	6N38	1E45	0h07E
Antequera, **Esp.**	37N01	4w34	0h18w	Athina, **Grc.**	38N00	23E44	1h35E
Antibes, **Fr.**	43N35	7E07	0h28E	Athlone, **Irl.**	53N25	7w56	0h32w
Antigua, **Guat.**	14N33	90w42	6h03w	Atlanta, Ga., **USA**	33N45	84w23	5h38w
Antioch, Ca., **USA**	38N01	121w49	8h07w	Atlantic City, NJ, **USA**	39N23	74w27	4h58w
Antipodes I., **Pac.O.**	49s45	179E00	11h56E	Aubagne, **Fr.**	43N17	5E35	0h22E
Antofagasta, **Chile**	23s40	70w23	4h42w	Aubenas, **Fr.**	44N37	4E24	0h18E
An-tong (Andong), **China**	40N08	124E24	8h18E	Auch, **Fr.**	43N40	0E36	0h02E
Antseranana, **Madag.**	12s19	49E17	3h17E	Auckland, **N.Zel.**	36s55	174E47	11h39E
Antsirabe, **Madag.**	19s51	47E01	3h08E	Auckland I., **Pac.O.**	51s00	166E00	11h04E
Antwerpen (Anvers), **Belg.**	51N13	4E25	0h18E	Audincourt, **Fr.**	47N29	6E50	0h27E
Anvers, → *Antwerpen,* **Belg.**				Augsburg, **BRD**	48N21	10E54	0h44E
Aomori, **Jap.**	40N50	140E43	9h23E	Augusta, Ga., **USA**	33N29	82w00	5h28w
Aosta, **Ital.**	45N43	7E19	0h29E	Augusta, Me., **USA**	44N17	69w48	4h39w
Apeldoorn, **Nth.**	52N13	5E57	0h24E	Aurangabad, Maharashtra, **Ind.**	19N52	75E22	5h01E
Appenzell, **Sui.**	47N22	9E25	0h38E	Aurillac, **Fr.**	44N56	2E26	0h10E
Aracaju, **Brasil**	10s54	37w07	2h28w	Aussig, → *Usti,* **Tch.**			
Arad, **Roum.**	46N10	21E19	1h25E	Austin, Tex., **USA**	30N18	97w47	6h31w
Aranda de Duero, **Esp.**	41N40	3w41	0h15w	Auxerre, **Fr.**	47N48	3E35	0h14E
Aransol, **Ind.**	23N40	86E59	5h48E	Aveiro, **Port.**	40N38	8w40	0h35w
Arbil, **Iraq**	36N12	44E01	2h56E	Avignon, **Fr.**	43N56	4E48	0h19E
Arbroath, **G.-B.**	56N34	2w35	0h10w	Avila, **Esp.**	40N39	4w42	0h19w
Arcachon, **Fr.**	44N40	1w11	0h05w	Ayacucho, **Peru**	13s10	74w15	4h57w
Arendal, **Nor.**	58N27	8E56	0h36E	Ayr, **G.-B.**	55N28	4w38	0h19w
Arequipa, **Peru**	16s25	71w32	4h46w	Azemmour, **Mar.**	33N20	8w25	0h34w
Arezzo, **Ital.**	43N28	11E53	0h48E	Azogues, **Ecuad.**	2s46	78w56	5h16w
Argel, → *Alger,* **Alg.**				Azul, **Arg.**	36s46	59w50	3h59w
Argentan, **Fr.**	48N45	0w01	0h00w				
Argenteuil, **Fr.**	48N57	2E13	0h09E				
Arhus, **Dan.**	56N10	10E13	0h41E	<center>*** B ***</center>			
Arica, **Chile**	18s30	70w20	4h41w				
Arkhangelsk, **URSS**	64N32	40E40	2h43E	Ba'albek (Balabakk), **Lbn**	34N00	36E12	2h25E
Arles, **Fr.**	43N41	4E38	0h19E	Bacau, **Roum.**	46N33	26E58	1h48E
Arlon, **Belg.**	49N41	5E49	0h23E	Bacolod, **Phil.**	10N38	122E58	8h12E
Armavir, **URSS**	44N59	41E10	2h45E	Badajoz, **Esp.**	38N53	6w58	0h28w
Armenia, **Col.**	4N32	75w40	5h03w	Badalona, **Esp.**	41N27	2E15	0h09E
Armentières, **Fr.**	50N41	2E53	0h12E	Baden, **Sui.**	47N28	8E19	0h33E
Arnhem, **Nth.**	52N00	5E53	0h24E	Baden-Baden, **BRD**	48N45	8E15	0h33E
Arras, **Fr.**	50N17	2E46	0h11E	Bad Homburg, **BRD**	50N13	8E37	0h34E
Artigas, **Urug.**	30s25	56w28	3h46w	Bad Ischl, **Aut.**	47N43	13E38	0h55E
Asahikawa, **Jap.**	43N46	142E23	9h30E	Bad Kreuznach, **BRD**	49N51	7E52	0h31E
Ascension I. (Georgetown), **Atl.O.**	7s56	14w25	0h58w	Bad Mergentheim, **BRD**	49N29	9E46	0h39E
Aschaffenburg, **BRD**	49N58	9E10	0h37E	Bad Oldesloe, **BRD**	53N49	10E22	0h41E
Aschersleben, **DDR**	51N46	11E28	0h46E	Bad Salzuflen, **BRD**	52N06	8E45	0h35E

City	Lat.	Long.	Time	City	Lat.	Long.	Time
Bafia, **Cam.**	4N49	11E14	0h45 E	Batavia, → *Jakarta*, **Indon.**			
Baghdad, **Iraq**	33N20	44E26	2h58 E	Bath, **G.-B.**	51N23	2w22	0h09w
Bahamas I. (Nassau), **Atl.O.**	25N05	77w20	5h09w	Bathurst, → *Banjul*, **Gamb.**			
Bahawalpur, **Pak.**	29N24	71E47	4h47 E	Batna, **Alg.**	35N34	6E10	0h25 E
Bahia, → *Salvador*, **Brasil**				Baton Rouge, La., **USA**	30N30	91w10	6h05w
Bahia Blanca, **Arg.**	38s45	62w15	4h09w	Batouri, **Cam.**	4N26	14E27	0h58 E
Baile Atha Cliath, → *Dublin*, **Irl.**				Batroun, **Lbn**	34N16	35E40	2h23 E
Bakersfield, Ca., **USA**	35N25	119w00	7h56w	Battambang, **Kamp.**	13N06	103E13	6h53 E
Baku (Bakou), **URSS**	40N22	49E53	3h20 E	Battleford, Sask., **Can.**	52N45	108w20	7h13w
Bâle, → *Basel*, **Sui.**				Batumi (Batoum), **URSS**	41N37	41E36	2h46 E
Balikesir, **Tur.**	39N37	27E51	1h51 E	Baubau, **Indon.**	5s30	122E37	8h10 E
Balikpapan, **Indon.**	1s15	116E50	7h47 E	Bauchi, **Nig.**	10N16	9E50	0h39 E
Ballarat, **Aust.**	37s36	143E58	9h36 E	Bauru, **Brasil**	22s19	49w07	3h16w
Baltimore, Md., **USA**	39N18	76w38	5h07w	Bautzen, **DDR**	51N11	14E29	0h58 E
Bamako, **Mali**	12N40	7w59	0h32w	Bawku, **Ghana**	11N05	0w11	0h01w
Bambari, **C.Afr.**	5N40	20E37	1h22 E	Bayamo, **Cuba**	20N23	76w39	5h07w
Bamberg, **BRD**	49N54	10E54	0h44 E	Bayonne, **Fr.**	43N30	1w28	0h06w
Bamenda, **Cam.**	5N55	10E09	0h41 E	Bayreuth, **BRD**	49N57	11E35	0h46 E
Banaba I., **Pac.O.**	0s52	169E35	11h18 E	Baza, **Esp.**	37N30	2w45	0h11w
Banbury, **USA**	52N04	1w20	0h05w	Beaumont, **Belg.**	50N14	4E14	0h17 E
Bandar Abbas, **Iran**	27N12	56E15	3h45 E	Beaumont, Tex., **USA**	30N04	94w06	6h16w
Bandar Seri Begawan, **Brunei**	4N56	114E58	7h40 E	Beauvais, **Fr.**	49N26	2E05	0h08 E
Bandung (Bandoeng), **Indon.**	6s57	107E34	7h10 E	Béchar (Bechard), **Alg.**	31N35	2w17	0h09w
Banfora, **H.Vol.**	10N36	4w45	0h19w	Bedford, **G.-B.**	52N08	0w29	0h02w
Bangalore, **Ind.**	12N58	77E35	5h10 E	Beersheba (Beer Sheva), **Isr.**	31N15	34E47	2h19 E
Bangkok, → *Krung Thep*, **Thai.**				Behbehan, **Iran**	30N34	50E18	3h21 E.
Bangor, Me., **USA**	44N49	68w47	4h35w	Beijing, → *Pe-king*, **China**			
Bangui, **C.Afr.**	4N23	18E37	1h14 E	Beira, → *Sofala*, **Moz.**			
Banja Luka, **Youg.**	44N47	17E11	1h09 E	Beirout (Bairut), **Lbn**	33N52	35E30	2h22 E
Banjarmasin (Bandjermassin),				Beja, **Port.**	38N01	7w52	0h31w
Indon.	3s22	114E33	7h38 E	Béja, **Tun.**	36N43	9E13	0h37 E
Banjul, **Gamb.**	13N28	16w39	1h07w	Bejaïa (Bougie), **Alg.**	36N49	5E03	0h20 E
Ban Me Thuot, **Viet.**	12N41	108E02	7h12 E	Bekescsaba, **Hong.**	46N40	21E05	1h24 E
Barahona, **Dom.**	18N13	71w07	4h44w	Belém (Para), **Brasil**	1s27	48w29	3h14w
Barbacena, Minas Gerais, **Brasil**	21s13	43w47	2h55w	Belfast, **Irl.**	54N35	5w55	0h24w
Barcelona, **Esp.**	41N25	2E10	0h09 E	Belfort, **Fr.**	47N38	6E52	0h27 E
Barcelona, **Ven.**	10N08	64w43	4h19w	Belgaum, **Ind.**	15N54	74E36	4h58 E
Bareilly (Bareli), **Ind.**	28N20	79E24	5h18 E	Belgorod (Bielgorod), **URSS**	50N38	36E36	2h26 E
Bari, **Ital.**	41N07	16E52	1h07 E	Belgrade, → *Beograd*, **Youg.**			
Barinas, **Ven.**	8N36	70w15	4h41w	Belize, **Belize**	17N29	88w10	5h53w
Barisal, **B.desh**	22N41	90E20	6h01 E	Bellinzona, **Sui.**	46N12	9E02	0h36 E
Bar-le-Duc, **Fr.**	48N46	5E10	0h21 E	Belmopan, **Belize**	17N13	88w48	5h55w
Barletta, **Ital.**	41N20	16E17	1h05 E	Belo Horizonte, M.Gerais, **Brasil**	19s54	43w54	2h56w
Barnaul (Barnaoul), **URSS**	53N21	83E45	5h35 E	Benares, → *Varanasi*, **Ind.**			
Barnsley, Yorks, **G.-B.**	53N34	1w28	0h06w	Bendigo, **Aust.**	36s48	144E21	9h37 E
Baroda, **Ind.**	22N19	73E14	4h53 E	Benevento, **Ital.**	41N08	14E46	0h59 E
Barquisimeto, **Ven.**	10N03	69w18	4h37w	Benghazi, **Lib.**	32N07	20E05	1h20 E
Barrancabermeja, **Col.**	7N06	73w54	4h56w	Benguela, **Angola**	12s34	13E24	0h54 E
Barranquilla, Atlántico, **Col.**	11N10	74w50	4h59w	Benicarló, **Esp.**	40N25	0E25	0h02 E
Barreiro, **Port.**	38N40	9w05	0h36w	Beni Mellal, **Mar.**	32N22	6w29	0h26w
Barrow in Furness, **G.-B.**	54N07	3w14	0h13w	Benin City, **Nig.**	6N19	5E41	0h23 E
Basel, **Sui.**	47N33	7E36	0h30 E	Beni Souef, **Egy.**	29N05	31E05	2h04 E
Basildon, **G.-B.**	51N34	0E25	0h02 E	Beograd (Belgrad), **Youg.**	44N50	20E30	1h22 E
Basingstoke, **G.-B.**	51N16	1w05	0h04w	Berbera, **Somal.**	10N28	45E02	3h00 E
Bassari (Bassar), **Togo**	9N18	0E53	0h04 E	Berbérati, **C.Afr.**	4N19	15E51	1h03 E
Bassein, **Birm.**	16N46	94E45	6h19 E	Berezniki, **URSS**	59N26	56E49	3h47 E
Basse Terre, Guadeloupe, **Ant.P.**	16N00	61w43	4h07w	Bergamo, **Ital.**	45N42	9E40	0h39 E
Basseterre, Saint Kitts, **Ant.P.**	17N17	62w43	4h11w	Bergen, **Nor.**	60N23	5E20	0h21 E
Bassorah (Basra), **Iraq**	30N30	47E50	3h11 E	Bergen op Zoom, **Nth.**	51N30	4E17	0h17 E
Bastia, Corse, **Fr.**	42N41	9E26	0h38 E	Bergerac, **Fr.**	44N50	0E29	0h02 E
Bastogne, **Belg.**	50N00	5E43	0h23 E	Berlin, **DDR**	52N32	13E25	0h54 E
Bata, **G.eq.**	1N51	9E49	0h39 E	Bermuda I. (Hamilton), **Atl.O.**	32N18	64w48	4h19w
Batangas, **Phil.**	13N46	121E01	8h04 E	Bern (Berne), **Sui.**	46N57	7E26	0h30 E

City	Lat.	Long.	Time	City	Lat.	Long.	Time
Bernburg, **DDR**	51N49	11E43	0h47E	Bolgatanga, **Ghana**	10N44	0w53	0h04w
Bertoua, **Cam.**	4N34	13E42	0h55E	Bologna, **Ital.**	44N30	11E20	0h45E
Berwick upon Tweed, **G.-B.**	55N46	2w00	0h08w	Bolton, **G.-B.**	53N35	2w26	0h10w
Besançon, **Fr.**	47N14	6E02	0h24E	Bolzano, **Ital.**	46N30	11E22	0h45E
Bethleem (Beit Lahm), **Jord.**	31N42	35E12	2h21E	Boma, **Zaire**	5s50	13E03	0h52E
Bethlehem, **S.Afr.**	28s15	28E19	1h53E	Bombay (Mumbaï), **Ind.**	18N56	72E51	4h51E
Bethlehem, Pa., **USA**	40N36	75w22	5h01w	Bonda, **Gabon**	0s50	12E43	0h51E
Béthune, **Fr.**	50N32	2E38	0h11E	Bondoukou, **C.Iv.**	8N03	2w45	0h11w
Beyla, **Guin.**	8N42	8w39	0h35w	Bône, → *Annaba,* **Alg.**			
Beyrouth, → *Beirout,* **Lbn**				Bongor, **Tchad**	10N18	15E20	1h01E
Béziers, **Fr.**	43N21	3E13	0h13E	Bonn, **BRD**	50N44	7E06	0h28E
Bezwada, → *Vijayavada,* **Ind.**				Boras, **Sue.**	57N44	12E55	0h52E
Bhagalpur, **Ind.**	25N14	86E59	5h48E	Bordeaux, **Fr.**	44N50	0w34	0h02w
Bhatpara, **Ind.**	22N51	88E31	5h54E	Borujerd, **Iran**	33N55	48E48	3h15E
Bhavnagar, **Ind.**	21N46	72E14	4h49E	Bossangoa, **C.Afr.**	6N27	17E21	1h09E
Bhopal, **Ind.**	23N17	77E28	5h10E	Boston, **G.-B.**	52N59	0w01	0h00w
Bialystok, **Pol.**	53N09	23E10	1h33E	Boston, Mass., **USA**	42N20	71w05	4h44w
Biarritz, **Fr.**	43N29	1w33	0h06w	Bottrop, **BRD**	51N31	6E55	0h28E
Bida, **Nig.**	9N06	5E59	0h24E	Bouaflé, **C.Iv.**	7N01	5w47	0h23w
Biel (Bienne), **Sui.**	47N09	7E16	0h29E	Bouaké, **C.Iv.**	7N42	5w00	0h20w
Bielefeld, **BRD**	52N02	8E32	0h34E	Bouar, **C.Afr.**	5N58	15E35	1h02E
Biella, **Ital.**	45N34	8E04	0h32E	Bouarfa, **Mar.**	32N30	1w59	0h08w
Bielsko-Biala, **Pol.**	49N50	19E00	1h16E	Bougouni, **Madag.**	11N25	7w28	0h30w
Bikaner, **Ind.**	28N01	73E22	4h53E	Boulogne-sur-Mer, **Fr.**	50N43	1E37	0h06E
Bilbao, **Esp.**	43N15	2w56	0h12w	Bourail, **N.Cal.**	21s34	165E29	11h02E
Billings, Mt., **USA**	45N47	108w30	7h14w	Bourg-en-Bresse, **Fr.**	46N12	5E13	0h21E
Binche, **Belg.**	50N25	4E10	0h17E	Bourges, **Fr.**	47N05	2E23	0h10E
Binghamton, NY, **USA**	42N06	75w55	5h04w	Bournemouth, **G.-B.**	50N43	1w54	0h08w
Binzert, **Tun.**	37N18	9E52	0h39E	Bowling Green, Ky., **USA**	37N00	86w29	5h46w
Birjand, **Iran**	32N55	59E10	3h57E	Bozoum, **C.Afr.**	6N16	16E22	1h05E
Birkenhead, **G.-B.**	53N24	3w02	0h12w	Bradford, Yorks, **G.-B.**	53N48	1w45	0h07w
Birmingham, **G.-B.**	52N30	1w50	0h07w	Braga, **Port.**	41N32	8w26	0h34w
Birmingham, Alab., **USA**	33N30	86w55	5h48w	Braila, **Roum.**	45N17	27E58	1h52E
Birnin Kebbi, **Nig.**	12N30	4E11	0h17E	Brandenburg, **DDR**	52N25	12E34	0h50E
Birni n'Konni, **Niger**	13N49	5E19	0h21E	Brandon, Man., **Can.**	49N50	99w57	6h40w
Biskra (Beskra), **Alg.**	34N50	5E41	0h23E	Brasilia, **Brasil**	15s45	47w57	3h12w
Bismarck, ND, **USA**	46N50	100w48	6h43w	Brasov, **Roum.**	45N39	25E35	1h42E
Bissau, **G.Bis.**	11N52	15w39	1h03w	Bratislava, **Tch.**	48N10	17E10	1h09E
Bitola (Monastir), **Youg.**	41N01	21E21	1h25E	Bratsk, **URSS**	56N20	101E50	6h47E
Biysk (Biisk), **URSS**	52N35	85E16	5h41E	Braunau am Inn, **Aut.**	48N16	13E03	0h52E
Bizerte, → *Binzert,* **Tun.**				Braunschweig, **BRD**	52N15	10E30	0h42E
Blackburn, Lancs, **G.-B.**	53N45	2w29	0h10w	Brazzaville, **Congo**	4s14	15E14	1h01E
Blackpool, **G.-B.**	53N50	3w03	0h12w	Breda, **Nth.**	51N35	4E46	0h19E
Blankenburg, **DDR**	51N48	10E58	0h44E	Bremen (Brême), **BRD**	53N05	8E48	0h35E
Blantyre, **Malawi**	15s46	35E00	2h20E	Bremerhaven, **BRD**	53N33	8E35	0h34E
Blida (El Boulaïda), **Alg.**	36N30	2E50	0h11E	Brescia, **Ital.**	45N33	10E13	0h41E
Bloemfontein, **S.Afr.**	29s07	26E14	1h45E	Breslau, → *Wroclaw,* **Pol.**			
Blois, **Fr.**	47N36	1E20	0h05E	Brest, **Fr.**	48N23	4w30	0h18w
Bloomington, Ill., **USA**	40N29	89w00	5h56w	Brest Litovsk, **URSS**	52N08	23E40	1h35E
Bludenz, **Aut.**	47N10	9E50	0h39E	Briançon, **Fr.**	44N53	6E39	0h27E
Blumenau, **Brasil**	26s55	49w07	3h16w	Bridgeport, Conn., **USA**	41N12	73w12	4h53w
Bo, **S.Leo.**	7N58	11w45	0h47w	Bridgetown, Barbados, **Ant.P.**	13N06	59w37	3h58w
Bobo-Dioulasso, **H.Vol.**	11N11	4w18	0h17w	Brig (Brigue), **Sui.**	46N19	8E00	0h32E
Bobruysk, **URSS**	53N08	29E10	1h57E	Brighton, **G.-B.**	50N50	0w10	0h01w
Bochum, **BRD**	51N28	7E11	0h29E	Brignoles, **Fr.**	43N25	6E03	0h24E
Boden, **Sue.**	65N50	21E44	1h27E	Brindisi, **Ital.**	40N37	17E57	1h12E
Boende, **Zaire**	0s15	20E51	1h23E	Brioude, **Fr.**	45N18	3E23	0h14E
Bogor, **Indon.**	6s34	106E45	7h07E	Brisbane, **Aust.**	27s30	153E00	10h12E
Bogotá, **Col.**	4N38	74w05	4h56w	Bristol, **G.-B.**	51N27	2w35	0h10w
Boise, Id., **USA**	43N38	116w12	7h45w	Brive-la-Gaillarde, **Fr.**	45N09	1E32	0h06E
Bois-le-Duc, → *'s-Hertogenbosch,* **Nth.**				Brno, **Tch.**	49N13	16E40	1h07E
				Broken Hill, **Aust.**	31s57	141E30	9h26E
Boké, **Guin.**	10N57	14w13	0h57w	Bromberg, → *Bydgoszcz,* **Pol.**			

City	Lat.	Long.	Time	City	Lat.	Long.	Time
Brousse, → *Bursa*, **Tur.**				Calarasi, **Roum.**	44N12	27E22	1h49E
Brownsville, Tex., **USA**	25N54	97w30	6h30w	Calatayud, **Esp.**	41N21	1w39	0h07w
Bruay-en-Artois, **Fr.**	50N29	2E33	0h10E	Calcutta (Kalikata), **Ind.**	22N30	88E20	5h53E
Brugge (Bruges), **Belg.**	51N13	3E14	0h13E	Calgary, Alb., **Can.**	51N05	114w05	7h36w
Brünn, → *Brno*, **Tch.**				Cali, **Col.**	3N24	76w30	5h06w
Brunswick, → *Braunschweig*, **BRD**				Calicut, → *Kozhikode*, **Ind.**			
Bruxelles (Brussel), **Belg.**	50N50	4E21	0h17E	Callao, **Peru**	12s05	77w08	5h09w
Bryansk (Briansk), **URSS**	53N15	34E09	2h17E	Caltanissetta, **Ital.**	37N29	14E04	0h56E
Bucaramanga, **Col.**	7N08	73w10	4h53w	Camagüey, **Cuba**	21N25	77w55	5h12w
Buchanan, **Liber.**	5N57	10w02	0h40w	Cambrai, **Fr.**	50N10	3E14	0h13E
Buckingham, **G.-B.**	52N00	1w00	0h04w	Cambridge, **G.-B.**	52N12	0w07	0h00w
Bucuresti (Bucarest), **Roum.**	44N25	26E07	1h44E	Camden, NJ, **USA**	39N52	75w07	5h00w
Budapest, **Hong.**	47N30	19E03	1h16E	Campbell I., **Pac.O.**	52s30	169E00	11h16E
Budweis, → *Ceske Budejovice*, **Tch.**				Campina Grande, **Brasil**	7s15	35w50	2h23w
Buenaventura, **Col.**	3N54	77w02	5h08w	Campinas, **Brasil**	22s54	47w06	3h08w
Buenos Aires, **Arg.**	34s40	58w30	3h54w	Campoalegre, **Col.**	2N49	75w19	5h01w
Buffalo, NY, **USA**	42N52	78w55	5h16w	Campo Grande, **Brasil**	20s24	54w35	3h38w
Buga, **Col.**	3N53	76w17	5h05w	Campos, **Brasil**	21s46	41w21	2h45w
Builth Wells, **G.-B.**	52N09	3w24	0h14w	Canberra, **Aust.**	35s18	149E08	9h57E
Bujumbura, **Bur.**	3s22	29E19	1h57E	Candie, → *Iráklio*, **Grc.**			
Bukama, **Zaire**	9s13	25E52	1h43E	Cannes, **Fr.**	43N33	7E00	0h28E
Bukavu, **Zaire**	2s30	28E50	1h55E	Canterbury, **G.-B.**	51N17	1E05	0h04E
Bukhara (Boukhara), **URSS**	39N47	64E26	4h18E	Canton, Oh., **USA**	40N48	81w23	5h26w
Bukittinggi, **Indon.**	0s18	100E20	6h41E	Canton, → *Kouang-tcheou*, **China**			
Bulawayo, **Zimb.**	20s10	28E43	1h55E	Cape Coast, **Ghana**	5N10	1w13	0h05w
Bulle, **Sui.**	46N37	7E04	0h28E	Cape Town, **S.Afr.**	33s56	18E28	1h14E
Bundaberg, **Aust.**	24s50	152E21	10h09E	Cape Verde I. (Praia), **Atl.O.**	14N56	23w31	1h34w
Burgas (Bourgas), **Bulg.**	42N30	27E29	1h50E	Cap-Haïtien, **Haiti**	19N47	72w17	4h49w
Burgdorf (Berthoud), **Sui.**	47N03	7E38	0h31E	Caracal, **Roum.**	44N07	24E18	1h37E
Burgos, **Esp.**	42N21	3w41	0h15w	Caracas, **Ven.**	10N35	66w56	4h28w
Burlington, Vt., **USA**	44N28	73w14	4h53w	Carcassonne, **Fr.**	43N13	2E21	0h09E
Burnley, **G.-B.**	53N48	2w14	0h09w	Cardiff, **G.-B.**	51N30	3w13	0h13w
Bursa, **Tur.**	40N12	29E04	1h56E	Cardigan, **G.-B.**	52N06	4w40	0h19w
Bûr Said, **Egy.**	31N17	32E18	2h09E	Carleton Place, Ont., **Can.**	45N08	76w09	5h05w
Burton on Trent, **G.-B.**	52N48	1w36	0h06w	Carlisle, **G.-B.**	54N54	2w55	0h12w
Bussum, **Nth.**	52N17	5E10	0h21E	Carlow, **Irl.**	52N50	6w55	0h28w
Busto Arsizio, **Ital.**	45N37	8E51	0h35E	Carmarthen, **G.-B.**	51N52	4w19	0h17w
Butare, **Rwanda**	2s35	29E44	1h59E	Carolina, **Brasil**	7s20	47w25	3h10w
Butte, Mt., **USA**	46N00	112w31	7h30w	Carolinas I., → *Truk + Palau*, **Pac.O.**			
Buzau, **Roum.**	45N09	26E49	1h47E	Carpentras, **Fr.**	44N03	5E03	0h20E
Bydgoszcz, **Pol.**	53N16	18E00	1h12E	Carrara, **Ital.**	44N04	10E06	0h40E
Bytom (Beuthen), **Pol.**	50N21	18E51	1h15E	Carson City, Nev., **USA**	39N10	119w46	7h59w
				Cartagena, **Col.**	10N24	75w33	5h02w
*** C ***				Cartagena (Carthagène), **Esp.**	37N36	0w59	0h04w
				Cartago, **Col.**	4N45	75w55	5h04w
Cabimas, **Ven.**	10N26	71w27	4h46w	Caruarú, **Brasil**	8s15	35w55	2h24w
Cabinda, **Angola**	5s34	12E12	0h49E	Carúpano, **Ven.**	10N39	63w14	4h13w
Cáceres, **Esp.**	39N29	6w23	0h26w	Casablanca, → *Dar el Beida*, **Mar.**			
Cádiz, **Esp.**	36N32	6w18	0h25w	Caserta, **Ital.**	41N04	14E20	0h57E
Caen, **Fr.**	49N11	0w22	0h01w	Casper, Wyo., **USA**	42N50	106w20	7h05w
Caernarfon, **G.-B.**	53N08	4w16	0h17w	Castellammare di Stabia, **Ital.**	40N47	14E29	0h58E
Cagliari, Sardegne, **Ital.**	39N13	9E08	0h37E	Castellane, **Fr.**	43N50	6E30	0h26E
Cahors, **Fr.**	44N28	1E26	0h06E	Castellón de la Plana, **Esp.**	39N59	0w03	0h00w
Cairns, **Aust.**	16s51	145E43	9h43E	Castelo Branco, **Port.**	39N50	7w30	0h30w
Cairo, Ill., **USA**	37N01	89w09	5h57w	Castres, **Fr.**	43N36	2E14	0h09E
Cairo, → *Al Qahira*, **Egy.**				Castries, Sainte-Lucie, **Ant.P.**	14N01	60w59	4h04w
Cajamarca, **Peru**	7s09	78w32	5h14w	Catamarca, **Arg.**	28s28	65w46	4h23w
Cajàzeiras, **Brasil**	6s52	38w31	2h34w	Catania (Catane), **Ital.**	37N31	15E06	1h00E
Calabar, **Nig.**	4N56	8E22	0h33E	Catanzaro, **Ital.**	38N54	16E36	1h06E
Calabozo, **Ven.**	8N58	67w28	4h30w	Cawnpore, → *Kanpur*, **Ind.**			
Calais, **Fr.**	50N57	1E52	0h07E	Cayambe, **Ecuad.**	0N02	78w08	5h13w
Calama, **Chile**	22s30	68w55	4h36w	Cayenne, **Gu.Fr.**	4N55	52w18	3h29w

City	Lat.	Long.	Time	City	Lat.	Long.	Time
Ceará, → *Fortaleza*, **Brasil**				Chinju, **Cor.S.**	35N10	128E06	8h32E
Cebu, **Phil.**	10N17	123E56	8h16E	Chiraz, → *Shiraz*, **Iran**			
Cedar Rapids, Ia., **USA**	41N59	91w39	6h07w	Chisinau, → *Kishinev*, **URSS**			
Celle, **BRD**	52N37	10E05	0h40E	Chita, **URSS**	52N03	113E35	7h34E
Cerignola, **Ital.**	41N16	15E54	1h04E	Chittagong, **B.desh**	22N20	91E48	6h07E
Cernauti, → *Chernovtsy*, **URSS**				Chivilcoy, **Arg.**	34s55	60w00	4h00w
Cerro de Pasco, **Peru**	10s43	76w15	5h05w	Choisy-le-Roi, **Fr.**	48N47	2E26	0h10E
Cesena, **Ital.**	44N09	12E15	0h49E	Cholet, **Fr.**	47N04	0w53	0h04w
Ceske Budejovice, **Tch.**	48N58	14E29	0h58E	Chongjin, **Cor.N.**	41N50	129E55	8h40E
Ceuta, **Mar.**	35N53	5w19	0h21w	Chongju, **Cor.S.**	35N39	127E27	8h30E
Chagos (Tchagos) I., **Ind.O.**	6s00	72E00	4h48E	Chorzow, **Pol.**	50N19	18E56	1h16E
Châlons-sur-Marne, **Fr.**	48N58	4E22	0h17E	Christchurch, **N.Zel.**	43s33	172E40	11h31E
Chalon-sur-Saône, **Fr.**	46N47	4E51	0h19E	Christiana, → *Oslo*, **Nor.**			
Chambéry, **Fr.**	45N34	5E55	0h24E	Christmas I., **Ind.O.**	10s30	105E40	7h03E
Chañaral, **Chile**	26s23	70w40	4h43w	Chur (Coire), **Sui.**	46N52	9E32	0h38E
Chang-hai (Shanghai), **China**	31N13	121E25	8h06E	Ciénaga, **Col.**	11N01	74w15	4h57w
Chang-hua (Tchang-houa), **Taiwan**	24N06	120E31	8h02E	Cienfuegos, **Cuba**	22N10	80w27	5h22w
Chan-teou (Shantou), **China**	23N23	116E39	7h47E	Cimpina, **Roum.**	45N08	25E44	1h43E
Chao-kouan, → *Shaoguan*, **China**				Cincinnati, Oh., **USA**	39N10	85w00	5h40w
Charleroi, **Belg.**	50N25	4E27	0h18E	Cirebon (Tjirebon), **Indon.**	6s46	108E33	7h14E
Charleston, SC, **USA**	32N48	79w58	5h20w	Ciudad Bolívar, **Ven.**	8N06	63w36	4h14w
Charleston, WV, **USA**	38N23	81w40	5h27w	Ciudad Camargo, Chihuahua, **Mex.**	27N41	105w10	7h01w
Charlestown, Nevis, **Ant.P.**	17N08	62w37	4h10w	Ciudadela, **Bal.I.**	40N00	3E50	0h15E
Charleville-Mézières, **Fr.**	49N46	4E43	0h19E	Ciudad Guyana, **Ven.**	8N22	62w37	4h10w
Charlotte, NC, **USA**	35N03	80w50	5h23w	Ciudad Juárez, **Mex.**	31N42	106w29	7h06w
Charlottesville, Va., **USA**	38N02	78w29	5h14w	Ciudad Obregón, **Mex.**	27N28	109w59	7h20w
Charlottetown, PE, **Can.**	46N19	63w09	4h13w	Ciudad Real, **Esp.**	38N59	3w55	0h16w
Chartres, **Fr.**	48N27	1E30	0h06E	Ciudad Trujillo, → *Santo-Domingo*, **Dom.**			
Chascomas, **Arg.**	35s34	58w00	3h52w	Ciudad Victoria, **Mex.**	23N43	99w10	6h37w
Châteaubriant, **Fr.**	47N43	1w22	0h05w	Clermont-Ferrand, **Fr.**	45N47	3E05	0h12E
Châteaudun, **Fr.**	48N04	1E20	0h05E	Cleveland, Oh., **USA**	41N30	81w41	5h27w
Châteauroux, Indre, **Fr.**	46N49	1E41	0h07E	Cliperton I., **Pac.O.**	10N20	109w13	7h17w
Château-Thierry, **Fr.**	49N03	3E24	0h14E	Cluj (Kolozsvar), **Roum.**	46N47	23E37	1h34E
Châtellerault, **Fr.**	46N49	0E33	0h02E	Coblence, → *Koblenz*, **BRD**			
Chatham, **G.-B.**	51N23	0E32	0h02E	Coburg, **BRD**	50N15	10E58	0h44E
Chatham I., **Pac.O.**	44s00	176w00	11h44w	Cochabamba, **Bol.**	17s26	66w10	4h25w
Chattanooga, Tenn., **USA**	35N02	85w18	5h41w	Cochin, **Ind.**	9N56	76E15	5h05E
Chaumont, **Fr.**	48N07	5E08	0h21E	Cochrane, Ont., **Can.**	49N04	81w02	5h24w
Cheboksary, **URSS**	56N08	47E12	3h09E	Cognac, **Fr.**	45N42	0w19	0h01w
Chelmsford, **G.-B.**	51N44	0E28	0h02E	Coimbatore, **Ind.**	11N00	76E57	5h08E
Cheltenham, **G.-B.**	51N54	2w04	0h08w	Coimbra (Coïmbre), **Port.**	40N12	8w25	0h34w
Chelyabinsk, **URSS**	55N12	61E25	4h06E	Colchester, **G.-B.**	51N54	0E54	0h04E
Chemnitz, → *Karl-Marx-Stadt*, **DDR**				Colmar, **Fr.**	48N05	7E21	0h29E
Chen-yang (Shenyang), **China**	41N50	123E26	8h14E	Cologne, → *Köln*, **BRD**			
Cherbourg, **Fr.**	49N38	1w37	0h06w	Colombo, **Sr.Lka**	6N55	79E52	5h19E
Cherepovets, **URSS**	59N09	37E50	2h31E	Colón, **Cuba**	22N42	81w54	5h28w
Cherkassy, **URSS**	49N27	32E04	2h08E	Colón, **Panama**	9N21	79w54	5h20w
Chernigov, **URSS**	51N30	31E18	2h05E	Colorado Springs, Colo., **USA**	38N50	104w50	6h59w
Chernovtsy, **URSS**	48N19	25E52	1h43E	Columbia, SC, **USA**	34N00	81w00	5h24w
Chester, **G.-B.**	53N12	2w54	0h12w	Columbus, Ga., **USA**	32N30	84w58	5h40w
Chesterfield, **G.-B.**	53N15	1w25	0h06w	Columbus, Miss., **USA**	33N30	88w27	5h54w
Cheyenne, Wyo., **USA**	41N08	104w50	6h59w	Columbus, Oh., **USA**	39N59	83w03	5h32w
Chiang Mai (Chiengmai), **Thai.**	18N48	98E59	6h36E	Colwyn Bay, **G.-B.**	53N18	3w43	0h15w
Chiba, **Jap.**	35N38	140E07	9h20E	Comilla, **B.desh**	23N28	91E10	6h05E
Chicago, Ill., **USA**	41N50	87w45	5h51w	Commandeur I., **Pac.O.**	55N04	166E13	11h05E
Chiclayo, **Peru**	6s47	79w47	5h19w	Como (Côme), **Ital.**	45N48	9E05	0h36E
Chicoutimi, Que., **Can.**	48N26	71w06	4h44w	Comodoro Rivadavia, **Arg.**	45s50	67w30	4h30w
Chihuahua, **Mex.**	28N40	106w06	7h04w	Comores I., **Ind.O.**	11s40	43E16	2h53E
Chillán, **Chile**	36s37	72w10	4h49w	Compiègne, **Fr.**	49N25	2E50	0h11E
Chi-lung (Tsilong), **Taiwan**	25N10	121E43	8h07E	Conakry, **Guin.**	9N30	13w43	0h55w
Chimay, **Belg.**	50N03	4E20	0h17E	Concepción, **Chile**	36s50	73w03	4h52w
Chimbote, **Peru**	9s04	78w34	5h14w	Concepción, **Parag.**	23s22	57w26	3h50w
Chimkent, **URSS**	42N16	69E05	4h36E				

City	Lat.	Long.	Time	City	Lat.	Long.	Time
Concepción del Uruguay, **Arg.**	32s30	58w15	3h53w	Da Nang, **Viet.**	16n04	108e14	7h13e
Concordia, **Arg.**	31s25	58w00	3h52w	Danzig, → *Gdansk, Pol.*			
Constance, → *Konstanz,* **BRD**				Darbhanga, **Ind.**	26n10	85e54	5h44e
Constanta (Constantza), **Roum.**	44n12	28e40	1h55e	Dar el Beida, **Mar.**	33n39	7w35	0h30w
Constantine, **Alg.**	36n22	6e40	0h27e	Dar es Salaam, **Tanz.**	6s51	39e18	2h37e
Constantinople, → *Istanbul, Tur.*				Darjeeling, **Ind.**	27n02	88e20	5h53e
Copenhague, → *Köbenhavn,* **Dan.**				Darlington, **G.-B.**	54n31	1w34	0h06w
Copiapó, **Chile**	27s20	70w23	4h42w	Darmstadt, **BRD**	49n52	8e39	0h35e
Córdoba, **Arg.**	31s25	64w11	4h17w	Darnah (Derna), **Lib.**	32n46	22e39	1h31e
Córdoba (Cordoue), **Esp.**	37n53	4w46	0h19w	Darwin, **Aust.**	12s23	130e44	8h43e
Corfu (Corfou), **Grc.**	39n38	19e55	1h20e	Datu Piang, **Phil.**	7n02	124e30	8h18e
Corinthe, → *Kórinthos,* **Grc.**				Daugavpils, **URSS**	55n52	26e31	1h46e
Cork, **Irl.**	51n54	8w28	0h34w	Davao, **Phil.**	7n05	125e38	8h23e
Corner Brook, TN, **Can.**	48n58	57w58	3h52w	Davenport, Ia., **USA**	41n32	90w36	6h02w
Cornwall, Ont., **Can.**	45n02	74w45	4h59w	David, **Panama**	8n26	82w26	5h30w
Coro, **Ven.**	11n27	69w41	4h39w	Dawson, Yukon, **Can.**	64n04	139w24	9h18w
Coroico, **Bol.**	16s09	67w45	4h31w	Dawson Creek, Br.Col., **Can.**	55n44	120w15	8h01w
Corpus Christi, Tex., **USA**	27n47	97w26	6h30w	Dayton, Oh., **USA**	39n45	84w10	5h37w
Corrientes, **Arg.**	27s30	58w48	3h55w	De Aar, **S.Afr.**	30s40	24e01	1h36e
Coruche, **Port.**	38n58	8w31	0h34w	Debrecen, **Hong.**	47n30	21e37	1h26e
Cosenza, **Ital.**	39n17	16e16	1h05e	Debre Markos, **Eth.**	10n19	37e41	2h31e
Cotagaita, **Bol.**	20s47	65w40	4h23w	Decatur, Alab., **USA**	34n36	87w00	5h48w
Cotonou, **Benin**	6n24	2e31	0h10e	Decatur, Ill., **USA**	39n51	88w57	5h56w
Cottbus, **DDR**	51n43	14e21	0h57e	Dédougou, **H.Vol.**	12n29	3w25	0h14w
Courtrai, → *Kortrijk,* **Belg.**				Dehra Dun, **Ind.**	30n19	78e03	5h12e
Coventry, **G.-B.**	52n25	1w30	0h06w	Deir es Zor, **Syr.**	35n20	40e08	2h41e
Covilhao, **Port.**	40n17	7w30	0h30w	Delémont, **Sui.**	47n22	7e21	0h29e
Cracovie, → *Krakow,* **Pol.**				Delft, **Nth.**	52n01	4e21	0h17e
Craiova, **Roum.**	44n18	23e47	1h35e	Delhi (Dilli), **Ind.**	28n40	77e14	5h09e
Creil, **Fr.**	49n16	2e29	0h10e	Delmenhorst, **BRD**	53n03	8e37	0h34e
Cremona, **Ital.**	45n08	10e01	0h40e	Demmin, **DDR**	53n55	13e03	0h52e
Créteil, **Fr.**	48n47	2e28	0h10e	Denain, **Fr.**	50n19	3e24	0h14e
Crewe, **G.-B.**	53n05	2w27	0h10w	Dendermonde (Termonde), **Belg.**	51n02	4e06	0h16e
Crozet I., **Ind.O.**	46s00	52e00	3h28e	Den Haag, **Nth.**	52n05	4e16	0h17e
Cruzeiro do Sul, **Brasil**	7s40	72w39	4h51w	Den Helder, **Nth.**	52n58	4e46	0h19e
Cúcuta, **Col.**	7n55	72w31	4h50w	Denpaser, **Indon.**	8s40	115e14	7h41e
Cuenca, **Ecuad.**	2s54	79w00	5h16w	Denver, Colo., **USA**	39n45	105w00	7h00w
Cuenca, **Esp.**	40n04	2w07	0h08w	Dera Ismail Khan, **Pak.**	31n51	70e56	4h44e
Cuernavaca, **Mex.**	18n57	99w15	6h37w	Derby, **G.-B.**	52n55	1w30	0h06w
Cuiabá, **Brasil**	15s32	56w05	3h44w	Des Moines, Ia., **USA**	41n35	93w35	6h14w
Culiacán, **Mex.**	24n50	107w23	7h10w	Dessau, **DDR**	51n51	12e15	0h49e
Cumana, **Ven.**	10n29	64w12	4h17w	Detmold, **BRD**	51n55	8e50	0h35e
Cumberland, Md., **USA**	39n40	78w47	5h15w	Detroit, Mich., **USA**	42n23	83w05	5h32w
Curitiba, **Brasil**	25s25	49w25	3h18w	Deva, **Roum.**	45n53	22e55	1h32e
Curvelo, **Brasil**	18s45	44w27	2h58w	Deventer, **Nth.**	52n15	6e10	0h25e
Cuttack (Kataka), **Ind.**	20n26	85e56	5h44e	Dibay (Doubaï), → *Dubay,* **E.A.U.**			
Cuxhaven, **BRD**	53n52	8e42	0h35e	Diego Suarez, → *Antseranana,*			
Cuzco (Cusco), **Peru**	13s32	71w57	4h48w	**Madag.**			
Czestochowa, **Pol.**	50n49	19e07	1h16e	Diepholz, **BRD**	52n37	8e22	0h33e
				Dieppe, **Fr.**	49n55	1e05	0h04e
*** D ***				Diest, **Belg.**	50n58	5e03	0h20e
				Dietikon, **Sui.**	47n24	8e25	0h34e
				Digne, **Fr.**	44n05	6e14	0h25e
Dabola, **Guin.**	10n48	11w02	0h44w	Dijon, **Fr.**	47n20	5e02	0h20e
Dacca, **B.desh**	23n42	90e22	6h01e	Dili, **Indon.**	8s35	125e35	8h22e
Dairen, → *Ta-lien,* **China**				Dimashq, → *Damas,* **Syr.**			
Dakar, **Seneg.**	14n38	17w27	1h10w	Dinant, **Belg.**	50n16	4e55	0h20e
Dalaba, **Guin.**	10n47	12w12	0h49w	Dingwall, **G.-B.**	57n35	4w26	0h18w
Dallas, Tex., **USA**	32n47	96w48	6h27w	Diourbel, **Seneg.**	14n39	16w12	1h05w
Daloa, **C.Iv.**	6n56	6w28	0h26w	Diredaoua (Dire Dawa), **Eth.**	9n35	41e50	2h47e
Damanhur, **Egy.**	31n03	30e28	2h02e	Disuq, **Egy.**	31n09	30e39	2h03e
Damas (Esh Sham), **Syr.**	33n30	36e19	2h25e	Diyarbakir, **Tur.**	37n55	40e14	2h41e
Damiette (Dumyat), **Egy.**	31n26	31e48	2h07e	Djakarta, → *Jakarta,* **Indon.**			

City	Lat.	Long.	Time	City	Lat.	Long.	Time
Djambi (Jambi), → *Telanaipura*, **Indon.**				Dzaudzhikau, → *Ordzhonikidze*, **URSS**			
Djedda, → *Jeddah,* **Ar.S.**				Dzhambul (Djamboul), **URSS**	42N50	71E25	4h46E
Djenné, **Mali**	13N55	4w31	0h18w				
Djibouti, **Djib.**	11N36	43E09	2h53E				
Djokjakarta, → *Yogyakarta,* **Indon.**				*** E ***			
Djougou, **Benin**	9N40	1E47	0h07E				
Dnepropetrovsk, **URSS**	48N29	35E00	2h20E	Eastbourne, **G.-B.**	50N46	0E17	0h01E
Dogondoutchi, **Niger**	13N36	4E03	0h16E	East London, **S.Afr.**	33s00	27E54	1h52E
Doha (Ad Dawhah), **Qatar**	25N15	51E36	3h26E	Eau Claire, Wis., **USA**	44N50	91w30	6h06w
Dôle, **Fr.**	47N05	5E30	0h22E	Eberswalde, **DDR**	52N50	13E50	0h55E
Dolores, **Arg.**	36s23	57w44	3h51w	Echo Bay, NT, **Can.**	66N04	118w00	7h52w
Doncaster, **G.-B.**	53N32	1w07	0h04w	Ede, **Nth.**	52N03	5E40	0h23E
Donetsk, **URSS**	48N00	37E50	2h31E	Edea, **Cam.**	3N47	10E13	0h41E
Dorchester, Dorset, **G.-B.**	50N43	2w26	0h10w	Edesse, → *Urfa,* **Tur.**			
Dordrecht, **Nth.**	51N48	4E40	0h19E	Edimburgh, **G.-B.**	55N57	3w13	0h13w
Dornbirn, **Aut.**	47N25	9E46	0h39E	Edmonton, Alb., **Can.**	53N34	113w25	7h34w
Dorpat, → *Tartu,* **URSS**				Edmundston, NB, **Can.**	47N22	68w20	4h33w
Dortmund, **BRD**	51N32	7E27	0h30E	Eindhoven, **Nth.**	51N26	5E30	0h22E
Dosso, **Niger**	13N03	3E10	0h13E	Eisenach, **DDR**	50N59	10E19	0h41E
Douai, **Fr.**	50N22	3E05	0h12E	Eisenerz, **Aut.**	47N33	14E53	1h00E
Douala, **Cam.**	4N04	9E43	0h39E	Eisenstadt, **Aut.**	47N50	16E32	1h06E
Douglas, Man I., **G.-B.**	54N09	4w29	0h18w	Eisleben, **DDR**	51N32	11E33	0h46E
Douna, **Mali**	13N13	5w55	0h24w	Elath (Eilat), **Isr.**	29N33	34E57	2h20E
Dover, Del., **USA**	39N10	75w32	5h02w	Elberfeld, → *Wuppertal,* **BRD**			
Dover (Douvres), **G.-B.**	51N08	1E19	0h05E	Elblag (Elbing), **Pol.**	54N10	19E25	1h18E
Drachten, **Nth.**	53N07	6E06	0h24E	Elche, **Esp.**	38N16	0w41	0h03w
Draguignan, **Fr.**	43N32	6E28	0h26E	El-Djazair, → *Alger,* **Alg.**			
Dráma, **Grc.**	41N10	24E11	1h37E	Eldoret, **Kenya**	0N31	35E17	2h21E
Drammen, **Nor.**	59N45	10E15	0h41E	El Faiyoum, **Egy.**	29N19	30E50	2h03E
Dresden (Dresde), **DDR**	51N03	13E45	0h55E	El Fasher, **Sudan**	13N37	25E22	1h41E
Dreux, **Fr.**	48N44	1E23	0h06E	El Ferrol, **Esp.**	43N29	8w14	0h33w
Drogheda, **Irl.**	53N43	6w21	0h25w	Elgin, **G.-B.**	57N39	3w20	0h13w
Drumheller, Alb., **Can.**	51N25	112w40	7h31w	Elisabethville, → *Lubumbashi,* **Zaire**			
Dubay, **E.A.U.**	25N14	55E17	3h41E	El Jadida, **Mar.**	33N19	8w35	0h34w
Dublin, **Irl.**	53N20	6w15	0h25w	El Kef, **Tun.**	36N10	8E40	0h35E
Dubrovnik, **Youg.**	42N40	18E07	1h12E	Elko, Nev., **USA**	40N50	115w46	7h43w
Dubuque, Ia., **USA**	42N31	90w41	6h03w	El Ladhiqiya (Latakieh), **Syr.**	35N31	35E47	2h23E
Dudley, **G.-B.**	52N30	2w05	0h08w	El Mahalla el Kubra, **Egy.**	30N59	31E10	2h05E
Duha, → *Doha,* **Qatar**				El Manzala, **Egy.**	31N10	31E56	2h08E
Duisburg, **BRD**	51N26	6E45	0h27E	El Minya, **Egy.**	28N06	30E45	2h03E
Duluth, Minn., **USA**	46N45	92w10	6h09w	Elmshorn, **BRD**	53N46	9E40	0h39E
Dumbarton, **G.-B.**	55N57	4w35	0h18w	El Obeid, **Sudan**	13N11	30E10	2h01E
Dum Dum, **Ind.**	22N37	88E25	5h54E	El Paso, Tex., **USA**	31N45	106w29	7h06w
Dumfries, **G.-B.**	55N04	3w37	0h14w	El Tigre, **Ven.**	8N44	64w18	4h17w
Dünaburg, → *Daugavpils,* **URSS**				Emden, **BRD**	53N23	7E13	0h29E
Dunaujváros, **Hong.**	47N00	18E55	1h16E	Emmen, **Nth.**	52N47	6E55	0h28E
Dundalk, **Irl.**	54N01	6w25	0h26w	Encarnación, **Parag.**	27s20	55w50	3h43w
Dundee, **G.-B.**	56N28	3w00	0h12w	Ende, **Indon.**	8s51	121E40	8h07E
Dunedin, **N.Zel.**	45s52	170E30	11h22E	Enns, **Aut.**	48N13	14E28	0h58E
Dunfermline, **G.-B.**	56N04	3w29	0h14w	Enschede, **Nth.**	52N13	6E55	0h28E
Dunkerque, **Fr.**	51N02	2E23	0h10E	Entebbe, **Uganda**	0N04	32E27	2h10E
Dunkwa, **Ghana**	5N59	1w45	0h07w	Enugu, **Nig.**	6N20	7E30	0h30E
Dun Laoghaire, **Irl.**	53N17	6w08	0h25w	Epernay, **Fr.**	49N02	3E58	0h16E
Durango, **Mex.**	24N01	104w40	6h59w	Epinal, **Fr.**	48N10	6E28	0h26E
Durazno, **Urug.**	33s22	56w31	3h46w	Erbil, → *Arbil,* **Iraq**			
Durban, **S.Afr.**	29s53	31E00	2h04E	Erfurt, **DDR**	50N58	11E02	0h44E
Düren, **BRD**	50N48	6E30	0h26E	Erie, Pa., **USA**	42N07	80w05	5h20w
Durham, **G.-B.**	54N47	1w34	0h06w	Erlangen, **BRD**	49N36	11E02	0h44E
Durham, NC, **USA**	36N00	78w54	5h16w	Ermoupoli, Siros, **Grc.**	37N26	24E55	1h40E
Dushanbe (Douchambe), **URSS**	38N38	68E51	4h35E	Ernakulam, **Ind.**	10N00	76E16	5h05E
Düsseldorf, **BRD**	51N13	6E47	0h27E	Erzincan, **Tur.**	39N44	39E30	2h38E
Dvinsk, → *Daugavpils,* **URSS**							

City	Lat.	Long.	Time	City	Lat.	Long.	Time
Erzurum (Erzeroum), **Tur.**	39N57	41E17	2h45E	Fort Dodge, Ia., **USA**	42N31	94w10	6h17w
Esbjerg, **Dan.**	55N28	8E28	0h34E	Fort Lamy, → **N'djamena, Tchad**			
Esch-sur-Alzette, **Luxem.**	49N30	5E59	0h24E	Fort Smith, Ark., **USA**	35N22	94w27	6h18w
Esfahan, → *Ispahan*, **Iran**				Fort Victoria, **Zimb.**	20s10	30E49	2h03E
Eskilstuna, **Sue.**	59N22	16E31	1h06E	Fort Wayne, Ind., **USA**	41N05	85w08	5h41w
Eskisehir, **Tur.**	39N46	30E30	2h02E	Fort William, → *Thunder Bay*,			
Esmeraldas, **Ecuad.**	0N56	79w40	5h19w	**Can.**			
Esquel, **Arg.**	42s55	71w20	4h45w	Fort Worth, Tex., **USA**	32N45	97w20	6h29w
Essaouira, **Mar.**	31N30	9w48	0h39w	Fou-chouen (Fushun), **China**	41N51	123E53	8h16E
Essen, Westfalen, **BRD**	51N27	6E57	0h28E	Fougères, **Fr.**	48N21	1w12	0h05w
Estremoz, **Port.**	38N50	7w35	0h30w	Foumban, **Cam.**	5N43	10E50	0h43E
Etampes, **Fr.**	48N26	2E10	0h09E	Fou-sin (Fuxin), **China**	42N04	121E39	8h07E
Eugene, Ore., **USA**	44N03	123w04	8h12w	Fou-tcheou (Fuzhou), **China**	26N09	119E17	7h57E
Eupen, **Belg.**	50N38	6E02	0h24E	Franceville, **Gabon**	.1s40	13E31	0h54E
Eureka, Ca., **USA**	40N49	124w10	8h17w	Francistown, **Bots.**	21s11	27E32	1h50E
Euskirchen, **BRD**	50N40	6E47	0h27E	Frankfort, Ky., **USA**	38N11	84w53	5h40w
Evansville, Ind., **USA**	38N00	87w33	5h50w	Frankfurt am Main, **BRD**	50N06	8E41	0h35E
Evora, **Port.**	38N34	7w54	0h32w	Frauenfeld, **Sui.**	47N34	8E54	0h36E
Evreux, **Fr.**	49N03	1E11	0h05E	Fredericton, NB, **Can.**	45N57	66w40	4h27w
Evry, **Fr.**	48N38	2E34	0h10E	Frederikshavn, **Dan.**	57N28	10E33	0h42E
Exeter, **G.-B.**	50N43	3w31	0h14w	Fredrikstad, **Nor.**	59N15	10E55	0h44E
				Freetown, **S.Leo.**	8N30	13w17	0h53w
				Freiberg, **DDR**	50N55	13E21	0h53E
*** F ***				Freiburg im Breisgau, **BRD**	48N00	7E52	0h31E
				Fréjus, **Fr.**	43N26	6E44	0h27E
Facatativá, **Col.**	4N48	74w32	4h58w	Fresno, Ca., **USA**	36N41	119w47	7h59w
Fada-N'Gourma, **H.Vol.**	12N05	0E26	0h02E	Freudenstadt, **BRD**	48N28	8E25	0h34E
Faenza, **Ital.**	44N17	11E53	0h48E	Fribourg, **Sui.**	46N50	7E10	0h29E
Fairbanks, Alas., **USA**	64N50	147w50	9h51w	Friedberg, Hessen, **BRD**	50N20	8E45	0h35E
Faisalabad, **Pak.**	31N25	73E09	4h53E	Frunze (Frounze), **URSS**	42N53	74E46	4h59E
Falkirk, **G.-B.**	56N00	3w48	0h15w	Fujisawa, **Jap.**	35N22	139E29	9h18E
Falkland I. (Stanley), **Atl.O.**	51s42	57w50	3h51w	Fukui, **Jap.**	36N04	136E12	9h05E
Fall River, Mass., **USA**	41N42	71w08	4h45w	Fukuoka, Kyushu, **Jap.**	33N39	130E21	8h41E
Fargo, ND, **USA**	47N00	97w00	6h28w	Fukushima, Honshu, **Jap.**	37N44	140E28	9h22E
Faro, **Port.**	37N01	7w56	0h32w	Fukuyama, Honshu, **Jap.**	34N29	133E21	8h53E
Feira de Santana, **Brasil**	12s17	38w53	2h36w	Fulda, **BRD**	50N33	9E41	0h39E
Feldkirch, **Aut.**	47N15	9E38	0h39E	Funtua, **Nig.**	11N34	7E17	0h29E
Ferkéssédougou, **C.Iv.**	9N30	5w10	0h21w	Futuna I., **Pac.O.**	14s25	178w20	11h53w
Feroe I. (Torshaven), **Atl.O.**	62N01	6w45	0h27w				
Ferrara, **Ital.**	44N50	11E38	0h47E				
Fes (Fez), **Mar.**	34N05	5w00	0h20w	*** G ***			
Fianarantsoa, **Madag.**	21s27	47E05	3h08E				
Fidji I. (Suva), **Pac.O.**	18s08	178E25	11h54E	Gabès, **Tun.**	33N52	10E06	0h40E
Figueras, **Esp.**	42N16	2E57	0h12E	Gaborone, **Bots.**	24s45	25E55	1h44E
Firenze (Florence), **Ital.**	43N47	11E15	0h45E	Gadsden, Alab., **USA**	34N00	86w00	5h44w
Fiume, → *Rijeka*, **Youg.**				Gafsa, **Tun.**	34N28	8E43	0h35E
Flagstaff, Ariz., **USA**	35N12	111w38	7h27w	Gagnoa, **C.Iv.**	6N04	5w55	0h24w
Flensburg, **BRD**	54N47	9E27	0h38E	Galapagos I., **Pac.O.**	1s00	91w00	6h04w
Flessingue, **Nth.**	51N27	3E35	0h14E	Galashiels, **G.-B.**	55N37	2w49	0h11w
Flint, Mich., **USA**	43N03	83w40	5h35w	Galati (Galatz), **Roum.**	45N27	28E02	1h52E
Florence, Alab., **USA**	34N48	87w40	5h51w	Galle, **Sr.Lka.**	6N01	80E13	5h21E
Florence, SC, **USA**	34N12	79w44	5h19w	Gällivare, **Sue.**	67N10	20E40	1h23E
Floriano, **Brasil**	6s45	43w00	2h52w	Galveston, Tex., **USA**	29N17	94w48	6h19w
Florianopólis, **Brasil**	27s35	48w31	3h14w	Galway, **Irl.**	53N16	9w03	0h36w
Florida, **Urug.**	34s04	56w14	3h45w	Gambier I., **Pac.O.**	23s07	134w57	9h00w
Focsani, **Roum.**	45N41	27E12	1h49E	Gamboma, **Congo**	1s50	15E58	1h04E
Foggia, **Ital.**	41N28	15E33	1h02E	Gand, → *Gent*, **Belg.**			
Fohnsdorf, **Aut.**	47N13	14E40	0h59E	Gander, TN, **Can.**	48N58	54w34	3h38w
Foix, **Fr.**	42N58	1E38	0h07E	Gangtok, **Ind.**	27N20	88E39	5h55E
Foligno, **Ital.**	42N57	12E43	0h51E	Gao, **Mali**	16N19	0w09	0h01w
Forli, **Ital.**	44N14	12E02	0h48E	Gap, **Fr.**	44N33	6E05	0h24E
Fortaleza (Ceará), **Brasil**	3s45	38w35	2h34w	Gardelegen, **DDR**	52N33	11E24	0h46E
Fort-de-France, Martinique, **Ant.P.**	14N36	61w05	4h04w	Garden City, Kans., **USA**	37N57	100w54	6h44w

City	Lat.	Long.	Time	City	Lat.	Long.	Time
Garoua (Garwa), **Cam.**	9N17	13E22	0h53E	Goundam, **Mali**	16N27	3w39	0h15w
Gary, Ind., **USA**	41N34	87w20	5h49w	Gouré, **Niger**	13N59	10E15	0h41E
Garzón, **Col.**	2N14	75w37	5h02w	Governador Valadares, **Brasil**	18s51	41w57	2h48w
Gävle, **Sue.**	60N41	17E10	1h09E	Goya, **Arg.**	29s10	59w15	3h57w
Gaya, **Ind.**	24N48	85E00	5h40E	Granada (Grenade), **Esp.**	37N10	3w35	0h14w
Gaza, **Egy.**	31N30	34E28	2h18E	Granby, Que., **Can.**	45N23	72w44	4h51w
Gaziantep, **Tur.**	37N04	37E21	2h29E	Grand Bassam, **C.Iv.**	5N14	3w45	0h15w
Gdansk, **Pol.**	54N22	18E41	1h15E	Grand Bourg, Marie Galante,			
Gdynia (Gdingen), **Pol.**	54N31	18E30	1h14E	**Ant.P.**	15N53	61w19	4h05w
Gedaref, **Sudan**	14N01	35E24	2h22E	Grande Prairie, Alb., **Can.**	55N10	118w52	7h55w
Geelong, **Aust.**	38s10	144E26	9h38E	Grand Forks, ND, **USA**	47N57	97w05	6h28w
Géla, **Ital.**	37N04	14E15	0h57E	Grand Island, Neb., **USA**	40N56	98w21	6h33w
Gelsenkirchen, **BRD**	51N30	7E05	0h28E	Grand Junction, Colo., **USA**	39N04	108w33	7h14w
Genève, **Sui.**	46N12	6E09	0h25E	Grand Rapids, Mich., **USA**	42N57	86w40	5h47w
Genova (Gênes), **Ital.**	44N24	8E56	0h36E	Granges (Grenchen), **Sui.**	47N13	7E24	0h30E
Gent, **Belg.**	51N02	3E42	0h15E	Granollers, **Esp.**	41N37	2E18	0h09E
Genthin, **DDR**	52N25	12E10	0h49E	Grantham, **G.-B.**	52N55	0w39	0h03w
Georgetown, **Guyana**	6N46	58w10	3h53w	Grasse, **Fr.**	43N40	6E56	0h28E
George Town, → *Penang,* **Malay.**				Graudenz, → *Grudziadz,* **Pol.**			
Gera, **DDR**	50N51	12E11	0h49E	Graz, **Aut.**	47N05	15E22	1h01E
Geraldton, **Aust.**	28s49	114E36	7h38E	Great Falls, Mt., **USA**	47N30	111w16	7h25w
Germiston, **S.Afr.**	26s15	28E10	1h53E	Great Yarmouth, **G.-B.**	52N37	1E44	0h07E
Gerona (Girona), **Esp.**	41N59	2E49	0h11E	Green Bay, Wis., **USA**	44N32	88w00	5h52w
Gex, **Fr.**	46N20	6E03	0h24E	Greenock, **G.-B.**	55N57	4w45	0h19w
Ghardaïa, **Alg.**	32N20	3E40	0h15E	Greensboro, NC, **USA**	36N03	79w50	5h19w
Ghazni, **Afg.**	33N33	68E28	4h34E	Greenville, SC, **USA**	34N52	82w25	5h30w
Gibraltar, **Esp.**	36N09	5w21	0h21w	Greenwich, **G.-B.**	51N29	0w00	0h00w
Giessen, **BRD**	50N35	8E42	0h35E	Greenwood, Miss., **USA**	33N31	90w10	6h01w
Gifu, **Jap.**	35N27	136E46	9h07E	Greifswald, **DDR**	54N06	13E24	0h54E
Gijón, **Esp.**	43N32	5w40	0h23w	Greiz, **DDR**	50N40	12E11	0h49E
Girardot, **Col.**	4N19	74w47	4h59w	Grenoble, **Fr.**	45N11	5E43	0h23E
Gisborne, **N.Zel.**	38s41	178E02	11h52E	Grimsby, **G.-B.**	53N35	0w05	0h00w
Giurgiu, **Roum.**	43N53	25E58	1h44E	Grodno, **URSS**	53N40	23E50	1h35E
Gizeh, → *Guizeh,* **Egy.**				Groningen, **Nth.**	53N13	6E35	0h26E
Gladbach, → *Mönchengladbach,*				Grosseto, **Ital.**	42N46	11E07	0h44E
BRD				Groznyi, **URSS**	43N21	45E42	3h03E
Glarus (Glaris), **Sui.**	47N03	9E04	0h36E	Grudziadz, **Pol.**	53N29	18E45	1h15E
Glasgow, **G.-B.**	55N53	4w15	0h17w	Guadalajara, **Esp.**	40N37	3w10	0h13w
Gliwice (Gleiwitz), **Pol.**	50N20	18E40	1h15E	Guadalajara, **Mex.**	20N40	103w20	6h53w
Gloucester, **G.-B.**	51N53	2w14	0h09w	Guadix, **Esp.**	37N19	3w08	0h13w
Gmünd, **Aut.**	48N47	14E59	1h00E	Gualeguay, **Arg.**	33s10	59w14	3h57w
Gmunden, **Aut.**	47N56	13E48	0h55E	Guam I., **Pac.O.**	13N30	144E45	9h39E
Gniezno, **Pol.**	52N32	17E32	1h10E	Guantánamo, **Cuba**	20N09	75w14	5h01w
Godthab (Groenland), **Dan.**	64N15	51w35	3h26w	Guaqui, **Bol.**	16s38	68w50	4h35w
Goiânia, **Brasil**	16s43	49w18	3h17w	Guaranda, **Ecuad.**	1s36	79w30	5h18w
Gomel, **URSS**	52N25	31E00	2h04E	Guarda, **Port.**	40N32	7w17	0h29w
Gonaïves, **Haiti**	19N29	72w42	4h51w	Guatemala, **Guat.**	14N38	90w22	6h01w
Gondar (Gonder), **Eth.**	12N39	37E29	2h30E	Guayaquil, **Ecuad.**	2s13	79w54	5h20w
Göppingen, **BRD**	48N43	9E39	0h39E	Guelma, **Alg.**	36N29	7E25	0h30E
Gorakhpur, **Ind.**	26N45	83E23	5h34E	Guelph, Ont., **Can.**	43N34	80w16	5h21w
Gore, **Eth.**	8N10	35E29	2h22E	Guéret, **Fr.**	46N10	1E52	0h07E
Gorgan, **Iran**	36N50	54E29	3h38E	Guildford, **G.-B.**	51N14	0w35	0h02w
Gorkiy, **URSS**	56N20	44E00	2h56E	Guizeh, **Egy.**	29N59	31E07	2h04E
Görlitz, **DDR**	51N09	15E00	1h00E	Gujranwala, **Pak.**	32N06	74E11	4h57E
Gorontalo, **Indon.**	0N33	123E05	8h12E	Gummersbach, **BRD**	51N02	7E34	0h30E
Gorzow Wielkopolski, **Pol.**	52N42	15E12	1h01E	Guntur, **Ind.**	16N20	80E27	5h22E
Goslar, **BRD**	51N55	10E25	0h42E	Guryev (Gouriev), **URSS**	47N08	51E59	3h28E
Göteborg, **Sue.**	57N45	12E00	0h48E	Gustavia, Saint-Barthélémy, **Ant.P.**	17N55	62w50	4h11w
Gotha, **DDR**	50N57	10E43	0h43E	Güstrow, **DDR**	53N48	12E11	0h49E
Göttingen, **BRD**	51N32	9E57	0h40E	Gütersloh, **BRD**	51N54	8E22	0h33E
Gottwaldov, **Tch.**	49N14	17E40	1h11E	Gwalior, **Ind.**	26N12	78E09	5h13E
Gouda, **Nth.**	52N01	4E43	0h19E	Gwelo, **Zimb.**	19s25	29E50	1h59E
Goulimine, **Mar.**	28N56	10w04	0h40w	Gyöngyös, **Hong.**	47N46	20E00	1h20E

City	Lat.	Long.	Time	City	Lat.	Long.	Time
Györ (Raab), **Hong.**	47N41	17E40	1h11E	Heard I., **Ind.O.**	53s10	73E30	4h54E
				Hebron (El Khalil), **Jord.**	31N32	35E06	2h20E
				Heerlen, **Nth.**	50N53	5E59	0h24E
*** H ***				Heidelberg, **BRD**	49N25	8E42	0h35E
				Heidenheim, Württemberg, **BRD**	48N41	10E10	0h41E
Haarlem, **Nth.**	52N23	4E38	0h19E	Heilbronn, **BRD**	49N08	9E14	0h37E
Hachinohe, **Jap.**	40N30	141E30	9h26E	Helena, Mt., **USA**	46N35	112w00	7h28w
Hadera, **Isr.**	32N26	34E55	2h20E	Heliopolis, **Egy.**	30N06	31E17	2h05E
Haderslev, **Dan.**	55N15	9E30	0h38E	Helmond, **Nth.**	51N28	5E40	0h23E
Haeju, **Cor.N.**	38N04	125E40	8h23E	Helsingborg, **Sue.**	56N05	12E45	0h51E
Hagen, Westfalen, **BRD**	51N22	7E27	0h30E	Helsingor (Elseneur), **Dan.**	56N03	12E38	0h51E
Hagerstown, Md., **USA**	39N39	77w44	5h11w	Helsinki (Helsingfors), **Finl.**	60N08	25E00	1h40E
Haidarabad, → *Hyderabad,* **Ind.**				Hengelo, **Nth.**	52N16	6E46	0h27E
Haïfa, **Isr.**	32N49	34E59	2h20E	Heng-yang, **China**	26N58	112E31	7h30E
Hai-keou (Haikou), **China**	20N05	110E25	7h22E	Henzada, **Birm.**	17N36	95E26	6h22E
Haïphong, **Viet.**	20N50	106E41	7h07E	Herat, **Afg.**	34N20	62E10	4h09E
Hakodate, **Jap.**	41N46	140E44	9h23E	Hereford, **G.-B.**	52N04	2w43	0h11w
Halab, **Syr.**	36N14	37E10	2h29E	Herford, **BRD**	52N07	8E40	0h35E
Halberstadt, **DDR**	51N54	11E04	0h44E	Herisau, **Sui.**	47N23	9E17	0h37E
Haldensleben, **DDR**	52N18	11E25	0h46E	Hermannstadt, → *Sibiu,* **Roum.**			
Halifax, NE, **Can.**	44N38	63w35	4h14w	Hermosillo, **Mex.**	29N15	110w59	7h24w
Halifax, **G.-B.**	53N44	1w52	0h07w	Herne, **BRD**	51N32	7E12	0h29E
Halle, **DDR**	51N28	11E58	0h48E	Herning, **Dan.**	56N08	8E59	0h36E
Halle (Hal), **Belg.**	50N44	4E14	0h17E	Hertford, **G.-B.**	51N48	0w05	0h00w
Hallein, **Aut.**	47N41	13E06	0h52E	Herzliya, **Isr.**	32N10	34E50	2h19E
Halmstad, **Sue.**	56N41	12E55	0h52E	Hexham, **G.-B.**	54N58	2w06	0h08w
Hama (Hamah), **Syr.**	35N09	36E44	2h27E	Hia-men (Xiamen), **China**	24N28	118E05	7h52E
Hamadhan, **Iran**	34N46	48E35	3h14E	Hildesheim, **BRD**	52N09	9E58	0h40E
Hamamatsu, **Jap.**	34N42	137E42	9h11E	Hilversum, **Nth.**	52N14	5E10	0h21E
Hamar, **Nor.**	60N57	10E55	0h44E	Himeji, **Jap.**	34N50	134E40	8h59E
Hamburg, **BRD**	53N33	10E00	0h40E	Hindenburg, → *Zabrze,* **Pol.**			
Hämeenlinna, **Finl.**	61N00	24E25	1h38E	Hiroshima, **Jap.**	34N23	132E27	8h50E
Hameln, **BRD**	52N07	9E22	0h37E	Hitachi, **Jap.**	36N35	140E40	9h23E
Hamhung, **Cor.N.**	39N54	127E35	8h30E	Hoa Binh, **Viet.**	20N49	105E20	7h01E
Hamilton, Ont., **Can.**	43N15	79w50	5h19w	Hobart, **Aust.**	42s54	147E18	9h49E
Hamilton, **G.-B.**	55N47	4w03	0h16w	Ho-Chi-Minh, **Viet.**	10N46	106E43	7h07E
Hamilton, **N.Zel.**	37s46	175E18	11h41E	Hof, **BRD**	50N19	11E56	0h48E
Hamm, **BRD**	51N40	7E49	0h31E	Ho-fei (Hefei), **China**	31N55	117E18	7h49E
Hang-tcheou (Hangzhou), **China**	30N18	120E07	8h00E	Holguín, **Cuba**	20N54	76w15	5h05w
Haniá (Khania), **Grc.**	35N30	24E04	1h36E	Hollandia, → *Jayapura,* **Indon.**			
Hannibal, Mo., **USA**	39N41	91w20	6h05w	Holyhead, **G.-B.**	53N19	4w38	0h19w
Hannover (Hanovre), **BRD**	52N23	9E44	0h39E	Homburg, Rheinland-Pfalz, **BRD**	49N20	7E20	0h29E
Hanoi, **Viet.**	21N01	105E52	7h03E	Homs, **Syr.**	34N44	36E43	2h27E
Han-yang, **China**	30N37	114E02	7h36E	Honda, **Col.**	5N15	74w50	4h59w
Hararé, **Zimb.**	17s43	31E05	2h04E	Hongkong, → *Kowloon + Victoria,*			
Harat, → *Herat,* **Afg.**				**H.K.**			
Harbin, **China**	45N45	126E41	8h27E	Honiara, **Sal.I.**	9s28	159E57	10h40E
Harer (Harar), **Eth.**	9N20	42E10	2h49E	Honolulu, Hawaii, **USA**	21N19	157w50	10h31w
Hargeisa, **Somal.**	9N31	44E02	2h56E	Hoogeveen, **Nth.**	52N43	6E29	0h26E
Harlem, → *Haarlem,* **Nth.**				Horsens, Vejle, **Dan.**	55N53	9E53	0h40E
Harrisburg, Pa., **USA**	40N18	76w49	5h07w	Horten, **Nor.**	59N25	10E30	0h42E
Harrogate, **G.-B.**	54N00	1w33	0h06w	Houston, Tex., **USA**	29N45	95w25	6h22w
Hartford, Conn., **USA**	41N45	72w42	4h51w	Howrah, **Ind.**	22N35	88E20	5h53E
Hartlepool, **G.-B.**	54N41	1w13	0h05w	Hradec Králové (Königgrätz), **Tch.**	50N13	15E50	1h03E
Harwich, **G.-B.**	51N57	1E17	0h05E	Hsin-chu (Sintchou), **Taiwan**	24N48	120E59	8h04E
Hasselt, **Belg.**	50N56	5E20	0h21E	Huacho, **Peru**	11s05	77w36	5h10w
Hastings, **G.-B.**	50N51	0E36	0h02E	Huambo, **Angola**	12s47	15E44	1h03E
Hastings, **N.Zel.**	39s39	176E52	11h47E	Huancayo, **Peru**	12s05	75w12	5h01w
Hattiesburg, Miss., **USA**	31N20	89w19	5h57w	Huánuco, **Peru**	9s55	76w11	5h05w
Hawick, **G.-B.**	55N25	2w47	0h11w	Huaráz, **Peru**	9s33	77w31	5h10w
Hawkesbury, Ont., **Can.**	45N36	74w38	4h59w	Hubli, **Ind.**	15N20	75E14	5h01E
Hay River, NT, **Can.**	60N51	115w42	7h43w	Huddersfield, **G.-B.**	53N39	1w47	0h07w
Hazelton, Br.Col., **Can.**	55N15	127w38	8h31w	Hudson Bay, Sask., **Can.**	52N51	102w23	6h50w

44

City	Lat.	Long.	Time	City	Lat.	Long.	Time
Huê, Viet.	16N28	107E35	7h10E	Islamabad, Pak.	33N40	73E08	4h53E
Huelva, Esp.	37N15	6w56	0h28w	Ismaïlia, Egy.	30N36	32E15	2h09E
Huesca, Esp.	42N08	0w25	0h02w	Ispahan, Iran	32N41	51E41	3h27E
Huhehot, China	40N49	111E37	7h26E	Issoudun, Fr.	46N57	1E59	0h08E
Hull, G.-B.	53N45	0w20	0h01w	Istanbul, Tur.	41N02	28E57	1h56E
Humaitá, Brasil	7s33	63w01	4h12w	Itzehoe, BRD	53N56	9E32	0h38E
Hungnam, Cor.N.	39N49	127E40	8h31E	Ivanovo, URSS	57N00	41E00	2h44E
Huntington, WV, USA	38N24	82w26	5h30w	Iwo, Nig.	7N38	4E11	0h17E
Huntsville, Alab., USA	34N44	86w35	5h46w	Izhevsk (Ijevsk), URSS	56N49	53E11	3h33E
Husavik, Isl.	66N03	17w17	1h09w	Izmir, Tur.	38N25	27E10	1h49E
Huttwill, Sui.	47N07	7E51	0h31E	Izmit, Tur.	40N47	29E55	2h00E
Huy (Hoei), Belg.	50N32	5E14	0h21E				
Hyderabad, Ind.	17N22	78E26	5h14E				
Hyderabad, Pak.	25N23	68E24	4h34E	*** J ***			
Hyères, Fr.	43N07	6E08	0h25E				
				Jabalpur, Ind.	23N10	79E59	5h20E
				Jackson, Miss., USA	32N20	90w11	6h01w
*** I ***				Jackson, Tenn., USA	35N37	88w50	5h55w
				Jacksonville, Fla., USA	30N20	81w40	5h27w
Iaroslav, → Yaroslav, URSS				Jacmel, Haiti	18N18	72w32	4h50w
Iasi (Jassy), Roum.	47N09	27E38	1h51E	Jaén, Esp.	37N46	3w48	0h15w
Ibadan, Nig.	7N23	3E56	0h16E	Jaffna, Sr.Lka	9N40	80E01	5h20E
Ibagué, Col.	4N25	75w20	5h01w	Jaipur, Rajasthan, Ind.	26N53	75E50	5h03E
Ibarra, Ecuad.	0N23	78w05	5h12w	Jakarta (Djakarta), Indon.	6s08	106E45	7h07E
Ibiza, Bal.I.	38N54	1E26	0h06E	Jalai Kut (Jalalabad), Afg.	34N26	70E25	4h42E
Ichikawa, Jap.	35N45	139E55	9h20E	Jalapa Enríquez, Mex.	19N32	96w56	6h28w
Iekaterinburg, → Sverdlovsk, URSS				Jamestown, ND, USA	46N54	98w42	6h35w
Iekaterinodar, → Krasnodar, URSS				Jamestown, NY, USA	42N05	79w15	5h17w
Iekaterinoslav, → Dnepropetrovsk, URSS				Jammu, Ind.	32N43	74E54	5h00E
				Jamnagar, Ind.	22N28	70E06	4h40E
Ielisavetgrad, → Kirovograd, URSS				Jamshedpur, Ind.	22N47	86E12	5h45E
Ieper (Ypres), Belg.	50N21	2E53	0h12E	Jan Mayen I., Atl.O.	71N00	8w10	0h33w
Ife, Nig.	7N33	4E34	0h18E	Jasper, Alb., Can.	52N55	118w05	7h52w
Ilesha, Nig.	7N39	4E38	0h19E	Jayapura (Djajapura), Indon.	2N28	140E38	9h23E
Ilhéus, Brasil	14s50	39w06	2h36w	Jeddah, Ar.S.	21N30	39E10	2h37E
Illapel, Chile	31s40	71w13	4h45w	Jefferson City, Mo., USA	38N33	92w10	-6h09w
Ilmenau, DDR	50N41	10E55	0h44E	Jelenia Gora, Pol.	50N55	15E45	1h03E
Iloilo, Phil.	10N41	122E33	8h10E	Jena (Iéna), DDR	50N56	11E35	0h46E
Ilorin, Nig.	8N32	4E34	0h18E	Jenin, Jord.	32N28	35E18	2h21E
Imbabah, Egy.	30N05	31E12	2h05E	Jequié, Brasil	13s52	40w06	2h40w
Imola, Ital.	44N22	11E43	0h47E	Jerez de la Frontera, Esp.	36N41	6w08	0h25w
Impfondo, Congo	1N36	18E00	1h12E	Jericho, Jord.	31N51	35E27	2h22E
Inchon, Cor.S.	37N30	126E38	8h27E	Jersey City, NJ, USA	40N43	74w03	4h56w
Indianapolis, Ind., USA	39N45	86w10	5h45w	Jerusalem (Yerushalayim), Isr.	31N47	35E13	2h21E
Indore (Indaor), Ind.	22N42	75E54	5h04E	Jhang Maghiana, Pak.	31N19	72E22	4h49E
Ingolstadt, BRD	48N46	11E27	0h46E	Jhansi, Ind.	25N27	78E34	5h14E
Inhambane, Moz.	23s51	35E29	2h22E	Jimma (Djimma), Eth.	7N39	36E47	2h27E
Innsbruck, Aut.	47N17	11E25	0h46E	Jinja-Bugembe, Uganda	0N27	33E14	2h13E
Inowroclaw, Pol.	52N49	18E12	1h13E	Jipijapa, Ecuad.	1s23	80w35	5h22w
Interlaken, Sui.	46N42	7E52	0h31E	Joao Pessoa (Paraiba), Brasil	7s06	34w53	2h20w
Invercargill, N.Zel.	46s26	168E21	11h13E	Jodhpur, Ind.	26N18	73E08	4h53E
Inverness, G.-B.	57N27	4w15	0h17w	Johannesburg, S.Afr.	26s10	28E02	1h52E
Ioánina, Grc.	39N40	20E51	1h23E	Johore Bharu, Malay.	1N29	103E44	6h55E
Ipoh, Malay.	4N36	101E02	6h44E	Jönköping, Sue.	57N45	14E10	0h57E
Ipswich, G.-B.	52N04	1E10	0h05E	Jonquière, Que., Can.	48N25	71w16	4h45w
Iquique, Chile	20s15	70w08	4h41w	Juan Fernandez I., Pac.O.	33s38	78w30	5h14w
Iquitos, Peru	3s51	73w13	4h53w	Juchitán, Mex.	16N27	95w05	6h20w
Iraklio (Heraklion), Grc.	35N20	25E08	1h41E	Judenburg, Aut.	47N10	14E40	0h59E
Irapuato, Mex.	20N40	101w30	6h46w	Juiz de Fora, Brasil	21s47	43w23	2h54w
Irbid, Jord.	32N33	35E51	2h23E	Jullundur, Ind.	31N18	75E40	5h03E
Irkutsk, URSS	52N18	104E15	6h57E	Junín, Buenos Aires, Arg.	34s34	60w55	4h04w
Iseyin, Nig.	7N59	3E40	0h15E	Jüterborg, DDR	51N59	13E05	0h52E
Iskenderun, Tur.	36N37	36E08	2h25E	Jyväskylä, Finl.	62N16	25E50	1h43E

City	Lat.	Long.	Time	City	Lat.	Long.	Time
				Kaunas, **URSS**	54N52	23E55	1h36 E
				Kaura Namoda, **Nig.**	12N39	6E38	0h27 E
*** K ***				Kavala, **Grc.**	40N57	24E28	1h38 E
Kabul, **Afg.**	34N30	69E10	4h37 E	Kawasaki, **Jap.**	35N32	139E41	9h19 E
Kaduna, **Nig.**	10N28	7E25	0h30 E	Kayes, **Mali**	14N26 ·	11w28	0h46 w
Kaédi, **Maur.**	16N12	13w32	0h54 w	Kayseri, **Tur.**	38N42	35E28	2h22 E
Kaesong, **Cor.N.**	37N59	126E30	8h26 E	Kazan, **URSS**	55N45	49E10	3h17 E
Kagoshima, **Jap.**	31N37	130E32	8h42 E	Kazanluk, **Bulg.**	42N37	25E23	1h42 E
Kai-fong (Kaifeng), **China**	34N47	114E20	7h37 E	Kecskemet, **Hong.**	46N56	19E43	1h19 E
Kairouan, **Tun.**	35N42	10E01	0h40 E	Kediri, **Indon.**	7s45	112E01	7h28 E
Kaiserlautern, **BRD**	49N27	7E47	0h31 E	Keetmanshoop, **Namib.**	26s36	18E08	1h13 E
Kajaani, **Finl.**	64N12	27E45	1h51 E	Kemerovo, **URSS**	55N25	86E05	5h44 E
Kalamáta, **Grc.**	37N02	22E07	1h28 E	Kemi, **Finl.**	65N46	24E34	1h38 E
Kalgan, → *Tchang-kia-keou,* **China**				Kempten, Bayern, **BRD**	47N44	10E19	0h41 E
Kalgoorlie, **Aust.**	30s49	121E29	8h06 E	Kenitra, **Mar.**	34N20	6w34	0h26 w
Kalinin, **URSS**	56N49	35E57	2h24 E	Kenora, Ont., **Can.**	49N47	94w26	6h18 w
Kaliningrad, **URSS**	54N40	20E30	1h22 E	Kerch, **URSS**	45N22	36E27	2h26 E
Kalisz, Poznan, **Pol.**	51N46	18E02	1h12 E	Kerguelen I., **Ind.O.**	49s33	69E49	4h39 E
Kalmar, **Sue.**	56N39	16E20	1h05 E	Kerkyra, → *Corfu,* **Grc.**			
Kaluga, **URSS**	54N31	36E16	2h25 E	Kermadec I., **Pac.O.**	30s00	178w00	11h52 w
Kamensk Uralskiy, **URSS**	56N29	61E49	4h07 E	Kerman, **Iran**	30N18	57E05	3h48 E
Kamina, **Zaire**	8s46	25E00	1h40 E	Kermanshah, **Iran**	34N19	47E04	3h08 E
Kamloops, Br.Col., **Can.**	50N39	120w24	8h02 w	Ketou, **Benin**	7N25	2E45	0h11 E
Kampala, **Uganda**	0N19	32E35	2h10 E	Kettering, **G.-B.**	52N24	0w44	0h03 w
Kamp-Lintfort, **BRD**	51N30	6E33	0h26 E	Khabarovsk, **URSS**	48N32	135E08	9h01 E
Kampot, **Kamp.**	10N37	104E11	6h57 E	Kharagpur, **Ind.**	22N23	87E22	5h49 E
Kananga, **Zaire**	5s53	22E26	1h30 E	Kharbin, → *Harbin,* **China**			
Kanazawa, **Jap.**	36N35	136E38	9h07 E	Kharkov, **URSS**	50N00	36E15	2h25 E
Kandahar, **Afg.**	31N36	65E47	4h23 E	Khartoum (El Khartum), **Sudan**	15N33	32E35	2h10 E
Kandi, **Benin**	11N05	2E59	0h12 E	Khaskovo, **Bulg.**	41N57	25E32	1h42 E
Kandy, **Sr.Lka**	7N17	80E40	5h23 E	Khenifra, **Mar.**	33N00	5w40	0h23 w
Kango, **Gabon**	0N15	10E11	0h41 E	Kherson, **URSS**	46N39	32E38	2h11 E
Kankan, **Guin.**	10N22	9w11	0h37 w	Khouribga, **Mar.**	32N54	6w57	0h28 w
Kano, **Nig.**	12N00	8E31	0h34 E	Kiang-men (Jiangmen), **China**	22N40	113E05	7h32 E
Kanpur, **Ind.**	26N27	80E14	5h21 E	Kidderminster, **G.-B.**	52N23	2w14	0h09 w
Kansas City, Kans., **USA**	39N05	94w37	6h18 w	Kiel, **BRD**	54N20	10E08	0h41 E
Kan-tcheou (Ganzhou), **China**	25N52	114E51	7h39 E	Kielce, **Pol.**	50N51	20E39	1h23 E
Kanye, **Bots.**	24s59	25E19	1h41 E	Kieta, **Pap.**	6s15	155E37	10h22 E
Kao-hsiung (Kaohiong), **Taiwan**	22N36	120E17	8h01 E	Kiev, → *Kiyev,* **URSS**			
Kaolack, **Seneg.**	14N09	16w08	1h05 w	Kigali, **Rwanda**	1s56	30E04	2h00 E
Kapfenberg, **Aut.**	47N27	15E18	1h01 E	Kilchu, **Cor.N.**	40N55	129E21	8h37 E
Kaposvar, **Hong.**	46N21	17E49	1h11 E	Kilkenny, **Irl.**	52N39	7w15	0h29 w
Karachi, **Pak.**	24N51	67E02	4h28 E	Killarney, **Irl.**	52N03	9w30	0h38 w
Karaganda, **URSS**	49N53	73E07	4h52 E	Kilmarnock, **G.-B.**	55N37	4w30	0h18 w
Karbala (Karbela), **Iraq**	32N37	44E03	2h56 E	Kimberley, **S.Afr.**	28s45	24E46	1h39 E
Karl-Marx-Stadt, **DDR**	50N50	12E55	0h52 E	Kindia, **Guin.**	10N03	12w49	0h51 w
Karlovac, **Youg.**	45N30	15E34	1h02 E	Kineshma, **URSS**	57N28	42E08	2h49 E
Karlsruhe, **BRD**	49N00	8E24	0h34 E	King's Lynn, **G.-B.**	52N45	0E24	0h02 E
Karlstad, **Sue.**	59N24	13E32	0h54 E	Kingston, Ont., **Can.**	44N14	76w30	5h06 w
Karvina, **Tch.**	49N50	18E30	1h14 E	Kingston, **Jama.**	17N58	76w48	5h07 w
Kasama, **Zamb.**	10s10	31E11	2h05 E	Kingston, NY, **USA**	41N55	74w00	4h56 w
Kasba Tadla, **Mar.**	32N34	6w18	0h25 w	Kingston upon Hull, → *Hull,* **G.-B.**			
Kaschau, → *Kosice,* **Tch.**				Kingstown, Saint-Vincent, **Ant.P.**	13N12	61w14	4h05 w
Kashan (Kachan), **Iran**	33N59	51E35	3h26 E	Kingstown, → *Dun Laoghaire,* **Irl.**			
Kashi (Kachgar), **China**	39N29	76E02	5h04 E	Kinshasa, **Zaire**	4s18	15E18	1h01 E
Kassala, **Sudan**	15N24	36E25	2h26 E	Kiribati (Gilbert) I., **Pac.O.**	0N00	174E00	11h36 E
Kassel (Cassel), **BRD**	51N18	9E30	0h38 E	Kirkcaldy, **G.-B.**	56N07	3w10	0h13 w
Kasserine, **Tun.**	35N13	8E43	0h35 E	Kirkuk, **Iraq**	36N28	44E26	2h58 E
Kastoria, **Grc.**	40N33	21E15	1h25 E	Kirkwall, Orkney, **G.-B.**	58N59	2w58	0h12 w
Kateríni, **Grc.**	40N15	22E30	1h30 E	Kirov, **URSS**	58N38	49E38	3h19 E
Kathmandu, **Nepal**	27N42	85E19	5h41 E	Kirovabad, **URSS**	40N39	46E20	3h05 E
Katiola, **C.Iv.**	8N11	5w04	0h20 w	Kirovograd, **URSS**	48N31	32E15	2h09 E
Katowice (Kattowitz), **Pol.**	50N15	18E59	1h16 E	Kiruna, **Sue.**	67N53	20E15	1h21 E
Katsina, **Nig.**	13N00	7E32	0h30 E				

City	Lat.	Long.	Time	City	Lat.	Long.	Time
Kisangani, **Zaire**	0N33	25E14	1h41E	Krakow, **Pol.**	50N03	19E55	1h20E
Kishinev (Kichinov), **URSS**	47N00	28E50	1h55E	Kramatorsk, **URSS**	48N43	37E33	2h30E
Kispest, **Hong.**	47N28	19E08	1h17E	Krasnodar, **URSS**	45N02	39E00	2h36E
Kisumu, **Kenya**	0s08	34E47	2h19E	Krasnoyarsk, **URSS**	56N05	92E46	6h11E
Kita-Kyushu, **Jap.**	33N52	130E49	8h43E	Krefeld, **BRD**	51N20	6E32	0h26E
Kitale, **Kenya**	1N01	35E01	2h20E	Kremenchug, **URSS**	49N03	33E25	2h14E
Kitchener, Ont., **Can.**	43N27	80w30	5h22w	Krems, **Aut.**	48N25	15E36	1h02E
Kitimat, Br.Col., **Can.**	54N05	128w38	8h35w	Kribi, **Cam.**	2N56	9E56	0h40E
Kiyev (Kiev), **URSS**	50N25	30E30	2h02E	Kristiansand, **Nor.**	58N08	8E01	0h32E
Klagenfurt, **Aut.**	46N38	14E20	0h57E	Kristianstad, **Sue.**	56N02	14E10	0h57E
Klaipeda, **URSS**	55N43	21E07	1h24E	Krivoy Rog, **URSS**	47N55	33E24	2h14E
Klamath Falls, Ore., **USA**	42N14	121w47	8h07w	Krugersdorp, **S.Afr.**	26s06	27E46	1h51E
Klausenburg, → *Cluj,* **Roum.**				Krung Thep, **Thai.**	13N44	100E30	6h42E
Knittelfeld, **Aut.**	47N14	14E50	0h59E	Kuala Lumpur, **Malay.**	3N08	101E42	6h47E
Knokke-Heist, **Belg.**	51N21	3E19	0h13E	Kuching, **Malay.**	1N32	110E20	7h21E
Knoxville, Tenn., **USA**	36N00	83w57	5h36w	Kufstein, **Aut.**	47N36	12E11	0h49E
Kobe, **Jap.**	34N40	135E12	9h01E	Kum, → *Qom,* **Iran**			
Köbenhavn, **Dan.**	55N43	12E34	0h50E	Kumamoto, **Jap.**	32N50	130E42	8h43E
Koblenz, **BRD**	50N21	7E36	0h30E	Kumanovo, **Youg.**	42N07	21E40	1h27E
Kochi, **Jap.**	33N33	133E32	8h54E	Kumasi, **Ghana**	6N45	1w35	0h06w
Koforidua, **Ghana**	6N01	0w12	0h01w	Kumba, **Cam.**	4N39	9E26	0h38E
Kofu, **Jap.**	35N42	138E34	9h14E	Kunsan, **Cor.S.**	35N57	126E42	8h27E
Kohat, **Pak.**	33N37	71E30	4h46E	Kuopio, **Finl.**	62N54	27E40	1h51E
Kokand, **URSS**	40N33	70E55	4h44E	Kupang, **Indon.**	10s13	123E38	8h15E
Kokkola, **Finl.**	63N50	23E10	1h33E	Kurashiki, **Jap.**	34N36	133E43	8h55E
Kolamba, → *Colombo,* **Sr.Lka**				Kure, **Jap.**	34N14	132E32	8h50E
Kolding, **Dan.**	55N29	9E30	0h38E	Kurgan (Kourgan), **URSS**	55N30	65E20	4h21E
Köln, **BRD**	50N56	6E57	0h28E	Kursk (Koursk), **URSS**	51N45	36E14	2h25E
Kolomna, **URSS**	55N05	38E45	2h35E	Kushiro, **Jap.**	42N58	144E24	9h38E
Komotiní, **Grc.**	41N06	25E25	1h42E	Kustanay (Koustanaï), **URSS**	53N15	63E40	4h15E
Kompong Cham, **Kamp.**	11N59	105E26	7h02E	Kutaisi (Koutaïssi), **URSS**	42N15	42E44	2h51E
Komsomolsk-na-Amure, **URSS**	50N32	136E59	9h08E	Kuwait (Al Kuwayt), **Kuwait**	29N20	48E00	3h12E
Kongolo, **Zaire**	5s20	27E00	1h48E	Kuybyshev (Kouïbichev), **URSS**	53N10	50E10	3h21E
Königsberg, → *Kaliningrad,* **URSS**				Kwangju, **Cor.S.**	35N07	126E52	8h27E
Königshütte, → *Chorzow,* **Pol.**				Kyongsong (Soul), **Cor.S.**	37N32	127E00	8h28E
Konstanz, **BRD**	47N40	9E10	0h37E	Kyoto, **Jap.**	35N02	135E45	9h03E
Konya, **Tur.**	37N51	32E30	2h10E	Kyustendil, **Bulg.**	42N16	22E40	1h31E
Korcë, **Alb.**	40N38	20E44	1h23E	Kzyl-Orda, **URSS**	44N52	65E28	4h22E
Korhogo, **C.Iv.**	9N22	5w31	0h22w				
Kórinthos, **Grc.**	37N56	22E55	1h32E				
Koriyama, **Jap.**	37N23	140E22	9h21E	*** L ***			
Kortrijk, **Belg.**	50N50	3E17	0h13E				
Kosice, **Tch.**	48N44	21E15	1h25E	Labé, **Guin.**	11N17	12w11	0h49w
Kosti, **Sudan**	13N11	32E38	2h11E	La Canée, → *Hania,* **Grc.**			
Kostroma, **URSS**	57N46	40E59	2h44E	La Chaux-de-Fonds, **Sui.**	47N07	6E51	0h27E
Koszalin, **Pol.**	54N10	16E10	1h05E	La Ciotat, **Fr.**	43N10	5E36	0h22E
Kota, Rajasthan, **Ind.**	25N11	75E58	5h04E	La Coruña, **Esp.**	43N22	8w24	0h34w
Kota Kinabalu (Jesselton), **Malay.**	5N59	116E04	7h44E	La Crosse, Wis., **USA**	43N48	91w15	6h05w
Kouang-tcheou (Guangzhou), **China**	23N08	113E20	7h33E	Lae, **Pap.**	6s45	147E00	9h48E
				Lafayette, Ind., **USA**	40N25	86w54	5h48w
Koudougou, **H.Vol.**	12N15	2w23	0h10w	Lafayette, La., **USA**	30N12	92w01	6h08w
Kouei-yang (Guiyang), **China**	26N35	106E40	7h07E	Laghouat, **Alg.**	33N49	2E55	0h12E
Kouen-ming (Kunming), **China**	25N04	102E41	6h51E	Lagos, **Nig.**	6N27	3E28	0h14E
Koumassi, → *Kumasi,* **Ghana**				La Habana (La Havane), **Cuba**	23N07	82w25	5h30w
Koupéla, **H.Vol.**	12N07	0w21	0h01w	La Haye, → *Den Haag,* **Nth.**			
Kourgan, → *Kurgan,* **URSS**				Lahn, **BRD**	50N33	8E40	0h35E
Kouroussa, **Guin.**	10N40	9w50	0h39w	Lahore, **Pak.**	31N34	74E22	4h57E
Kovno, → *Kaunas,* **URSS**				Lahti, **Finl.**	61N00	25E40	1h43E
Koweit, → *Kuwait,* **Kuwait**				Laibach, → *Ljubljana,* **Youg.**			
Kowloon, **H.K.**	22N20	114E15	7h37E	La Louvière, **Belg.**	50N29	4E12	0h17E
Kozáni, **Grc.**	40N18	21E48	1h27E	Lama-Kara, **Togo**	9N36	1E18	0h05E
Kozhikode, **Ind.**	11N15	75E45	5h03E	Lambarené, **Gabon**	0s41	10E13	0h41E
Kragujevac, **Youg.**	44N01	20E55	1h24E	La Mecque, → *Makkah,* **Ar.S.**			

City	Lat.	Long.	Time
Lamía, **Grc.**	38N55	22E26	1h30E
Lampang, **Thai.**	18N16	99E30	6h38E
Lancaster, **G.-B.**	54N03	2w48	0h11w
Landeck, **Aut.**	47N09	10E35	0h42E
Landshut, **BRD**	48N31	12E10	0h49E
Langenthal, **Sui.**	47N13	7E48	0h31E
Langres, **Fr.**	47N53	5E20	0h21E
Lansing, Mich., **USA**	42N44	85w34	5h42w
Lan-tcheou (Lanzhou), **China**	36N01	103E45	6h55E
Laoag, **Phil.**	18N14	120E36	8h02E
Laon, **Fr.**	49N34	3E37	0h14E
La Oroya, **Peru**	11s36	75w54	5h04w
La Paz, **Bol.**	16s30	68w10	4h33w
La Plata, **Arg.**	34s52	57w55	3h52w
L'Aquila, **Ital.**	42N21	13E24	0h54E
Larache (El Araich), **Mar.**	35N12	6w10	0h25w
Laredo, Tex., **USA**	27N32	99w22	6h37w
La Rioja, **Arg.**	29s26	66w50	4h27w
Lárisa, **Grc.**	39N38	22E25	1h30E
La Rochelle, **Fr.**	46N10	1w10	0h05w
La Roche-sur-Yon, **Fr.**	46N40	1w25	0h06w
La Roda, **Esp.**	39N13	2w10	0h09w
Larvik, **Nor.**	59N04	10E02	0h40E
La Serena, **Chile**	29s54	71w18	4h45w
Las Flores, Buenos Aires, **Arg.**	36s03	59w08	3h57w
Las Palmas, **Can.I.**	28N08	15w27	1h02w
La Spezia, **Ital.**	44N07	9E48	0h39E
Las Vegas, Nev., **USA**	36N10	115w10	7h41w
Latacunga, **Ecuad.**	0s58	78w36	5h14w
Latina, **Ital.**	41N28	12E53	0h52E
Lattaquié, → *El Ladhiqiya,* **Syr.**			
Lauenburg an der Elbe, **BRD**	53N23	10E33	0h42E
Launceston, **Aust.**	41s25	147E07	9h48E
Launceston, **G.-B.**	50N38	4w21	0h17w
Lausanne, **Sui.**	46N32	6E39	0h27E
Laval, **Fr.**	48N04	0w45	0h03w
La Valette, → *Valleta,* **Malta**			
La Vega, **Dom.**	19N15	70w33	4h42w
Lawton, Okla., **USA**	34N36	98w25	6h34w
Le Caire, → *Al Qahira,* **Egy.**			
Le Cap, → *Cape Town,* **S.Afr.**			
Lecce, **Ital.**	40N21	18E11	1h13E
Le Creusot, **Fr.**	46N48	4E27	0h18E
Leeds, **G.-B.**	53N50	1w35	0h06w
Leeuwarden, **Nth.**	53N12	5E48	0h23E
Legnica, **Pol.**	51N12	16E10	1h05E
Le Havre, **Fr.**	49N30	0E06	0h00E
Leicester, **G.-B.**	52N38	1w05	0h04w
Leiden, → *Leyde,* **Nth.**			
Leipzig, **DDR**	51N20	12E25	0h50E
Leith, **G.-B.**	55N59	3w10	0h13w
Le Locle, **Sui.**	47N04	6E45	0h27E
Le Mans, **Fr.**	48N00	0E12	0h01E
Lemberg, → *Lvov,* **URSS**			
Leninakan, **URSS**	40N47	43E49	2h55E
Leningrad, **URSS**	59N55	30E25	2h02E
Lens, **Fr.**	50N26	2E50	0h11E
Leoben, Steiermark, **Aut.**	47N23	15E06	1h00E
Leominster, **G.-B.**	52N14	2w45	0h11w
León, **Esp.**	42N35	5w34	0h22w
León, **Mex.**	21N10	101w42	6h47w
León, **Nicar.**	12N24	86w52	5h47w
Leopoldville, → *Kinshasa,* **Zaire**			

City	Lat.	Long.	Time
Le Pirée, → *Pireas,* **Grc.**			
Le Puy, **Fr.**	45N03	3E53	0h16E
Lérida (Lleida), **Esp.**	41N37	0E38	0h03E
Lerwick, Shetland I., **G.-B.**	60N09	1w09	0h05w
Les Cayes, **Haiti**	18N15	73w46	4h55w
Leszno, **Pol.**	51N51	16E35	1h06E
Lethbridge, Alb., **Can.**	49N43	112w48	7h31w
Leuven, **Belg.**	50N53	4E42	0h19E
Leuze, **Belg.**	50N36	3E37	0h14E
Leverkusen, **BRD**	51N02	6E59	0h28E
Lexington, Ky., **USA**	38N02	84w30	5h38w
Leyde, **Nth.**	52N10	4E30	0h18E
Lhassa, **China**	29N41	91E10	6h05E
Libau, → *Liepaja,* **URSS**			
Libourne, **Fr.**	44N55	0w14	0h01w
Libreville, **Gabon**	0N30	9E25	0h38E
Liège (Luik), **Belg.**	50N38	5E35	0h22E
Liegnitz, → *Legnica,* **Pol.**			
Lienz, **Aut.**	46N51	12E50	0h51E
Liepaja (Liepaïa), **URSS**	56N30	21E00	1h24E
Lierre (Lier), **Belg.**	51N08	4E35	0h18E
Liestal, **Sui.**	47N29	7E43	0h31E
Likasi, **Zaire**	10s58	26E47	1h47E
Lille, **Fr.**	50N39	3E05	0h12E
Lillehammer, **Nor.**	61N06	10E27	0h42E
Lilongwe, **Malawi**	13s58	33E49	2h15E
Lima, **Peru**	12s06	77w03	5h08w
Lima, Oh., **USA**	40N43	84w06	5h36w
Limburg, **BRD**	50N23	8E04	0h32E
Limerick, **Irl.**	52N40	8w38	0h35w
Limoges, **Fr.**	45N50	1E15	0h05E
Limón, **C.Rica**	10N00	83w01	5h32w
Linares, **Esp.**	38N05	3w38	0h15w
Lincoln, **G.-B.**	53N14	0w33	0h02w
Lincoln, Neb., **USA**	40N49	96w41	6h27w
Linköping, **Sue.**	58N25	15E35	1h02E
Linz, **Aut.**	48N19	14E18	0h57E
Lipetsk, **URSS**	52N37	39E36	2h38E
Lippstadt, **BRD**	51N41	8E20	0h33E
Lisboa (Lisbonne), **Port.**	38N44	9w08	0h37w
Lisieux, **Fr.**	49N09	0E14	0h01E
Lissabon, → *Lisboa,* **Port.**			
Little Rock, Ark., **USA**	34N42	92w17	6h09w
Liverpool, **G.-B.**	53N25	2w55	0h12w
Livorno (Livourne), **Ital.**	43N33	10E18	0h41E
Ljubljana, **Youg.**	46N04	14E30	0h58E
Lloydminster, Alb., **Can.**	53N18	110w00	7h20w
Loanda, → *Luanda,* **Angola**			
Lobatsi, **Bots.**	25s11	25E40	1h43E
Lobito, **Angola**	12s20	13E34	0h54E
Locarno, **Sui.**	46N10	8E48	0h35E
Lod (Lydda), **Isr.**	31N57	34E54	2h20E
Lodz (Lodsch), **Pol.**	51N49	19E28	1h18E
Logroño, **Esp.**	42N28	2w26	0h10w
Loja, **Ecuad.**	3s59	79w16	5h17w
Lokeren, **Belg.**	51N06	3E59	0h16E
Lomé, **Togo**	6N10	1E21	0h05E
London, Ont., **Can.**	42N58	81w15	5h25w
London (Londres), **G.-B.**	51N30	0w10	0h01w
Londonderry, **Irl.**	55N00	7w19	0h29w
Londrina, **Brasil**	23s18	51w13	3h25w
Long Beach, Ca., **USA**	33N47	118w15	7h53w
Lons-le-Saunier, **Fr.**	46N41	5E33	0h22E

City	Lat.	Long.	Time	City	Lat.	Long.	Time
Lorca, **Esp.**	37N40	1w41	0h07w	Maebashi, **Jap.**	36N24	139E04	9h16E
Lorient, **Fr.**	47N45	3w21	0h13w	Mafraq (Al Mafraq), **Jord.**	32N20	36E12	2h25E
Los Angeles, **Chile**	37s28	72w23	4h50w	Magdeburg, **DDR**	52N08	11E37	0h46E
Los Angeles, Ca., **USA**	34N00	118w15	7h53w	Magnitogorsk, **URSS**	53N28	59E06	3h56E
Los Mochis, **Mex.**	25N48	109w00	7h16w	Mahajanga, **Madag.**	15s40	46E20	3h05E
Loubomo, **Congo**	4s09	12E47	0h51E	Maidstone, **G.-B.**	51N17	0E32	0h02E
Louisville, Ky., **USA**	38N13	85w48	5h43w	Maiduguri, **Nig.**	11N53	13E16	0h53E
Lourenço-Marques, → *Maputo*, **Moz.**				Maimana, **Afg.**	35N54	64E43	4h19E
				Mainz (Mayence), **BRD**	50N00	8E16	0h33E
Louvain, → *Leuven*, **Belg.**				Majene, **Indon.**	3s33	118E59	7h56E
Lowestoft, **G.-B.**	52N29	1E45	0h07E	Makabana, **Congo**	3s25	12E41	0h51E
Lo-yang (Luoyang), **China**	34N47	112E26	7h30E	Makasar, → *Ujung Pandang*, **Indon.**			
Luanda, **Angola**	8s50	13E15	0h53E				
Luang Prabang, **Laos**	19N53	102E10	6h49E	Makeni, **S.Leo.**	8N57	12w02·	0h48w
Lübben, **DDR**	51N57	13E54	0h56E	Makeyevka, **URSS**	48N01	38E00	2h32E
Lubbock, Tex., **USA**	33N35	101w53	6h48w	Makhachkala, **URSS**	42N59	47E30	3h10E
Lübeck, **BRD**	53N52	10E40	0h43E	Makkah, **Ar.S.**	21N26	39E49	2h39E
Lublin, **Pol.**	51N18	22E31	1h30E	Makokou, **Gabon**	0N38	12E47	0h51E
Lubumbashi, **Zaire**	11s41	27E29	1h50E	Makurdi, **Nig.**	7N44	8E35	0h34E
Lucca, **Ital.**	43N50	10E30	0h42E	Malabo, **G.eq.**	3N45	8E48	0h35E
Lucerne, → *Luzern*, **Sui.**				Malacca (Melaka), **Malay.**	2N14	102E14	6h49E
Lucknow, **Ind.**	26N50	80E54	5h24E	Málaga, **Esp.**	36N43	4w25	0h18w
Lucques, → *Lucca*, **Ital.**				Malang, **Indon.**	7s59	112E45	7h31E
Lüdenscheid, **BRD**	51N13	7E38	0h31E	Malanje, **Angola**	9s36	16E21	1h05E
Ludhiana, **Ind.**	30N56	75E52	5h03E	Malatya, **Tur.**	38N22	38E18	2h33E
Ludwigsburg, **BRD**	48N54	9E12	0h37E	Maldive I. (Male), **Ind.O.**	4N10	73E30	4h54E
Ludwigshafen am Rhein, **BRD**	49N29	8E27	0h34E	Malegaon, **Ind.**	20N32	74E38	4h59E
Ludwigslust, **DDR**	53N20	11E30	0h46E	Malines, → *Mechelen*, **Belg.**			
Lugano, **Sui.**	46N01	8E57	0h36E	Malmö, **Sue.**	55N35	13E00	0h52E
Lugo, **Esp.**	43N00	7w33	0h30w	Mamou, **Guin.**	10N24	12w05	0h48w
Luimneach, → *Limerick*, **Irl.**				Man, **C.Iv.**	7N31	7w37	0h30w
Lulea, **Sue.**	65N35	22E10	1h29E	Manado, → *Menado*, **Indon.**			
Luluabourg, → *Kananga*, **Zaire**				Managua, **Nicar.**	12N06	86w18	5h45w
Lundazi, **Zamb.**	12s19	33E11	2h13E	Manaus (Manaos), **Brasil**	3s06	60w00	4h00w
Lüneburg, **BRD**	53N15	10E24	0h42E	Manchester, **G.-B.**	53N30	2w15	0h09w
Lünen, **BRD**	51N37	7E31	0h30E	Manchester, NH, **USA**	42N59	71w28	4h46w
Lusaka, **Zamb.**	15s26	28E20	1h53E	Mandalay, **Birm.**	21N57	96E04	6h24E
Luton, **G.-B.**	51N53	0w25	0h02w	Mangalore (Mangalur), **Ind.**	12N54	74E51	4h59E
Luxembourg, **Luxem.**	49N37	6E08	0h25E	Manila (Manille), **Phil.**	14N37	120E58	8h04E
Luzern, **Sui.**	47N03	8E17	0h33E	Manisa, **Tur.**	38N36	27E29	1h50E
Lvov (Lwow), **URSS**	49N50	24E00	1h36E	Manizales, **Col.**	5N03	75w32	5h02w
Lyon, **Fr.**	45N46	4E50	0h19E	Mankono, **C.Iv.**	8N01	6w09	0h25w
				Mannheim, **BRD**	49N30	8E28	0h34E
				Manresa, **Esp.**	41N43	1E50	0h07E
*** M ***				Mansfield, **G.-B.**	53N09	1w11	0h05w
				Mansfield, Oh., **USA**	40N46	82w31	5h30w
Ma'an, **Jord.**	30N11	35E45	2h23E	Mansourah (El Mansura), **Egy.**	31N03	31E23	2h06E
Maastricht, **Nth.**	50N51	5E42	0h23E	Manta, **Ecuad.**	0s59	80w44	5h23w
Macao, **China**	22N16	113E35	7h34E	Mantes-la-Jolie, **Fr.**	48N59	1E43	0h07E
Macapá, Amapá, **Brasil**	0N04	51w04	3h24w	Mantova (Mantoue), **Ital.**	45N10	10E47	0h43E
Maceió, **Brasil**	9s40	35w44	·2h23w	Manzanares, **Esp.**	39N00	3w23	0h14w
Machiques, **Ven.**	10N04	72w37	4h50w	Manzanillo, **Cuba**	20N21	77w21	5h09w
Mackay, **Aust.**	21s10	149E10	9h57E	Manzanillo, **Mex.**	19N00	104w20	6h57w
Mâcon, **Fr.**	46N18	4E50	0h19E	Maputo, **Moz.**	25s58	32E35	2h10E
Macon, Ga., **USA**	32N49	83w37	5h34w	Maracaibo, **Ven.**	10N44	71w37	4h46w
Macquarie I., **Pac.O.**	54s37	158E50	10h35E	Maracay, **Ven.**	10N20	67w28	4h30w
Madang, **Pap.**	5s14	145E45	9h43E	Maradi, **Niger**	13N29	7E10	0h29E
Madeira I. (Funchal), **Atl.O.**	32N40	16w55	1h08w	Maramba, **Zamb.**	17s50	25E53	1h44E
Madison, Wis., **USA**	43N04	89w22	5h57w	Marburg an der Lahn, **BRD**	50N49	8E36	0h34E
Madiun, **Indon.**	7s37	111E33	7h26E	Mar del Plata, **Arg.**	38s00	57w32	3h50w
Madras, **Ind.**	13N05	80E18	5h21E	Mariannes I., **Pac.O.**	15N00	146E00	9h44E
Madrid, **Esp.**	40N25	3w43	0h15w	Maribor (Marburg), **Youg.**	46N34	15E38	1h03E
Madurai, **Ind.**	9N55	78E07	5h12E	Marigot, Dominique, **Ant.P.**	15N32	61w18	4h05w

49

City	Lat.	Long.	Time	City	Lat.	Long.	Time
Marigot, Saint Martin, **Ant.P.**	18N06	63w06	4h12w	Meissen, **DDR**	51N50	13E28	0h54 E
Marília, **Brasil**	22s13	49w58	3h20w	Meknès, **Mar.**	33N53	5w37	0h22w
Maringá, **Brasil**	23s26	52w02	3h28w	Melbourne, **Aust.**	37s45	144E58	9h40 E
Marioupol, → *Zhdanov,* **URSS**				Melilla, **Mar.**	35N20	3w00	0h12w
Mariscal Estigarribia, **Parag.**	22s03	60w35	4h02w	Melitopol, **URSS**	46N51	35E22	2h21 E
Marl, **BRD**	51N38	7E06	0h28 E	Melo, **Urug.**	32s22	54w10	3h37w
Marmande, **Fr.**	44N30	0E10	0h01 E	Melun, **Fr.**	48N32	2E40	0h11 E
Maroua, **Cam.**	10N35	14E20	0h57 E	Memel, → *Klaipeda,* **URSS**			
Marquises I., **Pac.O.**	9s00	140w00	9h20w	Memmingen, **BRD**	47N59	10E11	0h41 E
Marrakech, **Mar.**	31N49	8w00	0h32w	Memphis, Tenn., **USA**	35N10	90w00	6h00w
Marsala, **Ital.**	37N48	12E27	0h50 E	Menado, **Indon.**	1N32	124E55	8h20 E
Marsa Matruh, **Egy.**	31N21	27E15	1h49 E	Mende, **Fr.**	44N32	3E30	0h14 E
Marseille, **Fr.**	43N18	5E22	0h21 E	Mendoza, **Arg.**	32s48	68w52	4h35w
Martigny, **Sui.**	46N06	7E04	0h28 E	Menen (Menin), **Belg.**	50N48	3E07	0h12 E
Martigues, **Fr.**	43N24	5E03	0h20 E	Menggala, **Indon.**	4s30	105E19	7h01 E
Masan, **Cor.S.**	35N10	128E35	8h34 E	Menton, **Fr.**	43N47	7E30	0h30 E
Masaya, **Nicar.**	11N59	86w03	5h44w	Merced, Ca., **USA**	37N17	120w29	8h02w
Mascara (Mouaskar), **Alg.**	35N20	0E09	0h01 E	Mercedes, Buenos Aires, **Arg.**	34s42	59w30	3h58w
Maseru, **Leso.**	29s19	27E29	1h50 E	Mercedes, Corrientes, **Arg.**	29s15	58w05	3h52w
Mashhad, → *Meched,* **Iran**				Mercedes, San Luis, **Arg.**	33s41	65w28	4h22w
Masqat (Maskat), **Oman**	23N37	58E38	3h55 E	Mercedes, **Urug.**	33s15	58w02	3h52w
Massa, **Ital.**	44N02	10E09	0h41 E	Mergui, **Birm.**	12N26	98E34	6h34 E
Massaoua (Massawa), **Eth.**	15N37	39E28	2h38 E	Mérida, **Esp.**	38N55	6w20	0h25w
Matadi, **Zaire**	5s50	13E32	0h54 E	Mérida, **Mex.**	20N59	89w39	5h59w
Matagalpa, **Nicar.**	12N52	85w58	5h44w	Mérida, **Ven.**	8N24	71w08	4h45w
Matanzas, **Cuba**	23N04	81w35	5h26w	Meridian, Miss., **USA**	32N21	88w42	5h55w
Mataró, **Esp.**	41N32	2E27	0h10 E	Mersin, **Tur.**	36N47	34E37	2h18 E
Matehuala, **Mex.**	23N40	100w40	6h43w	Merthyr Tydfil, **G.-B.**	51N46	3w23	0h14w
Mateur, **Tun.**	37N03	9E40	0h39 E	Messina, **Ital.**	38N13	15E33	1h02 E
Mathura, **Ind.**	27N30	77E42	5h11 E	Metz, **Fr.**	49N07	6E11	0h25 E
Matsue, **Jap.**	35N29	133E04	8h52 E	Mexicali, **Mex.**	32N38	115w27	7h42w
Matsuyama, **Jap.**	33N50	132E47	8h51 E	Mexico, **Mex.**	19N25	99w10	6h37w
Maturín, **Ven.**	9N45	63w10	4h13w	Miami, Fla., **USA**	25N45	80w15	5h21w
Maubeuge, **Fr.**	50N17	3E58	0h16 E	Middlesbrough, **G.-B.**	54N35	1w14	0h05w
Mayagüez, **P.Rico**	18N13	67w09	4h29w	Midland, Tex., **USA**	32N00	102w09	6h49w
Mayence, → *Mainz,* **BRD**				Mieres, **Esp.**	43N15	5w46	0h23w
Maykop (Maïkop), **URSS**	44N37	40E48	2h43 E	Mikhaylovgrad, **Bulg.**	43N25	23E11	1h33 E
Mayotte I., **Ind.O.**	12s50	45E10	3h01 E	Milagro, **Ecuad.**	2s11	79w36	5h18w
Mazar-i-Charif, **Afg.**	36N43	67E05	4h28 E	Milano, **Ital.**	45N28	9E12	0h37 E
Mazatenango, **Guat.**	14N31	91w30	6h06w	Millau, **Fr.**	44N06	3E05	0h12 E
Mazatlán, **Mex.**	23N11	106w25	7h06w	Milwaukee, Wis., **USA**	43N03	87w56	5h52w
Mbabane, **Swaz.**	26s20	31E08	2h05 E	Minas, **Urug.**	34s20	55w15	3h41w
Mbaïki, **C.Afr.**	3N53	18E01	1h12 E	Minden, **BRD**	52N18	8E54	0h36 E
Mbalmayo, **Cam.**	3N30	11E31	0h46 E	Minna, **Nig.**	9N39	6E32	0h26 E
Mbandaka, **Zaire**	0N03	18E28	1h14 E	Minneapolis, Minn., **USA**	45N00	93w15	6h13w
Mbanza-Ngungu, **Zaire**	5s17	14E51	0h59 E	Minot, ND, **USA**	48N16	101w19	6h45w
Mbeya, **Tanz.**	8s54	33E29	2h14 E	Minsk, **URSS**	53N51	27E30	1h50 E
Mbour, **Seneg.**	14N22	16w54	1h08w	Miranda de Ebro, **Esp.**	42N41	2w57	0h12w
Meaux, **Fr.**	48N58	2E54	0h12 E	Mirpur Khas, **Pak.**	25N33	69E05	4h36 E
Mecca, → *Makkah,* **Ar.S.**				Miskolc, **Hong.**	48N07	20E47	1h23 E
Meched, **Iran**	36N16	59E34	3h58 E	Missoula, Mt., **USA**	46N52	114w00	7h36w
Mechelen, **Belg.**	51N02	4E29	0h18 E	Miyazaki, **Jap.**	31N56	131E27	8h46 E
Medan, **Indon.**	3N35	98E39	6h35 E	Moanda, **Gabon**	1s32	13E17	0h53 E
Medellín, **Col.**	6N15	75w36	5h02w	Mobile, Alab., **USA**	30N40	88w05	5h52w
Medenine, **Tun.**	33N24	10E25	0h42 E	Mochudi, **Bots.**	24s28	26E05	1h44 E
Medford, Ore., **USA**	42N20	122w52	8h11w	Modena, **Ital.**	44N39	10E55	0h44 E
Medicine Hat, Alb., **Can.**	50N03	110w41	7h23w	Modesto, Ca., **USA**	37N37	121w00	8h04w
Medina (Al Medinah), **Ar.S.**	24N30	39E35	2h38 E	Moers, **BRD**	51N27	6E36	0h26 E
Medina del Campo, **Esp.**	41N18	4w55	0h20w	Mogadishu (Mogadiscio), **Somal.**	2N02	45E21	3h01 E
Meerut, **Ind.**	29N00	77E42	5h11 E	Mogador, → *Essaouira,* **Mar.**			
Meiktila, **Birm.**	20N53	95E54	6h24 E	Mogilev, **URSS**	53N54	30E20	2h01 E
Meiningen, **DDR**	50N34	10E25	0h42 E	Moknine, **Tun.**	35N39	10E53	0h44 E
Meiringen, **Sui.**	46N44	8E12	0h33 E	Mokolo, **Cam.**	10N49	13E54	0h56 E

City	Lat.	Long.	Time	City	Lat.	Long.	Time
Mokpo, **Cor.S.**	34N50	126E25	8h26 E	Multan, **Pak.**	30N10	71E36	4h46 E
Molfetta, **Ital.**	41N12	16E36	1h06 E	München (Munich), **BRD**	48N08	11E35	0h46 E
Mollendo, **Peru**	17s00	72w00	4h48 w	Münster, **BRD**	51N58	7E37	0h30 E
Molotov, → *Perm,* **URSS**				Murcia, **Esp.**	37N59	1w08	0h05 w
Molsheim, **Fr.**	48N33	7E30	0h30 E	Muriaé, **Brasil**	21s08	42w23	2h50 w
Mombasa, **Kenya**	4s04	39E40	2h39 E	Murmansk (Mourmansk), **URSS**	68N59	33E08	2h13 E
Mönchengladbach, **BRD**	51N12	6E25	0h26 E	Muroran, **Jap.**	42N21	140E59	9h24 E
Moncton, NB, **Can.**	46N04	64w50	4h19 w	Mürzzuschlag, **Aut.**	47N37	15E41	1h03 E
Monmouth, **G.-B.**	51N50	2w43	0h11 w	Mwanza, **Tanz.**	2s31	32E56	2h12 E
Monroe, La., **USA**	32N31	92w06	6h08 w	Mysore, **Ind.**	12N18	76E37	5h06 E
Monrovia, **Liber.**	6N20	10w46	0h43 w				
Mons (Bergen), **Belg.**	50N28	3E58	0h16 E				
Montauban, **Fr.**	44N01	1E20	0h05 E	*** N ***			
Montbéliard, **Fr.**	47N31	6E48	0h27 E				
Montceau-les-Mines, **Fr.**	46N40	4E23	0h18 E	Nabeul, **Tun.**	36N30	10E44	0h43 E
Mont-de-Marsan, **Fr.**	43N54	0w30	0h02 w	Nablus, **Jord.**	32N13	35E16	2h21 E
Monte-Carlo, **Monaco**	43N44	7E25	0h30 E	Nagano, **Jap.**	36N39	138E10	9h13 E
Montego Bay, **Jama.**	18N27	77w56	5h12 w	Nagaoka, **Jap.**	37N27	138E50	9h15 E
Montélimar, **Fr.**	44N33	4E45	0h19 E	Nagasaki, **Jap.**	32N45	129E52	8h39 E
Monterey, Ca., **USA**	36N35	121w55	8h08 w	Nagoya, **Jap.**	35N08	136E53	9h08 E
Montería, **Col.**	8N45	75w54	5h04 w	Nagpur, **Ind.**	21N10	79E12	5h17 E
Monterrey, **Mex.**	25N40	100w20	6h41 w	Nagy Varad, → *Oradea,* **Roum.**			
Montes Claros, **Brasil**	16s45	43w52	2h55 w	Naha, Okinawa, **Jap.**	26N10	127E40	8h31 E
Montevideo, **Urug.**	34s55	56w10	3h45 w	Nahariya, **Isr.**	33N01	35E05	2h20 E
Montgomery, Alab., **USA**	32N22	86w20	5h45 w	Nairobi, **Kenya**	1s17	36E50	2h27 E
Montijo, **Port.**	38N55	6w38	0h27 w	Najin, **Cor.N.**	42N10	130E20	8h41 E
Montluçon, **Fr.**	46N20	2E36	0h10 E	Nakhon Ratchasima (Khorat),			
Montpelier, Vt., **USA**	44N16	72w34	4h50 w	**Thai.**	15N00	102E06	6h48 E
Montpellier, **Fr.**	43N36	3E53	0h16 E	Nakina, Ont., **Can.**	50N11	86w43	5h47 w
Montréal, Que:, **Can.**	45N30	73w36	4h54 w	Nakuru, **Kenya**	0s16	36E04	2h24 E
Montreuil, Seine, **Fr.**	48N52	2E28	0h10 E	Nalchik, **URSS**	43N31	43E38	2h55 E
Montreux, **Sui.**	46N27	6E55	0h28 E	Namangan, **URSS**	40N59	71E41	4h47 E
Montrose, **G.-B.**	56N43	2w29	0h10 w	Nampula, **Moz.**	15s09	39E14	2h37 E
Monza, **Ital.**	45N35	9E16	0h37 E	Namsos, **Nor.**	64N28	11E30	0h46 E
Moose Jaw, Sask., **Can.**	50N23	105w35	7h02 w	Namur (Namen), **Belg.**	50N28	4E52	0h19 E
Mopti, **Mali**	14N29	4w10	0h17 w	Nanaimo, Br.Col., **Can.**	49N08	123w58	8h16 w
Moradabad, **Ind.**	28N50	78E45	5h15 E	Nancy, **Fr.**	48N42	6E12	0h25 E
Moratuwa, **Sr.Lka**	6N47	79E53	5h20 E	Nankin (Nanjing), **China**	32N03	118E47	7h55 E
Morelia, **Mex.**	19N40	101w11	6h45 w	Nan-ning, **China**	22N50	108E19	7h13 E
Morges, **Sui.**	46N31	6E30	0h26 E	Nan-tchang (Nanchang), **China**	28N33	115E58	7h44 E
Morioka, **Jap.**	39N43	141E08	9h25 E	Nantes, **Fr.**	47N14	1w35	0h06 w
Morlaix, **Fr.**	48N35	3w50	0h15 w	Nan-tong (Nantung), **China**	32N05	120E51	8h03 E
Morondava, **Madag.**	20s19	44E17	2h57 E	Nantua, **Fr.**	46N09	5E36	0h22 E
Moskva (Moscou), **URSS**	55N45	37E42	2h31 E	Naplouse, → *Nablus,* **Jord.**			
Mosseró, **Brasil**	5s10	37w18	2h29 w	Napoli (Naples), **Ital.**	40N50	14E15	0h57 E
Mossoul (Mosul), **Iraq**	36N21	43E08	2h53 E	Narbonne, **Fr.**	43N11	3E00	0h12 E
Most, **Tch.**	50N31	13E39	0h55 E	Narvik, **Nor.**	68N26	17E25	1h10 E
Mostaganem (Mestghanem), **Alg.**	35N54	0E05	0h00 E	Nashville, Tenn., **USA**	36N10	86w50	5h47 w
Mostar, **Youg.**	43N20	17E50	1h11 E	Nasik, **Ind.**	20N00	73E52	4h55 E
Motherwell, **G.-B.**	55N48	4w00	0h16 w	Natal, Rio Grande, **Brasil**	5s46	35w15	2h21 w
Moukden, → *Chen-yang,* **China**				National City, Ca., **USA**	32N39	117w06	7h48 w
Moulins, **Fr.**	46N34	3E20	0h13 E	Nauen, **DDR**	52N37	12E53	0h52 E
Moulmein, **Birm.**	16N30	97E39	6h31 E	Naumburg, **DDR**	51N09	11E48	0h47 E
Moundou, **Tchad**	8N35	16E01	1h04 E	Nauru I., **Pac.O.**	0s31	166E56	11h08 E
Mount Vernon, Ill., **USA**	38N19	88w52	5h55 w	Nawabshah, **Pak.**	26N15	68E26	4h34 E
Mouscron (Moeskroën), **Belg.**	50N44	3E14	0h13 E	Náxos, **Grc.**	37N06	25E24	1h42 E
Moutier, **Sui.**	47N18	7E23	0h30 E	Nazareth, **Isr.**	32N42	35E18	2h21 E
Moyobamba, **Peru**	6s04	76w56	5h08 w	Ndélé, **C.Afr.**	8N25	20E38	1h23 E
Mozambique, **Moz.**	15s03	40E42	2h43 E	N'djamena, **Tchad**	12N10	14E59	1h00 E
Mühldorf, **BRD**	48N14	12E33	0h50 E	Ndjolé, **Gabon**	0s07	10E45	0h43 E
Mühlhausen in Thüringen, **DDR**	51N13	10E28	0h42 E	Ndola, **Zamb.**	13s00	28E39	1h55 E
Mülheim an der Ruhr, **BRD**	51N25	6E50	0h27 E	Nefta, **Tun.**	33N53	7E50	0h31 E
Mulhouse, **Fr.**	47N45	7E21	0h29 E	Negombo, **Sr.Lka**	7N13	79E51	5h19 E

City	Lat.	Long.	Time	City	Lat.	Long.	Time
Neiva, **Col.**	2N58	75w15	5h01w	Northampton, **G.-B.**	52N14	0w54	0h04w
Nelson, **N.Zel.**	41s18	173E17	11h33E	North Bay, Ont., **Can.**	46N20	79w28	5h18w
Netanya, **Isr.**	32N20	34E51	2h19E	North Platte, Neb., **USA**	41N09	100w45	6h43w
Neubrandenburg, **DDR**	53N33	13E16	0h53E	Northwich, **G.-B.**	53N16	2w32	0h10w
Neuchâtel, **Sui.**	46N59	6E55	0h28E	Norwich, **G.-B.**	52N38	1E18	0h05E
Neumünster, **BRD**	54N04	9E58	0h40E	Nottingham, **G.-B.**	52N58	1w10	0h05w
Neunkirchen, Saar, **BRD**	49N21	7E12	0h29E	Nouakchott, **Maur.**	18N09	15w58	1h04w
Neuquén, **Arg.**	38s55	68w05	4h32w	Nouméa, **N.Cal.**	22s16	166E26	11h06E
Neuruppin, **DDR**	52N56	12E49	0h51E	Novara (Novare), **Ital.**	45N27	8E37	0h34E
Neusatz, → *Novi Sad,* **Youg.**				Nove Zamky, **Tch.**	48N00	18E10	1h13E
Neuss, **BRD**	51N12	6E42	0h27E	Novgorod, **URSS**	58N30	31E20	2h05E
Neustadt an der Weinstrasse, **BRD**	49N21	8E09	0h33E	Novi Sad, **Youg.**	45N15	19E51	1h19E
Neustrelitz, **DDR**	53N22	13E05	0h52E	Novokuznetsk, **URSS**	53N45	87E12	5h49E
Nevers, **Fr.**	47N00	3E09	0h13E	Novomoskovsk, **URSS**	54N06	38E15	2h33E
Newark, NJ, **USA**	40N44	74w12	4h57w	Novorossiysk, **URSS**	44N44	37E46	2h31E
New Bedford, Mass., **USA**	41N38	70w55	4h44w	Novosibirsk (Novonikolaïevsk),			
Newburgh, NY, **USA**	41N30	74w00	4h56w	**URSS**	55N04	83E05	5h32E
Newcastle, **Aust.**	32s55	151E46	10h07E	Nsawam, **Ghana**	5N47	0w19	0h01w
Newcastle upon Tyne, **G.-B.**	54N59	1w35	0h06w	Nueva Rosita, **Mex.**	27N58	101w11	6h45w
New Delhi, **Ind.**	28N37	77E13	5h09E	Nuevo Laredo, **Mex.**	27N30	99w30	6h38w
New Glasgow, NE, **Can.**	45N36	62w28	4h10w	Nukus (Noukous), **URSS**	42N28	59E07	3h56E
New Haven, Conn., **USA**	41N18	72w55	4h52w	Numazu, **Jap.**	35N08	138E50	9h15E
New Orleans, La., **USA**	30N00	90w03	6h00w	Nuneaton, **G.-B.**	52N32	1w28	0h06w
Newport, Gwent, **G.-B.**	51N35	3w00	0h12w	Nürnberg (Nuremberg), **BRD**	49N27	11E05	0h44E
Newport, Wight I., **G.-B.**	50N42	1w18	0h05w	Nyíregyháza, **Hong.**	47N57	21E43	1h27E
New York, NY, **USA**	40N40	73w50	4h55w	Nykobing, Storstrom, **Dan.**	54N47	11E53	0h48E
Ngan-chan, → *An-chan,* **China**				Nyon, **Sui.**	46N23	6E15	0h25E
Ngang-tong, → *An-tong,* **China**				Nyons, **Fr.**	44N22	5E08	0h21E
N'Gaoundéré, **Cam.**	7N20	13E35	0h54E				
Nguru, **Nig.**	12N53	10E30	0h42E				
Nha Trang, **Viet.**	12N15	109E10	7h17E	*** O ***			
Niamey, **Niger**	13N32	2E05	0h08E				
Nice, **Fr.**	43N42	7E16	0h29E	Oakland, Ca., **USA**	37N50	122w15	8h09w
Nicobar I. (Nankauri), **Ind.O.**	8N02	93E32	6h14E	Oaxaca, **Mex.**	17N05	96w41	6h27w
Nicosia, **Chyp.**	35N09	33E21	2h13E	Oban, **G.-B.**	56N25	5w29	0h22w
Nienburg, **BRD**	52N38	9E13	0h37E	Oberhausen, Westfalen, **BRD**	51N27	6E50	0h27E
Niigata, **Jap.**	37N58	139E02	9h16E	Obuasi, **Ghana**	6N15	1w36	0h06w
Nijmegen (Nimègue), **Nth.**	51N50	5E52	0h23E	Ocaña, **Esp.**	39N57	3w30	0h14w
Nikolayev, **URSS**	46N57	32E00	2h08E	Oceanside, Ca., **USA**	33N12	117w23	7h50w
Nikopol, **URSS**	47N34	34E25	2h18E	Oda, **Ghana**	5N55	0w56	0h04w
Nimègue, → *Nijmegen,* **Nth.**				Odense, **Dan.**	55N14	10E25	0h42E
Nîmes, **Fr.**	43N50	4E21	0h17E	Odessa, **URSS**	46N30	30E46	2h03E
Ning-po (Ningbo), **China**	29N54	121E33	8h06E	Odienné, **C.Iv.**	9N36	7w32	0h30w
Nioro du Sahel, **Mali**	15N12	9w35	0h38w	Oerebro, **Sue.**	59N18	15E05	1h00E
Niort, **Fr.**	46N19	0w27	0h02w	Oernsköldsvik, **Sue.**	63N19	18E45	1h15E
Nis (Nish), **Youg.**	43N20	21E54	1h28E	Oestersund, **Sue.**	63N10	14E40	0h59E
Niterói, **Brasil**	22s54	43w06	2h52w	Offenburg, **BRD**	48N29	7E57	0h32E
Niue I., **Pac.O.**	19s02	169w55	11h20w	Ogbomosho, **Nig.**	8N05	4E11	0h17E
Nivelles (Nijvel), **Belg.**	50N36	4E20	0h17E	Ogden, Ut., **USA**	41N14	111w59	7h28w
Nizhniy Novgorod, → *Gorkiy,*				Oita, **Jap.**	33N15	131E36	8h46E
URSS				Okayama, **Jap.**	34N40	133E54	8h56E
Nizhniy Tagil, **URSS**	58N00	59E58	4h00E	Oklahoma City, Okla., **USA**	35N28	97w33	6h30w
N'Kayi, **Congo**	4s07	13E17	0h53E	Oldenburg, **BRD**	53N08	8E13	0h33E
Nobeoka, **Jap.**	32N36	131E40	8h47E	Oldham, **G.-B.**	53N33	2w07	0h08w
Nogent-sur-Seine, **Fr.**	48N30	3E31	0h14E	Olmütz, → *Olomouc,* **Tch.**			
Norden, **BRD**	53N36	7E13	0h29E	Olomouc, **Tch.**	49N38	17E15	1h09E
Nordhausen, **DDR**	51N31	10E48	0h43E	Olsztyn, **Pol.**	53N48	20E29	1h22E
Nordhorn, **BRD**	52N27	7E05	0h28E	Olten, **Sui.**	47N22	7E55	0h32E
Nördlingen, **BRD**	48N51	10E31	0h42E	Olympia, Wash., **USA**	47N03	122w53	8h12w
Norfolk, Va., **USA**	36N54	76w18	5h05w	Omaha, Neb., **USA**	41N15	96w00	6h24w
Norfolk I., **Pac.O.**	29s00	168E00	11h12E	Omdurman, **Sudan**	15N37	32E29	2h10E
Norman Wells, NT, **Can.**	65N18	126w42	8h27w	Omiya, **Jap.**	35N54	139E39	9h19E
Norrköping, **Sue.**	58N35	16E10	1h05E	Omsk, **URSS**	55N00	73E22	4h53E

City	Lat.	Long.	Time	City	Lat.	Long.	Time
Omuta, **Jap.**	33N02	130E26	8h42E	Palma de Mallorca, **Bal.I.**	39N35	2E39	0h11E
Ondo, **Nig.**	7N05	4E55	0h20E	Palmerston North, **N.Zel.**	40s20	175E39	11h43E
Onitsha, **Nig.**	6N10	6E47	0h27E	Palmira, **Col.**	3N33	76w17	5h05w
Oostende, **Belg.**	51N13	2E55	0h12E	Palo Alto, Ca., **USA**	37N26	122w10	8h09w
Opole (Oppeln), **Pol.**	50N40	17E56	1h12E	Pamplona, **Col.**	7N24	72w38	4h51w
Oradea, **Roum.**	47N03	21E55	1h28E	Pamplona (Pampelune), **Esp.**	42N49	1w39	0h07w
Oran, **Alg.**	35N45	0w38	0h03w	Panaji (Panjim), **Ind.**	15N31	73E52	4h55E
Orange, **Fr.**	44N08	4E48	0h19E	Panamá, **Panama**	8N57	79w30	5h18w
Ordzhonikidze, **URSS**	43N02	44E43	2h59E	Pancevo, **Youg.**	44N52	20E40	1h23E
Orekhovo Zuyevo, **URSS**	55N47	39E00	2h36E	Pangkalpinang, **Indon.**	2s05	106E09	7h05E
Orël (Orol), **URSS**	52N58	36E04	2h24E	Pao-teou (Baotou), **China**	40N38	109E59	7h20E
Orenburg, **URSS**	51N50	55E00	3h40E	Pao-ting (Baoding), **China**	38N54	115E26	7h42E
Orense, **Esp.**	42N20	7w52	0h31w	Papeete, Tahiti I., **Pac.O.**	17s32	149w34	9h58w
Orihuela, **Esp.**	38N05	0w56	0h04w	Paraguarí, **Parag.**	25s36	57w06	3h48w
Orizaba, **Mex.**	18N51	97w08	6h29w	Parakou, **Benin**	9N23	2E40	0h11E
Orlando, Fla., **USA**	28N33	81w21	5h25w	Paramaribo, **Surin.**	5N52	55w14	3h41w
Orléans, **Fr.**	47N54	1E54	0h08E	Paraná, **Arg.**	31s45	60w30	4h02w
Orsk, **URSS**	51N13	58E35	3h54E	Pardubice, **Tch.**	50N03	15E45	1h03E
Oruro, **Bol.**	17s59	67w08	4h29w	Paris, **Fr.**	48N52	2E20	0h09E
Osaka, **Jap.**	34N42	135E23	9h02E	Parkersburg, WV, **USA**	39N17	81w33	5h26w
Oshawa, Ont., **Can.**	43N53	78w51	5h15w	Parma (Parme), **Ital.**	44N48	10E19	0h41E
Oshogbo, **Nig.**	7N50	4E35	0h18E	Parnaíba, **Brasil**	2s58	41w46	2h47w
Osijek, **Youg.**	45N33	18E41	1h15E	Pasadena, Ca., **USA**	34N10	118w09	7h53w
Oslo, **Nor.**	59N56	10E45	0h43E	Pascua (Pâques) I., **Pac.O.**	27s09	109w26	7h18w
Osnabrück, **BRD**	52N17	8E03	0h32E	Pasewalk, **DDR**	53N30	14E00	0h56E
Osorno, **Chile**	40s35	73w14	4h53w	Passau, **BRD**	48N35	13E28	0h54E
Ostende, → *Oostende,* **Belg.**				Passo Fundo, **Brasil**	28s16	52w20	3h29w
Osterode am Harz, **BRD**	51N44	10E15	0h41E	Pasto, **Col.**	1N12	77w17	5h09w
Ostrava, **Tch.**	49N50	18E15	1h13E	Paterson, NJ, **USA**	40N56	74w09	4h57w
Otaru, **Jap.**	43N14	140E59	9h24E	Pathankot, **Ind.**	32N16	75E43	5h03E
Ottawa, Ont., **Can.**	45N25	75w43	5h03w	Patiala, **Ind.**	30N21	76E27	5h06E
Ouagadougou, **H.Vol.**	12N20	1w40	0h07w	Patna, Bihar, **Ind.**	25N37	85E12	5h41E
Ouahigouya, **H.Vol.**	13N31	2w20	0h09w	Pátra (Patras), **Grc.**	38N14	21E44	1h27E
Oudenaarde (Audenarde), **Belg.**	50N50	3E37	0h14E	Pau, **Fr.**	43N18	0w22	0h01w
Oudtshoorn, **S.Afr.**	33s35	22E12	1h29E	Pavia (Pavie), **Ital.**	45N12	9E09	0h37E
Oued Zem, **Mar.**	32N55	6w33	0h26w	Pavlodar, **URSS**	52N21	76E59	5h08E
Ouesso, **Congo**	1N38	16E03	1h04E	Paysandú, **Urug.**	32s21	58w05	3h52w
Ouezzane, **Mar.**	34N52	5w35	0h22w	Pazardzhik, **Bulg.**	42N10	24E20	1h37E
Ouidah, **Benin**	6N23	2E08	0h09E	Peace River, Alb., **Can.**	56N15	117w18	7h49w
Oujda (Oudjda), **Mar.**	34N41	1w45	0h07w	Pecos, Tex., **USA**	31N25	103w30	6h54w
Oulan-Oude, → *Ulan-Ude,* **URSS**				Pecs, **Hong.**	46N04	18E15	1h13E
Oulu (Ouleaborg), **Finl.**	65N00	25E26	1h42E	Pedro Juan Caballero, **Parag.**	22s30	55w44	3h43w
Ourga, → *Ulaan Baatar,* **Mong.**				Peine, **BRD**	52N19	10E13	0h41E
Ourmia, → *Urumiyeh,* **Iran**				Pekanbaru (Pâkanbaru), **Indon.**	0N33	101E30	6h46E
Oviedo, **Esp.**	43N21	5w50	0h23w	Pe-king (Pekin), **China**	39N55	116E26	7h46E
Owerri, **Nig.**	5N29	7E02	0h28E	Pelotas, **Brasil**	31s45	52w20	3h29w
Oxford, **G.-B.**	51N46	1w15	0h05w	Pembroke, Ont., **Can.**	45N49	77w08	5h09w
Oyo, **Nig.**	7N50	3E55	0h16E	Penang, **Malay.**	5N30	100E28	6h42E
				Peng-pou (Bengbu), **China**	32N56	117E27	7h50E
				Pen-hsi (Benxi), **China**	41N20	123E45	8h15E
*** P ***				Penrith, **G.-B.**	54N40	2w44	0h11w
				Penticton, Br.Col., **Can.**	49N29	119w38	7h59w
Pachuca, **Mex.**	20N10	98w44	6h35w	Penza, **URSS**	53N11	45E00	3h00E
Padang, Sumatra, **Indon.**	1s00	100E21	6h41E	Penzance, **G.-B.**	50N07	5w33	0h22w
Paderborn, **BRD**	51N43	8E44	0h35E	Peoria, Ill., **USA**	40N43	89w38	5h59w
Padova (Padoue), **Ital.**	45N24	11E53	0h48E	Pereira, **Col.**	4N47	75w46	5h03w
Paisley, **G.-B.**	55N50	4w26	0h18w	Pergamino, **Arg.**	33s52	60w30	4h02w
Pakse, **Laos**	15N09	105E50	7h03E	Périgueux, **Fr.**	45N10	0E42	0h03E
Palau (Palos) I., **Pac.O.**	7N30	134E30	8h58E	Perm, **URSS**	58N00	56E10	3h45E
Palembang, **Indon.**	2s59	104E45	6h59E	Pernambuco, → *Recife,* **Brasil**			
Palencia, **Esp.**	42N01	4w32	0h18w	Pernik (Dimitrovo), **Bulg.**	42N36	23E03	1h32E
Palermo (Palerme), **Ital.**	38N08	13E23	0h54E	Perpignan, **Fr.**	42N42	2E54	0h12E
Palimé (Kpalimé), **Togo**	6N55	0E44	0h03E	Perth, **Aust.**	31s58	115E49	7h43E

City	Lat.	Long.	Time	City	Lat.	Long.	Time
Perth, Tayside, **G.-B.**	56N24	3w28	0h14w	Poona, **Ind.**	18N34	73E58	4h56E
Perugia (Pérouse), **Ital.**	43N07	12E23	0h50E	Popayán, **Col.**	2N27	76w32	5h06w
Pesaro, **Ital.**	43N54	12E54	0h52E	Poperinge, **Belg.**	50N52	2E44	0h11E
Pescara, **Ital.**	42N27	14E13	0h57E	Poplar Bluff, Mo., **USA**	36N46	90w25	6h02w
Pescia, **Ital.**	43N54	10E41	0h43E	Pori, **Finl.**	61N28	21E45	1h27E
Peshawar, **Pak.**	34N01	71E40	4h47E	Portachuelo, **Bol.**	17s20	53w23	3h34w
Petah Tiqva, **Isr.**	32N05	34E53	2h20E	Portalegre, **Port.**	39N17	7w25	0h30w
Peterborough, Ont., **Can.**	44N19	78w20	5h13w	Port Arthur, Tex., **USA**	29N55	93w56	6h16w
Peterborough, **G.-B.**	52N35	0w15	0h01w	Port Arthur, → *Thunder Bay,* **Can.**			
Petropavlovsk, **URSS**	54N53	69E13	4h37E	Port au Prince, **Haiti**	18N33	72w20	4h49w
Petropavlovsk Kamchatskiy, **URSS**	53N03	158E43	10h35E	Port Elizabeth, **S.Afr.**	33s58	25E36	1h42E
Petrópolis, **Brasil**	22s30	43w06	2h52w	Port Harcourt, **Nig.**	4N43	7E10	0h29E
Petrozavodsk, **URSS**	61N46	34E19	2h17E	Portland, Me., **USA**	43N41	70w18	4h41w
Pforzheim, **BRD**	48N53	8E41	0h35E	Portland, Ore., **USA**	45N32	122w40	8h11w
Philadelphia, Pa., **USA**	40N00	75w10	5h01w	Port Louis, **Mau.I.**	20s10	57E30	3h50E
Philippeville, **Belg.**	50N12	4E33	0h18E	Port Moresby, **Pap.**	9s30	147E07	9h48E
Phnom Penh, **Kamp.**	11N35	104E55	7h00E	Porto, **Port.**	41N09	8w37	0h34w
Phoenix, Ariz., **USA**	33N30	112w03	7h28w	Porto Alegre, Rio Grande, **Brasil**	30s03	51w10	3h25w
Phoenix I., **Pac.O.**	3s43	171w25	11h26w	Port of Spain, **T.Tob.**	10N38	61w31	4h06w
Piacenza, **Ital.**	45N03	9E41	0h39E	Porto Novo, **Benin**	6N30	2E47	0h11E
Piazza Armerina, **Ital.**	37N22	14E22	0h57E	Port Pirie, **Aust.**	33s11	138E01	9h12E
Pierre, SD, **USA**	44N23	100w20	6h41w	Port Saïd, → *Bûr Saïd,* **Egy.**			
Pietermaritzburg, **S.Afr.**	29s36	30E24	2h02E	Portsmouth, **G.-B.**	50N48	1w05	0h04w
Pietersburg, **S.Afr.**	23s54	29E23	1h58E	Portsmouth, Va., **USA**	36N50	76w20	5h05w
Pilar, **Parag.**	26s51	58w20	3h53w	Port Sudan, **Sudan**	19N38	37E07	2h28E
Pilsen, → *Plzen,* **Tch.**				Posadas, **Arg.**	27s27	55w50	3h43w
Pine Bluff, Ark., **USA**	34N13	92w00	6h08w	Possesion I., **Ind.O.**	46s35	51E50	3h27E
Piotrkow, Lodz, **Pol.**	51N27	19E40	1h19E	Potenza, **Ital.**	40N38	15E48	1h03E
Piracicaba, **Brasil**	22s45	47w40	3h11w	Potiskum, **Nig.**	11N40	11E03	0h44E
Piréas, **Grc.**	37N57	23E42	1h35E	Potosi, **Bol.**	19s34	65w45	4h23w
Pirmasens, **BRD**	49N12	7E37	0h30E	Potsdam, **DDR**	52N24	13E04	0h52E
Pisa (Pise), **Ital.**	43N43	10E24	0h42E	Poznan (Posen), **Pol.**	52N25	16E53	1h08E
Pisco, **Peru**	13s46	76w12	5h05w	Pozzuoli (Pouzzoles), **Ital.**	40N49	14E07	0h56E
Pistoia, **Ital.**	43N56	10E55	0h44E	Prague, → *Praha,* **Tch.**			
Pitcairn I., **Pac.O.**	25s04	130w06	8h40w	Praha, **Tch.**	50N06	14E26	0h58E
Pitea, **Sue.**	65N19	21E30	1h26E	Prato, **Ital.**	43N53	11E06	0h44E
Pitesti, **Roum.**	44N51	24E51	1h39E	Prenzlau, **DDR**	53N19	13E52	0h55E
Pithiviers, **Fr.**	48N10	2E15	0h09E	Presidente Prudente, **Brasil**	22s09	51w24	3h26w
Pittsburgh, Pa., **USA**	40N26	80w00	5h20w	Pressburg, → *Bratislava,* **Tch.**			
Piura, **Peru**	5s15	80w38	5h23w	Preston, Lancs, **G.-B.**	53N46	2w42	0h11w
Plaisance, → *Piacenza,* **Ital.**				Pretoria, **S.Afr.**	25s45	28E12	1h53E
Plauen, **DDR**	50N29	12E08	0h49E	Prince Albert, Sask., **Can.**	53N13	105w45	7h03w
Pleven, **Bulg.**	43N25	24E40	1h39E	Prince Edouard I., **Ind.O.**	46s50	37E45	2h31E
Ploiesti, **Roum.**	44N57	26E01	1h44E	Prince George, Br.Col., **Can.**	53N55	122w49	8h11w
Plovdiv, **Bulg.**	42N08	24E45	1h39E	Prince Rupert, Br.Col., **Can.**	54N18	130w17	8h41w
Plymouth, Montserrat, **Ant.P.**	16N44	62w14	4h09w	Pritzwalk, **DDR**	53N09	12E11	0h49E
Plymouth, **G.-B.**	50N23	4w10	0h17w	Privas, **Fr.**	44N44	4E36	0h18E
Plzen, **Tch.**	49N45	13E25	0h54E	Prokopyevsk, **URSS**	53N55	86E45	5h47E
Pobé, **Benin**	7N00	2E56	0h12E	Providence, RI, **USA**	41N50	71w28	4h46w
Pocatello, Id., **USA**	42N53	112w26	7h30w	Przemysl, **Pol.**	49N48	22E48	1h31E
Pointe-à-Pitre, Guadeloupe, **Ant.P.**	16N14	61w32	4h06w	Pskov, **URSS**	57N48	28E26	1h54E
Pointe Noire, **Congo**	4s46	11E53	0h48E	Puebla, **Mex.**	19N03	98w10	6h33w
Poitiers, **Fr.**	46N35	0E20	0h01E	Pueblo, Colo., **USA**	38N17	104w38	6h59w
Pokhara, **Nepal**	28N14	83E58	5h36E	Puertollano, **Esp.**	38N41	4w07	0h16w
Poltava, **URSS**	49N35	34E35	2h18E	Puerto Montt, **Chile**	41s28	73w00	4h52w
Ponce, **P.Rico**	18N01	66w36	4h26w	Puerto Plata, **Dom.**	19N48	70w41	4h43w
Pondichery, **Ind.**	11N59	79E50	5h19E	Pula, **Youg.**	44N52	13E52	0h55E
Ponferrada, **Esp.**	42N33	6w35	0h26w	Punakha, **Bhutan**	27N38	89E50	5h59E
Ponta Delgada, Açores I., **Atl.O.**	37N29	25w40	1h43w	Puno, **Peru**	15s53	70w03	4h40w
Ponta Grossa, **Brasil**	25s07	50w09	3h21w	Punta Arenas, **Chile**	53s10	70w56	4h44w
Pontevedra, **Esp.**	42N25	8w39	0h35w	Puntarenas, **C.Rica**	10N00	84w50	5h39w
Pontianak, **Indon.**	0s05	109E16	7h17E	Pursat, **Kamp.**	12N27	103E40	6h55E
Poole, **G.-B.**	50N43	1w59	0h08w	Pusan, **Cor.S.**	35N05	129E02	8h36E

City	Lat.	Long.	Time	City	Lat.	Long.	Time
Pyinmana, **Birm.**	19N45	96E12	6h25E	Reichenbach, **DDR**	50N36	12E18	0h49E
Pyongyang, **Cor.N.**	39N00	125E47	8h23E	Reims, **Fr.**	49N15	4E02	0h16E
				Remscheid, **BRD**	51N10	7E11	0h29E
				Rendsburg, **BRD**	54N19	9E39	0h39E
*** Q ***				Rennes, **Fr.**	48N06	1w40	0h07w
				Reno, Nev., **USA**	39N32	119w49	7h59w
Qacentina, → *Constantine,* **Alg.**				Requena, **Esp.**	39N29	1w08	0h05w-
Qazvin, **Iran**	36N16	50E00	3h20E	Resistencia, **Arg.**	27s28	59w00	3h56w
Qena, **Egy.**	26N08	32E42	2h11E	Resita, **Roum.**	45N16	21E55	1h28E
Qiryat Gat, **Isr.**	31N37	34E47	2h19E	Reutlingen, **BRD**	48N30	9E13	0h37E
Qiryat Shemona, **Isr.**	33N13	35E35	2h22E	Reval, → *Tallinn,* **URSS**			
Qom (Qum), **Iran**	34N39	50E57	3h24E	Reykjavik, **Isl.**	64N09	21w58	1h28w
Québec, Que., **Can.**	46N50	71w15	4h45w	Rheine, **BRD**	52N17	7E26	0h30E
Querétaro, **Mex.**	20N38	100w23	6h42w	Rhondda, **G.-B.**	51N40	3w30	0h14w
Quesnel, Br.Col., **Can.**	53N03	122w31	8h10w	Riad, → *Riyad,* **Ar.S.**			
Quetta, **Pak.**	30N15	66E55	4h28E	Ribeirao Prêto, **Brasil**	21s09	47w48	3h11w
Quezaltenango, **Guat.**	14N50	91w30	6h06w	Riberalta, **Bol.**	10s59	66w06	4h24w
Quezon City, **Phil.**	14N39	121E02	8h04E	Richland, Wash., **USA**	46N17	119w17	7h57w
Quimper, **Fr.**	48N00	4w06	0h16w	Richmond, Ca., **USA**	37N56	122w20	8h09w
Quito, **Ecuad.**	0s14	78w30	5h14w	Richmond, Ind., **USA**	39N50	84w51	5h39w
				Richmond, Va., **USA**	37N34	77w27	5h10w
				Ried im Innkreis, **Aut.**	48N13	13E29	0h54E
*** R ***				Riesa, **DDR**	51N18	13E18	0h53E
				Riga, **URSS**	56N53	24E08	1h37E
Raba, **Indon.**	8s27	118E45	7h55E	Rijeka, **Youg.**	45N20	14E27	0h58E
Rabat, **Mar.**	34N02	6w51	0h27w	Rimini, **Ital.**	44N03	12E34	0h50E
Rabaul, **Pap.**	4s13	152E11	10h09E	Riobamba, **Ecuad.**	1s44	78w40	5h15w
Radom, **Pol.**	51N26	21E10	1h25E	Rio Branco, **Brasil**	9s59	67w49	4h31w
Ragusa, **Ital.**	36N56	14E44	0h59E	Rio Cuarto, **Arg.**	33s08	64w20	4h17w
Raipur, **Ind.**	21N16	81E42	5h27E	Rio de Janeiro, **Brasil**	22s53	43w17	2h53w
Rajkot, **Ind.**	22N18	70E53	4h44E	Rio Gallegos, **Arg.**	51s35	69w15	4h37w
Raleigh, NC, **USA**	35N42	78w40	5h15w	Ríosucio, Caldas, **Col.**	5N26	75w44	5h03w
Rambouillet, **Fr.**	48N39	1E50	0h07E	Rishon le Zion, **Isr.**	31N57	34E48	2h19E
Ramla (Ramleh), **Isr.**	31N56	34E52	2h19E	Rivera, **Urug.**	31s00	55w50	3h43w
Rampur, Uttar Pradesh, **Ind.**	28N48	79E03	5h16E	Riverside, Ca., **USA**	33N59	117w22	7h49w
Ramtha (Ar-Ramtha), **Jord.**	32N34	36E00	2h24E	Riyad (Ar Riyad), **Ar.S.**	24N39	46E46	3h07E
Rancagua, **Chile**	34s10	70w45	4h43w	Roanne, **Fr.**	46N02	4E05	0h16E
Ranchi, **Ind.**	23N22	85E20	5h41E	Roanoke, Va., **USA**	37N15	79w58	5h20w
Randers, **Dan.**	56N28	10E03	0h40E	Rocha, **Urug.**	34s30	54w22	3h37w
Rangoon (Rangun), **Birm.**	16N47	96E10	6h25E	Rochdale, **G.-B.**	53N38	2w09	0h09w
Rangpur, **B.desh**	25N25	89E21	5h57E	Rochefort, **Fr.**	45N57	0w58	0h04w
Rapa Iti I., **Pac.O.**	27s35	144w20	9h37w	Rochester, NY, **USA**	43N12	77w37	5h10w
Rapid City, SD, **USA**	44N06	103w14	6h53w	Rockford, Ill., **USA**	42N16	89w06	5h56w
Rashid, **Egy.**	31N25	30E25	2h02E	Rockhampton, **Aust.**	23s22	150E32	10h02E
Rasht, **Iran**	37N18	49E38	3h19E	Rodez, **Fr.**	44N21	2E34	0h10E
Rathenow, **DDR**	52N37	12E21	0h49E	Rodos (Rhodes), **Grc.**	36N26	28E14	1h53E
Ratisbonne, → *Regensburg,* **BRD**				Rodriguez I., **Ind.O.**	19s40	63E26	4h14E
Ravenna, **Ital.**	44N25	12E12	0h49E	Roermond, **Nth.**	51N12	6E00	0h24E
Ravensburg, **BRD**	47N47	9E37	0h38E	Roeselare (Roulers), **Belg.**	50N57	3E08	0h13E
Rawalpindi, **Pak.**	33N40	73E08	4h53E	Roma (Rome), **Ital.**	41N53	12E30	0h50E
Razgrad, **Bulg.**	43N31	26E33	1h46E	Romans-sur-Isère, **Fr.**	45N03	5E03	0h20E
Reading, **G.-B.**	51N28	0w59	0h04w	Ronse (Renaix), **Belg.**	50N45	3E36	0h14E
Reading, Pa., **USA**	40N20	75w55	5h04w	Roosendaal, **Nth.**	51N32	4E28	0h18E
Recht, → *Rasht,* **Iran**				Rorschach, **Sui.**	47N28	9E30	0h38E
Recife, **Brasil**	8s06	34w53	2h20w	Rosario, Santa Fé, **Arg.**	33s00	60w40	4h03w
Recklinghausen, **BRD**	51N37	7E11	0h29E	Rosenheim, **BRD**	47N51	12E09	0h49E
Red Deer, Alb., **Can.**	52N15	113w48	7h35w	Rosetown, Sask., **Can.**	51N34	107w59	7h12w
Redding, Ca., **USA**	40N35	122w24	8h10w	Rosette, → *Rashid,* **Egy.**			
Regensburg, **BRD**	49N01	12E07	0h48E	Rostock, **DDR**	54N06	12E09	0h49E
Reggio Calabria, **Ital.**	38N06	15E39	1h03E	Rostov na Donu, **URSS**	47N15	39E45	2h39E
Reggio Emilia, **Ital.**	44N42	10E37	0h42E	Roswell, NM, **USA**	33N24	104w33	6h58w
Regina, Sask., **Can.**	50N30	104w38	6h59w	Rotherham, **G.-B.**	53N26	1w20	0h05w
Rehovot, **Isr.**	31N54	34E49	2h19E	Rotterdam, **Nth.**	51N55	4E29	0h18E

City	Lat.	Long.	Time	City	Lat.	Long.	Time
Rottweil, **BRD**	48N10	8E38	0h35E	Salamanca (Salamanque), **Esp.**	40N58	5w40	0h23w
Roubaix, **Fr.**	50N42	3E10	0h13E	Sala y Gómez I., **Pac.O.**	26s28	105w28	7h02w
Rouen, **Fr.**	49N26	1E05	0h04E	Salé, **Mar.**	34N04	6w50	0h27w
Rouyn, Que., **Can.**	48N15	79w00	5h16w	Salem, **Ind.**	11N38	78E08	5h13E
Royal Leamington Spa, **G.-B.**	52N18	1w31	0h06w	Salem, Ore., **USA**	44N57	123w01	8h12w
Rudolstadt, **DDR**	50N44	11E20	0h45E	Salerno, **Ital.**	40N40	14E46	0h59E
Rufino, **Arg.**	34s16	62w45	4h11w	Salisbury, **G.-B.**	51N05	1w48	0h07w
Rugby, **G.-B.**	52N23	1w15	0h05w	Salisbury, → *Hararé*, **Zimb.**			
Ruse (Ruschuk), **Bulg.**	43N50	25E59	1h44E	Salonique, → *Thessaloniki*, **Grc.**			
Rutland, Vt., **USA**	43N37	72w59	4h52w	Salt (As Salt), **Jord.**	32N03	35E44	2h23E
Ryazan (Riazan), **URSS**	54N37	39E43	2h39E	Salta, **Arg.**	24s46	65w28	4h22w
Rybinsk, **URSS**	58N01	38E52	2h35E	Saltillo, **Mex.**	25N30	101w00	6h44w
				Salt Lake City, Ut., **USA**	40N45	111w55	7h28w
				Salto, **Urug.**	31s27	57w50	3h51w
*** S ***				Salvador, **Brasil**	12s58	38w29	2h34w
				Salzburg (Salzbourg), **Aut.**	47N48	13E03	0h52E
Saalfeld, **DDR**	50N39	11E22	0h45E	Salzgitter, **BRD**	52N13	10E20	0h41E
Saanen (Gessenay), **Sui.**	46N30	7E16	0h29E	Salzwedel, **DDR**	52N51	11E10	0h45E
Saarbrücken, **BRD**	49N15	6E58	0h28E	Samara, → *Kuybyshev*, **URSS**			
Saarlouis (Sarrelouis), **BRD**	49N19	6E45	0h27E	Samarang, → *Semarang*, **Indon.**			
Sabadell, **Esp.**	41N33	2E07	0h08E	Samarkand, **URSS**	39N40	66E57	4h28E
Sacramento, Ca., **USA**	38N33	121w30	8h06w	Samoa I. (Apia), **Pac.O.**	13s48	171w45	11h27w
Safi, **Mar.**	32N18	9w20	0h37w	Samsun, **Tur.**	41N17	36E22	2h25E
Saginaw, Mich., **USA**	43N25	83w54	5h36w	San, **Mali**	13N21	4w57	0h20w
Saharanpur, **Ind.**	29N58	77E33	5h10E	Sana (Sanaa), **Yemen**	15N24	44E14	2h57E
Sahiwal, **Pak.**	30N14	73E10	4h53E	San Angelo, Tex., **USA**	31N28	100w28	6h42w
Saïgon, → *Ho-Chi-Minh*, **Viet.**				San Antonio, Tex., **USA**	29N25	98w30	6h34w
Saint Albans, **G.-B.**	51N46	0w21	0h01w	San Bernardino, Ca., **USA**	34N07	117w18	7h49w
Saint-Brieuc, **Fr.**	48N31	2w45	0h11w	San Cristóbal, **Arg.**	30s20	61w14	4h05w
Saint-Denis, **Reu.I.**	20s52	55E27	3h42E	San Cristóbal, **Ven.**	7N46	72w15	4h49w
Saint-Dizier, Haute-Marne, **Fr.**	48N38	4E58	0h20E	Sancti Spíritus, **Cuba**	21N55	79w28	5h18w
Saint-Domingue, → *Santo Domingo*, **Dom.**				Sandakan, **Malay.**	5N52	118E04	7h52E
Sainte-Menehould, **Fr.**	49N05	4E54	0h20E	San Diego, Ca., **USA**	32N45	117w10	7h49w
Saintes, **Fr.**	45N44	0w38	0h03w	San Felipe, **Chile**	32s45	70w42	4h43w
Saint-Etienne, Loire, **Fr.**	45N26	4E23	0h18E	San Felipe, **Ven.**	10N25	68w40	4h35w
Saint-Gall, → *Sankt Gallen*, **Sui.**				San Fernando, **Chile**	34s40	71w00	4h44w
Saint George's, Grenade, **Ant.P.**	12N04	61w44	4h07w	San Fernando, **T.Tob.**	10N16	61w28	4h06w
Saint Helena I., **Atl.O.**	15s57	5w42	0h23w	San Fernando, Ca., **USA**	34N17	118w27	7h54w
Saint Helens, **G.-B.**	53N28	2w44	0h11w	San Fernando de Apure, **Ven.**	7N53	67w15	4h29w
Saint Helier, Jersey, **G.-B.**	49N12	2w07	0h08w	San Francisco, Córdoba, **Arg.**	31s29	62w06	4h08w
Saint Hyacinthe, Que., **Can.**	45N38	72w57	4h52w	San Francisco, Ca., **USA**	37N45	122w27	8h10w
Saint John (Saint Jean), NB, **Can.**	45N16	66w03	4h24w	San Francisco de Macoris, **Dom.**	19N19	70w15	4h41w
Saint John's, Antigua, **Ant.P.**	17N08	61w50	4h07w	San José, **C.Rica**	9N59	84w04	5h36w
Saint John's (Saint Jean), TN, **Can.**	47N34	52w41	3h31w	San Jose, Ca., **USA**	37N20	121w55	8h08w
Saint Joseph, Mo., **USA**	39N46	94w52	6h19w	San Juan, **Arg.**	31s33	68w31	4h34w
Saint-Lô, **Fr.**	49N07	1w05	0h04w	San Juan, **P.Rico**	18N29	66w08	4h25w
Saint-Louis, **Reu.I.**	21s17	55E25	3h42E	San Juan de los Morros, **Ven.**	9N53	67w23	4h30w
Saint Louis, **Seneg.**	16N01	16w30	1h06w	Sankt Gallen, **Sui.**	47N25	9E23	0h38E
Saint Louis, Mo., **USA**	38N40	90w15	6h01w	Sankt Pölten, **Aut.**	48N13	15E37	1h02E
Saint-Malo, **Fr.**	48N39	2w00	0h08w	San Luis, **Arg.**	33s20	66w23	4h26w
Saint Moritz, **Sui.**	46N30	9E51	0h39E	San Luis Obispo, Ca., **USA**	35N16	120w40	8h03w
Saint-Nazaire, **Fr.**	47N17	2w12	0h09w	San Luis Potosí, **Mex.**	22N10	101w00	6h44w
Saint Paul, Minn., **USA**	45N00	93w10	6h13w	San Marino, San Marino, **Ital.**	43N56	12E26	0h50E
Saint Petersburg, Fla., **USA**	27N45	82w40	5h31w	San Mateo, Ca., **USA**	37N33	122w22	8h09w
Saint-Pierre, **Reu.I.**	21s20	55E29	3h42E	San Miguel, **Salv.**	13N28	88w10	5h53w
Saint-Pierre et Miquelon, **Atl.O.**	46N46	56w12	3h45w	San Miguel de Tucumán, **Arg.**	26s47	65w15	4h21w
Saint-Quentin, **Fr.**	49N51	3E17	0h13E	San Nicolas, **Arg.**	33s25	60w15	4h01w
Saint-Trond (St-Truiden), **Belg.**	50N49	5E11	0h21E	San Pedro Sula, **Hond.**	15N26	88w01	5h52w
Sakété, **Benin**	6N45	2E45	0h11E	San Rafael, **Arg.**	34s35	68w24	4h34w
Salaga, **Ghana**	8N34	0w28	0h02w	San Remo, **Ital.**	43N48	7E46	0h31E
Salalah, **Oman**	17N00	54E04	3h36E	San Salvador, **Salv.**	13N40	89w10	5h57w
				San Salvador de Jujuy, **Arg.**	24s10	65w48	4h23w
				Sansanné-Mango, **Togo**	10N23	0E35	0h02E

City	Lat.	Long.	Time	City	Lat.	Long.	Time
San Sebastián (Saint-Sébastien),				Schenectady, NY, **USA**	42N48	73w57	4h56w
Esp.	43N19	1w59	0h08w	Schiedam, **Nth.**	51N55	4E25	0h18E
San Severo, **Ital.**	41N41	15E23	1h02E	Schleiz, **DDR**	50N34	11E49	0h47E
Santa Ana, Beni, **Bol.**	13s46	65w37	4h22w	Schleswig, **BRD**	54N32	9E34	0h38E
Santa Ana, **Salv.**	14N00	89w31	5h58w	Schweinfurt, **BRD**	50N03	10E16	0h41E
Santa Ana, Ca., **USA**	33N44	117w54	7h52w	Schwenningen, **BRD**	48N03	8E32	0h34E
Santa Bárbara, **Mex.**	26N48	105w50	7h03w	Schwerin, **DDR**	53N38	11E25	0h46E
Santa Barbara, Ca., **USA**	34N25	119w41	7h59w	Schwyz, **Sui.**	47N02	8E39	0h35E
Santa Clara, **Cuba**	22N25	79w58	5h20w	Scranton, Pa., **USA**	41N25	75w40	5h03w
Santa Cruz, **Bol.**	17s45	63w14	4h13w	Scutari, → *Usküdar*, **Tur.**			
Santa Cruz, Ca., **USA**	36N58	122w03	8h08w	Seattle, Wash., **USA**	47N35	122w20	8h09w
Santa Cruz de Tenerife, **Can.I.**	28N28	16w15	1h05w	Sebastopol, → *Sevastopol*, **URSS**			
Santa Cruz I., **Pac.O.**	10s42	165E50	11h03E	Secunderabad, **Ind.**	17N27	78E27	5h14E
Santa Fé, **Arg.**	31s38	60w43	4h03w	Sedan, **Fr.**	49N42	4E57	0h20E
Santa Fe, NM, **USA**	35N41	105w57	7h04w	Sefrou, **Mar.**	33N50	4w50	0h19w
Santa Isabel, → *Malabo*, **G.eq.**				Segou, **Mali**	13N28	6w18	0h25w
Santa Maria, Rio Grande, **Brasil**	29s40	53w40	3h35w	Segovia, **Esp.**	40N57	4w07	0h16w
Santa Marta, **Col.**	11N18	74w10	4h57w	Sekondi, **Ghana**	4N59	1w43	0h07w
Santana do Livramento, **Brasil**	30s52	55w30	3h42w	Semarang, **Indon.**	6s58	110E29	7h22E
Santander, **Col.**	3N00	76w25	5h06w	Semipalatinsk, **URSS**	50N26	80E16	5h21E
Santander, **Esp.**	43N28	3w48	0h15w	Semnan, **Iran**	35N30	53E25	3h34E
Santarém, **Brasil**	2s26	54w41	3h39w	Sendai, Kyushu, **Jap.**	31N50	130E17	8h41E
Santarém, **Port.**	39N14	8w40	0h35w	Senlis, **Fr.**	49N12	2E35	0h10E
Santa Rosa, La Pampa, **Arg.**	36s37	64w17	4h17w	Sens, **Fr.**	48N12	3E18	0h13E
Santa Rosa, Ca., **USA**	38N26	122w43	8h11w	Seoul, → *Kyongsong*, **Cor.S.**			
Santiago, **Chile**	33s30	70w40	4h43w	Serang, **Indon.**	6s07	106E09	7h05E
Santiago, **Cuba**	20N00	75w49	5h03w	Serowe, **Bots.**	22s25	26E44	1h47E
Santiago, **Dom.**	19N30	70w42	4h43w	Serrai (Sérès), **Grc.**	41N03	23E33	1h34E
Santiago, **Panama**	8N08	80w59	5h24w	Sète, **Fr.**	43N25	3E43	0h15E
Santiago de Compostela, **Esp.**	42N52	8w33	0h34w	Setif (Stif), **Alg.**	36N11	5E24	0h22E
Santiago del Estero, **Arg.**	27s47	64w15	4h17w	Settat, **Mar.**	33N04	7w37	0h30w
Santo Domingo, **Dom.**	18N30	69w57	4h40w	Setúbal, **Port.**	38N31	8w54	0h36w
Santos, **Brasil**	23s56	46w22	3h05w	Sevastopol, **URSS**	44N36	33E31	2h14E
Sao José do Rio Prêto, **Brasil**	20s50	49w20	3h17w	Sevilla, **Col.**	4N16	75w58	5h04w
Sao Luis, Maranhao, **Brasil**	2s34	44w16	2h57w	Sevilla (Séville), **Esp.**	37N24	5w59	0h24w
Sao Paulo, **Brasil**	23s33	46w39	3h07w	Seychelles I. (Mahé), **Ind.O.**	4s38	55E28	3h42E
Sao Thome I., **Atl.O.**	0N19	6E43	0h27E	Sfax, **Tun.**	34N45	10E43	0h43E
Sapporo, **Jap.**	43N05	141E21	9h25E	's-Gravenhague, → *Den Haag*, **Nth.**			
Saragosse, → *Zaragoza*, **Esp.**				Shahjahanpur, **Ind.**	27N53	79E55	5h20E
Sarajevo, **Youg.**	43N52	18E26	1h14E	Shaki, **Nig.**	8N39	3E25	0h14E
Saransk, **URSS**	54N12	45E10	3h01E	Shangai, → *Chang-hai*, **China**			
Saratov, **URSS**	51N30	45E55	3h04E	Shaoguan, **China**	24N50	113E37	7h34E
Sarh, **Tchad**	9N08	18E22	1h13E	Shawinigan, Que., **Can.**	46N33	72w45	4h51w
Sarnen, **Sui.**	46N54	8E15	0h33E	Sheffield, **G.-B.**	53N23	1w30	0h06w
Sarnia, Ont., **Can.**	42N57	82w24	5h30w	Sherbrooke, Que., **Can.**	45N24	71w54	4h48w
Sarpsborg, **Nor.**	59N17	11E06	0h44E	Sheridan, Wyo., **USA**	44N48	106w57	7h08w
Sarrebourg, **Fr.**	48N44	7E03	0h28E	's-Hertogenbosch, **Nth.**	51N41	5E19	0h21E
Sarrebrück, → *Saarbrücken*, **BRD**				Shimizu, Honshu, **Jap.**	35N01	138E29	9h14E
Sasebo, **Jap.**	33N10	129E42	8h39E	Shimonoseki, **Jap.**	33N59	130E58	8h44E
Saskatoon, Sask., **Can.**	52N10	106w40	7h07w	Shiraz, **Iran**	29N38	52E34	3h30E
Sássari, Sardegne, **Ital.**	40N43	8E34	0h34E	Shizuoka, **Jap.**	34N59	138E24	9h14E
Satu-Mare, **Roum.**	47N48	22E52	1h31E	Shkodër (Scutari), **Alb.**	42N03	19E01	1h16E
Sault Sainte Marie, Ont., **Can.**	46N32	84w20	5h37w	Sholapur, **Ind.**	18N00	76E00	5h04E
Saumur, **Fr.**	47N16	0w05	0h00w	Shreveport, La., **USA**	32N30	93w46	6h15w
Savalou, **Benin**	7N59	2E03	0h08E	Shrewsbury, **G.-B.**	52N42	2w45	0h11w
Savannah, Ga., **USA**	32N04	81w07	5h24w	Shumen (Kolarovgrad), **Bulg.**	43N17	26E55	1h48E
Savannakhet, **Laos**	16N34	104E45	6h59E	Sialkot, **Pak.**	32N29	74E35	4h58E
Savé, **Benin**	8N04	2E37	0h10E	Siang-tan (Xiangtan), **China**	27N55	112E47	7h31E
Savona, **Ital.**	44N18	8E28	0h34E	Sibenik, **Youg.**	43N45	15E55	1h04E
Savonlinna, **Finl.**	61N54	28E55	1h56E	Sibiu, **Roum.**	45N46	24E09	1h37E
Sayda (Sidon), **Lbn**	33N32	35E22	2h21E	Sibolga, **Indon.**	1N42	98E48	6h35E
Scarborough, **G.-B.**	54N17	0w24	0h02w	Sicasica, **Bol.**	17s23	67w44	4h31w
Schaffhausen, **Sui.**	47N42	8E38	0h35E	Sidi-bel-Abbès, **Alg.**	35N15	0w39	0h03w

City	Lat.	Long.	Time	City	Lat.	Long.	Time
Sidi Ifni, **Mar.**	29N24	10w12	0h41w	Spokane, Wash., **USA**	47N40	117w25	7h50w
Sidi Kacem, **Mar.**	34N15	5w49	0h23w	Springfield, Ill., **USA**	39N49	89w39	5h59w
Siedlce, **Pol.**	52N10	22E18	1h29E	Springfield, Mass., **USA**	42N07	72w35	4h50w
Siegen, **BRD**	50N52	8E02	0h32E	Springfield, Mo., **USA**	37N11	93w19	6h13w
Siena (Sienne), **Ital.**	43N19	11E19	0h45E	Springfield, Oh., **USA**	39N50	83w48	5h35w
Sierre, **Sui.**	46N18	7E33	0h30E	Springfontein, **S.Afr.**	30s16	25E42	1h43E
Siguiri, **Guin.**	11N28	9w07	0h36w	Srinagar, **Ind.**	34N08	74E50	4h59E
Sikasso, **Mali**	11N18	5w38	0h23w	Stadthagen, **BRD**	52N19	9E13	0h37E
Simbirsk, → *Ulyanovsk,* **URSS**				Stafford, **G.-B.**	52N48	2w07	0h08w
Simferopol, **URSS**	44N57	34E05	2h16E	Stalinabad, → *Dushanbe,* **URSS**			
Sincelejo, **Col.**	9N17	75w23	5h02w	Stalingrad, → *Volgograd,* **URSS**			
Sinfra, **C.Iv.**	6N35	5w56	0h24w	Stalino, → *Donetsk,* **URSS**			
Si-ngan (Xi'an), **China**	34N16	108E54	7h16E	Stalinogorsk, → *Novomoskovsk,* **URSS**			
Singapore (Singapour), **Malay.**	1N19	103E49	6h55E				
Singkawang, **Indon.**	0N57	108E57	7h16E	Stalinsk, → *Novokuznetsk,* **URSS**			
Si-ning (Xining), **China**	36N35	101E55	6h48E	Stamford, **G.-B.**	52N39	0w29	0h02w
Sint-Niklaas (Saint-Nicolas), **Belg.**	51N10	4E09	0h17E	Stanleyville, → *Kisangani,* **Zaire**			
Sion, **Sui.**	46N14	7E22	0h29E	Stans, **Sui.**	46N57	8E23	0h34E
Sioux City, Ia., **USA**	42N30	96w28	6h26w	Stara Zagora, **Bulg.**	42N25	25E37	1h42E
Sioux Falls, SD, **USA**	43N34	96w42	6h27w	Stavanger, **Nor.**	58N58	5E45	0h23E
Siracusa (Syracuse), **Ital.**	37N04	15E18	1h01E	Stavropol, **URSS**	45N03	41E59	2h48E
Sittard, **Nth.**	51N00	5E52	0h23E	Stendal, **DDR**	52N36	11E52	0h47E
Sivas, **Tur.**	39N44	37E01	2h28E	Sterlitamak, **URSS**	53N40	55E59	3h44E
Skelleftea, **Sue.**	64N47	20E59	1h24E	Stettin, → *Szczecin,* **Pol.**			
Skien, **Nor.**	59N14	9E37	0h38E	Steyr, **Aut.**	48N04	14E25	0h58E
Skikda (Philippeville), **Alg.**	36N53	6E54	0h28E	Stirling, Central, **G.-B.**	56N07	3w57	0h16w
Skopje, **Youg.**	42N00	21E28	1h26E	Stockerau, **Aut.**	48N24	16E13	1h05E
Slagelse, **Dan.**	55N24	11E23	0h46E	Stockholm, **Sue.**	59N20	18E05	1h12E
Sligo, **Irl.**	54N17	8w28	0h34w	Stockport, **G.-B.**	53N25	2w10	0h09w
Sliven, **Bulg.**	42N40	26E19	1h45E	Stockton, Ca., **USA**	37N58	121w20	8h05w
Slupsk, **Pol.**	54N28	17E00	1h08E	Stockton on Tees, **G.-B.**	54N34	1w19	0h05w
Smolensk, **URSS**	54N49	32E04	2h08E	Stoke on Trent, **G.-B.**	53N00	2w10	0h09w
Smyrne, → *Izmir,* **Tur.**				Stralsund, **DDR**	54N18	13E06	0h52E
Socotra I., **Ind.O.**	12N30	54E00	3h36E	Stranraer, **G.-B.**	54N54	5w02	0h20w
Söderhamn, **Sue.**	61N19	17E10	1h09E	Strasbourg, **Fr.**	48N35	7E45	0h31E
Sofala, **Moz.**	19s49	34E52	2h19E	Stratford, Ont., **Can.**	43N22	81w00	5h24w
Sofiya (Sofia), **Bulg.**	42N40	23E18	1h33E	Straubing, **BRD**	48N53	12E35	0h50E
Sohag, **Egy.**	26N33	31E42	2h07E	Stuttgart, **BRD**	48N47	9E12	0h37E
Soignies (Zinnik), **Belg.**	50N35	4E04	0h16E	Subotica, **Youg.**	46N04	19E41	1h19E
Soissons, **Fr.**	49N23	3E20	0h13E	Sucre, **Bol.**	19s05	65w15	4h21w
Sokodé, **Togo**	8N59	1E11	0h05E	Sudbury, Ont., **Can.**	46N30	81w01	5h24w
Sokoto, **Nig.**	13N02	5E15	0h21E	Suez (As Suwais), **Egy.**	29N59	32E33	2h10E
Solingen, **BRD**	51N10	7E05	0h28E	Suhl, **DDR**	50N37	10E43	0h43E
Solothurn (Soleure), **Sui.**	47N13	7E32	0h30E	Sukarnopura, → *Jayapura,* **Indon.**			
Soltau, **BRD**	52N59	9E50	0h39E	Sukhumi (Soukhoumi), **URSS**	43N01	41E01	2h44E
Sopron, **Hong.**	47N40	16E35	1h06E	Sukkur, **Pak.**	27N42	68E54	4h36E
Soria, **Esp.**	41N46	2w28	0h10w	Sullana, **Peru**	4s52	80w39	5h23w
Sorocaba, **Brasil**	23s30	47w32	3h10w	Summit Lake, Br.Col., **Can.**	58N35	124w40	8h19w
Sosnowiec, **Pol.**	50N16	19E07	1h16E	Sumy (Soumy), **URSS**	50N55	34E49	2h19E
Sour, **Lbn**	33N16	35E12	2h21E	Sunderland, **G.-B.**	54N55	1w23	0h06w
Sousse, **Tun.**	35N50	10E38	0h43E	Sundsvall, **Sue.**	62N22	17E20	1h09E
Sou-tcheou (Suzhou), **China**	31N21	120E40	8h03E	Surabaya, **Indon.**	7s14	112E45	7h31E
Southampton, **G.-B.**	50N55	1w25	0h06w	Surakarta, **Indon.**	7s32	110E50	7h23E
South Bend, Ind., **USA**	41N40	86w15	5h45w	Surat, **Ind.**	21N10	72E54	4h52E
Southend on Sea, **G.-B.**	51N33	0E43	0h03E	Svendborg, **Dan.**	55N04	10E38	0h43E
South Georgia I., **Atl.O.**	54s16	36w32	2h26w	Sverdlovsk, **URSS**	56N52	60E35	4h02E
Southport, **G.-B.**	53N39	3w01	0h12w	Swansea, **G.-B.**	51N38	3w57	0h16w
South Shields, **G.-B.**	55N00	1w25	0h06w	Swatow, → *Chan-teou,* **China**			
Spartanburg, SC, **USA**	34N56	81w57	5h28w	Swift Current, Sask., **Can.**	50N17	107w49	7h11w
Speyer (Spire), **BRD**	49N18	8E26	0h34E	Swindon, **G.-B.**	51N34	1w47	0h07w
Spittal an der Drau, **Aut.**	46N48	13E30	0h54E	Sydney, **Aust.**	33s55	151E10	10h05E
Spitzberg (Svalbard) I., **Atl.O.**	78N00	17E00	1h08E	Sydney, NE, **Can.**	46N10	60w10	4h01w
Split (Spalato), **Youg.**	43N31	16E28	1h06E	Syktyvkar, **URSS**	61N42	50E45	3h23E

City	Lat.	Long.	Time
Syracuse, NY, **USA**	43N03	76w10	5h05w
Syzran, **URSS**	53N10	48E29	3h14E
Szczecin, **Pol.**	53N25	14E32	0h58E
Szeged, **Hong.**	46N15	20E09	1h21E
Székesfehérvár, **Hong.**	47N11	18E22	1h13E
Szekszárd, **Hong.**	46N21	18E41	1h15E
Szolnok, **Hong.**	47N10	20E10	1h21E
Szombathely, **Hong.**	47N14	16E38	1h07E

*** T ***

City	Lat.	Long.	Time
Tabora, **Tanz.**	5s02	32E57	2h12E
Tabriz, **Iran**	38N05	46E18	3h05E
Tacloban, **Phil.**	11N15	125E01	8h20E
Tacna, **Peru**	18s00	70w15	4h41w
Tacoma, Wash., **USA**	47N16	122w30	8h10w
Tacuarembó, **Urug.**	31s42	56w00	3h44w
Taegu, **Cor.S.**	35N52	128E36	8h34E
Taejon, **Cor.S.**	36N20	127E26	8h30E
Taganrog, **URSS**	47N14	38E55	2h36E
Tahoua, **Niger**	14N57	5E19	0h21E
T'ai-chung (Tai-tchong), **Taiwan**	24N09	120E40	8h03E
T'ai-nan, **Taiwan**	23N01	120E14	8h01E
T'ai-pei (Taipeh), **Taiwan**	25N05	121E32	8h06E
Tai-yuan, **China**	37N50	112E30	7h30E
Takamatsu, **Jap.**	34N20	134E01	8h56E
Takoradi, **Ghana**	4N55	1w45	0h07w
Talara, **Peru**	4s38	81w18	5h25w
Talca, **Chile**	35s28	71w40	4h47w
Ta-lien (Lüda), **China**	38N53	121E37	8h06E
Tallahassee, Fla., **USA**	30N26	84w19	5h37w
Tallinn, **URSS**	59N22	24E48	1h39E
Tamale, **Ghana**	9N26	0w49	0h03w
Tamatave, → *Toamasina*, **Madag.**			
Tambacounda, **Seneg.**	13N45	13w40	0h55w
Tambov, **URSS**	52N44	41E28	2h46E
Tampa, Fla., **USA**	27N58	82w38	5h31w
Tampere (Tammerfors), **Finl.**	61N32	23E45	1h35E
Tampico, **Mex.**	22N18	97w52	6h31w
Tananarive, → *Antananarivo*, **Madag.**			
Tandil, **Arg.**	37s18	59w10	3h57w
Tang-chan (Tangshan), **China**	39N37	118E05	7h52E
Tanger, **Mar.**	35N48	5w50	0h23w
Tanjungkarang, **Indon.**	5s22	105E18	7h01E
Tanout, **Niger**	15N05	8E50	0h35E
Tanta (Tantah), **Egy.**	30N48	31E00	2h04E
Taourirt, **Mar.**	34N25	2w53	0h12w
Tarabulus (Tripoli), **Lib.**	32N58	13E12	0h53E
Taranto (Tarente), **Ital.**	40N28	17E15	1h09E
Tarbes, **Fr.**	43N14	0E05	0h00E
Tarija, **Bol.**	21s33	64w45	4h19w
Tarkwa, **Ghana**	5N16	1w59	0h08w
Tarlac, **Phil.**	15N29	120E35	8h02E
Tarnow, **Pol.**	50N01	20E59	1h24E
Taroudannt, **Mar.**	30N31	8w55	0h36w
Tarragona, **Esp.**	41N07	1E15	0h05E
Tarrasa, **Esp.**	41N34	2E00	0h08E
Tartu, **URSS**	58N20	26E44	1h47E
Tartus, **Syr.**	34N55	35E52	2h23E
Tashkent (Tachkent), **URSS**	41N16	69E13	4h37E
Tatabanya, **Hong.**	47N31	18E25	1h14E

City	Lat.	Long.	Time
Ta-tong (Datong), **China**	40N12	113E12	7h33E
Taunton, **G.-B.**	51N01	3w06	0h12w
Tavua, **Fidji**	17s27	177E51	11h51E
Taza, **Mar.**	34N16	4w01	0h16w
Tbilisi, **URSS**	41N43	44E48	2h59E
Tch'ang-cha (Changsha), **China**	28N10	113E00	7h32E
Tchang-kia-keou (Zhangjiakou), **China**	40N59	114E59	7h40E
Tchang-tcheou (Zhangzhou), **China**	24N31	117E40	7h51E
Tch'ang-tch'ouen (Changchun), **China**	43N50	125E20	8h21E
Tcheng-tcheou (Zhengzhou), **China**	34N45	113E38	7h35E
Tch'eng-tou (Chengdu), **China**	30N37	104E06	6h56E
Tcherepovets, → *Cherepovets*, **URSS**			
Tchkalov, → *Orenburg*, **URSS**			
Tch'ong-K'ing (Chongqing), **China**	29N39	106E34	7h06E
Tczew, **Pol.**	54N05	18E46	1h15E
Tegucigalpa, **Hond.**	14N05	87w14	5h49w
Tehran (Teheran), **Iran**	35N40	51E26	3h26E
Telanaipura (Djambi), **Indon.**	1s36	103E39	6h55E
Tel Aviv-Jaffa, **Isr.**	32N05	34E46	2h19E
Telukbetung, **Indon.**	5s28	105E16	7h01E
Tema, **Ghana**	5N40	0w01	0h00w
Temesvar, → *Timisoara*, **Roum.**			
Temuco, **Chile**	38s45	72w40	4h51w
Tenkodogo, **H.Vol.**	11N54	0w19	0h01w
Teplice, **Tch.**	50N40	13E49	0h55E
Teresina, **Brasil**	5s09	42w46	2h51w
Ternate, **Indon.**	0N48	127E23	8h30E
Terni, **Ital.**	42N34	12E39	0h51E
Terre Haute, Ind., **USA**	39N27	87w24	5h50w
Teruel, **Esp.**	40N21	1w06	0h04w
Teterow, **DDR**	53N47	12E35	0h50E
Tetouan (Tetuan), **Mar.**	35N34	5w22	0h21w
Thessaloniki, **Grc.**	40N38	22E58	1h31E
Thiès, **Seneg.**	14N49	16w52	1h07w
Thimphu (Thimbu), **Bhutan**	27N32	89E43	5h59E
Thionville, **Fr.**	49N22	6E11	0h25E
Thonburi, **Thai.**	13N43	100E27	6h42E
Thonon-les-Bains, **Fr.**	46N22	6E30	0h26E
Thorn, → *Torun*, **Pol.**			
Thun (Thoune), **Sui.**	46N46	7E38	0h31E
Thunder Bay, Ont., **Can.**	48N27	89w12	5h57w
Thurso, **G.-B.**	58N35	3w32	0h14w
Tiaret (Tihert), **Alg.**	35N20	1E20	0h05E
Tiberiade, **Isr.**	32N48	35E32	2h22E
Tidjikdja, **Maur.**	18N29	11w31	0h46w
Tien-tsin (Tianjin), **China**	39N08	117E12	7h49E
Tiflis, → *Tbilisi*, **URSS**			
Ti-hua, → *Urümqi*, **China**			
Tijuana, **Mex.**	32N29	117w10	7h49w
Tilburg, **Nth.**	51N34	5E05	0h20E
Timaru, **N.Zel.**	44s23	171E14	11h25E
Timisoara, **Roum.**	45N45	21E15	1h25E
Timmins, Ont., **Can.**	48N30	81w20	5h25w
Tindouf, **Alg.**	27N42	8w10	0h33w
Tipperary, **Irl.**	52N29	8w10	0h33w
Tiranë (Tirana), **Alb.**	41N20	19E49	1h19E
Tiraspol, **URSS**	46N50	29E38	1h59E
Tîrgoviste, **Roum.**	44N56	25E27	1h42E
Tirgu-Mures, **Roum.**	46N33	24E34	1h38E
Tirlemont (Tienen), **Belg.**	50N48	4E56	0h20E

City	Lat.	Long.	Time	City	Lat.	Long.	Time
Tiruchirapalli, **Ind.**	10N50	78E43	5h15 E	Tristan da Cunha I., **Atl.O.**	37s03	12w19	0h49w
Titograd, **Youg.**	42N28	19E17	1h17 E	Trivandrum, **Ind.**	8N30	76E57	5h08 E
Titovo, **Youg.**	43N52	19E50	1h19 E	Trnava, **Tch.**	48N23	17E35	1h10 E
Tiznit, **Mar.**	29N43	9w44	0h39w	Trois Rivières, Que., **Can.**	46N21	72w34	4h50w
Tlemcen (Tilimsen), **Alg.**	34N53	1w21	0h05w	Trondheim (Trondhjem), **Nor.**	63N36	10E23	0h42 E
Toamasina, **Madag.**	18s10	49E23	3h18 E	Troyes, **Fr.**	48N18	4E05	0h16 E
Tocopilla, **Chile**	22s05	70w10	4h41w	Trujillo, **Peru**	8s06	79w00	5h16w
Tokelau I., **Pac.O.**	10s00	165w00	11h00w	Truk I., **Pac.O.**	7N25	151E45	10h07 E
Tokushima, **Jap.**	34N03	134E34	8h58 E	Tschenstochau, → *Czestochowa,*			
Tokyo, **Jap.**	35N40	139E45	9h19 E	**Pol.**			
Tolbukhin (Dobricht), **Bulg.**	43N34	27E51	1h51 E	Tselinograd, **URSS**	51N10	71E28	4h46 E
Toledo, **Esp.**	39N52	4w02	0h16w	Tsi-nan (Jinan), **China**	36N41	117E00	7h48 E
Toledo, Oh., **USA**	41N40	83w35	5h34w	Tsing-tao (Qingdao), **China**	36N04	120E22	8h01 E
Toliara, **Madag.**	23s20	43E41	2h55 E	Tsitsihar (Qiqihaer), **China**	47N23	124E00	8h16 E
Tolosa, **Esp.**	43N09	2w04	0h08w	Tuamotu I., **Pac.O.**	16s00	145w00	9h40w
Toluca, **Mex.**	19N20	99w40	6h39w	Tüblingen, **BRD**	48N32	9E04	0h36 E
Tombouctou, **Mali**	16N49	2w59	0h12w	Tubuaï (Australes) I., **Pac.O.**	23s23	149w27	9h58w
Tomsk, **URSS**	56N30	85E05	5h40 E	Tucson, Ariz., **USA**	32N15	110w57	7h24w
Tonga I., **Pac.O.**	21s10	175w10	11h41w	Tudela, **Esp.**	42N04	1w37	0h06w
Tong-leao (Tongliao), **China**	43N37	122E15	8h09 E	Tula (Toula), **URSS**	54N11	37E38	2h31 E
Topeka, Kans., **USA**	39N02	95w41	6h23w	Tulcan, **Ecuad.**	0N50	77w48	5h11w
Torbay, **G.-B.**	50N27	3w32	0h14w	Tulcea, **Roum.**	45N10	28E50	1h55 E
Torgau, **DDR**	51N34	13E01	0h52 E	Tulear, → *Toliara, Madag.*			
Torhout (Thourout), **Belg.**	51N04	3E06	0h12 E	Tulle, **Fr.**	45N16	1E46	0h07 E
Torino, **Ital.**	45N04	7E40	0h31 E	Tulsa; Okla., **USA**	36N07	95w58	6h24w
Toronto, Ont., **Can.**	43N42	79w25	5h18w	Tuluá, **Col.**	4N05	76w12	5h05w
Tororo, **Uganda**	0N42	34E12	2h17 E	Tumaco, **Col.**	1N51	78w46	5h15w
Torreón, **Mex.**	25N34	103w25	6h54w	Tunis, **Tun.**	36N50	10E13	0h41 E
Tortosa, **Esp.**	40N49	0E31	0h02 E	Tunja, **Col.**	5N33	73w23	4h54w
Torun, **Pol.**	53N01	18E35	1h14 E	Turda, **Roum.**	46N35	23E50	1h35 E
Totora, **Bol.**	17s40	65w10	4h21w	Turin, → *Torino, Ital.*			
Tottori, **Jap.**	35N32	134E12	8h57 E	Turku, **Finl.**	60N27	22E15	1h29 E
Touggourt, **Alg.**	33N08	6E04	0h24 E	Turnhout, **Belg.**	51N19	4E57	0h20 E
Toulon, **Fr.**	43N07	5E55	0h24 E	Turrialba, **C.Rica**	9N56	83w40	5h35w
Toulouse, **Fr.**	43N37	1E27	0h06 E	Tuttlingen, **BRD**	47N59	8E49	0h35 E
Tourane, → *Da Nang,* **Viet.**				Tuvalu (Ellice) I., **Pac.O.**	8s30	179E12	11h57 E
Tourcoing, **Fr.**	50N44	3E10	0h13 E	Tuzla, **Youg.**	44N33	18E41	1h15 E
Tournai (Doornik), **Belg.**	50N36	3E24	0h14 E	Tver, → *Kalinin,* **URSS**			
Tours, **Fr.**	47N23	0E42	0h03 E	Tynemouth, **G.-B.**	55N01	1w24	0h06w
Townsville, **Aust.**	19s13	146E48	9h47 E	Tyr, → *Sour,* **Lbn**			
Toyama, **Jap.**	36N42	137E14	9h09 E	Tyumen (Tioumen), **URSS**	57N00	65E18	4h21 E
Toyohashi, **Jap.**	34N46	137E22	9h09 E				
Trabzon (Trebizonde), **Tur.**	41N00	39E43	2h39 E				
Trail, Br.Col., **Can.**	49N04	117w39	7h51w	*** U ***			
Trápani, **Ital.**	38N02	12E32	0h50 E				
Treinta y Tres, **Urug.**	33s16	54w17	3h37w	Uberaba, **Brasil**	19s47	47w57	3h12w
Trelew, **Arg.**	43s13	65w15	4h21w	Uberlândia, **Brasil**	18s57	48w17	3h13w
Trencin, **Tch.**	48N53	18E00	1h12 E	Ubon Ratchathani, **Thai.**	15N15	104E50	6h59 E
Trenque Lauquén, **Arg.**	35s56	62w43	4h11w	Udaipur, **Ind.**	24N36	73E47	4h55 E
Trento (Trente), **Ital.**	46N04	11E08	0h45 E	Uddevalla, **Sue.**	58N20	11E56	0h48 E
Trenton, NJ, **USA**	40N15	74w43	4h59w	Udine, **Ital.**	46N04	13E14	0h53 E
Tres Arroyos, **Arg.**	38s26	60w17	4h01w	Udon Thani, **Thai.**	17N25	102E45	6h51 E
Treviso (Trévise), **Ital.**	45N40	12E15	0h49 E	Uelzen, **BRD**	52N58	10E34	0h42 E
Trichinopoly, → *Tiruchirapalli,* **Ind.**				Ufa (Oufa), **URSS**	54N45	55E58	3h44 E
Trier (Trèves), **BRD**	49N45	6E39	0h27 E	Ujjain, **Ind.**	23N11	75E50	5h03 E
Trieste, **Ital.**	45N39	13E47	0h55 E	Ujpest, **Hong.**	47N33	19E05	1h16 E
Tríkala, **Grc.**	39N33	21E46	1h27 E	Ujung Pandang (Macassar), **Indon.**	5s09	119E28	7h58 E
Trincomalee, **Sr.Lka**	8N34	81E13	5h25 E	Ulaan Baatar (Oulan Bator),			
Trinidad, **Bol.**	14s46	64w50	4h19w	**Mong.**	47N54	106E52	7h07 E
Trinidad, Colo., **USA**	37N11	104w31	6h58w	Ulan-Ude (Oulan-Oude), **URSS**	51N55	107E40	7h11 E
Trípoli, **Grc.**	37N31	22E22	1h29 E	Uleaborg, → *Oulu,* **Finl.**			
Tripoli (Trablous), **Lbn**	34N27	35E50	2h23 E	Ulhasnagar, **Ind.**	19N15	73E08	4h53 E
Tripoli, → *Tarabulus,* **Lib.**				Uliastay (Jirga lanta), **Mong.**	47N42	96E52	6h27 E

City	Lat.	Long.	Time	City	Lat.	Long.	Time
Ulm, **BRD**	48N24	10E00	0h40E	Victoria, **Arg.**	32s40	60w10	4h01w
Ulyanovsk (Oulianovsk), **URSS**	54N19	48E22	3h13E	Victoria, **Cam.**	4N01	9E12	0h37E
Umea, **Sue.**	63N50	20E15	1h21E	Victoria, Br.Col., **Can.**	48N25	123w22	8h13w
Umtali, **Zimb.**	19s00	32E40	2h11E	Victoria, **H.K.**	22N16	114E13	7h37E
Upington, **S.Afr.**	28s28	21E14	1h25E	Viedma, **Arg.**	40s45	63w00	4h12w
Uppsala (Upsal), **Sue.**	59N55	17E38	1h11E	Vienne, **Fr.**	45N32	4E54	0h20E
Uralsk (Ouralsk), **URSS**	51N19	51E20	3h25E	Vienne (Vienna), → *Wien,* **Aut.**			
Urawa, **Jap.**	35N52	139E40	9h19E	Vientiane, **Laos**	17N59	102E38	6h51E
Urfa, **Tur.**	37N08	38E45	2h35E	Vierzon, **Fr.**	47N14	2E03	0h08E
Urumiyeh (Rezaye), **Iran**	37N32	45E02	3h00E	Vigevano, **Ital.**	45N19	8E51	0h35E
Urümqi (Ouroumtsi), **China**	43N43	87E38	5h51E	Vigo, **Esp.**	42N15	8w44	0h35w
Usküdar, **Tur.**	41N01	29E03	1h56E	Vijayavada, **Ind.**	16N34	80E40	5h23E
Usti nad Labem, **Tch.**	50N41	14E00	0h56E	Vila Real, **Port.**	41N17	7w45	0h31w
Ust Kamenogorsk, **URSS**	49N58	82E36	5h30E	Villach (Bela), **Aut.**	46N37	13E51	0h55E
Usumbura, → *Bujumbura,* **Bur.**				Villahermosa, **Mex.**	18N00	92w53	6h12w
Utica, NY, **USA**	43N06	75w15	5h01w	Villa María, **Arg.**	32s25	63w15	4h13w
Utrecht, **Nth.**	52N06	5E07	0h20E	Villa Montes, **Bol.**	21s15	63w30	4h14w
Utsunomiya, **Jap.**	36N33	139E52	9h19E	Villarrica, **Parag.**	25s45	56w28	3h46w
Uyuni, **Bol.**	20s28	66w47	4h27w	Villefranche-sur-Saône, **Fr.**	46N00	4E43	0h19E
				Villeneuve-sur-Lot, **Fr.**	44N24	0E42	0h03E
				Villingen-Schwenningen, **BRD**	48N03	8E28	0h34E
*** V ***				Vilnius (Vilna), **URSS**	54N40	25E19	1h41E
				Vilvoorde, **Belg.**	50N56	4E25	0h18E
Vaasa, **Finl.**	63N06	21E36	1h26E	Vinh, **Viet.**	18N42	105E41	7h03E
Vadodara, **Ind.**	22N19	73E14	4h53E	Vinnitsa, **URSS**	49N11	28E30	1h54E
Vaduz, **Liech.**	47N08	9E32	0h38E	Vishakhapatnam, **Ind.**	17N42	83E24	5h34E
Valdepeñas, **Esp.**	38N46	3w24	0h14w	Vitebsk, **URSS**	55N10	30E14	2h01E
Valdivia, **Chile**	39s46	73w15	4h53w	Viterbo, **Ital.**	42N24	12E06	0h48E
Valence, Drôme, **Fr.**	44N56	4E54	0h20E	Vitória, **Brasil**	20s19	40w21	2h41w
Valencia, **Esp.**	39N29	0w24	0h02w	Vitoria, **Esp.**	42N51	2w40	0h11w
Valencia, **Ven.**	10N14	67w50	4h32w	Vlaardingen, **Nth.**	51N55	4E20	0h17E
Valenciennes, **Fr.**	50N22	3E32	0h14E	Vladikavkaz, → *Ordzhonikidze,*			
Valladolid, **Esp.**	41N39	4w45	0h19w	**URSS**			
Vallenar, **Chile**	28s36	70w45	4h43w	Vladimir, **URSS**	56N08	40E25	2h42E
Valleta, **Malta**	35N54	14E32	0h58E	Vladivostok, **URSS**	43N09	131E53	8h48E
Valleyfield, Que., **Can.**	45N15	74w08	4h57w	Vlissingen, → *Flessingue,* **Nth.**			
Valparaiso, **Chile**	33s05	71w40	4h47w	Vlorë (Valona), **Alb.**	40N29	19E29	1h18E
Vancouver, Br.Col., **Can.**	49N13	123w06	8h12w	Vogan, **Togo**	6N20	1E33	0h06E
Vannes, **Fr.**	47N40	2w44	0h11w	Volgograd, **URSS**	48N45	44E30	2h58E
Vanuatu I. (Vila), **Pac.O.**	17s45	168E18	11h13E	Vologda, **URSS**	59N10	39E55	2h40E
Varanasi, **Ind.**	25N20	83E00	5h32E	Vólos, **Grc.**	39N22	22E57	1h32E
Varese, **Ital.**	45N49	8E49	0h35E	Voronezh (Voronej), **URSS**	51N40	39E13	2h37E
Varna, **Bulg.**	43N12	27E57	1h52E	Voroshilovgrad, **URSS**	48N35	39E20	2h37E
Varsovie, → *Warszawa,* **Pol.**				Voroshilovsk, → *Stavropol,* **URSS**			
Västeräs, **Sue.**	59N36	16E32	1h06E	Vratsa, **Bulg.**	43N12	23E32	1h34E
Växjö, **Sue.**	56N52	14E50	0h59E				
Venezia (Venise), **Ital.**	45N26	12E20	0h49E				
Vénissieux, **Fr.**	45N42	4E46	0h19E	*** W ***			
Veracruz, **Mex.**	19N11	96w10	6h25w				
Vercelli, **Ital.**	45N19	8E26	0h34E	Waco, Tex., **USA**	31N33	97w10	6h29w
Verdun-sur-Meuse, **Fr.**	49N10	5E24	0h22E	Wad Medani, **Sudan**	14N24	33E30	2h14E
Vereeniging, **S.Afr.**	26s41	27E56	1h52E	Wakayama, **Jap.**	34N12	135E10	9h01E
Verona (Vérone), **Ital.**	45N26	11E00	0h44E	Wake I., **Pac.O.**	19N18	166E35	11h06E
Versailles, **Fr.**	48N48	2E08	0h09E	Walbrzych (Waldenburg), **Pol.**	50N48	16E19	1h05E
Verviers, **Belg.**	50N36	5E52	0h23E	Wallis I., **Pac.O.**	13s22	176w12	11h45w
Vervins, **Fr.**	49N50	3E55	0h16E	Walsall, **G.-B.**	52N35	1w58	0h08w
Vesoul, **Fr.**	47N38	6E09	0h25E	Wankie, **Zimb.**	18s20	26E25	1h46E
Vevey, **Sui.**	46N28	6E51	0h27E	Wanne-Eickel, **BRD**	51N31	7E09	0h29E
Viacha, **Bol.**	16s40	68w17	4h33w	Warangal, **Ind.**	18N00	79E35	5h18E
Viareggio, **Ital.**	43N52	10E15	0h41E	Warburg, **BRD**	51N28	9E10	0h37E
Viborg, **Dan.**	56N28	9E25	0h38E	Waren, **DDR**	53N32	12E42	0h51E
Vicenza (Vicence), **Ital.**	45N33	11E32	0h46E	Warendorf, **BRD**	51N57	8E00	0h32E
Vichy, **Fr.**	46N08	3E25	0h14E	Warrington, **G.-B.**	53N24	2w37	0h10w

City	Lat.	Long.	Time	City	Lat.	Long.	Time
Warszawa, **Pol.**	52N15	21E00	1h24E	Wrexham, **G.-B.**	53N03	3w00	0h12w
Warwick, **G.-B.**	52N17	1w34	0h06w	Wroclaw, **Pol.**	51N05	17E00	1h08E
Washington, DC, **USA**	38N55	77w00	5h08w	Wuppertal, **BRD**	51N15	7E10	0h29E
Waterbury, Conn., **USA**	41N33	73w03	4h52w	Würzburg, **BRD**	49N48	9E57	0h40E
Waterford, **Irl.**	52N15	7w06	0h28w				
Waterloo, Ia., **USA**	42N30	92w20	6h09w				
Watertown, NY, **USA**	43N57	75w56	5h04w	*** X ***			
Wavre (Waver), **Belg.**	50N43	4E37	0h18E				
Weiden in der Oberpfalz, **BRD**	49N40	12E10	0h49E	Xi'an, → *Si-ngan*, **China**			
Weimar, **DDR**	50N59	11E20	0h45E	Xieng Khouang, **Laos**	19N21	103E23	6h54E
Weissenfels, **DDR**	51N12	11E58	0h48E				
Wellington, **N.Zel.**	41s17	174E47	11h39E				
Wels, **Aut.**	48N10	14E02	0h56E	*** Y ***			
Wen-tcheou (Wenzhou), **China**	28N02	120E40	8h03E				
Wesel, **BRD**	51N39	6E37	0h26E	Yako, **H.Vol.**	12N59	2w15	0h09w
West Palm Beach, Fla., **USA**	26N42	80w05	5h20w	Yakutsk (Iakoutsk), **URSS**	62N10	129E50	8h39E
Westport, **N.Zel.**	41s46	171E38	11h27E	Yamagata, **Jap.**	38N16	140E19	9h21E
Wetaskiwin, Alb., **Can.**	52N57	113w20	7h33w	Yambol, **Bulg.**	42N28	26E30	1h46E
Wexford, **Irl.**	52N20	6w27	0h26w	Yaoundé, **Cam.**	3N51	11E31	0h46E
Weymouth, **G.-B.**	50N36	2w28	0h10w	Yaritagua, **Ven.**	10N05	69w07	4h36w
Wharan, → *Oran*, **Alg.**				Yarmouth, NE, **Can.**	43N50	66w08	4h25w
Wheeling, WV, **USA**	40N05	80w43	5h23w	Yaroslavl (Iaroslavl), **URSS**	57N34	39E52	2h39E
Whitehaven, **G.-B.**	54N33	3w35	0h14w	Yatsushiro, **Jap.**	32N32	130E35	8h42E
Whitehorse, Yukon, **Can.**	60N41	135w08	9h01w	Yazd (Yezd), **Iran**	31N55	54E22	3h37E
Wichita, Kans., **USA**	37N43	97w20	6h29w	Yellowknife, NT, **Can.**	62N30	114w29	7h38w
Wichita Falls, Tex., **USA**	33N55	98w30	6h34w	Yendi, **Ghana**	9N30	0w01	0h00w
Wien, **Aut.**	48N13	16E22	1h05E	Yeovil, **G.-B.**	50N57	2w39	0h11w
Wiener Neustadt, **Aut.**	47N49	16E15	1h05E	Yerevan (Erevan), **URSS**	40N10	44E31	2h58E
Wiesbaden, **BRD**	50N05	8E15	0h33E	Yin-tch'ouan (Yinchuan), **China**	38N30	106E19	7h05E
Wilhelmshaven, **BRD**	53N32	8E07	0h32E	Yogyakarta, **Indon.**	7s48	110E24	7h22E
Wilkes Barre, Pa., **USA**	41N15	75w50	5h03w	Yokkaichi, **Jap.**	34N58	136E38	9h07E
Willemstad, Curaçao, **Ant.P.**	12N12	68w56	4h36w	Yokohama, Kanagawa, **Jap.**	35N28	139E38	9h19E
Williamsport, Pa., **USA**	41N16	77w03	5h08w	Yokosuka, Kanagawa, **Jap.**	35N18	139E39	9h19E
Wilmington, Del., **USA**	39N46	75w31	5h02w	Yola, **Nig.**	9N14	12E32	0h50E
Wilmington, NC, **USA**	34N14	77w55	5h12w	Yonkers, NY, **USA**	40N57	73w52	4h55w
Winchester, **G.-B.**	51N04	1w19	0h05w	York, **G.-B.**	53N58	1w05	0h04w
Windhoek, **Namib.**	22s34	17E06	1h08E	Yorkton, Sask., **Can.**	51N12	102w29	6h50w
Windsor, Ont., **Can.**	42N18	83w00	5h32w	Youngstown, Oh., **USA**	41N05	80w40	5h23w
Windsor, **G.-B.**	51N29	0w38	0h03w	Yumen, **China**	39N54	97E43	6h31E
Winneba, **Ghana**	5N22	0w38	0h03w	Yverdon, **Sui.**	46N47	6E38	0h27E
Winnipeg, Man., **Can.**	49N53	97w10	6h29w				
Winston-Salem, NC, **USA**	36N05	80w18	5h21w				
Winterthur, **Sui.**	47N30	8E45	0h35E	*** Z ***			
Wismar, **DDR**	53N54	11E28	0h46E	Zaandam, **Nth.**	52N26	4E49	0h19E
Witten, **BRD**	51N25	7E19	0h29E	Zabrze, **Pol.**	50N18	18E47	1h15E
Wittenberg, **DDR**	51N53	12E39	0h51E	Zadar, **Youg.**	44N07	15E14	1h01E
Wittlich, **BRD**	49N59	6E54	0h28E	Zagazig, **Egy.**	30N35	31E30	2h06E
Wittstock, **DDR**	53N10	12E30	0h50E	Zagreb, **Youg.**	45N48	15E58	1h04E
Wloclawek, **Pol.**	52N39	19E01	1h16E	Zahedan (Duzdab), **Iran**	29N32	60E54	4h04E
Wohlen, **Sui.**	47N21	8E17	0h33E	Zahle, **Lbn**	33N50	35E55	2h24E
Wolfenbüttel, **BRD**	52N10	10E33	0h42E	Zalaegerszeg, **Hong.**	46N53	16E51	1h07E
Wolfsburg, **BRD**	52N27	10E49	0h43E	Zamora, **Esp.**	41N30	5w45	0h23w
Wollongong, **Aust.**	34s25	150E52	10h03E	Zanesville, Oh., **USA**	39N55	82w02	5h28w
Wolverhampton, **G.-B.**	52N36	2w08	0h09w	Zanzibar, **Tanz.**	6s10	39E12	2h37E
Wonsan, **Cor.N.**	39N07	127E26	8h30E	Zaporozhye, **URSS**	47N50	35E10	2h21E
Worcester, **G.-B.**	52N11	2w13	0h09w	Zaragoza, **Esp.**	41N39	0w54	0h04w
Worcester, **S.Afr.**	33s39	19E26	1h18E	Zárate, **Arg.**	34s07	59w00	3h56w
Worcester, Mass., **USA**	42N17	71w48	4h47w	Zaraza, **Ven.**	9N23	65w20	4h21w
Worms, **BRD**	49N38	8E23	0h34E	Zaria, **Nig.**	11N01	7E44	0h31E
Worthing, **G.-B.**	50N48	0w23	0h02w	Zarqa (Az-Zarqa), **Jord.**	32N04	36E06	2h24E
Wou-han (Wuhan), **China**	30N35	114E19	7h37E	Zefat (Safad), **Isr.**	32N57	35E27	2h22E
Wou-hou (Wuhu), **China**	31N23	118E25	7h54E	Zeitz, **DDR**	51N03	12E08	0h49E
Wou-si (Wuxi), **China**	31N35	120E19	8h01E	Zemio, **C.Afr.**	5N00	25E09	1h41E

City	Lat.	Long.	Time	City	Lat.	Long.	Time
Zenica, **Youg.**	44N11	17E53	1h12 E	Zofingen (Zofingue), **Sui.**	47N18	7E57	0h32 E
Zhdanov (Jdanov), **URSS**	47N05	37E34	2h30 E	Zomba, **Malawi**	15s22	35E22	2h21 E
Zhitomir (Jitomir), **URSS**	50N18	28E40	1h55 E	Zrenjanin (Petrovgrad), **Youg.**	45N22	20E23	1h22 E
Zielona Góra, **Pol.**	51N57	15E30	1h02 E	Zug (Zoug), **Sui.**	47N10	8E31	0h34 E
Ziguinchor, **Seneg.**	12N35	16w20	1h05w	Zürich, **Sui.**	47N23	8E33	0h34 E
Zinder, **Niger**	13N46	8E58	0h36 E	Zutphen, **Nth.**	52N08	6E12	0h25 E
Zlatoust, **URSS**	55N10	59E38	3h59 E	Zwickau, **DDR**	50N43	12E30	0h50 E
Zlin, → *Gottwaldov,* **Tch.**				Zwolle, **Nth.**	52N31	6E06	0h24 E

Notes

Notes

Notes

Notes

SIMPLIFIED
AMERICAN ATLAS

ATLAS AMEŔICAIN
SIMPLIFIÉ

VEREINFACHTER
AMERIKANISCHER ATLAS

ATLAS AMERICANO
SIMPLIFICADO

In this section are listed 4000 principal American cities including all county seats with their longitudes, latitudes, and the time difference with Greenwich. Longitudes and latitudes are adjusted to the nearest exact degree so that the student can easily refer to the next section of the Tables of Houses and use the appropriate column for latitudes without the need for interpolation.

Dans cette section, 4000 principales villes des Etats-Unis comprenant tous les chefs-lieux de canton sont listés avec leurs longitudes, leurs latitudes, et leurs différences horaires avec Greenwich. Ces longitudes et latitudes sont arrondies au degré le plus proche afin que l'étudiant puisse se référer, dans les Tables des Maisons, à la colonne des latitudes qui convient sans avoir à faire d'interpolation.

In diesem Gebiet sin 4000 Americanische Stätde eingezeichnet, einschliesslich der Bezirke mit Längen- und Breiten- und der Differenzzeit von Greenwich. Längen- und Breiten-Grade sind festgelegt zu ihrem genauesten Grad, sodass der Student nur zur am nächsten liegenden Spalte der Häusertabelle greifen und die Werte für die Breintengrade ohne weitere Berechnung benutzen kann.

En esta sección se nombran 4000 de la prìncipales ciudades Americanas, incluyendo todas las capitales de los condados con sus longitudes, latitudes y la diferencia de tiempo con Greenwich. Las longitudes y latitudes están ajustadas al grado exacto más próximo a fin que el estudiante pueda fácilmente trasladarse a la siguiente sección de la Tabla de Casas y usar la columna apropiada para las latitudes sin necesidad de interpolación.

CITY ALABAMA	LAT N.	LONG W.	TIME h m	CITY	LAT N.	LONG W.	TIME h m
				Phenix City	32	85	5:40
ALABAMA (AL)				Prattville	32	86	5:44
				Prichard	31	88	5:52
Abbeville	32	85	5:40	Rockford	33	86	5:44
Alexander City	33	86	5:44	Russellville	35	88	5:52
Andalusia	31	86	5:44	Scottsboro	35	86	5:44
Anniston	34	86	5:44	Selma	32	87	5:48
Ashland	33	86	5:44	Sheffield	35	88	5:52
Athens	35	87	5:48	Sylacauga	33	86	5:44
Auburn	33	85	5:40	Talladega	33	86	5:44
Bay Minette	31	88	5:52	Troy	32	86	5:44
Bessemer	33	87	5:48	Tuscaloosa	33	88	5:52
Birmingham	34	87	5:48	Tuscumbia	35	88	5:52
Brewton	31	87	5:48	Tuskegee	32	86	5:44
Butler	32	88	5:52	Union Springs	32	86	5:44
Camden	32	87	5:48	Vernon	34	88	5:52
Carrollton	33	88	5:52	Wedowee	33	85	5:40
Centre	34	86	5:44	Wetumpka	33	86	5:44
Centreville	33	87	5:48				
Chatom	31	88	5:52	ALASKA (AK)			
Clanton	33	87	5:48				
Clayton	32	85	5:40	Anchorage	61	150	10:00
Columbiana	33	87	5:48	Cordova	61	146	9:44
Cullman	34	87	5:48	Fairbanks	65	148	9:52
Dadeville	33	86	5:44	Juneau	58	134	8:56
Decatur	35	87	5:48	Ketchikan	55	132	8:48
Dothan	31	85	5:40	Nome	65	165	11:00
Double Springs	34	87	5:48	Petersburg	57	133	8:52
Elba	31	86	5:44	Sitka	57	135	9:00
Enterprise	31	86	5:44	Valdez	61	146	9:44
Eufaula	32	85	5:40				
Eutaw	33	88	5:52	ARIZONA (AZ)			
Evergreen	31	87	5:48				
Fairfield	33	87	5:48	Bisbee	31	110	7:20
Fayette	34	88	5:52	Casa Grande	33	112	7:28
Florence	35	88	5:52	Clifton	33	109	7:16
Fort Payne	34	86	5:44	Douglas	31	110	7:20
Gadsden	34	86	5:44	Flagstaff	35	112	7:28
Geneva	31	86	5:44	Florence	33	111	7:24
Greensboro	33	88	5:52	Glendale	34	112	7:28
Greenville	32	87	5:48	Globe	33	111	7:24
Grove Hill	32	88	5:52	Holbrook	35	110	7:20
Guntersville	34	86	5:44	Kingman	35	114	7:36
Hamilton	34	88	5:52	Mesa	33	112	7:28
Hayneville	32	87	5:48	Nogales	31	111	7:24
Heflin	34	86	5:44	Phoenix	33	112	7:28
Huntsville	35	87	5:48	Prescott	35	112	7:28
Jasper	34	87	5:48	Safford	33	110	7:20
Lafayette	33	85	5:40	St Johns	35	109	7:16
Linden	32	88	5:52	Scottsdale	33	112	7:28
Livingston	33	88	5:52	Tempe	33	112	7:28
Luverne	32	86	5:44	Tucson	32	111	7:24
Marion	33	87	5:48	Yuma	33	115	7:40
Mobile	31	88	5:52				
Montgomery	32	86	5:44	ARKANSAS (AR)			
Monroeville	32	87	5:48				
Moulton	34	87	5:48	Arkadelphia	34	93	6:12
Oneonta	34	86	5:44	Arkansas City	34	91	6:04
Opelika	33	85	5:40	Ashdown	34	94	6:16
Ozark	31	86	5:44	Augusta	35	91	6:04
Pell City	34	86	5:44	Batesville	36	92	6:08

CITY ARKANSAS	LAT N.	LONG W.	TIME h m	CITY	LAT N.	LONG W.	TIME h m
Benton	35	93	6:12	Osceola	36	90	6:00
Bentonville	36	94	6:16	Ozark	35	94	6:16
Berryville	36	94	6:16	Paragould	36	90	6:00
Blytheville	36	90	6:00	Paris	35	94	6:16
Booneville	35	94	6:16	Perryville	35	93	6:12
Camden	34	93	6:12	Piggott	36	90	6:00
Charleston	35	94	6:16	Pine Bluff	34	92	6:08
Clarendon	35	91	6:04	Pocahontas	36	91	6:04
Clarksville	35	93	6:12	Powhatan	36	91	6:04
Clinton	36	92	6:08	Prescott	34	93	6:12
Conway	35	92	6:08	Rison	34	92	6:08
Corning	36	91	6:04	Rogers	36	94	6:16
Danville	35	93	6:12	Russellville	35	93	6:12
Dardanelle	35	93	6:12	Salem	36	92	6:08
De Queen	34	94	6:16	Searcy	35	92	6:08
Des Arc	35	92	6:08	Sheridan	34	92	6:08
De Valls Bluff	35	91	6:04	Springdale	36	94	6:16
De Witt	34	91	6:04	Star City	34	92	6:08
El Dorado	33	93	6:12	Stuttgart	35	92	6:08
Eureka Springs	36	94	6:16	Texarkana	33	94	6:16
Evening Shade	36	92	6:08	Van Buren	35	94	6:16
Fayetteville	36	94	6:16	Waldron	35	94	6:16
Fordyce	34	92	6:08	Walnut Ridge	36	91	6:04
Forrest City	35	91	6:04	Warren	34	92	6:08
Fort Smith	35	94	6:16	West Memphis	35	90	6:00
Greenwood	35	94	6:16	Wynne	35	91	6:04
Hamburg	33	92	6:08	Yellville	36	93	6:12
Hampton	34	92	6:08				
Hardy	36	91	6:04	CALIFORNIA (CA)			
Harrisburg	36	91	6:04				
Harrison	36	93	6:12	Alameda	38	122	8:08
Heber Springs	36	92	6:08	Alhambra	34	118	7:52
Helena	35	91	6:04	Altadena	34	118	7:52
Hope	34	94	6:16	Alturas	41	121	8:04
Hot Springs	35	93	6:12	Anaheim	34	118	7:52
Hot Springs Nat Park	35	93	6:12	Antioch	38	122	8:08
Huntsville	36	94	6:16	Arcade	39	121	8:04
Jacksonville	35	92	6:08	Arcadia	34	118	7:52
Jasper	36	93	6:12	Arden	39	121	8:04
Jonesboro	36	91	6:04	Auburn	39	121	8:04
Lake City	36	90	6:00	Azusa	34	118	7:52
Lake Village	33	91	6:04	Bakersfield	35	119	7:56
Lewisville	33	94	6:16	Baldwin Park	34	118	7:52
Little Rock	35	92	6:08	Banning	34	117	7:48
Lonoke	35	92	6:08	Barstow	35	117	7:48
Magnolia	33	93	6:12	Bell	34	118	7:52
Malvern	34	93	6:12	Bell Gardens	34	118	7:52
Marianna	35	91	6:04	Bellflower	34	118	7:52
Marion	35	90	6:00	Belmont	38	122	8:08
Marshall	36	93	6:12	Berkeley	38	122	8:08
Melbourne	36	92	6:08	Beverly Hills	34	118	7:52
Mena	35	94	6:16	Brawley	33	116	7:44
Monticello	34	92	6:08	Bridgeport	38	119	7:56
Morrilton	35	93	6:12	Buena Park	34	118	7:52
Mountain Home	36	92	6:08	Burbank	34	118	7:52
Mountain View	36	92	6:08	Burlingame	38	122	8:08
Mount Ida	35	94	6:16	Calexico	33	116	7:44
Murfreesboro	34	94	6:16	Campbell	37	122	8:08
Nashville	34	94	6:16	Carmichael	39	121	8:04
Newport	36	91	6:04	Carson	34	118	7:52
North Little Rock	35	92	6:08	Castro Valley	38	122	8:08

CITY CALIFORNIA	LAT N.	LONG W.	TIME h m	CITY	LAT N.	LONG W.	TIME h m
Chico	40	122	8:08	Lancaster	35	118	7:52
Chino	34	118	7:52	La Puente	34	118	7:52
Chula Vista	33	117	7:48	Lawndale	34	118	7:52
Citrus Heights	39	121	8:04	Lemon Grove	33	117	7:48
Claremont	34	118	7:52	Livermore	38	122	8:08
Colton	34	117	7:48	Lodi	38	121	8:04
Colusa	39	122	8:08	Lompoc	35	120	8:00
Compton	34	118	7:52	Long Beach	34	118	7:52
Concord	38	122	8:08	Los Altos	37	122	8:08
Corona	34	118	7:52	Los Angeles	34	118	7:52
Coronado	33	117	7:48	Los Gatos	37	122	8:08
Costa Mesa	34	118	7:52	Lynwood	34	118	7:52
Covina	34	118	7:52	Madera	37	120	8:00
Crescent City	42	124	8:16	Manhattan Beach	34	118	7:52
Culver City	34	118	7:52	Mariposa	37	120	8:00
Cypress	34	118	7:52	Markleeville	39	120	8:00
Daly City	38	122	8:08	Martinez	38	122	8:08
Davis	39	122	8:08	Marysville	39	121	8:04
Delano	36	119	7:56	Menlo Park	37	122	8:08
Downey	34	118	7:52	Merced	37	120	8:00
Downieville	40	121	8:04	Millbrae	38	122	8:08
East Los Angeles	34	118	7:52	Milpitas	37	122	8:08
El Cajon	33	117	7:48	Modesto	38	121	8:04
El Centro	33	116	7:44	Monrovia	34	118	7:52
El Cerrito	38	122	8:08	Montclair	34	118	7:52
El Monte	34	118	7:52	Montebello	34	118	7:52
Escondido	33	117	7:48	Monterey	37	122	8:08
Eureka	41	124	8:16	Monterey Park	34	118	7:52
Fairfield	38	122	8:08	Mountain View	37	122	8:08
Florence	34	118	7:52	Napa	38	122	8:08
Fontana	34	117	7:48	National City	33	117	7:48
Fountain Valley	34	118	7:52	Nevada City	39	121	8:04
Fremont	38	122	8:08	Newark	38	122	8:08
Fresno	37	120	8:00	Newport Beach	34	118	7:52
Fullerton	34	118	7:52	North Highlands	39	121	8:04
Garden Grove	34	118	7:52	Norwalk	34	118	7:52
Gardena	34	118	7:52	Novato	38	123	8:12
Gilroy	37	122	8:08	Oakland	38	122	8:08
Glendale	34	118	7:52	Oceanside	33	117	7:48
Glendora	34	118	7:52	Oildale	35	119	7:56
Hacienda Heights	34	118	7:52	Ontario	34	118	7:52
Hanford	36	120	8:00	Orange	34	118	7:52
Hawthorne	34	118	7:52	Oroville	40	122	8:08
Hayward	38	122	8:08	Oxnard	34	119	7:56
Hemet	34	117	7:48	Pacifica	38	123	8:12
Hillcrest Center	35	119	7:56	Palm Springs	34	117	7:48
Hollister	37	121	8:04	Palo Alto	37	122	8:08
Huntington Beach	34	118	7:52	Paramount	34	118	7:52
Huntington Park	34	118	7:52	Pasadena	34	118	7:52
Imperial Beach	33	117	7:48	Petaluma	38	123	8:12
Independence	37	118	7:52	Pico Rivera	34	118	7:52
Indio	34	116	7:44	Pittsburg	38	122	8:08
Inglewood	34	118	7:52	Placentia	34	118	7:52
Jackson	38	121	8:04	Placerville	39	121	8:04
Lafayette	38	122	8:08	Pleasant Hill	38	122	8:08
Laguna Beach	34	118	7:52	Pomona	34	118	7:52
La Habra	34	118	7:52	Porterville	36	119	7:56
Lakeport	39	123	8:12	Quincy	40	121	8:04
Lakewood	34	118	7:52	Rancho Cordova	39	121	8:04
La Mesa	33	117	7:48	Red Bluff	40	122	8:08
La Mirada	34	118	7:52	Redlands	34	117	7:48

CITY CALIFORNIA	LAT N.	LONG W.	TIME h m	CITY	LAT N.	LONG W.	TIME h m
Redding	41	122	8:08	Walnut Creek	38	122	8:08
Redondo Beach	34	118	7:52	Watsonville	37	122	8:08
Redwood City	38	122	8:08	Weaverville	41	123	8:12
Rialto	34	117	7:48	West Covina	34	118	7:52
Richmond	38	122	8:08	West Hollywood	34	118	7:52
Riverside	34	117	7:48	Westminster	34	118	7:52
Rosemead	34	118	7:52	Whittier	34	118	7:52
Roseville	39	121	8:04	Willow Brook	34	118	7:52
Sacramento	39	121	8:04	Willows	40	122	8:08
Salinas	37	122	8:08	Woodland	39	122	8:08
San Andreas	38	121	8:04	Yreka	42	123	8:12
San Bernardino	34	117	7:48	Yuba City	39	122	8:08
San Bruno	38	122	8:08				
San Carlos	38	122	8:08	COLORADO (CO)			
San Diego	33	117	7:48				
San Fernando	34	118	7:52	Akron	40	103	6:52
San Francisco	38	122	8:08	Alamosa	37	106	7:04
San Gabriel	34	118	7:52	Arvada	40	105	7:00
San Jose	37	122	8:08	Aspen	39	107	7:08
San Leandro	38	122	8:08	Aurora	40	105	7:00
San Lorenzo	38	122	8:08	Boulder	40	105	7:00
San Luis Obispo	35	121	8:04	Breckenridge	39	106	7:04
San Mateo	38	122	8:08	Brighton	40	105	7:00
San Rafael	38	123	8:12	Burlington	39	102	6:48
Santa Ana	34	118	7:52	Canon City	38	105	7:00
Santa Barbara	34	120	8:00	Castle Rock	39	105	7:00
Santa Clara	37	122	8:08	Central City	40	106	7:04
Santa Cruz	37	122	8:08	Cheyenne Wells	39	102	6:48
Santa Maria	35	120	8:00	Colorado Springs	39	105	7:00
Santa Monica	34	118	7:52	Conejos	37	106	7:04
Santa Paula	34	119	7:56	Cortez	37	109	7:16
Santa Rosa	38	123	8:12	Craig	41	108	7:12
Saratoga	37	122	8:08	Creede	38	107	7:08
Seal Beach	34	118	7:52	Cripple Creek	39	105	7:00
Seaside	37	122	8:08	Del Norte	38	106	7:04
Simi	34	119	7:56	Delta	39	108	7:12
Sonora	38	120	8:00	Denver	40	105	7:00
South Gate	34	118	7:52	Dove Creek	38	109	7:16
South Lake Tahoe	39	120	8:00	Durango	37	108	7:12
South Pasadena	34	118	7:52	Eads	38	103	6:52
South San Francisco	38	122	8:08	Eagle	40	107	7:08
South Whittier	34	118	7:52	Englewood	40	105	7:00
Spring Valley	33	117	7:48	Fairplay	39	106	7:04
Stockton	38	121	8:04	Fort Collins	41	105	7:00
Susanville	40	121	8:04	Fort Morgan	40	104	6:56
Sunnyvale	37	122	8:08	Georgetown	40	106	7:04
Temple City	34	118	7:52	Glenwood Springs	40	107	7:08
Thousand Oaks	34	119	7:56	Golden	40	105	7:00
Torrance	34	118	7:52	Grand Junction	39	109	7:16
Tracy	38	121	8:04	Greeley	40	105	7:00
Tulare	36	119	7:56	Gunnison	39	107	7:08
Tustin	34	118	7:52	Holyoke	41	102	6:48
Ukiah	39	123	8:12	Hot Sulphur Springs	40	106	7:04
Upland	34	118	7:52	Hugo	39	103	6:52
Vacaville	38	122	8:08	Julesburg	41	102	6:48
Vallejo	38	122	8:08	Kiowa	39	104	6:56
Van Nuys	34	118	7:52	La Junta	38	104	6:56
Ventura	34	119	7:56	Lake City	38	107	7:08
Victorville	35	117	7:48	Lakewood	40	105	7:00
Visalia	36	119	7:56	Lamar	38	103	6:52
Vista	33	117	7:48	Las Animas	38	103	6:52

CITY COLORADO	LAT N.	LONG W.	TIME h m	CITY	LAT N.	LONG W.	TIME h m
Leadville	39	106	7:04	Waterbury	42	73	4:52
Littleton	40	105	7:00	West Hartford	42	73	4:52
Longmont	40	105	7:00	West Haven	41	73	4:52
Loveland	40	105	7:00	Westport	41	73	4:52
Meeker	40	108	7:12	Wethersfield	42	73	4:52
Montrose	38	108	7:12	Willimantic	42	72	4:48
Northglenn	40	105	7:00	Windsor	42	73	4:52
Ordway	38	104	6:56				
Ouray	38	108	7:12	DELAWARE (DE)			
Pagosa Springs	37	107	7:08				
Pueblo	38	105	7:00	Dover	39	76	5:04
Saguache	38	106	7:04	Georgetown	39	75	5:00
Salida	39	106	7:04	Wilmington	40	76	5:04
San Luis	37	105	7:00				
Silverton	38	108	7:12	DISTRICT OF COLUMBIA (DC)			
Springfield	37	103	6:52				
Steamboat Springs	40	107	7:08	Washington	39	77	5:08
Sterling	41	103	6:52				
Telluride	38	108	7:12	FLORIDA (FL)			
Trinidad	37	105	7:00				
Walden	41	106	7:04	Apalachicola	30	85	5:40
Walsenburg	38	105	7:00	Arcadia	27	82	5:28
Westcliffe	38	105	7:00	Bartow	28	82	5:28
Wheat Ridge	40	105	7:00	Belle Glade	27	81	5:24
Wray	40	102	6:48	Blountstown	30	85	5:40
				Boca Raton	26	80	5:20
CONNECTICUT (CT)				Bonifay	31	86	5:44
				Bradenton	28	83	5:32
Ansonia	41	73	4:52	Bristol	30	85	5:40
Bridgeport	41	73	4:52	Bronson	29	83	5:32
Bristol	42	73	4:52	Brooksville	29	82	5:28
Danbury	41	73	4:52	Bunnell	29	81	5:24
East Hartford	42	73	4:52	Bushnell	29	82	5:28
East Haven	41	73	4:52	Carol City	26	80	5:20
Fairfield	41	73	4:52	Chipley	31	86	5:44
Greenwich	41	74	4:56	Clearwater	28	83	5:32
Hamden	41	73	4:52	Cocoa	28	81	5:24
Hartford	42	73	4:52	Coral Gables	26	80	5:20
Litchfield	42	73	4:52	Crawfordville	30	84	5:36
Manchester	42	73	4:52	Crestview	31	87	5:48
Meriden	42	73	4:52	Cross City	30	83	5:32
Middletown	42	73	4:52	Dade City	28	82	5:28
Milford	41	73	4:52	Daytona Beach	29	81	5:24
New Britain	42	73	4:52	De Funiak Springs	31	86	5:44
New Milford	42	73	4:52	De Land	29	81	5:24
New Haven	41	73	4:52	Fernandina Beach	31	81	5:24
Newington	42	73	4:52	Fort Lauderdale	26	80	5:20
New London	41	72	4:48	Fort Myers	27	82	5:28
Norwalk	41	73	4:52	Fort Pierce	27	80	5:20
Norwich	42	72	4:48	Fort Walton Beach	30	87	5:48
Putnam	42	72	4:48	Gainesville	30	82	5:28
Rockville	42	72	4:48	Green Cove Springs	30	82	5:28
Seymour	41	73	4:52	Hialeah	26	80	5:20
Shelton	41	73	4:52	Hollywood	26	80	5:20
Southington	42	73	4:52	Inverness	29	82	5:28
Stamford	41	74	4:56	Jacksonville	30	82	5:28
Stratford	41	73	4:52	Jasper	31	83	5:32
Torrington	42	73	4:52	Kendall	26	80	5:20
Trumbull	41	73	4:52	Key West	25	82	5:28
Vernon	42	72	4:48	Kissimmee	28	81	5:24
Wallingford	41	73	4:52	La Belle	27	81	5:24

CITY FLORIDA	LAT N.	LONG W.	TIME h m	CITY	LAT N.	LONG W.	TIME h m
Lake Butler	30	82	5:28	Augusta	33	82	5:28
Lake City	30	83	5:32	Bainbridge	31	85	5:40
Lake Worth	27	80	5:20	Barnesville	33	84	5:36
Lakeland	28	82	5:28	Baxley	32	82	5:28
Leesburg	29	82	5:28	Blackshear	31	82	5:28
Live Oak	30	83	5:32	Blairsville	35	84	5:36
Macclenny	30	82	5:28	Blakely	31	85	5:40
Madison	30	83	5:32	Blue Ridge	35	84	5:36
Marianna	31	85	5:40	Brunswick	31	82	5:28
Mayo	30	83	5:32	Buchanan	34	85	5:40
Melbourne	28	81	5:24	Buena Vista	32	85	5:40
Merritt Island	28	81	5:24	Butler	33	84	5:36
Miami	26	80	5:20	Cairo	31	84	5:36
Miami Beach	26	80	5:20	Calhoun	35	85	5:40
Milton	31	87	5:48	Camilla	31	84	5:36
Monticello	31	84	5:36	Canton	34	84	5:36
Moore Haven	27	81	5:24	Carnesville	34	83	5:32
Naples	26	82	5:28	Carrollton	34	85	5:40
North Miami	26	80	5:20	Cartersville	34	85	5:40
North Miami Beach	26	80	5:20	Cedartown	34	85	5:40
Ocala	29	82	5:28	Chatsworth	35	85	5:40
Okeechobee	27	81	5:24	Clarkesville	35	84	5:36
Orlando	29	81	5:24	Claxton	32	82	5:28
Palatka	30	82	5:28	Clayton	35	83	5:32
Panama City	30	86	5:44	Cleveland	35	84	5:36
Pensacola	30	87	5:48	Cochran	32	83	5:32
Perry	30	84	5:36	Colquitt	31	85	5:40
Pompano Beach	26	80	5:20	Columbus	32	85	5:40
Punta Gorda	27	82	5:28	Conyers	34	84	5:36
Quincy	31	85	5:40	Cordele	32	84	5:36
Saint Augustine	30	81	5:24	Covington	34	84	5:36
Saint Petersburg	28	83	5:32	Crawfordville	34	83	5:32
Sanford	29	81	5:24	Cumming	34	84	5:36
Sarasota	27	83	5:32	Cusseta	32	85	5:40
Sebring	27	81	5:24	Cuthbert	32	85	5:40
Starke	30	82	5:28	Dahlonega	35	84	5:36
Stuart	27	80	5:20	Dallas	34	85	5:40
Tallahassee	30	84	5:36	Dalton	35	85	5:40
Tampa	28	82	5:28	Danielsville	34	83	5:32
Tavares	29	82	5:28	Darien	31	81	5:24
Titusville	29	81	5:24	Dawson	32	84	5:36
Trenton	30	83	5:32	Dawsonville	34	84	5:36
Vero Beach	28	80	5:20	Decatur	34	84	5:36
Wauchula	28	82	5:28	Donalsonville	31	85	5:40
West Palm Beach	27	80	5:20	Douglas	32	83	5:32
Wewahitchka	30	85	5:40	Douglasville	34	85	5:40
Winter Haven	28	82	5:28	Dublin	33	83	5:32
Winter Park	29	81	5:24	Eastman	32	83	5:32
				East Point	34	84	5:36
GEORGIA (GA)				Eatonton	33	83	5:32
				Elberton	34	83	5:32
Abbeville	32	83	5:32	Ellaville	32	84	5:36
Adel	31	83	5:32	Ellijay	35	84	5:36
Alamo	32	83	5:32	Fayetteville	33	84	5:36
Albany	32	84	5:36	Fitzgerald	32	83	5:32
Alma	32	82	5:28	Folkston	31	82	5:28
Americus	32	84	5:36	Forsyth	33	84	5:36
Appling	34	82	5:28	Fort Gaines	32	85	5:40
Ashburn	32	84	5:36	Fort Valley	33	84	5:36
Athens	34	83	5:32	Franklin	33	85	5:40
Atlanta	34	84	5:36	Gainesville	34	84	5:36

CITY GEORGIA	LAT N.	LONG W.	TIME h m	CITY	LAT N.	LONG W.	TIME h m
Georgetown	32	85	5:40	Savannah	32	81	5:24
Gibson	33	83	5:32	Soperton	32	83	5:32
Gray	33	84	5:36	Sparta	33	83	5:32
Greensboro	34	83	5:32	Springfield	32	81	5:24
Greenville	33	85	5:40	Statenville	31	83	5:32
Griffin	33	84	5:36	Statesboro	32	82	5:28
Hamilton	33	85	5:40	Summerville	34	85	5:40
Hartwell	34	83	5:32	Swainsboro	33	82	5:28
Hawkinsville	32	83	5:32	Sylvania	33	82	5:28
Hazlehurst	32	83	5:32	Sylvester	32	84	5:36
Hiawassee	35	84	5:36	Talbotton	33	85	5:40
Hinesville	32	82	5:28	Thomaston	33	84	5:36
Homer	34	84	5:36	Thomasville	31	84	5:36
Homerville	31	83	5:32	Thomson	33	83	5:32
Irwinton	33	83	5:32	Tifton	31	84	5:36
Jackson	33	84	5:36	Toccoa	35	83	5:32
Jasper	34	84	5:36	Trenton	35	86	5:44
Jefferson	34	84	5:36	Valdosta	31	83	5:32
Jeffersonville	33	83	5:32	Vienna	32	84	5:36
Jesup	32	82	5:28	Warrenton	33	83	5:32
Jonesboro	34	84	5:36	Warner Robins	33	84	5:36
Knoxville	33	84	5:36	Washington	34	83	5:32
La Fayette	35	85	5:40	Watkinsville	34	83	5:32
La Grange	33	85	5:40	Waycross	31	82	5:28
Lakeland	31	83	5:32	Waynesboro	33	82	5:28
Lawrenceville	34	84	5:36	Winder	34	84	5:36
Leesburg	32	84	5:36	Woodbine	31	82	5:28
Lexington	34	83	5:32	Wrightsville	33	83	5:32
Lincolnton	34	82	5:28	Zebulon	33	84	5:36
Louisville	33	82	5:28				
Ludowici	32	82	5:28	HAWAII (HI)			
Lumpkin	32	85	5:40				
Lyons	32	82	5:28	Hilo	20	155	10:20
Macon	33	84	5:36	Honolulu	21	158	10:32
Marietta	34	85	5:40	Kailua	21	158	10:32
McDonough	33	84	5:36	Kaneohe	21	158	10:32
McRae	32	83	5:32	Lihue	22	159	10:36
Madison	34	83	5:32	Wahiawa	22	158	10:32
Metter	32	82	5:28	Wailuku	21	157	10:28
Milledgeville	33	83	5:32				
Millen	33	82	5:28	IDAHO (ID)			
Monroe	34	84	5:36				
Monticello	33	84	5:36	American Falls	43	113	7:32
Morgan	32	85	5:40	Arco	44	113	7:32
Moultrie	31	84	5:36	Blackfoot	43	112	7:28
Mount Vernon	32	83	5:32	Boise	44	116	7:44
Nahunta	31	82	5:28	Bonners Ferry	49	116	7:44
Nashville	31	83	5:32	Burley	43	114	7:36
Newnan	33	85	5:40	Caldwell	44	117	7:48
Newton	31	84	5:36	Cascade	45	116	7:44
Ocilla	32	83	5:32	Challis	45	114	7:36
Oglethorpe	32	84	5:36	Coeur d'Alene	48	117	7:48
Pearson	31	83	5:32	Council	45	116	7:44
Pembroke	32	82	5:28	Driggs	44	111	7:24
Perry	32	84	5:36	Dubois	44	112	7:28
Preston	32	85	5:40	Emmett	44	117	7:48
Quitman	31	84	5:36	Fairfield	43	115	7:40
Reidsville	32	82	5:28	Gooding	43	115	7:40
Ringgold	35	85	5:40	Grangeville	46	116	7:44
Rome	34	85	5:40	Hailey	44	114	7:36
Sandersville	33	83	5:32	Idaho City	44	116	7:44

CITY	LAT N.	LONG W.	TIME h m	CITY	LAT N.	LONG W.	TIME h m
IDAHO				Des Plaines	42	88	5:52
Idaho Falls	44	112	7:28	Dixon	42	89	5:56
Jerome	43	115	7:40	Dolton	42	88	5:52
Lewiston	46	117	7:48	Downers Grove	42	88	5:52
Malad City	42	112	7:28	East Saint Louis	39	90	6:00
Moscow	47	117	7:48	Edwardsville	39	90	6:00
Mountain Home	43	116	7:44	Effingham	39	89	5:56
Murphy	43	117	7:48	Elgin	42	88	5:52
Nampa	44	117	7:48	Elizabethtown	37	88	5:52
Nezperce	46	116	7:44	Elmhurst	42	88	5:52
Orofino	46	116	7:44	Elmwood Park	42	88	5:52
Paris	42	111	7:24	Eureka	41	89	5:56
Payette	44	117	7:48	Evanston	42	88	5:52
Pocatello	43	112	7:28	Evergreen Park	42	88	5:52
Preston	42	112	7:28	Fairfield	38	88	5:52
Rexburg	44	112	7:28	Freeport	42	90	6:00
Rigby	44	112	7:28	Galena	42	90	6:00
Rupert	43	114	7:36	Galesburg	41	90	6:00
Saint Anthony	44	112	7:28	Geneva	42	88	5:52
Saint Maries	47	117	7:48	Golconda	37	88	5:52
Salmon	45	114	7:36	Granite City	39	90	6:00
Sandpoint	48	117	7:48	Greenville	39	89	5:56
Shoshone	43	114	7:36	Hardin	39	91	6:04
Soda Springs	43	112	7:28	Harrisburg	38	89	5:56
Twin Falls	43	114	7:36	Harvey	42	88	5:52
Wallace	47	116	7:44	Havana	40	90	6:00
Weiser	45	117	7:48	Hennepin	41	89	5:56
				Highland Park	42	88	5:52
ILLINOIS (IL)				Hillsboro	39	89	5:56
Albion	38	88	5:52	Jacksonville	40	90	6:00
Aledo	41	91	6:04	Jerseyville	39	90	6:00
Alton	39	90	6:00	Joliet	42	88	5:52
Arlington Heights	42	88	5:52	Jonesboro	37	89	5:56
Aurora	42	88	5:52	Kankakee	41	88	5:52
Belleville	39	90	6:00	Kewanee	41	90	6:00
Belvidere	42	89	5:56	Lacon	41	89	5:56
Benton	38	89	5:56	La Grange	42	88	5:52
Berwyn	42	88	5:52	La Salle	41	89	5:56
Bloomington	40	89	5:56	Lansing	42	88	5:52
Burbank	42	88	5:52	Lawrenceville	39	88	5:52
Cairo	37	89	5:56	Lewistown	40	90	6:00
Calumet City	42	88	5:52	Lincoln	40	89	5:56
Cambridge	41	90	6:00	Lombard	42	88	5:52
Canton	41	90	6:00	Louisville	39	89	5:56
Carbondale	38	89	5:56	Macomb	40	91	6:04
Carlinville	39	90	6:00	Marion	38	89	5:56
Carlyle	39	89	5:56	Marshall	39	88	5:52
Carmi	38	88	5:52	Mattoon	39	88	5:52
Carrollton	39	90	6:00	Maywood	42	88	5:52
Carthage	40	91	6:04	McLeansboro	38	89	5:56
Centralia	39	89	5:56	Metropolis	37	89	5:56
Champaign	40	88	5:52	Moline	42	91	6:04
Charleston	40	88	5:52	Monmouth	41	91	6:04
Chester	38	90	6:00	Monticello	40	89	5:56
Chicago	42	88	5:52	Morris	41	88	5:52
Chicago Heights	42	88	5:52	Morrison	42	90	6:00
Cicero	42	88	5:52	Morton Grove	42	88	5:52
Clinton	40	89	5:56	Mound City	37	89	5:56
Danville	40	88	5:52	Mount Carmel	38	88	5:52
De Kalb	42	89	5:56	Mount Carroll	42	90	6:00
Decatur	40	89	5:56	Mount Prospect	42	88	5:52

CITY ILLINOIS	LAT N.	LONG W.	TIME h m	CITY	LAT N.	LONG W.	TIME h m
Mount Sterling	40	91	6:04	INDIANA (IN)			
Mount Vernon	38	89	5:56				
Murphysboro	38	89	5:56	Albion	41	85	5:40
Nashville	38	89	5:56	Anderson	40	86	5:44
Newton	39	88	5:52	Angola	42	85	5:40
Niles	42	88	5:52	Auburn	41	85	5:40
Normal	41	89	5:56	Bedford	39	86	5:44
Northbrook	42	88	5:52	Bloomfield	39	87	5:48
North Chicago	42	88	5:52	Bloomington	39	87	5:48
Oak Lawn	40	88	5:52	Bluffton	41	85	5:40
Oak Park	42	88	5:52	Boonville	38	87	5:48
Olney	39	88	5:52	Brazil	40	87	5:48
Oquawka	41	91	6:04	Brookville	39	85	5:40
Oregon	42	89	5:56	Brownstown	39	86	5:44
Ottawa	41	89	5:56	Cannelton	38	87	5:48
Palatine	42	88	5:52	Columbia City	41	85	5:40
Paris	40	88	5:52	Columbus	39	86	5:44
Park Forest	41	88	5:52	Connersville	40	85	5:40
Park Ridge	42	88	5:52	Corydon	38	86	5:44
Paxton	40	88	5:52	Covington	40	87	5:48
Pekin	41	90	6:00	Crawfordsville	40	87	5:48
Peoria	41	90	6:00	Crown Point	41	87	5:48
Petersburg	40	90	6:00	Danville	40	87	5:48
Pinckneyville	38	89	5:56	Decatur	41	85	5:40
Pittsfield	40	91	6:04	Delphi	41	87	5:48
Pontiac	41	89	5:56	East Chicago	42	87	5:48
Princeton	41	89	5:56	Elkhart	42	86	5:44
Quincy	40	91	6:04	Elwood	40	86	5:44
Rantoul	40	88	5:52	English	38	86	5:44
Robinson	39	88	5:52	Evansville	38	88	5:52
Rockford	42	89	5:56	Fort Wayne	41	85	5:40
Rock Island	42	91	6:04	Fowler	41	87	5:48
Rushville	40	91	6:04	Frankfort	40	87	5:48
Salem	39	89	5:56	Franklin	39	86	5:44
Shawneetown	38	88	5:52	Gary	42	87	5:48
Shelbyville	39	89	5:56	Goshen	42	86	5:44
Skokie	42	88	5:52	Greencastle	40	87	5:48
Springfield	40	90	6:00	Greenfield	40	86	5:44
Sterling	42	90	6:00	Greensburg	39	85	5:40
Streator	41	89	5:56	Greenwood	40	86	5:44
Sullivan	40	89	5:56	Hammond	42	88	5:52
Sycamore	42	89	5:56	Hartford City	40	85	5:40
Taylorville	40	89	5:56	Huntington	41	86	5:44
Toledo	39	88	5:52	Indianapolis	40	86	5:44
Toulon	41	90	6:00	Jasper	38	87	5:48
Tuscola	40	88	5:52	Jeffersonville	38	86	5:44
Urbana	40	88	5:52	Kentland	41	87	5:48
Vandalia	39	89	5:56	Knox	41	87	5:48
Vienna	37	89	5:56	Kokomo	40	86	5:44
Villa Park	42	88	5:52	Lafayette	40	87	5:48
Virginia	40	90	6:00	Lagrange	42	85	5:40
Waterloo	38	90	6:00	La Porte	42	87	5:48
Watseka	41	88	5:52	Lawrenceburg	39	85	5:40
Waukegan	42	88	5:52	Lebanon	40	86	5:44
Wheaton	42	88	5:52	Liberty	40	85	5:40
Wilmette	42	88	5:52	Logansport	41	86	5:44
Winchester	40	90	6:00	Madison	39	85	5:40
Winnetka	42	88	5:52	Marion	41	86	5:44
Woodstock	42	88	5:52	Martinsville	39	86	5:44
Yorkville	42	88	5:52	Michigan City	42	87	5:48
				Mishawaka	42	86	5:44

CITY INDIANA	LAT N.	LONG W.	TIME h m	CITY	LAT N.	LONG W.	TIME h m
Monticello	41	87	5:48	Chariton	41	93	6:12
Mount Vernon	38	88	5:52	Charles City	43	93	6:12
Muncie	40	85	5:40	Cherokee	43	96	6:24
Nashville	39	86	5:44	Clarinda	41	95	6:20
New Albany	38	86	5:44	Clarion	43	94	6:16
New Castle	40	85	5:40	Clinton	42	90	6:00
Newport	40	87	5:48	Corning	41	95	6:20
Noblesville	40	86	5:44	Corydon	41	93	6:12
Paoli	39	86	5:44	Council Bluffs	41	96	6:24
Peru	41	86	5:44	Cresco	43	92	6:08
Petersburg	39	87	5:48	Creston	41	94	6:16
Plymouth	41	86	5:44	Dakota City	43	94	6:16
Portland	40	85	5:40	Davenport	42	91	6:04
Princeton	38	88	5:52	Decorah	43	92	6:08
Rensselaer	41	87	5:48	Denison	42	95	6:20
Richmond	40	85	5:40	Des Moines	42	94	6:16
Rising Sun	39	85	5:40	Dubuque	43	91	6:04
Rochester	41	86	5:44	Eldora	42	93	6:12
Rockport	38	87	5:48	Elkader	43	91	6:04
Rockville	40	87	5:48	Emmetsburg	43	95	6:20
Rushville	40	85	5:40	Estherville	43	95	6:20
Salem	39	86	5:44	Fairfield	41	92	6:08
Scottsburg	39	86	5:44	Forest City	43	94	6:16
Seymour	39	86	5:44	Fort Dodge	43	94	6:16
Shelbyville	40	86	5:44	Fort Madison	41	91	6:04
Shoals	39	87	5:48	Garner	43	94	6:16
South Bend	42	86	5:44	Glenwood	41	96	6:24
Spencer	39	87	5:48	Greenfield	41	94	6:16
Sullivan	39	87	5:48	Grundy Center	42	93	6:12
Terre Haute	39	87	5:48	Guthrie Center	42	95	6:20
Tipton	40	86	5:44	Hampton	43	93	6:12
Valparaiso	41	87	5:48	Harlan	42	95	6:20
Vernon	39	86	5:44	Ida Grove	42	95	6:20
Versailles	39	85	5:40	Independence	42	92	6:08
Vevay	39	85	5:40	Indianola	41	94	6:16
Vincennes	39	88	5:52	Iowa City	42	92	6:08
Wabash	41	86	5:44	Jefferson	42	94	6:16
Warsaw	41	86	5:44	Keokuk	40	91	6:04
Washington	39	87	5:48	Keosauqua	41	92	6:08
Williamsport	40	87	5:48	Knoxville	41	93	6:12
Winamac	41	87	5:48	Le Mars	43	96	6:24
Winchester	40	85	5:40	Leon	41	94	6:16
				Logan	42	96	6:24
IOWA (IA)				Manchester	42	91	6:04
				Maquoketa	42	91	6:04
Adel	42	94	6:16	Marengo	42	92	6:08
Albia	41	93	6:12	Marshalltown	42	93	6:12
Algona	43	94	6:16	Mason City	43	93	6:12
Allison	43	93	6:12	Montezuma	42	93	6:12
Ames	42	94	6:16	Mount Ayr	41	94	6:16
Anamosa	42	91	6:04	Mount Pleasant	41	92	6:08
Atlantic	41	95	6:20	Muscatine	41	91	6:04
Audubon	42	95	6:20	Nevada	42	93	6:12
Bedford	41	95	6:20	New Hampton	43	92	6:08
Bloomfield	41	92	6:08	Newton	42	93	6:12
Boone	42	94	6:16	Northwood	43	93	6:12
Burlington	41	91	6:04	Onawa	42	96	6:24
Carroll	42	95	6:20	Orange City	43	96	6:24
Cedar Falls	43	92	6:08	Osage	43	93	6:12
Cedar Rapids	42	92	6:08	Osceola	41	94	6:16
Centerville	41	93	6:12	Oskaloosa	41	93	6:12

CITY	LAT N.	LONG W.	TIME h m	CITY	LAT N.	LONG W.	TIME h m
IOWA							
Ottumwa	41	92	6:08	Goodland	39	102	6:48
Pocahontas	43	95	6:20	Gove	39	100	6:40
Primghar	43	96	6:24	Great Bend	38	99	6:36
Red Oak	41	95	6:20	Greensburg	38	99	6:36
Rock Rapids	43	96	6:24	Hays	39	99	6:36
Rockwell City	42	95	6:20	Hiawatha	40	96	6:24
Sac City	42	95	6:20	Hill City	39	100	6:40
Sibley	43	96	6:24	Holton	39	96	6:24
Sidney	41	96	6:24	Howard	37	96	6:24
Sigourney	41	92	6:08	Hoxie	39	100	6:40
Sioux City	43	96	6:24	Hugoton	37	101	6:44
Spencer	43	95	6:20	Hutchinson	38	98	6:32
Spirit Lake	43	95	6:20	Independence	37	96	6:24
Storm Lake	43	95	6:20	Iola	38	95	6:20
Tipton	42	91	6:04	Jetmore	38	100	6:40
Toledo	42	93	6:12	Johnson	38	102	6:48
Vinton	42	92	6:08	Junction City	39	97	6:28
Wapello	41	91	6:04	Kansas City	39	95	6:20
Washington	41	92	6:08	Kingman	38	98	6:32
Waterloo	43	92	6:08	Kinsley	38	99	6:36
Waukon	43	91	6:04	La Crosse	39	99	6:36
Waverly	43	92	6:08	Lakin	38	101	6:44
Webster City	42	94	6:16	Larned	38	99	6:36
West Union	43	92	6:08	Lawrence	39	95	6:20
Winterset	41	94	6:16	Leavenworth	39	95	6:20
				Leoti	38	101	6:44
KANSAS (KS)				Liberal	37	101	6:44
				Lincoln	39	98	6:32
Abilene	39	97	6:28	Lyndon	39	96	6:24
Alma	39	96	6:24	Lyons	38	98	6:32
Anthony	37	98	6:32	Manhattan	39	97	6:28
Arkansas City	37	97	6:28	Mankato	40	98	6:32
Ashland	37	100	6:40	Marion	38	97	6:28
Atchison	40	95	6:20	Marysville	40	97	6:28
Atwood	40	101	6:44	McPherson	38	98	6:32
Belleville	40	98	6:32	Meade	37	100	6:40
Beloit	39	98	6:32	Medicine Lodge	37	99	6:36
Burlington	38	96	6:24	Minneapolis	39	98	6:32
Chanute	38	95	6:20	Mound City	38	95	6:20
Cimarron	38	100	6:40	Ness City	38	100	6:40
Clay Center	39	97	6:28	Newton	38	97	6:28
Coffeyville	37	96	6:24	Norton	40	100	6:40
Colby	39	101	6:44	Oakley	39	101	6:44
Coldwater	37	99	6:36	Oberlin	40	101	6:44
Columbus	37	95	6:20	Olathe	39	95	6:20
Concordia	40	98	6:32	Osborne	39	99	6:36
Cottonwood Falls	38	97	6:28	Oskaloosa	39	95	6:20
Council Grove	39	96	6:24	Oswego	37	95	6:20
Dighton	38	100	6:40	Ottawa	39	95	6:20
Dodge City	38	100	6:40	Overland Park	39	95	6:20
El Dorado	38	97	6:28	Paola	39	95	6:20
Elkhart	37	102	6:48	Parsons	37	95	6:20
Ellsworth	39	98	6:32	Phillipsburg	40	99	6:36
Emporia	38	96	6:24	Pittsburg	37	95	6:20
Erie	38	95	6:20	Prairie Village	39	95	6:20
Eureka	38	96	6:24	Pratt	38	99	6:36
Fort Scott	38	95	6:20	Russell	39	99	6:36
Fredonia	38	96	6:24	Saint Francis	40	102	6:48
Garden City	38	101	6:44	Saint John	38	99	6:36
Garnett	38	95	6:20	Salina	39	98	6:32
Girard	38	95	6:20	Scott City	38	101	6:44

CITY	LAT N.	LONG W.	TIME h m	CITY	LAT N.	LONG W.	TIME h m
KANSAS							
Sedan	37	96	6:24	Grayson	38	83	5:32
Seneca	40	96	6:24	Greensburg	37	86	5:44
Sharon Springs	39	102	6:48	Greenup	39	83	5:32
Smith Center	40	99	6:36	Greenville	37	87	5:48
Stockton	39	99	6:36	Hardinsburg	38	86	5:44
Sublette	37	101	6:44	Harlan	37	83	5:32
Syracuse	38	102	6:48	Harrodsburg	38	85	5:40
Topeka	39	96	6:24	Hartford	37	87	5:48
Tribune	38	102	6:48	Hazard	37	83	5:32
Troy	40	95	6:20	Hawesville	38	87	5:48
Ulysses	38	101	6:44	Henderson	38	88	5:52
Wa Keeney	39	100	6:40	Hickman	37	89	5:56
Washington	40	97	6:28	Hindman	37	83	5:32
Wellington	37	97	6:28	Hodgenville	38	86	5:44
Westmoreland	39	96	6:24	Hopkinsville	37	87	5:48
Wichita	38	97	6:28	Hyden	37	83	5:32
Winfield	37	97	6:28	Independence	39	85	5:40
Yates Center	38	96	6:24	Inez	38	83	5:32
				Irvine	38	84	5:36
KENTUCKY (KY)				Jackson	38	83	5:32
				Jamestown	37	85	5:40
Albany	37	85	5:40	La Grange	38	85	5:40
Alexandria	39	84	5:36	Lancaster	38	85	5:40
Ashland	38	83	5:32	Lawrenceburg	38	85	5:40
Barbourville	37	84	5:36	Lebanon	38	85	5:40
Bardstown	38	85	5:40	Leitchfield	37	86	5:44
Bardwell	37	89	5:56	Lexington	38	85	5:40
Beattyville	38	84	5:36	Liberty	37	85	5:40
Bedford	39	85	5:40	London	37	84	5:36
Benton	37	88	5:52	Louisa	38	83	5:32
Booneville	37	84	5:36	Louisville	38	86	5:44
Bowling Green	37	86	5:44	McKee	37	84	5:36
Brandenburg	38	86	5:44	Madisonville	37	88	5:52
Brooksville	39	84	5:36	Manchester	37	84	5:36
Brownsville	37	86	5:44	Marion	37	88	5:52
Burkesville	37	85	5:40	Mayfield	37	89	5:56
Burlington	39	85	5:40	Maysville	39	84	5:36
Cadiz	37	88	5:52	Middlesboro	37	84	5:36
Calhoun	38	87	5:48	Monticello	37	85	5:40
Campbellsville	37	85	5:40	Morehead	38	83	5:32
Campton	38	84	5:36	Morganfield	38	88	5:52
Carlisle	38	84	5:36	Morgantown	37	87	5:48
Carrollton	39	85	5:40	Mount Olivet	39	84	5:36
Catlettsburg	38	83	5:32	Mount Sterling	38	84	5:36
Clinton	37	89	5:56	Mount Vernon	37	84	5:36
Columbia	37	85	5:40	Munfordville	37	86	5:44
Covington	39	85	5:40	Murray	37	88	5:52
Cynthiana	38	84	5:36	New Castle	38	85	5:40
Danville	38	85	5:40	Newport	39	85	5:40
Dixon	38	88	5:52	Nicholasville	38	85	5:40
Eddyville	37	88	5:52	Owensboro	38	87	5:48
Edmonton	37	86	5:44	Owenton	39	85	5:40
Elizabethtown	38	86	5:44	Owingsville	38	84	5:36
Elkton	37	87	5:48	Paducah	37	89	5:56
Falmouth	39	84	5:36	Paintsville	38	83	5:32
Flemingsburg	38	84	5:36	Paris	38	84	5:36
Frankfort	38	85	5:40	Pikeville	37	83	5:32
Franklin	37	87	5:48	Pineville	37	84	5:36
Frenchburg	38	84	5:36	Prestonsburg	38	83	5:32
Georgetown	38	85	5:40	Princeton	37	88	5:52
Glasgow	37	86	5:44	Richmond	38	84	5:36

CITY	LAT N.	LONG W.	TIME h m
KENTUCKY			
Russellville	37	87	5:48
Salyersville	38	83	5:32
Sandy Hook	38	83	5:32
Scottsville	37	86	5:44
Shelbyville	38	85	5:40
Shepherdsville	38	86	5:44
Smithland	37	88	5:52
Somerset	37	85	5:40
Springfield	38	85	5:40
Stanford	38	85	5:40
Stanton	38	84	5:36
Taylorsville	38	85	5:40
Tompkinsville	37	86	5:44
Vanceburg	39	83	5:32
Versailles	38	85	5:40
Warsaw	39	85	5:40
West Liberty	38	83	5:32
Whitesburg	37	83	5:32
Whitley City	37	84	5:36
Wickliffe	37	89	5:56
Williamsburg	37	84	5:36
Williamstown	39	85	5:40
Winchester	38	84	5:36
LOUISIANA (LA)			
Abbeville	30	92	6:08
Alexandria	31	92	6:08
Amite	31	91	6:04
Arcadia	33	93	6:12
Bastrop	33	92	6:08
Baton Rouge	30	91	6:04
Benton	33	94	6:16
Bogalusa	31	90	6:00
Bossier City	33	94	6:16
Cameron	30	93	6:12
Chalmette	30	90	6:00
Clinton	31	91	6:04
Colfax	32	93	6:12
Columbia	32	92	6:08
Convent	30	91	6:04
Coushatta	32	93	6:12
Covington	30	90	6:00
Crowley	30	92	6:08
De Ridder	31	93	6:12
Donaldsonville	30	91	6:04
Edgard	30	91	6:04
Eunice	31	92	6:08
Farmerville	33	92	6:08
Franklin	30	92	6:08
Franklinton	31	90	6:00
Greensburg	31	91	6:04
Gretna	30	90	6:00
Hahnville	30	90	6:00
Hammond	31	90	6:00
Harrisonburg	32	92	6:08
Homer	33	93	6:12
Houma	30	91	6:04
Jena	32	92	6:08
Jennings	30	93	6:12
Jonesboro	32	93	6:12

CITY	LAT N.	LONG W.	TIME h m
Kenner	30	90	6:00
Lafayette	30	92	6:08
Lake Charles	30	93	6:12
Lake Providence	33	91	6:04
Leesville	31	93	6:12
Livingston	31	91	6:04
Mansfield	32	94	6:16
Many	32	93	6:12
Marksville	31	92	6:08
Marrero	30	90	6:00
Metairie	30	90	6:00
Minden	33	93	6:12
Monroe	33	92	6:08
Morgan City	30	91	6:04
Napoleonville	30	91	6:04
Natchitoches	32	93	6:12
New Iberia	30	92	6:08
New Orleans	30	90	6:00
New Roads	31	91	6:04
Oak Grove	33	91	6:04
Oberlin	31	93	6:12
Opelousas	31	92	6:08
Plaquemine	30	91	6:04
Pointe A La Hache	30	90	6:00
Port Allen	30	91	6:04
Rayville	32	92	6:08
Ruston	33	93	6:12
Saint Francisville	31	91	6:04
Saint Joseph	32	91	6:04
Saint Martinville	30	92	6:08
Shreveport	33	94	6:16
Tallulah	32	91	6:04
Thibodaux	30	91	6:04
Vidalia	32	91	6:04
Ville Platte	31	92	6:08
Winnfield	32	93	6:12
Winnsboro	32	92	6:08
MAINE (ME)			
Alfred	43	71	4:44
Auburn	44	70	4:40
Augusta	44	70	4:40
Bangor	45	69	4:36
Bath	44	70	4:40
Belfast	44	69	4:36
Biddeford	44	70	4:40
Brunswick	44	70	4:40
Dover-Foxcroft	45	69	4:36
Ellsworth	45	68	4:32
Farmington	45	70	4:40
Houlton	46	68	4:32
Kittery	43	71	4:44
Lewiston	44	70	4:40
Machias	45	67	4:28
Portland	44	70	4:40
Presque Isle	47	68	4:32
Rockland	44	69	4:36
Sanford	43	71	4:44
Skowhegan	45	70	4:40
South Paris	44	71	4:44

CITY MAINE	LAT N.	LONG W.	TIME h m	CITY	LAT N.	LONG W.	TIME h m
Waterville	45	70	4:40	Chicopee	42	73	4:52
Westbrook	44	70	4:40	Clinton	42	72	4:48
Wiscasset	44	70	4:40	Concord	42	71	4:44
				Danvers	43	71	4:44
MARYLAND (MD)				Dedham	42	71	4:44
				Easthampton	42	73	4:52
Aberdeen	40	76	5:04	Edgartown	41	71	4:44
Annapolis	39	77	5:08	Everett	42	71	4:44
Baltimore	39	77	5:08	Fall River	42	71	4:44
Bel Air	40	76	5:04	Fitchburg	43	72	4:48
Bethesda	39	77	5:08	Framingham	42	71	4:44
Bowie	39	77	5:08	Gardner	43	72	4:48
Cambridge	39	76	5:04	Gloucester	43	71	4:44
Catonsville	39	77	5:08	Greenfield	43	73	4:52
Centreville	39	76	5:04	Haverhill	43	71	4:44
Chestertown	39	76	5:04	Holyoke	42	73	4:52
College Park	39	77	5:08	Lawrence	43	71	4:44
Cumberland	40	79	5:16	Leominster	43	72	4:48
Denton	39	76	5:04	Lexington	42	71	4:44
Dundalk	39	77	5:08	Lowell	43	71	4:44
Easton	39	76	5:04	Lynn	42	71	4:44
Elkton	40	76	5:04	Malden	42	71	4:44
Ellicott City	39	77	5:08	Marlboro	43	71	4:44
Essex	39	76	5:04	Medford	42	71	4:44
Frederick	39	77	5:08	Melrose	42	71	4:44
Glen Burnie	39	77	5:08	Methuen	43	71	4:44
Hagerstown	40	78	5:12	Middleborough	42	71	4:44
Hyattsville	39	77	5:08	Milford	42	72	4:48
La Plata	39	77	5:08	Milton	42	71	4:44
Leonardtown	38	77	5:08	Nantucket	41	70	4:40
Oakland	39	79	5:16	Natick	42	71	4:44
Parkville	39	77	5:08	Needham	42	71	4:44
Prince Frederick	39	77	5:08	New Bedford	42	71	4:44
Princess Anne	38	76	5:04	Newburyport	43	71	4:44
Rockville	39	77	5:08	Newton	42	71	4:44
Salisbury	38	76	5:04	Northampton	42	73	4:52
Silver Spring	39	77	5:08	North Adams	43	73	4:52
Snow Hill	38	75	5:00	North Attleboro	42	71	4:44
Suitland	39	77	5:08	Northbridge	42	72	4:48
Towson	39	77	5:08	Norwood	42	71	4:44
Upper Marlboro	39	77	5:08	Peabody	43	71	4:44
Westminster	40	77	5:08	Pittsfield	42	73	4:52
Wheaton	39	77	5:08	Plymouth	42	71	4:44
				Quincy	42	71	4:44
MASSACHUSETTS (MA)				Randolph	42	71	4:44
				Reading	43	71	4:44
Amesbury	43	71	4:44	Revere	42	71	4:44
Amherst	42	73	4:52	Salem	43	71	4:44
Andover	43	71	4:44	Saugus	42	71	4:44
Arlington	42	71	4:44	Somerville	42	71	4:44
Athol	43	72	4:48	Southbridge	42	72	4:48
Attleboro	42	71	4:44	Springfield	42	73	4:52
Barnstable	42	70	4:40	Stoughton	42	71	4:44
Belmont	42	71	4:44	Taunton	42	71	4:44
Beverly	43	71	4:44	Wakefield	43	71	4:44
Boston	42	71	4:44	Walpole	42	71	4:44
Braintree	42	71	4:44	Waltham	42	71	4:44
Brockton	42	71	4:44	Watertown	42	71	4:44
Brookline	42	71	4:44	Webster	42	72	4:48
Cambridge	42	71	4:44	Wellesley	42	71	4:44
Chelsea	42	71	4:44	Westfield	42	73	4:52

CITY	LAT N.	LONG W.	TIME h m	CITY	LAT N.	LONG W.	TIME h m
MASSACHUSETTS				Ionia	43	85	5:40
West Springfield	42	73	4:52	Iron Mountain	46	88	5:52
Weymouth	42	71	4:44	Ironwood	46	90	6:00
Woburn	42	71	4:44	Ithaca	43	85	5:40
Worcester	42	72	4:48	Jackson	42	84	5:36
				Kalamazoo	42	86	5:44
MICHIGAN (MI)				Kalkaska	45	85	5:40
Adrian	42	84	5:36	Lake City	44	85	5:40
Albion	42	85	5:40	L'Anse	47	88	5:52
Allegan	43	86	5:44	Lansing	43	85	5:40
Allen Park	42	83	5:32	Lapeer	43	83	5:32
Alpena	45	83	5:32	Leland	45	86	5:44
Ann Arbor	42	84	5:36	Lincoln Park	42	83	5:32
Atlanta	45	84	5:36	Livonia	42	83	5:32
Bad Axe	44	83	5:32	Ludington	44	86	5:44
Baldwin	44	86	5:44	Madison Heights	43	83	5:32
Battle Creek	42	85	5:40	Manistee	44	86	5:44
Bay City	44	84	5:36	Manistique	46	86	5:44
Bellaire	45	85	5:40	Marquette	47	87	5:48
Benton Harbor	42	86	5:44	Marshall	42	85	5:40
Bessemer	46	90	6:00	Mason	43	84	5:36
Beulah	45	86	5:44	Menominee	45	88	5:52
Big Rapids	44	85	5:40	Midland	44	84	5:36
Birmingham	43	83	5:32	Mio	45	84	5:36
Cadillac	44	85	5:40	Monroe	42	83	5:32
Caro	43	83	5:32	Mount Clemens	43	83	5:32
Cassopolis	42	86	5:44	Mount Pleasant	44	85	5:40
Centreville	42	86	5:44	Munising	46	87	5:48
Charlevoix	45	85	5:40	Muskegon	43	86	5:44
Charlotte	43	85	5:40	Newberry	46	86	5:44
Cheboygan	46	84	5:36	Niles	42	86	5:44
Clinton Township	42	84	5:36	Oak Park	42	83	5:32
Coldwater	42	85	5:40	Ontonagon	47	89	5:56
Corunna	43	84	5:36	Owosso	43	84	5:36
Crystal Falls	46	88	5:52	Paw Paw	42	86	5:44
Dearborn	42	83	5:32	Petoskey	45	85	5:40
Dearborn Heights	42	83	5:32	Pontiac	43	83	5:32
Detroit	42	83	5:32	Portage	42	86	5:44
Eagle River	47	88	5:52	Port Huron	43	82	5:28
East Detroit	42	83	5:32	Redford	42	83	5:32
East Lansing	43	84	5:36	Reed City	44	86	5:44
Escanaba	46	87	5:48	Rogers City	45	84	5:36
Ferndale	42	83	5:32	Roscommon	45	85	5:40
Flint	43	84	5:36	Roseville	43	83	5:32
Garden City	42	83	5:32	Royal Oak	43	83	5:32
Gaylord	45	85	5:40	Saginaw	43	84	5:36
Gladwin	44	84	5:36	Saint Clair Shores	43	83	5:32
Grand Haven	43	86	5:44	Saint Ignace	46	85	5:40
Grand Rapids	43	86	5:44	Saint Johns	43	85	5:40
Grayling	45	85	5:40	Saint Joseph	42	86	5:44
Hamtramck	42	83	5:32	Sandusky	43	83	5:32
Harrison	44	85	5:40	Sault Sainte Marie	47	84	5:36
Harrisville	45	83	5:32	Southfield	42	83	5:32
Hart	44	86	5:44	Southgate	42	83	5:32
Hastings	43	85	5:40	Standish	44	84	5:36
Highland Park	42	83	5:32	Stanton	43	85	5:40
Hillsdale	42	85	5:40	Sterling Heights	43	83	5:32
Holland	43	86	5:44	Taylor	42	83	5:32
Houghton	47	89	5:56	Tawas City	44	84	5:36
Howell	43	84	5:36	Traverse City	45	86	5:44
Inkster	42	83	5:32	Troy	43	83	5:32

CITY	LAT N.	LONG W.	TIME h m	CITY	LAT N.	LONG W.	TIME h m
MICHIGAN							
Warren	43	83	5:32	Luverne	44	96	6:24
West Branch	44	84	5:36	Madison	45	96	6:24
Westland	42	83	5:32	Mahnomen	47	96	6:24
White Cloud	44	86	5:44	Mankato	44	94	6:16
Wyandotte	42	83	5:32	Mantorville	44	93	6:12
Wyoming	43	86	5:44	Maplewood	45	93	6:12
Ypsilanti	42	84	5:36	Marshall	44	96	6:24
				Milaca	46	94	6:16
MINNESOTA (MN)				Minneapolis	45	93	6:12
				Minnetonka	45	93	6:12
Ada	47	97	6:28	Montevideo	45	96	6:24
Aitkin	47	94	6:16	Moorhead	47	97	6:28
Albert Lea	44	93	6:12	Mora	46	93	6:12
Alexandria	46	95	6:20	Morris	46	96	6:24
Anoka	45	93	6:12	New Ulm	44	94	6:16
Austin	44	93	6:12	Olivia	45	95	6:20
Bagley	48	95	6:20	Ortonville	45	96	6:24
Baudette	49	95	6:20	Owatonna	44	93	6:12
Bemidji	47	95	6:20	Park Rapids	47	95	6:20
Benson	45	96	6:24	Pine City	46	93	6:12
Bloomington	45	93	6:12	Pipestone	44	96	6:24
Blue Earth	44	94	6:16	Preston	44	92	6:08
Brainerd	46	94	6:16	Red Lake Falls	48	96	6:24
Breckenridge	46	97	6:28	Red Wing	45	93	6:12
Brooklyn Center	45	93	6:12	Redwood Falls	45	95	6:20
Brooklyn Park	45	93	6:12	Richfield	45	93	6:12
Buffalo	45	94	6:16	Rochester	44	92	6:08
Caledonia	44	92	6:08	Roseau	49	96	6:24
Cambridge	46	93	6:12	Roseville	45	93	6:12
Carlton	47	92	6:08	Saint Cloud	46	94	6:16
Center City	45	93	6:12	Saint James	44	95	6:20
Chaska	45	94	6:16	Saint Louis Park	45	93	6:12
Coon Rapids	45	93	6:12	Saint Paul	45	93	6:12
Crookston	48	97	6:28	Saint Peter	44	94	6:16
Crystal	45	93	6:12	Shakopee	45	94	6:16
Detroit Lakes	47	96	6:24	Slayton	44	96	6:24
Duluth	47	92	6:08	Stillwater	45	93	6:12
Edina	45	93	6:12	South Saint Paul	45	93	6:12
Elbow Lake	46	96	6:24	Thief River Falls	48	96	6:24
Elk River	45	94	6:16	Two Harbors	47	92	6:08
Fairmont	44	94	6:16	Virginia	48	93	6:12
Faribault	44	93	6:12	Wabasha	44	92	6:08
Fergus Falls	46	96	6:24	Wadena	46	95	6:20
Foley	46	94	6:16	Walker	47	95	6:20
Fridley	45	93	6:12	Warren	48	97	6:28
Gaylord	45	94	6:16	Waseca	44	94	6:16
Glencoe	45	94	6:16	Wheaton	46	97	6:28
Glenwood	46	95	6:20	Willmar	45	95	6:20
Grand Marais	48	90	6:00	Windom	44	95	6:20
Grand Rapids	47	94	6:16	Winona	44	92	6:08
Granite Falls	45	96	6:24	Worthington	44	96	6:24
Hallock	49	97	6:28				
Hastings	45	93	6:12	**MISSISSIPPI (MS)**			
Hibbing	47	93	6:12				
International Falls	49	93	6:12	Aberdeen	34	89	5:56
Ivanhoe	44	96	6:24	Ackerman	33	89	5:56
Jackson	44	95	6:20	Ashland	35	89	5:56
Le Center	44	94	6:16	Batesville	34	90	6:00
Litchfield	45	95	6:20	Bay Saint Louis	30	89	5:56
Little Falls	46	94	6:16	Bay Springs	32	89	5:56
Long Prairie	46	95	6:20	Belzoni	33	90	6:00

CITY MISSISSIPPI	LAT N.	LONG W.	TIME h m	CITY	LAT N.	LONG W.	TIME h m
Biloxi	30	89	5:56	Poplarville	31	90	6:00
Booneville	35	89	5:56	Port Gibson	32	91	6:04
Brandon	32	90	6:00	Prentiss	32	90	6:00
Brookhaven	32	90	6:00	Purvis	31	89	5:56
Canton	33	90	6:00	Quitman	32	89	5:56
Carrollton	34	90	6:00	Raleigh	32	90	6:00
Carthage	33	90	6:00	Raymond	32	90	6:00
Charleston	34	90	6:00	Ripley	35	89	5:56
Clarksdale	34	91	6:04	Rolling Fork	33	91	6:04
Cleveland	34	91	6:04	Rosedale	34	91	6:04
Coffeeville	34	90	6:00	Sardis	34	90	6:00
Collins	32	90	6:00	Senatobia	35	90	6:00
Columbia	31	90	6:00	Starkville	33	89	5:56
Columbus	34	88	5:52	Sumner	34	90	6:00
Corinth	35	89	5:56	Tunica	35	90	6:00
Decatur	32	89	5:56	Tupelo	34	89	5:56
De Kalb	33	89	5:56	Tylertown	31	90	6:00
Ellisville	32	89	5:56	Vaiden	33	90	6:00
Fayette	32	91	6:04	Vicksburg	32	91	6:04
Forest	32	89	5:56	Walthall	34	89	5:56
Fulton	34	88	5:52	Water Valley	34	90	6:00
Greenville	33	91	6:04	Waynesboro	32	89	5:56
Greenwood	34	90	6:00	West Point	34	89	5:56
Grenada	34	90	6:00	Wiggins	31	89	5:56
Gulfport	30	89	5:56	Winona	33	90	6:00
Hattiesburg	31	89	5:56	Woodville	31	91	6:04
Hazlehurst	32	90	6:00	Yazoo City	33	90	6:00
Hernando	35	90	6:00				
Holly Springs	35	89	5:56	MISSOURI (MO)			
Houston	34	89	5:56				
Indianola	33	91	6:04	Albany	40	94	6:16
Iuka	35	88	5:52	Alton	37	91	6:04
Jackson	32	90	6:00	Ava	37	93	6:12
Kosciusko	33	90	6:00	Benton	37	90	6:00
Laurel	32	89	5:56	Bethany	40	94	6:16
Leakesville	31	89	5:56	Bloomfield	37	90	6:00
Lexington	33	90	6:00	Bolivar	38	93	6:12
Liberty	31	91	6:04	Boonville	39	93	6:12
Louisville	33	89	5:56	Bowling Green	39	91	6:04
Lucedale	31	89	5:56	Buffalo	38	93	6:12
McComb	31	90	6:00	Butler	38	94	6:16
Macon	33	89	5:56	California	39	93	6:12
Magnolia	31	90	6:00	Camdenton	38	93	6:12
Marks	34	90	6:00	Cape Girardeau	37	90	6:00
Mayersville	33	91	6:04	Carrollton	39	94	6:16
Meadville	31	91	6:04	Carthage	37	94	6:16
Mendenhall	32	90	6:00	Caruthersville	36	90	6:00
Meridian	32	89	5:56	Cassville	37	94	6:16
Monticello	32	90	6:00	Centerville	37	91	6:04
Moss Point	30	89	5:56	Charleston	37	89	5:56
Natchez	32	91	6:04	Chillicothe	40	94	6:16
New Albany	34	89	5:56	Clayton	39	90	6:00
New Augusta	31	89	5:56	Clinton	38	94	6:16
Okolona	34	89	5:56	Columbia	39	92	6:08
Oxford	34	90	6:00	Doniphan	37	91	6:04
Pascagoula	30	89	5:56	Edina	40	92	6:08
Paulding	32	89	5:56	Eminence	37	91	6:04
Philadelphia	33	89	5:56	Farmington	38	90	6:00
Picayune	31	90	6:00	Fayette	39	93	6:12
Pittsboro	34	89	5:56	Ferguson	39	90	6:00
Pontotoc	34	89	5:56	Florissant	39	90	6:00

CITY MISSOURI	LAT N.	LONG W.	TIME h m	CITY	LAT N.	LONG W.	TIME h m
Forsyth	37	93	6:12	Platte City	39	95	6:20
Fredericktown	38	90	6:00	Plattsburg	40	94	6:16
Fulton	39	92	6:08	Poplar Bluff	37	90	6:00
Gainesville	37	92	6:08	Potosi	38	91	6:04
Galena	37	93	6:12	Princeton	40	94	6:16
Gallatin	40	94	6:16	Raytown	39	94	6:16
Grant City	40	94	6:16	Richmond	39	94	6:16
Greenfield	37	94	6:16	Rock Port	40	96	6:24
Greenville	37	90	6:00	Rolla	38	92	6:08
Hannibal	40	91	6:04	Saint Charles	39	90	6:00
Harrisonville	39	94	6:16	Saint Joseph	40	95	6:20
Hartville	37	93	6:12	Saint Louis	39	90	6:00
Hermann	39	91	6:04	Salem	38	92	6:08
Hermitage	38	93	6:12	Savannah	40	95	6:20
Hillsboro	38	91	6:04	Sedalia	39	93	6:12
Houston	37	92	6:08	Shelbyville	40	92	6:08
Huntsville	39	93	6:12	Sikeston	37	90	6:00
Independence	39	94	6:16	Springfield	37	93	6:12
Ironton	38	91	6:04	Steelville	38	91	6:04
Jackson	37	90	6:00	Stockton	38	94	6:16
Jefferson City	39	92	6:08	Trenton	40	94	6:16
Joplin	37	95	6:20	Troy	39	91	6:04
Kahoka	40	92	6:08	Tuscumbia	38	92	6:08
Kansas City	39	95	6:20	Union	38	91	6:04
Kennett	36	90	6:00	Unionville	40	93	6:12
Keytesville	39	93	6:12	University City	39	90	6:00
Kingston	40	94	6:16	Van Buren	37	91	6:04
Kirksville	40	93	6:12	Webster Groves	39	90	6:00
Kirkwood	39	90	6:00	Versailles	38	93	6:12
Lamar	38	94	6:16	Vienna	38	92	6:08
Lancaster	41	93	6:12	Warrensburg	39	94	6:16
Lebanon	38	93	6:12	Warrenton	39	91	6:04
Lemay	39	90	6:00	Warsaw	38	93	6:12
Lexington	39	94	6:16	Waynesville	38	92	6:08
Liberty	39	92	6:08	West Plains	37	92	6:08
Linn	38	92	6:08				
Linneus	40	93	6:12	MONTANA (MT)			
Macon	40	92	6:08				
Marble Hill	37	90	6:00	Anaconda	46	113	7:32
Marshall	39	93	6:12	Baker	46	104	6:56
Marshfield	37	93	6:12	Big Timber	46	110	7:20
Maryville	40	95	6:20	Billings	46	109	7:16
Maysville	40	94	6:16	Boulder	46	112	7:28
Memphis	40	92	6:08	Bozeman	46	111	7:24
Mexico	39	92	6:08	Broadus	45	105	7:00
Milan	40	93	6:12	Butte	46	113	7:32
Moberly	39	92	6:08	Chester	49	111	7:24
Montgomery City	39	92	6:08	Chinook	49	109	7:16
Monticello	40	92	6:08	Choteau	48	112	7:28
Mount Vernon	37	94	6:16	Circle	47	106	7:04
Neosho	37	94	6:16	Columbus	46	109	7:16
Nevada	38	94	6:16	Conrad	48	112	7:28
New London	40	91	6:04	Cut Bank	49	112	7:28
New Madrid	37	90	6:00	Deer Lodge	46	113	7:32
Oregon	40	95	6:20	Dillon	45	113	7:32
Osceola	38	94	6:16	Ekalaka	46	105	7:00
Ozark	37	93	6:12	Forsyth	46	107	7:08
Palmyra	40	92	6:08	Fort Benton	48	111	7:24
Paris	39	92	6:08	Glasgow	48	107	7:08
Perryville	38	90	6:00	Glendive	47	105	7:00
Pineville	37	94	6:16	Great Falls	48	111	7:24

CITY	LAT N.	LONG W.	TIME h m	CITY	LAT N.	LONG W.	TIME h m
MONTANA							
Hamilton	46	114	7:36	David City	41	97	6:28
Hardin	46	108	7:12	Elwood	41	100	6:40
Harlowton	46	110	7:20	Fairbury	40	97	6:28
Havre	49	110	7:20	Falls City	40	96	6:24
Helena	47	112	7:28	Franklin	40	99	6:36
Hysham	46	107	7:08	Fremont	41	97	6:28
Jordan	47	107	7:08	Fullerton	41	98	6:32
Kalispell	48	114	7:36	Geneva	41	98	6:32
Lewistown	47	109	7:16	Gering	42	104	6:56
Libby	48	116	7:44	Grand Island	41	98	6:32
Livingston	46	111	7:24	Grant	41	102	6:48
Malta	48	108	7:12	Greeley	42	99	6:36
Miles City	46	106	7:04	Harrisburg	42	104	6:56
Missoula	47	114	7:36	Harrison	43	104	6:56
Philipsburg	46	113	7:32	Hartington	43	97	6:28
Plentywood	49	105	7:00	Hastings	41	98	6:32
Polson	48	114	7:36	Hayes Center	41	101	6:44
Red Lodge	45	109	7:16	Hebron	40	98	6:32
Roundup	46	109	7:16	Holdrege	40	99	6:36
Ryegate	46	109	7:16	Hyannis	42	102	6:48
Scobey	49	105	7:00	Imperial	41	102	6:48
Shelby	49	112	7:28	Kearney	41	99	6:36
Sidney	48	104	6:56	Kimball	41	104	6:56
Stanford	47	110	7:20	Lexington	41	100	6:40
Superior	47	115	7:40	Lincoln	41	97	6:28
Terry	47	105	7:00	Loup City	41	99	6:36
Thompson Falls	48	115	7:40	McCook	40	101	6:44
Townsend	46	112	7:28	Madison	42	97	6:28
Virginia City	45	112	7:28	Minden	41	99	6:36
White Sulphur Springs	47	111	7:24	Mullen	42	101	6:44
Wibaux	47	104	6:56	Nebraska City	41	96	6:24
Winnett	47	108	7:12	Neligh	42	98	6:32
Wolf Point	48	106	7:04	Nelson	40	98	6:32
				Norfolk	42	97	6:28
NEBRASKA (NE)				North Platte	41	101	6:44
				Ogallala	41	102	6:48
Ainsworth	43	100	6:40	Omaha	41	96	6:24
Albion	42	98	6:32	O'Neill	42	99	6:36
Alliance	42	103	6:52	Ord	42	99	6:36
Alma	40	99	6:36	Osceola	41	98	6:32
Arthur	42	102	6:48	Oshkosh	41	102	6:48
Auburn	40	96	6:24	Papillion	41	96	6:24
Aurora	41	98	6:32	Pawnee City	40	96	6:24
Bartlett	42	99	6:36	Pender	42	97	6:28
Bassett	43	100	6:40	Pierce	42	98	6:32
Beatrice	40	97	6:28	Plattsmouth	41	96	6:24
Beaver City	40	100	6:40	Ponca	43	97	6:28
Benkelman	40	102	6:48	Red Cloud	40	99	6:36
Blair	42	96	6:24	Rushville	43	102	6:48
Brewster	42	100	6:40	Saint Paul	41	98	6:32
Bridgeport	42	103	6:52	Schuyler	41	97	6:28
Broken Bow	41	100	6:40	Scottsbluff	42	104	6:56
Burwell	42	99	6:36	Seward	41	97	6:28
Butte	43	99	6:36	Sidney	41	103	6:52
Center	43	98	6:32	Springview	43	100	6:40
Central City	41	98	6:32	Stanton	42	97	6:28
Chadron	43	103	6:52	Stapleton	41	101	6:44
Chappell	41	102	6:48	Stockville	41	100	6:40
Clay Center	41	98	6:32	Taylor	42	99	6:36
Columbus	41	97	6:28	Tecumseh	40	96	6:24
Dakota City	42	96	6:24	Tekamah	42	96	6:24

88

CITY	LAT N.	LONG W.	TIME h m	CITY	LAT N.	LONG W.	TIME h m
NEBRASKA							
Thedford	42	101	6:44	Bergenfield	41	74	4:56
Trenton	40	101	6:44	Bloomfield	41	74	4:56
Tryon	42	101	6:44	Bound Brook	41	75	5:00
Valentine	43	101	6:44	Bridgeton	39	75	5:00
Wahoo	41	97	6:28	Burlington	40	75	5:00
Wayne	42	97	6:28	Camden	40	75	5:00
West Point	42	97	6:28	Cape May Court House	39	75	5:00
Wilber	40	97	6:28	Cherry Hill	40	75	5:00
York	41	98	6:32	Clifton	41	74	4:56
				Cranford	41	74	4:56
NEVADA (NV)				Dover	41	75	5:00
				East Brunswick	40	74	4:56
Austin	40	117	7:48	East Orange	41	74	4:56
Carson City	39	120	8:00	Edison	41	74	4:56
Elko	41	116	7:44	Elizabeth	41	74	4:56
Ely	39	115	7:40	Fair Lawn	41	74	4:56
Eureka	40	116	7:44	Flemington	41	75	5:00
Fallon	39	119	7:56	Fort Lee	41	74	4:56
Goldfield	38	117	7:48	Freehold	40	74	4:56
Hawthorne	39	119	7:56	Garfield	41	74	4:56
Henderson	36	115	7:40	Glassboro	40	75	5:00
Las Vegas	36	115	7:40	Hackensack	41	74	4:56
Lovelock	40	118	7:52	Hammonton	40	75	5:00
Minden	39	120	8:00	Hoboken	41	74	4:56
North Las Vegas	36	115	7:40	Irvington	41	74	4:56
Pioche	38	114	7:36	Jersey City	41	74	4:56
Reno	40	120	8:00	Kearny	41	74	4:56
Tonopah	38	117	7:48	Lakewood	40	74	4:56
Virginia City	39	120	8:00	Linden	41	74	4:56
Winnemucca	41	118	7:52	Livingston	41	74	4:56
Yerington	39	119	7:56	Lodi	41	74	4:56
				Long Branch	40	74	4:56
NEW HAMPSHIRE (NH)				Madison	41	74	4:56
				Manville	41	75	5:00
Berlin	44	71	4:44	Mays Landing	39	75	5:00
Claremont	43	72	4:48	Metuchen	41	74	4:56
Concord	43	72	4:48	Millville	39	75	5:00
Derry	43	71	4:44	Montclair	41	74	4:56
Dover	43	71	4:44	Morristown	41	74	4:56
Exeter	43	71	4:44	Mount Holly	40	75	5:00
Keene	43	72	4:48	Newark	41	74	4:56
Laconia	44	71	4:44	New Brunswick	41	74	4:56
Lancaster	44	72	4:48	Newton	41	75	5:00
Lebanon	44	72	4:48	North Bergen	41	74	4:56
Manchester	43	71	4:44	Nutley	41	74	4:56
Nashua	43	71	4:44	Ocean City	39	75	5:00
Newport	43	72	4:48	Orange	41	74	4:56
Ossipee	44	71	4:44	Paramus	41	74	4:56
Portsmouth	43	71	4:44	Passaic	41	74	4:56
Rochester	43	71	4:44	Paterson	41	74	4:56
Salem	43	71	4:44	Pennsauken	40	75	5:00
Somersworth	43	71	4:44	Perth Amboy	41	74	4:56
Woodsville	44	72	4:48	Phillipsburg	41	75	5:00
				Piscataway	41	74	4:56
NEW JERSEY (NJ)				Plainfield	41	74	4:56
				Pleasantville	39	75	5:00
Asbury Park	40	74	4:56	Princeton	40	75	5:00
Atlantic City	39	74	4:56	Rahway	41	74	4:56
Bayonne	41	74	4:56	Red Bank	40	74	4:56
Belleville	41	74	4:56	Ridgewood	41	74	4:56
Belvidere	41	75	5:00	Salem	40	75	5:00

CITY NEW JERSEY	LAT N.	LONG W.	TIME h m	CITY	LAT N.	LONG W.	TIME h m
Sayreville	40	74	4:56	Baldwin	41	74	4:56
Somerville	40	75	5:00	Ballston Spa	43	74	4:56
South River	40	74	4:56	Batavia	43	78	5:12
Summit	41	74	4:56	Bath	42	77	5:08
Teaneck	41	74	4:56	Bay Shore	41	73	4:52
Toms River	40	74	4:56	Bayside	41	74	4:56
Trenton	40	75	5:00	Beacon	42	74	4:56
Union	41	74	4:56	Belmont	42	78	5:12
Union City	41	74	4:56	Bethpage	41	74	4:56
Vineland	39	75	5:00	Binghamton	42	76	5:04
Wayne	41	74	4:56	Brentwood	41	73	4:52
Westfield	41	74	4:56	Brighton	43	78	5:12
West New York	41	74	4:56	Bronx	41	74	4:56
West Orange	41	74	4:56	Brooklyn	41	74	4:56
Willingboro	40	75	5:00	Buffalo	43	79	5:16
Woodbury	40	75	5:00	Canandaigua	43	77	5:08
				Canton	45	75	5:00
NEW MEXICO (NM)				Carmel	41	74	4:56
				Catskill	42	74	4:56
Alamogordo	33	106	7:04	Central Islip	41	73	4:52
Albuquerque	35	107	7:08	Cheektowaga	43	79	5:16
Aztec	37	108	7:12	Cohoes	43	74	4:56
Bernalillo	35	107	7:08	Cooperstown	43	75	5:00
Carlsbad	32	104	6:56	Corning	42	77	5:08
Carrizozo	34	106	7:04	Corona	41	74	4:56
Clayton	36	103	6:52	Cortland	43	76	5:04
Clovis	34	103	6:52	Deer Park	41	73	4:52
Deming	32	108	7:12	Delhi	42	75	5:00
Estancia	35	106	7:04	Dunkirk	42	79	5:16
Fort Sumner	34	104	6:56	East Meadow	41	74	4:56
Gallup	36	109	7:16	Elizabethtown	44	74	4:56
Hobbs	33	103	6:52	Elmira	42	77	5:08
Las Cruces	32	107	7:08	Elmont	41	74	4:56
Las Vegas	36	105	7:00	Flushing	41	74	4:56
Lordsburg	32	109	7:16	Fonda	43	74	4:56
Los Alamos	36	106	7:04	Forest Hills	41	74	4:56
Los Lunas	35	107	7:08	Franklin Square	41	74	4:56
Lovington	33	103	6:52	Freeport	41	74	4:56
Mora	36	105	7:00	Fulton	43	76	5:04
Mosquero	36	104	6:56	Garden City	41	74	4:56
Portales	34	103	6:52	Gates	43	78	5:12
Raton	37	104	6:56	Geneseo	43	78	5:12
Reserve	34	109	7:16	Geneva	43	77	5:08
Roswell	33	105	7:00	Glen Cove	41	74	4:56
Santa Fe	36	106	7:04	Glens Falls	43	74	4:56
Santa Rosa	35	105	7:00	Gloversville	43	74	4:56
Silver City	33	108	7:12	Goshen	41	74	4:56
Socorro	34	107	7:08	Greece	43	78	5:12
Taos	36	106	7:04	Hempstead	41	74	4:56
Tierra Amarilla	37	107	7:08	Herkimer	43	75	5:00
Truth Or Consequences	33	107	7:08	Hicksville	41	74	4:56
Tucumcari	35	104	6:56	Hornell	42	78	5:12
				Hudson	42	74	4:56
NEW YORK (NY)				Hudson Falls	43	74	4:56
				Huntington Station	41	73	4:52
Albany	43	74	4:56	Irondequoit	43	78	5:12
Albion	43	78	5:12	Ithaca	42	77	5:08
Amherst	43	79	5:16	Jamaica	41	74	4:56
Amsterdam	43	74	4:56	Jamestown	42	79	5:16
Astoria	41	74	4:56	Johnstown	43	74	4:56
Auburn	43	77	5:08	Kew Gardens	41	74	4:56

CITY NEW YORK	LAT N.	LONG W.	TIME h m	CITY	LAT N.	LONG W.	TIME h m
Kingston	42	74	4:56	Wampsville	43	76	5:04
Lackawanna	43	79	5:16	Warsaw	43	78	5:12
Lake George	43	74	4:56	Waterloo	43	77	5:08
Lake Pleasant	43	74	4:56	Watertown	44	76	5:04
Levittown	41	74	4:56	Watkins Glen	42	77	5:08
Lindenhurst	41	73	4:52	West Babylon	41	73	4:52
Little Falls	43	75	5:00	West Hempstead	41	74	4:56
Little Valley	42	79	5:16	West Islip	41	73	4:52
Lockport	43	79	5:16	West Seneca	43	79	5:16
Long Beach	41	74	4:56	White Plains	41	74	4:56
Lowville	44	75	5:00	Woodside	41	74	4:56
Lyons	43	77	5:08	Yonkers	41	74	4:56
Malone	45	74	4:56				
Massapequa	41	73	4:52	NORTH CAROLINA (NC)			
Massena	45	75	5:00				
Mayville	42	80	5:20	Albemarle	35	80	5:20
Merrick	41	74	4:56	Asheboro	36	80	5:20
Middletown	41	74	4:56	Asheville	36	83	5:32
Mineola	41	74	4:56	Bakersville	36	82	5:28
Monticello	42	75	5:00	Bayboro	35	77	5:08
Mount Vernon	41	74	4:56	Beaufort	35	77	5:08
Newburgh	42	74	4:56	Boone	36	82	5:28
New City	41	74	4:56	Brevard	35	83	5:32
New Rochelle	41	74	4:56	Bryson City	35	83	5:32
New York	41	74	4:56	Burgaw	35	78	5:12
Niagara Falls	43	79	5:16	Burlington	36	79	5:16
North Babylon	41	73	4:52	Burnsville	36	82	5:28
North Tonawanda	43	79	5:16	Camden	36	76	5:04
Norwich	43	76	5:04	Carthage	35	79	5:16
Oceanside	41	74	4:56	Chapel Hill	36	79	5:16
Ogdensburg	45	76	5:04	Charlotte	35	81	5:24
Olean	42	78	5:12	Clinton	35	78	5:12
Oneida	43	76	5:04	Columbia	36	76	5:04
Oneonta	42	75	5:00	Columbus	35	82	5:28
Ossining	41	74	4:56	Concord	35	81	5:24
Oswego	43	77	5:08	Currituck	36	76	5:04
Ovid	43	77	5:08	Danbury	36	80	5:20
Owego	42	76	5:04	Dobson	36	81	5:24
Peekskill	41	74	4:56	Durham	36	79	5:16
Penn Yan	43	77	5:08	Edenton	36	77	5:08
Plainview	41	73	4:52	Elizabeth City	36	76	5:04
Plattsburgh	45	73	4:52	Elizabethtown	35	79	5:16
Port Chester	41	74	4:56	Fayetteville	35	79	5:16
Poughkeepsie	42	74	4:56	Franklin	35	83	5:32
Queens	41	74	4:56	Gastonia	35	81	5:24
Rego Park	41	74	4:56	Gatesville	36	77	5:08
Riverhead	41	73	4:52	Goldsboro	35	78	5:12
Rochester	43	78	5:12	Graham	36	79	5:16
Rockville Centre	41	74	4:56	Greensboro	36	80	5:20
Rome	43	75	5:00	Greenville	36	77	5:08
Rotterdam	43	74	4:56	Halifax	36	78	5:12
Saint George	41	74	4:56	Hayesville	35	84	5:36
Saratoga Springs	43	74	4:56	Henderson	36	78	5:12
Schenectady	43	74	4:56	Hendersonville	35	82	5:28
Schoharie	43	74	4:56	Hertford	36	76	5:04
Staten Island	41	74	4:56	Hickory	36	81	5:24
Syracuse	43	76	5:04	High Point	36	80	5:20
Town Of Tonawanda	43	79	5:16	Hillsboro	36	79	5:16
Troy	43	74	4:56	Jackson	36	77	5:08
Utica	43	75	5:00	Jacksonville	35	77	5:08
Valley Stream	41	74	4:56	Jefferson	36	81	5:24

91

CITY NORTH CAROLINA	LAT N.	LONG W.	TIME h m	CITY	LAT N.	LONG W.	TIME h m
Kannapolis	36	81	5:24	Yadkinville	36	81	5:24
Kenansville	35	78	5:12	Yanceyville	36	79	5:16
Kinston	35	78	5:12				
Laurinburg	35	79	5:16	NORTH DAKOTA (ND)			
Lenoir	36	82	5:28				
Lexington	36	80	5:20	Amidon	46	103	6:52
Lillington	35	79	5:16	Ashley	46	99	6:36
Lincolnton	35	81	5:24	Beach	47	104	6:56
Louisburg	36	78	5:12	Bismarck	47	101	6:44
Lumberton	35	79	5:16	Bottineau	49	100	6:40
Manteo	36	76	5:04	Bowbells	49	102	6:48
Marion	36	82	5:28	Bowman	46	103	6:52
Marshall	36	83	5:32	Cando	49	99	6:36
Mocksville	36	81	5:24	Carrington	47	99	6:36
Monroe	35	81	5:24	Carson	46	102	6:48
Morganton	36	82	5:28	Cavalier	49	98	6:32
Murphy	35	84	5:36	Center	47	101	6:44
Nashville	36	78	5:12	Cooperstown	47	98	6:32
New Bern	35	77	5:08	Crosby	49	103	6:52
Newland	36	82	5:28	Devils Lake	48	99	6:36
Newton	36	81	5:24	Dickinson	47	103	6:52
Oxford	36	79	5:16	Ellendale	46	99	6:36
Pittsboro	36	79	5:16	Fargo	47	97	6:28
Plymouth	36	77	5:08	Fessenden	48	100	6:40
Raeford	35	79	5:16	Finley	48	98	6:32
Raleigh	36	79	5:16	Forman	46	98	6:32
Reidsville	36	80	5:20	Fort Yates	46	101	6:44
Roanoke Rapids	36	78	5:12	Grafton	48	97	6:28
Robbinsville	35	84	5:36	Grand Forks	48	97	6:28
Rockingham	35	80	5:20	Hettinger	46	103	6:52
Rocky Mount	36	78	5:12	Hillsboro	47	97	6:28
Roxboro	36	79	5:16	Jamestown	47	99	6:36
Rutherfordton	35	82	5:28	Lakota	48	98	6:32
Salisbury	36	80	5:20	La Moure	46	98	6:32
Sanford	35	79	5:16	Langdon	49	98	6:32
Shelby	35	82	5:28	Linton	46	100	6:40
Smithfield	36	78	5:12	Lisbon	46	98	6:32
Snow Hill	35	78	5:12	McClusky	47	100	6:40
Southport	34	78	5:12	Mandan	47	101	6:44
Sparta	37	81	5:24	Manning	47	103	6:52
Statesville	36	81	5:24	Medora	47	104	6:56
Swanquarter	35	76	5:04	Minnewaukan	48	99	6:36
Sylva	35	83	5:32	Minot	48	101	6:44
Tarboro	36	78	5:12	Mohall	49	102	6:48
Taylorsville	36	81	5:24	Mott	46	102	6:48
Thomasville	36	80	5:20	Napoleon	47	100	6:40
Trenton	35	77	5:08	New Rockford	48	99	6:36
Troy	35	80	5:20	Rolla	49	100	6:40
Wadesboro	35	80	5:20	Rugby	48	100	6:40
Warrenton	36	78	5:12	Stanley	48	102	6:48
Washington	36	77	5:08	Stanton	47	101	6:44
Waynesville	35	83	5:32	Steele	47	100	6:40
Wentworth	36	80	5:20	Towner	48	100	6:40
Whiteville	34	79	5:16	Valley City	47	98	6:32
Wilkesboro	36	81	5:24	Wahpeton	46	97	6:28
Williamston	36	77	5:08	Washburn	47	101	6:44
Wilmington	34	78	5:12	Watford City	48	103	6:52
Wilson	36	78	5:12	Williston	48	104	6:56
Windsor	36	77	5:08				
Winston-Salem	36	80	5:20				
Winton	36	77	5:08				

CITY OHIO	LAT N.	LONG W.	TIME h m	CITY	LAT N.	LONG W.	TIME h m
OHIO (OH)				Logan	40	82	5:28
				London	40	83	5:32
Akron	41	82	5:28	Lorain	41	82	5:28
Alliance	41	81	5:24	Mansfield	41	83	5:32
Ashland	41	82	5:28	Maple Heights	41	82	5:28
Ashtabula	42	81	5:24	Marietta	39	81	5:24
Athens	39	82	5:28	Marion	41	83	5:32
Barberton	41	82	5:28	Martins Ferry	40	81	5:24
Batavia	39	84	5:36	Marysville	40	83	5:32
Bellaire	40	81	5:24	Massillon	41	82	5:28
Bellefontaine	40	84	5:36	McArthur	39	82	5:28
Berea	41	82	5:28	McConnelsville	40	82	5:28
Boardman	41	81	5:24	Medina	41	82	5:28
Bowling Green	41	84	5:36	Mentor	42	81	5:24
Brook Park	41	81	5:24	Middletown	40	84	5:36
Bryan	41	85	5:40	Millersburg	41	82	5:28
Bucyrus	41	83	5:32	Mount Gilead	41	83	5:32
Cadiz	40	81	5:24	Mount Vernon	40	82	5:28
Caldwell	40	82	5:28	Napoleon	41	84	5:36
Cambridge	40	82	5:28	New Lexington	40	82	5:28
Canton	41	81	5:24	New Philadelphia	41	81	5:24
Carrollton	41	81	5:24	Newark	40	82	5:28
Celina	41	85	5:40	North Olmsted	41	82	5:28
Chardon	42	81	5:24	Norwalk	41	83	5:32
Chillicothe	39	83	5:32	Norwood	39	84	5:36
Cincinnati	39	85	5:40	Ottawa	41	84	5:36
Circleville	40	83	5:32	Painesville	42	81	5:24
Cleveland	42	82	5:28	Parma	41	82	5:28
Cleveland Heights	42	82	5:28	Parma Heights	41	82	5:28
Columbus	40	83	5:32	Paulding	41	85	5:40
Coshocton	40	82	5:28	Piqua	40	84	5:36
Cuyahoga Falls	41	81	5:24	Pomeroy	39	82	5:28
Dayton	40	84	5:36	Port Clinton	42	83	5:32
Defiance	41	84	5:36	Portsmouth	39	83	5:32
Delaware	40	83	5:32	Ravenna	41	81	5:24
East Cleveland	42	82	5:28	Saint Clairsville	40	81	5:24
East Liverpool	41	81	5:24	Salem	41	81	5:24
Eaton	40	85	5:40	Sandusky	41	83	5:32
Euclid	42	82	5:28	Shaker Heights	41	82	5:28
Elyria	41	82	5:28	Sidney	40	84	5:36
Fairborn	40	84	5:36	South Euclid	42	82	5:28
Findlay	41	84	5:36	Springfield	40	84	5:36
Fostoria	41	83	5:32	Steubenville	40	81	5:24
Fremont	41	83	5:32	Tiffin	41	83	5:32
Gallipolis	39	82	5:28	Toledo	42	84	5:36
Garfield Heights	41	82	5:28	Troy	40	84	5:36
Georgetown	39	84	5:36	Upper Arlington	40	83	5:32
Greenville	40	85	5:40	Upper Sandusky	41	83	5:32
Hamilton	39	85	5:40	Urbana	40	84	5:36
Hillsboro	39	84	5:36	Van Wert	41	85	5:40
Ironton	39	83	5:32	Wapakoneta	41	84	5:36
Jackson	39	83	5:32	Warren	41	81	5:24
Jefferson	42	81	5:24	Washington Court House	40	83	5:32
Kent	41	81	5:24	Wauseon	42	84	5:36
Kenton	41	84	5:36	Waverly	39	83	5:32
Kettering	40	84	5:36	West Union	39	84	5:36
Lakewood	41	82	5:28	Whitehall	40	83	5:32
Lancaster	40	83	5:32	Wilmington	39	84	5:36
Lebanon	39	84	5:36	Woodsfield	40	81	5:24
Lima	41	84	5:36	Wooster	41	82	5:28
Lisbon	41	81	5:24	Xenia	40	84	5:36

CITY	LAT N.	LONG W.	TIME h m	CITY	LAT N.	LONG W.	TIME h m
OHIO				Pawhuska	37	96	6:24
Youngstown	41	81	5:24	Pawnee	36	97	6:28
Zanesville	40	82	5:28	Perry	36	97	6:28
				Ponca City	37	97	6:28
OKLAHOMA (OK)				Poteau	35	95	6:20
Ada	35	97	6:28	Pryor	36	95	6:20
Altus	35	99	6:36	Purcell	35	97	6:28
Alva	37	99	6:36	Sallisaw	35	95	6:20
Anadarko	35	98	6:32	Sapulpa	36	96	6:24
Antlers	34	96	6:24	Sayre	35	100	6:40
Arapaho	36	99	6:36	Shawnee	35	97	6:28
Ardmore	34	97	6:28	Stigler	35	95	6:20
Arnett	36	100	6:40	Stillwater	36	97	6:28
Atoka	34	96	6:24	Stilwell	36	95	6:20
Bartlesville	37	96	6:24	Sulphur	35	97	6:28
Beaver	37	101	6:44	Tahlequah	36	95	6:20
Blackwell	37	97	6:28	Taloga	36	99	6:36
Boise City	37	103	6:52	Tishomingo	34	97	6:28
Broken Arrow	36	96	6:24	Tulsa	36	96	6:24
Buffalo	37	100	6:40	Vinita	37	95	6:20
Chandler	36	97	6:28	Wagoner	36	95	6:20
Cherokee	37	98	6:32	Walters	34	98	6:32
Cheyenne	36	100	6:40	Watonga	36	98	6:32
Chickasha	35	98	6:32	Waurika	34	98	6:32
Claremore	36	96	6:24	Wewoka	35	97	6:28
Coalgate	35	96	6:24	Wilburton	35	95	6:20
Cordell	35	99	6:36	Woodward	36	99	6:36
Del City	35	97	6:28				
Duncan	35	98	6:32	**OREGON (OR)**			
Durant	34	96	6:24	Albany	45	123	8:12
Edmond	36	97	6:28	Ashland	42	123	8:12
El Reno	36	98	6:32	Astoria	46	124	8:16
Enid	36	98	6:32	Baker	45	118	7:52
Eufaula	35	96	6:24	Bend	44	121	8:04
Fairview	36	98	6:32	Burns	44	119	7:56
Frederick	34	99	6:36	Canyon City	44	119	7:56
Guthrie	36	97	6:28	Condon	45	120	8:00
Guymon	37	101	6:44	Coos Bay	43	124	8:16
Hobart	35	99	6:36	Coquille	43	124	8:16
Holdenville	35	96	6:24	Corvallis	45	123	8:12
Hollis	35	100	6:40	Dallas	45	123	8:12
Hugo	34	96	6:24	Enterprise	45	117	7:48
Idabel	34	95	6:20	Eugene	44	123	8:12
Jay	36	95	6:20	Fossil	45	120	8:00
Kingfisher	36	98	6:32	Gold Beach	42	124	8:16
Lawton	35	98	6:32	Grants Pass	42	123	8:12
McAlester	35	96	6:24	Heppner	45	120	8:00
Madill	34	97	6:28	Hillsboro	46	123	8:12
Mangum	35	100	6:40	Hood River	46	122	8:08
Marietta	34	97	6:28	Klamath Falls	42	122	8:08
Medford	37	98	6:32	La Grande	45	118	7:52
Miami	37	95	6:20	Lakeview	42	120	8:00
Midwest City	35	97	6:28	Madras	45	121	8:04
Muskogee	36	95	6:20	McMinnville	45	123	8:12
Newkirk	37	97	6:28	Medford	42	123	8:12
Norman	35	97	6:28	Moro	45	121	8:04
Nowata	37	96	6:24	Newport	45	124	8:16
Okemah	35	96	6:24	Oregon City	45	123	8:12
Oklahoma City	36	98	6:32	Pendleton	46	119	7:56
Okmulgee	36	96	6:24	Portland	46	123	8:12
Pauls Valley	35	97	6:28				

CITY	LAT N.	LONG W.	TIME h m		CITY	LAT N.	LONG W.	TIME h m
OREGON					Lancaster	40	76	5:04
Prineville	44	121	8:04		Lansdale	40	75	5:00
Roseburg	43	123	8:12		Laporte	41	77	5:08
Saint Helens	46	123	8:12		Latrobe	40	79	5:16
Salem	45	123	8:12		Lebanon	40	76	5:04
Springfield	44	123	8:12		Levittown	40	75	5:00
The Dalles	46	121	8:04		Lewisburg	41	77	5:08
Tillamook	45	124	8:16		Lewistown	41	78	5:12
Vale	44	117	7:48		Lock Haven	41	77	5:08
					McConnellsburg	40	78	5:12
PENNSYLVANIA (PA)					McKeesport	40	80	5:20
					Meadville	42	80	5:20
Aliquippa	41	80	5:20		Media	40	75	5:00
Allentown	41	75	5:00		Mercer	41	80	5:20
Altoona	41	78	5:12		Middleburg	41	77	5:08
Baldwin	40	80	5:20		Mifflintown	41	77	5:08
Beaver	41	80	5:20		Milford	41	75	5:00
Bedford	40	79	5:16		Monessen	40	80	5:20
Bellefonte	41	78	5:12		Monroeville	40	80	5:20
Berwick	41	76	5:04		Montrose	42	76	5:04
Bethel Park	40	80	5:20		Mount Lebanon	40	80	5:20
Bethlehem	41	75	5:00		Nanticoke	41	76	5:04
Bloomsburg	41	76	5:04		New Bloomfield	40	77	5:08
Bradford	42	79	5:16		New Castle	41	80	5:20
Brookville	41	79	5:16		New Kensington	41	80	5:20
Broomall	40	75	5:00		Norristown	40	75	5:00
Butler	41	80	5:20		Oil City	41	80	5:20
Canonsburg	40	80	5:20		Penn Hills	40	80	5:20
Carbondale	42	76	5:04		Philadelphia	40	75	5:00
Carlisle	40	77	5:08		Phoenixville	40	76	5:04
Chambersburg	40	78	5:12		Pittsburgh	40	80	5:20
Chester	40	75	5:00		Pottstown	40	76	5:04
Clairton	40	80	5:20		Pottsville	41	76	5:04
Clarion	41	79	5:16		Reading	40	76	5:04
Clearfield	41	78	5:12		Ridgway	41	79	5:16
Coatesville	40	76	5:04		Scranton	41	76	5:04
Columbia	40	77	5:08		Shamokin	41	77	5:08
Connellsville	40	80	5:20		Sharon	41	81	5:24
Coudersport	42	78	5:12		Shenandoah	41	76	5:04
Danville	41	77	5:08		Smethport	42	78	5:12
Doylestown	40	75	5:00		Somerset	40	79	5:16
Drexel Hill	40	75	5:00		Springfield-Delaware	40	75	5:00
Du Bois	41	79	5:16		State College	41	78	5:12
Easton	41	75	5:00		Stroudsburg	41	75	5:00
Ebensburg	40	79	5:16		Sunbury	41	77	5:08
Emporium	42	78	5:12		Tionesta	42	79	5:16
Erie	42	80	5:20		Towanda	42	76	5:04
Franklin	41	80	5:20		Tunkhannock	42	76	5:04
Gettysburg	40	77	5:08		Uniontown	40	80	5:20
Greensburg	40	80	5:20		Upper Darby	40	75	5:00
Hanover	40	77	5:08		Warminster	40	75	5:00
Harrisburg	40	77	5:08		Warren	42	79	5:16
Havertown	40	75	5:00		Washington	40	80	5:20
Hazleton	41	76	5:04		Waynesburg	40	80	5:20
Hollidaysburg	40	78	5:12		Wellsboro	42	77	5:08
Honesdale	42	75	5:00		West Chester	40	76	5:04
Huntingdon	41	78	5:12		West Mifflin	40	80	5:20
Indiana	41	79	5:16		Wilkes-Barre	41	76	5:04
Jeannette	40	80	5:20		Wilkinsburg	40	80	5:20
Jim Thorpe	41	76	5:04		Williamsport	41	77	5:08
Johnstown	40	79	5:16		York	40	77	5:08
Kittanning	41	80	5:20					

CITY RHODE ISLAND	LAT N.	LONG W.	TIME h m	CITY	LAT N.	LONG W.	TIME h m
				Rock Hill	35	81	5:24
RHODE ISLAND (RI)				Saint George	33	81	5:24
				Saint Matthews	34	81	5:24
Bristol	42	71	4:44	Saluda	34	82	5:28
Coventry	42	72	4:48	Spartanburg	35	82	5:28
Cranston	42	71	4:44	Sumter	34	80	5:20
East Greenwich	42	71	4:44	Union	35	82	5:28
East Providence	42	71	4:44	Walhalla	35	83	5:32
Middletown	42	71	4:44	Walterboro	33	81	5:24
Newport	41	71	4:44	Winnsboro	34	81	5:24
Pawtucket	42	71	4:44	York	35	81	5:24
Providence	42	71	4:44				
Tiverton	42	71	4:44	SOUTH DAKOTA (SD)			
Warwick	42	71	4:44				
Westerly	41	72	4:48	Aberdeen	45	98	6:32
West Kingston	41	72	4:48	Alexandria	44	98	6:32
West Warwick	42	72	4:48	Armour	43	98	6:32
Woonsocket	42	72	4:48	Belle Fourche	45	104	6:56
				Bison	46	102	6:48
SOUTH CAROLINA (SC)				Britton	46	98	6:32
				Brookings	44	97	6:28
Abbeville	34	82	5:28	Buffalo	46	104	6:56
Aiken	34	82	5:28	Burke	43	99	6:36
Allendale	33	81	5:24	Canton	43	97	6:28
Anderson	35	83	5:32	Chamberlain	44	99	6:36
Bamberg	33	81	5:24	Clark	45	98	6:32
Barnwell	33	81	5:24	Clear Lake	45	97	6:28
Beaufort	32	81	5:24	Custer	44	104	6:56
Bennettsville	35	80	5:20	Deadwood	44	104	6:56
Bishopville	34	80	5:20	De Smet	44	98	6:32
Camden	34	81	5:24	Dupree	45	102	6:48
Charleston	33	80	5:20	Elk Point	43	97	6:28
Charleston Heights	33	80	5:20	Faulkton	45	99	6:36
Chester	35	81	5:24	Flandreau	44	97	6:28
Chesterfield	35	80	5:20	Fort Pierre	44	100	6:40
Columbia	34	81	5:24	Gannvalley	44	99	6:36
Conway	34	79	5:16	Gettysburg	45	100	6:40
Darlington	34	80	5:20	Hayti	45	97	6:28
Dillon	34	79	5:16	Highmore	45	99	6:36
Easley	35	83	5:32	Hot Springs	43	103	6:52
Edgefield	34	82	5:28	Howard	44	98	6:32
Florence	34	80	5:20	Huron	44	98	6:32
Gaffney	35	82	5:28	Ipswich	45	99	6:36
Georgetown	33	79	5:16	Kadoka	44	102	6:48
Greenville	35	82	5:28	Kennebec	44	100	6:40
Greenwood	34	82	5:28	Lake Andes	43	99	6:36
Greer	35	82	5:28	Leola	46	99	6:36
Hampton	33	81	5:24	McIntosh	46	101	6:44
Hartsville	34	80	5:20	Madison	44	97	6:28
Kingstree	34	80	5:20	Martin	43	102	6:48
Lancaster	35	81	5:24	Milbank	45	97	6:28
Laurens	35	82	5:28	Miller	45	99	6:36
Lexington	34	81	5:24	Mitchell	44	98	6:32
McCormick	34	82	5:28	Mound City	46	100	6:40
Manning	34	80	5:20	Murdo	44	101	6:44
Marion	34	79	5:16	Olivet	43	98	6:32
Moncks Corner	33	80	5:20	Onida	45	100	6:40
Newberry	34	82	5:28	Parker	43	97	6:28
Orangeburg	34	81	5:24	Philip	44	102	6:48
Pickens	35	83	5:32	Pierre	44	100	6:40
Ridgeland	32	81	5:24	Plankinton	44	98	6:32

CITY SOUTH DAKOTA	LAT N.	LONG W.	TIME h m	CITY	LAT N.	LONG W.	TIME h m
Rapid City	44	103	6:52	Hohenwald	36	88	5:52
Redfield	45	99	6:36	Humboldt	36	89	5:56
Salem	44	97	6:28	Huntingdon	36	88	5:52
Selby	46	100	6:40	Huntsville	36	84	5:36
Sioux Falls	44	97	6:28	Jacksboro	36	84	5:36
Sisseton	46	97	6:28	Jackson	36	89	5:56
Sturgis	44	104	6:56	Jamestown	36	85	5:40
Timber Lake	45	101	6:44	Jasper	35	86	5:44
Tyndall	43	98	6:32	Johnson City	36	82	5:28
Vermillion	43	97	6:28	Jonesboro	36	82	5:28
Watertown	45	97	6:28	Kingsport	37	83	5:32
Webster	45	98	6:32	Kingston	36	85	5:40
Wessington Springs	44	99	6:36	Knoxville	36	84	5:36
White River	44	101	6:44	Lafayette	37	86	5:44
Winner	43	100	6:40	Lawrenceburg	35	87	5:48
Woonsocket	44	98	6:32	Lebanon	36	86	5:44
Yankton	43	97	6:28	Lewisburg	35	87	5:48
				Lexington	36	88	5:52
TENNESSEE (TN)				Linden	36	88	5:52
				Livingston	36	85	5:40
Alamo	36	89	5:56	Loudon	36	84	5:36
Altamont	35	86	5:44	Lynchburg	35	86	5:44
Ashland City	36	87	5:48	Madisonville	36	84	5:36
Athens	35	85	5:40	Manchester	35	86	5:44
Benton	35	85	5:40	Maryville	36	84	5:36
Blountville	37	82	5:28	Maynardville	36	84	5:36
Bolivar	35	89	5:56	McMinnville	36	86	5:44
Bristol	37	82	5:28	Memphis	35	90	6:00
Brownsville	36	89	5:56	Millington	35	90	6:00
Byrdstown	37	85	5:40	Morristown	36	83	5:32
Camden	36	88	5:52	Mountain City	36	82	5:28
Carthage	36	86	5:44	Murfreesboro	36	86	5:44
Celina	37	86	5:44	Nashville	36	87	5:48
Centerville	36	87	5:48	Newport	36	83	5:32
Charlotte	36	87	5:48	Oak Ridge	36	84	5:36
Chattanooga	35	85	5:40	Paris	36	88	5:52
Clarksville	37	87	5:48	Pikeville	36	85	5:40
Cleveland	35	85	5:40	Pulaski	35	87	5:48
Clinton	36	84	5:36	Ripley	36	90	6:00
Columbia	36	87	5:48	Rogersville	36	83	5:32
Cookeville	36	86	5:44	Rutledge	36	84	5:36
Covington	36	90	6:00	Savannah	35	88	5:52
Crossville	36	85	5:40	Selmer	35	89	5:56
Dandridge	36	83	5:32	Sevierville	36	84	5:36
Dayton	36	85	5:40	Shelbyville	35	86	5:44
Decatur	36	85	5:40	Smithville	36	86	5:44
Decaturville	36	88	5:52	Sneedville	37	83	5:32
Dover	36	88	5:52	Somerville	35	89	5:56
Dresden	36	89	5:56	Sparta	36	85	5:40
Dunlap	35	85	5:40	Spencer	36	85	5:40
Dyersburg	36	89	5:56	Springfield	37	87	5:48
Elizabethton	36	82	5:28	Tazewell	36	84	5:36
Erin	36	88	5:52	Tiptonville	36	89	5:56
Erwin	36	82	5:28	Trenton	36	89	5:56
Fayetteville	35	87	5:48	Tullahoma	35	86	5:44
Franklin	36	87	5:48	Union City	36	89	5:56
Gainesboro	36	86	5:44	Wartburg	36	85	5:40
Gallatin	36	86	5:44	Waverly	36	88	5:52
Greeneville	36	83	5:32	Waynesboro	35	88	5:52
Hartsville	36	86	5:44	Winchester	35	86	5:44
Henderson	35	89	5:56	Woodbury	36	86	5:44

CITY TEXAS	LAT N.	LONG W.	TIME h m	CITY	LAT N.	LONG W.	TIME h m
TEXAS (TX)				Coleman	32	99	6:36
				Colorado City	32	101	6:44
				Columbus	30	97	6:28
Abilene	32	100	6:40	Comanche	32	99	6:36
Albany	33	99	6:36	Conroe	30	95	6:20
Alice	28	98	6:32	Cooper	33	96	6:24
Alpine	30	104	6:56	Corpus Christi	28	97	6:28
Alvin	29	95	6:20	Corsicana	32	96	6:24
Amarillo	35	102	6:48	Cotulla	28	99	6:36
Anahuac	30	95	6:20	Crane	31	102	6:48
Anderson	30	96	6:24	Crockett	31	95	6:20
Andrews	32	103	6:52	Crosbyton	34	101	6:44
Angleton	29	95	6:20	Crowell	34	100	6:40
Anson	33	100	6:40	Crystal City	29	100	6:40
Archer City	34	99	6:36	Cuero	29	97	6:28
Arlington	33	97	6:28	Daingerfield	33	95	6:20
Aspermont	33	100	6:40	Dalhart	36	103	6:52
Athens	32	96	6:24	Dallas	33	97	6:28
Austin	30	98	6:32	Decatur	33	98	6:32
Baird	32	99	6:36	Del Rio	29	101	6:44
Ballinger	32	100	6:40	Denison	34	97	6:28
Bandera	30	99	6:36	Denton	33	97	6:28
Bastrop	30	97	6:28	Dickens	34	101	6:44
Bay City	29	96	6:24	Dimmitt	35	102	6:48
Baytown	30	95	6:20	Dumas	36	102	6:48
Beaumont	30	94	6:16	Eagle Pass	29	101	6:44
Beeville	28	98	6:32	Eastland	32	99	6:36
Bellville	30	96	6:24	Edinburg	26	98	6:32
Belton	31	97	6:28	Edna	29	97	6:28
Benjamin	34	100	6:40	El Paso	32	106	7:04
Big Lake	31	101	6:44	Eldorado	31	101	6:44
Big Spring	32	101	6:44	Emory	33	96	6:24
Boerne	30	99	6:36	Ennis	32	97	6:28
Bonham	34	96	6:24	Fairfield	32	96	6:24
Borger	36	101	6:44	Falfurrias	27	98	6:32
Boston	33	94	6:16	Farmers Branch	33	97	6:28
Brackettville	29	100	6:40	Farwell	34	103	6:52
Brady	31	99	6:36	Floresville	29	98	6:32
Breckenridge	33	99	6:36	Floydada	34	101	6:44
Brenham	30	96	6:24	Fort Davis	31	104	6:56
Brownfield	33	102	6:48	Fort Stockton	31	103	6:52
Brownsville	26	98	6:32	Fort Worth	33	97	6:28
Brownwood	32	99	6:36	Franklin	31	96	6:24
Bryan	31	96	6:24	Fredericksburg	30	99	6:36
Burnet	31	98	6:32	Gail	33	101	6:44
Caldwell	31	97	6:28	Gainesville	34	97	6:28
Cameron	31	97	6:28	Galveston	29	95	6:20
Canadian	36	100	6:40	Garden City	32	101	6:44
Canton	33	96	6:24	Garland	33	97	6:28
Canyon	35	102	6:48	Gatesville	31	98	6:32
Carrizo Springs	29	100	6:40	Georgetown	31	98	6:32
Carthage	32	94	6:16	George West	28	98	6:32
Center	32	94	6:16	Giddings	30	97	6:28
Centerville	31	96	6:24	Gilmer	33	95	6:20
Channing	36	102	6:48	Glen Rose	32	98	6:32
Childress	34	100	6:40	Goldthwaite	31	99	6:36
Clarendon	35	101	6:44	Goliad	29	97	6:28
Clarksville	34	95	6:20	Gonzales	30	97	6:28
Claude	35	101	6:44	Graham	33	99	6:36
Cleburne	32	97	6:28	Granbury	32	98	6:32
Coldspring	31	95	6:20	Grand Prairie	33	97	6:28

CITY TEXAS	LAT N.	LONG W.	TIME h m	CITY	LAT N.	LONG W.	TIME h m
Greenville	33	96	6:24	Menard	31	100	6:40
Groesbeck	32	97	6:28	Mentone	32	104	6:56
Groveton	31	95	6:20	Meridian	32	98	6:32
Guthrie	34	100	6:40	Mertzon	31	101	6:44
Hallettsville	29	97	6:28	Mesquite	33	97	6:28
Haltom City	33	97	6:28	Miami	36	101	6:44
Hamilton	32	98	6:32	Midland	32	102	6:48
Harlingen	26	98	6:32	Mineral Wells	33	98	6:32
Haskell	33	100	6:40	Monahans	32	103	6:52
Hebbronville	27	99	6:36	Montague	34	98	6:32
Hemphill	31	94	6:16	Morton	34	103	6:52
Hempstead	30	96	6:24	Mount Pleasant	33	95	6:20
Henderson	32	95	6:20	Mount Vernon	33	95	6:20
Henrietta	34	98	6:32	Muleshoe	34	103	6:52
Hereford	35	102	6:48	Nacogdoches	32	95	6:20
Hillsboro	32	97	6:28	New Braunfels	30	98	6:32
Hondo	29	99	6:36	Newton	31	94	6:16
Houston	30	95	6:20	Odessa	32	102	6:48
Huntsville	31	96	6:24	Orange	30	94	6:16
Hurst	33	97	6:28	Ozona	31	101	6:44
Irving	33	97	6:28	Paducah	34	100	6:40
Jacksboro	33	98	6:32	Paint Rock	32	100	6:40
Jasper	31	94	6:16	Palestine	32	96	6:24
Jayton	33	101	6:44	Palo Pinto	33	98	6:32
Jefferson	33	94	6:16	Pampa	36	101	6:44
Johnson City	30	98	6:32	Panhandle	35	101	6:44
Jourdanton	29	99	6:36	Paris	34	96	6:24
Junction	30	100	6:40	Pasadena	30	95	6:20
Karnes City	29	98	6:32	Pearsall	29	99	6:36
Kaufman	33	96	6:24	Pecos	31	104	6:56
Kermit	32	103	6:52	Perryton	36	101	6:44
Kerrville	30	99	6:36	Pittsburg	33	95	6:20
Killeen	31	98	6:32	Plains	33	103	6:52
Kingsville	28	98	6:32	Plainview	34	102	6:48
Kountze	30	94	6:16	Port Arthur	30	94	6:16
La Grange	30	97	6:28	Port Lavaca	29	97	6:28
Lake Jackson	29	95	6:20	Post	33	101	6:44
Lamesa	33	102	6:48	Quanah	34	100	6:40
Lampasas	31	98	6:32	Quitman	33	95	6:20
Laredo	28	100	6:40	Rankin	31	102	6:48
Leakey	30	100	6:40	Raymondville	26	98	6:32
Levelland	34	102	6:48	Refugio	28	97	6:28
Liberty	30	95	6:20	Richardson	33	97	6:28
Linden	33	94	6:16	Richmond	30	96	6:24
Lipscomb	36	100	6:40	Rio Grande City	26	99	6:36
Littlefield	34	102	6:48	Robert Lee	32	100	6:40
Livingston	31	95	6:20	Robstown	28	98	6:32
Llano	31	99	6:36	Roby	33	100	6:40
Lockhart	30	98	6:32	Rockport	28	97	6:28
Longview	33	95	6:20	Rocksprings	30	100	6:40
Lubbock	34	102	6:48	Rockwall	33	96	6:24
Lufkin	31	95	6:20	Rusk	32	95	6:20
Madisonville	31	96	6:24	San Angelo	31	100	6:40
Marfa	30	104	6:56	San Antonio	29	99	6:36
Marlin	31	97	6:28	San Augustine	32	94	6:16
Marshall	33	94	6:16	San Diego	28	98	6:32
Mason	31	99	6:36	San Marcos	30	98	6:32
Matador	34	101	6:44	San Saba	31	99	6:36
McAllen	26	98	6:32	Sanderson	30	102	6:48
McKinney	33	97	6:28	Sarita	27	98	6:32
Memphis	35	101	6:44	Seguin	30	98	6:32

CITY	LAT N.	LONG W.	TIME h m	CITY	LAT N.	LONG W.	TIME h m
TEXAS				Murray	41	112	7:28
Seminole	33	103	6:52	Nephi	40	112	7:28
Seymour	34	99	6:36	Ogden	41	112	7:28
Sherman	34	97	6:28	Orem	40	112	7:28
Sierra Blanca	31	105	7:00	Panguitch	38	112	7:28
Silverton	34	101	6:44	Parowan	38	113	7:32
Sinton	28	98	6:32	Price	40	111	7:24
Snyder	33	101	6:44	Provo	40	112	7:28
Sonora	31	101	6:44	Randolph	42	111	7:24
Spearman	36	101	6:44	Richfield	39	112	7:28
Stanton	32	102	6:48	Saint George	37	114	7:36
Stephenville	32	98	6:32	Salt Lake City	41	112	7:28
Sterling City	32	101	6:44	Tooele	41	112	7:28
Stinnett	36	101	6:44	Vernal	40	110	7:20
Stratford	36	102	6:48				
Sulphur Springs	33	96	6:24	**VERMONT (VT)**			
Sweetwater	32	100	6:40				
Tahoka	33	102	6:48	Barre	44	73	4:52
Temple	31	97	6:28	Bennington	43	73	4:52
Terrell	33	96	6:24	Brattleboro	43	73	4:52
Texarkana	33	94	6:16	Burlington	44	73	4:52
Texas City	29	95	6:20	Chelsea	44	72	4:48
Throckmorton	33	99	6:36	Guildhall	45	72	4:48
Tilden	28	99	6:36	Hyde Park	45	73	4:52
Tulia	35	102	6:48	Middlebury	44	73	4:52
Tyler	32	95	6:20	Montpelier	44	73	4:52
Uvalde	29	100	6:40	Newfane	43	73	4:52
Van Horn	31	105	7:00	Newport	45	72	4:48
Vega	35	102	6:48	North Hero	45	73	4:52
Vernon	34	99	6:36	Rutland	44	73	4:52
Victoria	29	97	6:28	Saint Albans	45	73	4:52
Waco	32	97	6:28	Saint Johnsbury	44	72	4:48
Waxahachie	32	97	6:28	Springfield	43	72	4:48
Weatherford	33	98	6:32	Woodstock	44	73	4:52
Wellington	35	100	6:40				
Wharton	29	96	6:24	**VIRGINIA (VA)**			
Wheeler	35	100	6:40				
Wichita Falls	34	99	6:36	Abingdon	37	82	5:28
Woodville	31	94	6:16	Accomac	38	76	5:04
Zapata	27	99	6:36	Alexandria	39	77	5:08
				Amelia Court House	37	78	5:12
UTAH (UT)				Amherst	38	79	5:16
				Annandale	39	77	5:08
Beaver	38	113	7:32	Appomattox	37	79	5:16
Bountiful	41	112	7:28	Arlington	37	77	5:08
Brigham City	42	112	7:28	Bedford	37	80	5:20
Castle Dale	39	111	7:24	Berryville	39	78	5:12
Coalville	41	111	7:24	Bland	37	81	5:24
Duchesne	40	110	7:20	Bowling Green	38	77	5:08
Farmington	41	112	7:28	Boydton	37	78	5:12
Fillmore	39	112	7:28	Bristol	37	82	5:28
Heber City	40	111	7:24	Buckingham	38	79	5:16
Junction	38	112	7:28	Charles City	37	77	5:08
Kanab	37	113	7:32	Charlotte Court House	37	79	5:16
Loa	38	112	7:28	Charlottesville	38	79	5:16
Logan	42	112	7:28	Chatham	37	79	5:16
Manila	41	110	7:20	Chesapeake	37	76	5:04
Manti	39	112	7:28	Chesterfield	37	78	5:12
Millcreek	41	112	7:28	Christiansburg	37	80	5:20
Moab	39	110	7:20	Clintwood	37	82	5:28
Monticello	38	109	7:16	Courtland	37	77	5:08
Morgan	41	112	7:28				

CITY	LAT N.	LONG W.	TIME h m	CITY	LAT N.	LONG W.	TIME h m
VIRGINIA							
Covington	38	80	5:20	Radford	37	81	5:24
Culpeper	38	78	5:12	Richmond	38	77	5:08
Cumberland	38	78	5:12	Roanoke	37	80	5:20
Danville	37	79	5:16	Rocky Mount	37	80	5:20
Dinwiddie	37	78	5:12	Rustburg	37	79	5:16
Eastville	37	76	5:04	Salem	37	80	5:20
Emporia	37	78	5:12	Saluda	38	77	5:08
Fairfax	39	77	5:08	Spotsylvania	38	78	5:12
Farmville	37	78	5:12	Stafford	38	77	5:08
Fincastle	38	80	5:20	Stanardsville	38	78	5:12
Floyd	37	80	5:20	Staunton	38	79	5:16
Fredericksburg	38	77	5:08	Stuart	37	80	5:20
Front Royal	39	78	5:12	Suffolk	37	77	5:08
Gate City	37	83	5:32	Surry	37	77	5:08
Gloucester	37	77	5:08	Sussex	37	77	5:08
Goochland	38	78	5:12	Tappahannock	38	77	5:08
Grundy	37	82	5:28	Tazewell	37	82	5:28
Halifax	37	79	5:16	Vienna	39	77	5:08
Hampton	37	76	5:04	Virginia Beach	37	76	5:04
Hanover	38	77	5:08	Warm Springs	38	80	5:20
Harrisonburg	38	79	5:16	Warrenton	39	78	5:12
Heathsville	38	76	5:04	Warsaw	38	77	5:08
Hillsville	37	81	5:24	Washington	39	78	5:12
Hopewell	37	77	5:08	Waynesboro	38	79	5:16
Independence	37	81	5:24	Williamsburg	37	77	5:08
Isle Of Wight	37	77	5:08	Winchester	39	78	5:12
Jonesville	37	83	5:32	Wise	37	83	5:32
King And Queen Court	38	77	5:08	Woodbridge	39	77	5:08
King George	38	77	5:08	Woodstock	39	79	5:16
King William	38	77	5:08	Wytheville	37	81	5:24
Lancaster	38	76	5:04	Yorktown	37	77	5:08
Lawrenceville	37	78	5:12				
Lebanon	37	82	5:28	**WASHINGTON (WA)**			
Leesburg	39	78	5:12				
Lexington	38	79	5:16	Aberdeen	47	124	8:16
Louisa	38	78	5:12	Asotin	46	117	7:48
Lovingston	38	79	5:16	Auburn	47	122	8:08
Lunenburg	37	78	5:12	Bellevue	48	122	8:08
Luray	39	78	5:12	Bellingham	49	122	8:08
Lynchburg	37	79	5:16	Bremerton	48	123	8:12
Madison	38	78	5:12	Cathlamet	46	123	8:12
Manassas	39	77	5:08	Chehalis	47	123	8:12
Marion	37	82	5:28	Colfax	47	117	7:48
Martinsville	37	80	5:20	Colville	49	118	7:52
Mathews	37	76	5:04	Coupeville	48	123	8:12
Monterey	38	80	5:20	Davenport	48	118	7:52
Montross	38	77	5:08	Dayton	46	118	7:52
Nansemond	37	77	5:08	Edmonds	48	122	8:08
New Castle	38	80	5:20	Ellensburg	47	121	8:04
New Kent	38	77	5:08	Ephrata	47	120	8:00
Newport News	37	76	5:04	Everett	48	122	8:08
Norfolk	37	76	5:04	Friday Harbor	49	123	8:12
Nottoway	37	78	5:12	Goldendale	46	121	8:04
Orange	38	78	5:12	Kennewick	46	119	7:56
Palmyra	38	78	5:12	Kent	47	122	8:08
Pearisburg	37	81	5:24	Kelso	46	123	8:12
Petersburg	37	77	5:08	Lakewood Center	47	123	8:12
Portsmouth	37	76	5:04	Longview	46	123	8:12
Powhatan	38	78	5:12	Montesano	47	124	8:16
Prince George	37	77	5:08	Mount Vernon	48	122	8:08
Pulaski	37	81	5:24	Newport	48	117	7:48

101

CITY WASHINGTON	LAT N.	LONG W.	TIME h m	CITY	LAT N.	LONG W.	TIME h m
Okanogan	48	120	8:00	Parkersburg	39	82	5:28
Olympia	47	123	8:12	Parsons	39	80	5:20
Pasco	46	119	7:56	Petersburg	39	79	5:16
Pomeroy	46	118	7:52	Philippi	39	80	5:20
Port Angeles	48	123	8:12	Pineville	38	82	5:28
Port Orchard	48	123	8:12	Point Pleasant	39	82	5:28
Port Townsend	48	123	8:12	Princeton	37	81	5:24
Prosser	46	120	8:00	Ripley	39	82	5:28
Pullman	47	117	7:48	Romney	39	79	5:16
Renton	47	122	8:08	Saint Albans	38	82	5:28
Republic	49	119	7:56	Saint Marys	39	81	5:24
Richland	46	119	7:56	Spencer	39	81	5:24
Ritzville	47	118	7:52	Summersville	38	81	5:24
Riverton Heights	47	122	8:08	Sutton	39	81	5:24
Seattle	48	122	8:08	Union	38	81	5:24
Shelton	47	123	8:12	Wayne	38	82	5:28
South Bend	47	124	8:16	Webster Springs	38	80	5:20
Spokane	48	117	7:48	Weirton	40	81	5:24
Stevenson	46	122	8:08	Welch	37	82	5:28
Tacoma	47	122	8:08	Wellsburg	40	81	5:24
Vancouver	46	123	8:12	Weston	39	80	5:20
Walla Walla	46	118	7:52	West Union	39	81	5:24
Waterville	48	120	8:00	Wheeling	40	81	5:24
Wenatchee	47	120	8:00	Williamson	38	82	5:28
Yakima	47	121	8:04	Winfield	39	82	5:28

WEST VIRGINIA (WV)

WISCONSIN (WI)

Beckley	38	81	5:24	Alma	44	92	6:08
Berkeley Springs	40	78	5:12	Antigo	45	89	5:56
Bluefield	37	81	5:24	Appleton	44	88	5:52
Buckhannon	39	80	5:20	Ashland	47	91	6:04
Charleston	38	82	5:28	Balsam Lake	45	92	6:08
Charles Town	39	78	5:12	Baraboo	43	90	6:00
Clarksburg	39	80	5:20	Barron	45	92	6:08
Clay	38	81	5:24	Beaver Dam	43	89	5:56
Elizabeth	39	81	5:24	Beloit	43	89	5:56
Elkins	39	80	5:20	Black River Falls	44	91	6:04
Fairmont	39	80	5:20	Brookfield	43	88	5:52
Fayetteville	38	81	5:24	Chilton	44	88	5:52
Franklin	39	79	5:16	Chippewa Falls	45	91	6:04
Glenville	39	81	5:24	Crandon	46	89	5:56
Grafton	39	80	5:20	Darlington	43	90	6:00
Grantsville	39	81	5:24	Dodgeville	43	90	6:00
Hamlin	38	82	5:28	Durand	45	92	6:08
Harrisville	39	81	5:24	Eagle River	46	89	5:56
Hinton	38	81	5:24	Eau Claire	45	92	6:08
Huntington	38	82	5:28	Elkhorn	43	89	5:56
Keyser	39	79	5:16	Ellsworth	45	92	6:08
Kingwood	39	80	5:20	Florence	46	88	5:52
Lewisburg	38	80	5:20	Fond Du Lac	44	88	5:52
Logan	38	82	5:28	Friendship	44	90	6:00
Madison	38	82	5:28	Grantsburg	46	93	6:12
Marlinton	38	80	5:20	Green Bay	45	88	5:52
Martinsburg	39	78	5:12	Green Lake	44	89	5:56
Middlebourne	40	81	5:24	Hayward	46	91	6:04
Moorefield	39	79	5:16	Hudson	45	93	6:12
Morgantown	40	80	5:20	Hurley	46	90	6:00
Moundsville	40	81	5:24	Janesville	43	89	5:56
New Cumberland	41	81	5:24	Jefferson	43	89	5:56
New Martinsville	40	81	5:24	Juneau	43	89	5:56

CITY WISCONSIN	LAT N.	LONG W.	TIME h m	CITY	LAT N.	LONG W.	TIME h m
Kaukauna	44	88	5:52	Evanston	41	111	7:24
Kenosha	43	88	5:52	Gillette	44	106	7:04
Keshena	45	89	5:56	Green River	42	109	7:16
Kewaunee	44	88	5:52	Jackson	43	111	7:24
La Crosse	44	91	6:04	Kemmerer	42	111	7:24
Ladysmith	45	91	6:04	Lander	43	109	7:16
Lancaster	43	91	6:04	Laramie	41	106	7:04
Madison	43	89	5:56	Lusk	43	104	6:56
Manitowoc	44	88	5:52	Newcastle	44	104	6:56
Marinette	45	88	5:52	Pinedale	43	110	7:20
Marshfield	45	90	6:00	Rawlins	42	107	7:08
Mauston	44	90	6:00	Rock Springs	42	109	7:16
Medford	45	90	6:00	Sheridan	45	107	7:08
Menomonee Falls	43	88	5:52	Sundance	44	104	6:56
Menomonie	45	92	6:08	Thermopolis	44	108	7:12
Merrill	45	90	6:00	Torrington	42	104	6:56
Milwaukee	43	88	5:52	Wheatland	42	105	7:00
Monroe	43	90	6:00	Worland	44	108	7:12
Montello	44	89	5:56				
Neenah	44	88	5:52				
Neillsville	45	91	6:04				
New Berlin	43	88	5:52				
Oconto	45	88	5:52				
Oshkosh	44	89	5:56				
Phillips	46	90	6:00				
Portage	44	89	5:56				
Port Washington	43	88	5:52				
Prairie Du Chien	43	91	6:04				
Racine	43	88	5:52				
Rhinelander	46	89	5:56				
Richland Center	43	90	6:00				
Shawano	45	89	5:56				
Sheboygan	44	88	5:52				
Shell Lake	46	92	6:08				
Sparta	44	91	6:04				
Stevens Point	45	90	6:00				
Sturgeon Bay	45	87	5:48				
Superior	47	92	6:08				
Two Rivers	44	88	5:52				
Viroqua	44	91	6:04				
Washburn	47	91	6:04				
Watertown	43	89	5:56				
Waukesha	43	88	5:52				
Waupaca	44	89	5:56				
Wausau	45	90	6:00				
Wautoma	44	89	5:56				
Wauwatosa	43	88	5:52				
West Allis	43	88	5:52				
West Bend	43	88	5:52				
Whitehall	44	91	6:04				
Whitewater	43	89	5:56				
Wisconsin Rapids	44	90	6:00				
WYOMING (WY)							
Basin	44	108	7:12				
Buffalo	44	107	7:08				
Casper	43	106	7:04				
Cheyenne	41	105	7:00				
Cody	45	109	7:16				
Douglas	43	105	7:00				

CITY	LAT	LONG	TIME h m	CITY	LAT	LONG	TIME h m
Aachen, W Germany	51N	6E	-0:24	An Najaf, Iraq	32N	44E	-2:56
Aalborg, Denmark	57N	10E	-0:40	Ancona, Italy	44N	14E	-0:56
Aarhus, Denmark	57N	10E	-0:40	Andizhan, USSR	41N	72E	-4:48
Abadan, Iran	30N	48E	-3:12	Angers, France	47N	1W	0:04
Abeokuta, Nigeria	7N	3E	-0:12	Angouleme, France	46N	0E	0:00
Aberdeen, G Britain	57N	2W	0:08	Ankara, Turkey	40N	33E	-2:12
Abidjan, Ivory Coast	5N	4W	0:16	Annaba, Algeria	37N	8E	-0:32
Abo, Finland	60N	22E	-1:28	Annecy, France	46N	6E	-0:24
Acapulco, Mexico	17N	100W	6:40	Anshan, China	41N	123E	-8:12
Accra, Ghana	6N	0W	0:00	Antalya, Turkey	37N	31E	-2:04
Ad Dawhah, Qatar	25N	52E	-3:28	Antofagasta, Chile	24S	70W	4:40
Adalia, Turkey	37N	31E	-2:04	Antung, China	40N	124E	-8:16
Adana, Turkey	37N	35E	-2:20	Antwerpen (Anvers) Belgium	51N	4E	-0:16
Adapazari, Turkey	41N	30E	-2:00	Aomori, Japan	41N	141E	-9:24
Addis Ababa, Ethiopia	9N	39E	-2:36	Apeldoorn, Netherlands	52N	6E	-0:24
Adelaide, Australia	35S	139E	-9:16	Apia, W Samoa	14S	172W	11:28
Aden, Yemen	13N	45E	-3:00	Ar Riyad, Saudi Arabia	25N	47E	-3:08
Agana, Guam	13N	145E	-9:40	Aracaju, Brazil	11S	37W	2:28
Agra, India	27N	78E	-5:12	Arad, Rumania	46N	21E	-1:24
Agram, Yugoslavia	46N	16E	-1:04	Arak, Iran	34N	50E	-3:20
Aguadilla, Puerto Rico	18N	67W	4:28	Arbela (Arbil), Iraq	36N	44E	-2:56
Aguascalientes, Mexico	22N	102W	6:48	Archangel, USSR	65N	41E	-2:44
Ahmadabad, India	23N	73E	-4:52	Ardabil, Iran	38N	48E	-3:12
Ahvaz, Iran	31N	49E	-3:16	Arecibo, Puerto Rico	18N	67W	4:28
Aix En Provence, France	44N	5E	-0:20	Arequipa, Peru	16S	72W	4:48
Ajaccio, France (Corsica)	42N	9E	-0:36	Arhus, Denmark	57N	10E	-0:40
Ajmer, India	26N	75E	-5:00	Arkhangelsk, USSR	65N	41E	-2:44
Akita, Japan	40N	140E	-9:20	Armavir, USSR	45N	41E	-2:44
Aktyubinsk, USSR	50N	57E	-3:48	Arnhem, Netherlands	52N	6E	-0:24
Al Basrah, Iraq	31N	48E	-3:12	Arras, France	50N	3E	-0:12
Al Hillah, Iraq	32N	44E	-2:56	As Sulaymaniyah, Iraq	35N	45E	-3:00
Al Hufuf, Saudi Arabia	25N	50E	-3:20	Asahigawa, Japan	44N	142E	-9:28
Al Khurtum, Sudan	16N	33E	-2:12	Asansol, India	24N	87E	-5:48
Al Kuwayt, Kuwait	29N	48E	-3:12	Aschaffenburg, W Germany	50N	9E	-0:36
Al Ladhiqiyah, Syria	36N	36E	-2:24	Ashkhabad, USSR	38N	58E	-3:52
Al Madinah, Saudi Arabia	24N	40E	-2:40	Asmara (Asmera), Ethiopia	15N	39E	-2:36
Al Manamah. Bahrain	26N	51E	-3:24	Astrakhan, USSR	46N	48E	-3:12
Al Mawsil, Iraq	36N	43E	-2:52	Asuncion, Paraguay	25S	58W	3:52
Albacete, Spain	39N	2W	0:08	Aswan, Egypt	24N	33E	-2:12
Alborg, Denmark	57N	10E	-0:40	Asyut, Egypt	27N	31E	-2:04
Aldershot, G Britain	51N	1W	0:00	Athens (Athinai) Greece	38N	24E	-1:36
Aleksandropol (Leninakan)	50N	39E	-2:36	Auckland, N Zealand	37S	175E	-11:40
Aleksandrovsk (Zaporozhye)	41N	44E	-2:56	Augsburg, W Germany	48N	11E	-0:44
Aleppo, Syria	36N	37E	-2:28	Aussig, Czechoslovakia	51N	14E	-0:56
Alessandria, Italy	45N	9E	-0:36	Avignon, France	44N	5E	-0:20
Alexandretta, Turkey	37N	36E	-2:24	Aviles, Spain	44N	6W	0:24
Alexandria, Egypt	31N	30E	-2:00	Az Zaqazik, Egypt	31N	32E	-2:08
Algeciras, Spain	36N	5W	0:20	Bacau, Rumania	47N	27E	-1:48
Alger (Algiers) Algeria	37N	3E	-0:12	Bacolod, Philippines	11N	123E	-8:12
Alicante, Spain	38N	0W	0:00	Badajoz, Spain	39N	7W	0:28
Alkmaar, Netherlands	53N	5E	-0:20	Baghdad, Iraq	33N	44E	-2:56
Allahabad, India	25N	82E	-5:28	Bahia, Brazil	13S	39W	2:36
Allenstein, Poland	54N	20E	-1:20	Bahia Blanca, Argentina	39S	62W	4:08
Alma Ata, USSR	43N	77E	-5:08	Baia Mare, Rumania	48N	24E	-1:36
Almeria, Spain	37N	2W	0:08	Baile Atha Cliath, Ireland	53N	6W	0:24
Amagasaki, Japan	35N	135E	-9:00	Baku, USSR	40N	50E	-3:20
Ambon (Amboina) Indonesia	4S	128E	-8:32	Balikpapan, Indonesia	1S	117E	-7:48
Amersfoort, Netherlands	52N	5E	-0:20	Bamako, Mali	13N	8W	0:32
Amiens, France	50N	2E	-0:08	Banaras, India	25N	83E	-5:32
Amman, Jordan	32N	36E	-2:24	Bandar Seri Begawan, Brunei	5N	115E	-7:40
Amoy, China	24N	118E	-7:52	Bandjarmasin, Indonesia	3S	115E	-7:40
Amritsar, India	32N	75E	-5:00	Bandung, Indonesia	7S	108E	-7:12
Amsterdam, Netherlands	52N	5E	-0:20	Bangalore, India	13N	78E	-5:12

CITY	LAT	LONG	TIME h m	CITY	LAT	LONG	TIME h m
Banghazi, Libya	32N	20E	-1:20	Blantyre, Malawi	16S	35E	-2:20
Bangkok, Thailand	14N	101E	-6:44	Blida, Algeria	37N	3E	-0:12
Bangui, Central Afr Repub	4N	19E	-1:16	Bloemfontein, S Africa	29S	26E	-1:44
Baranovichi, USSR	53N	26E	-1:44	Bobruysk (Bobrujsk), USSR	53N	29E	-1:56
Barcelona, Spain	41N	2E	-0:08	Bochum, W Germany	51N	7E	-0:28
Bareilly, India	28N	79E	-5:16	Bodo, Norway	67N	14E	-0:56
Bari, Italy	41N	17E	-1:08	Bogor, Indonesia	7S	107E	-7:08
Barnaul, USSR	53N	84E	-5:36	Bogota, Colombia	5N	74W	4:56
Barnsley, G Britain	54N	1W	0:04	Bologna, Italy	44N	11E	-0:44
Baroda, India	22N	73E	-4:52	Bolton, G Britain	54N	2W	0:08
Barquisimeto, Venezuela	10N	69W	4:36	Bolzano, Italy	47N	11E	-0:44
Barranquilla, Colombia	11N	75W	5:00	Bombay, India	19N	73E	-4:52
Basel, Switzerland	48N	8E	-0:32	Bone, Algeria	37N	8E	-0:32
Basra (Bassorah) Iraq	31N	48E	-3:12	Bonn, W Germany	51N	7E	-0:28
Bastia, France (Corsica)	43N	9E	-0:36	Boras, Sweden	58N	13E	-0:52
Batangas, Philippines	14N	121E	-8:04	Bordeaux, France	45N	1W	0:04
Batavia, Indonesia	6S	107E	-7:08	Borisov, USSR	54N	29E	-1:56
Bath, G Britain	51N	2W	0:08	Boulogne Sur Mer, France	51N	2E	-0:08
Bathurst, Gambia	13N	17W	1:08	Bournemouth, G Britain	51N	2W	0:08
Batumi (Batum) USSR	42N	42E	-2:48	Bradford, G Britain	54N	2W	0:08
Bauru, Brazil	22S	49W	3:16	Braila, Rumania	45N	28E	-1:52
Bayamon, Puerto Rico	18N	66W	4:24	Brasilia, Brazil	16S	48W	3:12
Bayonne, France	43N	1W	0:04	Brasov, Rumania	46N	26E	-1:44
Bayrut, Lebanon	34N	36E	-2:24	Bratislava, Czech	48N	17E	-1:08
BeerSheva(Beersheba)Israel	31N	35E	-2:20	Bratsk, USSR	56N	102E	-6:48
Beira, Mozambique	20S	35E	-2:20	Braunschweig, W Germany	52N	11E	-0:44
Beirut, Lebanon	34N	36E	-2:24	Brazzaville, Congo	4S	15E	-1:00
Belaya Tserkov, USSR	50N	30E	-2:00	Breda, Netherlands	52N	5E	-0:20
Belem, Brazil	1S	48W	3:12	Bremen, W Germany	53N	9E	-0:36
Belfast, N Ireland	55N	6W	0:24	Bremerhaven, W Germany	54N	9E	-0:36
Belfort, France	48N	7E	-0:28	Brescia, Italy	46N	10E	-0:40
Belgorod, USSR	51N	37E	-2:28	Breslau, Poland	51N	17E	-1:08
Belgrade, Yugoslavia	45N	20E	-1:20	Brest, France	48N	4W	0:16
Belize City, Belize	17N	88W	5:52	Brest Litovsk, USSR	52N	24E	-1:36
Belmopan, Belize	17N	89W	5:56	Bridgetown, Barbados	13N	60W	4:00
Belo Horizonte, Brazil	20S	44W	2:56	Brighton, G Britain	51N	0W	0:00
Beltsy, USSR	48N	28E	-1:52	Brindisi, Italy	41N	18E	-1:12
Benares, India	25N	83E	-5:32	Brisbane, Australia	27S	153E	-10:12
Benghazi, Libya	32N	20E	-1:20	Bristol, G Britain	51N	3W	0:12
Benin City, Nigeria	6N	6E	-0:24	Brno, Czech	49N	17E	-1:08
Beograd, Yugoslavia	45N	20E	-1:20	Bromberg, Poland	53N	18E	-1:12
Berezniki, USSR	59N	57E	-3:48	Brousse (Bursa), Turkey	40N	29E	-1:56
Bergamo, Italy	46N	10E	-0:40	Brugge, (Bruges) Belgium	51N	3E	-0:12
Bergen, Norway	60N	5E	-0:20	Brunei, Brunei	5N	115E	-7:40
Berlin, Germany	53N	13E	-0:52	Brunswick, W Germany	52N	11E	-0:44
Bern, Switzerland	47N	7E	-0:28	Bruxelles(Brussels)Belgium	51N	4E	-0:16
Besancon, France	47N	6E	-0:24	Bryansk, USSR	53N	34E	-2:16
Beuthen, Poland	50N	19E	-1:16	Bucaramanga, Columbia	7N	73W	4:52
Beyrouth, Lebanon	34N	36E	-2:24	Bucuresti(Bucharest)Rumania	44N	26E	-1:44
Beziers, France	43N	3E	-0:12	Budapest, Hungary	48N	19E	-1:16
Bhopal, India	23N	77E	-5:08	Budweis, Czech	49N	14E	-0:56
Bialystok, Poland	53N	23E	-1:32	Buenaventura, Columbia	4N	77W	5:08
Biel, Switzerland	47N	7E	-0:28	Buenos Aires, Argentina	35S	58W	3:52
Bielefeld, W Germany	52N	9E	-0:36	Buitenzorg, Indonesia	7S	107E	-7:08
Bielsko-Biala, Poland	50N	19E	-1:16	Bujumbura, Burundi	3S	29E	-1:56
Bikaner, India	28N	73E	-4:52	Bukhara, USSR	40N	64E	-4:16
Bilbao, Spain	43N	3W	0:12	Bulawayo, Zimbabwe	20S	29E	-1:56
Birmingham, G Britain	53N	2W	0:08	Bur Said, Egypt	31N	32E	-2:08
Bissau, Port Guinea	12N	16W	1:04	Burgas, Bulgaria	43N	27E	-1:48
Bitterfeld, E Germany	52N	12E	-0:48	Burgos, Spain	42N	4W	0:16
Biysk, USSR	53N	85E	-5:40	Burnley, G Britain	54N	2W	0:08
Blackburn, G Britain	54N	2W	0:08	Bursa, Turkey	40N	29E	-1:56
Blackpool, G Britain	54N	3W	0:12	Butuan, Philippines	9N	126E	-8:24

CITY	LAT	LONG	TIME h m	CITY	LAT	LONG	TIME h m
Bydgoszcz, Poland	53N	18E	-1:12	Chernovtsy, USSR	48N	26E	-1:44
Bytom, Poland	50N	19E	-1:16	Chesterfield, G Britain	53N	1W	0:04
Cabimas, Venezuela	10N	71W	4:44	Chiai, Taiwan	23N	120E	-8:00
Cadiz, Spain	37N	6W	0:24	Chiang Mai, Thailand	19N	99E	-6:36
Caen, France	49N	0W	0:00	Chiaotso, China	35N	113E	-7:32
Cagliari, Italy	39N	9E	-0:36	Chiba, Japan	36N	140E	-9:20
Caguas, Puerto Rico	18N	66W	4:24	Chichihaerh, China	47N	124E	-8:16
Cairo, Egypt	30N	31E	-2:04	Chiclayo, Peru	7S	80W	5:20
Calais, France	51N	2E	-0:08	Chicoutimi, Canada	48N	71W	4:44
Calcutta, India	23N	88E	-5:52	Chihsi, China	45N	131E	-8:44
Calgary, Canada	51N	114W	7:36	Chihuahua, Mexico	29N	106W	7:04
Cali, Colombia	3N	77W	5:08	Chilin, China	44N	127E	-8:28
Calicut, India	11N	76E	-5:04	Chillan, Chile	37S	72W	4:48
Camaguey, Cuba	21N	78W	5:12	Chilung, Taiwan	25N	122E	-8:00
Cambridge, G Britain	52N	0E	0:00	Chimkent, USSR	42N	70E	-4:40
Campina Grande, Brazil	7S	36W	2:24	Chinan, China	37N	117E	-7:48
Campinas, Brazil	23S	47W	3:08	Chinchou, China	41N	121E	-8:04
Campos, Brazil	22S	41W	2:44	Chingtao, China	36N	120E	-8:00
Canberra, Australia	35S	149E	-9:56	Chingtechen, China	29N	117E	-7:48
Candia, Greece	35N	25E	-1:40	Chisinau, USSR	47N	29E	-1:56
Canea, Greece	36N	24E	-1:36	Chita, USSR	52N	114E	-7:36
Cannes, France	44N	7E	-0:28	Chittagong, Bangladesh	22N	92E	-6:08
Canton, China	23N	113E	-7:32	Chkalov, USSR	52N	55E	-3:40
Cap Haitien, Haiti	20N	72W	4:48	Chongjin, N Korea	42N	130E	-8:40
Cape Town, S Africa	34S	18E	-1:12	Chonju, S Korea	36N	127E	-8:28
Caracas, Venezuela	11N	67W	4:28	Chorzow, Poland	50N	19E	-1:16
Cardiff, G Britain	51N	3W	0:12	Christchurch, N Zealand	44S	173E	-11:32
Carolina, Puerto Rico	18N	66W	4:24	Christiania, Norway	60N	11E	-0:44
Cartagena, Colombia	10N	76W	5:04	Chungchin (Chungking) China	30N	107E	-7:08
Cartagena, Spain	38N	1W	0:04	Cienfuegos, Cuba	22N	80W	5:20
Casablanca, Morocco	34N	8W	0:32	Ciudad Guayana, Venezuela	8N	63W	4:12
Castellon De La Plana,Spain	40N	0W	0:00	Ciudad Juarez, Mexico	32N	106W	7:04
Cataneo, Puerto Rico	18N	66W	4:24	Ciudad Obregon, Mexico	27N	110W	7:20
Catania, Italy	38N	15E	-1:00	Ciudad Trujillo, Dom Rep	18N	70W	4:40
Catanzaro, Italy	39N	17E	-1:08	Ciudad Victoria, Mexico	24N	99W	6:36
Cawnpore, India	26N	80E	-5:20	Clermont-Ferrand, France	46N	3E	-0:12
Cayenne, Fr Guiana	5N	52W	3:28	Cluj, Rumania	47N	24E	-1:36
Cayey, Puerto Rico	18N	66W	4:24	Cochabamba, Bolivia	17S	66W	4:24
Ceara, Brazil	4S	39W	2:36	Cochin, India	10N	76E	-5:04
Cebu, Phillipines	10N	124E	-8:16	Coimbatore, India	11N	77E	-5:08
Celaya, Mexico	21N	101W	6:44	Colchester, G Britain	52N	1E	-0:04
Cernauti, USSR	48N	26E	-1:44	Cologne, W Germany	51N	7E	-0:28
Ceske Budejovice, Czech	49N	14E	-0:56	Colombo, Sri Lanka	7N	80E	-5:20
Ceuta, Sp Morocco	36N	5W	0:20	Colon, Panama	9N	80W	5:20
Chambery, France	46N	6E	-0:24	Como, Italy	46N	9E	-0:36
Changchiakou, China	41N	115E	-7:40	Conakry, Guinea	10N	14W	0:56
Changchow, China	32N	120E	-8:00	Concepcion, Chile	37S	73W	4:52
Changchun, China	44N	125E	-8:20	Concordia, Argentina	31S	58W	3:52
Changsha, China	28N	113E	-7:32	Constanta, Rumania	44N	29E	-1:56
Charleroi, Belgium	50N	4E	-0:16	Constantine, Algeria	36N	7E	-0:28
Charlotte Amalie, Vir Isl	18N	65W	4:20	Constantinople, Turkey	41N	29E	-1:56
Charlottetown, Canada	46N	63W	4:12	Copenhague, Denmark	56N	13E	-0:52
Chatham, G Britain	51N	1E	-0:04	Corcaigh, Ireland	52N	8W	0:32
Cheboksary, USSR	56N	47E	-3:08	Cordoba, Argentina	31S	64W	4:16
Cheltenham, G Britain	52N	2W	0:08	Cordoba, Spain	38N	5W	0:20
Chelyabinsk, USSR	55N	61E	-4:04	Corfu, Greece	40N	20E	-1:20
Chemnitz, E Germany	51N	13E	-0:52	Cork, Ireland	52N	8W	0:32
Chengchou, China	35N	114E	-7:36	Corrientes, Argentina	27S	59W	3:56
Chengtu, China	31N	104E	-6:56	Cosenza, Italy	39N	16E	-1:04
Cherbourg, France	50N	2W	0:08	Cotonou, Dahomey	6N	2E	-0:08
Cherepovets, USSR	59N	38E	-2:32	Cottbus, E Germany	52N	14E	-0:56
Cherkassy, USSR	49N	32E	-2:08	Courtrai, Belgium	51N	3E	-0:12
Chernigov, USSR	52N	31E	-2:04	Coventry, G Britain	52N	2W	0:08

CITY	LAT	LONG	TIME h m	CITY	LAT	LONG	TIME h m
Cracow, Poland	50N	20E	-1:20	Dun Laoghaire, Ireland	53N	6W	0:24
Craiova, Rumania	44N	24E	-1:36	Dunaburg, USSR	56N	27E	-1:48
Cremona, Italy	45N	10E	-0:40	Dundee, G Britain	56N	3W	0:12
Cucuta, Colombia	8N	73W	4:52	Dunedin, N Zealand	46S	171E	-11:24
Cuenca, Ecuador	3S	79W	5:16	Dunkerque (Dunkirk) France	51N	2E	-0:08
Culiacan, Mexico	25N	107W	7:08	Durango, Mexico	24N	105W	7:00
Cumana, Venezuela	10N	64W	4:16	Durban, S Africa	30S	31E	-2:04
Curitiba, Brazil	25S	49W	3:16	Dushanbe, USSR	39N	69E	-4:36
Cuzco, (Cusco) Peru	14S	72W	4:48	Dusseldorf, W Germany	51N	7E	-0:28
Czestochowa, Poland	51N	19E	-1:16	Dvinsk, USSR	56N	27E	-1:48
Da Nang, Vietnam	16N	108E	-7:12	Dzaudzhikau, USSR	43N	45E	-3:00
Dacca, Bangladesh	24N	90E	-6:00	Dzhambul, USSR	43N	71E	-4:44
Dagupan, Philippines	16N	120E	-8:00	East London, S Africa	33S	28E	-1:52
Dairen, China	39N	122E	-8:08	Ede, Nigeria	8N	4E	-0:16
Dakar, Senegal	15N	17W	1:08	Edessa, Greece	41N	22E	-1:28
Damanhur, Egypt	31N	30E	-2:00	Edinburgh, G Britain	56N	3W	0:12
Damascus, Syria	34N	36E	-2:24	Edmonton, Canada	54N	113W	7:32
Damietta, Egypt	31N	32E	-2:08	Eindhoven, Netherlands	51N	5E	-0:20
Danzig, Poland	54N	19E	-1:16	Ekaterinburg, USSR	57N	61E	-4:04
Dar Es Salaam, Tanzania	7S	39E	-2:36	Ekaterinodar, USSR	45N	39E	-2:36
Darlington, G Britain	55N	2W	0:08	Ekaterinoslav, USSR	48N	35E	-2:20
Darmstadt, W Germany	50N	9E	-0:36	El Faiyum, Egypt	29N	31E	-2:04
Darwin, Australia	12S	131E	-8:44	El Ferrol, Spain	43N	8W	0:32
Daugavpils, USSR	56N	27E	-1:48	El Giza, Egypt	30N	31E	-2:04
Davao, Philippines	7N	126E	-8:24	El Iskandariya, Egypt	31N	30E	-2:00
Debrecen, Hungary	48N	22E	-1:28	El Mahalla El Kubra, Egypt	31N	31E	-2:04
Dehra Dun, India	30N	78E	-5:12	El Mansura, Egypt	31N	31E	-2:04
Delft, Netherlands	52N	4E	-0:16	El Minya, Egypt	28N	31E	-2:04
Delhi, India	29N	77E	-5:08	El Qahira, Egypt	30N	31E	-2:04
Den Haag, Netherlands	52N	4E	-0:16	El Suweis, Egypt	30N	33E	-2:12
Den Helder, Netherlands	53N	5E	-0:20	Elat, Israel	30N	35E	-2:20
Denain, France	50N	3E	-0:12	Elberfeld, W Germany	51N	7E	-0:28
Denpasar, Indonesia	9S	115E	-7:40	Elblag (Elbing) Poland	54N	19E	-1:16
Derby, G Britain	53N	1W	0:04	Elche, Spain	38N	1W	0:04
Dessau, E Germany	52N	12E	-0:48	Elisabethville, Zaire	12S	27E	-1:48
Dezful, Iran	32N	48E	-3:12	Elizavetgrad, USSR	57N	60E	-4:00
Diego Suarez, Mal R	12S	49E	-3:16	Enschede, Netherlands	52N	7E	-0:28
Dijon, France	47N	5E	-0:20	Enugu, Nigeria	6N	7E	-0:28
Dili, Port Timor	9S	126E	-8:24	Erfurt, E Germany	51N	11E	-0:44
Dimashq, Syria	34N	36E	-2:24	Erivan, USSR	40N	45E	-3:00
Diredawa, Ethiopia	10N	42E	-2:48	Erlangen, W Germany	50N	11E	-0:44
Diyarbakir, Turkey	38N	40E	-2:40	Erzurum, Turkey	40N	41E	-2:44
Djajapura, Indonesia	3S	141E	-9:24	Esbjerg, Denmark	55N	8E	-0:32
Djakarta, Indonesia	6S	107E	-7:08	Esch Sur Alzette,Luxembourg	50N	6E	-0:24
Djambi, Indonesia	2S	104E	-6:56	Esfahan, Iran	32N	52E	-3:28
Djibouti, Rep. of Djibouti	12N	43E	-2:52	Eskilstuna, Sweden	59N	17E	-1:08
Dnepropetrovsk, USSR	48N	35E	-2:20	Eskisehir, Turkey	40N	31E	-2:04
Doha, Qatar	25N	52E	-3:28	Essen, W Germany	51N	7E	-0:28
Doncaster, G Britain	54N	1W	0:04	Esslingen, W Germany	49N	9E	-0:36
Donetsk, USSR	48N	38E	-2:32	Exeter, G Britain	51N	4W	0:16
Dordrecht, Netherlands	52N	5E	-0:20	Fayum, Egypt	29N	31E	-2:04
Dorpat, USSR	58N	27E	-1:48	Ferrara, Italy	45N	12E	-0:48
Dortmund, W Germany	52N	7E	-0:28	Fes (Fez) Morocco	34N	5W	0:20
Douai, France	50N	3E	-0:12	Fianarantsoa, Malagasy Rep	21S	47E	-3:08
Douala, Cameroun	4N	10E	-0:40	Firenze, Italy	44N	11E	-0:44
Douglas, G Britain	54N	4W	0:16	Fiume, Yugoslavia	45N	14E	-0:56
Drammen, Norway	60N	10E	-0:40	Flensburg, W Germany	55N	9E	-0:36
Dresden, E Germany	51N	14E	-0:56	Florence, Italy	44N	11E	-0:44
Dubayy, U.A. Emirates	25N	55E	-3:40	Florianopolis, Brazil	28S	49W	3:16
Dublin, Ireland	53N	6W	0:24	Foggia, Italy	41N	16E	-1:04
Dudley, G Britain	53N	2W	0:08	Foochow, China	26N	119E	-7:56
Duisburg, W Germany	51N	7E	-0:28	Forli, Italy	44N	12E	-0:48
Dumyat, Egypt	31N	32E	-2:08	Fort De France, Martinique	15N	61W	4:04

CITY	LAT	LONG	TIME h m	CITY	LAT	LONG	TIME h m
Fort Lamy, Chad	12N	15E	-1:00	Groningen, Netherlands	53N	7E	-0:28
Fort William, Canada	48N	89W	5:56	Groznyy, USSR	43N	46E	-3:04
Fortaleza, Brazil	4S	39W	2:36	Grudziadz, Poland	53N	19E	-1:16
Fowliang, China	29N	117E	-7:48	Guadalajara, Mexico	21N	103W	6:52
Frankfurt Am Main, W Germany	50N	9E	-0:36	Guantanamo, Cuba	20N	75W	5:00
Fredrikstad, Norway	59N	11E	-0:44	Guatemala, Guatemala	15N	91W	6:04
Freetown, Sierra Leone	9N	13W	0:52	Guayama, Puerto Rico	18N	66W	4:24
Freiburg, W Germany	48N	8E	-0:32	Guayana, Venezuela	8N	63W	4:12
Frunze, USSR	43N	75E	-5:00	Guayaquil, Ecuador	2S	80W	5:20
Fuchou, China	26N	119E	-7:56	Guaynabo, Puerto Rico	18N	66W	4:24
Fuhsin, China	42N	122E	-8:08	Gujranwala, Pakistan	32N	75E	-5:00
Fuji, Japan	35N	139E	-9:16	Guryev, USSR	47N	52E	-3:28
Fujisawa, Japan	35N	139E	-9:16	Gwalior, India	26N	78E	-5:12
Fukui, Japan	36N	136E	-9:04	Gyor, Hungary	48N	18E	-1:12
Fukuoka, Japan	34N	130E	-8:40	Haarlem, Netherlands	52N	5E	-0:20
Fukushima, Japan	38N	140E	-9:20	Habana, Cuba	23N	82W	5:28
Fukuyama, Japan	34N	133E	-8:52	Hachinohe, Japan	41N	141E	-9:24
Funchal, Portugal	33N	17W	1:08	Haderslev, Denmark	55N	9E	-0:36
Furth, W Germany	49N	11E	-0:44	Haerhpin, China	46N	127E	-8:28
Fusan, S Korea	35N	129E	-8:36	Hagen, W Germany	51N	7E	-0:28
Fushun, China	42N	124E	-8:16	Haifa, Israel	33N	35E	-2:20
Fusin, China	42N	122E	-8:08	Haikou, China	20N	110E	-7:20
Gaborone, Botswana	25S	26E	-1:44	Haiphong, Vietnam	21N	107E	-7:08
Galati (Galatz) Rumania	45N	28E	-1:52	Hakodate, Japan	42N	141E	-9:24
Gand, Belgium	51N	4E	-0:16	Halab, Syria	36N	37E	-2:28
Gavle, Sweden	61N	17E	-1:08	Halifax, Canada	45N	64W	4:16
Gaza, Gaza Strip	31N	34E	-2:16	Halifax, G Britain	54N	2W	0:08
Gaziantep, Turkey	37N	37E	-2:28	Halle, E Germany	51N	12E	-0:48
Gdansk, Poland	54N	19E	-1:16	Halmstad, Sweden	57N	13E	-0:52
Gdynia, Poland	55N	19E	-1:16	Halsingborg, Sweden	56N	13E	-0:52
Geelong, Australia	38S	144E	-9:36	Hamadan, Iran	35N	49E	-3:16
Gelsenkirchen, W Germany	52N	7E	-0:28	Hamah, Syria	35N	37E	-2:28
Geneve (Geneva) Switzerland	46N	6E	-0:24	Hamamatsu, Japan	35N	138E	-9:12
Genova, (Genoa) Italy	44N	9E	-0:36	Hamburg, W Germany	54N	10E	-0:40
Gent, Belgium	51N	4E	-0:16	Hamilton, Canada	43N	80W	5:20
George Town, Malaysia	5N	100E	-6:40	Hamm, W Germany	52N	8E	-0:32
Georgetown, Guyana	7N	58W	3:52	Hangchou, China	30N	120E	-8:00
Gera, E Germany	51N	12E	-0:48	Hankou, China	31N	114E	-7:36
Ghent, Belgium	51N	4E	-0:16	Hannover, W Germany	52N	10E	-0:40
Gibraltar, Gibraltar	36N	5W	0:20	Hanoi, Vietnam	21N	106E	-7:04
Giessen, W Germany	51N	9E	-0:36	Hantan, China	37N	114E	-7:36
Gifu, Japan	35N	137E	-9:08	Hanyang, China	31N	114E	-7:36
Gijon, Spain	44N	6W	0:24	Harbin, China	46N	127E	-8:28
Giza, Egypt	30N	31E	-2:04	Hartlepool, G Britain	55N	1W	0:04
Gladbach, W Germany	51N	6E	-0:24	Havana, Cuba	23N	82W	5:28
Glasgow, G Britain	56N	4W	0:16	Heerlen, Netherlands	51N	6E	-0:24
Gliwice (Gleiwitz) Poland	50N	19E	-1:16	Heidelberg, W Germany	49N	9E	-0:36
Gloucester, G Britain	52N	2W	0:08	Heilbronn, W Germany	49N	9E	-0:36
Goiania, Brazil	17S	49W	3:16	Helsingborg, Sweden	56N	13E	-0:52
Gomel, USSR	52N	31E	-2:04	Helsinki (Helsingfors) Fin	60N	25E	-1:40
Gorkiy (Gorki) USSR	56N	44E	-2:56	Hengyang, China	27N	113E	-7:32
Gorlitz, E Germany	51N	15E	-1:00	Herat, Afghanistan	34N	62E	-4:08
Goteborg (Gothenburg) Sweden	58N	12E	-0:48	Herford, W Germany	52N	9E	-0:36
Gottingen, W Germany	52N	10E	-0:40	Hermannstadt, Rumania	46N	24E	-1:36
Gottwaldov, Czech	49N	18E	-1:12	Hermosillo, Mexico	29N	111W	7:24
Granada, Spain	37N	4W	0:16	Hildesheim, W Germany	52N	10E	-0:40
Graudenz, Poland	53N	19E	-1:16	Hilversum, Netherlands	52N	5E	-0:20
Graz, Austria	47N	15E	-1:00	Himeji, Japan	35N	135E	-9:00
Greenock, G Britain	56N	5W	0:20	Hims, Syria	35N	37E	-2:28
Greenwich, G Britain	51N	0W	0:00	Hindenburg, Poland	50N	19E	-1:16
Grenoble, France	45N	6E	-0:24	Hiroshima, Japan	34N	132E	-8:48
Grimsby, G Britain	54N	0W	0:00	Ho Chi Minh (Saigon) Vietnam	11N	107E	-7:08
Grodno, USSR	54N	24E	-1:36	Hobart, Australia	43S	147E	-9:48

CITY	LAT	LONG	TIME h m	CITY	LAT	LONG	TIME h m
Hofei, China	32N	117E	-7:48	Jena, E Germany	51N	12E	-0:48
Hofuf, Saudi Arabia	25N	50E	-3:20	Jerez De La Frontera, Spain	37N	6W	0:24
Hoihow, China	20N	110E	-7:20	Jerusalem, Israel	32N	35E	-2:20
Holguin, Cuba	21N	76W	5:04	Joao Pessoa, Brazil	7S	35W	2:20
Hollandia, Indonesia	3S	141E	-9:24	Jodhpur, India	26N	73E	-4:52
Homs, Syria	35N	37E	-2:28	Jogjakarta, Indonesia	8S	110E	-7:20
Hongkong, Hongkong T	22N	114E	-7:36	Johannesburg, S Africa	26S	28E	-1:52
Hradec Kralove, Czech	50N	16E	-1:04	Johore Baharu, Malaysia	1N	104E	-6:56
Hsiamen, China	24N	118E	-7:52	Jonkoping, Sweden	58N	14E	-0:56
Hsian, China	34N	109E	-7:16	Juddah, Saudi Arabia	21N	39E	-2:36
Hsiangtan, China	28N	113E	-7:32	Juiz De Fora, Brazil	22S	43W	2:52
Hsining, China	37N	102E	-6:48	Jullundur, India	31N	76E	-5:04
Hsinking, China	44N	125E	-8:20	Kabul, Afghanistan	35N	69E	-4:36
Hsuchou, China	34N	117E	-7:48	Kadiyevka, USSR	49N	39E	-2:36
Huddersfield, G Britain	54N	2W	0:08	Kaduna, Nigeria	11N	7E	-0:28
Hue, Vietnam	16N	108E	-7:12	Kaesong, N Korea	38N	127E	-8:28
Huelva, Spain	37N	7W	0:28	Kagoshima, Japan	32N	131E	-8:44
Huhohaote (Huhehot) China	41N	112E	-7:28	Kaifeng, China	35N	114E	-7:36
Hull, G Britain	54N	0W	0:00	Kaiserslautern, W Germany	49N	8E	-0:32
Humacao, Puerto Rico	18N	66W	4:24	Kalgan, China	41N	115E	-7:40
Hunedoara, Rumania	46N	23E	-1:32	Kalinin, USSR	57N	36E	-2:24
Hyderabad, India	17N	78E	-5:12	Kaliningrad, USSR	55N	21E	-1:24
Hyderabad, Pakistan	25N	68E	-4:32	Kalisz, Poland	52N	18E	-1:12
Iasi, Rumania	47N	28E	-1:52	Kaluga, USSR	55N	36E	-2:24
Ibadan, Nigeria	7N	4E	-0:16	Kamensk Uralskiy, USSR	56N	62E	-4:08
Ibague, Colombia	4N	75W	5:00	Kampala, Uganda	0N	33E	-2:12
Ife, Nigeria	8N	5E	-0:20	Kanazawa, Japan	37N	137E	-9:08
Ilesha, Nigeria	8N	5E	-0:20	Kandahar, Afghanistan	32N	66E	-4:24
Iloilo, Philippines	11N	123E	-8:12	Kano, Nigeria	12N	9E	-0:36
Ilorin, Nigeria	9N	5E	-0:20	Kanpur, India	26N	80E	-5:20
Inchon, S Korea	37N	127E	-8:28	Kaohsiung, Taiwan	23N	120E	-8:00
Indore, India	23N	76E	-5:04	Kaolack, Senegal	14N	16W	1:04
Inhambane, Mozambique	24S	35E	-2:20	Karachi, Pakistan	25N	67E	-4:28
Innsbruck, Austria	47N	11E	-0:44	Karaganda, USSR	50N	73E	-4:52
Invercargill, N Zealand	46S	168E	-11:12	Karbala, Iraq	33N	44E	-2:56
Ipoh, Malaysia	5N	101E	-6:44	Karl Marx Stadt, W Germany	51N	13E	-0:52
Ipswich, G Britain	52N	1E	-0:04	Karlsruhe, W Germany	49N	8E	-0:32
Iquique, Chile	20S	70W	4:40	Karlstad, Sweden	59N	14E	-0:56
Iraklion, Greece	35N	25E	-1:40	Kashih (Kashgar) China	39N	76E	-5:04
Irbil, Iraq	36N	44E	-2:56	Kassala, Sudan	15N	36E	-2:24
Irkutsk, USSR	52N	104E	-6:56	Kassel, W Germany	51N	9E	-0:36
Isfahan, Iran	33N	52E	-3:28	Kathmandu, Nepal	28N	85E	-5:40
Iskenderun, Turkey	37N	36E	-2:24	Katowice (Kattowitz) Poland	50N	19E	-1:16
Islamabad, Pakistan	34N	73E	-4:52	Kaunas, USSR	55N	24E	-1:36
Ismailya, Egypt	31N	32E	-2:08	Kavala, Greece	41N	24E	-1:36
Ispahan, Iran	33N	52E	-3:28	Kayseri, Turkey	39N	36E	-2:24
Istanbul, Turkey	41N	29E	-1:56	Kazan, USSR	56N	49E	-3:16
Ivano Frankovsk, USSR	49N	25E	-1:40	Kediri, Indonesia	8S	112E	-7:28
Ivanovo, USSR	57N	41E	-2:44	Keelung, Taiwan	25N	122E	-8:08
Iwaki, Japan	37N	141E	-9:24	Kelang, Malaysia	3N	101E	-6:44
Iwo, Nigeria	8N	4E	-0:16	Kemerovo, USSR	55N	86E	-5:44
Izhevsk, USSR	57N	53E	-3:32	Kenitra, Morocco	34N	7W	0:28
Izmir, Turkey	38N	27E	-1:48	Kerch, USSR	45N	36E	-2:24
Izmit, Turkey	41N	30E	-2:00	Kerkira, Greece	40N	20E	-1:20
Jabalpur, India	23N	80E	-5:20	Kerman, Iran	30N	57E	-3:48
Jaen, Spain	38N	4W	0:16	Kermanshah, Iran	34N	47E	-3:08
Jaffna, Ceylon	10N	80E	-5:20	Khabarovsk, USSR	48N	135E	-9:00
Jaipur, India	27N	76E	-5:04	Khania, Greece	36N	24E	-1:36
Jakarta, Indonesia	6S	107E	-7:08	Khanty Mansiysk, USSR	61N	69E	-4:36
Jalapa Enriquez, Mexico	20N	97W	6:28	Kharkov, USSR	50N	36E	-2:24
Jamshedpur, India	23N	86E	-5:44	Khartoum, Sudan	16N	33E	-2:12
Jeddah(Jidda),Saudi Arabia	21N	39E	-2:36	Khemelnitskiy, USSR	49N	27E	-1:48
Jelenia Gora, Poland	51N	16E	-1:04	Kherson, USSR	47N	33E	-2:12

CITY	LAT	LONG	TIME h m	CITY	LAT	LONG	TIME h m
Kiel, W Germany	54N	10E	-0:40	Kuching, Malaysia	2N	110E	-7:20
Kielce, Poland	51N	21E	-1:24	Kueiyang, China	27N	107E	-7:08
Kiev, USSR	50N	31E	-2:04	Kumamoto, Japan	33N	131E	-8:44
Kigali, Rwanda	2S	30E	-2:00	Kumasi, Ghana	7N	2W	0:08
Kimberley, S Africa	29S	25E	-1:40	Kunming, China	25N	103E	-6:52
Kineshma, USSR	57N	42E	-2:48	Kuopio, Finland	63N	28E	-1:52
Kingston Upon Hull,GBritain	54N	0W	0:00	Kure, Japan	34N	133E	-8:52
Kingston, Canada	44N	77W	5:08	Kurgan, USSR	55N	65E	-4:20
Kingston, Jamaica	18N	77W	5:08	Kursk, USSR	52N	36E	-2:24
Kingstown, Ireland	53N	6W	0:24	Kustanay, USSR	53N	64E	-4:16
Kingstown, St Vincent	13N	61W	4:04	Kutaisi, USSR	42N	43E	-2:52
Kinshasa, Zaire	4S	15E	-1:00	Kuwait, Kuwait	29N	48E	-3:12
Kirin, China	44N	127E	-8:28	Kuybyshev, USSR	53N	50E	-3:20
Kirkuk, Iraq	35N	44E	-2:56	Kwangju, S Korea	35N	127E	-8:28
Kirkwall, G Britain	59N	3W	0:12	Kyongsong, S Korea	38N	127E	-8:28
Kirov, USSR	59N	50E	-3:20	Kyoto, Japan	35N	136E	-9:04
Kirovabad, USSR	41N	46E	-3:04	Kzyl Orda, USSR	45N	65E	-4:20
Kirovgrad, USSR	57N	60E	-4:00	La Coruna, Spain	43N	8W	0:32
Kirovograd, USSR	49N	32E	-2:08	La Paz, Bolivia	17S	68W	4:32
Kirovsk, USSR	68N	34E	-2:16	La Plata, Argentina	35S	58W	3:52
Kisangani, Zaire	0N	25E	-1:40	La Rochelle, France	46N	1W	0:04
Kishinev, USSR	47N	29E	-1:56	La Serena, Chile	30S	71W	4:44
Kita Kyushu, Japan	34N	131E	-8:44	La Spezia, Italy	44N	10E	-0:40
Kitchener, Canada	43N	80W	5:20	Lagos, Nigeria	6N	3E	-0:12
Kitwe, Zambia	13S	28E	-1:52	Lahore, Pakistan	32N	74E	-4:56
Kiyev, USSR	50N	31E	-2:04	Lahti, Finland	61N	26E	-1:44
Klagenfurt, Austria	47N	14E	-0:56	Laibach, Yugoslavia	46N	15E	-1:00
Klaipeda, USSR	56N	21E	-1:24	Lancaster, G Britain	54N	3W	0:12
Klausenburg, Rumania	47N	24E	-1:36	Lanchou (Lanchow), China	36N	104E	-6:56
Kobe, Japan	35N	135E	-9:00	Larisa, Greece	40N	22E	-1:28
Kobenhavn, Denmark	56N	13E	-0:52	Las Palmas De Gran Canaria	28N	15W	1:00
Koblenz, W Germany	50N	8E	-0:32	Lasa, China	30N	91E	-6:04
Kochi, Japan	34N	134E	-8:56	Latakia, Syria	36N	36E	-2:24
Kofu, Japan	36N	139E	-9:16	Launceston, Australia	41S	147E	-9:48
Kokand, USSR	41N	71E	-4:44	Lausanne, Switzerland	47N	7E	-0:28
Koln, W Germany	51N	7E	-0:28	Le Havre, France	50N	0E	0:00
Kolomna, USSR	55N	39E	-2:36	Le Mans, France	48N	0E	0:00
Komsomolsk, USSR	51N	137E	-9:08	Lecce, Italy	40N	18E	-1:12
Konigsberg, USSR	55N	21E	-1:24	Leeds, G Britain	54N	2W	0:08
Konigshutte, Poland	50N	19E	-1:16	Leeuwarden, Netherlands	53N	6E	-0:24
Konya, Turkey	38N	33E	-2:12	Leghorn, Italy	44N	10E	-0:40
Korce, Albania	41N	21E	-1:24	Legnica, Poland	51N	16E	-1:04
Koriyama, Japan	37N	140E	-9:20	Leicester, G Britain	53N	1W	0:04
Kortrijk, Belgium	51N	3E	-0:12	Leiden, Netherlands	52N	5E	-0:20
Kosice, Czech	49N	21E	-1:24	Leipzig, E Germany	51N	12E	-0:48
Kostroma, USSR	58N	41E	-2:44	Lemberg, Poland	50N	24E	-1:36
Kota Kinabalu, Malaysia	6N	116E	-7:44	Leninakan, USSR	41N	44E	-2:56
Kovno, USSR	55N	24E	-1:36	Leningrad, USSR	60N	30E	-2:00
Koweit, Kuwait	29N	48E	-3:12	Lens, France	50N	3E	-0:12
Kowloon, Hongkong	22N	114E	-7:36	Leon, Mexico	21N	102W	6:48
Kozhikode, India	11N	76E	-5:04	Leon, Spain	43N	6W	0:24
Krakow, Poland	50N	20E	-1:20	Leopoldville, Zaire	4S	15E	-1:00
Kramatorsk, USSR	49N	38E	-2:32	Lerwick, G Britain	60N	1W	0:04
Krasnodar, USSR	45N	39E	-2:36	Leuven, Belgium	51N	5E	-0:20
Krasnovodsk-Ufra, USSR	40N	53E	-3:32	Leyden, Netherlands	52N	5E	-0:20
Krasnoyarsk, USSR	56N	93E	-6:12	Lhasa, China	30N	91E	-6:04
Krefeld, W Germany	51N	7E	-0:28	Libau, USSR	57N	21E	-1:24
Kremenchug, USSR	49N	33E	-2:12	Libreville, Gabon	0N	9E	-0:36
Kristiansand, Norway	58N	8E	-0:32	Liege, Belgium	51N	6E	-0:24
Krivoy Rog, USSR	48N	33E	-2:12	Liegnitz, Poland	51N	16E	-1:04
Krung Thep, Thailand	14N	101E	-6:44	Liepaja, USSR	57N	21E	-1:24
Kuala Lumpur, Malaysia	3N	102E	-6:48	Lille, France	51N	3E	-0:12
Kuangchou, China	23N	113E	-7:32	Lima, Peru	12S	77W	5:08

CITY	LAT	LONG	TIME h m	CITY	LAT	LONG	TIME h m
Limerick, Ireland	53N	9W	0:36	Makasar, Indonesia	5S	119E	-7:56
Limoges, France	46N	1E	-0:04	Makeyevka, USSR	48N	38E	-2:32
Lincoln, G Britain	53N	1W	0:04	Makkah, Saudi Arabia	21N	40E	-2:40
Linkoping, Sweden	58N	16E	-1:04	Malacca, Malaysia	2N	102E	-6:48
Linz, Austria	48N	14E	-0:56	Malaga, Spain	37N	4W	0:16
Lipetsk, USSR	53N	40E	-2:40	Malang, Indonesia	8S	113E	-7:32
Lisboa (Lisbon) Portugal	39N	9W	0:36	Malatya, Turkey	38N	38E	-2:32
Liverpool, G Britain	53N	3W	0:12	Malmo, Sweden	56N	13E	-0:52
Livorno, Italy	44N	10E	-0:40	Manado, Indonesia	1N	125E	-8:20
Ljubljana, Yugoslavia	46N	15E	-1:00	Managua, Nicaragua	12N	86W	5:44
Lodz, Poland	52N	19E	-1:16	Manama, Bahrain	26N	51E	-3:24
Logrono, Spain	42N	2W	0:08	Manaus, Brazil	3S	60W	4:00
Lome, Togo	6N	1E	-0:04	Manchester, G Britain	54N	2W	0:08
London, Canada	43N	81W	5:24	Mandalay, Burma	22N	96E	-6:24
London, G Britain	52N	0W	0:00	Mangalore, India	13N	75E	-5:00
Londonderry, N Ireland	55N	7W	0:28	Manila, Philippines	15N	121E	-8:04
Longwy, France	50N	6E	-0:24	Manizales, Colombia	5N	76W	5:04
Lorient, France	48N	3W	0:12	Mannheim, W Germany	49N	8E	-0:32
Lourenco Marques,Mozambique	26S	33E	-2:12	Mansfield, G Britain	53N	1W	0:04
Louvain, Belgium	51N	5E	-0:20	Mansura, Egypt	31N	31E	-2:04
Loyang, China	35N	112E	-7:28	Mantova (Mantua) Italy	45N	11E	-0:44
Luanda, Angola	9S	13E	-0:52	Manzanillo, Cuba	20N	77W	5:08
Luang Prabang, Laos	20N	102E	-6:48	Mar Del Plata, Argentina	38S	58W	3:52
Lubeck, W Germany	54N	11E	-0:44	Maracaibo, Venezuela	11N	72W	4:48
Lublin, Poland	51N	23E	-1:32	Maracay, Venezuela	10N	68W	4:32
Lubumbashi, Zaire	12S	27E	-1:48	Maribor (Marburg)Yugoslavia	47N	16E	-1:04
Lucca, Italy	44N	10E	-0:40	Mariupol, USSR	47N	38E	-2:32
Lucerne, Switzerland	47N	8E	-0:32	Marrakech, Morocco	32N	8W	0:32
Luck, USSR	51N	25E	-1:40	Marseille, France	43N	5E	-0:20
Lucknow, India	27N	81E	-5:24	Maseru, Lesotho	29S	28E	-1:52
Ludhiana, India	31N	76E	-5:04	Mashhad, Iran	36N	60E	-4:00
Ludwigsburg, W Germany	49N	9E	-0:36	Massa, Italy	44N	10E	-0:40
Ludwigshafen, W Germany	49N	8E	-0:32	Matadi, Zaire	6S	13E	-0:52
Lugansk, USSR	49N	39E	-2:36	Matanzas, Cuba	23N	82W	5:28
Luimneach, Ireland	53N	9W	0:36	Matsuyama, Japan	34N	133E	-8:52
Lulea, Sweden	66N	22E	-1:28	Maubeuge, France	50N	4E	-0:16
Luluabourg, Zaire	6S	22E	-1:28	Mayaguez, Puerto Rico	18N	67W	4:28
Lusaka, Zambia	15S	28E	-1:52	Maykop, USSR	45N	40E	-2:40
Lushun-Luta, China	39N	121E	-8:04	Mazatlan, Mexico	23N	106W	7:04
Luton, G Britain	52N	0W	0:00	Mbabane, Swaziland	26S	31E	-2:04
Lutsk, USSR	51N	25E	-1:40	Mecca, Saudi Arabia	21N	40E	-2:40
Luxembourg, Luxembourg	50N	6E	-0:24	Medan, Indonesia	4N	99E	-6:36
Luzern, Switzerland	47N	8E	-0:32	Medellin, Colombia	6N	76W	5:04
Lvov (Lwow) USSR	50N	24E	-1:36	Medina, Saudi Arabia	24N	40E	-2:40
Lyallpur, Pakistan	31N	73E	-4:52	Meerut, India	29N	78E	-5:12
Lyon, France	46N	5E	-0:20	Meknes, Morocco	34N	6W	0:24
Maastricht, Netherlands	51N	6E	-0:24	Melbourne, Australia	38S	145E	-9:40
Macao, Macao	22N	114E	-7:36	Melilla, Sp Morocco	35N	3W	0:12
Macassar, Indonesia	5S	119E	-7:56	Melitopol, USSR	47N	35E	-2:20
Maceio, Brazil	10S	36W	2:24	Memel, USSR	56N	21E	-1:24
Madiun, Indonesia	8S	112E	-7:28	Mendoza, Argentina	33S	69W	4:36
Madras, India	13N	80E	-5:20	Merida, Mexico	21N	90W	6:00
Madrid, Spain	40N	4W	0:16	Mersin, Turkey	37N	35E	-2:20
Madurai, India	10N	78E	-5:12	Meshed, Iran	36N	60E	-4:00
Maebashi, Japan	36N	139E	-9:16	Messina, Italy	38N	16E	-1:04
Magallanes, Chile	53S	71W	4:44	Metz, France	49N	6E	-0:24
Magdeburg, E Germany	52N	12E	-0:48	Mexicali, Mexico	33N	115W	7:40
Magnitogorsk, USSR	53N	59E	-3:56	Mexico City, Mexico	19N	99W	6:36
Mahon, Spain	40N	4E	-0:16	Middlesbrough, G Britain	55N	1W	0:04
Maiduguri, Nigeria	12N	13E	-0:52	Milano (Milan), Italy	45N	9E	-0:36
Mainz, W Germany	50N	8E	-0:32	Minden, W Germany	52N	9E	-0:36
Majunga, Malagasy Rep	16S	46E	-3:04	Minhow, China	26N	119E	-7:56
Makachkala, USSR	43N	47E	-3:08	Minsk, USSR	54N	28E	-1:52

CITY	LAT	LONG	TIME h m
Miskolc, Hungary	48N	21E	-1:24
Miyazaki, Japan	32N	131E	-8:44
Modena, Italy	45N	11E	-0:44
Mogadishu(Mogadiscio)Somali	2N	45E	-3:00
Mogilev, USSR	54N	30E	-2:00
Molotov, USSR	58N	56E	-3:44
Mombasa, Kenya	4S	40E	-2:40
Monaco, Monaco	44N	7E	-0:28
Monchen-Gladbach, W Germany	51N	6E	-0:24
Monrovia, Liberia	6N	11W	0:44
Mons, Belgium	50N	4E	-0:16
Monte Carlo, Monaco	44N	7E	-0:28
Monteria, Colombia	9N	76W	5:04
Monterrey, Mexico	26N	100W	6:40
Montevideo, Uruguay	35S	56W	3:44
Montpellier, France	44N	4E	-0:16
Montreal, Canada	46N	74W	4:56
Moradabad, India	29N	79E	-5:16
Morelia, Mexico	20N	101W	6:44
Moskva (Moscow), USSR	56N	38E	-2:32
Mostaganem, Algeria	36N	0E	0:00
Mosul, Iraq	36N	43E	-2:52
Moulmein, Burma	17N	98E	-6:32
Mufulira, Zambia	13S	28E	-1:52
Mukden, China	42N	123E	-8:12
Mulheim, W Germany	51N	7E	-0:28
Mulhouse, France	48N	7E	-0:28
Multan, Pakistan	30N	72E	-4:48
Munchen (Munich) W Germany	48N	12E	-0:48
Munster, W Germany	52N	8E	-0:32
Murcia, Spain	38N	1W	0:04
Murmansk, USSR	69N	33E	-2:12
Muroran, Japan	42N	141E	-9:24
Mutanchjang, China	45N	130E	-8:40
My Tho, Vietnam	10N	106E	-7:04
Mysore, India	12N	77E	-5:08
Nagano, Japan	37N	138E	-9:12
Nagasaki, Japan	33N	130E	-8:40
Nagoya, Japan	35N	137E	-9:08
Nagpur, India	21N	79E	-5:16
Naha, Okinawa	26N	128E	-8:32
Nairobi, Kenya	1S	37E	-2:28
Nalchik, USSR	44N	44E	-2:56
Namangan, USSR	41N	72E	-4:48
Nampula, Mozambique	15S	39E	-2:36
Namur, Belgium	50N	5E	-0:20
Nanchang, China	29N	116E	-7:44
Nanching (Nanking), China	32N	119E	-7:56
Nancy, France	49N	6E	-0:24
Nanning, China	23N	108E	-7:12
Nantes, France	47N	2W	0:08
Nantung, China	32N	121E	-8:04
Napier-Hastings, N Zealand	39S	177E	-11:48
Napoli (Naples), Italy	41N	14E	-0:56
Nasik, India	20N	74E	-4:56
Nassau, Bahamas	25N	77W	5:08
Natal, Brazil	6S	35W	2:20
Ndola, Zambia	13S	29E	-1:56
Neiva, Colombia	3N	75W	5:00
Neusatz, Yugoslavia	45N	20E	-1:20
Neuss, W Germany	51N	7E	-0:28
New Delhi, India	29N	77E	-5:08
Newcastle Upon Tyne, G Brit	55N	2W	0:08
Newcastle, Australia	33S	152E	-10:08
Newport, G Britain	52N	3W	0:12
Niamey, Niger	14N	2E	-0:08
Nice, France	44N	7E	-0:28
Nicosia, Cyprus	35N	33E	-2:12
Niigata, Japan	38N	139E	-9:16
Nijmegen, Netherlands	52N	6E	-0:24
Nikolayev, USSR	47N	32E	-2:08
Nikopol, USSR	48N	34E	-2:16
Nimes, France	44N	4E	-0:16
Ningpo, China	30N	122E	-8:08
Ningsia, China	39N	106E	-7:04
Nis, Yugoslavia	43N	22E	-1:28
Niteroi, Brazil	23S	43W	2:52
Nizhni Novgorod, USSR	56N	44E	-2:56
Nizhniy Tagil, USSR	58N	60E	-4:00
Norrkoping, Sweden	59N	16E	-1:04
Northampton, G Brtain	52N	1W	0:04
Norwich, G Britain	53N	1E	-0:04
Nottingham, G Britain	53N	1W	0:04
Nouakchott, Mauretania	18N	16W	1:04
Noumea, N Caledonia	22S	166E	-11:04
Novara, Italy	45N	9E	-0:36
Novgorod, USSR	59N	31E	-2:04
Novi Sad, Yugoslavia	45N	20E	-1:20
Novokuznetsk, USSR	54N	87E	-5:48
Novomoskovsk, USSR	54N	38E	-2:32
Novonikolayevsk, USSR	55N	83E	-5:32
Novorossiysk, USSR	45N	38E	-2:32
Novosibirsk, USSR	55N	83E	-5:32
Nuevo Laredo, Mexico	28N	100W	6:40
Nukualofa, Tonga	21S	175W	11:40
Nukus, USSR	42N	60E	-4:00
Numazu, Japan	35N	139E	-9:16
Nurnberg (Nuremberg) W Ger	49N	11E	-0:44
Oaxaca, Mexico	17N	97W	6:28
Oberhausen, W Germany	52N	7E	-0:28
Odense, Denmark	55N	10E	-0:40
Odessa, USSR	47N	31E	-2:04
Ogbomosho, Nigeria	8N	4E	-0:16
Oita, Japan	33N	132E	-8:48
Okayama, Japan	35N	134E	-8:56
Oldenburg, W Germany	53N	8E	-0:32
Oldham, G Britain	54N	2W	0:08
Olomouc (Olmutz), Czech	50N	17E	-1:08
Olsztyn, Poland	54N	20E	-1:20
Omdurman, Sudan	16N	32E	-2:08
Omsk, USSR	55N	73E	-4:52
Omuta, Japan	33N	130E	-8:40
Onitsha, Nigeria	6N	7E	-0:28
Oostende, Belgium	51N	3E	-0:12
Opole (Oppeln), Poland	51N	18E	-1:12
Oporto, Portugal	41N	9W	0:36
Oradea, Rumania	47N	22E	-1:28
Oran, Algeria	36N	1W	0:04
Ordzhonikidze, USSR	43N	45E	-3:00
Orebro, Sweden	59N	15E	-1:00
Orekhovo Zuyevo, USSR	56N	39E	-2:36
Orel, USSR	53N	36E	-2:24
Orenburg, USSR	52N	55E	-3:40
Orizaba, Mexico	19N	97W	6:28
Orleans, France	48N	2E	-0:08
Orsk, USSR	51N	59E	-3:56

CITY	LAT	LONG	TIME h m	CITY	LAT	LONG	TIME h m
Oruro, Bolivia	18S	67W	4:28	Petropavlovsk Kamchatskiy	53N	159E	-10:36
Osaka, Japan	35N	135E	-9:00	Petropavlovsk, USSR	55N	69E	-4:36
Osh, USSR	41N	73E	-4:52	Petrozavodsk, USSR	62N	34E	-2:16
Oshawa, Canada	44N	79W	5:16	Pforzheim, W Germany	49N	9E	-0:36
Oshogbo, Nigeria	8N	5E	-0:20	Philippeville, Algeria	37N	7E	-0:28
Oslo, Norway	60N	11E	-0:44	Phnom Penh, Cambodia	12N	105E	-7:00
Osnabruck, W Germany	52N	8E	-0:32	Piacenza, Italy	45N	10E	-0:40
Osorno, Chile	41S	73W	4:52	Piatigorsk, USSR	44N	43E	-2:52
Ostend, Belgium	51N	3E	-0:12	Pietermaritzburg, S Africa	30S	30E	-2:00
Ostiako Vogulsk, USSR	61N	69E	-4:36	Pilsen, Czech	50N	13E	-0:52
Ostrava, Czech	50N	18E	-1:12	Pinang, Malaysia	5N	100E	-6:40
Otaru, Japan	43N	141E	-9:24	Pinar Del Rio, Cuba	22N	84W	5:36
Ottawa, Canada	45N	76W	5:04	Piraievs (Piraeus), Greece	38N	24E	-1:36
Ouagadougou, Up Volta	12N	2W	0:08	Pisa, Italy	44N	10E	-0:40
Oujda, Morocco	35N	2W	0:08	Pishpek, USSR	43N	75E	-5:00
Oulu, Finland	65N	25E	-1:40	Piura, Peru	5S	81W	5:24
Oviedo, Spain	43N	6W	0:24	Plauen, E Germany	50N	12E	-0:48
Oxford, G Britain	52N	1W	0:04	Pleven, Bulgaria	43N	25E	-1:40
Ozorkow, Poland	52N	19E	-1:16	Ploiesti, Rumania	45N	26E	-1:44
Pachuca, Mexico	20N	99W	6:36	Plovdiv, Bulgaria	42N	25E	-1:40
Padang, Indonesia	1S	100E	-6:40	Plymouth, G Britain	50N	4W	0:16
Padova (Padua), Italy	45N	12E	-0:48	Plzen, Czech	50N	13E	-0:52
Pago Pago, American Samoa	14S	171W	11:24	Pointe A Pitre, Guadeloupe	16N	62W	4:08
Palembang, Indonesia	3S	105E	-7:00	Pointe Noire, Congo	5S	12E	-0:48
Palermo, Italy	38N	13E	-0:52	Poltava, USSR	50N	35E	-2:20
Palma De Mallorca, Spain	40N	3E	-0:12	Poltoratsk, USSR	38N	58E	-3:52
Pamplona, Spain	43N	2W	0:08	Ponce, Puerto Rico	18N	67W	4:28
Panama, Panama	9N	80W	5:20	Ponta Delgada, Azores	38N	26W	1:44
Panevezys, USSR	56N	24E	-1:36	Ponta Grossa, Brazil	25S	50W	3:20
Pangpu, China	33N	117E	-7:48	Pontianak, Indonesia	0S	109E	-7:16
Paoting, China	39N	115E	-7:40	Poole, G Britain	51N	2W	0:08
Paotou (Paotow), China	41N	110E	-7:20	Poona, India	19N	74E	-4:56
Papeete, Tahiti	18S	150W	10:00	Pori, Finland	61N	22E	-1:28
Papenburg, W Germany	53N	7E	-0:28	Port Arthur, Canada	48N	89W	5:56
Para, Brazil	1S	48W	3:12	Port Arthur-Dairen, China	39N	121E	-8:04
Paramaribo, Surinam	6N	55W	3:40	Port Au Prince, Haiti	19N	72W	4:48
Parana, Argentina	32S	61W	4:04	Port Elizabeth, S Africa	34S	26E	-1:44
Pardubice, Czech	50N	16E	-1:04	Port Harcourt, Nigeria	5N	7E	-0:28
Paris, France	49N	2E	-0:08	Port Louis, Mauritius	20S	58E	-3:52
Parma, Italy	45N	10E	-0:40	Port Moresby, Papua	10S	147E	-9:48
Pasto, Colombia	1N	77W	5:08	Port Of Spain, Trinidad	11N	62W	4:08
Patna, India	26N	85E	-5:40	Port Said, Egypt	31N	32E	-2:08
Patrai (Patras), Greece	38N	22E	-1:28	Port Sudan, Sudan	20N	37E	-2:28
Pau, France	43N	0W	0:00	Port Talbot, G Britain	52N	4W	0:16
Pavia, Italy	45N	9E	-0:36	Porto Alegre, Brazil	30S	51W	3:24
Pavlodar, USSR	52N	77E	-5:08	Porto Novo, Dahomey	6N	3E	-0:12
Paysandu, Uruguay	32S	58W	3:52	Porto, Portugal	41N	9W	0:36
Pecs, Hungary	46N	18E	-1:12	Portsmouth, G Britain	51N	1W	0:04
Peking, (Peiping), China	40N	116E	-7:44	Posadas, Argentina	27S	56W	3:44
Pelotas, Brazil	32S	52W	3:28	Posen, Poland	52N	17E	-1:08
Penang, Malaysia	5N	100E	-6:40	Poshan, China	36N	118E	-7:52
Penchi (Penki), China	41N	124E	-8:16	Potosi, Bolivia	20S	66W	4:24
Penza, USSR	53N	45E	-3:00	Poznan, Poland	52N	17E	-1:08
Pereira, Colombia	5N	76W	5:04	Praha (Prague), Czech	50N	14E	-0:56
Perm, USSR	58N	56E	-3:44	Praia, Cabo Verde	15N	24W	1:36
Permskoye, USSR	51N	137E	-9:08	Prato, Italy	44N	11E	-0:44
Pernambuco, Brazil	8S	35W	2:20	Preston, G Britain	54N	3W	0:12
Perpignan, France	43N	3E	-0:12	Pretoria, S Africa	26S	28E	-1:52
Perth, Australia	32S	116E	-7:44	Prokopyevsk, USSR	54N	87E	-5:48
Perugia, Italy	43N	12E	-0:48	Proskurov, USSR	49N	27E	-1:48
Pescara, Italy	42N	14E	-0:56	Pskov, USSR	58N	28E	-1:52
Peshawar, Pakistan	34N	72E	-4:48	Puebla, Mexico	19N	98W	6:32
Petah Tiqwa, Israel	32N	35E	-2:20	Puerto Montt, Chile	41S	73W	4:52

CITY	LAT	LONG	TIME h m	CITY	LAT	LONG	TIME h m
unta Arenas, Chile	53S	71W	4:44	Rovno, USSR	51N	26E	-1:44
usan, S Korea	35N	129E	-8:36	Ruse (Ruschuk), Bulgaria	44N	26E	-1:44
yatigorsk, USSR	44N	43E	-2:52	Ryazan, USSR	55N	40E	-2:40
yongyang, N Korea	39N	126E	-8:24	Rybinsk, USSR	58N	39E	-2:36
azvin, Iran	36N	50E	-3:20	Saarbrucken, W Germany	49N	7E	-0:28
om, Iran	35N	51E	-3:24	Sabadell, Spain	42N	2E	-0:08
uebec, Canada	47N	71W	4:44	Safi, Morocco	32N	9W	0:36
ueretaro, Mexico	21N	100W	6:40	Saigon, Vietnam	11N	107E	-7:08
uetta, Pakistan	30N	67E	-4:28	Saint Catharines, Canada	43N	79W	5:16
uezaltenango, Guatemala	15N	92W	6:08	Saint Denis, Reunion	21S	55E	-3:40
uezon City, Philippines	15N	121E	-8:04	Saint Etienne, France	45N	4E	-0:16
uito, Ecuador	0S	79W	5:16	Saint Gall, Switzerland	47N	9E	-0:36
um, Iram	35N	51E	-3:24	Saint Helens, G Britain	53N	3W	0:12
abat, Morocco	34N	7W	0:28	Saint Helier, G Britain	49N	2W	0:08
abaul, New Guinea	4S	152E	-10:08	Saint John, Canada	45N	66W	4:24
adom, Poland	51N	21E	-1:24	Saint John's, Canada	48N	53W	3:32
ajkot, India	22N	71E	-4:44	Saint Louis, Senegal	16N	17W	1:08
ancagua, Chile	34S	71W	4:44	Saint Nazaire, France	47N	2W	0:08
anders, Denmark	56N	10E	-0:40	Salamanca, Spain	41N	6W	0:24
angoon, Burma	17N	96E	-6:24	Salem, India	12N	78E	-5:12
asht, Iran	37N	50E	-3:20	Salerno, Italy	41N	15E	-1:00
avenna, Italy	44N	12E	-0:48	Salisbury, Zimbabwe	18S	31E	-2:04
awalpindi, Pakistan	34N	73E	-4:52	Salonica, Greece	41N	23E	-1:32
awson, Argentina	43S	65W	4:20	Salta, Argentina	25S	65W	4:20
eading, G Britain	51N	1W	0:04	Saltillo, Mexico	25N	101W	6:44
ecife, Brazil	8S	35W	2:20	Salto, Uruguay	31S	58W	3:52
ecklinghausen, W Germany	52N	7E	-0:28	Salvador, Brazil	13S	39W	2:36
egensburg, W Germany	49N	12E	-0:48	Salzburg, Austria	48N	13E	-0:52
eggio Calabria, Italy	38N	16E	-1:04	Salzgitter, W Germany	52N	10E	-0:40
eggio Emilia, Italy	45N	11E	-0:44	Samara, USSR	53N	50E	-3:20
egina, Canada	50N	105W	7:00	Samarang, Indonesia	7S	110E	-7:20
eims, France	49N	4E	-0:16	Samarkand, USSR	40N	67E	-4:28
emscheid, W Germany	51N	7E	-0:28	Samsun, Turkey	41N	36E	-2:24
ennes, France	48N	2W	0:08	San Cristobal, Venezuela	8N	72W	4:48
esistencia, Argentina	27S	59W	3:56	San Fernando, Trinidad	10N	61W	4:04
esita, Rumania	45N	22E	-1:28	San Jose, Costa Rica	10N	84W	5:36
eutlingen, W Germany	48N	9E	-0:36	San Juan, Argentina	31S	69W	4:36
eval, USSR	59N	25E	-1:40	San Juan, Puerto Rico	18N	66W	4:24
eykjavik, Iceland	64N	22W	1:28	San Luis Potosi, Mexico	22N	101W	6:44
ezaiyeh, Iran	38N	45E	-3:00	San Marino, San Marino	44N	12E	-0:48
heims, France	49N	4E	-0:16	San Miguel De Tucuman, Arg	27S	65W	4:20
hodes (Rodhos), Greece	36N	28E	-1:52	San Salvador, El Salvador	14N	89W	5:56
hondda, G Britain	52N	3W	0:12	San Sebastian, Spain	43N	2W	0:08
ibeirao Preto, Brazil	21S	48W	3:12	Sana (Sana'a), Yemen	15N	44E	-2:56
iga, USSR	57N	24E	-1:36	Sancti Spiritus, Cuba	22N	79W	5:16
ijeka, Yugoslavia	45N	14E	-0:56	Sankt Gallen, Switzerland	47N	9E	-0:36
imini, Italy	44N	13E	-0:52	Santa Ana, El Salvador	14N	90W	6:00
io De Janeiro, Brazil	23S	43W	2:52	Santa Clara, Cuba	22N	80W	5:20
io Grande, Brazil	32S	52W	3:28	Santa Cruz De Tenerife, Sp	28N	16W	1:04
iyadh, Saudi Arabia	25N	47E	-3:08	Santa Cruz, Bolivia	18S	63W	4:12
oanne, France	46N	4E	-0:16	Santa Fe, Argentina	32S	61W	4:04
ochdale, G Britain	54N	2W	0:08	Santa Isabel, Eq Guinea	4N	9E	-0:36
ochester, G Britain	51N	1E	-0:04	Santa Maria, Brazil	30S	54W	3:36
odhos, Greece	36N	28E	-1:52	Santa Marta, Colombia	11N	74W	4:56
oma (Rome), Italy	42N	12E	-0:48	Santander, Spain	43N	4W	0:16
onne, Denmark	55N	15E	-1:00	Santiago De Cuba, Cuba	20N	76W	5:04
osario, Argentina	33S	61W	4:04	Santiago Del Estero, Argen	28S	64W	4:16
ostock, E Germany	54N	12E	-0:48	Santiago, Chile	33S	71W	4:44
ostov Na Donu, USSR	47N	40E	-2:40	Santiago, Dominican Rep	19N	71W	4:44
otherham, G Britain	53N	1W	0:04	Santo Domingo, Dominican Rep	18N	70W	4:40
otterdam, Netherlands	52N	4E	-0:16	Santo Tome De Guayana, Ven	8N	63W	4:12
oubaix, France	51N	3E	-0:12	Santos, Brazil	24S	46W	3:04
ouen, France	49N	1E	-0:04	Sao Luis, Brazil	3S	44W	2:56

CITY	LAT	LONG	TIME h m	CITY	LAT	LONG	TIME h m
Sao Paulo De Loanda, Angola	9S	13E	-0:52	Sosnowiec, Poland	50N	19E	-1:16
Sao Paulo, Brazil	24S	47W	3:08	Soul, S Korea	38N	127E	-8:28
Sapporo, Japan	43N	141E	-9:24	South Shields, G Britain	55N	1W	0:04
Saragossa, Spain	42N	1W	0:04	Southampton, G Britain	51N	1W	0:04
Sarajevo, Yugoslavia	44N	18E	-1:12	Southend On Sea, G Britain	52N	1E	-0:04
Saransk, USSR	54N	45E	-3:00	Southport, G Britain	54N	3W	0:12
Saratov, USSR	52N	46E	-3:04	Split (Spalato) Yugoslavia	44N	16E	-1:04
Sasebo, Japan	33N	130E	-8:40	Springs, S Africa	26S	28E	-1:52
Saskatoon, Canada	52N	107W	7:08	Srinagar, India	34N	75E	-5:00
Sassari, Italy	41N	9E	-0:36	Stalinabad, USSR	39N	69E	-4:36
Sault Sainte Marie, Canada	47N	84W	5:36	Stalingrad, USSR	49N	44E	-2:56
Savona, Italy	44N	8E	-0:32	Stalino, USSR	48N	38E	-2:32
Schweinfurt, W Germany	50N	10E	-0:40	Stalinogorsk, USSR	54N	38E	-2:32
Schwerin, E Germany	54N	11E	-0:44	Stalinsk, USSR	54N	87E	-5:48
Scutari, Albania	42N	19E	-1:16	Stanleyville, Zaire	0N	25E	-1:40
Scutari, Turkey	41N	29E	-1:56	Stara Zagora, Bulgaria	42N	26E	-1:44
Sebastopol, USSR	45N	34E	-2:16	Stavanger, Norway	59N	6E	-0:24
Sekondi-Takoradi, Ghana	5N	2W	0:08	Stavropol, USSR	45N	42E	-2:48
Semarang, Indonesia	7S	110E	-7:20	Sterlitamak, USSR	54N	56E	-3:44
Semipalatinsk, USSR	50N	80E	-5:20	Stettin, Poland	53N	15E	-1:00
Sendai, Japan	38N	141E	-9:24	Stockholm , Sweden	59N	18E	-1:12
Seoul, S Korea	38N	127E	-8:28	Stockton On Tees, G Britain	55N	1W	0:04
Setif, Algeria	36N	5E	-0:20	Stoke On Trent, G Britain	53N	2W	0:08
Sevastopol, USSR	45N	34E	-2:16	Strasbourg, France	49N	8E	-0:32
Sevilla (Seville), Spain	37N	6W	0:24	Stuttgart, W Germany	49N	9E	-0:36
Sfax, Tunisia	35N	11E	-0:44	Subotica, Yugoslavia	46N	20E	-1:20
's Gravenhage, Netherlands	52N	4E	-0:16	Suchow, China	34N	117E	-7:48
Shanghai, China	31N	121E	-8:04	Sucre, Bolivia	19S	65W	4:20
Shantou, China	23N	117E	-7:48	Sudbury, Canada	47N	81W	5:24
Shawinigan, Canada	47N	73W	4:52	Suez, Egypt	30N	33E	-2:12
Sheffield, G Britain	53N	2W	0:08	Sukarnapura, Indonesia	3S	141E	-9:24
Shenyang, China	42N	123E	-8:12	Sukhumi, USSR	43N	41E	-2:44
Sherbrooke, Canada	45N	72W	4:48	Sultanabad, Iran	34N	50E	-3:20
's Hertogenbosch,Netherland	52N	5E	-0:20	Sumy, USSR	51N	35E	-2:20
Shihchiachuang, China	38N	114E	-7:36	Sunderland, G Britain	55N	1W	0:04
Shimizu, Japan	35N	138E	-9:12	Sundsvall, Sweden	62N	17E	-1:08
Shimonoseki, Japan	34N	131E	-8:44	Surabaja, Indonesia	7S	113E	-7:32
Shiraz, Iran	30N	53E	-3:32	Surakarta, Indonesia	8S	111E	-7:24
Shizuoka, Japan	35N	138E	-9:12	Surat, India	21N	73E	-4:52
Shkoder, Albania	42N	19E	-1:16	Suva, Fiji	18S	178E	-11:52
Sholapur, India	18N	76E	-5:04	Sverdlovsk, USSR	57N	61E	-4:04
Sian, China	34N	109E	-7:16	Swansea, G Britain	52N	4W	0:16
Siangtan, China	28N	113E	-7:32	Swatow, China	23N	117E	-7:48
Siauliai, USSR	56N	23E	-1:32	Swindon, G Britain	52N	2W	0:08
Sibiu, Rumania	46N	24E	-1:36	Sydney, Australia	34S	151E	-10:04
Sidi Bel Abbes, Algeria	35N	1W	0:04	Sydney, Canada	46N	60W	4:00
Siegen, W Germany	51N	8E	-0:32	Syktyvkar, USSR	62N	51E	-3:24
Simbirsk, USSR	54N	48E	-3:12	Syracuse, Italy	37N	15E	-1:00
Simferopol, USSR	45N	34E	-2:16	Syzran, USSR	53N	48E	-3:12
Singapore, Singapore	1N	104E	-6:56	Szczecin, Poland	53N	15E	-1:00
Sining, China	37N	102E	-6:48	Szeged (Szegedin), Hungary	46N	20E	-1:20
Siracusa, Italy	37N	15E	-1:00	Szekesfehervar, Hungary	47N	18E	-1:12
Sivas, Turkey	40N	37E	-2:28	Tabriz, Iran	38N	46E	-3:04
Skien, Norway	59N	10E	-0:40	Taegu, S Korea	36N	129E	-8:36
Skikda, Algeria	37N	7E	-0:28	Taejon, S Korea	36N	127E	-8:28
Skopje (Skoplje), Yug	42N	21E	-1:24	Taganrog, USSR	47N	39E	-2:36
Smolensk, USSR	55N	32E	-2:08	Taichung, Taiwan	24N	121E	-8:04
Smyrna, Turkey	38N	27E	-1:48	Tainan, Taiwan	23N	120E	-8:00
Sochi, USSR	44N	40E	-2:40	Taipei, Taiwan	25N	122E	-8:08
Sofiya (Sofia), Bulgaria	43N	23E	-1:32	Taiyuan, China	38N	113E	-7:32
Solingen, W Germany	51N	7E	-0:28	Takamatsu, Japan	34N	134E	-8:56
Soochow, China	31N	121E	-8:04	Talca, Chile	35S	72W	4:48
Sorocaba, Brazil	23S	47W	3:08	Tallinn, USSR	59N	25E	-1:40

CITY	LAT	LONG	TIME h m	CITY	LAT	LONG	TIME h m
Tamatave, Malagasy Rep	18S	49E	-3:16	Tours, France	47N	1E	-0:04
Tambov, USSR	53N	41E	-2:44	Toyama, Japan	37N	137E	-9:08
Tampere(Tammersfors)Finland	62N	24E	-1:36	Toyohashi, Japan	35N	137E	-9:08
Tampico, Mexico	22N	98W	6:32	Trento, Italy	46N	11E	-0:44
Tananarive, Malagasy Rep	19S	48E	-3:12	Treves, W Germany	50N	7E	-0:28
Tanga, Tanzania	5S	39E	-2:36	Treviso, Italy	46N	12E	-0:48
Tanger (Tangier), Morocco	36N	6W	0:24	Trichinopoly, India	11N	79E	-5:16
Tangshan, China	40N	118E	-7:52	Trier, W Germany	50N	7E	-0:28
Tanta, Egypt	31N	31E	-2:04	Trieste, Italy	46N	14E	-0:56
Tantung, China	40N	124E	-8:16	Tripoli, Lebanon	34N	36E	-2:24
Tarabulus, Lebanon	34N	36E	-2:24	Tripoli, Libya	33N	13E	-0:52
Tarabulus, Libya	33N	13E	-0:52	Trivandrum, India	8N	77E	-5:08
Taranto, Italy	40N	17E	-1:08	Trois Rivieres, Canada	46N	73W	4:52
Tarbes, France	43N	0E	0:00	Tromso, Norway	70N	19E	-1:16
Tarlac, Philippines	15N	121E	-8:04	Trondheim, Norway	63N	10E	-0:40
Tarnopol, USSR	50N	26E	-1:44	Troyes, France	48N	4E	-0:16
Tarnow, Poland	50N	21E	-1:24	Trujillo, Peru	8S	79W	5:16
Tarrasa, Spain	42N	2E	-0:08	Tsaritsyn, USSR	49N	44E	-2:56
Tartu, USSR	58N	27E	-1:48	Tschenstochau, Poland	51N	19E	-1:16
Tashkent, USSR	41N	69E	-4:36	Tselinograd, USSR	51N	72E	-4:48
Tasikmalaja, Indonesnia	7S	108E	-7:12	Tsinan, China	37N	117E	-7:48
Tatung, China	40N	113E	-7:32	Tsingtao, China	36N	120E	-8:00
Tbilisi, USSR	42N	45E	-3:00	Tsingyuan, China	39N	115E	-7:40
Tegucigalpa, Honduras	14N	87W	5:48	Tsitsihar, China	47N	124E	-8:16
Tehran (Teheran), Iran	36N	51E	-3:24	Tsuni, China	28N	107E	-7:08
Tel Aviv, Israel	32N	35E	-2:20	Tucuman, Argentina	27S	65W	4:20
Telukbetung, Indonesia	5S	105E	-7:00	Tula, USSR	54N	38E	-2:32
Temesvar, Rumania	46N	21E	-1:24	Tulear, Malagasy Rep	23S	44E	-2:56
Temuco, Chile	39S	73W	4:52	Tunis, Tunesia	37N	10E	-0:40
Tepic, Mexico	22N	105W	7:00	Turin, Italy	45N	8E	-0:32
Teresina, Brazil	5S	43W	2:52	Turku, Finland	60N	22E	-1:28
Terni, Italy	43N	13E	-0:52	Tver, USSR	57N	36E	-2:24
Ternopol, USSR	50N	26E	-1:44	Tyumen, USSR	57N	66E	-4:24
Tetouan, Morocco	36N	5W	0:20	Tzukung (Tzekung), China	29N	105E	-7:00
The Hague, Netherlands	52N	4E	-0:16	Ube, Japan	34N	131E	-8:44
Thessaloniki, Greece	41N	23E	-1:32	Uberaba, Brazil	20S	48W	3:12
Thimbu, Bhutan	27N	90E	-6:00	Udine, Italy	46N	13E	-0:52
Three Rivers, Canada	46N	73W	4:52	Ufa, USSR	55N	56E	-3:44
Thunder Bay, Canada	48N	89W	5:56	Ulaanbaatar, Mong Rep	48N	107E	-7:08
Tienching (Tientsin), China	39N	117E	-7:48	Ulaangom, Mong Rep	50N	92E	-6:08
Tiflis, USSR	42N	45E	-3:00	Ulan-Ude, USSR	52N	108E	-7:12
Tihwa, China	44N	88E	-5:52	Uleaborg, Finland	65N	25E	-1:40
Tijuana, Mexico	33N	117W	7:48	Ulm, W Germany	48N	10E	-0:40
Tilburg, Netherlands	52N	5E	-0:20	Ulyanovsk, USSR	54N	48E	-3:12
Timisoara, Rumania	46N	21E	-1:24	Umea, Sweden	64N	20E	-1:20
Tirane (Tirana), Albania	41N	20E	-1:20	Uppsala, Sweden	60N	18E	-1:12
Tiraspol, USSR	47N	30E	-2:00	Uralsk, USSR	51N	51E	-3:24
Tirgu Mures, Rumania	47N	25E	-1:40	Urawa, Japan	36N	140E	-9:20
Tiruchchirappalli, India	11N	79E	-5:16	Urfa, Turkey	37N	39E	-2:36
Tjirebon, Indonesia	7S	109E	-7:16	Urga, Mongolian Rep	48N	107E	-7:08
Tlemcen, Algeria	35N	1W	0:04	Urmia, Iran	38N	45E	-3:00
Tokushima, Japan	34N	135E	-9:00	Urumchi, China	44N	88E	-5:52
Tokyo, Japan	36N	140E	-9:20	Uskudar, Turkey	41N	29E	-1:56
Toluca, Mexico	19N	100W	6:40	Ust Kamengorsk, USSR	50N	83E	-5:32
Tomsk, USSR	57N	85E	-5:40	Ust Sykolsk, USSR	62N	51E	-3:24
Torino, Italy	45N	8E	-0:32	Usti, Czech	51N	14E	-0:56
Toronto, Canada	44N	79W	5:16	Usumbura, Burundi	3S	29E	-1:56
Torquay, G Britain	50N	4W	0:16	Utrecht, Netherlands	52N	5E	-0:20
Torreon, Mexico	26N	103W	6:52	Utsunomiya, Japan	37N	140E	-9:20
Torun, Poland	53N	19E	-1:16	Vaasa, Finland	63N	22E	-1:28
Toulon, France	43N	6E	-0:24	Vaduz, Liechtenstein	47N	10E	-0:40
Toulouse, France	44N	1E	-0:04	Valdivia, Chile	40S	73W	4:52
Tourane, Vietnam	16N	108E	-7:12	Valence, France	45N	5E	-0:20

CITY	LAT	LONG	TIME h m	CITY	LAT	LONG	TIME h m
Valencia, Spain	39N	0W	0:00	Windhoek, S Africa	23S	17E	-1:08
Valencia, Venezuela	10N	68W	4:32	Windsor, Canada	42N	83W	5:32
Valenciennes, France	50N	4E	-0:16	Winnipeg, Canada	50N	97W	6:28
Valetta, Malta	36N	15E	-1:00	Winterthur, Switzerland	48N	9E	-0:36
Valladolid, Spain	42N	5W	0:20	Wloclawek, Poland	53N	19E	-1:16
Valledupar, Colombia	10N	73W	4:52	Wolfsburg, W Germany	52N	11E	-0:44
Valparaiso, Chile	33S	72W	4:48	Wollongong, Australia	34S	151E	-10:04
Vancouver, Canada	49N	123W	8:12	Wolverhampton, G Britain	53N	2W	0:08
Varanasi, India	25N	83E	-5:32	Worms, W Germany	50N	8E	-0:32
Varese, Italy	46N	9E	-0:36	Wroclaw, Poland	51N	17E	-1:08
Varna, Bulgaria	43N	28E	-1:52	Wuhan (Wuchang), China	31N	114E	-7:36
Vasteras, Sweden	60N	17E	-1:08	Wuhsi (Wuhsien), China	32N	120E	-8:00
Velikiye Luki, USSR	56N	31E	-2:04	Wuhu, China	31N	118E	-7:52
Venezia (Venice), Italy	45N	12E	-0:48	Wulumuchi, China	44N	88E	-5:52
Venlo, Netherlands	51N	6E	-0:24	Wuppertal, W Germany	51N	7E	-0:28
Veracruz, Mexico	19N	96W	6:24	Wurzburg, W Germany	50N	10E	-0:40
Verkhne Udinsk, USSR	52N	108E	-7:12	Yakutsk, USSR	62N	130E	-8:40
Verona, Italy	45N	11E	-0:44	Yamagata, Japan	38N	140E	-9:20
Versailles, France	49N	2E	-0:08	Yangchuan, China	38N	114E	-7:36
Verviers, Belgium	51N	6E	-0:24	Yangku, China	38N	113E	-7:32
Vevey Montreux,Switzerland	46N	7E	-0:28	Yaounde, Cameroun	4N	12E	-0:48
Vicenza, Italy	46N	12E	-0:48	Yaroslavl, USSR	58N	40E	-2:40
Victoria, Canada	48N	123W	8:12	Yazd, Iran	32N	54E	-3:36
Victoria, Hong Kong Terr	22N	114E	-7:36	Yelets, USSR	53N	39E	-2:36
Vienna, Austria	48N	16E	-1:04	Yerevan, USSR	40N	45E	-3:00
Vientiane, Laos	18N	103E	-6:52	Yezd, Iran	32N	54E	-3:36
Vigo, Spain	42N	9W	0:36	Yinchuan, China	39N	106E	-7:04
Viipuri, USSR	61N	29E	-1:56	Yokkaichi, Japan	35N	137E	-9:08
Vijayawada, India	17N	81E	-5:24	Yokohama, Japan	35N	140E	-9:20
Vila, New Hebrides	18S	168E	-11:12	Yokosuka, Japan	35N	140E	-9:20
Villahermosa, Mexico	18N	93W	6:12	York, G Britain	54N	1W	0:04
Vilnius, USSR	55N	25E	-1:40	Yoshkar Ola, USSR	57N	48E	-3:12
Vinnitsa, USSR	49N	28E	-1:52	Yumen, China	40N	98E	-6:32
Vitebsk, USSR	55N	30E	-2:00	Yungkia, China	28N	121E	-8:04
Vitoria, Brazil	20S	40W	2:40	Yungning, China	23N	108E	-7:12
Vitoria, Spain	43N	3W	0:12	Yunnan(Yunnanfou)China	25N	103E	-6:52
Vladikavkaz, USSR	43N	45E	-3:00	Yuzhno Sakhalinsk, USSR	47N	143E	-9:32
Vladimir, USSR	56N	40E	-2:40	Yuzovka, USSR	48N	38E	-2:32
Vladivostok, USSR	43N	132E	-8:48	Zabrze, Poland	50N	19E	-1:16
Volgograd, USSR	49N	44E	-2:56	Zagazig, Egypt	31N	32E	-2:08
Vologda, USSR	59N	40E	-2:40	Zagreb, Yugoslavia	46N	16E	-1:04
Volos, Greece	39N	23E	-1:32	Zahedan, Iran	30N	61E	-4:04
Voronezh, USSR	52N	39E	-2:36	Zamboanga, Philippines	7N	122E	-8:08
Voroshilovgrad, USSR	49N	39E	-2:36	Zanzibar, Tanzania	6S	39E	-2:36
Voroshilov (Ussuriysk)USSR	44N	132E	-8:48	Zaporozhye, USSR	48N	35E	-2:20
Voroshilovsk, USSR	45N	42E	-2:48	Zaragoza, Spain	42N	1W	0:04
Vyatka, USSR	59N	50E	-3:20	Zaria, Nigeria	11N	8E	-0:32
Vyborg, USSR	61N	29E	-1:56	Zhdanov, USSR	47N	38E	-2:32
Wad Medani, Sudan	14N	33E	-2:12	Zhitomir, USSR	50N	29E	-1:56
Wakayama, Japan	34N	135E	-9:00	Zlatoust, USSR	55N	60E	-4:00
Walbrzych(Waldenburg)Poland	51N	16E	-1:04	Zlin, Czech	49N	18E	-1:12
Walsall, G Britain	53N	2W	0:08	Zomba, Malawi	15S	35E	-2:20
Wanchuan, China	41N	115E	-7:40	Zurich, Switzerland	47N	9E	-0:36
Warrington, G Britain	53N	3W	0:12	Zwickau, E Germany	51N	13E	-0:52
Warszawa (Warsaw), Poland	52N	21E	-1:24	Zwolle, Netherlands	53N	6E	-0:24
Welkom, S Africa	28S	27E	-1:48				
Wellington, N Zealand	41S	175E	-11:40				
Wenchou, China	28N	121E	-8:04				
Wien, Austria	48N	16E	-1:04				
Wiesbaden, W Germany	50N	8E	-0:32				
Wilhelmshaven, W Germany	54N	8E	-0:32				
Willemstad, Curacao	12N	69W	4:36				
Wilno, USSR	55N	25E	-1:40				

TABLES OF HOUSES

TABLES DES MAISONS

HÄUSERTABELLEN

TABLAS DE CASAS

LATITUDE 1° N.   LATITUDE 2° N.   LATITUDE 3° N.

Columns for each latitude block: **10 ♈ | 11 ♉ | 12 ♊ | ASC ♋ | 2 ♋ | 3 ♌**

SIDEREAL TIME (H M S)	10 ♈	11 ♉	12 ♊	ASC ♋	2 ♋	3 ♌	10 ♈	11 ♉	12 ♊	ASC ♋	2 ♋	3 ♌	10 ♈	11 ♉	12 ♊	ASC ♋	2 ♋	3 ♌
0 0 0	0	2	2	0 24	28	28	0	2	3	0 48	28	28	0	2	3	1 12	29	28
0 3 40	1	3	3	1 14	29	29	1	3	3	1 38	29	29	1	3	4	2 2	29	29
0 7 20	2	4	4	2 5	♌	♍	2	4	4	2 29	♌	♍	2	4	5	2 53	♌	♍
0 11 1	3	5	5	2 55	1	1	3	5	5	3 19	1	1	3	5	5	3 43	1	1
0 14 41	4	6	6	3 46	2	2	4	6	6	4 10	2	2	4	6	6	4 34	2	2
0 18 21	5	7	7	4 37	3	3	5	7	7	5 0	3	3	5	7	7	5 24	3	3
0 22 2	6	8	8	5 27	3	4	6	8	8	5 51	4	4	6	8	8	6 15	4	4
0 25 43	7	9	8	6 18	4	5	7	9	9	6 42	5	5	7	9	9	7 5	5	5
0 29 23	8	10	9	7 8	5	6	8	10	10	7 32	5	6	8	10	10	7 56	6	6
0 33 4	9	11	10	7 59	6	7	9	11	10	8 23	6	7	9	11	11	8 47	7	7
0 36 45	10	12	11	8 50	7	8	10	12	11	9 14	7	8	10	12	12	9 37	7	8
0 40 27	11	13	12	9 41	8	9	11	13	12	10 5	8	9	11	13	12	10 28	8	9
0 44 8	12	14	13	10 32	9	10	12	14	13	10 56	9	10	12	14	13	11 19	9	10
0 47 50	13	15	14	11 23	10	11	13	15	14	11 47	10	11	13	15	14	12 10	10	11
0 51 32	14	15	14	12 15	11	11	14	16	15	12 38	11	12	14	16	15	13 1	11	12
0 55 15	15	16	15	13 6	12	12	15	16	16	13 29	12	13	15	17	16	13 52	12	13
0 58 57	16	17	16	13 57	12	13	16	17	16	14 21	13	14	16	18	17	14 44	13	14
1 2 40	17	18	17	14 49	13	14	17	18	17	15 12	14	15	17	18	18	15 35	14	15
1 6 24	18	19	18	15 41	14	15	18	19	18	16 4	15	16	18	19	18	16 27	15	16
1 10 8	19	20	19	16 33	15	16	19	20	19	16 56	15	17	19	20	19	17 19	16	17
1 13 52	20	21	20	17 25	16	17	20	21	20	17 48	16	18	20	21	20	18 11	17	18
1 17 36	21	22	21	18 17	17	19	21	22	21	18 40	17	19	21	22	21	19 3	18	19
1 21 21	22	23	21	19 10	18	20	22	23	22	19 32	18	20	22	23	22	19 55	18	20
1 25 7	23	24	22	20 2	19	21	23	24	23	20 25	19	21	23	24	23	20 47	19	21
1 28 52	24	25	23	20 55	20	22	24	25	23	21 18	20	22	24	25	24	21 40	20	22
1 32 39	25	26	24	21 48	21	23	25	26	24	22 11	21	23	25	26	25	22 33	21	23
1 36 26	26	27	25	22 41	22	24	26	27	25	23 4	22	24	26	27	25	23 26	22	24
1 40 13	27	27	26	23 35	23	25	27	28	26	23 57	23	25	27	28	26	24 19	23	25
1 44 1	28	28	27	24 29	24	26	28	28	27	24 51	24	26	28	29	27	25 12	24	26
1 47 49	29	29	27	25 23	25	27	29	29	28	25 44	25	27	29	♊	28	26 6	25	27
1 51 38	♉	♊	28	26 17	26	28	♉	♊	29	26 39	26	28	♉	0	29	27 0	26	28
1 55 28	1	1	29	27 11	27	29	1	1	29	27 33	27	29	1	1	♋	27 54	27	29
1 59 18	2	2	♋	28 6	28	♎	2	2	♋	28 27	28	♎	2	2	1	28 49	28	♎
2 3 9	3	3	1	29 1	29	1	3	3	1	29 22	29	1	3	3	2	29 43	29	1
2 7 0	4	4	2	29 56	♍	2	4	4	2	0♌ 17	♍	2	4	4	2	0♌ 38	♍	2
2 10 52	5	5	3	0♌ 52	1	3	5	5	3	1 13	1	3	5	5	3	1 33	1	3
2 14 45	6	6	4	1 48	2	4	6	6	4	2 8	2	4	6	6	4	2 29	2	4
2 18 38	7	7	5	2 44	3	5	7	7	5	3 4	3	5	7	7	5	3 25	3	5
2 22 32	8	8	5	3 40	4	6	8	8	6	4 0	4	6	8	8	6	4 21	4	6
2 26 26	9	8	6	4 37	5	7	9	9	7	4 57	5	7	9	9	7	5 17	5	7
2 30 22	10	9	7	5 34	6	8	10	10	7	5 54	6	8	10	10	8	6 14	6	8
2 34 17	11	10	8	6 31	7	9	11	10	8	6 51	7	9	11	11	9	7 10	7	9
2 38 14	12	11	9	7 29	8	10	12	11	9	7 48	8	10	12	12	10	8 8	8	10
2 42 11	13	12	10	8 27	9	11	13	12	10	8 46	9	11	13	12	10	9 5	9	11
2 46 10	14	13	11	9 25	10	13	14	13	11	9 44	10	12	14	13	11	10 3	10	12
HOUSES	4	5	6	7	8	9	4	5	6	7	8	9	4	5	6	7	8	9

LATITUDE 1° S.   LATITUDE 2° S.   LATITUDE 3° S.

LATITUDE 1° N.   LATITUDE 2° N.   LATITUDE 3° N.

SIDEREAL TIME	10 ♉	11 ♊	12 ♋	ASC ♌	2 ♍	3 ♎	10 ♉	11 ♊	12 ♋	ASC ♌	2 ♍	3 ♎	10 ♉	11 ♊	12 ♋	ASC ♌	2 ♍	3 ♎
H M S	°	°	°	° '	°	°	°	°	°	° '	°	°	°	°	°	° '	°	°
2 50 8	15	14	12	10 24	11	14	15	14	12	10 43	11	14	15	14	12	11 1	11	14
2 54 8	16	15	13	11 23	12	15	16	15	13	11 42	12	15	16	15	13	12 0	12	15
2 58 8	17	16	14	12 23	13	16	17	16	14	12 41	13	16	17	16	14	12 59	13	16
3 2 9	18	17	15	13 22	14	17	18	17	15	13 40	14	17	18	17	15	13 58	15	17
3 6 10	19	18	16	14 22	15	18	19	18	16	14 40	16	18	19	18	16	14 58	16	18
3 10 13	20	19	16	15 23	17	19	20	19	17	15 40	17	19	20	19	17	15 57	17	19
3 14 16	21	20	17	16 24	18	20	21	20	18	16 41	18	20	21	20	18	16 58	18	20
3 18 20	22	21	18	17 25	19	21	22	21	19	17 42	19	21	22	21	19	17 58	19	21
3 22 24	23	21	19	18 26	20	22	23	22	20	18 43	20	22	23	22	20	18 59	20	22
3 26 30	24	22	20	19 28	21	23	24	23	20	19 44	21	23	24	23	21	20 0	21	23
3 30 36	25	23	21	20 31	22	24	25	24	21	20 46	22	24	25	24	22	21 2	22	24
3 34 42	26	24	22	21 33	23	25	26	24	22	21 49	23	25	26	25	23	22 4	23	25
3 38 50	27	25	23	22 36	24	27	27	25	23	22 51	24	27	27	26	24	23 6	24	26
3 42 58	28	26	24	23 40	25	28	28	26	24	23 54	25	28	28	26	25	24 9	25	28
3 47 7	29	27	25	24 43	27	29	29	27	25	24 58	27	29	29	27	26	25 12	27	29
3 51 16	♊	28	26	25 47	28	♏	♊	28	26	26 1	28	♏	♊	28	27	26 15	28	♏
3 55 26	1	29	27	26 52	29	1	1	29	27	27 6	29	1	1	29	28	27 19	29	1
3 59 37	2	♋	28	27 57	♎	2	2	♋	28	28 10	♎	2	2	♋	29	28 23	♎	2
4 3 49	3	1	29	29 2	1	3	3	1	29	29 15	1	3	3	1	♌	29 28	1	3
4 8 1	4	2	♌	0♍ 7	2	4	4	2	♌	0♍ 20	2	4	4	2	1	0♍ 32	2	4
4 12 14	5	3	1	1 13	3	5	5	3	1	1 25	3	5	5	3	2	1 37	3	5
4 16 27	6	4	2	2 19	4	6	6	4	2	2 31	4	6	6	4	3	2 43	4	6
4 20 41	7	5	3	3 26	6	7	7	5	3	3 37	6	7	7	5	4	3 48	6	7
4 24 56	8	6	4	4 33	7	9	8	6	4	4 43	7	8	8	6	5	4 54	7	8
4 29 11	9	7	5	5 40	8	10	9	7	5	5 50	8	10	9	7	6	6 0	8	9
4 33 27	10	8	6	6 47	9	11	10	8	6	6 57	9	11	10	8	7	7 7	9	11
4 37 43	11	9	7	7 55	10	12	11	9	7	8 4	10	12	11	9	8	8 14	10	12
4 41 59	12	10	8	9 3	11	13	12	10	9	9 12	11	13	12	10	9	9 21	11	13
4 46 17	13	11	9	10 11	13	14	13	11	10	10 20	12	14	13	11	10	10 28	12	14
4 50 34	14	12	10	11 19	14	15	14	12	11	11 28	14	15	14	12	11	11 36	14	15
4 54 53	15	13	11	12 28	15	16	15	13	12	12 36	15	16	15	13	12	12 44	15	16
4 59 11	16	14	13	13 37	16	17	16	14	13	13 44	16	17	16	14	13	13 52	16	17
5 3 30	17	15	14	14 46	17	18	17	15	14	14 53	17	18	17	15	14	15 0	17	18
5 7 49	18	16	15	15 56	18	19	18	16	15	16 2	18	19	18	16	15	16 8	18	19
5 12 9	19	17	16	17 6	19	20	19	17	16	17 11	19	20	19	17	16	17 17	19	20
5 16 29	20	18	17	18 15	21	21	20	18	17	18 21	21	21	20	18	17	18 26	20	21
5 20 49	21	19	18	19 25	22	23	21	19	18	19 30	22	22	21	19	18	19 35	22	22
5 25 10	22	20	19	20 35	23	24	22	20	19	20 40	23	23	22	20	19	20 44	23	23
5 29 31	23	21	20	21 46	24	25	23	21	20	21 49	24	25	23	21	21	21 53	24	24
5 33 51	24	22	21	22 56	25	26	24	22	21	22 59	25	26	24	22	22	23 2	25	25
5 38 13	25	23	22	24 7	26	27	25	23	23	24 9	26	27	25	23	23	24 12	26	27
5 42 34	26	24	23	25 17	27	28	26	24	24	25 19	27	28	26	24	24	25 21	27	28
5 46 55	27	25	25	26 28	29	29	27	25	25	26 29	28	29	27	25	25	26 31	28	29
5 51 17	28	26	26	27 39	♏	♐	28	26	26	27 40	♏	♐	28	26	26	27 41	29	♐
5 55 38	29	27	27	28 49	1	1	29	27	27	28 50	1	1	29	27	27	28 50	♏	1
HOUSES	4	5	6	7	8	9	4	5	6	7	8	9	4	5	6	7	8	9

LATITUDE 1° S.   LATITUDE 2° S.   LATITUDE 3° S.

LATITUDE 1° N. LATITUDE 2° N. LATITUDE 3° N.

SIDEREAL TIME	10 ♋	11 ♋	12 ♌	ASC ♎	2 ♏	3 ♐	10 ♋	11 ♋	12 ♌	ASC ♎	2 ♏	3 ♐	10 ♋	11 ♋	12 ♌	ASC ♎	2 ♏	3 ♐
H M S	°	°	°	° ′	°	°	°	°	°	° ′	°	°	°	°	°	° ′	°	°
6 0 0	0	28	28	0 0	2	2	0	28	28	0 0	2	2	0	28	28	0 0	2	2
6 4 22	1	29	29	1 11	3	3	1	29	29	1 10	3	3	1	29	29	1 10	3	3
6 8 43	2	Ω	m	2 21	4	4	2	Ω	m	2 20	4	4	2	Ω	m	2 19	4	4
6 13 5	3	1	1	3 32	5	5	3	1	2	3 31	5	5	3	1	2	3 29	5	5
6 17 26	4	2	3	4 43	7	6	4	2	3	4 41	6	6	4	2	3	4 39	6	6
6 21 47	5	3	4	5 53	8	7	5	3	4	5 51	7	7	5	3	4	5 48	7	7
6 26 9	6	4	5	7 4	9	8	6	4	5	7 1	9	8	6	5	5	6 58	8	8
6 30 29	7	5	6	8 14	10	9	7	5	6	8 11	10	9	7	6	6	8 7	9	9
6 34 50	8	6	7	9 25	11	10	8	7	7	9 20	11	10	8	7	7	9 16	11	10
6 39 11	9	7	8	10 35	12	11	9	8	8	10 30	12	11	9	8	8	10 25	12	11
6 43 31	10	9	9	11 45	13	12	10	9	9	11 39	13	12	10	9	10	11 34	13	12
6 47 51	11	10	11	12 54	14	13	11	10	11	12 49	14	13	11	10	11	12 43	14	13
6 52 11	12	11	12	14 4	15	14	12	11	12	13 58	15	14	12	11	12	13 52	15	14
6 56 30	13	12	13	15 14	16	15	13	12	13	15 7	16	15	13	12	13	15 0	16	15
7 0 49	14	13	14	16 23	17	16	14	13	14	16 16	17	16	14	13	14	16 8	17	16
7 5 7	15	14	15	17 32	19	17	15	14	15	17 24	18	17	15	14	15	17 16	18	17
7 9 26	16	15	16	18 41	20	18	16	15	16	18 32	19	18	16	15	16	18 24	19	18
7 13 43	17	16	17	19 49	21	19	17	16	18	19 40	20	19	17	16	18	19 32	20	19
7 18 0	18	17	19	20 57	22	20	18	17	19	20 48	21	20	18	17	19	20 39	21	20
7 22 17	19	18	20	22 5	23	21	19	18	20	21 56	23	21	19	18	20	21 46	22	21
7 26 33	20	19	21	23 13	24	22	20	19	21	23 3	24	22	20	19	21	22 53	23	22
7 30 49	21	20	22	24 20	25	23	21	20	22	24 10	25	23	21	21	22	24 0	24	23
7 35 4	22	21	23	25 27	26	24	22	22	23	25 17	26	24	22	22	23	25 6	25	24
7 39 19	23	23	24	26 34	27	25	23	23	24	26 23	27	25	23	23	24	26 12	26	25
7 43 33	24	24	26	27 41	28	26	24	24	26	27 29	28	26	24	24	26	27 17	27	26
7 47 46	25	25	27	28 47	29	27	25	25	27	28 35	29	27	25	25	27	28 23	28	27
7 51 59	26	26	28	29 53	♐	28	26	26	28	29 40	♐	28	26	26	28	29 28	29	28
7 56 11	27	27	29	0m 58	1	29	27	27	29	0m 45	1	29	27	27	29	0m 32	♐	29
8 0 23	28	28	♎	2 3	2	♑	28	28	♎	1 50	2	♑	28	28	♎	1 37	1	♑
8 4 34	29	29	1	3 8	3	1	29	29	1	2 54	3	1	29	29	1	2 41	2	1
8 8 44	Ω	m	2	4 13	4	2	Ω	m	2	3 59	4	2	Ω	m	2	3 45	3	2
8 12 53	1	1	3	5 17	5	3	1	1	3	5 2	5	3	1	1	3	4 48	4	3
8 17 2	2	2	5	6 20	6	4	2	2	5	6 6	6	4	2	2	5	5 51	5	4
8 21 10	3	3	6	7 24	7	5	3	3	6	7 9	7	5	3	4	6	6 54	6	4
8 25 18	4	5	7	8 27	8	6	4	5	7	8 11	8	6	4	5	7	7 56	7	5
8 29 24	5	6	8	9 29	9	7	5	6	8	9 14	9	6	5	6	8	8 58	8	6
8 33 30	6	7	9	10 32	10	8	6	7	9	10 16	10	7	6	7	9	10 0	9	7
8 37 36	7	8	10	11 34	11	9	7	8	10	11 17	10	8	7	8	10	11 1	10	8
8 41 40	8	9	11	12 35	12	9	8	9	11	12 18	11	9	8	9	11	12 2	11	9
8 45 44	9	10	12	13 36	13	10	9	10	12	13 19	12	10	9	10	12	13 2	12	10
8 49 47	10	11	13	14 37	14	11	10	11	13	14 20	13	11	10	11	13	14 3	13	11
8 53 50	11	12	15	15 38	14	12	11	12	14	15 20	14	12	11	12	14	15 2	14	12
8 57 51	12	13	16	16 38	15	13	12	13	16	16 20	15	13	12	13	15	16 2	15	13
9 1 52	13	14	17	17 37	16	14	13	14	17	17 19	16	14	13	14	17	17 1	16	14
9 5 52	14	15	18	18 37	17	15	14	15	18	18 18	17	15	14	15	18	18 0	17	15
HOUSES	4	5	6	7	8	9	4	5	6	7	8	9	4	5	6	7	8	9

LATITUDE 1° S. LATITUDE 2° S. LATITUDE 3° S.

LATITUDE 1° N.

SIDEREAL TIME (H M S)	10 Ω	11 ♍	12 ♎	ASC ♏ (° ')		2 ♐	3 ♑
9 9 52	15	16	19	19	36	18	16
9 13 50	16	17	20	20	35	19	17
9 17 49	17	19	21	21	33	20	18
9 21 46	18	20	22	22	31	21	19
9 25 42	19	21	23	23	29	22	20
9 29 38	20	22	24	24	26	23	21
9 33 34	21	23	25	25	23	24	22
9 37 28	22	24	26	26	20	25	22
9 41 22	23	25	27	27	16	25	23
9 45 15	24	26	28	28	12	26	24
9 49 8	25	27	29	29	8	27	25
9 53 0	26	28	♏	0♐	4	28	26
9 56 51	27	29	1	0	59	29	27
10 0 42	28	♎	2	1	54	♑	28
10 4 32	29	1	3	2	49	1	29
10 8 22	♍	2	4	3	43	2	♒
10 12 11	1	3	5	4	37	3	1
10 15 59	2	4	6	5	31	3	2
10 19 47	3	5	7	6	25	4	3
10 23 34	4	6	8	7	19	5	3
10 27 21	5	7	9	8	12	6	4
10 31 8	6	8	10	9	5	7	5
10 34 53	7	9	11	9	58	8	6
10 38 39	8	10	12	10	50	9	7
10 42 24	9	11	13	11	43	9	8
10 46 8	10	13	14	12	35	10	9
10 49 52	11	14	15	13	27	11	10
10 53 36	12	15	16	14	19	12	11
10 57 20	13	16	17	15	11	13	12
11 1 3	14	17	18	16	3	14	13
11 4 45	15	18	18	16	54	15	14
11 8 28	16	19	19	17	45	16	15
11 12 10	17	19	20	18	37	16	15
11 15 52	18	20	21	19	28	17	16
11 19 33	19	21	22	20	19	18	17
11 23 15	20	22	23	21	10	19	18
11 26 56	21	23	24	22	1	20	19
11 30 37	22	24	25	22	52	21	20
11 34 17	23	25	26	23	42	22	21
11 37 58	24	26	27	24	33	22	22
11 41 39	25	27	27	25	23	23	23
11 45 19	26	28	28	26	14	24	24
11 48 59	27	29	29	27	5	25	25
11 52 40	28	♏	♐	27	55	26	26
11 56 20	29	1	1	28	46	27	27
HOUSES	4	5	6	7		8	9

LATITUDE 2° N.

SIDEREAL TIME (H M S)	10 Ω	11 ♍	12 ♎	ASC ♏ (° ')		2 ♐	3 ♑
9 9 52	15	16	19	19	17	18	16
9 13 50	16	18	20	20	16	19	17
9 17 49	17	19	21	21	14	20	18
9 21 46	18	20	22	22	12	21	19
9 25 42	19	21	23	23	9	22	20
9 29 38	20	22	24	24	6	23	20
9 33 34	21	23	25	25	3	23	21
9 37 28	22	24	26	26	0	24	22
9 41 22	23	25	27	26	56	25	23
9 45 15	24	26	28	27	52	26	24
9 49 8	25	27	29	28	47	27	25
9 53 0	26	28	♏	29	43	28	26
9 56 51	27	29	1	0♐	38	29	27
10 0 42	28	♎	2	1	33	♑	28
10 4 32	29	1	3	2	27	1	29
10 8 22	♍	2	4	3	21	1	♒
10 12 11	1	3	5	4	16	2	1
10 15 59	2	4	6	5	9	3	2
10 19 47	3	5	7	6	3	4	2
10 23 34	4	6	8	6	56	5	3
10 27 21	5	7	9	7	49	6	4
10 31 8	6	8	10	8	42	7	5
10 34 53	7	9	11	9	35	7	6
10 38 39	8	10	12	10	28	8	7
10 42 24	9	11	13	11	20	9	8
10 46 8	10	12	14	12	12	10	9
10 49 52	11	13	15	13	4	11	10
10 53 36	12	14	15	13	56	12	11
10 57 20	13	15	16	14	48	13	12
11 1 3	14	16	17	15	39	14	13
11 4 45	15	17	18	16	31	14	14
11 8 28	16	18	19	17	22	15	14
11 12 10	17	19	20	18	13	16	15
11 15 52	18	20	21	19	4	17	16
11 19 33	19	21	22	19	55	18	17
11 23 15	20	22	23	20	46	19	18
11 26 56	21	23	24	21	37	20	19
11 30 37	22	24	25	22	28	20	20
11 34 17	23	25	25	23	18	21	21
11 37 58	24	26	26	24	9	22	22
11 41 39	25	27	27	25	0	23	23
11 45 19	26	28	28	25	50	24	24
11 48 59	27	29	29	26	41	25	25
11 52 40	28	♏	♐	27	31	26	26
11 56 20	29	1	1	28	22	27	27
HOUSES	4	5	6	7		8	9

LATITUDE 3° N.

SIDEREAL TIME (H M S)	10 Ω	11 ♍	12 ♎	ASC ♏ (° ')		2 ♐	3 ♑
9 9 52	15	16	19	18	59	18	16
9 13 50	16	18	20	19	57	19	17
9 17 49	17	19	21	20	55	20	18
9 21 46	18	20	22	21	52	20	18
9 25 42	19	21	23	22	50	21	19
9 29 38	20	22	24	23	46	22	20
9 33 34	21	23	25	24	43	23	21
9 37 28	22	24	26	25	39	24	22
9 41 22	23	25	27	26	35	25	23
9 45 15	24	26	28	27	31	26	24
9 49 8	25	27	29	28	27	27	25
9 53 0	26	28	♏	29	22	28	26
9 56 51	27	29	1	0♐	17	28	27
10 0 42	28	♎	2	1	11	29	28
10 4 32	29	1	3	2	6	♑	29
10 8 22	♍	2	4	3	0	1	♒
10 12 11	1	3	5	3	54	2	0
10 15 59	2	4	6	4	48	3	1
10 19 47	3	5	7	5	41	4	2
10 23 34	4	6	8	6	34	5	3
10 27 21	5	7	9	7	27	5	4
10 31 8	6	8	10	8	20	6	5
10 34 53	7	9	11	9	13	7	6
10 38 39	8	10	12	10	5	8	7
10 42 24	9	11	12	10	57	9	8
10 46 8	10	12	13	11	49	10	9
10 49 52	11	13	14	12	41	11	10
10 53 36	12	14	15	13	33	12	11
10 57 20	13	15	16	14	25	12	12
11 1 3	14	16	17	15	16	13	12
11 4 45	15	17	18	16	8	14	13
11 8 28	16	18	19	16	59	15	14
11 12 10	17	19	20	17	50	16	15
11 15 52	18	20	21	18	41	17	16
11 19 33	19	21	22	19	32	18	17
11 23 15	20	22	23	20	23	18	18
11 26 56	21	23	23	21	13	19	19
11 30 37	22	24	24	22	4	20	20
11 34 17	23	25	25	22	55	21	21
11 37 58	24	26	26	23	45	22	22
11 41 39	25	27	27	24	36	23	23
11 45 19	26	28	28	25	26	24	24
11 48 59	27	29	29	26	17	25	25
11 52 40	28	♏	♐	27	7	25	26
11 56 20	29	1	1	27	58	26	27
HOUSES	4	5	6	7		8	9

LATITUDE 1° S.   LATITUDE 2° S.   LATITUDE 3° S.

	LATITUDE 1° N.						LATITUDE 2° N.						LATITUDE 3° N.					
SIDEREAL TIME	10 ♎	11 ♏	12 ♐	ASC ♐	2 ♑	3 ♒	10 ♎	11 ♏	12 ♐	ASC ♐	2 ♑	3 ♒	10 ♎	11 ♏	12 ♐	ASC ♐	2 ♑	3 ♒
H M S	°	°	°	° '	°	°	°	°	°	° '	°	°	°	°	°	° '	°	°
12 0 0	0	2	2	29 36	28	28	0	2	2	29 12	27	28	0	2	1	28 48	27	28
12 3 40	1	3	3	0♑ 27	29	29	1	3	2	0♑ 3	28	29	1	3	2	29 39	28	29
12 7 20	2	4	4	1 17	29	♓	2	4	3	0 53	29	♓	2	4	3	0♑ 29	29	♓
12 11 1	3	5	4	2 8	♒	1	3	5	4	1 44	♒	1	3	5	4	1 20	♒	0
12 14 41	4	6	5	2 58	1	2	4	6	5	2 34	1	2	4	6	5	2 10	1	1
12 18 21	5	7	6	3 49	2	3	5	7	6	3 25	2	2	5	7	6	3 1	2	2
12 22 2	6	8	7	4 40	3	4	6	8	7	4 16	3	3	6	8	7	3 52	3	3
12 25 42	7	9	8	5 30	4	5	7	9	8	5 6	4	4	7	9	7	4 43	3	4
12 29 23	8	10	9	6 21	5	5	8	10	9	5 57	5	5	8	9	8	5 33	4	5
12 33 4	9	11	10	7 12	6	6	9	11	9	6 48	5	6	9	10	9	6 24	5	6
12 36 45	10	12	11	8 3	7	7	10	11	10	7 39	6	7	10	11	10	7 15	6	7
12 40 27	11	12	11	8 54	7	8	11	12	11	8 30	7	8	11	12	11	8 6	7	8
12 44 8	12	13	12	9 45	8	9	12	13	12	9 21	8	9	12	13	12	8 58	8	9
12 47 50	13	14	13	10 36	9	10	13	14	13	10 13	9	10	13	14	13	9 49	9	10
12 51 32	14	15	14	11 28	10	11	14	15	14	11 4	10	11	14	15	13	10 40	10	11
12 55 15	15	16	15	12 19	11	12	15	16	15	11 56	11	12	15	16	14	11 32	11	12
12 58 57	16	17	16	13 11	12	13	16	17	15	12 47	12	13	16	17	15	12 24	12	13
13 2 40	17	18	17	14 3	13	14	17	18	16	13 39	13	14	17	18	16	13 16	13	14
13 6 24	18	19	17	14 54	14	15	18	19	17	14 31	14	15	18	19	17	14 8	14	15
13 10 8	19	20	18	15 47	15	16	19	20	18	15 23	15	16	19	20	18	15 0	14	16
13 13 52	20	21	19	16 39	16	17	20	21	19	16 16	16	17	20	21	19	15 52	15	17
13 17 36	21	22	20	17 31	17	18	21	22	20	17 8	17	18	21	21	19	16 45	16	18
13 21 21	22	22	21	18 24	18	19	22	23	21	18 1	18	19	22	22	20	17 38	17	19
13 25 7	23	24	22	19 17	19	20	23	23	21	18 54	18	20	23	23	21	18 31	18	20
13 28 52	24	24	23	20 10	20	22	24	24	22	19 47	19	21	24	24	22	19 24	19	21
13 32 39	25	25	23	21 3	21	23	25	25	23	20 41	20	23	25	25	23	20 18	20	22
13 36 26	26	26	24	21 57	22	24	26	26	24	21 34	21	24	26	26	24	21 11	21	24
13 40 13	27	27	25	22 50	23	25	27	27	25	22 28	22	25	27	27	25	22 5	22	25
13 44 1	28	28	26	23 44	24	26	28	28	26	23 22	23	26	28	28	26	23 0	23	26
13 47 49	29	29	27	24 39	24	27	29	29	27	24 16	24	27	29	29	26	23 54	24	27
13 51 38	♏	♐	28	25 33	25	28	♏	♐	28	25 11	25	28	♏	♐	27	24 49	25	28
13 55 28	1	1	29	26 28	26	29	1	1	28	26 6	26	29	1	1	28	25 44	26	29
13 59 18	2	2	♑	27 23	27	♈	2	2	29	27 1	27	♈	2	2	29	26 39	27	♈
14 3 9	3	3	0	28 18	28	1	3	3	♑	27 57	28	1	3	2	♑	27 35	28	1
14 7 0	4	4	1	29 14	29	2	4	4	1	28 52	29	2	4	3	1	28 31	29	2
14 10 52	5	5	2	0♒ 10	♓	3	5	4	2	29 48	♓	3	5	4	2	29 27	♓	3
14 14 45	6	5	3	1 6	2	4	6	5	3	0♒ 45	1	4	6	5	3	0♒ 23	1	4
14 18 38	7	6	4	2 2	3	5	7	6	4	1 41	2	5	7	6	3	1 20	2	5
14 22 32	8	7	5	2 59	4	6	8	7	5	2 38	3	6	8	7	4	2 17	3	6
14 26 26	9	8	6	3 56	5	7	9	8	6	3 36	5	7	9	8	5	3 15	4	7
14 30 22	10	9	7	4 54	6	8	10	9	6	4 33	6	8	10	9	6	4 13	5	8
14 34 17	11	10	8	5 52	7	9	11	10	7	5 31	7	9	11	10	7	5 11	6	9
14 38 14	12	11	9	6 50	8	10	12	11	8	6 30	8	10	12	11	8	6 10	8	10
14 42 11	13	12	9	7 48	9	12	13	12	9	7 28	9	12	13	12	9	7 9	9	12
14 46 10	14	13	10	8 47	10	13	14	13	10	8 27	10	13	14	13	10	8 8	10	13
HOUSES	4	5	6	7	8	9	4	5	6	7	8	9	4	5	6	7	8	9

LATITUDE 1° S.   LATITUDE 2° S.   LATITUDE 3° S.

	LATITUDE 1° N.						LATITUDE 2° N.						LATITUDE 3° N.					
SIDEREAL TIME	10 ♏	11 ♐	12 ♑	ASC ♒		2 ♓	3 ♈	10 ♏	11 ♐	12 ♑	ASC ♒		2 ♓	3 ♈	10 ♏	11 ♐	12 ♑	ASC ♒
H M S	°	°	°	°	′	°	°	°	°	°	°	′	°	°	°	°	°	° ′	° °
14 50 8	15	14	11	9	46	11	14	15	14	11	9	27	11	14	15	14	11	9 7	11 14
14 54 8	16	15	12	10	46	12	15	16	15	12	10	27	12	15	16	14	12	10 8	12 15
14 58 8	17	16	13	11	46	13	16	17	15	13	11	27	13	16	17	15	13	11 8	13 16
15 2 9	18	17	14	12	46	14	17	18	16	14	12	27	14	17	18	16	14	12 9	14 17
15 6 10	19	17	15	13	47	15	18	19	17	15	13	28	15	18	19	17	14	13 10	15 18
15 10 13	20	18	16	14	48	16	19	20	18	16	14	30	16	19	20	18	15	14 12	16 19
15 14 16	21	19	17	15	49	18	20	21	19	17	15	31	17	20	21	19	16	15 14	17 20
15 18 20	22	20	18	16	51	19	21	22	20	18	16	33	19	21	22	20	17	16 16	18 21
15 22 24	23	21	19	17	53	20	22	23	21	19	17	36	20	22	23	21	18	17 19	20 22
15 26 30	24	22	20	18	55	21	23	24	22	19	18	39	21	23	24	22	19	18 22	21 24
15 30 36	25	23	21	19	58	22	25	25	23	20	19	42	22	25	25	23	20	19 25	22 25
15 34 42	26	24	22	21	2	23	26	26	24	21	20	46	23	26	26	24	21	20 29	23 26
15 38 50	27	25	23	22	5	24	27	27	25	22	21	50	24	27	27	25	22	21 34	24 27
15 42 58	28	26	24	23	9	25	28	28	26	23	22	54	25	28	28	26	23	22 39	25 28
15 47 7	29	27	25	24	14	26	29	29	27	24	23	59	26	29	29	27	24	23 44	26 29
15 51 16	♐	28	26	25	19	28	♉	♐	28	25	25	4	28	♉	♐	28	25	24 49	28 ♉
15 55 26	1	29	27	26	24	29	1	1	29	26	26	10	29	1	1	29	26	25 55	29 1
15 59 37	2	♑	28	27	29	♈	2	2	♑	27	27	16	♈	2	2	♑	27	27 2	♈ 2
16 3 49	3	1	29	28	35	1	3	3	1	28	28	22	1	3	3	0	28	28 8	1 3
16 8 1	4	2	♒	29	42	2	4	4	2	29	29	29	2	4	4	1	29	29 15	2 5
16 12 14	5	3	1	0♓	48	3	5	5	3	♒	0♓	36	3	6	5	2	♒	0♓ 23	3 6
16 16 27	6	4	2	1	55	5	7	6	4	1	1	43	5	7	6	3	1	1 31	5 7
16 20 41	7	5	3	3	3	6	8	7	4	2	2	51	6	8	7	4	2	2 39	6 8
16 24 56	8	6	4	4	10	7	9	8	5	3	3	59	7	9	8	5	3	3 47	7 9
16 29 11	9	7	5	5	18	8	10	9	6	4	5	7	8	10	9	6	4	4 56	8 10
16 33 27	10	8	6	6	27	9	11	10	7	6	6	16	9	11	10	7	5	6 6	9 11
16 37 43	11	9	7	7	35	10	12	11	8	7	7	25	10	12	11	8	6	7 15	10 12
16 41 59	12	10	8	8	44	11	13	12	9	8	8	35	12	13	12	9	7	8 25	12 13
16 46 17	13	11	9	9	53	13	14	13	10	9	9	44	13	14	13	10	8	9 35	13 14
16 50 34	14	11	10	11	3	14	15	14	11	10	10	54	14	15	14	11	10	10 46	14 15
16 54 53	15	12	11	12	13	15	16	15	12	11	12	5	15	16	15	12	11	11 56	15 16
16 59 11	16	13	12	13	23	16	17	16	13	12	13	15	16	17	16	13	12	13 7	16 18
17 3 30	17	14	13	14	33	17	18	17	14	13	14	26	17	19	17	14	13	14 19	17 19
17 7 49	18	15	14	15	43	18	20	18	15	14	15	37	19	20	18	15	14	15 30	19 20
17 12 9	19	17	15	16	54	20	21	19	16	15	16	48	20	21	19	16	15	16 42	20 21
17 16 29	20	18	16	18	5	21	22	20	17	16	17	59	21	22	20	17	16	17 54	21 22
17 20 49	21	19	18	19	16	22	23	21	18	17	19	11	22	23	21	18	17	19 6	22 23
17 25 10	22	20	19	20	27	23	24	22	19	18	20	23	23	24	22	19	18	20 18	23 24
17 29 31	23	21	20	21	38	24	25	23	20	20	21	34	24	25	23	20	19	21 31	25 25
17 33 51	24	22	21	22	50	25	26	24	21	21	22	46	26	26	24	21	21	22 43	26 26
17 38 13	25	23	22	24	1	27	27	25	22	22	23	58	27	27	25	22	22	23 56	27 27
17 42 34	26	24	23	25	13	28	28	26	24	23	25	11	28	28	26	23	23	25 8	28 28
17 46 55	27	25	24	26	25	29	29	27	25	24	26	23	29	29	27	24	24	26 21	29 29
17 51 17	28	26	25	27	36	♉	♊	28	26	25	27	35	♉	♊	28	25	25	27 34	♉ ♊
17 55 38	29	27	27	28	48	1	1	29	27	26	28	48	1	1	29	27	26	28 47	1 1
HOUSES	4	5	6	7		8	9	4	5	6	7		8	9	4	5	6	7	8 9

LATITUDE 1° S.   LATITUDE 2° S.   LATITUDE 3° S.

	LATITUDE 1° N.						LATITUDE 2° N.						LATITUDE 3° N.					
SIDEREAL TIME	10 ♑	11 ♑	12 ♒	ASC ♈	2 ♉	3 ♊	10 ♑	11 ♑	12 ♒	ASC ♈	2 ♉	3 ♊	10 ♑	11 ♑	12 ♒	ASC ♈	2 ♉	3 ♊
H M S	°	°	°	° '	°	°	°	°	°	° '	°	°	°	°	°	° '	°	°
18 0 0	0	28	28	0 0	2	2	0	28	28	0 0	2	2	0	28	27	0 0	3	2
18 4 22	1	29	29	1 12	3	3	1	29	29	1 12	4	3	1	29	29	1 13	4	3
18 8 43	2	♒	♓	2 24	5	4	2	♒	♓	2 25	5	4	2	♒	♓	2 26	5	5
18 13 5	3	1	1	3 35	6	5	3	1	1	3 37	6	5	3	1	1	3 39	6	6
18 17 26	4	2	2	4 47	7	6	4	2	2	4 49	7	6	4	2	2	4 52	7	7
18 21 47	5	3	3	5 59	8	7	5	3	3	6 2	8	8	5	3	3	6 4	8	8
18 26 9	6	4	5	7 10	9	8	6	4	4	7 14	9	9	6	4	4	7 17	9	9
18 30 29	7	5	6	8 22	10	9	7	5	6	8 26	10	10	7	5	5	8 29	11	10
18 34 50	8	6	7	9 33	11	10	8	6	7	9 37	12	11	8	6	7	9 42	12	11
18 39 11	9	7	8	10 44	12	11	9	7	8	10 49	13	12	9	7	8	10 54	13	12
18 43 31	10	8	9	11 55	14	12	10	8	9	12 1	14	13	10	8	9	12 6	14	13
18 47 51	11	9	10	13 6	15	13	11	9	10	13 12	15	14	11	9	10	13 18	15	14
18 52 11	12	10	12	14 17	16	15	12	10	11	14 23	16	15	12	10	11	14 30	16	15
18 56 30	13	12	13	15 27	17	16	13	11	13	15 34	17	16	13	11	13	15 41	17	16
19 0 49	14	13	14	16 37	18	17	14	13	14	16 45	18	17	14	12	14	16 53	18	17
19 5 7	15	14	15	17 47	19	18	15	14	15	17 55	19	18	15	14	15	18 4	19	18
19 9 26	16	15	16	18 57	20	19	16	15	16	19 6	20	19	16	15	16	19 14	20	19
19 13 43	17	16	17	20 7	21	19	17	16	17	20 16	21	20	17	16	17	20 25	22	20
19 18 0	18	17	19	21 16	22	20	18	17	18	21 25	22	21	18	17	18	21 35	23	21
19 22 17	19	18	20	22 25	23	21	19	18	20	22 35	23	22	19	18	20	22 45	24	22
19 26 33	20	19	21	23 33	24	22	20	19	21	23 44	24	23	20	19	21	23 54	25	23
19 30 49	21	20	22	24 42	25	23	21	20	22	24 53	26	24	21	20	22	25 4	26	24
19 35 4	22	21	23	25 50	26	24	22	21	23	26 1	27	25	22	21	23	26 13	27	25
19 39 19	23	22	24	26 57	27	25	23	22	24	27 9	28	26	23	22	24	27 21	28	26
19 43 33	24	23	25	28 5	28	26	24	23	25	28 17	29	26	24	23	25	28 29	29	27
19 47 46	25	25	27	29 12	29	27	25	24	27	29 24	Ⅱ	27	25	24	27	29 37	Ⅱ	28
19 51 59	26	26	28	0♉ 18	Ⅱ	28	26	26	28	0♉ 31	1	28	26	25	28	0♉ 45	1	29
19 56 11	27	27	29	1 25	1	29	27	27	29	1 38	2	29	27	27	29	1 52	2	♋
20 0 23	28	28	♈	2 31	2	♋	28	28	♈	2 44	3	♋	28	28	♈	2 58	3	0
20 4 34	29	29	1	3 36	3	1	29	29	1	3 50	4	1	29	29	1	4 5	4	1
20 8 44	♒	♓	2	4 41	4	2	♒	♓	2	4 56	5	2	♒	♓	2	5 11	5	2
20 12 53	1	1	4	5 46	5	3	1	1	4	6 1	6	3	1	1	4	6 16	6	3
20 17 2	2	2	5	6 51	6	4	2	2	5	7 6	7	4	2	2	5	7 21	7	4
20 21 10	3	3	6	7 55	7	5	3	3	6	8 10	8	5	3	3	6	8 26	8	5
20 25 18	4	4	7	8 58	8	6	4	4	7	9 14	9	6	4	4	7	9 31	9	6
20 29 24	5	5	8	10 2	9	7	5	5	8	10 18	10	7	5	5	8	10 35	10	7
20 33 30	6	7	9	11 5	10	8	6	7	9	11 21	11	8	6	6	9	11 38	11	8
20 37 36	7	8	10	12 7	11	9	7	8	10	12 24	11	9	7	8	10	12 41	12	9
20 41 40	8	9	11	13 9	12	10	8	9	11	13 27	12	10	8	9	12	13 44	13	10
20 45 44	9	10	12	14 11	13	11	9	10	13	14 29	13	11	9	10	13	14 46	14	11
20 49 47	10	11	14	15 12	14	12	10	11	14	15 30	14	12	10	11	14	15 48	15	12
20 53 50	11	12	15	16 13	15	13	11	12	15	16 32	15	13	11	12	15	16 50	16	13
20 57 51	12	13	16	17 14	16	13	12	13	16	17 33	16	14	12	13	16	17 51	16	14
21 1 52	13	14	17	18 14	17	14	13	14	17	18 33	17	15	13	14	17	18 52	17	15
21 5 52	14	15	18	19 14	18	15	14	15	18	19 33	18	15	14	15	18	19 52	18	16
HOUSES	4	5	6	7	8	9	4	5	6	7	8	9	4	5	6	7	8	9

	LATITUDE 1° N.						LATITUDE 2° N.						LATITUDE 3° N.					
SIDEREAL TIME	10 ♒	11 ♓	12 ♈	ASC ♉	2 ♊	3 ♋	10 ♒	11 ♓	12 ♈	ASC ♉	2 ♊	3 ♋	10 ♒	11 ♓	12 ♈	ASC ♉	2 ♊	3 ♋
H M S	°	°	°	° '	°	°	°	°	°	° '	°	°	°	°	°	° '	°	°
21 9 52	15	16	19	20 14	19	16	15	16	19	20 33	19	16	15	16	19	20 53	19	16
21 13 50	16	17	20	21 13	20	17	16	17	20	21 33	20	17	16	17	20	21 52	20	17
21 17 49	17	18	21	22 12	21	18	17	18	21	22 32	21	18	17	18	21	22 51	21	18
21 21 46	18	20	22	23 10	21	19	18	20	22	23 30	22	19	18	20	22	23 50	22	19
21 25 42	19	21	23	24 8	22	20	19	21	23	24 29	23	20	19	21	24	24 49	23	20
21 29 38	20	22	24	25 6	23	21	20	22	24	25 27	24	21	20	22	25	25 47	24	21
21 33 34	21	23	25	26 4	24	22	21	23	25	26 24	24	22	21	23	26	26 45	25	22
21 37 28	22	24	26	27 1	25	23	22	24	27	27 22	25	23	22	24	27	27 43	26	23
21 41 22	23	25	27	27 58	26	24	23	25	28	28 19	26	24	23	25	28	28 40	27	24
21 45 15	24	26	28	28 54	27	25	24	26	29	29 15	27	25	24	26	29	29 37	27	25
21 49 8	25	27	29	29 50	28	25	25	27	♉	0♊ 12	28	26	25	27	♉	0♊ 33	28	26
21 53 0	26	28	♉	0♊ 46	29	26	26	28	1	1 8	29	26	26	28	1	1 29	29	27
21 56 51	27	29	2	1 42	♋	27	27	29	2	2 3	♋	27	27	29	2	2 25	♋	28
22 0 42	28	♈	3	2 37	0	28	28	♈	3	2 59	1	28	28	♈	3	3 21	1	28
22 4 32	29	1	4	3 32	1	29	29	1	4	3 54	2	29	29	1	4	4 16	2	29
22 8 22	♓	2	5	4 27	2	♌	♓	2	5	4 49	2	♌	♓	2	5	5 11	3	♌
22 12 11	1	3	6	5 21	3	1	1	3	6	5 44	3	1	1	3	6	6 6	4	1
22 15 59	2	4	6	6 16	4	2	2	4	7	6 38	4	2	2	4	7	7 0	4	2
22 19 47	3	5	7	7 10	5	3	3	5	8	7 32	5	3	3	5	8	7 55	5	3
22 23 34	4	6	8	8 3	6	4	4	6	9	8 26	6	4	4	6	9	8 49	6	4
22 27 21	5	7	9	8 57	7	5	5	7	10	9 19	7	5	5	8	10	9 42	7	5
22 31 8	6	8	10	9 50	7	6	6	9	11	10 13	8	6	6	9	11	10 36	8	6
22 34 53	7	10	11	10 43	8	6	7	10	12	11 6	9	7	7	10	12	11 29	9	7
22 38 39	8	11	12	11 36	9	7	8	11	12	11 59	9	7	8	11	13	12 22	10	8
22 42 24	9	12	13	12 29	10	8	9	12	13	12 52	10	8	9	12	14	13 15	11	9
22 46 8	10	13	14	13 21	11	9	10	13	14	13 44	11	9	10	13	15	14 8	11	9
22 49 52	11	14	15	14 13	12	10	11	14	15	14 37	12	10	11	14	16	15 0	12	10
22 53 36	12	15	16	15 6	13	11	12	15	16	15 29	13	11	12	15	16	15 52	13	11
22 57 20	13	16	17	15 57	13	12	13	16	17	16 21	14	12	13	16	17	16 44	14	12
23 1 3	14	17	18	16 49	14	13	14	17	18	17 13	15	13	14	17	18	17 36	15	13
23 4 45	15	18	19	17 41	15	14	15	18	19	18 4	15	14	15	18	19	18 28	16	14
23 8 28	16	19	20	18 32	16	15	16	19	20	18 56	16	15	16	19	20	19 20	17	15
23 12 10	17	20	21	19 24	17	16	17	20	21	19 47	17	16	17	20	21	20 11	17	16
23 15 52	18	21	22	20 15	18	17	18	21	22	20 39	18	17	18	21	22	21 2	18	17
23 19 33	19	22	23	21 6	19	18	19	22	23	21 30	19	18	19	22	23	21 54	19	18
23 23 15	20	23	23	21 57	19	18	20	23	24	22 21	20	19	20	23	24	22 45	20	19
23 26 56	21	24	24	22 48	20	19	21	24	25	23 12	21	19	21	24	25	23 36	21	20
23 30 37	22	25	25	23 39	21	20	22	25	25	24 3	21	20	22	25	26	24 27	22	21
23 34 17	23	25	26	24 30	22	21	23	26	26	24 54	22	21	23	26	27	25 17	23	21
23 37 58	24	26	27	25 20	23	22	24	27	27	25 44	23	22	24	27	27	26 8	23	22
23 41 39	25	27	28	26 11	24	23	25	28	28	26 35	24	23	25	28	28	26 59	24	23
23 45 19	26	28	29	27 2	25	24	26	28	29	27 26	25	24	26	29	29	27 50	25	24
23 48 59	27	29	♊	27 52	26	25	27	29	♊	28 16	26	25	27	♉	♊	28 40	26	25
23 52 40	28	♉	1	28 43	26	26	28	♉	1	29 7	27	26	28	0	1	29 31	27	26
23 56 20	29	1	1	29 33	27	27	29	1	2	29 57	28	27	29	1	2	0♋ 21	28	27
HOUSES	4	5	6	7	8	9	4	5	6	7	8	9	4	5	6	7	8	9

LATITUDE 1° S.   LATITUDE 2° S.   LATITUDE 3° S.

	LATITUDE 4° N.						LATITUDE 5° N.						LATITUDE 6° N.					
SIDEREAL TIME	10 ♈	11 ♉	12 ♊	ASC ♋	2 ♋	3 ♌	10 ♈	11 ♉	12 ♊	ASC ♋	2 ♋	3 ♌	10 ♈	11 ♉	12 ♊	ASC ♋	2 ♋	3 ♌
H M S	°	°	°	° '	°	°	°	°	°	° '	°	°	°	°	°	° '	°	°
0 0 0	0	2	3	1 36	29	28	0	3	3	2 0	29	28	0	3	4	2 24	29	28
0 3 40	1	3	4	2 26	♌	29	1	4	4	2 50	♌	29	1	4	4	3 14	♌	29
0 7 20	2	4	5	3 17	1	♍	2	4	5	3 40	1	♍	2	5	5	4 4	1	♍
0 11 1	3	5	6	4 7	1	1	3	5	6	4 31	2	1	3	6	6	4 55	2	1
0 14 41	4	6	7	4 57	2	2	4	6	7	5 21	3	2	4	6	7	5 45	3	2
0 18 21	5	7	7	5 48	3	3	5	7	8	6 12	3	3	5	7	8	6 36	4	3
0 22 2	6	8	8	6 38	4	4	6	8	9	7 2	4	4	6	8	9	7 26	5	4
0 25 43	7	9	9	7 29	5	5	7	9	9	7 53	5	5	7	9	10	8 16	5	5
0 29 23	8	10	10	8 20	6	6	8	10	10	8 43	6	6	8	10	11	9 7	6	6
0 33 4	9	11	11	9 10	7	7	9	11	11	9 34	7	7	9	11	11	9 57	7	7
0 36 45	10	12	12	10 1	8	8	10	12	12	10 24	8	8	10	12	12	10 48	8	8
0 40 27	11	13	13	10 52	9	9	11	13	13	11 15	9	9	11	13	13	11 39	9	9
0 44 8	12	14	14	11 43	9	10	12	14	14	12 6	10	10	12	14	14	12 29	10	10
0 47 50	13	15	14	12 33	10	11	13	15	15	12 57	11	11	13	15	15	13 20	11	11
0 51 32	14	16	15	13 25	11	12	14	16	16	13 48	11	12	14	16	16	14 11	12	12
0 55 15	15	17	16	14 16	12	13	15	17	16	14 39	12	13	15	17	17	15 2	13	13
0 58 57	16	18	17	15 7	13	14	16	18	17	15 30	13	14	16	18	18	15 53	13	14
1 2 40	17	19	18	15 58	14	15	17	19	18	16 21	14	15	17	19	18	16 44	14	15
1 6 24	18	19	19	16 50	15	16	18	20	19	17 13	15	16	18	20	19	17 36	15	16
1 10 8	19	20	20	17 42	16	17	19	21	20	18 4	16	17	19	21	20	18 27	16	17
1 13 52	20	21	20	18 33	17	18	20	21	21	18 56	17	18	20	22	21	19 19	17	18
1 17 36	21	22	21	19 25	18	19	21	22	22	19 48	18	19	21	22	22	20 10	18	19
1 21 21	22	23	22	20 17	19	20	22	23	22	20 40	19	20	22	23	23	21 2	19	20
1 25 7	23	24	23	21 10	20	21	23	24	23	21 32	20	21	23	24	24	21 54	20	21
1 28 52	24	25	24	22 2	21	22	24	25	24	22 25	21	22	24	25	24	22 47	21	22
1 32 39	25	26	25	22 55	21	23	25	26	25	23 17	22	23	25	26	25	23 39	22	23
1 36 26	26	27	26	23 48	22	24	26	27	26	24 10	23	24	26	27	26	24 32	23	24
1 40 13	27	28	27	24 41	23	25	27	28	27	25 3	24	25	27	28	27	25 25	24	25
1 44 1	28	29	27	25 34	24	26	28	29	28	25 56	24	26	28	29	28	26 18	25	26
1 47 49	29	♊	28	26 28	25	27	29	♊	29	26 49	25	27	29	♊	29	27 11	26	27
1 51 38	♉	1	29	27 22	26	28	♉	1	29	27 43	26	28	♉	1	♋	28 4	27	28
1 55 28	1	1	♋	28 16	27	29	1	2	♋	28 37	27	29	1	2	1	28 58	28	29
1 59 18	2	2	1	29 10	28	♎	2	3	1	29 31	28	♎	2	3	1	29 52	29	♎
2 3 9	3	3	2	0♌ 4	29	1	3	3	2	0♌ 25	29	1	3	4	2	0♌ 46	♍	1
2 7 0	4	4	3	0 59	♍	2	4	4	3	1 20	♍	2	4	4	3	1 40	0	2
2 10 52	5	5	4	1 54	1	3	5	5	4	2 14	1	3	5	5	4	2 35	1	3
2 14 45	6	6	4	2 49	2	4	6	6	5	3 10	2	4	6	6	5	3 30	2	4
2 18 38	7	7	5	3 45	3	5	7	7	6	4 5	3	5	7	7	6	4 25	3	5
2 22 32	8	8	6	4 41	4	6	8	8	6	5 1	4	6	8	8	7	5 20	4	6
2 26 26	9	9	7	5 37	5	7	9	9	7	5 56	5	7	9	9	8	6 16	5	7
2 30 22	10	10	8	6 33	6	8	10	10	8	6 53	6	8	10	10	9	7 12	6	8
2 34 17	11	11	9	7 30	7	9	11	11	9	7 49	7	9	11	11	9	8 8	7	9
2 38 14	12	12	10	8 27	8	10	12	12	10	8 46	8	10	12	12	10	9 5	9	10
2 42 11	13	13	11	9 24	9	11	13	13	11	9 43	9	11	13	13	11	10 2	10	11
2 46 10	14	13	12	10 22	10	12	14	14	12	10 40	10	12	14	14	12	10 59	11	12
HOUSES	4	5	6	7	8	9	4	5	6	7	8	9	4	5	6	7	8	9

LATITUDE 4° S.   LATITUDE 5° S.   LATITUDE 6° S.

LATITUDE 4° N.   LATITUDE 5° N.   LATITUDE 6° N.

SIDEREAL TIME	10 ♉	11 ♊	12 ♋	ASC ♌	2 ♍	3 ♎	10 ♉	11 ♊	12 ♋	ASC ♌	2 ♍	3 ♎	10 ♉	11 ♊	12 ♋	ASC ♌	2 ♍	3 ♎
H M S	°	°	°	° '	°	°	°	°	°	° '	°	°	°	°	°	° '	°	°
2 50 8	15	14	13	11 20	11	13	15	15	13	11 38	12	13	15	15	13	11 56	12	13
2 54 8	16	15	13	12 18	12	15	16	15	14	12 36	13	15	16	16	14	12 54	13	14
2 58 8	17	16	14	13 17	14	16	17	16	15	13 34	14	16	17	17	15	13 52	14	16
3 2 9	18	17	15	14 16	15	17	18	17	16	14 33	15	17	18	18	16	14 51	15	17
3 6 10	19	18	16	15 15	16	18	19	18	17	15 32	16	18	19	18	17	15 49	16	18
3 10 13	20	19	17	16 15	17	19	20	19	17	16 31	17	19	20	19	18	16 48	17	19
3 14 16	21	20	18	17 14	18	20	21	20	18	17 31	18	20	21	20	19	17 48	18	20
3 18 20	22	21	19	18 15	19	21	22	21	19	18 31	19	21	22	21	20	18 47	19	21
3 22 24	23	22	20	19 15	20	22	23	22	20	19 31	20	22	23	22	21	19 47	20	22
3 26 30	24	23	21	20 16	21	23	24	23	21	20 32	21	23	24	23	21	20 48	21	23
3 30 36	25	24	22	21 18	22	24	25	24	22	21 33	22	24	25	24	22	21 48	22	24
3 34 42	26	25	23	22 19	23	25	26	25	23	22 34	23	25	26	25	23	22 49	23	25
3 38 50	27	26	24	23 21	24	26	27	26	24	23 36	24	26	27	26	24	23 51	24	26
3 42 58	28	27	25	24 24	25	27	28	27	25	24 38	25	27	28	27	25	24 52	25	27
3 47 7	29	28	26	25 26	27	29	29	28	26	25 40	27	28	29	28	26	25 54	27	28
3 51 16	♊	29	27	26 29	28	♏	♊	29	27	26 43	28	♏	♊	29	27	26 56	28	29
3 55 26	1	29	28	27 33	29	1	1	♋	28	27 46	29	1	1	♋	28	27 59	29	♏
3 59 37	2	♋	29	28 36	♎	2	2	1	29	28 49	♎	2	2	1	29	29 2	♎	2
4 3 49	3	1	♌	29 40	1	3	3	2	♌	29 53	1	3	3	2	♌	0♍ 5	1	3
4 8 1	4	2	1	0♍ 44	2	4	4	3	1	0♍ 57	2	4	4	3	1	1 9	2	4
4 12 14	5	3	2	1 49	3	5	5	3	2	2 1	3	5	5	4	2	2 12	3	5
4 16 27	6	4	3	2 54	4	6	6	4	3	3 5	4	6	6	5	3	3 17	4	6
4 20 41	7	5	4	3 59	6	7	7	5	4	4 10	5	7	7	6	4	4 21	5	7
4 24 56	8	6	5	5 5	7	8	8	6	5	5 15	7	8	8	7	5	5 26	7	8
4 29 11	9	7	6	6 11	8	9	9	7	6	6 21	8	9	9	7	6	6 31	8	9
4 33 27	10	8	7	7 17	9	10	10	8	7	7 26	9	10	10	8	7	7 36	9	10
4 37 43	11	9	8	8 23	10	11	11	9	8	8 32	10	11	11	9	8	8 41	10	11
4 41 59	12	10	9	9 30	11	13	12	10	9	9 38	11	12	12	10	9	9 47	11	12
4 46 17	13	11	10	10 37	12	14	13	11	10	10 45	12	14	13	11	10	10 53	12	13
4 50 34	14	12	11	11 44	13	15	14	12	11	11 52	13	15	14	12	11	11 59	13	15
4 54 53	15	13	12	12 51	15	16	15	13	12	12 58	15	16	15	13	12	13 6	14	16
4 59 11	16	14	13	13 59	16	17	16	14	13	14 5	16	17	16	14	14	14 12	16	17
5 3 30	17	15	14	15 6	17	18	17	15	14	15 13	17	18	17	15	15	15 19	17	18
5 7 49	18	16	15	16 14	18	19	18	16	15	16 20	18	19	18	16	16	16 26	18	19
5 12 9	19	17	16	17 22	19	20	19	17	17	17 28	19	20	19	17	17	17 33	19	20
5 16 29	20	18	17	18 31	20	21	20	18	18	18 36	20	21	20	18	18	18 41	20	21
5 20 49	21	19	19	19 39	21	22	21	19	19	19 44	21	22	21	19	19	19 48	21	22
5 25 10	22	20	20	20 48	23	23	22	20	20	20 52	22	23	22	20	20	20 56	22	23
5 29 31	23	21	21	21 57	24	24	23	21	21	22 0	24	24	23	21	21	22 4	23	24
5 33 51	24	22	22	23 5	25	25	24	22	22	23 8	25	25	24	22	22	23 11	25	25
5 38 13	25	23	23	24 14	26	26	25	23	23	24 17	26	26	25	23	23	24 19	26	26
5 42 34	26	24	24	25 23	27	27	26	24	24	25 25	27	27	26	25	24	25 27	27	27
5 46 55	27	25	25	26 33	28	28	27	25	25	26 34	28	28	27	26	25	26 36	28	28
5 51 17	28	26	26	27 42	29	♐	28	26	26	27 43	29	♐	28	27	26	27 44	29	29
5 55 38	29	27	27	28 51	♏	1	29	27	27	28 51	♏	♐	29	28	28	28 52	♏	♐
HOUSES	4	5	6	7	8	9	4	5	6	7	8	9	4	5	6	7	8	9

LATITUDE 4° S.   LATITUDE 5° S.   LATITUDE 6° S.

	LATITUDE 4° N.						LATITUDE 5° N.						LATITUDE 6° N.					
SIDEREAL TIME	10 ♋	11 ♋	12 ♌	ASC ♎	2 ♏	3 ♐	10 ♋	11 ♋	12 ♌	ASC ♎	2 ♏	3 ♐	10 ♋	11 ♋	12 ♌	ASC ♎	2 ♏	3 ♐
H M S	°	°	°	° '	°	°	°	°	°	° '	°	°	°	°	°	° '	°	°
6 0 0	0	28	28	0 0	2	2	0	29	29	0 0	1	1	0	29	29	0 0	1	1
6 4 22	1	29	♍	1 9	3	3	1	♌	♍	1 9	3	3	1	♌	♍	1 8	2	2
6 8 43	2	♌	1	2 18	4	4	2	1	1	2 17	4	4	2	1	1	2 16	4	3
6 13 5	3	2	2	3 27	5	5	3	2	2	3 26	5	5	3	2	2	3 24	5	4
6 17 26	4	3	3	4 37	6	6	4	3	3	4 35	6	6	4	3	3	4 33	6	5
6 21 47	5	4	4	5 46	7	7	5	4	4	5 43	7	7	5	4	4	5 41	7	7
6 26 9	6	5	5	6 55	8	8	6	5	5	6 52	8	8	6	5	5	6 49	8	8
6 30 29	7	6	6	8 3	9	9	7	6	6	8 0	9	9	7	6	7	7 56	9	9
6 34 50	8	7	7	9 12	10	10	8	7	8	9 8	10	10	8	7	8	9 4	10	10
6 39 11	9	8	9	10 21	11	11	9	8	9	10 16	11	11	9	8	9	10 12	11	11
6 43 31	10	9	10	11 29	13	12	10	9	10	11 24	12	12	10	9	10	11 19	12	12
6 47 51	11	10	11	12 38	14	13	11	10	11	12 32	13	13	11	10	11	12 27	13	13
6 52 11	12	11	12	13 46	15	14	12	11	12	13 40	15	14	12	11	12	13 34	14	14
6 56 30	13	12	13	14 54	16	15	13	12	13	14 47	16	15	13	12	13	14 41	15	15
7 0 49	14	13	14	16 1	17	16	14	13	14	15 55	17	16	14	13	14	15 48	16	16
7 5 7	15	14	15	17 9	18	17	15	14	15	17 2	18	17	15	14	16	16 54	18	17
7 9 26	16	15	17	18 16	19	18	16	15	17	18 8	19	18	16	15	17	18 1	19	18
7 13 43	17	16	18	19 23	20	19	17	16	18	19 15	20	19	17	17	18	19 7	20	19
7 18 0	18	17	19	20 30	21	20	18	18	19	20 22	21	20	18	18	19	20 13	21	20
7 22 17	19	19	20	21 37	22	21	19	19	20	21 28	22	21	19	19	20	21 19	22	21
7 26 33	20	20	21	22 43	23	22	20	20	21	22 34	23	22	20	20	21	22 24	23	22
7 30 49	21	21	22	23 49	24	23	21	21	22	23 39	24	23	21	21	22	23 29	24	23
7 35 4	22	22	23	24 55	25	24	22	22	23	24 45	25	24	22	22	23	24 34	25	23
7 39 19	23	23	24	26 1	26	25	23	23	25	25 50	26	25	23	23	25	25 39	26	24
7 43 33	24	24	26	27 6	27	26	24	24	26	26 55	27	26	24	24	26	26 43	27	25
7 47 46	25	25	27	28 11	28	27	25	25	27	27 59	28	27	25	25	27	27 48	28	26
7 51 59	26	26	28	29 16	29	28	26	26	28	29 3	29	27	26	26	28	28 51	29	27
7 56 11	27	27	29	0♍ 20	♐	29	27	27	29	0♍ 7	♐	28	27	27	29	29 55	♐	28
8 0 23	28	28	♎	1 24	1	♑	28	28	♎	1 11	1	29	28	28	♎	0♍ 58	1	29
8 4 34	29	29	1	2 27	2	1	29	29	1	2 14	2	♑	29	29	1	2 1	2	♑
8 8 44	♌	♍	2	3 31	3	1	♌	♍	2	3 17	3	1	♌	♍	2	3 4	3	1
8 12 53	1	1	3	4 34	4	2	1	2	3	4 20	4	2	1	2	3	4 6	4	2
8 17 2	2	3	5	5 36	5	3	2	3	5	5 22	5	3	2	3	5	5 8	5	3
8 21 10	3	4	6	6 39	6	4	3	4	6	6 24	6	4	3	4	6	6 9	6	4
8 25 18	4	5	7	7 41	7	5	4	5	7	7 26	7	5	4	5	7	7 11	7	5
8 29 24	5	6	8	8 42	8	6	5	6	8	8 27	8	6	5	6	8	8 12	8	6
8 33 30	6	7	9	9 44	9	7	6	7	9	9 28	9	7	6	7	9	9 12	9	7
8 37 36	7	8	10	10 45	10	8	7	8	10	10 29	10	8	7	8	10	10 13	9	8
8 41 40	8	9	11	11 45	11	9	8	9	11	11 29	11	9	8	9	11	11 13	10	9
8 45 44	9	10	12	12 46	12	10	9	10	12	12 29	12	10	9	10	12	12 12	11	10
8 49 47	10	11	13	13 45	13	11	10	11	13	13 29	13	11	10	11	13	13 12	12	11
8 53 50	11	12	14	14 45	14	12	11	12	14	14 28	13	12	11	12	14	14 11	13	12
8 57 51	12	13	15	15 44	15	13	12	13	15	15 27	14	13	12	13	15	15 9	14	13
9 1 52	13	14	16	16 43	16	14	13	14	16	16 26	15	14	13	14	16	16 8	15	13
9 5 52	14	15	18	17 42	17	15	14	15	17	17 24	16	15	14	16	17	17 6	16	14
HOUSES	4	5	6	7	8	9	4	5	6	7	8	9	4	5	6	7	8	9

LATITUDE 4° S.   LATITUDE 5° S.   LATITUDE 6° S.

	LATITUDE 4° N.						LATITUDE 5° N.						LATITUDE 6° N.					
SIDEREAL TIME	10 Ω	11 ♍	12 ⚎	ASC ♏	2 ♐	3 ♑	10 Ω	11 ♍	12 ⚎	ASC ♏	2 ♐	3 ♑	10 Ω	11 ♍	12 ⚎	ASC ♏	2 ♐	3 ♑
H M S	°	°	°	° '	°	°	°	°	°	° '	°	°	°	°	°	° '	°	°
9 9 52	15	17	19	18 40	17	16	15	17	18	18 22	17	15	15	17	18	18 4	17	15
9 13 50	16	18	20	19 38	18	17	16	18	20	19 20	18	16	16	18	19	19 1	18	16
9 17 49	17	19	21	20 36	19	17	17	19	21	20 17	19	17	17	19	20	19 58	19	17
9 21 46	18	20	22	21 33	20	18	18	20	22	21 14	20	18	18	20	21	20 55	20	18
9 25 42	19	21	23	22 30	21	19	19	21	23	22 11	21	19	19	21	23	21 52	21	19
9 29 38	20	22	24	23 27	22	20	20	22	24	23 7	22	20	20	22	24	22 48	21	20
9 33 34	21	23	25	24 23	23	21	21	23	25	24 4	23	21	21	23	25	23 44	22	21
9 37 28	22	24	26	25 19	24	22	22	24	26	24 59	24	22	22	24	26	24 40	23	22
9 41 22	23	25	27	26 15	25	23	23	25	27	25 55	24	23	23	25	27	25 35	24	23
9 45 15	24	26	28	27 11	26	24	24	26	28	26 50	25	24	24	26	28	26 30	25	24
9 49 8	25	27	29	28 6	26	25	25	27	29	27 46	26	25	25	27	29	27 25	26	25
9 53 0	26	28	♏	29 1	27	26	26	28	♏	28 40	27	26	26	28	♏	28 20	27	26
9 56 51	27	29	1	29 56	28	27	27	29	1	29 35	28	27	27	29	0	29 14	28	26
10 0 42	28	⚎	2	0♐ 50	29	28	28	⚎	2	0♐ 29	29	27	28	⚎	1	0♐ 8	29	27
10 4 32	29	1	3	1 44	♑	29	29	1	3	1 23	♑	28	29	1	2	1 2	29	28
10 8 22	♏	2	4	2 38	1	29	♏	2	4	2 17	1	29	♏	2	3	1 56	♑	29
10 12 11	1	3	5	3 32	2	♒	1	3	5	3 11	2	♒	1	3	4	2 49	1	♒
10 15 59	2	4	6	4 26	3	1	2	4	6	4 4	3	1	2	4	5	3 42	2	1
10 19 47	3	5	7	5 19	3	2	3	5	6	4 57	3	2	3	5	6	4 35	3	2
10 23 34	4	6	8	6 12	4	3	4	6	7	5 50	4	3	4	6	7	5 28	4	3
10 27 21	5	7	9	7 5	5	4	5	7	8	6 43	5	4	5	7	8	6 21	5	4
10 31 8	6	8	9	7 58	6	5	6	8	9	7 35	6	5	6	8	9	7 13	6	5
10 34 53	7	9	10	8 50	7	6	7	9	10	8 28	7	6	7	9	10	8 6	6	6
10 38 39	8	10	11	9 43	8	7	8	10	11	9 20	8	7	8	10	11	8 58	7	7
10 42 24	9	11	12	10 35	9	8	9	11	12	10 12	8	8	9	11	12	9 50	8	8
10 46 8	10	12	13	11 27	10	9	10	12	13	11 4	9	9	10	12	13	10 41	9	8
10 49 52	11	13	14	12 18	10	10	11	13	14	11 56	10	9	11	13	14	11 33	10	9
10 53 36	12	14	15	13 10	11	11	12	14	15	12 47	11	10	12	14	15	12 24	11	10
10 57 20	13	15	16	14 2	12	11	13	15	16	13 39	12	11	13	15	16	13 16	12	11
11 1 3	14	16	17	14 53	13	12	14	16	17	14 30	13	12	14	16	17	14 7	12	12
11 4 45	15	17	18	15 44	14	13	15	17	18	15 21	14	13	15	17	17	14 58	13	13
11 8 28	16	18	19	16 35	15	14	16	18	19	16 12	14	14	16	18	18	15 49	14	14
11 12 10	17	19	20	17 27	16	15	17	19	19	17 3	15	15	17	19	19	16 40	15	15
11 15 52	18	20	21	18 17	16	16	18	20	20	17 54	16	16	18	20	20	17 31	16	16
11 19 33	19	21	21	19 8	17	17	19	21	21	18 45	17	17	19	21	21	18 21	17	17
11 23 15	20	22	22	19 59	18	18	20	22	22	19 36	18	18	20	22	22	19 12	18	18
11 26 56	21	23	23	20 50	19	19	21	23	23	20 26	19	19	21	23	23	20 3	19	19
11 30 37	22	24	24	21 40	20	20	22	24	24	21 17	20	20	22	24	24	20 53	19	20
11 34 17	23	25	25	22 31	21	21	23	25	25	22 7	21	21	23	25	25	21 44	20	21
11 37 58	24	26	26	23 22	22	22	24	26	26	22 58	21	22	24	26	25	22 34	21	22
11 41 39	25	27	27	24 12	23	23	25	27	27	23 48	22	23	25	27	26	23 24	22	23
11 45 19	26	28	28	25 3	23	24	26	28	27	24 39	23	24	26	28	27	24 15	23	24
11 48 59	27	29	29	25 53	24	25	27	29	28	25 29	24	25	27	29	28	25 5	24	24
11 52 40	28	♏	29	26 43	25	26	28	♏	29	26 20	25	26	28	♏	29	25 56	25	25
11 56 20	29	1	♐	27 34	26	27	29	1	♐	27 10	26	26	29	1	♐	26 46	26	26
HOUSES	4	5	6	7	8	9	4	5	6	7	8	9	4	5	6	7	8	9

LATITUDE 4° S. LATITUDE 5° S. LATITUDE 6° S.

	LATITUDE 4° N.						LATITUDE 5° N.						LATITUDE 6° N.					
SIDEREAL TIME	10 ♎	11 ♏	12 ♐	ASC ♐	2 ♑	3 ♒	10 ♎	11 ♏	12 ♐	ASC ♐	2 ♑	3 ♒	10 ♎	11 ♏	12 ♐	ASC ♐	2 ♑	3 ♒
H M S	°	°	°	° '	°	°	°	°	°	° '	°	°	°	°	°	° '	°	°
12 0 0	0	2	1	28 24	27	28	0	2	1	28 0	27	27	0	2	1	27 36	26	27
12 3 40	1	3	2	29 15	28	28	1	3	2	28 51	28	28	1	3	2	28 27	27	28
12 7 20	2	4	3	0♑ 5	29	29	2	4	3	29 41	28	29	2	4	3	29 17	28	29
12 11 1	3	5	4	0 56	♒	♓	3	5	4	0♑ 32	29	♓	3	5	3	0♑ 8	29	♓
12 14 41	4	6	5	1 46	0	1	4	6	4	1 22	♒	1	4	5	4	0 58	♒	1
12 18 21	5	7	5	2 37	1	2	5	7	5	2 13	1	2	5	6	5	1 49	1	2
12 22 2	6	8	6	3 28	2	3	6	7	6	3 4	2	3	6	7	6	2 40	2	3
12 25 42	7	8	7	4 19	3	4	7	8	7	3 54	3	4	7	8	7	3 30	3	4
12 29 23	8	9	8	5 9	4	5	8	9	8	4 45	4	5	8	9	8	4 21	4	5
12 33 4	9	10	9	6 0	5	6	9	10	9	5 36	5	6	9	10	8	5 12	5	6
12 36 45	10	11	10	6 51	6	7	10	11	10	6 27	6	7	10	11	9	6 3	5	7
12 40 27	11	12	11	7 42	7	8	11	12	10	7 18	7	8	11	12	10	6 54	6	8
12 44 8	12	13	11	8 34	8	9	12	13	11	8 10	8	9	12	13	11	7 46	7	9
12 47 50	13	14	12	9 25	9	10	13	14	12	9 1	8	10	13	14	12	8 37	8	10
12 51 32	14	15	13	10 17	10	11	14	15	13	9 53	9	11	14	15	13	9 29	9	11
12 55 15	15	16	14	11 8	11	12	15	16	14	10 44	10	12	15	16	14	10 20	10	12
12 58 57	16	17	15	12 0	11	13	16	17	15	11 36	11	13	16	17	14	11 12	11	13
13 2 40	17	18	16	12 52	12	14	17	18	16	12 28	12	14	17	18	15	12 4	12	14
13 6 24	18	19	17	13 44	13	15	18	19	16	13 21	13	15	18	19	16	12 57	13	15
13 10 8	19	20	17	14 37	14	16	19	19	17	14 13	14	16	19	19	17	13 49	14	16
13 13 52	20	20	18	15 29	15	17	20	20	18	15 5	15	17	20	20	18	14 42	15	17
13 17 36	21	21	19	16 22	16	18	21	21	19	15 58	16	18	21	21	19	15 35	16	18
13 21 21	22	22	20	17 15	17	19	22	22	20	16 51	17	19	22	22	20	16 28	17	19
13 25 7	23	23	21	18 8	18	20	23	23	21	17 44	18	20	23	23	20	17 21	18	20
13 28 52	24	24	22	19 1	19	21	24	24	22	18 38	19	21	24	24	21	18 14	19	21
13 32 39	25	25	23	19 55	20	22	25	25	22	19 32	20	22	25	25	22	19 8	20	22
13 36 26	26	26	24	20 49	21	24	26	26	23	20 25	21	23	26	26	23	20 2	21	23
13 40 13	27	27	24	21 43	22	25	27	27	24	21 20	22	25	27	27	24	20 57	22	25
13 44 1	28	28	25	22 37	23	26	28	28	25	22 14	23	26	28	28	25	21 51	23	26
13 47 49	29	29	26	23 32	24	27	29	29	26	23 9	24	27	29	28	26	22 46	24	27
13 51 38	♏	♐	27	24 26	25	28	♏	♐	27	24 4	25	28	♏	29	26	23 41	25	28
13 55 28	1	1	28	25 22	26	29	1	0	28	24 59	26	29	1	♐	27	24 36	26	29
13 59 18	2	1	29	26 17	27	♈	2	1	29	25 55	27	♈	2	1	28	25 32	27	♈
14 3 9	3	2	♑	27 13	28	1	3	2	29	26 51	28	1	3	2	29	26 28	28	1
14 7 0	4	3	1	28 9	29	2	4	3	♑	27 47	29	2	4	3	♑	27 25	29	2
14 10 52	5	4	1	29 5	♓	3	5	4	1	28 43	♓	3	5	4	1	28 21	♓	3
14 14 45	6	5	2	0♒ 2	1	4	6	5	2	29 40	1	4	6	5	2	29 18	1	4
14 18 38	7	6	3	0 59	2	5	7	6	3	0♒ 37	2	5	7	6	3	0♒ 16	2	5
14 22 32	8	7	4	1 56	3	6	8	7	4	1 35	3	6	8	7	4	1 13	3	6
14 26 26	9	8	5	2 54	4	7	9	8	5	2 33	4	7	9	8	4	2 11	4	7
14 30 22	10	9	6	3 52	5	8	10	9	6	3 31	5	8	10	9	5	3 10	5	8
14 34 17	11	10	7	4 50	6	9	11	10	7	4 30	6	9	11	9	6	4 9	6	9
14 38 14	12	11	8	5 49	7	11	12	10	7	5 29	7	11	12	10	7	5 8	7	11
14 42 11	13	12	9	6 48	9	12	13	11	8	6 28	8	12	13	11	8	6 7	8	12
14 46 10	14	12	10	7 48	10	13	14	12	9	7 28	10	13	14	12	9	7 7	9	13
HOUSES	4	5	6	7	8	9	4	5	6	7	8	9	4	5	6	7	8	9

LATITUDE 4° S.   LATITUDE 5° S.   LATITUDE 6° S.

LATITUDE 4° N.

SIDEREAL TIME (H M S)	10 ♏	11 ♐	12 ♑	ASC ♒ (° ')	2 ♓	3 ♈
14 50 8	15	13	10	8 48	11	14
14 54 8	16	14	11	9 48	12	15
14 58 8	17	15	12	10 49	13	16
15 2 9	18	16	13	11 50	14	17
15 6 10	19	17	14	12 51	15	18
15 10 13	20	18	15	13 53	16	19
15 14 16	21	19	16	14 55	17	20
15 18 20	22	20	17	15 58	18	21
15 22 24	23	21	18	17 1	20	22
15 26 30	24	22	19	18 5	21	24
15 30 36	25	23	20	19 9	22	25
15 34 42	26	24	21	20 13	23	26
15 38 50	27	25	22	21 18	24	27
15 42 58	28	26	23	22 23	25	28
15 47 7	29	27	24	23 28	26	29
15 51 16	♐	27	25	24 34	28	♉
15 55 26	1	28	26	25 41	29	1
15 59 37	2	29	27	26 47	♈	2
16 3 49	3	♑	28	27 54	1	3
16 8 1	4	1	29	29 2	2	5
16 12 14	5	2	♒	0♓ 10	3	6
16 16 27	6	3	1	1 18	5	7
16 20 41	7	4	2	2 27	6	8
16 24 56	8	5	3	3 36	7	9
16 29 11	9	6	4	4 45	8	10
16 33 27	10	7	5	5 55	9	11
16 37 43	11	8	6	7 5	10	12
16 41 59	12	9	7	8 15	12	13
16 46 17	13	10	8	9 26	13	14
16 50 34	14	11	9	10 37	14	16
16 54 53	15	12	10	11 48	15	17
16 59 11	16	13	12	13 0	16	18
17 3 30	17	14	13	14 11	18	19
17 7 49	18	15	14	15 23	19	20
17 12 9	19	16	15	16 36	20	21
17 16 29	20	17	16	17 48	21	22
17 20 49	21	18	17	19 1	22	23
17 25 10	22	19	18	20 14	23	24
17 29 31	23	20	19	21 27	25	25
17 33 51	24	21	20	22 40	26	26
17 38 13	25	22	21	23 53	27	27
17 42 34	26	23	23	25 6	28	28
17 46 55	27	24	24	26 20	29	29
17 51 17	28	25	25	27 33	♉	♊
17 55 38	29	26	26	28 46	2	2

LATITUDE 5° N.

SIDEREAL TIME (H M S)	10 ♏	11 ♐	12 ♑	ASC ♒ (° ')	2 ♓	3 ♈
14 50 8	15	13	10	8 28	11	14
14 54 8	16	14	11	9 28	12	15
14 58 8	17	15	12	10 29	13	16
15 2 9	18	16	13	11 31	14	17
15 6 10	19	17	14	12 32	15	18
15 10 13	20	18	15	13 35	16	19
15 14 16	21	19	16	14 37	17	20
15 18 20	22	20	17	15 40	18	21
15 22 24	23	21	18	16 44	20	23
15 26 30	24	22	19	17 47	21	24
15 30 36	25	23	20	18 52	22	25
15 34 42	26	24	21	19 56	23	26
15 38 50	27	24	22	21 1	24	27
15 42 58	28	25	23	22 7	25	28
15 47 7	29	26	24	23 13	26	29
15 51 16	♐	27	25	24 19	28	♉
15 55 26	1	28	26	25 26	29	1
15 59 37	2	29	27	26 33	♈	2
16 3 49	3	♑	28	27 40	1	4
16 8 1	4	1	29	28 48	2	5
16 12 14	5	2	♒	29 57	3	6
16 16 27	6	3	1	1♓ 5	5	7
16 20 41	7	4	2	2 14	6	8
16 24 56	8	5	3	3 24	7	9
16 29 11	9	6	4	4 34	8	10
16 33 27	10	7	5	5 44	9	11
16 37 43	11	8	6	6 54	11	12
16 41 59	12	9	7	8 5	12	13
16 46 17	13	10	8	9 17	13	15
16 50 34	14	11	9	10 28	14	16
16 54 53	15	12	10	11 40	15	17
16 59 11	16	13	11	12 52	16	18
17 3 30	17	14	12	14 4	18	19
17 7 49	18	15	13	15 17	19	20
17 12 9	19	16	15	16 29	20	21
17 16 29	20	17	16	17 42	21	22
17 20 49	21	18	17	18 56	22	23
17 25 10	22	19	18	20 9	24	24
17 29 31	23	20	19	21 22	25	25
17 33 51	24	21	20	22 36	26	26
17 38 13	25	22	21	23 50	27	27
17 42 34	26	23	22	25 4	28	28
17 46 55	27	24	24	26 18	29	♊
17 51 17	28	25	25	27 32	♉	1
17 55 38	29	26	26	28 46	2	2

LATITUDE 6° N.

SIDEREAL TIME (H M S)	10 ♏	11 ♐	12 ♑	ASC ♒ (° ')	2 ♓	3 ♈
14 50 8	15	13	10	8 8	10	14
14 54 8	16	14	11	9 9	12	15
14 58 8	17	15	12	10 10	13	16
15 2 9	18	16	13	11 11	14	17
15 6 10	19	17	14	12 13	15	18
15 10 13	20	18	15	13 16	16	19
15 14 16	21	19	16	14 19	17	20
15 18 20	22	20	17	15 22	18	22
15 22 24	23	21	17	16 26	19	23
15 26 30	24	22	18	17 30	21	24
15 30 36	25	22	19	18 34	22	25
15 34 42	26	23	20	19 39	23	26
15 38 50	27	24	21	20 45	24	27
15 42 58	28	25	22	21 51	25	28
15 47 7	29	26	23	22 57	26	29
15 51 16	♐	27	24	24 4	28	♉
15 55 26	1	28	25	25 11	29	1
15 59 37	2	29	26	26 18	♈	3
16 3 49	3	♑	27	27 26	1	4
16 8 1	4	1	28	28 34	2	5
16 12 14	5	2	29	29 43	3	6
16 16 27	6	3	♒	0♓ 52	5	7
16 20 41	7	4	1	2 2	6	8
16 24 56	8	5	3	3 12	7	9
16 29 11	9	6	4	4 22	8	10
16 33 27	10	7	5	5 33	9	11
16 37 43	11	8	6	6 44	11	12
16 41 59	12	9	7	7 55	12	14
16 46 17	13	10	8	9 7	13	15
16 50 34	14	11	9	10 19	14	16
16 54 53	15	12	10	11 31	15	17
16 59 11	16	13	11	12 44	17	18
17 3 30	17	14	12	13 57	18	19
17 7 49	18	15	13	15 10	19	20
17 12 9	19	16	14	16 23	20	21
17 16 29	20	17	15	17 37	21	22
17 20 49	21	18	17	18 50	23	23
17 25 10	22	19	18	20 4	24	24
17 29 31	23	20	19	21 18	25	25
17 33 51	24	21	20	22 33	26	26
17 38 13	25	22	21	23 47	27	28
17 42 34	26	23	22	25 1	28	29
17 46 55	27	24	23	26 16	♉	♊
17 51 17	28	25	25	27 31	1	1
17 55 38	29	26	26	28 45	2	2

HOUSES	4	5	6	7	8	9

LATITUDE 4° S. LATITUDE 5° S. LATITUDE 6° S.

	LATITUDE 4° N.						LATITUDE 5° N.						LATITUDE 6° N.					
SIDEREAL TIME	10 ♑	11 ♑	12 ♒	ASC ♈	2 ♉	3 ♊	10 ♑	11 ♑	12 ♒	ASC ♈	2 ♉	3 ♊	10 ♑	11 ♑	12 ♒	ASC ♈	2 ♉	3 ♊
H M S	°	°	°	° '	°	°	°	°	°	° '	°	°	°	°	°	° '	°	°
18 0 0	0	27	27	0 0	3	3	0	27	27	0 0	3	3	0	27	27	0 0	3	3
18 4 22	1	28	28	1 14	4	4	1	28	28	1 14	4	4	1	28	28	1 15	4	4
18 8 43	2	≈	♓	2 27	5	5	2	29	29	2 28	5	5	2	29	29	2 29	5	5
18 13 5	3	1	1	3 40	6	6	3	≈	♓	3 42	6	6	3	≈	♓	3 44	7	6
18 17 26	4	2	2	4 54	7	7	4	2	2	4 56	8	7	4	1	2	4 59	8	7
18 21 47	5	3	3	6 7	9	8	5	3	3	6 10	9	8	5	2	3	6 13	9	8
18 26 9	6	4	4	7 20	10	9	6	4	4	7 24	10	9	6	4	4	7 27	10	9
18 30 29	7	5	5	8 33	11	10	7	5	5	8 38	11	10	7	5	5	8 42	11	10
18 34 50	8	6	7	9 46	12	11	8	6	6	9 51	12	11	8	6	6	9 56	12	11
18 39 11	9	7	8	10 59	13	12	9	7	8	11 4	13	12	9	7	7	11 10	13	12
18 43 31	10	8	9	12 12	14	13	10	8	9	12 18	14	13	10	8	9	12 23	15	13
18 47 51	11	9	10	13 24	15	14	11	9	10	13 31	15	14	11	9	10	13 37	16	14
18 52 11	12	10	11	14 37	16	15	12	10	11	14 43	17	15	12	10	11	14 50	17	15
18 56 30	13	11	12	15 49	17	16	13	11	12	15 56	18	16	13	11	12	16 3	18	16
19 0 49	14	12	14	17 0	18	17	14	12	14	17 8	19	17	14	12	13	17 16	19	17
19 5 7	15	13	15	18 12	20	18	15	13	15	18 20	20	18	15	13	15	18 29	20	18
19 9 26	16	14	16	19 23	21	19	16	14	16	19 32	21	19	16	14	16	19 41	21	19
19 13 43	17	16	17	20 34	22	20	17	15	17	20 43	22	20	17	15	17	20 53	22	20
19 18 0	18	17	18	21 45	23	21	18	17	18	21 55	23	21	18	16	18	22 5	23	21
19 22 17	19	18	20	22 55	24	22	19	18	19	23 6	24	22	19	18	19	23 16	24	22
19 26 33	20	19	21	24 5	25	23	20	19	21	24 16	25	23	20	19	21	24 27	25	23
19 30 49	21	20	22	25 15	26	24	21	20	22	25 26	26	24	21	20	22	25 38	26	24
19 35 4	22	21	23	26 24	27	25	22	21	23	26 36	27	25	22	21	23	26 48	27	25
19 39 19	23	22	24	27 33	28	26	23	22	24	27 46	28	26	23	22	24	27 58	29	26
19 43 33	24	23	25	28 42	29	27	24	23	25	28 55	29	27	24	23	25	29 8	Ⅱ	27
19 47 46	25	24	27	29 50	Ⅱ	28	25	24	27	0♉ 3	Ⅱ	28	25	24	27	0♉ 17	1	28
19 51 59	26	25	28	0♉ 58	1	29	26	25	28	1 12	1	29	26	25	28	1 26	2	29
19 56 11	27	27	29	2 6	2	♋	27	26	29	2 20	2	♋	27	26	29	2 34	3	♋
20 0 23	28	28	♈	3 13	3	1	28	28	♈	3 27	3	1	28	27	♈	3 42	4	1
20 4 34	29	29	1	4 19	4	2	29	29	1	4 34	4	2	29	29	1	4 49	5	2
20 8 44	≈	♓	2	5 26	5	3	≈	♓	2	5 41	5	3	≈	♓	2	5 56	6	3
20 12 53	1	1	4	6 32	6	3	1	1	4	6 47	6	4	1	1	4	7 3	7	4
20 17 2	2	2	5	7 37	7	4	2	2	5	7 53	7	5	2	2	5	8 9	8	5
20 21 10	3	3	6	8 42	8	5	3	3	6	8 59	8	6	3	3	6	9 15	9	6
20 25 18	4	4	7	9 47	9	6	4	4	7	10 4	9	6	4	4	7	10 21	10	7
20 29 24	5	5	8	10 51	10	7	5	5	8	11 8	10	7	5	5	8	11 26	11	8
20 33 30	6	6	9	11 55	11	8	6	6	9	12 13	11	8	6	6	9	12 30	12	8
20 37 36	7	8	10	12 59	12	9	7	7	10	13 16	12	9	7	7	11	13 34	13	9
20 41 40	8	9	12	14 2	13	10	8	9	12	14 20	13	10	8	8	12	14 38	13	10
20 45 44	9	10	13	15 5	14	11	9	10	13	15 23	14	11	9	10	13	15 41	14	11
20 49 47	10	11	14	16 7	15	12	10	11	14	16 25	15	12	10	11	14	16 44	15	12
20 53 50	11	12	15	17 9	16	13	11	12	15	17 28	16	13	11	12	15	17 47	16	13
20 57 51	12	13	16	18 10	17	14	12	13	16	18 29	17	14	12	13	16	18 49	17	14
21 1 52	13	14	17	19 11	18	15	13	14	17	19 31	18	15	13	14	17	19 50	18	15
21 5 52	14	15	18	20 12	19	16	14	15	18	20 32	19	16	14	15	18	20 51	19	16
HOUSES	4	5	6	7	8	9	4	5	6	7	8	9	4	5	6	7	8	9

LATITUDE 4° S.   LATITUDE 5° S.   LATITUDE 6° S.

LATITUDE 4° N. LATITUDE 5° N. LATITUDE 6° N.

LATITUDE 4° N.

SIDEREAL TIME (H M S)	10 ♒	11 ♓	12 ♈	ASC ♉	2 ♊	3 ♋
21 9 52	15	16	19	21 12	20	17
21 13 50	16	17	20	22 12	20	18
21 17 49	17	18	21	23 12	21	18
21 21 46	18	19	23	24 11	22	19
21 25 42	19	21	24	25 10	23	20
21 29 38	20	22	25	26 8	24	21
21 33 34	21	23	26	27 6	25	22
21 37 28	22	24	27	28 4	26	23
21 41 22	23	25	28	29 1	27	24
21 45 15	24	26	29	29 58	28	25
21 49 8	25	27	♉	0♊ 55	29	26
21 53 0	26	28	1	1 51	29	27
21 56 51	27	29	2	2 47	♋	28
22 0 42	28	♈	3	3 43	1	29
22 4 32	29	1	4	4 38	2	29
22 8 22	♓	2	5	5 34	3	♌
22 12 11	1	3	6	6 28	4	1
22 15 59	2	4	7	7 23	5	2
22 19 47	3	5	8	8 17	6	3
22 23 34	4	6	9	9 11	6	4
22 27 21	5	8	10	10 5	7	5
22 31 8	6	9	11	10 59	8	6
22 34 53	7	10	12	11 52	9	7
22 38 39	8	11	13	12 45	10	8
22 42 24	9	12	14	13 38	11	9
22 46 8	10	13	15	14 31	12	10
22 49 52	11	14	16	15 23	13	10
22 53 36	12	15	17	16 16	13	11
22 57 20	13	16	18	17 8	14	12
23 1 3	14	17	19	18 0	15	13
23 4 45	15	18	19	18 52	16	14
23 8 28	16	19	20	19 43	17	15
23 12 10	17	20	21	20 35	18	16
23 15 52	18	21	22	21 26	19	17
23 19 33	19	22	23	22 18	19	18
23 23 15	20	23	24	23 9	20	19
23 26 56	21	24	25	24 0	21	20
23 30 37	22	25	26	24 51	22	21
23 34 17	23	26	27	25 41	23	22
23 37 58	24	27	28	26 32	24	23
23 41 39	25	28	29	27 23	25	23
23 45 19	26	29	♊	28 14	25	24
23 48 59	27	♉	0	29 4	26	25
23 52 40	28	1	1	29 55	27	26
23 56 20	29	2	2	0♋ 45	28	27

LATITUDE 5° N.

SIDEREAL TIME (H M S)	10 ♒	11 ♓	12 ♈	ASC ♉	2 ♊	3 ♋
21 9 52	15	16	19	21 32	20	17
21 13 50	16	17	20	22 32	21	18
21 17 49	17	18	22	23 32	22	19
21 21 46	18	19	23	24 31	23	20
21 25 42	19	21	24	25 30	23	20
21 29 38	20	22	25	26 29	24	21
21 33 34	21	23	26	27 27	25	22
21 37 28	22	24	27	28 25	26	23
21 41 22	23	25	28	29 23	27	24
21 45 15	24	26	29	0♊ 20	28	25
21 49 8	25	27	♉	1 17	29	26
21 53 0	26	28	1	2 13	♋	27
21 56 51	27	29	2	3 9	1	28
22 0 42	28	♈	3	4 5	1	29
22 4 32	29	1	4	5 1	2	♌
22 8 22	♓	2	5	5 56	3	0
22 12 11	1	3	6	6 51	4	1
22 15 59	2	4	7	7 46	5	2
22 19 47	3	5	8	8 40	6	3
22 23 34	4	7	9	9 35	7	4
22 27 21	5	8	10	10 28	8	5
22 31 8	6	9	11	11 22	8	6
22 34 53	7	10	12	12 16	9	7
22 38 39	8	11	13	13 9	10	8
22 42 24	9	12	14	14 2	11	9
22 46 8	10	13	15	14 55	12	10
22 49 52	11	14	16	15 47	13	11
22 53 36	12	15	17	16 39	14	11
22 57 20	13	16	18	17 32	14	12
23 1 3	14	17	19	18 24	15	13
23 4 45	15	18	20	19 16	16	14
23 8 28	16	19	21	20 7	17	15
23 12 10	17	20	22	20 59	18	16
23 15 52	18	21	22	21 50	19	17
23 19 33	19	22	23	22 42	20	18
23 23 15	20	23	24	23 33	20	19
23 26 56	21	24	25	24 24	21	20
23 30 37	22	25	26	25 15	22	21
23 34 17	23	26	27	26 6	23	22
23 37 58	24	27	28	26 56	24	23
23 41 39	25	28	29	27 47	25	23
23 45 19	26	29	♊	28 38	26	24
23 48 59	27	♉	1	29 28	26	25
23 52 40	28	1	2	0♋ 19	27	26
23 56 20	29	2	2	1 9	28	27

LATITUDE 6° N.

SIDEREAL TIME (H M S)	10 ♒	11 ♓	12 ♈	ASC ♉	2 ♊	3 ♋
21 9 52	15	16	20	21 52	20	17
21 13 50	16	17	21	22 53	21	18
21 17 49	17	18	22	23 53	22	19
21 21 46	18	19	23	24 52	23	20
21 25 42	19	21	24	25 51	24	21
21 29 38	20	22	25	26 50	25	22
21 33 34	21	23	26	27 49	26	22
21 37 28	22	24	27	28 47	26	23
21 41 22	23	25	28	29 44	27	24
21 45 15	24	26	29	0♊ 42	28	25
21 49 8	25	27	♉	1 39	29	26
21 53 0	26	28	1	2 35	♋	27
21 56 51	27	29	2	3 32	1	28
22 0 42	28	♈	3	4 28	2	29
22 4 32	29	1	4	5 24	3	♌
22 8 22	♓	2	5	6 19	4	1
22 12 11	1	3	6	7 14	4	2
22 15 59	2	4	7	8 9	5	2
22 19 47	3	5	8	9 3	6	3
22 23 34	4	7	9	9 58	7	4
22 27 21	5	8	10	10 52	8	5
22 31 8	6	9	11	11 46	9	6
22 34 53	7	10	12	12 39	10	7
22 38 39	8	11	13	13 32	10	8
22 42 24	9	12	14	14 25	11	9
22 46 8	10	13	15	15 18	12	10
22 49 52	11	14	16	16 11	13	11
22 53 36	12	15	17	17 3	14	12
22 57 20	13	16	18	17 56	15	12
23 1 3	14	17	19	18 48	16	13
23 4 45	15	18	20	19 40	16	14
23 8 28	16	19	21	20 31	17	15
23 12 10	17	20	22	21 23	18	16
23 15 52	18	21	23	22 14	19	17
23 19 33	19	22	24	23 6	20	18
23 23 15	20	23	25	23 57	21	19
23 26 56	21	24	25	24 48	22	20
23 30 37	22	25	26	25 39	22	21
23 34 17	23	26	27	26 30	23	22
23 37 58	24	27	28	27 20	24	23
23 41 39	25	28	29	28 11	25	24
23 45 19	26	29	♊	29 2	26	25
23 48 59	27	♉	1	29 52	27	25
23 52 40	28	1	2	0♋ 43	28	26
23 56 20	29	2	3	1 33	28	27

HOUSES | 4 | 5 | 6 | 7 | 8 | 9

LATITUDE 4° S. LATITUDE 5° S. LATITUDE 6° S.

LATITUDE 7° N. LATITUDE 8° N. LATITUDE 9° N.

SIDEREAL TIME H M S	10 ♈	11 ♉	12 ♊	ASC ♋	2 ♌	3 ♌	10 ♈	11 ♉	12 ♊	ASC ♋	2 ♌	3 ♌	10 ♈	11 ♉	12 ♊	ASC ♋	2 ♌	3 ♌
0 0 0	0	3	4	2 48	0	28	0	3	4	3 12	0	28	0	3	4	3 36	0	28
0 3 40	1	4	5	3 38	0	29	1	4	5	4 2	1	29	1	4	5	4 27	1	29
0 7 20	2	5	6	4 29	1	♏	2	5	6	4 53	2	♏	2	5	6	5 17	2	♏
0 11 1	3	6	6	5 19	2	1	3	6	7	5 43	2	1	3	6	7	6 7	3	1
0 14 41	4	7	7	6 9	3	2	4	7	8	6 33	3	2	4	7	8	6 57	3	2
0 18 21	5	8	8	7 0	4	3	5	8	8	7 24	4	3	5	8	9	7 48	4	3
0 22 2	6	8	9	7 50	5	4	6	9	9	8 14	5	4	6	9	10	8 38	5	4
0 25 43	7	9	10	8 40	6	5	7	10	10	9 4	6	5	7	10	10	9 28	6	5
0 29 23	8	10	11	9 31	7	6	8	10	11	9 54	7	6	8	11	11	10 18	7	6
0 33 4	9	11	12	10 21	7	7	9	11	12	10 45	8	7	9	12	12	11 9	8	7
0 36 45	10	12	13	11 12	8	8	10	12	13	11 35	9	8	10	12	13	11 59	9	8
0 40 27	11	13	13	12 2	9	9	11	13	14	12 26	9	9	11	13	14	12 49	10	9
0 44 8	12	14	14	12 53	10	10	12	14	15	13 16	10	10	12	14	15	13 40	11	10
0 47 50	13	15	15	13 44	11	11	13	15	15	14 7	11	11	13	15	16	14 30	11	11
0 51 32	14	16	16	14 34	12	12	14	16	16	14 58	12	12	14	16	17	15 21	12	12
0 55 15	15	17	17	15 25	13	13	15	17	17	15 48	13	13	15	17	17	16 12	13	13
0 58 57	16	18	18	16 16	14	14	16	18	18	16 39	14	14	16	18	18	17 2	14	14
1 2 40	17	19	19	17 7	15	15	17	19	19	17 30	15	15	17	19	19	17 53	15	15
1 6 24	18	20	20	17 59	15	16	18	20	20	18 21	16	16	18	20	20	18 44	16	16
1 10 8	19	21	20	18 50	16	17	19	21	21	19 13	17	17	19	21	21	19 35	17	17
1 13 52	20	22	21	19 41	17	18	20	22	22	20 4	18	18	20	22	22	20 27	18	18
1 17 36	21	23	22	20 33	18	19	21	23	22	20 56	18	19	21	23	23	21 18	19	19
1 21 21	22	24	23	21 25	19	20	22	24	23	21 47	19	20	22	24	24	22 10	20	20
1 25 7	23	24	24	22 17	20	21	23	25	24	22 39	20	21	23	25	24	23 1	20	21
1 28 52	24	25	25	23 9	21	22	24	25	25	23 31	21	22	24	26	25	23 53	21	22
1 32 39	25	26	26	24 1	22	23	25	26	26	24 23	22	23	25	27	26	24 45	22	23
1 36 26	26	27	26	24 54	23	24	26	27	27	25 15	23	24	26	27	27	25 37	23	24
1 40 13	27	28	27	25 46	24	25	27	28	28	26 8	24	25	27	28	28	26 30	24	25
1 44 1	28	29	28	26 39	25	26	28	29	28	27 1	25	26	28	29	29	27 22	25	26
1 47 49	29	♊	29	27 32	26	27	29	♊	29	27 54	26	27	29	♊	♋	28 15	26	27
1 51 38	♉	1	♋	28 25	27	28	♉	1	♋	28 47	27	28	♉	1	0	29 8	27	28
1 55 28	1	2	1	29 19	28	29	1	2	1	29 40	28	29	1	2	1	0♌ 1	28	29
1 59 18	2	3	2	0♌ 13	29	♎	2	3	2	0♌ 33	29	♎	2	3	2	0 54	29	♎
2 3 9	3	4	3	1 7	♏	1	3	4	3	1 27	♏	1	3	4	3	1 48	♏	1
2 7 0	4	5	3	2 1	1	2	4	5	4	2 21	1	2	4	5	4	2 42	1	2
2 10 52	5	6	4	2 55	2	3	5	6	5	3 15	2	3	5	6	5	3 36	2	3
2 14 45	6	6	5	3 50	3	4	6	7	6	4 10	3	4	6	7	6	4 30	3	4
2 18 38	7	7	6	4 45	4	5	7	8	6	5 5	4	5	7	8	7	5 24	4	5
2 22 32	8	8	7	5 40	5	6	8	8	7	6 0	5	6	8	9	8	6 19	5	6
2 26 26	9	9	8	6 36	6	7	9	9	8	6 55	6	7	9	9	8	7 14	6	7
2 30 22	10	10	9	7 31	7	8	10	10	9	7 50	7	8	10	10	9	8 10	7	8
2 34 17	11	11	10	8 27	8	9	11	11	10	8 46	8	9	11	11	10	9 5	8	9
2 38 14	12	12	11	9 24	9	10	12	12	11	9 42	9	10	12	12	11	10 1	9	10
2 42 11	13	13	12	10 20	10	11	13	13	12	10 39	10	11	13	13	12	10 57	10	11
2 46 10	14	14	12	11 17	11	12	14	14	13	11 35	11	12	14	14	13	11 54	11	12
HOUSES	4	5	6	7	8	9	4	5	6	7	8	9	4	5	6	7	8	9

LATITUDE 7° S. LATITUDE 8° S. LATITUDE 9° S.

LATITUDE 7° N. LATITUDE 8° N. LATITUDE 9° N.

SIDEREAL TIME	10 ♉	11 ♊	12 ♋	ASC ♌ °	ASC '	2 ♍	3 ♎	10 ♉	11 ♊	12 ♋	ASC ♌ °	ASC '	2 ♍	3 ♎	10 ♉	11 ♊	12 ♋	ASC ♌ °	ASC '	2 ♍	3 ♎
H M S																					
2 50 8	15	15	13	12	14	12	13	15	15	14	12	32	12	13	15	15	14	12	50	12	13
2 54 8	16	16	14	13	12	13	14	16	16	15	13	30	13	14	16	16	15	13	47	13	14
2 58 8	17	17	15	14	10	14	16	17	17	15	14	27	14	15	17	17	16	14	44	14	15
3 2 9	18	18	16	15	8	15	17	18	18	16	15	25	15	17	18	18	17	15	42	15	16
3 6 10	19	19	17	16	6	16	18	19	19	17	16	23	16	18	19	19	18	16	40	16	18
3 10 13	20	19	18	17	5	17	19	20	20	18	17	22	17	19	20	20	18	17	38	17	19
3 14 16	21	20	19	18	4	18	20	21	21	19	18	20	18	20	21	21	19	18	37	18	20
3 18 20	22	21	20	19	3	19	21	22	21	20	19	19	19	21	22	22	20	19	35	19	21
3 22 24	23	22	21	20	3	20	22	23	22	21	20	19	20	22	23	23	21	20	34	20	22
3 26 30	24	23	22	21	3	21	23	24	23	22	21	18	21	23	24	24	22	21	34	21	23
3 30 36	25	24	23	22	3	22	24	25	24	23	22	18	22	24	25	24	23	22	33	22	24
3 34 42	26	25	24	23	4	23	25	26	25	24	23	19	23	25	26	25	24	23	33	23	25
3 38 50	27	26	25	24	5	24	26	27	26	25	24	19	24	26	27	26	25	24	34	24	26
3 42 58	28	27	26	25	6	26	27	28	27	26	25	20	26	27	28	27	26	25	34	26	27
3 47 7	29	28	27	26	8	27	28	29	28	27	26	22	27	28	29	28	27	26	35	27	28
3 51 16	♊	29	28	27	10	28	29	♊	29	28	27	23	28	29	♊	29	28	27	36	28	29
3 55 26	1	♋	28	28	12	29	♏	1	♋	29	28	25	29	♏	1	♋	29	28	38	29	♏
3 59 37	2	1	29	29	15	♎	2	2	1	♌	29	27	♎	1	2	1	♌	29	40	♎	1
4 3 49	3	2	♌	0♍	17	1	3	3	2	1	0♍	30	1	3	3	2	1	0♍	42	1	2
4 8 1	4	3	1	1	21	2	4	4	3	2	1	32	2	4	4	3	2	1	44	2	4
4 12 14	5	4	2	2	24	3	5	5	4	3	2	35	3	5	5	4	3	2	47	3	5
4 16 27	6	5	3	3	28	4	6	6	5	4	3	39	4	6	6	5	4	3	50	4	6
4 20 41	7	6	4	4	32	5	7	7	6	5	4	42	5	7	7	6	5	4	53	5	7
4 24 56	8	7	5	5	36	7	8	8	7	6	5	46	7	8	8	7	6	5	56	6	8
4 29 11	9	8	6	6	41	8	9	9	8	7	6	50	8	9	9	8	7	7	0	8	9
4 33 27	10	9	8	7	45	9	10	10	9	8	7	55	9	10	10	9	8	8	4	9	10
4 37 43	11	10	9	8	50	10	11	11	10	9	8	59	10	11	11	10	9	9	8	10	11
4 41 59	12	11	10	9	56	11	12	12	11	10	10	4	11	12	12	11	10	10	13	11	12
4 46 17	13	12	11	11	1	12	13	13	12	11	11	9	12	13	13	12	11	11	17	12	13
4 50 34	14	13	12	12	7	13	14	14	13	12	12	15	13	14	14	13	12	12	22	13	14
4 54 53	15	14	13	13	13	14	15	15	14	13	13	20	14	15	15	14	13	13	27	14	15
4 59 11	16	15	14	14	19	16	17	16	15	14	14	26	15	16	16	15	14	14	33	15	16
5 3 30	17	16	15	15	26	17	18	17	16	15	15	32	17	18	17	16	15	15	38	16	17
5 7 49	18	17	16	16	32	18	19	18	17	16	16	38	18	19	18	17	16	16	44	18	18
5 12 9	19	18	17	17	39	19	20	19	18	17	17	44	19	20	19	18	17	17	49	19	20
5 16 29	20	19	18	18	46	20	21	20	19	18	18	51	20	21	20	19	18	18	55	20	21
5 20 49	21	20	19	19	53	21	22	21	20	19	19	57	21	22	21	20	19	20	1	21	22
5 25 10	22	21	20	21	0	22	23	22	21	20	21	4	22	23	22	21	20	21	8	22	23
5 29 31	23	22	21	22	7	23	24	23	22	21	22	10	23	24	23	22	22	22	14	23	24
5 33 51	24	23	22	23	14	24	25	24	23	22	23	17	24	25	24	23	23	23	20	24	25
5 38 13	25	24	23	24	22	26	26	25	24	24	24	24	25	26	25	24	24	24	27	25	26
5 42 34	26	25	24	25	29	27	27	26	25	25	25	31	27	27	26	25	25	25	33	26	27
5 46 55	27	26	25	26	37	28	28	27	26	26	26	38	28	28	27	26	26	26	40	28	28
5 51 17	28	27	27	27	45	29	29	28	27	27	27	46	29	29	28	27	27	27	47	29	29
5 55 38	29	28	28	28	52	♏	♐	29	28	28	28	53	♏	♐	29	28	28	28	53	♏	♐
HOUSES	4	5	6	7		8	9	4	5	6	7		8	9	4	5	6	7		8	9

LATITUDE 7° S. LATITUDE 8° S. LATITUDE 9° S.

LATITUDE 7° N. LATITUDE 8° N. LATITUDE 9° N.

SIDEREAL TIME	10 S	11 S	12 Ω	ASC ≈		2 ♏	3 ♐	10 S	11 S	12 Ω	ASC ≈		2 ♏	3 ♐	10 S	11 S	12 Ω	ASC ≈		2 ♏	3 ♐
H M S	°	°	°	°	′	°	°	°	°	°	°	′	°	°	°	°	°	°	′	°	°
6 0 0	0	29	29	0	0	1	1	0	29	29	0	0	1	1	0	29	29	0	0	1	1
6 4 22	1	Ω	♏	1	8	2	2	1	Ω	♏	1	7	2	2	1	Ω	♏	1	7	2	2
6 8 43	2	1	1	2	15	3	3	2	1	1	2	14	3	3	2	1	1	2	13	3	3
6 13 5	3	2	2	3	23	4	4	3	2	2	3	22	4	4	3	2	2	3	20	4	4
6 17 26	4	3	3	4	31	6	5	4	3	3	4	29	5	5	4	3	4	4	27	5	5
6 21 47	5	4	4	5	38	7	6	5	4	5	5	36	6	6	5	4	5	5	33	6	6
6 26 9	6	5	6	6	46	8	7	6	5	6	6	43	8	7	6	5	6	6	40	7	7
6 30 29	7	6	7	7	53	9	8	7	6	7	7	49	9	8	7	6	7	7	46	8	8
6 34 50	8	7	8	9	0	10	9	8	7	8	8	56	10	9	8	7	8	8	52	10	9
6 39 11	9	8	9	10	7	11	10	9	8	9	10	3	11	10	9	8	9	9	59	11	10
6 43 31	10	9	10	11	14	12	11	10	9	10	11	9	12	11	10	9	10	11	5	12	11
6 47 51	11	10	11	12	21	13	12	11	10	11	12	16	13	12	11	10	11	12	11	13	12
6 52 11	12	11	12	13	28	14	13	12	11	12	13	22	14	13	12	12	12	13	16	14	13
6 56 30	13	12	13	14	34	15	14	13	12	13	14	28	15	14	13	13	14	14	22	15	14
7 0 49	14	13	14	15	41	16	15	14	14	15	15	34	16	15	14	14	15	15	27	16	15
7 5 7	15	15	16	16	47	17	16	15	15	16	16	40	17	16	15	15	16	16	33	17	16
7 9 26	16	16	17	17	53	18	17	16	16	17	17	45	18	17	16	16	17	17	38	18	17
7 13 43	17	17	18	18	59	19	18	17	17	18	18	51	19	18	17	17	18	18	43	19	18
7 18 0	18	18	19	20	4	20	19	18	18	19	19	56	20	19	18	18	19	19	47	20	19
7 22 17	19	19	20	21	10	21	20	19	19	20	21	1	21	20	19	19	20	20	52	21	20
7 26 33	20	20	21	22	15	22	21	20	20	21	22	5	22	21	20	20	21	21	56	22	21
7 30 49	21	21	22	23	19	24	22	21	21	22	23	10	23	22	21	21	22	23	0	23	22
7 35 4	22	22	23	24	24	25	23	22	22	23	24	14	24	23	22	22	24	24	4	24	23
7 39 19	23	23	25	25	28	26	24	23	23	25	25	18	25	24	23	23	25	25	7	25	24
7 43 33	24	24	26	26	32	27	25	24	24	26	26	21	26	25	24	24	26	26	10	26	25
7 47 46	25	25	27	27	36	28	26	25	25	27	27	25	27	26	25	25	27	27	13	27	26
7 51 59	26	26	28	28	39	29	27	26	26	28	28	28	28	27	26	26	28	28	16	28	27
7 56 11	27	27	29	29	43	♐	28	27	27	29	29	30	29	28	27	28	29	29	18	29	28
8 0 23	28	28	≈	0♏	45	1	29	28	29	≈	0♏	33	♐	29	28	29	≈	0♏	20	♐	29
8 4 34	29	♏	1	1	48	2	♑	29	♏	1	1	35	1	♑	29	♏	1	1	22	1	♑
8 8 44	Ω	1	2	2	50	2	1	Ω	1	2	2	37	2	1	Ω	1	2	2	24	2	1
8 12 53	1	2	3	3	52	3	2	1	2	3	3	38	3	2	1	2	3	3	25	3	2
8 17 2	2	3	4	4	54	4	3	2	3	4	4	40	4	3	2	3	4	4	26	4	3
8 21 10	3	4	6	5	55	5	4	3	4	6	5	41	5	4	3	4	6	5	26	5	4
8 25 18	4	5	7	6	56	6	5	4	5	7	6	41	6	5	4	5	7	6	27	6	5
8 29 24	5	6	8	7	57	7	6	5	6	8	7	42	7	6	5	6	8	7	27	7	6
8 33 30	6	7	9	8	57	8	7	6	7	9	8	42	8	7	6	7	9	8	26	8	6
8 37 36	7	8	10	9	57	9	8	7	8	10	9	41	9	8	7	8	10	9	26	9	7
8 41 40	8	9	11	10	57	10	9	8	9	11	10	41	10	9	8	9	11	10	25	10	8
8 45 44	9	10	12	11	56	11	10	9	10	12	11	40	11	10	9	10	12	11	23	11	9
8 49 47	10	11	13	12	55	12	11	10	11	13	12	38	12	10	10	11	13	12	22	12	10
8 53 50	11	12	14	13	54	13	11	11	12	14	13	37	13	11	11	12	14	13	20	12	11
8 57 51	12	13	15	14	52	14	12	12	13	15	14	35	14	12	12	14	15	14	18	13	12
9 1 52	13	14	16	15	50	15	13	13	15	16	15	33	15	13	13	15	16	15	16	14	13
9 5 52	14	16	17	16	48	16	14	14	16	17	16	30	15	14	14	16	17	16	13	15	14
HOUSES	4	5	6	7		8	9	4	5	6	7		8	9	4	5	6	7		8	9

LATITUDE 7° S. LATITUDE 8° S. LATITUDE 9° S.

LATITUDE 7° N. LATITUDE 8° N. LATITUDE 9° N.

SIDEREAL TIME	10 ♌	11 ♍	12 ♎	ASC ♏	2 ♐	3 ♑	10 ♌	11 ♍	12 ♎	ASC ♏	2 ♐	3 ♑	10 ♌	11 ♍	12 ♎	ASC ♏	2 ♐	3 ♑
H M S																		
9 9 52	15	17	18	17 46	17	15	15	17	18	17 28	16	15	15	17	18	17 10	16	15
9 13 50	16	18	19	18 43	18	16	16	18	19	18 25	17	16	16	18	19	18 6	17	16
9 17 49	17	19	20	19 40	18	17	17	19	20	19 21	18	17	17	19	20	19 3	18	17
9 21 46	18	20	21	20 36	19	18	18	20	21	20 18	19	18	18	20	21	19 59	19	18
9 25 42	19	21	22	21 33	20	19	19	21	22	21 14	20	19	19	21	22	20 55	20	19
9 29 38	20	22	23	22 29	21	20	20	22	23	22 10	21	20	20	22	23	21 50	21	20
9 33 34	21	23	24	23 24	22	21	21	23	24	23 5	22	21	21	23	24	22 46	22	21
9 37 28	22	24	25	24 20	23	22	22	24	25	24 0	23	22	22	24	25	23 41	22	21
9 41 22	23	25	26	25 15	24	23	23	25	26	24 55	24	22	23	25	26	24 36	23	22
9 45 15	24	26	27	26 10	25	24	24	26	27	25 50	24	23	24	26	27	25 30	24	23
9 49 8	25	27	28	27 5	26	24	25	27	28	26 45	25	24	25	27	28	26 24	25	24
9 53 0	26	28	29	27 59	27	25	26	28	29	27 39	26	25	26	28	29	27 18	26	25
9 56 51	27	29	♏	28 53	27	26	27	29	♏	28 33	27	26	27	29	♏	28 12	27	26
10 0 42	28	♎	1	29 47	28	27	28	♎	1	29 27	28	27	28	♎	1	29 6	28	27
10 4 32	29	1	2	0♐ 41	29	28	29	1	2	0♐ 20	29	28	29	1	2	29 59	29	28
10 8 22	♏	2	3	1 35	♑	29	♏	2	3	1 13	♑	29	♏	2	3	0♐ 52	♑	29
10 12 11	1	3	4	2 28	1	♒	1	3	4	2 6	1	♒	1	3	4	1 45	0	♒
10 15 59	2	4	5	3 21	2	1	2	4	5	2 59	2	1	2	4	5	2 38	1	1
10 19 47	3	5	6	4 14	3	2	3	5	6	3 52	2	2	3	5	6	3 30	2	2
10 23 34	4	6	7	5 6	4	3	4	6	7	4 45	3	3	4	6	7	4 23	3	3
10 27 21	5	7	8	5 59	4	4	5	7	8	5 37	4	4	5	7	8	5 15	4	3
10 31 8	6	8	9	6 51	5	5	6	8	9	6 29	5	5	6	8	9	6 7	5	4
10 34 53	7	9	10	7 43	6	6	7	9	10	7 21	6	5	7	9	10	6 59	6	5
10 38 39	8	10	11	8 35	7	6	8	10	11	8 13	7	6	8	10	10	7 50	6	6
10 42 24	9	11	12	9 27	8	7	9	11	12	9 4	8	7	9	11	11	8 42	7	7
10 46 8	10	12	13	10 19	9	8	10	12	12	9 56	8	8	10	12	12	9 33	8	8
10 49 52	11	13	14	11 10	10	9	11	13	13	10 47	9	9	11	13	13	10 25	9	9
10 53 36	12	14	15	12 1	10	10	12	14	14	11 39	10	10	12	14	14	11 16	10	10
10 57 20	13	15	15	12 53	11	11	13	15	15	12 30	11	11	13	15	15	12 7	11	11
11 1 3	14	16	16	13 44	12	12	14	16	16	13 21	12	12	14	16	16	12 58	12	12
11 4 45	15	17	17	14 35	13	13	15	17	17	14 12	13	13	15	17	17	13 48	13	13
11 8 28	16	18	18	15 26	14	14	16	18	18	15 2	14	14	16	18	18	14 39	13	14
11 12 10	17	19	19	16 16	15	15	17	19	19	15 53	15	15	17	19	19	15 30	14	15
11 15 52	18	20	20	17 7	16	16	18	20	20	16 44	15	16	18	20	19	16 20	15	16
11 19 33	19	21	21	17 58	17	17	19	21	21	17 34	16	17	19	21	20	17 11	16	17
11 23 15	20	22	22	18 48	17	18	20	22	21	18 25	17	18	20	22	21	18 1	17	18
11 26 56	21	23	23	19 39	18	19	21	23	22	19 15	18	19	21	23	22	18 51	18	18
11 30 37	22	24	24	20 29	19	20	22	24	23	20 6	19	20	22	24	23	19 42	19	19
11 34 17	23	25	25	21 20	20	21	23	25	24	20 56	20	20	23	25	24	20 32	20	20
11 37 58	24	26	25	22 10	21	22	24	26	25	21 46	21	21	24	26	25	21 22	20	21
11 41 39	25	27	26	23 0	22	22	25	27	26	22 36	22	22	25	27	26	22 12	21	22
11 45 19	26	28	27	23 51	23	23	26	28	27	23 27	22	23	26	28	27	23 3	22	23
11 48 59	27	29	28	24 41	24	24	27	29	28	24 17	23	24	27	29	27	23 53	23	24
11 52 40	28	♏	29	25 31	24	25	28	♏	28	25 7	24	25	28	♏	28	24 43	24	25
11 56 20	29	1	♐	26 22	25	26	29	1	29	25 58	25	26	29	1	29	25 33	25	26
HOUSES	4	5	6	7	8	9	4	5	6	7	8	9	4	5	6	7	8	9

LATITUDE 7° N. LATITUDE 8° N. LATITUDE 9° N.

SIDEREAL TIME	10 ♎	11 ♏	12 ♐	ASC ♐	2 ♑	3 ♒	10 ♎	11 ♏	12 ♐	ASC ♐	2 ♑	3 ♒	10 ♎	11 ♏	12 ♐	ASC ♐	2 ♑	3 ♒
H M S	°	°	°	° '	°	°	°	°	°	° '	°	°	°	°	°	° '	°	°
12 0 0	0	2	0	27 12	26	27	0	2	0	26 48	26	27	0	2	0	26 24	26	27
12 3 40	1	3	1	28 3	27	28	1	3	1	27 38	27	28	1	2	1	27 14	27	28
12 7 20	2	4	2	28 53	28	29	2	3	2	28 29	28	29	2	3	2	28 4	27	29
12 11 1	3	4	3	29 44	29	♓	3	4	3	29 19	29	♓	3	4	3	28 55	28	♓
12 14 41	4	5	4	0♑ 34	♒	1	4	5	4	0♑ 10	♒	1	4	5	3	29 45	29	1
12 18 21	5	6	5	1 25	1	2	5	6	4	1 0	0	2	5	6	4	0♑ 36	♒	2
12 22 2	6	7	6	2 15	2	3	6	7	5	1 51	1	3	6	7	5	1 26	1	3
12 25 42	7	8	6	3 6	2	4	7	8	6	2 42	2	4	7	8	6	2 17	2	4
12 29 23	8	9	7	3 57	3	5	8	9	7	3 33	3	5	8	9	7	3 8	3	5
12 33 4	9	10	8	4 48	4	6	9	10	8	4 24	4	6	9	10	8	3 59	4	5
12 36 45	10	11	9	5 39	5	7	10	11	9	5 15	5	7	10	11	9	4 50	5	7
12 40 27	11	12	10	6 30	6	8	11	12	10	6 6	6	8	11	12	9	5 41	6	8
12 44 8	12	13	11	7 21	7	9	12	13	10	6 57	7	9	12	13	10	6 33	7	9
12 47 50	13	14	12	8 13	8	10	13	14	11	7 49	8	10	13	14	11	7 24	8	10
12 51 32	14	15	12	9 5	9	11	14	15	12	8 40	9	11	14	14	12	8 16	8	11
12 55 15	15	16	13	9 56	10	12	15	15	13	9 32	10	12	15	15	13	9 8	9	12
12 58 57	16	16	14	10 48	11	13	16	16	14	10 24	11	13	16	16	14	10 0	10	13
13 2 40	17	17	15	11 40	12	14	17	17	15	11 16	12	14	17	17	14	10 52	11	14
13 6 24	18	18	16	12 33	13	15	18	18	16	12 8	12	15	18	18	15	11 44	12	15
13 10 8	19	19	17	13 25	14	16	19	19	16	13 1	13	16	19	19	16	12 37	13	16
13 13 52	20	20	18	14 18	15	17	20	20	17	13 54	14	17	20	20	17	13 29	14	17
13 17 36	21	21	18	15 11	16	18	21	21	18	14 47	15	18	21	21	18	14 22	15	18
13 21 21	22	22	19	16 4	17	19	22	22	19	15 40	16	19	22	22	19	15 16	16	19
13 25 7	23	23	20	16 57	18	20	23	23	20	16 33	17	20	23	23	20	16 9	17	20
13 28 52	24	24	21	17 51	19	21	24	24	21	17 27	18	21	24	24	20	17 3	18	21
13 32 39	25	25	22	18 45	19	22	25	25	22	18 21	19	22	25	24	21	17 57	19	22
13 36 26	26	26	23	19 39	20	23	26	26	22	19 15	20	23	26	25	22	18 51	20	23
13 40 13	27	27	24	20 33	21	25	27	26	23	20 10	21	25	27	26	23	19 46	21	24
13 44 1	28	27	24	21 28	22	26	28	27	24	21 4	22	26	28	27	24	20 41	22	26
13 47 49	29	28	25	22 23	23	27	29	28	25	21 59	23	27	29	28	25	21 36	23	27
13 51 38	♏	29	26	23 18	24	28	♏	29	26	22 55	24	28	♏	29	26	22 31	24	28
13 55 28	1	♐	27	24 14	26	29	1	♐	27	23 50	25	29	1	♐	27	23 27	25	29
13 59 18	2	1	28	25 9	27	♈	2	1	28	24 46	26	♈	2	1	27	24 23	26	♈
14 3 9	3	2	29	26 6	28	1	3	2	29	25 43	27	1	3	2	28	25 20	27	1
14 7 0	4	3	♑	27 2	29	2	4	3	29	26 39	28	2	4	3	29	26 16	28	2
14 10 52	5	4	1	27 59	♓	3	5	4	♑	27 36	29	3	5	4	♑	27 13	29	3
14 14 45	6	5	2	28 56	1	4	6	5	1	28 34	♓	4	6	4	1	28 11	♓	4
14 18 38	7	6	2	29 54	2	5	7	6	2	29 31	2	5	7	5	2	29 9	1	5
14 22 32	8	7	3	0♒ 51	3	6	8	6	3	0♒ 29	3	6	8	6	3	0♒ 7	3	6
14 26 26	9	7	4	1 50	4	7	9	7	4	1 28	4	7	9	7	4	1 6	4	7
14 30 22	10	8	5	2 48	5	8	10	8	5	2 27	5	8	10	8	5	2 5	5	8
14 34 17	11	9	6	3 47	6	9	11	9	6	3 26	6	10	11	9	5	3 4	6	10
14 38 14	12	10	7	4 47	7	11	12	10	7	4 25	7	11	12	10	6	4 4	7	11
14 42 11	13	11	8	5 47	8	12	13	11	8	5 25	8	12	13	11	7	5 4	8	12
14 46 10	14	12	9	6 47	9	13	14	12	8	6 26	9	13	14	12	8	6 5	9	13
HOUSES	4	5	6	7	8	9	4	5	6	7	8	9	4	5	6	7	8	9

LATITUDE 7° S. LATITUDE 8° S. LATITUDE 9° S.

	LATITUDE 7° N.						LATITUDE 8° N.						LATITUDE 9° N.					
SIDEREAL TIME	10 ♏	11 ♐	12 ♑	ASC ♒	2 ♓	3 ♈	10 ♏	11 ♐	12 ♑	ASC ♒	2 ♓	3 ♈	10 ♏	11 ♐	12 ♑	ASC ♒	2 ♓	3 ♈
H M S	°	°	°	° '	°	°	°	°	°	° '	°	°	°	°	°	° '	°	°
14 50 8	15	13	10	7 47	10	14	15	13	9	7 27	10	14	15	13	9	7 6	10	14
14 54 8	16	14	11	8 48	12	15	16	14	10	8 28	11	15	16	14	10	8 7	11	15
14 58 8	17	15	12	9 50	13	16	17	15	11	9 30	13	16	17	15	11	9 9	12	16
15 2 9	18	16	12	10 52	14	17	18	16	12	10 32	14	17	18	16	12	10 12	14	17
15 6 10	19	17	13	11 54	15	18	19	17	13	11 34	15	18	19	16	13	11 14	15	18
15 10 13	20	18	14	12 57	16	19	20	18	14	12 37	16	19	20	17	14	12 18	16	19
15 14 16	21	19	15	14 0	17	20	21	18	15	13 41	17	21	21	18	15	13 21	17	21
15 18 20	22	20	16	15 3	18	22	22	19	16	14 45	18	22	22	19	16	14 25	18	22
15 22 24	23	20	17	16 7	19	23	23	20	17	15 49	19	23	23	20	17	15 30	19	23
15 26 30	24	21	18	17 12	21	24	24	21	18	16 54	20	24	24	21	18	16 35	20	24
15 30 36	25	22	19	18 17	22	25	25	22	19	17 59	22	25	25	22	19	17 41	22	25
15 34 42	26	23	20	19 22	23	26	26	23	20	19 5	23	26	26	23	20	18 47	23	26
15 38 50	27	24	21	20 28	24	27	27	24	21	20 11	24	27	27	24	21	19 53	24	27
15 42 58	28	25	22	21 34	25	28	28	25	22	21 17	25	28	28	25	22	21 0	25	28
15 47 7	29	26	23	22 41	26	29	29	26	23	22 24	26	29	29	26	23	22 8	26	29
15 51 16	♐	27	24	23 48	28	♉	♐	27	24	23 32	28	♉	♐	27	24	23 15	28	♉
15 55 26	1	28	25	24 55	29	2	1	28	25	24 40	29	2	1	28	25	24 24	29	2
15 59 37	2	29	26	26 3	♈	3	2	29	26	25 48	♈	3	2	29	26	25 33	♈	3
16 3 49	3	♑	27	27 12	1	4	3	♑	27	26 57	1	4	3	♑	27	26 42	1	4
16 8 1	4	1	28	28 20	2	5	4	1	28	28 6	2	5	4	1	28	27 51	2	5
16 12 14	5	2	29	29 30	3	6	5	2	29	29 16	3	6	5	2	29	29 2	3	6
16 16 27	6	3	♒	0♓ 39	5	7	6	3	♒	0♓ 26	5	7	6	3	♒	0♓ 12	5	7
16 20 41	7	4	1	1 49	6	8	7	4	1	1 36	6	8	7	4	1	1 23	6	8
16 24 56	8	5	2	3 0	7	9	8	5	2	2 47	7	9	8	5	2	2 34	7	9
16 29 11	9	6	3	4 10	8	10	9	6	3	3 58	8	10	9	5	3	3 46	8	11
16 33 27	10	7	4	5 22	9	11	10	7	4	5 10	9	12	10	6	4	4 58	10	12
16 37 43	11	8	5	6 33	11	13	11	8	5	6 22	11	13	11	7	5	6 11	11	13
16 41 59	12	9	7	7 45	12	14	12	9	6	7 34	12	14	12	8	6	7 24	12	14
16 46 17	13	10	8	8 57	13	15	13	10	7	8 47	13	15	13	9	7	8 37	13	15
16 50 34	14	11	9	10 10	14	16	14	11	8	10 0	14	16	14	10	8	9 51	14	16
16 54 53	15	12	10	11 22	15	17	15	12	10	11 13	16	17	15	11	9	11 4	16	17
16 59 11	16	13	11	12 36	17	18	16	13	11	12 27	17	18	16	12	10	12 19	17	18
17 3 30	17	14	12	13 49	18	19	17	14	12	13 41	18	19	17	13	12	13 33	18	19
17 7 49	18	15	13	15 3	19	20	18	15	13	14 55	19	20	18	14	13	14 48	19	20
17 12 9	19	16	14	16 17	20	21	19	16	14	16 10	20	21	19	15	14	16 3	20	21
17 16 29	20	17	15	17 31	21	22	20	17	15	17 25	22	22	20	16	15	17 18	22	23
17 20 49	21	18	16	18 45	23	23	21	18	16	18 39	23	23	21	17	16	18 34	23	24
17 25 10	22	19	18	19 59	24	24	22	19	17	19 55	24	25	22	19	17	19 50	24	25
17 29 31	23	20	19	21 14	25	26	23	20	18	21 10	25	26	23	20	18	21 6	25	26
17 33 51	24	21	20	22 29	26	27	24	21	20	22 25	26	27	24	21	19	22 22	26	27
17 38 13	25	22	21	23 44	27	28	25	22	21	23 41	28	28	25	22	21	23 38	28	28
17 42 34	26	23	22	24 59	29	29	26	23	22	24 57	29	29	26	23	22	24 54	29	29
17 46 55	27	24	23	26 14	♉	♊	27	24	23	26 12	♉	♊	27	24	23	26 10	♉	♊
17 51 17	28	25	24	27 29	1	1	28	25	24	27 28	1	1	28	25	24	27 27	1	1
17 55 38	29	26	26	28 45	2	2	29	26	25	28 44	2	2	29	26	25	28 43	2	2
HOUSES	4	5	6	7	8	9	4	5	6	7	8	9	4	5	6	7	8	9

LATITUDE 7° S.   LATITUDE 8° S.   LATITUDE 9° S.

LATITUDE 7° N.   LATITUDE 8° N.   LATITUDE 9° N.

SIDEREAL TIME H	M	S	10 ♑	11 ♑	12 ♒	ASC ♈	2 ♉	3 ♊	10 ♑	11 ♑	12 ♒	ASC ♈	2 ♉	3 ♊	10 ♑	11 ♑	12 ♒	ASC ♈	2 ♉	3 ♊
18	0	0	0	27	27	0 0	3	3	0	27	27	0 0	3	3	0	27	26	0 0	4	3
18	4	22	1	28	28	1 15	4	4	1	28	28	1 16	5	4	1	28	28	1 17	5	4
18	8	43	2	29	29	2 31	6	5	2	29	29	2 32	6	5	2	29	29	2 33	6	5
18	13	5	3	♒	♓	3 46	7	6	3	♒	♓	3 48	7	6	3	♒	♓	3 50	7	6
18	17	26	4	1	1	5 1	8	7	4	1	1	5 3	8	7	4	1	1	5 6	8	7
18	21	47	5	2	3	6 16	9	8	5	2	2	6 19	9	8	5	2	2	6 22	9	8
18	26	9	6	3	4	7 31	10	9	6	3	4	7 35	10	9	6	3	4	7 38	11	9
18	30	29	7	4	5	8 46	11	10	7	4	5	8 50	12	10	7	4	5	8 54	12	10
18	34	50	8	6	6	10 1	12	11	8	5	6	10 5	13	11	8	5	6	10 10	13	11
18	39	11	9	7	7	11 15	14	12	9	7	7	11 21	14	12	9	6	7	11 26	14	13
18	43	31	10	8	9	12 29	15	13	10	8	8	12 35	15	13	10	7	8	12 42	15	14
18	47	51	11	9	10	13 43	16	14	11	9	10	13 50	16	14	11	9	10	13 57	16	15
18	52	11	12	10	11	14 57	17	15	12	10	11	15 5	17	15	12	10	11	15 12	17	16
18	56	30	13	11	12	16 11	18	16	13	11	12	16 19	18	16	13	11	12	16 27	18	17
19	0	49	14	12	13	17 24	19	17	14	12	13	17 33	19	17	14	12	13	17 41	20	18
19	5	7	15	13	15	18 38	20	18	15	13	14	18 46	20	18	15	13	14	18 56	21	19
19	9	26	16	14	16	19 50	21	19	16	14	16	20 0	22	19	16	14	16	20 9	22	20
19	13	43	17	15	17	21 3	22	20	17	15	17	21 13	23	20	17	15	17	21 23	23	21
19	18	0	18	16	18	22 15	23	21	18	16	18	22 26	24	21	18	16	18	22 36	24	22
19	22	17	19	17	19	23 27	25	22	19	17	19	23 38	25	22	19	17	19	23 49	25	23
19	26	33	20	19	21	24 38	26	23	20	18	21	24 50	26	23	20	18	20	25 2	26	24
19	30	49	21	20	22	25 50	27	24	21	20	22	26 2	27	24	21	19	22	26 14	27	25
19	35	4	22	21	23	27 0	28	25	22	21	23	27 13	28	25	22	21	23	27 26	28	25
19	39	19	23	22	24	28 11	29	26	23	22	24	28 24	29	26	23	22	24	28 37	29	26
19	43	33	24	23	25	29 21	♊	27	24	23	25	29 34	♊	27	24	23	25	29 48	♊	27
19	47	46	25	24	27	♉ 30	1	28	25	24	27	♉ 44	1	28	25	24	27	♉ 58	1	28
19	51	59	26	25	28	1 40	2	29	26	25	28	1 54	2	29	26	25	28	2 9	2	29
19	56	11	27	26	29	2 48	3	♋	27	26	29	3 3	3	♋	27	26	29	3 18	3	♋
20	0	23	28	27	♈	3 57	4	1	28	27	♈	4 12	4	1	28	27	♈	4 27	4	1
20	4	34	29	28	1	5 5	5	2	29	28	1	5 20	5	2	29	28	1	5 36	5	2
20	8	44	♒	♓	2	6 12	6	3	♒	♓	2	6 28	6	3	♒	29	2	6 45	6	3
20	12	53	1	1	4	7 19	7	4	1	1	4	7 36	7	4	1	♓	4	7 52	7	4
20	17	2	2	2	5	8 26	8	5	2	2	5	8 43	8	5	2	2	5	9 0	8	5
20	21	10	3	3	6	9 32	9	6	3	3	6	9 49	9	6	3	3	6	10 7	9	6
20	25	18	4	4	7	10 38	10	7	4	4	7	10 55	10	7	4	4	7	11 13	10	7
20	29	24	5	5	8	11 43	11	8	5	5	8	12 1	11	8	5	5	8	12 19	11	8
20	33	30	6	6	9	12 48	12	9	6	6	10	13 6	12	9	6	6	10	13 25	12	9
20	37	36	7	7	11	13 53	13	10	7	7	11	14 11	13	10	7	7	11	14 30	13	10
20	41	40	8	8	12	14 57	14	10	8	8	12	15 15	14	11	8	8	12	15 35	14	11
20	45	44	9	10	13	16 0	15	11	9	9	13	16 19	15	12	9	9	13	16 39	15	12
20	49	47	10	11	14	17 3	16	12	10	11	14	17 23	16	12	10	11	14	17 42	16	13
20	53	50	11	12	15	18 6	17	13	11	12	15	18 26	17	13	11	12	15	18 46	17	14
20	57	51	12	13	16	19 8	18	14	12	13	16	19 28	18	14	12	13	16	19 48	18	14
21	1	52	13	14	17	20 10	18	15	13	14	17	20 30	19	15	13	14	18	20 51	19	15
21	5	52	14	15	18	21 12	19	16	14	15	19	21 32	20	16	14	15	19	21 53	20	16
HOUSES			4	5	6	7	8	9	4	5	6	7	8	9	4	5	6	7	8	9

LATITUDE 7° S.   LATITUDE 8° S.   LATITUDE 9° S.

	LATITUDE 7° N.						LATITUDE 8° N.						LATITUDE 9° N.					
SIDEREAL TIME	10 ♒	11 ♓	12 ♈	ASC ♉	2 ♊	3 ♋	10 ♒	11 ♓	12 ♈	ASC ♉	2 ♊	3 ♋	10 ♒	11 ♓	12 ♈	ASC ♉	2 ♊	3 ♋
H M S	°	°	°	° '	°	°	°	°	°	° '	°	°	°	°	°	° '	°	°
21 9 52	15	16	20	22 13	20	17	15	16	20	22 33	21	17	15	16	20	22 54	21	17
21 13 50	16	17	21	23 13	21	18	16	17	21	23 34	22	18	16	17	21	23 55	22	18
21 17 49	17	18	22	24 13	22	19	17	18	22	24 35	22	19	17	18	22	24 56	23	19
21 21 46	18	19	23	25 13	23	20	18	19	23	25 35	23	20	18	19	23	25 56	24	20
21 25 42	19	21	24	26 13	24	21	19	20	24	26 34	24	21	19	20	24	26 56	25	21
21 29 38	20	22	25	27 12	25	22	20	22	25	27 33	25	22	20	22	25	27 55	25	22
21 33 34	21	23	26	28 10	26	23	21	23	26	28 32	26	23	21	23	26	28 54	26	23
21 37 28	22	24	27	29 9	27	23	22	24	27	29 31	27	24	22	24	27	29 53	27	24
21 41 22	23	25	28	0♊ 6	28	24	23	25	28	0♊ 29	28	24	23	25	29	0♊ 51	28	25
21 45 15	24	26	29	1 4	28	25	24	26	29	1 26	29	25	24	26	♉	1 49	29	26
21 49 8	25	27	♉	2 1	29	26	25	27	♉	2 24	♋	26	25	27	1	2 47	♋	26
21 53 0	26	28	1	2 58	♋	27	26	28	2	3 21	1	27	26	28	2	3 44	1	27
21 56 51	27	29	2	3 54	1	28	27	29	3	4 17	1	28	27	29	3	4 40	2	28
22 0 42	28	♈	3	4 51	2	29	28	♈	4	5 14	2	29	28	♈	4	5 37	3	29
22 4 32	29	1	4	5 46	3	♌	29	1	5	6 10	3	♌	29	1	5	6 33	3	♌
22 8 22	♓	2	6	6 42	4	1	♓	2	6	7 5	4	1	♓	2	6	7 29	4	1
22 12 11	1	3	7	7 37	5	2	1	3	7	8 1	5	2	1	3	7	8 24	5	2
22 15 59	2	4	8	8 32	6	3	2	4	8	8 56	6	3	2	4	8	9 19	6	3
22 19 47	3	5	9	9 27	6	3	3	5	9	9 50	7	4	3	6	9	10 14	7	4
22 23 34	4	7	10	10 21	7	4	4	7	10	10 45	8	4	4	7	10	11 9	8	5
22 27 21	5	8	11	11 15	8	5	5	8	11	11 39	8	5	5	8	11	12 3	9	6
22 31 8	6	9	11	12 9	9	6	6	9	12	12 33	9	6	6	9	12	12 57	10	6
22 34 53	7	10	12	13 3	10	7	7	10	13	13 27	10	7	7	10	13	13 51	10	7
22 38 39	8	11	13	13 56	11	8	8	11	14	14 20	11	8	8	11	14	14 44	11	8
22 42 24	9	12	14	14 49	12	9	9	12	15	15 13	12	9	9	12	15	15 38	12	9
22 46 8	10	13	15	15 42	12	10	10	13	16	16 6	13	10	10	13	16	16 31	13	10
22 49 52	11	14	16	16 35	13	11	11	14	17	16 59	14	11	11	14	17	17 23	14	11
22 53 36	12	15	17	17 27	14	12	12	15	18	17 52	14	12	12	15	18	18 16	15	12
22 57 20	13	16	18	18 20	15	13	13	16	18	18 44	15	13	13	16	19	19 8	16	13
23 1 3	14	17	19	19 12	16	14	14	17	19	19 36	16	14	14	17	20	20 0	16	14
23 4 45	15	18	20	20 4	17	14	15	18	20	20 28	17	15	15	18	21	20 52	17	15
23 8 28	16	19	21	20 55	18	15	16	19	21	21 20	18	15	16	19	22	21 44	18	16
23 12 10	17	20	22	21 47	18	16	17	20	22	22 11	19	16	17	20	22	22 36	19	16
23 15 52	18	21	23	22 39	19	17	18	21	23	23 3	20	17	18	21	23	23 27	20	17
23 19 33	19	22	24	23 30	20	18	19	22	24	23 54	20	18	19	22	24	24 19	21	18
23 23 15	20	23	25	24 21	21	19	20	23	25	24 45	21	19	20	23	25	25 10	21	19
23 26 56	21	24	26	25 12	22	20	21	24	26	25 36	22	20	21	24	26	26 1	22	20
23 30 37	22	25	27	26 3	23	21	22	25	27	26 27	23	21	22	25	27	26 52	23	21
23 34 17	23	26	28	26 54	24	22	23	26	28	27 18	24	22	23	26	28	27 43	24	22
23 37 58	24	27	28	27 45	24	23	24	27	29	28 9	25	23	24	27	29	28 34	25	23
23 41 39	25	28	29	28 35	25	24	25	28	♊	29 0	26	24	25	28	♊	29 24	26	24
23 45 19	26	29	♊	29 26	26	25	26	29	0	29 50	26	25	26	29	1	0♋ 15	27	25
23 48 59	27	♉	1	0♋ 16	27	26	27	♉	1	0♋ 41	27	26	27	♉	2	1 5	27	26
23 52 40	28	1	2	1 7	28	26	28	1	2	1 31	28	27	28	1	3	1 56	28	27
23 56 20	29	2	3	1 57	29	27	29	2	3	2 22	29	27	29	2	3	2 46	29	28
HOUSES	4	5	6	7	8	9	4	5	6	7	8	9	4	5	6	7	8	9

LATITUDE 7° S. LATITUDE 8° S. LATITUDE 9° S.

LATITUDE 10° N.　　　LATITUDE 11° N.　　　LATITUDE 12° N.

SIDEREAL TIME (H M S)	10 ♈	11 ♉	12 ♊	ASC ♋	2 ♌	3 ♌	10 ♈	11 ♉	12 ♊	ASC ♋	2 ♌	3 ♌	10 ♈	11 ♉	12 ♊	ASC ♋	2 ♌	3 ♌
0 0 0	0	3	5	4 1	0	29	0	3	5	4 25	1	29	0	3	5	4 50	1	29
0 3 40	1	4	5	4 51	1	29	1	4	6	5 16	1	♍	1	4	6	5 40	2	♍
0 7 20	2	5	6	5 41	2	♍	2	5	7	6 6	2	1	2	5	7	6 30	2	1
0 11 1	3	6	7	6 31	3	1	3	6	7	6 56	3	1	3	6	8	7 20	3	2
0 14 41	4	7	8	7 22	4	2	4	7	8	7 46	4	2	4	7	9	8 10	4	2
0 18 21	5	8	9	8 12	5	3	5	8	9	8 36	5	3	5	8	10	9 0	5	3
0 22 2	6	9	10	9 2	5	4	6	9	10	9 26	6	4	6	9	10	9 50	6	4
0 25 43	7	10	11	9 52	6	5	7	10	11	10 16	7	5	7	10	11	10 40	7	5
0 29 23	8	11	12	10 42	7	6	8	11	12	11 6	7	6	8	11	12	11 30	8	6
0 33 4	9	12	12	11 32	8	7	9	12	13	11 56	8	7	9	12	13	12 20	9	7
0 36 45	10	13	13	12 23	9	8	10	13	14	12 47	9	8	10	13	14	13 10	9	8
0 40 27	11	14	14	13 13	10	9	11	14	15	13 37	10	9	11	14	15	14 1	10	9
0 44 8	12	14	15	14 3	11	10	12	15	15	14 27	11	10	12	15	16	14 51	11	10
0 47 50	13	15	16	14 54	12	11	13	16	16	15 17	12	11	13	16	17	15 41	12	11
0 51 32	14	16	17	15 44	12	12	14	16	17	16 8	13	12	14	17	17	16 31	13	12
0 55 15	15	17	18	16 35	13	13	15	17	18	16 58	14	13	15	18	18	17 22	14	13
0 58 57	16	18	19	17 26	14	14	16	18	19	17 49	14	14	16	18	19	18 12	15	14
1 2 40	17	19	19	18 16	15	15	17	19	20	18 39	15	15	17	19	20	19 3	16	15
1 6 24	18	20	20	19 7	16	16	18	20	21	19 30	16	16	18	20	21	19 53	16	16
1 10 8	19	21	21	19 58	17	17	19	21	21	20 21	17	17	19	21	22	20 44	17	17
1 13 52	20	22	22	20 49	18	18	20	22	22	21 12	18	18	20	22	23	21 35	18	18
1 17 36	21	23	23	21 41	19	19	21	23	23	22 3	19	19	21	23	23	22 26	19	19
1 21 21	22	24	24	22 32	20	20	22	24	24	22 54	20	20	22	24	24	23 17	20	20
1 25 7	23	25	25	23 23	21	21	23	25	25	23 46	21	21	23	25	25	24 8	21	21
1 28 52	24	26	26	24 15	22	22	24	26	26	24 37	22	22	24	26	26	24 59	22	22
1 32 39	25	27	26	25 7	22	23	25	27	27	25 29	23	23	25	27	27	25 51	23	23
1 36 26	26	28	27	25 59	23	24	26	28	28	26 21	24	24	26	28	28	26 43	24	24
1 40 13	27	29	28	26 51	24	25	27	29	28	27 13	25	25	27	29	29	27 34	25	25
1 44 1	28	29	29	27 44	25	26	28	♊	29	28 5	25	26	28	♊	♋	28 26	26	26
1 47 49	29	♊	♋	28 36	26	27	29	0	♋	28 57	26	27	29	1	0	29 19	27	27
1 51 38	♉	1	1	29 29	27	28	♉	1	1	29 50	27	28	♉	2	1	0♌ 11	27	28
1 55 28	1	2	2	0♌ 22	28	29	1	2	2	0♌ 43	28	29	1	2	2	1 4	28	29
1 59 18	2	3	3	1 15	29	♎	2	3	3	1 36	29	♎	2	3	3	1 56	29	♎
2 3 9	3	4	3	2 8	♍	1	3	4	4	2 29	♍	1	3	4	4	2 49	♍	1
2 7 0	4	5	4	3 2	1	2	4	5	5	3 22	1	2	4	5	5	3 43	1	2
2 10 52	5	6	5	3 56	2	3	5	6	5	4 16	2	3	5	6	6	4 36	2	3
2 14 45	6	7	6	4 50	3	4	6	7	6	5 10	3	4	6	7	7	5 30	3	4
2 18 38	7	8	7	5 44	4	5	7	8	7	6 4	4	5	7	8	7	6 24	4	5
2 22 32	8	9	8	6 39	5	6	8	9	8	6 58	5	6	8	9	8	7 18	5	6
2 26 26	9	10	9	7 34	6	7	9	10	9	7 53	6	7	9	10	9	8 12	6	7
2 30 22	10	11	10	8 29	7	8	10	11	10	8 48	7	8	10	11	10	9 7	7	8
2 34 17	11	11	11	9 24	8	9	11	12	11	9 43	8	9	11	12	11	10 2	8	9
2 38 14	12	12	11	10 20	9	10	12	13	12	10 38	9	10	12	13	12	10 57	9	10
2 42 11	13	13	12	11 15	10	11	13	13	13	11 34	10	11	13	14	13	11 52	10	11
2 46 10	14	14	13	12 12	11	12	14	14	14	12 30	11	12	14	15	14	12 48	11	12
HOUSES	4	5	6	7	8	9	4	5	6	7	8	9	4	5	6	7	8	9

LATITUDE 10° S.　　　LATITUDE 11° S.　　　LATITUDE 12° S.

SIDEREAL TIME	10 ♉	11 ♊	12 ♋	ASC ♌	2 ♍	3 ♎	10 ♉	11 ♊	12 ♋	ASC ♌	2 ♍	3 ♎	10 ♉	11 ♊	12 ♋	ASC ♌	2 ♍	3 ♎
H M S	°	°	°	° '	°	°	°	°	°	° '	°	°	°	°	°	° '	°	°
2 50 8	15	15	14	13 8	12	13	15	15	14	13 26	12	13	15	15	15	13 44	12	13
2 54 8	16	16	15	14 5	13	14	16	16	15	14 22	13	14	16	16	16	14 40	13	14
2 58 8	17	17	16	15 2	14	15	17	17	16	15 19	14	15	17	17	16	15 36	14	15
3 2 9	18	18	17	15 59	15	16	18	18	17	16 16	15	16	18	18	17	16 33	15	16
3 6 10	19	19	18	16 57	16	18	19	19	18	17 13	16	17	19	19	18	17 30	16	17
3 10 13	20	20	19	17 54	17	19	20	20	19	18 11	17	19	20	20	19	18 27	17	18
3 14 16	21	21	20	18 53	18	20	21	21	20	19 9	18	20	21	21	20	19 25	18	20
3 18 20	22	22	21	19 51	19	21	22	22	21	20 7	19	21	22	22	21	20 23	19	21
3 22 24	23	23	22	20 50	20	22	23	23	22	21 5	20	22	23	23	22	21 21	20	22
3 26 30	24	24	22	21 49	21	23	24	24	23	22 4	21	23	24	24	23	22 19	21	23
3 30 36	25	25	23	22 48	22	24	25	25	24	23 3	22	24	25	25	24	23 18	22	24
3 34 42	26	26	24	23 48	23	25	26	26	25	24 2	23	25	26	26	25	24 17	24	25
3 38 50	27	26	25	24 48	25	26	27	27	26	25 2	25	26	27	27	26	25 16	25	26
3 42 58	28	27	26	25 48	26	27	28	28	27	26 2	26	27	28	28	27	26 16	26	27
3 47 7	29	28	27	26 49	27	28	29	29	28	27 2	27	28	29	29	28	27 15	27	28
3 51 16	♊	29	28	27 50	28	29	♊	29	28	28 3	28	29	♊	♋	29	28 16	28	29
3 55 26	1	♋	29	28 51	29	♍	1	♋	29	29 3	29	♍	1	1	♌	29 16	29	♍
3 59 37	2	1	♌	29 52	♎	1	2	1	♌	0♍ 4	♎	1	2	2	1	0♍ 17	♎	1
4 3 49	3	2	1	0♍ 54	1	2	3	2	1	1 6	1	2	3	2	2	1 18	1	2
4 8 1	4	3	2	1 56	2	3	4	3	2	2 7	2	3	4	3	3	2 19	2	3
4 12 14	5	4	3	2 58	3	5	5	4	3	3 9	3	4	5	4	4	3 20	3	4
4 16 27	6	5	4	4 1	4	6	6	5	4	4 11	4	6	6	5	5	4 22	4	5
4 20 41	7	6	5	5 3	5	7	7	6	5	5 14	5	7	7	6	6	5 24	5	7
4 24 56	8	7	6	6 6	6	8	8	7	6	6 16	6	8	8	7	7	6 26	6	8
4 29 11	9	8	7	7 10	8	9	9	8	7	7 19	7	9	9	8	8	7 29	7	9
4 33 27	10	9	8	8 13	9	10	10	9	8	8 22	9	10	10	9	9	8 31	9	10
4 37 43	11	10	9	9 17	10	11	11	10	9	9 26	10	11	11	10	10	9 34	10	11
4 41 59	12	11	10	10 21	11	12	12	11	10	10 29	11	12	12	11	11	10 38	11	12
4 46 17	13	12	11	11 25	12	13	13	12	11	11 33	12	13	13	12	12	11 41	12	13
4 50 34	14	13	12	12 30	13	14	14	13	12	12 37	13	14	14	13	13	12 44	13	14
4 54 53	15	14	13	13 34	14	15	15	14	13	13 41	14	15	15	14	14	13 48	14	15
4 59 11	16	15	14	14 39	15	16	16	15	14	14 46	15	16	16	15	15	14 52	15	16
5 3 30	17	16	15	15 44	16	17	17	16	15	15 50	16	17	17	16	16	15 56	16	17
5 7 49	18	17	16	16 49	18	18	18	17	17	16 55	17	18	18	17	17	17 1	17	18
5 12 9	19	18	17	17 55	19	19	19	18	18	18 0	19	19	19	18	18	18 5	18	19
5 16 29	20	19	19	19 0	20	20	20	19	19	19 5	20	20	20	19	19	19 10	20	20
5 20 49	21	20	20	20 6	21	22	21	20	20	20 10	21	21	21	20	20	20 14	21	21
5 25 10	22	21	21	21 11	22	23	22	21	21	21 15	22	22	22	21	21	21 19	22	22
5 29 31	23	22	22	22 17	23	24	23	22	22	22 21	23	24	23	22	22	22 24	23	23
5 33 51	24	23	23	23 23	24	25	24	23	23	23 26	24	25	24	23	23	23 29	24	24
5 38 13	25	24	24	24 29	25	26	25	24	24	24 32	25	26	25	24	24	24 34	25	25
5 42 34	26	25	25	25 35	26	27	26	25	25	25 37	26	27	26	25	25	25 39	26	27
5 46 55	27	26	26	26 41	27	28	27	26	26	26 43	27	28	27	26	26	26 44	27	28
5 51 17	28	27	27	27 48	29	29	28	27	27	27 49	28	29	28	27	27	27 49	28	29
5 55 38	29	28	28	28 54	♏	♐	29	28	28	28 54	29	♐	29	28	28	28 55	29	♐
HOUSES	4	5	6	7	8	9	4	5	6	7	8	9	4	5	6	7	8	9

LATITUDE 10° N.   LATITUDE 11° N.   LATITUDE 12° N.

SIDEREAL TIME	10 ♋	11 ♋	12 ♌	ASC ♎		2 ♏	3 ♐	10 ♋	11 ♋	12 ♌	ASC ♎		2 ♏	3 ♐	10 ♋	11 ♋	12 ♍	ASC ♎		2 ♏	3 ♐
H M S	°	°	°	°	'	°	°	°	°	°	°	'	°	°	°	°	°	°	'	°	°
6 0 0	0	29	29	0	0	1	1	0	29	29	0	0	1	1	0	29	0	0	0	0	1
6 4 22	1	♌	♍	1	6	2	2	1	♌	♍	1	6	2	2	1	♌	1	1	5	2	2
6 8 43	2	1	1	2	12	3	3	2	1	2	2	11	3	3	2	1	2	2	11	3	3
6 13 5	3	2	3	3	19	4	4	3	2	3	3	17	4	4	3	2	3	3	16	4	4
6 17 26	4	3	4	4	25	5	5	4	3	4	4	23	5	5	4	3	4	4	21	5	5
6 21 47	5	4	5	5	31	6	6	5	4	5	5	28	6	6	5	5	5	5	26	6	6
6 26 9	6	5	6	6	37	7	7	6	5	6	6	34	7	7	6	6	6	6	31	7	7
6 30 29	7	6	7	7	43	8	8	7	6	7	7	39	8	8	7	7	7	7	36	8	8
6 34 50	8	7	8	8	49	9	9	8	8	8	8	45	9	9	8	8	8	8	41	9	9
6 39 11	9	8	9	9	54	10	10	9	9	9	9	50	10	10	9	9	9	9	46	10	10
6 43 31	10	10	10	11	0	11	11	10	10	10	10	55	11	11	10	10	10	10	51	11	11
6 47 51	11	11	11	12	5	13	12	11	11	11	12	0	12	12	11	11	12	11	55	12	12
6 52 11	12	12	12	13	11	14	13	12	12	13	13	5	13	13	12	12	13	12	59	13	13
6 56 30	13	13	14	14	16	15	14	13	13	14	14	10	14	14	13	13	14	14	4	14	14
7 0 49	14	14	15	15	21	16	15	14	14	15	15	14	15	15	14	14	15	15	8	15	15
7 5 7	15	15	16	16	26	17	16	15	15	16	16	19	17	16	15	15	16	16	12	16	16
7 9 26	16	16	17	17	30	18	17	16	16	17	17	23	18	17	16	16	17	17	16	17	17
7 13 43	17	17	18	18	35	19	18	17	17	18	18	27	19	18	17	17	18	18	19	18	18
7 18 0	18	18	19	19	39	20	19	18	18	19	19	31	20	19	18	18	19	19	22	19	19
7 22 17	19	19	20	20	43	21	20	19	19	20	20	34	21	20	19	19	20	20	26	20	20
7 26 33	20	20	21	21	47	22	21	20	20	21	21	38	22	21	20	20	21	21	29	21	21
7 30 49	21	21	22	22	50	23	22	21	21	22	22	41	23	22	21	21	23	22	31	22	22
7 35 4	22	22	24	23	54	24	23	22	22	24	23	44	24	23	22	22	24	23	34	23	23
7 39 19	23	23	25	24	57	25	24	23	23	25	24	46	25	24	23	23	25	24	36	24	24
7 43 33	24	24	26	25	59	26	25	24	24	26	25	49	26	25	24	25	26	25	38	25	25
7 47 46	25	25	27	27	2	27	26	25	26	27	26	51	27	26	25	26	27	26	40	26	26
7 51 59	26	27	28	28	4	28	27	26	27	28	27	53	28	27	26	27	28	27	41	27	27
7 56 11	27	28	29	29	6	29	28	27	28	29	28	54	29	28	27	28	29	28	42	28	28
8 0 23	28	29	♎	♏	8	♐	29	28	29	♎	29	56	♐	29	28	29	♎	29	43	29	28
8 4 34	29	♍	1	1	9	1	♑	29	♍	1	♏	57	1	♑	29	♍	1	♏	44	♐	29
8 8 44	♌	1	2	2	10	2	1	♌	1	2	1	57	2	1	♌	1	2	1	44	1	♑
8 12 53	1	2	3	3	11	3	2	1	2	3	2	58	2	1	1	2	3	2	45	2	1
8 17 2	2	3	4	4	12	4	3	2	3	4	3	58	3	2	2	3	4	3	44	3	2
8 21 10	3	4	5	5	12	5	4	3	4	5	4	58	4	3	3	4	5	4	44	4	3
8 25 18	4	5	7	6	12	6	4	4	5	7	5	58	5	4	4	5	6	5	43	5	4
8 29 24	5	6	8	7	12	7	5	5	6	8	6	57	6	5	5	6	8	6	42	6	5
8 33 30	6	7	9	8	11	8	6	6	7	9	7	56	7	6	6	7	9	7	41	7	6
8 37 36	7	8	10	9	10	8	7	7	8	10	8	55	8	7	7	8	10	8	39	8	7
8 41 40	8	9	11	10	9	9	8	8	9	11	9	53	9	8	8	9	11	9	37	9	8
8 45 44	9	10	12	11	7	10	9	9	10	12	10	51	10	9	9	10	12	10	35	10	9
8 49 47	10	11	13	12	6	11	10	10	11	13	11	49	11	10	10	12	13	11	33	11	10
8 53 50	11	12	14	13	3	12	11	11	13	14	12	47	12	11	11	13	14	12	30	12	11
8 57 51	12	14	15	14	1	13	12	12	14	15	13	44	13	12	12	14	15	13	27	13	12
9 1 52	13	15	16	14	58	14	13	13	15	16	14	41	14	13	13	15	16	14	24	14	13
9 5 52	14	16	17	15	55	15	14	14	16	17	15	38	15	14	14	16	17	15	20	14	14
HOUSES	4	5	6	7		8	9	4	5	6	7		8	9	4	5	6	7		8	9

LATITUDE 10° S.   LATITUDE 11° S.   LATITUDE 12° S.

LATITUDE 10° N. LATITUDE 11° N. LATITUDE 12° N.

LATITUDE 10° N.

SIDEREAL TIME	10 ♌	11 ♍	12 ♎	ASC ♏	2 ♐	3 ♈
H M S	°	°	°	° '	°	°
9 9 52	15	17	18	16 52	16	15
9 13 50	16	18	19	17 48	17	16
9 17 49	17	19	20	18 45	18	17
9 21 46	18	20	21	19 40	19	18
9 25 42	19	21	22	20 36	19	18
9 29 38	20	22	23	21 31	20	19
9 33 34	21	23	24	22 26	21	20
9 37 28	22	24	25	23 21	22	21
9 41 22	23	25	26	24 16	23	22
9 45 15	24	26	27	25 10	24	23
9 49 8	25	27	28	26 4	25	24
9 53 0	26	28	29	26 58	26	25
9 56 51	27	29	♏	27 52	27	26
10 0 42	28	♎	1	28 45	27	27
10 4 32	29	1	2	29 38	28	28
10 8 22	♏	2	3	0♐31	29	29
10 12 11	1	3	4	1 24	♑	♒
10 15 59	2	4	5	2 16	1	1
10 19 47	3	5	6	3 9	2	1
10 23 34	4	6	7	4 1	3	2
10 27 21	5	7	8	4 53	4	3
10 31 8	6	8	8	5 45	4	4
10 34 53	7	9	9	6 37	5	5
10 38 39	8	10	10	7 28	6	6
10 42 24	9	11	11	8 19	7	7
10 46 8	10	12	12	9 11	8	8
10 49 52	11	13	13	10 2	9	9
10 53 36	12	14	14	10 53	10	10
10 57 20	13	15	15	11 44	11	11
11 1 3	14	16	16	12 34	11	12
11 4 45	15	17	17	13 25	12	13
11 8 28	16	18	18	14 16	13	14
11 12 10	17	19	18	15 6	14	15
11 15 52	18	20	19	15 57	15	16
11 19 33	19	21	20	16 47	16	16
11 23 15	20	22	21	17 37	17	17
11 26 56	21	23	22	18 28	18	18
11 30 37	22	24	23	19 18	18	19
11 34 17	23	25	24	20 8	19	20
11 37 58	24	26	25	20 58	20	21
11 41 39	25	27	25	21 48	21	22
11 45 19	26	28	26	22 38	22	23
11 48 59	27	29	27	23 29	23	24
11 52 40	28	♏	28	24 19	24	25
11 56 20	29	1	29	25 9	25	26
HOUSES	4	5	6	7	8	9

LATITUDE 11° N.

SIDEREAL TIME	10 ♌	11 ♍	12 ♎	ASC ♏	2 ♐	3 ♈
H M S	°	°	°	° '	°	°
9 9 52	15	17	18	16 34	16	15
9 13 50	16	18	19	17 30	17	16
9 17 49	17	19	20	18 26	17	17
9 21 46	18	20	21	19 22	18	17
9 25 42	19	21	22	20 17	19	18
9 29 38	20	22	23	21 12	20	19
9 33 34	21	23	24	22 7	21	20
9 37 28	22	24	25	23 2	22	21
9 41 22	23	25	26	23 56	23	22
9 45 15	24	26	27	24 50	24	23
9 49 8	25	27	28	25 44	25	24
9 53 0	26	28	29	26 38	25	25
9 56 51	27	29	♏	27 31	26	26
10 0 42	28	♎	1	28 24	27	27
10 4 32	29	1	2	29 17	28	28
10 8 22	♏	2	3	0♐10	29	29
10 12 11	1	3	4	1 3	♑	♒
10 15 59	2	4	5	1 55	1	0
10 19 47	3	5	5	2 47	2	1
10 23 34	4	6	6	3 39	2	2
10 27 21	5	7	7	4 31	3	3
10 31 8	6	8	8	5 23	4	4
10 34 53	7	9	9	6 14	5	5
10 38 39	8	10	10	7 6	6	6
10 42 24	9	11	11	7 57	7	7
10 46 8	10	12	12	8 48	8	8
10 49 52	11	13	13	9 39	9	9
10 53 36	12	14	14	10 30	9	10
10 57 20	13	15	15	11 21	10	11
11 1 3	14	16	16	12 11	11	12
11 4 45	15	17	16	13 2	12	13
11 8 28	16	18	17	13 52	13	14
11 12 10	17	19	18	14 43	14	14
11 15 52	18	20	19	15 33	15	15
11 19 33	19	21	20	16 23	15	16
11 23 15	20	22	21	17 13	16	17
11 26 56	21	23	22	18 4	17	18
11 30 37	22	24	23	18 54	18	19
11 34 17	23	25	23	19 44	19	20
11 37 58	24	26	24	20 34	20	21
11 41 39	25	27	25	21 24	21	22
11 45 19	26	28	26	22 14	22	23
11 48 59	27	29	27	23 4	23	24
11 52 40	28	29	28	23 54	23	25
11 56 20	29	♏	29	24 44	24	26
HOUSES	4	5	6	7	8	9

LATITUDE 12° N.

SIDEREAL TIME	10 ♌	11 ♍	12 ♎	ASC ♏	2 ♐	3 ♈
H M S	°	°	°	° '	°	°
9 9 52	15	17	18	16 16	15	15
9 13 50	16	18	19	17 12	16	15
9 17 49	17	19	20	18 8	17	16
9 21 46	18	20	21	19 3	18	17
9 25 42	19	21	22	19 58	19	18
9 29 38	20	22	23	20 53	20	19
9 33 34	21	23	24	21 48	21	20
9 37 28	22	24	25	22 42	22	21
9 41 22	23	25	26	23 36	23	22
9 45 15	24	26	27	24 30	23	23
9 49 8	25	27	28	25 24	24	24
9 53 0	26	28	29	26 17	25	25
9 56 51	27	29	♏	27 11	26	26
10 0 42	28	♎	1	28 4	27	27
10 4 32	29	1	2	28 56	28	28
10 8 22	♏	2	3	29 49	29	28
10 12 11	1	3	3	0♐41	♑	29
10 15 59	2	4	4	1 34	0	♒
10 19 47	3	5	5	2 26	1	2
10 23 34	4	6	6	3 17	2	2
10 27 21	5	7	7	4 9	3	3
10 31 8	6	8	8	5 1	4	4
10 34 53	7	9	9	5 52	5	5
10 38 39	8	10	10	6 43	6	6
10 42 24	9	11	11	7 34	7	7
10 46 8	10	12	12	8 25	7	8
10 49 52	11	13	13	9 16	8	9
10 53 36	12	14	14	10 7	9	10
10 57 20	13	15	14	10 57	10	11
11 1 3	14	16	15	11 48	11	12
11 4 45	15	17	16	12 38	12	12
11 8 28	16	18	17	13 29	13	13
11 12 10	17	19	18	14 19	13	14
11 15 52	18	20	19	15 9	14	15
11 19 33	19	21	20	15 59	15	16
11 23 15	20	22	21	16 50	16	17
11 26 56	21	23	21	17 40	17	18
11 30 37	22	24	22	18 30	18	19
11 34 17	23	25	23	19 20	19	20
11 37 58	24	26	24	20 10	20	21
11 41 39	25	27	25	21 0	20	22
11 45 19	26	28	26	21 50	21	23
11 48 59	27	28	27	22 40	22	24
11 52 40	28	29	28	23 30	23	25
11 56 20	29	♏	28	24 20	24	26
HOUSES	4	5	6	7	8	9

LATITUDE 10° S. LATITUDE 11° S. LATITUDE 12° S.

LATITUDE 10° N. LATITUDE 11° N. LATITUDE 12° N.

SIDEREAL TIME (H M S)	10 ♎	11 ♏	12 ♐	ASC ♐	2 ♑	3 ♒	10 ♎	11 ♏	12 ♏	ASC ♐	2 ♑	3 ♒	10 ♎	11 ♏	12 ♏	ASC ♐	2 ♑	3 ♒
12 0 0	0	1	0	25 59	25	27	0	1	29	25 35	25	27	0	1	29	25 10	25	27
12 3 40	1	2	1	26 49	26	28	1	2	♐	26 25	26	28	1	2	♐	26 0	26	28
12 7 20	2	3	1	27 40	27	29	2	3	1	27 15	27	29	2	3	1	26 50	27	29
12 11 1	3	4	2	28 30	28	♓	3	4	2	28 6	28	♓	3	4	2	27 41	28	♓
12 14 41	4	5	3	29 21	29	1	4	5	3	28 56	29	1	4	5	3	28 31	29	1
12 18 21	5	6	4	0♑ 11	♒	2	5	6	4	29 46	♒	2	5	6	4	29 21	29	2
12 22 2	6	7	5	1 2	1	3	6	7	5	0♑ 37	1	3	6	7	4	0♑ 12	♒	3
12 25 42	7	8	6	1 53	2	4	7	8	5	1 28	2	4	7	8	5	1 3	1	4
12 29 23	8	9	7	2 43	3	5	8	9	6	2 19	2	5	8	9	6	1 53	2	5
12 33 4	9	10	7	3 34	4	6	9	10	7	3 9	3	6	9	10	7	2 44	3	6
12 36 45	10	11	8	4 25	5	7	10	11	8	4 0	4	7	10	11	8	3 35	4	7
12 40 27	11	12	9	5 17	5	8	11	12	9	4 52	5	8	11	11	9	4 27	5	8
12 44 8	12	13	10	6 8	6	9	12	12	10	5 43	6	9	12	12	9	5 18	6	9
12 47 50	13	13	11	6 59	7	10	13	13	11	6 35	7	10	13	13	10	6 9	7	10
12 51 32	14	14	12	7 51	8	11	14	14	11	7 26	8	11	14	14	11	7 1	8	11
12 55 15	15	15	13	8 43	9	12	15	15	12	8 18	9	12	15	15	12	7 53	9	12
12 58 57	16	16	13	9 35	10	13	16	16	13	9 10	10	13	16	16	13	8 45	10	13
13 2 40	17	17	14	10 27	11	14	17	17	14	10 2	11	14	17	17	14	9 37	11	14
13 6 24	18	18	15	11 20	12	15	18	18	15	10 55	12	15	18	18	15	10 30	12	15
13 10 8	19	19	16	12 12	13	16	19	19	16	11 47	13	16	19	19	15	11 22	13	16
13 13 52	20	20	17	13 5	14	17	20	20	17	12 40	14	17	20	20	16	12 15	14	17
13 17 36	21	21	18	13 58	15	18	21	21	17	13 33	15	18	21	21	17	13 8	15	18
13 21 21	22	22	18	14 51	16	19	22	22	18	14 27	16	19	22	21	18	14 2	16	19
13 25 7	23	23	19	15 45	17	20	23	22	19	15 20	17	20	23	22	19	14 55	17	20
13 28 52	24	23	20	16 39	18	21	24	23	20	16 14	18	21	24	23	20	15 49	18	21
13 32 39	25	24	21	17 33	19	22	25	24	21	17 8	19	22	25	24	21	16 44	19	22
13 36 26	26	25	22	18 27	20	23	26	25	22	18 3	20	23	26	25	21	17 38	20	23
13 40 13	27	26	23	19 22	21	24	27	26	23	18 57	21	24	27	26	22	18 33	21	24
13 44 1	28	27	24	20 17	22	26	28	27	23	19 52	22	26	28	27	23	19 28	22	26
13 47 49	29	28	25	21 12	23	27	29	28	24	20 48	23	27	29	28	24	20 23	23	27
13 51 38	♏	29	25	22 7	24	28	♏	29	25	21 43	24	28	♏	29	25	21 19	24	28
13 55 28	1	♐	26	23 3	25	29	1	♐	26	22 39	25	29	1	♐	26	22 15	25	29
13 59 18	2	1	27	24 0	26	♈	2	1	27	23 36	26	♈	2	0	27	23 12	26	♈
14 3 9	3	2	28	24 56	27	1	3	2	28	24 32	27	1	3	1	27	24 8	27	1
14 7 0	4	3	29	25 53	28	2	4	2	29	25 29	28	2	4	2	28	25 6	28	2
14 10 52	5	3	♑	26 50	29	3	5	3	♑	26 27	29	3	5	3	29	26 3	29	3
14 14 45	6	4	1	27 48	♓	4	6	4	0	27 25	♓	4	6	4	♑	27 1	♓	4
14 18 38	7	5	2	28 46	1	5	7	5	1	28 23	1	5	7	5	1	27 59	1	5
14 22 32	8	6	2	29 44	2	6	8	6	2	29 21	2	6	8	6	2	28 58	2	6
14 26 26	9	7	3	0♒ 43	3	7	9	7	3	0♒ 20	3	7	9	7	3	29 57	3	7
14 30 22	10	8	4	1 42	5	8	10	8	4	1 20	4	9	10	8	4	0♒ 57	4	9
14 34 17	11	9	5	2 42	6	10	11	9	5	2 19	6	10	11	9	5	1 57	5	10
14 38 14	12	10	6	3 42	7	11	12	10	6	3 20	7	11	12	10	6	2 57	7	11
14 42 11	13	11	7	4 42	8	12	13	11	7	4 20	8	12	13	11	6	3 58	8	12
14 46 10	14	12	8	5 43	9	13	14	12	8	5 21	9	13	14	11	7	4 59	9	13
HOUSES	4	5	6	7	8	9	4	5	6	7	8	9	4	5	6	7	8	9

LATITUDE 10° S. LATITUDE 11° S. LATITUDE 12° S.

LATITUDE 10° N. LATITUDE 11° N. LATITUDE 12° N.

SIDEREAL TIME	10 ♏	11 ♐	12 ♑	ASC ♒		2 ♓	3 ♈	10 ♏	11 ♐	12 ♑	ASC ♒		2 ♓	3 ♈	10 ♏	11 ♐	12 ♑	ASC ♒		2 ♓	3 ♈
H M S	°	°	°	°	'	°	°	°	°	°	°	'	°	°	°	°	°	°	'	°	°
14 50 8	15	13	9	6	44	10	14	15	12	9	6	23	10	14	15	12	8	6	1	10	14
14 54 8	16	14	10	7	46	11	15	16	13	10	7	25	11	15	16	13	9	7	3	11	15
14 58 8	17	14	11	8	48	12	16	17	14	10	8	27	12	16	17	14	10	8	6	12	16
15 2 9	18	15	12	9	51	13	17	18	15	11	9	30	13	17	18	15	11	9	9	13	17
15 6 10	19	16	13	10	54	15	18	19	16	12	10	33	15	18	19	16	12	10	12	14	18
15 10 13	20	17	14	11	58	16	20	20	17	13	11	37	16	20	20	17	13	11	17	16	20
15 14 16	21	18	15	13	2	17	21	21	18	14	12	42	17	21	21	18	14	12	21	17	21
15 18 20	22	19	15	14	6	18	22	22	19	15	13	46	18	22	22	19	15	13	26	18	22
15 22 24	23	20	16	15	11	19	23	23	20	16	14	52	19	23	23	20	16	14	32	19	23
15 26 30	24	21	17	16	16	20	24	24	21	17	15	57	20	24	24	21	17	15	38	20	24
15 30 36	25	22	18	17	22	22	25	25	22	18	17	4	22	25	25	22	18	16	44	21	25
15 34 42	26	23	19	18	29	23	26	26	23	19	18	10	23	26	26	23	19	17	51	23	26
15 38 50	27	24	20	19	36	24	27	27	24	20	19	17	24	27	27	24	20	18	59	24	27
15 42 58	28	25	21	20	43	25	28	28	25	21	20	25	25	28	28	24	21	20	7	25	29
15 47 7	29	26	22	21	51	26	♉	29	26	22	21	33	26	♉	29	25	22	21	16	26	♉
15 51 16	♐	27	23	22	59	27	1	♐	27	23	22	42	27	1	♐	26	23	22	25	27	1
15 55 26	1	28	24	24	8	29	2	1	27	24	23	51	29	2	1	27	24	23	34	29	2
15 59 37	2	29	25	25	17	♈	3	2	28	25	25	1	♈	3	2	28	25	24	44	♈	3
16 3 49	3	♑	26	26	26	1	4	3	29	26	26	11	1	4	3	29	26	25	55	1	4
16 8 1	4	0	27	27	37	2	5	4	♑	27	27	21	2	5	4	♑	27	27	6	2	5
16 12 14	5	1	28	28	47	4	6	5	1	28	28	32	4	6	5	1	28	28	17	4	6
16 16 27	6	2	29	29	58	5	7	6	2	29	29	44	5	7	6	2	29	29	29	5	7
16 20 41	7	3	♒	1♓	9	6	8	7	3	♒	0♓	56	6	9	7	3	♒	0♓	42	6	9
16 24 56	8	4	2	2	21	7	10	8	4	1	2	8	7	10	8	4	1	1	54	7	10
16 29 11	9	5	3	3	34	8	11	9	5	2	3	21	8	11	9	5	2	3	8	8	11
16 33 27	10	6	4	4	46	10	12	10	6	3	4	34	10	12	10	6	3	4	21	10	12
16 37 43	11	7	5	5	59	11	13	11	7	5	5	48	11	13	11	7	4	5	36	11	13
16 41 59	12	8	6	7	13	12	14	12	8	6	7	2	12	14	12	8	5	6	50	12	14
16 46 17	13	9	7	8	27	13	15	13	9	7	8	16	13	15	13	9	6	8	5	13	15
16 50 34	14	10	8	9	41	14	16	14	10	8	9	31	15	16	14	10	8	9	20	15	16
16 54 53	15	11	9	10	55	16	17	15	11	9	10	46	16	17	15	11	9	10	36	16	17
16 59 11	16	12	10	12	10	17	18	16	12	10	12	1	17	18	16	12	10	11	52	17	19
17 3 30	17	13	11	13	25	18	19	17	13	11	13	17	18	20	17	13	11	13	8	18	20
17 7 49	18	14	12	14	40	19	20	18	14	12	14	33	19	21	18	14	12	14	25	20	21
17 12 9	19	15	14	15	56	21	22	19	15	13	15	49	21	22	19	15	13	15	42	21	22
17 16 29	20	16	15	17	12	22	23	20	16	14	17	6	22	23	20	16	14	16	59	22	23
17 20 49	21	17	16	18	28	23	24	21	17	16	18	22	23	24	21	17	15	18	16	23	24
17 25 10	22	18	17	19	45	24	25	22	18	17	19	39	24	25	22	18	17	19	34	24	25
17 29 31	23	19	18	21	1	25	26	23	19	18	20	56	26	26	23	19	18	20	52	26	26
17 33 51	24	20	19	22	18	27	27	24	20	19	22	14	27	27	24	20	19	22	10	27	27
17 38 13	25	21	20	23	35	28	28	25	21	20	23	31	28	28	25	21	20	23	28	28	28
17 42 34	26	23	22	24	52	29	29	26	22	21	24	49	29	29	26	22	21	24	46	29	29
17 46 55	27	24	23	26	9	♉	♊	27	23	23	26	7	♉	♊	27	23	22	26	5	♉	♊
17 51 17	28	25	24	27	26	1	1	28	24	24	27	24	2	1	28	24	24	27	23	2	1
17 55 38	29	26	25	28	43	3	2	29	26	25	28	42	3	2	29	25	25	28	41	3	3
HOUSES	4	5	6	7		8	9	4	5	6	7		8	9	4	5	6	7		8	9

LATITUDE 10° S. LATITUDE 11° S. LATITUDE 12° S.

LATITUDE 10° N.   LATITUDE 11° N.   LATITUDE 12° N.

SIDEREAL TIME	10 ♑	11 ♑	12 ♒	ASC ♈	2 ♉	3 ♊	10 ♑	11 ♑	12 ♒	ASC ♈	2 ♉	3 ♊	10 ♑	11 ♑	12 ♒	ASC ♈	2 ♉	3 ♊
H M S	°	°	°	° '	°	°	°	°	°	° '	°	°	°	°	°	° '	°	°
18 0 0	0	27	26	0 0	4	3	0	27	26	0 0	4	3	0	26	26	0 0	4	4
18 4 22	1	28	27	1 17	5	4	1	28	27	1 18	5	4	1	27	27	1 19	5	5
18 8 43	2	29	29	2 34	6	5	2	29	28	2 36	6	6	2	29	28	2 37	6	6
18 13 5	3	♒	♓	3 51	7	6	3	♒	♓	3 53	7	7	3	♒	29	3 55	8	7
18 17 26	4	1	1	5 8	8	7	4	1	1	5 11	9	8	4	1	♓	5 14	9	8
18 21 47	5	2	2	6 25	10	9	5	2	2	6 29	10	9	5	2	2	6 32	10	9
18 26 9	6	3	3	7 42	11	10	6	3	3	7 46	11	10	6	3	3	7 50	11	10
18 30 29	7	4	5	8 59	12	11	7	4	4	9 4	12	11	7	4	4	9 8	12	11
18 34 50	8	5	6	10 15	13	12	8	5	6	10 21	13	12	8	5	6	10 26	13	12
18 39 11	9	6	7	11 32	14	13	9	6	7	11 38	14	13	9	6	7	11 44	15	13
18 43 31	10	7	8	12 48	15	14	10	7	8	12 54	16	14	10	7	8	13 1	16	14
18 47 51	11	8	9	14 4	16	15	11	8	9	14 11	17	15	11	8	9	14 18	17	15
18 52 11	12	10	11	15 20	18	16	12	9	11	15 27	18	16	12	9	10	15 35	18	16
18 56 30	13	11	12	16 35	19	17	13	10	12	16 43	19	17	13	10	12	16 52	19	17
19 0 49	14	12	13	17 50	20	18	14	12	13	17 59	20	18	14	11	13	18 8	20	18
19 5 7	15	13	14	19 5	21	19	15	13	14	19 14	21	19	15	13	14	19 24	21	19
19 9 26	16	14	16	20 19	22	20	16	14	15	20 29	22	20	16	14	15	20 40	22	20
19 13 43	17	15	17	21 33	23	21	17	15	17	21 44	23	21	17	15	17	21 55	24	21
19 18 0	18	16	18	22 47	24	22	18	16	18	22 58	24	22	18	16	18	23 10	25	22
19 22 17	19	17	19	24 1	25	23	19	17	19	24 12	25	23	19	17	19	24 24	26	23
19 26 33	20	18	20	25 14	26	24	20	18	20	25 26	27	24	20	18	20	25 39	27	24
19 30 49	21	19	22	26 26	27	25	21	19	22	26 39	28	25	21	19	22	26 52	28	25
19 35 4	22	20	23	27 39	28	26	22	20	23	27 52	29	26	22	20	23	28 6	29	26
19 39 19	23	22	24	28 51	29	27	23	21	24	29 4	♊	27	23	21	24	29 18	♊	27
19 43 33	24	23	25	♉ 2	♊	28	24	23	25	♉ 16	1	28	24	23	25	♉ 31	1	28
19 47 46	25	24	26	1 13	2	29	25	24	26	1 28	2	29	25	24	26	1 43	2	29
19 51 59	26	25	28	2 23	3	♋	26	25	28	2 39	3	♋	26	25	28	2 54	3	♋
19 56 11	27	26	29	3 34	4	0	27	26	29	3 49	4	1	27	26	29	4 5	4	1
20 0 23	28	27	♈	4 43	5	1	28	27	♈	4 59	5	2	28	27	♈	5 16	5	2
20 4 34	29	28	1	5 52	6	2	29	28	1	6 9	6	3	29	28	1	6 26	6	3
20 8 44	♒	29	3	7 1	7	3	♒	29	3	7 18	7	3	♒	29	3	7 35	7	4
20 12 53	1	♓	4	8 9	8	4	1	♓	4	8 27	8	4	1	♓	4	8 44	8	5
20 17 2	2	2	5	9 17	9	5	2	2	5	9 35	9	5	2	1	5	9 53	9	6
20 21 10	3	3	6	10 24	10	6	3	3	6	10 43	10	6	3	3	6	11 1	10	6
20 25 18	4	4	7	11 31	11	7	4	4	7	11 50	11	7	4	4	7	12 9	11	7
20 29 24	5	5	8	12 38	12	8	5	5	8	12 56	12	8	5	5	9	13 16	12	8
20 33 30	6	6	10	13 44	13	9	6	6	10	14 3	13	9	6	6	10	14 22	13	9
20 37 36	7	7	11	14 49	14	10	7	7	11	15 8	14	10	7	7	11	15 28	14	10
20 41 40	8	8	12	15 54	15	11	8	8	12	16 14	15	11	8	8	12	16 34	15	11
20 45 44	9	9	13	16 58	15	12	9	9	13	17 18	16	12	9	9	13	17 39	16	12
20 49 47	10	10	14	18 2	16	13	10	10	14	18 23	17	13	10	10	14	18 43	17	13
20 53 50	11	12	15	19 6	17	14	11	12	15	19 27	18	14	11	12	16	19 48	18	14
20 57 51	12	13	17	20 9	18	15	12	13	17	20 30	19	15	12	13	17	20 51	19	15
21 1 52	13	14	18	21 12	19	16	13	14	18	21 33	20	16	13	14	18	21 54	20	16
21 5 52	14	15	19	22 14	20	16	14	15	19	22 35	20	17	14	15	19	22 57	21	17
HOUSES	4	5	6	7	8	9	4	5	6	7	8	9	4	5	6	7	8	9

LATITUDE 10° S.   LATITUDE 11° S.   LATITUDE 12° S.

LATITUDE 10° N. LATITUDE 11° N. LATITUDE 12° N.

SIDEREAL TIME			10 ≈	11 ♓	12 ♈	ASC ♉		2 Ⅱ	3 ♋	10 ≈	11 ♓	12 ♈	ASC ♉		2 Ⅱ	3 ♋	10 ≈	11 ♓	12 ♈	ASC ♉		2 Ⅱ	3 ♋
H	M	S	°	°	°	°	′	°	°	°	°	°	°	′	°	°	°	°	°	°	′	°	°
21	9	52	15	16	20	23	16	21	17	15	16	20	23	37	21	18	15	16	20	23	59	22	18
21	13	50	16	17	21	24	17	22	18	16	17	21	24	39	22	18	16	17	21	25	1	23	19
21	17	49	17	18	22	25	18	23	19	17	18	22	25	40	23	19	17	18	22	26	2	24	19
21	21	46	18	19	23	26	18	24	20	18	19	23	26	40	24	20	18	19	23	27	3	24	20
21	25	42	19	20	24	27	18	25	21	19	20	24	27	41	25	21	19	20	25	28	3	25	21
21	29	38	20	22	25	28	18	26	22	20	21	26	28	40	26	22	20	21	26	29	3	26	22
21	33	34	21	23	27	29	17	27	23	21	23	27	29	40	27	23	21	23	27	0Ⅱ	3	27	23
21	37	28	22	24	28	0Ⅱ	16	28	24	22	24	28	0Ⅱ	39	28	24	22	24	28	1	2	28	24
21	41	22	23	25	29	1	14	28	25	23	25	29	1	37	29	25	23	25	29	2	1	29	25
21	45	15	24	26	♉	2	12	29	26	24	26	♉	2	35	♋	26	24	26	♉	2	59	♋	26
21	49	8	25	27	1	3	10	♋	27	25	27	1	3	33	0	27	25	27	1	3	57	1	27
21	53	0	26	28	2	4	7	1	27	26	28	2	4	31	1	28	26	28	2	4	54	2	28
21	56	51	27	29	3	5	4	2	28	27	29	3	5	28	2	28	27	29	3	5	52	3	29
22	0	42	28	♈	4	6	0	3	29	28	♈	4	6	24	3	29	28	♈	4	6	48	3	♌
22	4	32	29	1	5	6	57	4	♌	29	1	5	7	21	4	♌	29	1	5	7	45	4	0
22	8	22	♓	2	6	7	53	5	1	♓	2	6	8	17	5	1	♓	2	6	8	41	5	1
22	12	11	1	3	7	8	48	5	2	1	3	7	9	12	6	2	1	3	7	9	37	6	2
22	15	59	2	4	8	9	43	6	3	2	4	8	10	8	7	3	2	4	8	10	32	7	3
22	19	47	3	6	9	10	38	7	4	3	6	9	11	3	7	4	3	6	9	11	27	8	4
22	23	34	4	7	10	11	33	8	5	4	7	10	11	57	8	5	4	7	10	12	22	9	5
22	27	21	5	8	11	12	27	9	6	5	8	11	12	52	9	6	5	8	11	13	16	9	6
22	31	8	6	9	12	13	21	10	7	6	9	12	13	46	10	7	6	9	12	14	11	10	7
22	34	53	7	10	13	14	15	11	7	7	10	13	14	40	11	8	7	10	13	15	5	11	8
22	38	39	8	11	14	15	9	12	8	8	11	14	15	33	12	8	8	11	14	15	58	12	9
22	42	24	9	12	15	16	2	12	9	9	12	15	16	27	13	9	9	12	15	16	52	13	9
22	46	8	10	13	16	16	55	13	10	10	13	16	17	20	13	10	10	13	16	17	45	14	10
22	49	52	11	14	17	17	48	14	11	11	14	17	18	13	14	11	11	14	17	18	38	15	11
22	53	36	12	15	18	18	40	15	12	12	15	18	19	5	15	12	12	15	18	19	30	15	12
22	57	20	13	16	19	19	33	16	13	13	16	19	19	58	16	13	13	16	19	20	23	16	13
23	1	3	14	17	20	20	25	17	14	14	17	20	20	50	17	14	14	17	20	21	15	17	14
23	4	45	15	18	21	21	17	17	15	15	18	21	21	42	18	15	15	18	21	22	7	18	15
23	8	28	16	19	22	22	9	18	16	16	19	22	22	34	19	16	16	19	22	22	59	19	16
23	12	10	17	20	23	23	1	19	17	17	20	23	23	25	19	17	17	20	23	23	51	20	17
23	15	52	18	21	24	23	52	20	17	18	21	24	24	17	20	18	18	21	24	24	42	21	18
23	19	33	19	22	25	24	43	21	18	19	22	25	25	8	21	18	19	22	25	25	33	21	19
23	23	15	20	23	25	25	35	22	19	20	23	26	26	0	22	19	20	23	26	26	25	22	19
23	26	56	21	24	26	26	26	23	20	21	24	27	26	51	23	20	21	24	27	27	16	23	20
23	30	37	22	25	27	27	17	23	21	22	25	28	27	41	24	21	22	25	28	28	7	24	21
23	34	17	23	26	28	28	7	24	22	23	26	28	28	32	25	22	23	26	29	28	57	25	22
23	37	58	24	27	29	28	58	25	23	24	27	29	29	23	25	23	24	27	Ⅱ	29	48	26	23
23	41	39	25	28	Ⅱ	29	49	26	24	25	28	Ⅱ	0♋	14	26	24	25	28	1	0♋	39	26	24
23	45	19	26	29	1	0♋	39	27	25	26	29	1	1	4	27	25	26	29	1	1	29	27	25
23	48	59	27	♉	2	1	30	28	26	27	♉	2	1	54	28	26	27	♉	2	2	19	28	26
23	52	40	28	1	3	2	20	29	27	28	1	3	2	45	29	27	28	1	3	3	10	29	27
23	56	20	29	2	4	3	11	29	28	29	2	4	3	35	♌	28	29	2	4	4	0	♌	28
HOUSES			4	5	6	7		8	9	4	5	6	7		8	9	4	5	6	7		8	9

LATITUDE 10° S. LATITUDE 11° S. LATITUDE 12° S.

LATITUDE 13° N.   LATITUDE 14° N.   LATITUDE 15° N.

SIDEREAL TIME	10 ♈	11 ♉	12 ♊	ASC ♋	2 ♌	3 ♌	10 ♈	11 ♉	12 ♊	ASC ♋	2 ♌	3 ♌	10 ♈	11 ♉	12 ♊	ASC ♋	2 ♌	3 ♌
H M S	°	°	°	° '	°	°	°	°	°	° '	°	°	°	°	°	° '	°	°
0 0 0	0	3	5	5 15	1	29	0	3	6	5 40	1	29	0	3	6	6 5	1	29
0 3 40	1	4	6	6 5	2	♏	1	4	7	6 30	2	♏	1	4	7	6 55	2	♏
0 7 20	2	5	7	6 55	3	1	2	5	7	7 20	3	1	2	5	8	7 45	3	1
0 11 1	3	6	8	7 45	4	2	3	6	8	8 10	4	2	3	6	9	8 35	4	2
0 14 41	4	7	9	8 35	4	3	4	7	9	9 0	5	3	4	7	9	9 24	5	3
0 18 21	5	8	10	9 25	5	3	5	8	10	9 49	5	4	5	8	10	10 14	6	4
0 22 2	6	9	11	10 15	6	4	6	9	11	10 39	6	4	6	9	11	11 4	7	5
0 25 43	7	10	12	11 5	7	5	7	10	12	11 29	7	5	7	10	12	11 54	7	5
0 29 23	8	11	12	11 55	8	6	8	11	13	12 19	8	6	8	11	13	12 43	8	6
0 33 4	9	12	13	12 45	9	7	9	12	14	13 9	9	7	9	12	14	13 33	9	7
0 36 45	10	13	14	13 35	10	8	10	13	14	13 59	10	8	10	13	15	14 23	10	8
0 40 27	11	14	15	14 25	10	9	11	14	15	14 49	11	9	11	14	16	15 13	11	9
0 44 8	12	15	16	15 15	11	10	12	15	16	15 38	12	10	12	15	17	16 2	12	10
0 47 50	13	16	17	16 5	12	11	13	16	17	16 28	12	11	13	16	17	16 52	13	11
0 51 32	14	17	18	16 55	13	12	14	17	18	17 18	13	12	14	17	18	17 42	14	12
0 55 15	15	18	19	17 45	14	13	15	18	19	18 9	14	13	15	18	19	18 32	14	13
0 58 57	16	19	19	18 35	15	14	16	19	20	18 59	15	14	16	19	20	19 22	15	14
1 2 40	17	20	20	19 26	16	15	17	20	21	19 49	16	15	17	20	21	20 12	16	15
1 6 24	18	20	21	20 16	17	16	18	21	21	20 39	17	16	18	21	22	21 3	17	16
1 10 8	19	21	22	21 7	18	17	19	22	22	21 30	18	17	19	22	23	21 53	18	17
1 13 52	20	22	23	21 58	18	18	20	22	23	22 20	19	18	20	23	23	22 43	19	18
1 17 36	21	23	24	22 48	19	19	21	23	24	23 11	20	19	21	24	24	23 34	20	19
1 21 21	22	24	25	23 39	20	20	22	24	25	24 2	20	20	22	24	25	24 24	21	20
1 25 7	23	25	25	24 30	21	21	23	25	26	24 53	21	21	23	25	26	25 15	22	21
1 28 52	24	26	26	25 22	22	22	24	26	27	25 44	22	22	24	26	27	26 6	22	22
1 32 39	25	27	27	26 13	23	23	25	27	28	26 35	23	23	25	27	28	26 57	23	23
1 36 26	26	28	28	27 4	24	24	26	28	28	27 26	24	24	26	28	29	27 48	24	24
1 40 13	27	29	29	27 56	25	25	27	29	29	28 18	25	25	27	29	♋	28 40	25	25
1 44 1	28	♊	♋	28 48	26	26	28	♊	♋	29 9	26	26	28	♊	0	29 31	26	26
1 47 49	29	1	1	29 40	27	27	29	1	1	0♌ 1	27	27	29	1	1	0♌ 23	27	27
1 51 38	♉	2	2	0♌ 32	28	28	♉	2	2	0 53	28	28	♉	2	2	1 14	28	28
1 55 28	1	3	2	1 25	29	29	1	3	3	1 45	29	29	1	3	3	2 6	29	29
1 59 18	2	4	3	2 17	♏	♎	2	4	4	2 38	♏	♎	2	4	4	2 59	♏	♎
2 3 9	3	4	4	3 10	0	1	3	5	5	3 30	1	1	3	5	5	3 51	1	1
2 7 0	4	5	5	4 3	1	2	4	6	5	4 23	2	2	4	6	6	4 44	2	2
2 10 52	5	6	6	4 56	2	3	5	6	6	5 16	3	3	5	7	7	5 36	3	3
2 14 45	6	7	7	5 50	3	4	6	7	7	6 9	3	4	6	8	7	6 29	4	4
2 18 38	7	8	8	6 43	4	5	7	8	8	7 3	4	5	7	8	8	7 23	5	5
2 22 32	8	9	9	7 37	5	6	8	9	9	7 57	5	6	8	9	9	8 16	6	6
2 26 26	9	10	10	8 31	6	7	9	10	10	8 50	6	7	9	10	10	9 10	7	7
2 30 22	10	11	10	9 26	7	8	10	11	11	9 45	7	8	10	11	11	10 3	7	8
2 34 17	11	12	11	10 20	8	9	11	12	12	10 39	8	9	11	12	12	10 58	8	9
2 38 14	12	13	12	11 15	9	10	12	13	12	11 33	9	10	12	13	13	11 52	9	10
2 42 11	13	14	13	12 10	10	11	13	14	13	12 28	10	11	13	14	14	12 46	10	11
2 46 10	14	15	14	13 6	11	12	14	15	14	13 23	11	12	14	15	15	13 41	11	12
HOUSES	4	5	6	7	8	9	4	5	6	7	8	9	4	5	6	7	8	9

LATITUDE 13° S.   LATITUDE 14° S.   LATITUDE 15° S.

LATITUDE 13° N. LATITUDE 14° N. LATITUDE 15° N.

SIDEREAL TIME	10 ♉	11 ♊	12 ♋	ASC ♌		2 ♍	3 ♎	10 ♉	11 ♊	12 ♋	ASC ♌		2 ♍	3 ♎	10 ♉	11 ♊	12 ♋	ASC ♌		2 ♍	3 ♎
H M S	°	°	°	°	'	°	°	°	°	°	°	'	°	°	°	°	°	°	'	°	°
2 50 8	15	16	15	14	1	12	13	15	16	15	14	19	12	13	15	16	15	14	36	12	13
2 54 8	16	17	16	14	57	13	14	16	17	16	15	14	13	14	16	17	16	15	32	13	14
2 58 8	17	17	17	15	53	14	15	17	18	17	16	10	14	15	17	18	17	16	27	14	15
3 2 9	18	18	18	16	50	15	16	18	19	18	17	6	15	16	18	19	18	17	23	15	16
3 6 10	19	19	19	17	46	16	17	19	19	19	18	3	16	17	19	20	19	18	19	16	17
3 10 13	20	20	20	18	43	17	18	20	20	20	19	0	17	18	20	21	20	19	16	17	18
3 14 16	21	21	20	19	41	18	19	21	21	21	19	57	18	19	21	22	21	20	12	18	19
3 18 20	22	22	21	20	38	19	21	22	22	22	20	54	19	20	22	22	22	21	9	19	20
3 22 24	23	23	22	21	36	20	22	23	23	23	21	51	20	22	23	23	23	22	6	21	21
3 26 30	24	24	23	22	34	21	23	24	24	24	22	49	21	23	24	24	24	23	4	22	23
3 30 36	25	25	24	23	32	22	24	25	25	24	23	47	23	24	25	25	25	24	2	23	24
3 34 42	26	26	25	24	31	24	25	26	26	25	24	45	24	25	26	26	26	25	0	24	25
3 38 50	27	27	26	25	30	25	26	27	27	26	25	44	25	26	27	27	27	25	58	25	26
3 42 58	28	28	27	26	29	26	27	28	28	27	26	43	26	27	28	28	28	26	56	26	27
3 47 7	29	29	28	27	29	27	28	29	29	28	27	42	27	28	29	29	28	27	55	27	28
3 51 16	♊	♋	29	28	29	28	29	♊	♋	29	28	41	28	29	♊	♋	29	28	54	28	29
3 55 26	1	1	♌	29	29	29	♏	1	1	♌	29	41	29	♏	1	1	♌	29	54	29	♏
3 59 37	2	2	1	0♍	29	♎	1	2	2	1	0♍	41	♎	1	2	2	1	0♍	53	♎	1
4 3 49	3	3	2	1	29	1	2	3	3	2	1	41	1	2	3	3	3	1	53	1	2
4 8 1	4	4	3	2	30	2	3	4	4	3	2	42	2	3	4	4	3	2	53	2	3
4 12 14	5	5	4	3	31	3	4	5	5	4	3	42	3	4	5	5	4	3	53	3	4
4 16 27	6	6	5	4	33	4	5	6	6	5	4	43	4	5	6	6	5	4	54	4	5
4 20 41	7	6	6	5	34	5	6	7	7	6	5	45	5	6	7	7	6	5	55	5	6
4 24 56	8	7	7	6	36	6	7	8	8	7	6	46	6	7	8	8	7	6	56	6	7
4 29 11	9	8	8	7	38	7	9	9	9	8	7	48	7	8	9	9	8	7	57	7	8
4 33 27	10	9	9	8	41	9	10	10	10	9	8	50	8	10	10	10	9	8	58	8	9
4 37 43	11	10	10	9	43	10	11	11	11	10	9	52	10	11	11	11	10	10	0	10	10
4 41 59	12	11	11	10	46	11	12	12	12	11	10	54	11	12	12	12	11	11	2	11	12
4 46 17	13	12	12	11	49	12	13	13	12	12	11	56	12	13	13	13	12	12	4	12	13
4 50 34	14	13	13	12	52	13	14	14	13	13	12	59	13	14	14	14	13	13	6	13	14
4 54 53	15	14	14	13	55	14	15	15	14	14	14	2	14	15	15	15	14	14	9	14	15
4 59 11	16	15	15	14	59	15	16	16	15	15	15	5	15	16	16	16	15	15	11	15	16
5 3 30	17	16	16	16	2	16	17	17	16	16	16	8	16	17	17	17	16	16	14	16	17
5 7 49	18	17	17	17	6	17	18	18	17	17	17	12	17	18	18	18	17	17	17	17	18
5 12 9	19	18	18	18	10	18	19	19	18	18	18	15	18	19	19	19	18	18	20	18	19
5 16 29	20	19	19	19	14	19	20	20	19	19	19	19	19	20	20	20	19	19	23	19	20
5 20 49	21	20	20	20	18	21	21	21	20	20	20	23	20	21	21	21	20	20	27	20	21
5 25 10	22	21	21	21	23	22	22	22	21	21	21	26	22	22	22	22	21	21	30	21	22
5 29 31	23	22	22	22	27	23	23	23	22	22	22	30	23	23	23	23	23	22	34	22	23
5 33 51	24	23	23	23	32	24	24	24	23	23	23	34	24	24	24	24	24	23	37	24	24
5 38 13	25	24	24	24	36	25	25	25	24	25	24	39	25	25	25	25	25	24	41	25	25
5 42 34	26	25	25	25	41	26	26	26	26	26	25	43	26	26	26	26	26	25	45	26	26
5 46 55	27	26	26	26	46	27	27	27	27	27	26	47	27	27	27	27	27	26	48	27	27
5 51 17	28	27	28	27	50	28	28	28	28	28	27	51	28	28	28	28	28	27	52	28	28
5 55 38	29	28	29	28	55	29	♐	29	29	29	28	56	29	29	29	29	29	28	56	29	29
HOUSES	4	5	6	7		8	9	4	5	6	7		8	9	4	5	6	7		8	9

LATITUDE 13° S. LATITUDE 14° S. LATITUDE 15° S.

LATITUDE 13° N.   LATITUDE 14° N.   LATITUDE 15° N.

SIDEREAL TIME H M S	10 S	11 S	12 ♍	ASC ≏	2 ♏	3 ♐	10 S	11 Ω	12 ♍	ASC ≏	2 ♏	3 ♐	10 S	11 Ω	12 ♍	ASC ≏	2 ♏	3 ♐
6 0 0	0	29	0	0 0	0	1	0	0	0	0 0	0	0	0	0	0	0 0	0	0
6 4 22	1	Ω	1	1 5	1	2	1	1	1	1 4	1	1	1	1	1	1 4	1	1
6 8 43	2	2	2	2 10	2	3	2	2	2	2 9	2	2	2	2	2	2 8	2	2
6 13 5	3	3	3	3 14	4	4	3	3	3	3 13	3	3	3	3	3	3 12	3	3
6 17 26	4	4	4	4 19	5	5	4	4	4	4 17	4	4	4	4	4	4 15	4	4
6 21 47	5	5	5	5 24	6	6	5	5	5	5 21	5	6	5	5	5	5 19	5	5
6 26 9	6	6	6	6 28	7	7	6	6	6	6 26	7	7	6	6	6	6 23	6	6
6 30 29	7	7	7	7 33	8	8	7	7	7	7 30	8	8	7	7	8	7 26	7	7
6 34 50	8	8	8	8 37	9	9	8	8	8	8 34	9	9	8	8	9	8 30	8	8
6 39 11	9	9	9	9 42	10	10	9	9	10	9 37	10	10	9	9	10	9 33	10	9
6 43 31	10	10	11	10 46	11	11	10	10	11	10 41	11	11	10	10	11	10 37	11	10
6 47 51	11	11	12	11 50	12	12	11	11	12	11 45	12	12	11	11	12	11 40	12	11
6 52 11	12	12	13	12 54	13	13	12	12	13	12 48	13	13	12	12	13	12 43	13	12
6 56 30	13	13	14	13 58	14	14	13	13	14	13 52	14	14	13	13	14	13 46	14	13
7 0 49	14	14	15	15 1	15	15	14	14	15	14 55	15	15	14	14	15	14 49	15	14
7 5 7	15	15	16	16 5	16	16	15	15	16	15 58	16	16	15	15	16	15 51	16	15
7 9 26	16	16	17	17 8	17	17	16	16	17	17 1	17	17	16	16	17	16 54	17	16
7 13 43	17	17	18	18 11	18	18	17	17	18	18 4	18	18	17	17	18	17 56	18	17
7 18 0	18	18	19	19 14	19	19	18	18	19	19 6	19	18	18	18	19	18 58	19	18
7 22 17	19	19	20	20 17	20	20	19	19	20	20 8	20	19	19	20	20	20 0	20	19
7 26 33	20	20	21	21 19	21	21	20	20	22	21 10	21	20	20	21	22	21 2	21	20
7 30 49	21	21	23	22 22	22	22	21	22	23	22 12	22	21	21	22	23	22 3	22	21
7 35 4	22	23	24	23 24	23	23	22	23	24	23 14	23	22	22	23	24	23 4	23	22
7 39 19	23	24	25	24 26	24	24	23	24	25	24 15	24	23	23	24	25	24 5	24	23
7 43 33	24	25	26	25 27	25	24	24	25	26	25 17	25	24	24	25	26	25 6	25	24
7 47 46	25	26	27	26 29	26	25	25	26	27	26 18	26	25	25	26	27	26 7	26	25
7 51 59	26	27	28	27 30	27	26	26	27	28	27 18	27	26	26	27	28	27 7	27	26
7 56 11	27	28	29	28 31	28	27	27	28	29	28 19	28	27	27	28	29	28 7	28	27
8 0 23	28	29	≏	29 31	29	28	28	29	≏	29 19	29	28	28	29	≏	29 7	29	28
8 4 34	29	♏	1	0♏ 31	♐	29	29	♏	1	0♏ 19	♐	29	29	♏	1	0♏ 6	♐	29
8 8 44	Ω	1	2	1 31	1	♑	Ω	1	2	1 19	1	♑	Ω	1	2	1 6	1	♑
8 12 53	1	2	3	2 31	2	1	1	2	3	2 18	2	1	1	2	3	2 5	2	1
8 17 2	2	3	4	3 31	3	2	2	3	4	3 17	3	2	2	3	4	3 4	3	2
8 21 10	3	4	5	4 30	4	3	3	4	5	4 16	4	3	3	4	5	4 2	4	3
8 25 18	4	5	6	5 29	5	4	4	5	6	5 15	5	4	4	5	6	5 0	5	4
8 29 24	5	6	8	6 28	6	5	5	6	7	6 13	6	5	5	6	7	5 58	5	5
8 33 30	6	7	9	7 26	7	6	6	7	9	7 11	6	6	6	7	8	6 56	6	6
8 37 36	7	8	10	8 24	8	7	7	8	10	8 9	7	7	7	8	9	7 54	7	7
8 41 40	8	9	11	9 22	9	8	8	10	11	9 6	8	8	8	10	11	8 51	8	8
8 45 44	9	11	12	10 19	10	9	9	11	12	10 3	9	9	9	11	12	9 48	9	8
8 49 47	10	12	13	11 17	10	10	10	12	13	11 0	10	10	10	12	13	10 44	10	9
8 53 50	11	13	14	12 14	11	11	11	13	14	11 57	11	11	11	13	14	11 41	11	10
8 57 51	12	14	15	13 10	12	12	12	14	15	12 54	12	11	12	14	15	12 37	12	11
9 1 52	13	15	16	14 7	13	13	13	15	16	13 50	13	12	13	15	16	13 33	13	12
9 5 52	14	16	17	15 3	14	13	14	16	17	14 46	14	13	14	16	17	14 28	14	13
HOUSES	4	5	6	7	8	9	4	5	6	7	8	9	4	5	6	7	8	9

LATITUDE 13° S.   LATITUDE 14° S.   LATITUDE 15° S.

LATITUDE 13° N. LATITUDE 14° N. LATITUDE 15° N.

SIDEREAL TIME	10 ♌	11 ♍	12 ♎	ASC ♏		2 ✗	3 ♑	10 ♌	11 ♍	12 ♎	ASC ♏		2 ✗	3 ♑	10 ♌	11 ♍	12 ♎	ASC ♏		2 ✗	3 ♑
H M S	°	°	°	°	′	°	°	°	°	°	°	′	°	°	°	°	°	°	′	°	°
9 9 52	15	17	18	15	59	15	14	15	17	18	15	41	15	14	15	17	18	15	24	15	14
9 13 50	16	18	19	16	54	16	15	16	18	19	16	37	16	15	16	18	19	16	19	15	15
9 17 49	17	19	20	17	50	17	16	17	19	20	17	32	17	16	17	19	20	17	14	16	16
9 21 46	18	20	21	18	45	18	17	18	20	21	18	27	18	17	18	20	21	18	8	17	17
9 25 42	19	21	22	19	40	19	18	19	21	22	19	21	18	18	19	21	22	19	2	18	18
9 29 38	20	22	23	20	34	20	19	20	22	23	20	15	19	19	20	22	23	19	57	19	19
9 33 34	21	23	24	21	29	20	20	21	23	24	21	10	20	20	21	23	23	20	50	20	20
9 37 28	22	24	25	22	23	21	21	22	24	25	22	3	21	21	22	24	24	21	44	21	21
9 41 22	23	25	26	23	17	22	22	23	25	26	22	57	22	22	23	25	25	22	37	22	22
9 45 15	24	26	27	24	10	23	23	24	26	27	23	51	23	23	24	26	26	23	31	23	22
9 49 8	25	27	28	25	4	24	24	25	27	27	24	44	24	24	25	27	27	24	24	23	23
9 53 0	26	28	29	25	57	25	25	26	28	28	25	37	25	24	26	28	28	25	16	24	24
9 56 51	27	29	♏	26	50	26	26	27	29	29	26	30	25	25	27	29	29	26	9	25	25
10 0 42	28	♎	0	27	43	27	26	28	♎	♏	27	22	26	26	28	♎	♏	27	1	26	26
10 4 32	29	1	1	28	35	28	27	29	1	1	28	15	27	27	29	1	1	27	54	27	27
10 8 22	♏	2	2	29	28	28	28	♏	2	2	29	7	28	28	♏	2	2	28	46	28	28
10 12 11	1	3	3	0✗	20	29	29	1	3	3	29	59	29	29	1	3	3	29	37	29	29
10 15 59	2	4	4	1	12	♑	♒	2	4	4	0✗	51	♑	♒	2	4	4	0✗	29	♑	♒
10 19 47	3	5	5	2	4	1	1	3	5	5	1	42	1	1	3	5	5	1	20	0	1
10 23 34	4	6	6	2	56	2	2	4	6	6	2	34	2	2	4	6	6	2	12	1	2
10 27 21	5	7	7	3	47	3	3	5	7	7	3	25	2	3	5	7	7	3	3	2	3
10 31 8	6	8	8	4	38	4	4	6	8	8	4	16	3	4	6	8	8	3	54	3	4
10 34 53	7	9	9	5	30	5	5	7	9	9	5	7	4	5	7	9	9	4	45	4	5
10 38 39	8	10	10	6	21	5	6	8	10	10	5	58	5	6	8	10	9	5	36	5	6
10 42 24	9	11	11	7	12	6	7	9	11	10	6	49	6	7	9	11	10	6	26	6	6
10 46 8	10	12	12	8	2	7	8	10	12	11	7	40	7	8	10	12	11	7	17	7	7
10 49 52	11	13	12	8	53	8	9	11	13	12	8	30	8	8	11	13	12	8	7	8	8
10 53 36	12	14	13	9	44	9	10	12	14	13	9	21	9	9	12	14	13	8	57	9	9
10 57 20	13	15	14	10	34	10	10	13	15	14	10	11	9	10	13	15	14	9	48	9	10
11 1 3	14	16	15	11	25	11	11	14	16	15	11	1	10	11	14	16	15	10	38	10	11
11 4 45	15	17	16	12	15	11	12	15	17	16	11	51	11	12	15	17	16	11	28	11	12
11 8 28	16	18	17	13	5	12	13	16	18	17	12	42	12	13	16	18	16	12	18	12	13
11 12 10	17	19	18	13	55	13	14	17	19	18	13	32	13	14	17	19	17	13	8	13	14
11 15 52	18	20	19	14	45	14	15	18	20	18	14	22	14	15	18	20	18	13	58	13	15
11 19 33	19	21	20	15	35	15	16	19	21	19	15	11	15	16	19	21	19	14	47	14	16
11 23 15	20	22	20	16	25	16	17	20	22	20	16	1	16	17	20	22	20	15	37	15	17
11 26 56	21	23	21	17	15	17	18	21	23	21	16	51	16	18	21	23	21	16	27	16	18
11 30 37	22	24	22	18	5	18	19	22	24	22	17	41	17	19	22	24	22	17	17	17	19
11 34 17	23	25	23	18	55	18	20	23	25	23	18	31	18	20	23	25	23	18	6	18	20
11 37 58	24	26	24	19	45	19	21	24	26	24	19	21	19	21	24	25	23	18	56	19	21
11 41 39	25	27	25	20	35	20	22	25	26	25	20	11	20	22	25	26	24	19	46	20	22
11 45 19	26	27	26	21	25	21	23	26	27	25	21	0	21	23	26	27	25	20	36	21	23
11 48 59	27	28	26	22	15	22	24	27	28	26	21	50	22	24	27	28	26	21	25	21	24
11 52 40	28	29	27	23	5	23	25	28	29	27	22	40	23	25	28	29	27	22	15	22	25
11 56 20	29	♏	28	23	55	24	26	29	♏	28	23	30	23	26	29	♏	28	23	5	23	26
HOUSES	4	5	6	7		8	9	4	5	6	7		8	9	4	5	6	7		8	9

LATITUDE 13° S. LATITUDE 14° S. LATITUDE 15° S.

LATITUDE 13° N. LATITUDE 14° N. LATITUDE 15° N.

SIDEREAL TIME	10 ♎	11 ♏	12 ♏	ASC ♐	2 ♑	3 ♒	10 ♎	11 ♏	12 ♏	ASC ♐	2 ♑	3 ♒	10 ♎	11 ♏	12 ♏	ASC ♐	2 ♑	3 ♒
12 0 0	0	1	29	24 45	25	27	0	1	29	24 20	24	27	0	1	29	23 55	24	27
12 3 40	1	2	♐	25 35	26	28	1	2	♐	25 10	25	28	1	2	29	24 45	25	28
12 7 20	2	3	1	26 25	26	29	2	3	0	26 0	26	29	2	3	♐	25 35	26	29
12 11 1	3	4	2	27 16	27	♓	3	4	1	26 50	27	♓	3	4	1	26 25	27	♓
12 14 41	4	5	2	28 6	28	1	4	5	2	27 41	28	1	4	5	2	27 15	28	1
12 18 21	5	6	3	28 56	29	2	5	6	3	28 31	29	2	5	6	3	28 6	29	2
12 22 2	6	7	4	29 47	♒	3	6	7	4	29 22	♒	3	6	7	4	28 56	♒	3
12 25 42	7	8	5	0♑ 37	1	4	7	8	5	0♑ 12	1	4	7	8	4	29 46	0	4
12 29 23	8	9	6	1 28	2	5	8	9	6	1 3	2	5	8	8	5	0♑ 37	1	5
12 33 4	9	10	7	2 19	3	6	9	9	6	1 54	3	6	9	9	6	1 28	2	6
12 36 45	10	10	7	3 10	4	7	10	10	7	2 45	4	7	10	10	7	2 19	3	7
12 40 27	11	11	8	4 1	5	8	11	11	8	3 36	4	8	11	11	8	3 10	4	8
12 44 8	12	12	9	4 53	6	9	12	12	9	4 27	5	9	12	12	9	4 1	5	9
12 47 50	13	13	10	5 44	7	10	13	13	10	5 19	6	10	13	13	10	4 53	6	10
12 51 32	14	14	11	6 36	8	11	14	14	11	6 10	7	11	14	14	10	5 44	7	11
12 55 15	15	15	12	7 28	8	12	15	15	11	7 2	8	12	15	15	11	6 36	8	12
12 58 57	16	16	13	8 20	9	13	16	16	12	7 54	9	13	16	16	12	7 28	9	13
13 2 40	17	17	13	9 12	10	14	17	17	13	8 46	10	14	17	17	13	8 20	10	14
13 6 24	18	18	14	10 4	11	15	18	18	14	9 39	11	15	18	17	14	9 13	11	15
13 10 8	19	19	15	10 57	12	16	19	19	15	10 31	12	16	19	18	15	10 6	12	16
13 13 52	20	20	16	11 50	13	17	20	19	16	11 24	13	17	20	19	15	10 59	13	17
13 17 36	21	20	17	12 43	14	18	21	20	17	12 18	14	18	21	20	16	11 52	14	18
13 21 21	22	21	18	13 37	15	19	22	21	17	13 11	15	19	22	21	17	12 45	15	19
13 25 7	23	22	19	14 30	16	20	23	22	18	14 5	16	20	23	22	18	13 39	16	20
13 28 52	24	23	19	15 24	17	21	24	23	19	14 59	17	21	24	23	19	14 33	17	21
13 32 39	25	24	20	16 18	18	22	25	24	20	15 53	18	22	25	24	20	15 27	18	22
13 36 26	26	25	21	17 13	19	23	26	25	21	16 48	19	23	26	25	21	16 22	19	23
13 40 13	27	26	22	18 8	20	24	27	26	22	17 43	20	24	27	26	21	17 17	20	24
13 44 1	28	27	23	19 3	21	25	28	27	23	18 38	21	25	28	27	22	18 12	21	25
13 47 49	29	28	24	19 59	22	27	29	28	23	19 33	22	27	29	27	23	19 8	22	27
13 51 38	♏	29	25	20 54	23	28	♏	28	24	20 29	23	28	♏	28	24	20 4	23	28
13 55 28	1	29	25	21 51	24	29	1	29	25	21 26	24	29	1	29	25	21 0	24	29
13 59 18	2	♐	26	22 47	26	♈	2	♐	26	22 22	25	♈	2	♐	26	21 57	25	♈
14 3 9	3	1	27	23 44	27	1	3	1	27	23 19	26	1	3	1	27	22 54	26	1
14 7 0	4	2	28	24 41	28	2	4	2	28	24 17	27	2	4	2	28	23 52	27	2
14 10 52	5	3	29	25 39	29	3	5	3	29	25 14	29	3	5	3	28	24 50	28	3
14 14 45	6	4	♑	26 37	♓	4	6	4	♑	26 13	♓	4	6	4	29	25 48	29	4
14 18 38	7	5	1	27 35	1	5	7	5	0	27 11	1	5	7	5	♑	26 47	♓	5
14 22 32	8	6	2	28 34	2	6	8	6	1	28 10	2	6	8	6	1	27 46	2	6
14 26 26	9	7	3	29 34	3	7	9	7	2	29 10	3	7	9	6	2	28 45	3	7
14 30 22	10	8	3	0♒ 33	4	9	10	8	3	0♒ 10	4	9	10	7	3	29 45	4	9
14 34 17	11	9	4	1 33	5	10	11	8	4	1 10	5	10	11	8	4	0♒ 46	5	10
14 38 14	12	9	5	2 34	6	11	12	9	5	2 11	6	11	12	9	5	1 47	6	11
14 42 11	13	10	6	3 35	7	12	13	10	6	3 12	7	12	13	10	6	2 48	7	12
14 46 10	14	11	7	4 37	9	13	14	11	7	4 14	9	13	14	11	7	3 50	8	13
HOUSES	4	5	6	7	8	9	4	5	6	7	8	9	4	5	6	7	8	9

LATITUDE 13° S. LATITUDE 14° S. LATITUDE 15° S.

LATITUDE 13° N.   LATITUDE 14° N.   LATITUDE 15° N.

SIDEREAL TIME	10 ♏	11 ♐	12 ♑	ASC ♒	2 ♓	3 ♈	10 ♏	11 ♐	12 ♑	ASC ♒	2 ♓	3 ♈	10 ♏	11 ♐	12 ♑	ASC ♒	2 ♓	3 ♈
H M S	°	°	°	° '	°	°	°	°	°	° '	°	°	°	°	°	° '	°	°
14 50 8	15	12	8	5 39	10	14	15	12	8	5 16	10	14	15	12	7	4 53	10	14
14 54 8	16	13	9	6 41	11	15	16	13	9	6 18	11	15	16	13	8	5 55	11	15
14 58 8	17	14	10	7 44	12	16	17	14	10	7 22	12	16	17	14	9	6 59	12	16
15 2 9	18	15	11	8 47	13	17	18	15	11	8 25	13	17	18	15	10	8 3	13	18
15 6 10	19	16	12	9 51	14	19	19	16	12	9 29	14	19	19	16	11	9 7	14	19
15 10 13	20	17	13	10 55	16	20	20	17	12	10 34	15	20	20	17	12	10 12	15	20
15 14 16	21	18	14	12 0	17	21	21	18	13	11 39	17	21	21	17	13	11 18	17	21
15 18 20	22	19	15	13 6	18	22	22	19	14	12 45	18	22	22	18	14	12 24	18	22
15 22 24	23	20	16	14 12	19	23	23	19	15	13 51	19	23	23	19	15	13 30	19	23
15 26 30	24	21	17	15 18	20	24	24	20	16	14 58	20	24	24	20	16	14 37	20	24
15 30 36	25	22	18	16 25	21	25	25	21	17	16 5	21	25	25	21	17	15 45	21	25
15 34 42	26	22	19	17 32	23	26	26	22	18	17 13	23	26	26	22	18	16 53	23	27
15 38 50	27	23	20	18 40	24	28	27	23	19	18 21	24	28	27	23	19	18 1	24	28
15 42 58	28	24	21	19 49	25	29	28	24	20	19 30	25	29	28	24	20	19 11	25	29
15 47 7	29	25	22	20 58	26	♉	29	25	21	20 39	26	♉	29	25	21	20 20	26	♉
15 51 16	♐	26	23	22 7	27	1	♐	26	22	21 49	27	1	♐	26	22	21 31	27	1
15 55 26	1	27	24	23 17	29	2	1	27	23	22 59	29	2	1	27	23	22 41	29	2
15 59 37	2	28	25	24 28	♈	3	2	28	24	24 10	♈	3	2	28	24	23 53	♈	3
16 3 49	3	29	26	25 38	1	4	3	29	25	25 22	1	4	3	29	25	25 5	1	4
16 8 1	4	♑	27	26 50	2	5	4	♑	26	26 34	2	5	4	♑	26	26 17	2	6
16 12 14	5	1	28	28 2	4	6	5	1	27	27 46	4	7	5	1	27	27 30	4	7
16 16 27	6	2	29	29 14	5	8	6	2	28	28 59	5	8	6	2	28	28 43	5	8
16 20 41	7	3	♒	0♓ 27	6	9	7	3	29	0♓ 12	6	9	7	3	29	29 57	6	9
16 24 56	8	4	1	1 41	7	10	8	4	♒	1 26	7	10	8	4	♒	1♓ 12	7	10
16 29 11	9	5	2	2 54	9	11	9	5	1	2 41	9	11	9	5	1	2 27	9	11
16 33 27	10	6	3	4 9	10	12	10	6	3	3 56	10	12	10	6	2	3 42	10	12
16 37 43	11	7	4	5 23	11	13	11	7	4	5 11	11	13	11	7	4	4 58	11	13
16 41 59	12	8	5	6 38	12	14	12	8	5	6 26	12	14	12	8	5	6 14	12	14
16 46 17	13	9	6	7 54	13	15	13	9	6	7 43	14	15	13	9	6	7 31	14	16
16 50 34	14	10	7	9 10	15	16	14	10	7	8 59	15	17	14	10	7	8 48	15	17
16 54 53	15	11	8	10 26	16	18	15	11	8	10 16	16	18	15	11	8	10 5	16	18
16 59 11	16	12	10	11 43	17	19	16	12	9	11 33	17	19	16	12	9	11 23	17	19
17 3 30	17	13	11	13 0	18	20	17	13	10	12 51	19	20	17	13	10	12 41	19	20
17 7 49	18	14	12	14 17	20	21	18	14	12	14 9	20	21	18	14	11	14 0	20	21
17 12 9	19	15	13	15 34	21	22	19	15	13	15 27	21	22	19	15	12	15 19	21	22
17 16 29	20	16	14	16 52	22	23	20	16	14	16 45	22	23	20	16	14	16 38	22	23
17 20 49	21	17	15	18 10	23	24	21	17	15	18 4	23	24	21	17	15	17 57	24	24
17 25 10	22	18	16	19 28	25	25	22	18	16	19 23	25	25	22	18	16	19 17	25	25
17 29 31	23	19	17	20 47	26	26	23	19	17	20 42	26	26	23	19	17	20 37	26	26
17 33 51	24	20	19	22 6	27	27	24	20	18	22 1	27	27	24	20	18	21 57	27	28
17 38 13	25	21	20	23 24	28	28	25	21	20	23 21	28	29	25	21	19	23 17	29	29
17 42 34	26	22	21	24 43	29	29	26	22	21	24 41	♉	♊	26	22	21	24 38	♉	♊
17 46 55	27	23	22	26 2	♉	♊	27	23	22	26 0	1	1	27	23	22	25 58	1	1
17 51 17	28	24	23	27 22	2	2	28	24	23	27 20	2	2	28	24	23	27 19	2	2
17 55 38	29	25	25	28 41	3	3	29	25	24	28 40	3	3	29	25	24	28 39	3	3
HOUSES	4	5	6	7	8	9	4	5	6	7	8	9	4	5	6	7	8	9

LATITUDE 13° S.   LATITUDE 14° S.   LATITUDE 15° S.

LATITUDE 13° N. LATITUDE 14° N. LATITUDE 15° N.

LATITUDE 13° N.

SIDEREAL TIME (H M S)	10 ♑	11 ♑	12 ♒	ASC ♈		2 ♉	3 ♊
18 0 0	0	26	26	0	0	4	4
18 4 22	1	27	27	1	19	5	5
18 8 43	2	28	28	2	38	7	6
18 13 5	3	29	29	3	58	8	7
18 17 26	4	♒	♓	5	17	9	8
18 21 47	5	2	2	6	36	10	9
18 26 9	6	3	3	7	54	11	10
18 30 29	7	4	4	9	13	13	11
18 34 50	8	5	5	10	32	14	12
18 39 11	9	6	7	11	50	15	13
18 43 31	10	7	8	13	8	16	14
18 47 51	11	8	9	14	26	17	15
18 52 11	12	9	10	15	43	18	16
18 56 30	13	10	12	17	0	19	17
19 0 49	14	11	13	18	17	20	18
19 5 7	15	12	14	19	34	22	19
19 9 26	16	14	15	20	50	23	20
19 13 43	17	15	17	22	6	24	21
19 18 0	18	16	18	23	22	25	22
19 22 17	19	17	19	24	37	26	23
19 26 33	20	18	20	25	51	27	24
19 30 49	21	19	21	27	6	28	25
19 35 4	22	20	23	28	19	29	26
19 39 19	23	21	24	29	33	♊	27
19 43 33	24	22	25	0♉	46	1	28
19 47 46	25	24	26	1	58	2	29
19 51 59	26	25	28	3	10	3	♋
19 56 11	27	26	29	4	22	4	1
20 0 23	28	27	♈	5	32	5	2
20 4 34	29	28	1	6	43	6	3
20 8 44	♒	29	3	7	53	7	4
20 12 53	1	♓	4	9	2	8	5
20 17 2	2	1	5	10	11	9	6
20 21 10	3	2	6	11	20	10	7
20 25 18	4	4	7	12	28	11	8
20 29 24	5	5	9	13	35	12	8
20 33 30	6	6	10	14	42	13	9
20 37 36	7	7	11	15	48	14	10
20 41 40	8	8	12	16	54	15	11
20 45 44	9	9	13	18	0	16	12
20 49 47	10	10	14	19	5	17	13
20 53 50	11	11	16	20	9	18	14
20 57 51	12	13	17	21	13	19	15
21 1 52	13	14	18	22	16	20	16
21 5 52	14	15	19	23	19	21	17

LATITUDE 14° N.

SIDEREAL TIME (H M S)	10 ♑	11 ♑	12 ♒	ASC ♈		2 ♉	3 ♊
18 0 0	0	26	26	0	0	4	4
18 4 22	1	27	27	1	20	6	5
18 8 43	2	28	28	2	40	7	6
18 13 5	3	29	29	4	0	8	7
18 17 26	4	♒	♓	5	19	9	8
18 21 47	5	1	2	6	39	10	9
18 26 9	6	3	3	7	59	12	10
18 30 29	7	4	4	9	18	13	11
18 34 50	8	5	5	10	37	14	12
18 39 11	9	6	7	11	56	15	13
18 43 31	10	7	8	13	15	16	14
18 47 51	11	8	9	14	33	17	15
18 52 11	12	9	10	15	51	18	16
18 56 30	13	10	11	17	9	20	17
19 0 49	14	11	13	18	27	21	18
19 5 7	15	12	14	19	44	22	19
19 9 26	16	13	15	21	1	23	20
19 13 43	17	15	16	22	17	24	21
19 18 0	18	16	18	23	34	25	22
19 22 17	19	17	19	24	49	26	23
19 26 33	20	18	20	26	4	27	24
19 30 49	21	19	21	27	19	28	25
19 35 4	22	20	23	28	34	29	26
19 39 19	23	21	24	29	48	♊	27
19 43 33	24	22	25	1♉	1	2	28
19 47 46	25	23	26	2	14	3	29
19 51 59	26	25	28	3	26	4	♋
19 56 11	27	26	29	4	38	5	1
20 0 23	28	27	♈	5	50	6	2
20 4 34	29	28	1	7	1	7	3
20 8 44	♒	29	3	8	11	8	4
20 12 53	1	♓	4	9	21	9	5
20 17 2	2	1	5	10	30	10	6
20 21 10	3	2	6	11	39	11	7
20 25 18	4	4	7	12	47	12	8
20 29 24	5	5	9	13	55	13	9
20 33 30	6	6	10	15	2	14	10
20 37 36	7	7	11	16	9	15	11
20 41 40	8	8	12	17	15	16	11
20 45 44	9	9	13	18	21	17	12
20 49 47	10	10	15	19	26	18	13
20 53 50	11	11	16	20	31	18	14
20 57 51	12	13	17	21	35	19	15
21 1 52	13	14	18	22	38	20	16
21 5 52	14	15	19	23	42	21	17

LATITUDE 15° N.

SIDEREAL TIME (H M S)	10 ♑	11 ♑	12 ♒	ASC ♈		2 ♉	3 ♊
18 0 0	0	26	25	0	0	5	4
18 4 22	1	27	27	1	21	6	5
18 8 43	2	28	28	2	41	7	6
18 13 5	3	29	29	4	2	8	7
18 17 26	4	♒	♓	5	22	9	8
18 21 47	5	1	1	6	43	11	9
18 26 9	6	2	3	8	3	12	10
18 30 29	7	4	4	9	23	13	11
18 34 50	8	5	5	10	43	14	12
18 39 11	9	6	6	12	3	15	13
18 43 31	10	7	8	13	22	16	14
18 47 51	11	8	9	14	41	18	15
18 52 11	12	9	10	16	0	19	16
18 56 30	13	10	11	17	19	20	17
19 0 49	14	11	13	18	37	21	18
19 5 7	15	12	14	19	55	22	19
19 9 26	16	13	15	21	12	23	20
19 13 43	17	14	16	22	29	24	21
19 18 0	18	16	18	23	46	25	22
19 22 17	19	17	19	25	2	26	23
19 26 33	20	18	20	26	18	28	24
19 30 49	21	19	21	27	33	29	25
19 35 4	22	20	23	28	48	♊	26
19 39 19	23	21	24	0♉	3	1	27
19 43 33	24	22	25	1	17	2	28
19 47 46	25	23	26	2	30	3	29
19 51 59	26	24	28	3	43	4	♋
19 56 11	27	26	29	4	55	5	1
20 0 23	28	27	♈	6	7	6	2
20 4 34	29	28	1	7	19	7	3
20 8 44	♒	29	3	8	29	8	4
20 12 53	1	♓	4	9	40	9	5
20 17 2	2	1	5	10	49	10	6
20 21 10	3	2	6	11	59	11	7
20 25 18	4	3	7	13	7	12	8
20 29 24	5	5	9	14	15	13	9
20 33 30	6	6	10	15	23	14	10
20 37 36	7	7	11	16	30	15	11
20 41 40	8	8	12	17	36	16	12
20 45 44	9	9	13	18	42	17	13
20 49 47	10	10	15	19	48	18	13
20 53 50	11	11	16	20	53	19	14
20 57 51	12	12	17	21	57	20	15
21 1 52	13	14	18	23	1	21	16
21 5 52	14	15	19	24	5	22	17

HOUSES	4	5	6	7	8	9

LATITUDE 13° N.

SIDEREAL TIME H M S	10 ♒	11 ♓	12 ♈	ASC ♉		2 ♊	3 ♋
21 9 52	15	16	20	24	21	22	18
21 13 50	16	17	21	25	23	23	19
21 17 49	17	18	23	26	25	24	20
21 21 46	18	19	24	27	26	25	21
21 25 42	19	20	25	28	27	26	21
21 29 38	20	21	26	29	27	27	22
21 33 34	21	23	27	0♊	26	27	23
21 37 28	22	24	28	1	26	28	24
21 41 22	23	25	29	2	25	29	25
21 45 15	24	26	♉	3	23	♋	26
21 49 8	25	27	1	4	21	1	27
21 53 0	26	28	2	5	19	2	28
21 56 51	27	29	3	6	16	3	29
22 0 42	28	♈	4	7	13	4	♌
22 4 32	29	1	6	8	9	5	1
22 8 22	♓	2	7	9	6	5	1
22 12 11	1	3	8	10	1	6	2
22 15 59	2	5	9	10	57	7	3
22 19 47	3	6	10	11	52	8	4
22 23 34	4	7	11	12	47	9	5
22 27 21	5	8	12	13	42	10	6
22 31 8	6	9	13	14	36	11	7
22 34 53	7	10	14	15	30	11	8
22 38 39	8	11	15	16	23	12	9
22 42 24	9	12	16	17	17	13	10
22 46 8	10	13	17	18	10	14	10
22 49 52	11	14	18	19	3	15	11
22 53 36	12	15	19	19	56	16	12
22 57 20	13	16	20	20	48	17	13
23 1 3	14	17	21	21	40	17	14
23 4 45	15	18	22	22	32	18	15
23 8 28	16	19	22	23	24	19	16
23 12 10	17	20	23	24	16	20	17
23 15 52	18	21	24	25	7	21	18
23 19 33	19	22	25	25	59	22	19
23 23 15	20	23	26	26	50	23	20
23 26 56	21	24	27	27	41	23	20
23 30 37	22	25	28	28	32	24	21
23 34 17	23	26	29	29	23	25	22
23 37 58	24	27	♊	0♋	13	26	23
23 41 39	25	28	1	1	4	27	24
23 45 19	26	29	2	1	54	28	25
23 48 59	27	♉	3	2	44	28	26
23 52 40	28	1	4	3	35	29	27
23 56 20	29	2	4	4	25	♌	28
HOUSES	4	5	6	7		8	9

LATITUDE 14° N.

SIDEREAL TIME H M S	10 ♒	11 ♓	12 ♈	ASC ♉		2 ♊	3 ♋
21 9 52	15	16	20	24	44	22	18
21 13 50	16	17	21	25	46	23	19
21 17 49	17	18	23	26	48	24	20
21 21 46	18	19	24	27	49	25	21
21 25 42	19	20	25	28	50	26	22
21 29 38	20	21	26	29	50	27	22
21 33 34	21	23	27	0♊	50	28	23
21 37 28	22	24	28	1	50	29	24
21 41 22	23	25	29	2	49	♋	25
21 45 15	24	26	♉	3	47	0	26
21 49 8	25	27	1	4	46	1	27
21 53 0	26	28	3	5	43	2	28
21 56 51	27	29	4	6	41	3	29
22 0 42	28	♈	5	7	38	4	♌
22 4 32	29	1	6	8	34	5	1
22 8 22	♓	2	7	9	31	6	2
22 12 11	1	3	8	10	27	7	2
22 15 59	2	5	9	11	22	7	3
22 19 47	3	6	10	12	17	8	4
22 23 34	4	7	11	13	12	9	5
22 27 21	5	8	12	14	7	10	6
22 31 8	6	9	13	15	1	11	7
22 34 53	7	10	14	15	55	12	8
22 38 39	8	11	15	16	49	13	9
22 42 24	9	12	16	17	42	13	10
22 46 8	10	13	17	18	36	14	11
22 49 52	11	14	18	19	29	15	11
22 53 36	12	15	19	20	21	16	12
22 57 20	13	16	20	21	14	17	13
23 1 3	14	17	21	22	6	18	14
23 4 45	15	18	22	22	58	19	15
23 8 28	16	19	23	23	50	19	16
23 12 10	17	20	24	24	41	20	17
23 15 52	18	21	25	25	33	21	18
23 19 33	19	22	26	26	24	22	19
23 23 15	20	23	26	27	15	23	20
23 26 56	21	24	27	28	6	24	21
23 30 37	22	25	28	28	57	24	21
23 34 17	23	26	29	29	48	25	22
23 37 58	24	27	♊	0♋	38	26	23
23 41 39	25	28	1	1	29	27	24
23 45 19	26	29	2	2	19	28	25
23 48 59	27	♉	3	3	10	29	26
23 52 40	28	1	4	4	0	♌	27
23 56 20	29	2	5	4	50	0	28
HOUSES	4	5	6	7		8	9

LATITUDE 15° N.

SIDEREAL TIME H M S	10 ♒	11 ♓	12 ♈	ASC ♉		2 ♊	3 ♋
21 9 52	15	16	20	25	7	23	18
21 13 50	16	17	22	26	10	23	19
21 17 49	17	18	23	27	12	24	20
21 21 46	18	19	24	28	13	25	21
21 25 42	19	20	25	29	14	26	22
21 29 38	20	21	26	0♊	15	27	23
21 33 34	21	23	27	1	15	28	24
21 37 28	22	24	28	2	14	29	24
21 41 22	23	25	29	3	13	♋	25
21 45 15	24	26	♉	4	12	1	26
21 49 8	25	27	2	5	10	2	27
21 53 0	26	28	3	6	8	2	28
21 56 51	27	29	4	7	6	3	29
22 0 42	28	♈	5	8	3	4	♌
22 4 32	29	1	6	9	0	5	1
22 8 22	♓	2	7	9	56	6	2
22 12 11	1	3	8	10	52	7	3
22 15 59	2	5	9	11	48	8	3
22 19 47	3	6	10	12	43	9	4
22 23 34	4	7	11	13	38	9	5
22 27 21	5	8	12	14	33	10	6
22 31 8	6	9	13	15	27	11	7
22 34 53	7	10	14	16	21	12	8
22 38 39	8	11	15	17	15	13	9
22 42 24	9	12	16	18	8	14	10
22 46 8	10	13	17	19	1	15	11
22 49 52	11	14	18	19	54	15	12
22 53 36	12	15	19	20	47	16	13
22 57 20	13	16	20	21	40	17	13
23 1 3	14	17	21	22	32	18	14
23 4 45	15	18	22	23	24	19	15
23 8 28	16	19	23	24	16	20	16
23 12 10	17	20	24	25	7	20	17
23 15 52	18	21	25	25	59	21	18
23 19 33	19	22	26	26	50	22	19
23 23 15	20	23	27	27	41	23	20
23 26 56	21	24	28	28	32	24	21
23 30 37	22	25	29	29	23	25	22
23 34 17	23	26	♊	0♋	14	26	22
23 37 58	24	27	0	1	4	26	23
23 41 39	25	28	1	1	54	27	24
23 45 19	26	29	2	2	45	28	25
23 48 59	27	♉	3	3	35	29	26
23 52 40	28	1	4	4	25	♌	27
23 56 20	29	2	5	5	15	1	28
HOUSES	4	5	6	7		8	9

LATITUDE 13° S.   LATITUDE 14° S.   LATITUDE 15° S.

LATITUDE 16° N.						LATITUDE 17° N.						LATITUDE 18° N.					

SIDEREAL TIME	10 ♈	11 ♉	12 ♊	ASC ♋	2 ♌	3 ♌	10 ♈	11 ♉	12 ♊	ASC ♋	2 ♌	3 ♌	10 ♈	11 ♉	12 ♊	ASC ♋	2 ♌	3 ♌
H M S	°	°	°	° '	°	°	°	°	°	° '	°	°	°	°	°	° '	°	°
0 0 0	0	3	6	6 31	2	29	0	4	6	6 56	2	29	0	4	7	7 22	2	29
0 3 40	1	4	7	7 20	3	♏	1	5	7	7 46	3	♏	1	5	8	8 12	3	♏
0 7 20	2	5	8	8 10	3	1	2	6	8	8 36	4	1	2	6	9	9 1	4	1
0 11 1	3	6	9	9 0	4	2	3	7	9	9 25	4	2	3	7	9	9 51	5	2
0 14 41	4	7	10	9 50	5	3	4	7	10	10 15	5	3	4	8	10	10 40	6	3
0 18 21	5	8	11	10 39	6	4	5	8	11	11 4	6	4	5	9	11	11 30	6	4
0 22 2	6	9	12	11 29	7	5	6	9	12	11 54	7	5	6	10	12	12 19	7	5
0 25 43	7	10	12	12 18	8	6	7	10	13	12 43	8	6	7	11	13	13 8	8	6
0 29 23	8	11	13	13 8	9	6	8	11	14	13 33	9	7	8	11	14	13 58	9	7
0 33 4	9	12	14	13 58	9	7	9	12	14	14 22	10	7	9	12	15	14 47	10	8
0 36 45	10	13	15	14 47	10	8	10	13	15	15 12	10	8	10	13	15	15 37	11	8
0 40 27	11	14	16	15 37	11	9	11	14	16	16 1	11	9	11	14	16	16 26	12	9
0 44 8	12	15	17	16 27	12	10	12	15	17	16 51	12	10	12	15	17	17 15	12	10
0 47 50	13	16	18	17 16	13	11	13	16	18	17 41	13	11	13	16	18	18 5	13	11
0 51 32	14	17	19	18 6	14	12	14	17	19	18 30	14	12	14	17	19	18 54	14	12
0 55 15	15	18	19	18 56	15	13	15	18	20	19 20	15	13	15	18	20	19 44	15	13
0 58 57	16	19	20	19 46	15	14	16	19	21	20 10	16	14	16	19	21	20 33	16	14
1 2 40	17	20	21	20 36	16	15	17	20	21	20 59	17	15	17	20	22	21 23	17	15
1 6 24	18	21	22	21 26	17	16	18	21	22	21 49	17	16	18	21	23	22 13	18	16
1 10 8	19	22	23	22 16	18	17	19	22	23	22 39	18	17	19	22	23	23 3	18	17
1 13 52	20	23	24	23 6	19	18	20	23	24	23 29	19	18	20	23	24	23 53	19	18
1 17 36	21	24	25	23 57	20	19	21	24	25	24 20	20	19	21	24	25	24 43	20	19
1 21 21	22	25	25	24 47	21	20	22	25	26	25 10	21	20	22	25	26	25 33	21	20
1 25 7	23	26	26	25 38	22	21	23	26	27	26 0	22	21	23	26	27	26 23	22	21
1 28 52	24	26	27	26 28	23	22	24	27	28	26 51	23	22	24	27	28	27 13	23	22
1 32 39	25	27	28	27 19	24	23	25	28	28	27 41	24	23	25	28	29	28 4	24	23
1 36 26	26	28	29	28 10	24	24	26	28	29	28 32	25	24	26	29	♋	28 54	25	24
1 40 13	27	29	♋	29 1	25	25	27	29	♋	29 23	25	25	27	♋	0	29 45	26	25
1 44 1	28	♊	1	29 53	26	26	28	♊	1	0♌ 14	26	26	28	0	1	0♌ 36	26	26
1 47 49	29	1	2	0♌ 44	27	27	29	1	2	1 5	27	27	29	1	2	1 27	27	27
1 51 38	♉	2	2	1 36	28	28	♉	2	3	1 57	28	28	♉	2	3	2 18	28	28
1 55 28	1	3	3	2 27	29	29	1	3	4	2 48	29	29	1	3	4	3 10	29	29
1 59 18	2	4	4	3 19	♏	♎	2	4	4	3 40	♏	♎	2	4	5	4 1	♏	♎
2 3 9	3	5	5	4 12	1	1	3	5	5	4 32	1	1	3	5	6	4 53	1	1
2 7 0	4	6	6	5 4	2	2	4	6	6	5 24	2	2	4	6	7	5 45	2	2
2 10 52	5	7	7	5 56	3	3	5	7	7	6 17	3	3	5	7	7	6 37	3	3
2 14 45	6	8	8	6 49	4	4	6	8	8	7 9	4	4	6	8	8	7 29	4	4
2 18 38	7	9	9	7 42	5	5	7	9	9	8 2	5	5	7	9	9	8 22	5	5
2 22 32	8	10	9	8 35	6	6	8	10	10	8 55	6	6	8	10	10	9 14	6	6
2 26 26	9	10	10	9 29	7	7	9	11	11	9 48	7	7	9	11	11	10 7	7	7
2 30 22	10	11	11	10 22	8	8	10	12	12	10 41	8	8	10	12	12	11 0	8	8
2 34 17	11	12	12	11 16	9	9	11	12	12	11 35	9	9	11	13	13	11 54	9	9
2 38 14	12	13	13	12 10	10	10	12	13	13	12 29	10	10	12	14	14	12 47	10	10
2 42 11	13	14	14	13 5	11	11	13	14	14	13 23	11	11	13	14	15	13 41	11	11
2 46 10	14	15	15	13 59	11	12	14	15	15	14 17	12	12	14	15	15	14 35	12	12
HOUSES	4	5	6	7	8	9	4	5	6	7	8	9	4	5	6	7	8	9

LATITUDE 16° S.   LATITUDE 17° S.   LATITUDE 18° S.

	LATITUDE 16° N.							LATITUDE 17° N.							LATITUDE 18° N.						
SIDEREAL TIME	10 ♉	11 ♊	12 ♋	ASC ♌		2 ♍	3 ♎	10 ♉	11 ♊	12 ♋	ASC ♌		2 ♍	3 ♎	10 ♉	11 ♊	12 ♋	ASC ♌		2 ♍	3 ♎
H M S	°	°	°	°	'	°	°	°	°	°	°	'	°	°	°	°	°	°	'	°	°
2 50 8	15	16	16	14	54	12	13	15	16	16	15	12	13	13	15	16	16	15	29	13	13
2 54 8	16	17	17	15	49	13	14	16	17	17	16	6	14	14	16	17	17	16	24	14	14
2 58 8	17	18	18	16	44	14	15	17	18	18	17	1	15	15	17	18	18	17	18	15	15
3 2 9	18	19	18	17	40	15	16	18	19	19	17	57	16	16	18	19	19	18	13	16	16
3 6 10	19	20	19	18	36	16	17	19	20	20	18	52	17	17	19	20	20	19	9	17	17
3 10 13	20	21	20	19	32	17	18	20	21	21	19	48	18	18	20	21	21	20	4	18	18
3 14 16	21	22	21	20	28	19	19	21	22	21	20	44	19	19	21	22	22	21	0	19	19
3 18 20	22	23	22	21	25	20	20	22	23	22	21	40	20	20	22	23	23	21	56	20	20
3 22 24	23	24	23	22	22	21	21	23	24	23	22	37	21	21	23	24	24	22	52	21	21
3 26 30	24	24	24	23	19	22	22	24	25	24	23	34	22	22	24	25	25	23	48	22	22
3 30 36	25	25	25	24	16	23	24	25	26	25	24	31	23	23	25	26	25	24	45	23	23
3 34 42	26	26	26	25	14	24	25	26	27	26	25	28	24	25	26	27	26	25	42	24	24
3 38 50	27	27	27	26	12	25	26	27	27	27	26	26	25	26	27	28	27	26	39	25	25
3 42 58	28	28	28	27	10	26	27	28	28	28	27	23	26	27	28	29	28	27	37	26	27
3 47 7	29	29	29	28	8	27	28	29	29	29	28	22	27	28	29	♋	29	28	35	27	28
3 51 16	♊	♋	♌	29	7	28	29	♊	♋	♌	29	20	28	29	♊	0	♌	29	33	28	29
3 55 26	1	1	1	0♍	6	29	♏	1	1	1	0♍	18	29	♏	1	1	1	0♍	31	29	♏
3 59 37	2	2	2	1	5	♎	1	2	2	2	1	17	♎	1	2	2	2	1	29	♎	1
4 3 49	3	3	3	2	5	1	2	3	3	3	2	16	1	2	3	3	3	2	28	1	2
4 8 1	4	4	4	3	4	2	3	4	4	4	3	16	2	3	4	4	4	3	27	2	3
4 12 14	5	5	5	4	4	3	4	5	5	5	4	15	3	4	5	5	5	4	26	3	4
4 16 27	6	6	6	5	4	4	5	6	6	6	5	15	4	5	6	6	6	5	25	4	5
4 20 41	7	7	6	6	5	5	6	7	7	7	6	15	5	6	7	7	7	6	25	5	6
4 24 56	8	8	7	7	5	6	7	8	8	8	7	15	6	7	8	8	8	7	25	6	7
4 29 11	9	9	8	8	6	7	8	9	9	9	8	16	7	8	9	9	9	8	25	7	8
4 33 27	10	10	9	9	7	8	9	10	10	10	9	16	8	9	10	10	10	9	25	8	9
4 37 43	11	11	10	10	9	9	10	11	11	11	10	17	9	10	11	11	11	10	26	9	10
4 41 59	12	12	11	11	10	11	11	12	12	12	11	18	10	11	12	12	12	11	26	10	11
4 46 17	13	13	12	12	12	12	12	13	13	13	12	19	12	12	13	13	13	12	27	12	12
4 50 34	14	14	13	13	14	13	14	14	14	14	13	21	13	13	14	14	14	13	28	13	13
4 54 53	15	15	14	14	16	14	15	15	15	15	14	22	14	14	15	15	15	14	29	14	14
4 59 11	16	16	16	15	18	15	16	16	16	16	15	24	15	16	16	16	16	15	30	15	15
5 3 30	17	17	17	16	20	16	17	17	17	17	16	26	16	17	17	17	17	16	32	16	16
5 7 49	18	18	18	17	23	17	18	18	18	18	17	28	17	18	18	18	18	17	34	17	18
5 12 9	19	19	19	18	25	18	19	19	19	19	18	30	18	19	19	19	19	18	35	18	19
5 16 29	20	20	20	19	28	19	20	20	20	20	19	33	19	20	20	20	20	19	37	19	20
5 20 49	21	21	21	20	31	20	21	21	21	21	20	35	20	21	21	21	21	20	39	20	21
5 25 10	22	22	22	21	34	21	22	22	22	22	21	37	21	22	22	22	22	21	41	21	22
5 29 31	23	23	23	22	37	22	23	23	23	23	22	40	22	23	23	23	23	22	43	22	23
5 33 51	24	24	24	23	40	23	24	24	24	24	23	43	23	24	24	24	24	23	46	23	24
5 38 13	25	25	25	24	43	25	25	25	25	25	24	46	24	25	25	25	25	24	48	24	25
5 42 34	26	26	26	25	47	26	26	26	26	26	25	48	25	26	26	26	26	25	50	25	26
5 46 55	27	27	27	26	50	27	27	27	27	27	26	51	27	27	27	27	27	26	53	26	27
5 51 17	28	28	28	27	53	28	28	28	28	28	27	54	28	28	28	28	28	27	55	27	28
5 55 38	29	29	29	28	57	29	29	29	29	29	28	57	29	29	29	29	29	28	58	29	29
HOUSES	4	5	6	7		8	9	4	5	6	7		8	9	4	5	6	7		8	9

LATITUDE 16° N.   LATITUDE 17° N.   LATITUDE 18° N.

SIDEREAL TIME (H M S)	10 ♋	11 ♌	12 ♍	ASC ♎		2 ♏	3 ♐	10 ♋	11 ♌	12 ♍	ASC ♎		2 ♏	3 ♐	10 ♋	11 ♌	12 ♍	ASC ♎		2 ♏	3 ♐
6 0 0	0	0	0	0	0	0	0	0	0	0	0	0	0	0	0	0	0	0	0	0	0
6 4 22	1	1	1	1	3	1	1	1	1	1	1	3	1	1	1	1	1	1	2	1	1
6 8 43	2	2	2	2	7	2	2	2	2	2	2	6	2	2	2	2	3	2	5	2	2
6 13 5	3	3	3	3	10	3	3	3	3	3	3	9	3	3	3	3	4	3	7	3	3
6 17 26	4	4	4	4	13	4	4	4	4	5	4	12	4	4	4	4	5	4	10	4	4
6 21 47	5	5	5	5	17	5	5	5	5	6	5	14	5	5	5	5	6	5	12	5	5
6 26 9	6	6	7	6	20	6	6	6	6	7	6	17	6	6	6	6	7	6	14	6	6
6 30 29	7	7	8	7	23	7	7	7	7	8	7	20	7	7	7	7	8	7	17	7	7
6 34 50	8	8	9	8	26	8	8	8	8	9	8	23	8	8	8	8	9	8	19	8	8
6 39 11	9	9	10	9	29	9	9	9	9	10	9	25	9	9	9	9	10	9	21	9	9
6 43 31	10	10	11	10	32	10	10	10	10	11	10	27	10	10	10	10	11	10	23	10	10
6 47 51	11	11	12	11	35	11	11	11	11	12	11	30	11	11	11	11	12	11	25	11	11
6 52 11	12	12	13	12	37	12	12	12	12	13	12	32	12	12	12	12	13	12	26	12	12
6 56 30	13	13	14	13	40	13	13	13	13	14	13	34	13	13	13	14	14	13	28	13	13
7 0 49	14	14	15	14	42	14	14	14	14	15	14	36	14	14	14	15	15	14	30	14	14
7 5 7	15	15	16	15	44	16	15	15	16	16	15	38	15	15	15	16	16	15	31	15	15
7 9 26	16	16	17	16	46	17	16	16	17	17	16	39	16	16	16	17	17	16	32	16	16
7 13 43	17	18	18	17	48	18	17	17	18	18	17	41	17	17	17	18	18	17	33	17	17
7 18 0	18	19	19	18	50	19	18	18	19	20	18	42	18	18	18	19	20	18	34	18	18
7 22 17	19	20	21	19	51	20	19	19	20	21	19	43	19	19	19	20	21	19	34	19	19
7 26 33	20	21	22	20	53	21	20	20	21	22	20	44	20	20	20	21	22	20	35	20	20
7 30 49	21	22	23	21	54	22	21	21	22	23	21	44	21	21	21	22	23	21	35	21	21
7 35 4	22	23	24	22	55	23	22	22	23	24	22	45	22	22	22	23	24	22	35	22	22
7 39 19	23	24	25	23	55	24	23	23	24	25	23	45	23	23	23	24	25	23	35	23	23
7 43 33	24	25	26	24	56	24	24	24	25	26	24	45	24	24	24	25	26	24	35	24	24
7 47 46	25	26	27	25	56	25	25	25	26	27	25	45	25	25	25	26	27	25	34	25	25
7 51 59	26	27	28	26	56	26	26	26	27	28	26	44	26	26	26	27	28	26	33	26	26
7 56 11	27	28	29	27	55	27	27	27	28	29	27	44	27	27	27	28	29	27	32	27	27
8 0 23	28	29	♎	28	55	28	28	28	29	♎	28	43	28	28	28	29	♎	28	31	28	28
8 4 34	29	♏	1	29	54	29	29	29	♏	1	29	42	29	29	29	♏	1	29	29	29	29
8 8 44	♌	1	2	0♏	53	♐	♑	♌	1	2	0♏	40	♐	♑	♌	1	2	0♏	27	♐	♑
8 12 53	1	2	3	1	52	1	1	1	2	3	1	38	1	1	1	2	3	1	25	1	0
8 17 2	2	3	4	2	50	2	2	2	3	4	2	37	2	2	2	3	4	2	23	2	1
8 21 10	3	4	5	3	48	3	3	3	4	5	3	34	3	3	3	5	5	3	21	3	2
8 25 18	4	5	6	4	46	4	4	4	5	6	4	32	4	3	4	6	6	4	18	4	3
8 29 24	5	6	7	5	44	5	5	5	7	7	5	29	5	4	5	7	7	5	15	5	4
8 33 30	6	8	8	6	41	6	6	6	8	8	6	26	6	5	6	8	8	6	12	5	5
8 37 36	7	9	9	7	38	7	6	7	9	9	7	23	7	6	7	9	9	7	8	6	6
8 41 40	8	10	10	8	35	8	7	8	10	10	8	20	8	7	8	10	10	8	4	7	7
8 45 44	9	11	11	9	32	9	8	9	11	11	9	16	9	8	9	11	11	9	0	8	8
8 49 47	10	12	13	10	28	10	9	10	12	12	10	12	9	9	10	12	12	9	56	9	9
8 53 50	11	13	14	11	24	11	10	11	13	13	11	8	10	10	11	13	13	10	51	10	10
8 57 51	12	14	15	12	20	12	11	12	14	14	12	3	11	11	12	14	14	11	47	11	11
9 1 52	13	15	16	13	16	12	12	13	15	15	12	59	12	12	13	15	15	12	42	12	12
9 5 52	14	16	17	14	11	13	13	14	16	16	13	54	13	13	14	16	16	13	36	13	13
HOUSES	4	5	6	7		8	9	4	5	6	7		8	9	4	5	6	7		8	9

LATITUDE 16° S.   LATITUDE 17° S.   LATITUDE 18° S.

LATITUDE 16° N.   LATITUDE 17° N.   LATITUDE 18° N.

LATITUDE 16° N.

SIDEREAL TIME (H M S)	10 Ω	11 ♍	12 ♎	ASC ♏	2 ♐	3 ♑
9 9 52	15	17	18	15 6	14	14
9 13 50	16	18	19	16 1	15	15
9 17 49	17	19	19	16 55	16	16
9 21 46	18	20	20	17 50	17	17
9 25 42	19	21	21	18 44	18	18
9 29 38	20	22	22	19 38	19	19
9 33 34	21	23	23	20 31	20	20
9 37 28	22	24	24	21 25	21	20
9 41 22	23	25	25	22 18	21	21
9 45 15	24	26	26	23 11	22	22
9 49 8	25	27	27	24 4	23	23
9 53 0	26	28	28	24 56	24	24
9 56 51	27	29	29	25 48	25	25
10 0 42	28	♎	♏	26 41	26	26
10 4 32	29	1	1	27 33	27	27
10 8 22	♍	2	2	28 24	28	28
10 12 11	1	3	3	29 16	28	29
10 15 59	2	4	4	0♐ 7	29	♒
10 19 47	3	5	5	0 59	♑	1
10 23 34	4	6	6	1 50	1	2
10 27 21	5	7	6	2 41	2	3
10 31 8	6	8	7	3 32	3	4
10 34 53	7	9	8	4 22	4	4
10 38 39	8	10	9	5 13	5	5
10 42 24	9	11	10	6 3	5	6
10 46 8	10	12	11	6 54	6	7
10 49 52	11	13	12	7 44	7	8
10 53 36	12	14	13	8 34	8	9
10 57 20	13	15	14	9 24	9	10
11 1 3	14	16	15	10 14	10	11
11 4 45	15	17	15	11 4	11	12
11 8 28	16	18	16	11 54	11	13
11 12 10	17	19	17	12 44	12	14
11 15 52	18	20	18	13 33	13	15
11 19 33	19	21	19	14 23	14	16
11 23 15	20	22	20	15 13	15	17
11 26 56	21	23	21	16 2	16	18
11 30 37	22	24	21	16 52	17	19
11 34 17	23	24	22	17 42	18	20
11 37 58	24	25	23	18 31	18	21
11 41 39	25	26	24	19 21	19	22
11 45 19	26	27	25	20 10	20	23
11 48 59	27	28	26	21 0	21	24
11 52 40	28	29	27	21 50	22	25
11 56 20	29	♏	27	22 40	23	26

LATITUDE 17° N.

SIDEREAL TIME (H M S)	10 Ω	11 ♍	12 ♎	ASC ♏	2 ♐	3 ♑
9 9 52	15	17	17	14 48	14	14
9 13 50	16	18	18	15 43	15	15
9 17 49	17	19	19	16 37	16	16
9 21 46	18	20	20	17 31	17	17
9 25 42	19	21	21	18 25	18	18
9 29 38	20	22	22	19 19	18	18
9 33 34	21	23	23	20 12	19	19
9 37 28	22	24	24	21 5	20	20
9 41 22	23	25	25	21 58	21	21
9 45 15	24	26	26	22 51	22	22
9 49 8	25	27	27	23 43	23	23
9 53 0	26	28	28	24 36	24	24
9 56 51	27	29	29	25 28	25	25
10 0 42	28	♎	♏	26 20	26	26
10 4 32	29	1	1	27 12	26	27
10 8 22	♍	2	2	28 3	27	28
10 12 11	1	3	3	28 55	28	29
10 15 59	2	4	4	29 46	29	♒
10 19 47	3	5	5	0♐ 37	♑	1
10 23 34	4	6	5	1 28	1	2
10 27 21	5	7	6	2 19	2	2
10 31 8	6	8	7	3 9	2	3
10 34 53	7	9	8	4 0	3	4
10 38 39	8	10	9	4 50	4	5
10 42 24	9	11	10	5 40	5	6
10 46 8	10	12	11	6 31	6	7
10 49 52	11	13	12	7 21	7	8
10 53 36	12	14	13	8 11	8	9
10 57 20	13	15	13	9 1	9	10
11 1 3	14	16	14	9 50	9	11
11 4 45	15	17	15	10 40	10	12
11 8 28	16	18	16	11 30	11	13
11 12 10	17	19	17	12 19	12	14
11 15 52	18	20	18	13 9	13	15
11 19 33	19	21	19	13 59	14	16
11 23 15	20	22	20	14 48	15	17
11 26 56	21	23	20	15 38	16	18
11 30 37	22	23	21	16 27	16	19
11 34 17	23	24	22	17 17	17	20
11 37 58	24	25	23	18 6	18	21
11 41 39	25	26	24	18 56	19	22
11 45 19	26	27	25	19 45	20	23
11 48 59	27	28	26	20 35	21	23
11 52 40	28	29	26	21 24	22	24
11 56 20	29	♏	27	22 14	23	25

LATITUDE 18° N.

SIDEREAL TIME (H M S)	10 Ω	11 ♍	12 ♎	ASC ♏	2 ♐	3 ♑
9 9 52	15	17	17	14 31	14	14
9 13 50	16	18	18	15 25	15	15
9 17 49	17	19	19	16 19	15	16
9 21 46	18	20	20	17 13	16	16
9 25 42	19	21	21	18 6	17	17
9 29 38	20	22	22	19 0	18	18
9 33 34	21	23	23	19 53	19	19
9 37 28	22	24	24	20 46	20	20
9 41 22	23	25	25	21 38	21	21
9 45 15	24	26	26	22 31	22	22
9 49 8	25	27	27	23 23	23	23
9 53 0	26	28	28	24 15	23	24
9 56 51	27	29	29	25 7	24	25
10 0 42	28	♎	♏	25 59	25	26
10 4 32	29	1	1	26 50	26	27
10 8 22	♍	2	2	27 42	27	28
10 12 11	1	3	3	28 33	28	29
10 15 59	2	4	3	29 24	29	♒
10 19 47	3	5	4	0♐ 15	♑	0
10 23 34	4	6	5	1 6	0	1
10 27 21	5	7	6	1 56	1	2
10 31 8	6	8	7	2 47	2	3
10 34 53	7	9	8	3 37	3	4
10 38 39	8	10	9	4 27	4	5
10 42 24	9	11	10	5 17	5	6
10 46 8	10	12	11	6 7	6	7
10 49 52	11	13	12	6 57	7	8
10 53 36	12	14	12	7 47	7	9
10 57 20	13	15	13	8 37	8	10
11 1 3	14	16	14	9 27	9	11
11 4 45	15	17	15	10 16	10	12
11 8 28	16	18	16	11 6	11	13
11 12 10	17	19	17	11 55	12	14
11 15 52	18	20	18	12 45	13	15
11 19 33	19	21	18	13 34	14	16
11 23 15	20	22	19	14 23	14	17
11 26 56	21	22	20	15 13	15	18
11 30 37	22	23	21	16 2	16	19
11 34 17	23	24	22	16 52	17	19
11 37 58	24	25	23	17 41	18	20
11 41 39	25	26	24	18 30	19	21
11 45 19	26	27	24	19 20	20	22
11 48 59	27	28	25	20 9	21	23
11 52 40	28	29	26	20 59	21	24
11 56 20	29	♏	27	21 48	22	25

HOUSES	4	5	6	7	8	9

LATITUDE 16° S.   LATITUDE 17° S.   LATITUDE 18° S.

LATITUDE 16° N. LATITUDE 17° N. LATITUDE 18° N.

SIDEREAL TIME (H M S)	10 ♑	11 ♑	12 ♒	ASC ♈	2 ♉	3 ♊	10 ♑	11 ♑	12 ♒	ASC ♈	2 ♉	3 ♊	10 ♑	11 ♑	12 ♒	ASC ♈	2 ♉	3 ♊
18 0 0	0	26	25	0 0	5	4	0	26	25	0 0	5	4	0	26	25	0 0	5	4
18 4 22	1	27	26	1 21	6	5	1	27	26	1 22	6	5	1	27	26	1 23	6	5
18 8 43	2	28	28	2 43	7	6	2	28	27	2 44	7	6	2	28	27	2 46	8	6
18 13 5	3	29	29	4 4	8	7	3	29	29	4 6	9	7	3	29	28	4 9	9	8
18 17 26	4	♒	♓	5 25	10	8	4	♒	♓	5 28	10	8	4	♒	♓	5 32	10	9
18 21 47	5	1	1	6 46	11	9	5	1	1	6 50	11	9	5	1	1	6 54	11	10
18 26 9	6	2	3	8 7	12	10	6	2	2	8 12	12	11	6	2	2	8 17	12	11
18 30 29	7	3	4	9 28	13	11	7	3	4	9 34	13	12	7	3	3	9 39	14	12
18 34 50	8	4	5	10 49	14	12	8	4	5	10 55	15	13	8	4	5	11 1	15	13
18 39 11	9	6	6	12 9	16	13	9	5	6	12 16	16	14	9	5	6	12 23	16	14
18 43 31	10	7	7	13 29	17	14	10	7	7	13 37	17	15	10	6	7	13 45	17	15
18 47 51	11	8	9	14 49	18	15	11	8	9	14 57	18	16	11	7	9	15 6	18	16
18 52 11	12	9	10	16 9	19	17	12	9	10	16 18	19	17	12	9	10	16 27	19	17
18 56 30	13	10	11	17 28	20	18	13	10	11	17 38	20	18	13	10	11	17 48	21	18
19 0 49	14	11	13	18 47	21	19	14	11	12	18 57	21	19	14	11	12	19 8	22	19
19 5 7	15	12	14	20 5	22	20	15	12	14	20 16	23	20	15	12	14	20 28	23	20
19 9 26	16	13	15	21 23	23	21	16	13	15	21 35	24	21	16	13	15	21 47	24	21
19 13 43	17	14	16	22 41	25	22	17	14	16	22 54	25	22	17	14	16	23 6	25	22
19 18 0	18	15	18	23 58	26	23	18	15	17	24 11	26	23	18	15	17	24 25	26	23
19 22 17	19	17	19	25 15	27	24	19	16	19	25 29	27	24	19	16	19	25 43	27	24
19 26 33	20	18	20	26 32	28	24	20	18	20	26 46	28	25	20	17	20	27 0	28	25
19 30 49	21	19	21	27 48	29	25	21	19	21	28 2	29	26	21	19	21	28 18	29	26
19 35 4	22	20	23	29 3	♊	26	22	20	23	29 18	♊	27	22	20	23	29 34	♊	27
19 39 19	23	21	24	0♉ 18	1	27	23	21	24	0♉ 34	1	28	23	21	24	0♉ 50	2	28
19 43 33	24	22	25	1 33	2	28	24	22	25	1 49	2	29	24	22	25	2 6	3	29
19 47 46	25	23	26	2 46	3	29	25	23	26	3 3	3	♋	25	23	26	3 21	4	♋
19 51 59	26	24	28	4 0	4	♋	26	24	28	4 17	4	0	26	24	28	4 35	5	1
19 56 11	27	26	29	5 13	5	1	27	25	29	5 31	6	1	27	25	29	5 49	6	2
20 0 23	28	27	♈	6 25	6	2	28	27	♈	6 43	7	2	28	26	♈	7 2	7	3
20 4 34	29	28	1	7 37	7	3	29	28	1	7 56	8	3	29	28	1	8 15	8	4
20 8 44	♒	29	3	8 48	8	4	♒	29	3	9 7	9	4	♒	29	3	9 27	9	4
20 12 53	1	♓	4	9 59	9	5	1	♓	4	10 19	10	5	1	♓	4	10 39	10	5
20 17 2	2	1	5	11 9	10	6	2	1	5	11 29	11	6	2	1	5	11 50	11	6
20 21 10	3	2	6	12 19	11	7	3	2	6	12 39	12	7	3	2	6	13 0	12	7
20 25 18	4	3	8	13 28	12	8	4	3	8	13 48	13	8	4	3	8	14 10	13	8
20 29 24	5	5	9	14 36	13	9	5	4	9	14 57	14	9	5	4	9	15 19	14	9
20 33 30	6	6	10	15 44	14	10	6	6	10	16 6	15	10	6	6	10	16 28	15	10
20 37 36	7	7	11	16 51	15	11	7	7	11	17 13	16	11	7	7	11	17 36	16	11
20 41 40	8	8	12	17 58	16	12	8	8	12	18 20	16	12	8	8	12	18 43	17	12
20 45 44	9	9	14	19 4	17	13	9	9	14	19 27	17	13	9	9	14	19 50	18	13
20 49 47	10	10	15	20 10	18	14	10	10	15	20 33	18	14	10	10	15	20 56	19	14
20 53 50	11	11	16	21 15	19	15	11	11	16	21 39	19	15	11	11	16	22 2	20	15
20 57 51	12	12	17	22 20	20	15	12	12	17	22 43	20	16	12	12	17	23 7	21	16
21 1 52	13	14	18	23 24	21	16	13	14	18	23 48	21	16	13	13	18	24 12	22	17
21 5 52	14	15	19	24 28	22	17	14	15	20	24 52	22	17	14	15	20	25 16	22	18
HOUSES	4	5	6	7	8	9	4	5	6	7	8	9	4	5	6	7	8	9

LATITUDE 16° S. LATITUDE 17° S. LATITUDE 18° S.

LATITUDE 16° N.   LATITUDE 17° N.   LATITUDE 18° N.

SIDEREAL TIME H M S	10 ♒	11 ♓	12 ♈	ASC ♉ °	ASC '	2 ♊	3 ♋	10 ♒	11 ♓	12 ♈	ASC ♉ °	ASC '	2 ♊	3 ♋	10 ♒	11 ♓	12 ♈	ASC ♉ °	ASC '	2 ♊	3 ♋
21 9 52	15	16	21	25	31	23	18	15	16	21	25	55	23	18	15	16	21	26	20	23	18
21 13 50	16	17	22	26	34	24	19	16	17	22	26	58	24	19	16	17	22	27	23	24	19
21 17 49	17	18	23	27	36	25	20	17	18	23	28	0	25	20	17	18	23	28	25	25	20
21 21 46	18	19	24	28	37	26	21	18	19	24	29	2	26	21	18	19	24	29	27	26	21
21 25 42	19	20	25	29	38	26	22	19	20	25	0♊	3	27	22	19	20	25	0♊	29	27	22
21 29 38	20	21	26	0♊	39	27	23	20	21	26	1	4	28	23	20	21	27	1	30	28	23
21 33 34	21	22	27	1	39	28	24	21	22	28	2	4	29	24	21	22	28	2	30	29	24
21 37 28	22	24	28	2	39	29	25	22	24	29	3	4	29	25	22	24	29	3	30	♋	25
21 41 22	23	25	29	3	38	♋	25	23	25	♉	4	4	♋	26	23	25	♉	4	30	1	26
21 45 15	24	26	1	4	37	1	26	24	26	1	5	3	1	27	24	26	1	5	29	2	27
21 49 8	25	27	2	5	36	2	27	25	27	2	6	1	2	27	25	27	2	6	27	2	28
21 53 0	26	28	3	6	34	3	28	26	28	3	6	59	3	28	26	28	3	7	26	3	28
21 56 51	27	29	4	7	31	4	29	27	29	4	7	57	4	29	27	29	4	8	23	4	29
22 0 42	28	♈	5	8	28	5	♌	28	♈	5	8	54	5	♌	28	♈	5	9	21	5	♌
22 4 32	29	1	6	9	25	5	1	29	1	6	9	51	6	1	29	1	6	10	18	6	1
22 8 22	♓	2	7	10	22	6	2	♓	2	7	10	48	7	2	♓	2	8	11	14	7	2
22 12 11	1	3	8	11	18	7	3	1	3	8	11	44	7	3	1	3	9	12	11	8	3
22 15 59	2	5	9	12	13	8	4	2	5	9	12	40	8	4	2	5	10	13	6	9	4
22 19 47	3	6	10	13	9	9	5	3	6	10	13	35	9	5	3	6	11	14	2	9	5
22 23 34	4	7	11	14	4	10	5	4	7	12	14	30	10	6	4	7	12	14	57	10	6
22 27 21	5	8	12	14	59	11	6	5	8	13	15	25	11	6	5	8	13	15	52	11	7
22 31 8	6	9	13	15	53	11	7	6	9	14	16	19	12	7	6	9	14	16	46	12	7
22 34 53	7	10	14	16	47	12	8	7	10	15	17	14	13	8	7	10	15	17	40	13	8
22 38 39	8	11	15	17	41	13	9	8	11	16	18	7	13	9	8	11	16	18	34	14	9
22 42 24	9	12	16	18	34	14	10	9	12	17	19	1	14	10	9	12	17	19	28	15	10
22 46 8	10	13	17	19	28	15	11	10	13	18	19	54	15	11	10	13	18	20	21	15	11
22 49 52	11	14	18	20	21	16	12	11	14	19	20	47	16	12	11	14	19	21	14	16	12
22 53 36	12	15	19	21	13	17	13	12	15	20	21	40	17	13	12	15	20	22	7	17	13
22 57 20	13	16	20	22	6	17	14	13	16	21	22	32	18	14	13	16	21	22	59	18	14
23 1 3	14	17	21	22	58	18	14	14	17	22	23	24	18	15	14	17	22	23	51	19	15
23 4 45	15	18	22	23	50	19	15	15	18	22	24	16	19	15	15	18	23	24	43	20	16
23 8 28	16	19	23	24	42	20	16	16	19	23	25	8	20	16	16	19	24	25	35	20	16
23 12 10	17	20	24	25	33	21	17	17	20	24	26	0	21	17	17	20	25	26	27	21	17
23 15 52	18	21	25	26	25	22	18	18	21	25	26	51	22	18	18	22	26	27	18	22	18
23 19 33	19	22	26	27	16	22	19	19	22	26	27	42	23	19	19	23	27	28	9	23	19
23 23 15	20	23	27	28	7	23	20	20	24	27	28	33	24	20	20	24	28	29	0	24	20
23 26 56	21	24	28	28	58	24	21	21	25	28	29	24	24	21	21	25	28	29	51	25	21
23 30 37	22	25	29	29	49	25	22	22	26	29	0♋	15	25	22	22	26	29	0♋	41	25	22
23 34 17	23	26	♊	0♋	39	26	23	23	27	♊	1	6	26	23	23	27	♊	1	32	26	23
23 37 58	24	27	1	1	30	27	23	24	28	1	1	56	27	24	24	28	1	2	22	27	24
23 41 39	25	28	2	2	20	27	24	25	29	2	2	46	28	24	25	29	2	3	13	28	25
23 45 19	26	29	3	3	10	28	25	26	♉	3	3	36	29	25	26	♉	3	4	3	29	25
23 48 59	27	♉	3	4	1	29	26	27	1	4	4	26	29	26	27	1	4	4	53	♌	26
23 52 40	28	1	4	4	51	♌	27	28	2	5	5	16	♌	27	28	2	5	5	42	1	27
23 56 20	29	2	5	5	41	1	28	29	3	6	6	6	1	28	29	3	6	6	32	1	28
HOUSES	4	5	6	7		8	9	4	5	6	7		8	9	4	5	6	7		8	9

LATITUDE 16° S.   LATITUDE 17° S.   LATITUDE 18° S.

LATITUDE 19° N. LATITUDE 20° N. LATITUDE 21° N.

LATITUDE 19° N.

SIDEREAL TIME (H M S)	10 ♌	11 ♌	12 ♍	ASC ♎	2 ♎	3 ♐
6 0 0	0	0	1	0 0	29	0
6 4 22	1	1	2	1 2	♏	1
6 8 43	2	2	3	2 4	2	2
6 13 5	3	3	4	3 6	3	3
6 17 26	4	4	5	4 8	4	4
6 21 47	5	5	6	5 10	5	5
6 26 9	6	6	7	6 12	6	6
6 30 29	7	7	8	7 14	7	7
6 34 50	8	8	9	8 15	8	8
6 39 11	9	9	10	9 17	9	9
6 43 31	10	11	11	10 18	10	10
6 47 51	11	12	12	11 20	11	11
6 52 11	12	13	13	12 21	12	12
6 56 30	13	14	14	13 22	13	13
7 0 49	14	15	15	14 23	14	14
7 5 7	15	16	16	15 24	15	15
7 9 26	16	17	17	16 25	16	16
7 13 43	17	18	19	17 25	17	17
7 18 0	18	19	20	18 26	18	18
7 22 17	19	20	21	19 26	19	19
7 26 33	20	21	22	20 26	20	20
7 30 49	21	22	23	21 26	21	21
7 35 4	22	23	24	22 25	22	22
7 39 19	23	24	25	23 25	23	23
7 43 33	24	25	26	24 24	24	24
7 47 46	25	26	27	25 23	25	25
7 51 59	26	27	28	26 22	26	26
7 56 11	27	28	29	27 20	27	27
8 0 23	28	29	≏	28 19	28	27
8 4 34	29	♏	1	29 17	29	28
8 8 44	♌	1	2	0♏ 15	♐	29
8 12 53	1	2	3	1 12	1	♑
8 17 2	2	4	4	2 10	1	1
8 21 10	3	5	5	3 7	2	2
8 25 18	4	6	6	4 4	3	3
8 29 24	5	7	7	5 0	4	4
8 33 30	6	8	8	5 57	5	5
8 37 36	7	9	9	6 53	6	6
8 41 40	8	10	10	7 49	7	7
8 45 44	9	11	11	8 44	8	8
8 49 47	10	12	12	9 40	9	9
8 53 50	11	13	13	10 35	10	10
8 57 51	12	14	14	11 30	11	11
9 1 52	13	15	15	12 25	12	12
9 5 52	14	16	16	13 19	13	13

LATITUDE 20° N.

SIDEREAL TIME (H M S)	10 ♌	11 ♌	12 ♍	ASC ♎	2 ♎	3 ♐
6 0 0	0	0	1	0 0	29	0
6 4 22	1	1	2	1 2	♏	1
6 8 43	2	2	3	2 3	1	2
6 13 5	3	3	4	3 5	2	3
6 17 26	4	4	5	4 6	3	4
6 21 47	5	5	6	5 8	4	5
6 26 9	6	6	7	6 9	6	6
6 30 29	7	8	8	7 10	7	7
6 34 50	8	9	9	8 12	8	8
6 39 11	9	10	10	9 13	9	9
6 43 31	10	11	11	10 14	10	10
6 47 51	11	12	12	11 15	11	11
6 52 11	12	13	13	12 16	12	12
6 56 30	13	14	14	13 16	13	13
7 0 49	14	15	15	14 17	14	14
7 5 7	15	16	16	15 17	15	15
7 9 26	16	17	18	16 18	16	16
7 13 43	17	18	19	17 18	17	17
7 18 0	18	19	20	18 18	18	18
7 22 17	19	20	21	19 18	19	19
7 26 33	20	21	22	20 17	20	20
7 30 49	21	22	23	21 17	21	21
7 35 4	22	23	24	22 16	22	22
7 39 19	23	24	25	23 15	22	22
7 43 33	24	25	26	24 14	24	23
7 47 46	25	26	27	25 12	25	24
7 51 59	26	27	28	26 11	25	25
7 56 11	27	28	29	27 9	26	26
8 0 23	28	29	≏	28 7	27	27
8 4 34	29	♏	1	29 5	28	28
8 8 44	♌	2	2	0♏ 2	29	29
8 12 53	1	3	3	0 59	♐	♑
8 17 2	2	4	4	1 56	1	1
8 21 10	3	5	5	2 53	2	2
8 25 18	4	6	6	3 50	3	3
8 29 24	5	7	7	4 46	4	4
8 33 30	6	8	8	5 42	5	5
8 37 36	7	9	9	6 38	6	6
8 41 40	8	10	10	7 33	7	7
8 45 44	9	11	11	8 29	8	8
8 49 47	10	12	12	9 24	9	9
8 53 50	11	13	13	10 19	10	10
8 57 51	12	14	14	11 13	10	11
9 1 52	13	15	15	12 7	11	12
9 5 52	14	16	16	13 2	12	12

LATITUDE 21° N.

SIDEREAL TIME (H M S)	10 ♌	11 ♌	12 ♍	ASC ♎	2 ♎	3 ♐
6 0 0	0	0	1	0 0	29	0
6 4 22	1	2	2	1 1	♏	1
6 8 43	2	3	3	2 2	1	2
6 13 5	3	4	4	3 3	2	3
6 17 26	4	5	5	4 4	3	4
6 21 47	5	6	6	5 5	4	5
6 26 9	6	7	7	6 6	5	6
6 30 29	7	8	8	7 7	6	7
6 34 50	8	9	9	8 8	7	8
6 39 11	9	10	10	9 9	8	9
6 43 31	10	11	11	10 9	9	10
6 47 51	11	12	12	11 10	10	11
6 52 11	12	13	13	12 10	11	12
6 56 30	13	14	14	13 11	12	13
7 0 49	14	15	16	14 11	13	14
7 5 7	15	16	17	15 11	14	15
7 9 26	16	17	18	16 11	15	16
7 13 43	17	18	19	17 10	16	17
7 18 0	18	19	20	18 10	17	17
7 22 17	19	20	21	19 9	18	18
7 26 33	20	21	22	20 8	19	19
7 30 49	21	22	23	21 7	20	20
7 35 4	22	23	24	22 6	21	21
7 39 19	23	24	25	23 5	22	22
7 43 33	24	25	26	24 3	23	23
7 47 46	25	26	27	25 1	24	24
7 51 59	26	27	28	25 59	25	25
7 56 11	27	28	29	26 57	26	26
8 0 23	28	29	≏	27 55	27	27
8 4 34	29	♏	1	28 52	28	28
8 8 44	♌	2	2	29 49	29	29
8 12 53	1	3	3	0♏ 46	♐	♑
8 17 2	2	4	4	1 43	1	1
8 21 10	3	5	5	2 39	2	2
8 25 18	4	6	6	3 35	3	3
8 29 24	5	7	7	4 31	4	4
8 33 30	6	8	8	5 27	5	5
8 37 36	7	9	9	6 23	6	6
8 41 40	8	10	10	7 18	7	7
8 45 44	9	11	11	8 13	7	8
8 49 47	10	12	12	9 8	8	9
8 53 50	11	13	13	10 2	9	9
8 57 51	12	14	14	10 56	10	10
9 1 52	13	15	15	11 50	11	11
9 5 52	14	16	16	12 44	12	12

HOUSES	4	5	6	7	8	9

LATITUDE 19° S. LATITUDE 20° S. LATITUDE 21° S.

	LATITUDE 19° N.						LATITUDE 20° N.						LATITUDE 21° N.					
SIDEREAL TIME	10 Ω	11 ♍	12 ♎	ASC ♏	2 ♐	3 ♑	10 Ω	11 ♍	12 ♎	ASC ♏	2 ♐	3 ♑	10 Ω	11 ♍	12 ♎	ASC ♏	2 ♐	3 ♑
H M S	°	°	°	° '	°	°	°	°	°	° '	°	°	°	°	°	° '	°	°
9 9 52	15	17	17	14 13	13	14	15	17	17	13 56	13	13	15	17	17	13 38	13	13
9 13 50	16	18	18	15 7	14	14	16	18	18	14 49	14	14	16	18	18	14 31	14	14
9 17 49	17	19	19	16 1	15	15	17	19	19	15 43	15	15	17	19	19	15 24	15	15
9 21 46	18	20	20	16 54	16	16	18	20	20	16 36	16	16	18	20	20	16 17	16	16
9 25 42	19	21	21	17 48	17	17	19	21	21	17 29	17	17	19	21	21	17 10	16	17
9 29 38	20	22	22	18 41	18	18	20	22	22	18 22	18	18	20	22	22	18 3	17	18
9 33 34	21	23	23	19 34	19	19	21	23	23	19 14	18	19	21	23	23	18 55	18	19
9 37 28	22	24	24	20 26	20	20	22	24	24	20 7	19	20	22	24	24	19 47	19	20
9 41 22	23	25	25	21 19	21	21	23	25	25	20 59	20	21	23	25	25	20 39	20	21
9 45 15	24	26	26	22 11	21	22	24	26	26	21 51	21	22	24	26	26	21 31	21	22
9 49 8	25	27	27	23 3	22	23	25	27	27	22 43	22	23	25	27	27	22 22	22	23
9 53 0	26	28	28	23 55	23	24	26	28	28	23 34	23	24	26	28	27	23 14	23	24
9 56 51	27	29	29	24 47	24	25	27	29	29	24 26	24	25	27	29	28	24 5	23	24
10 0 42	28	♎	♏	25 38	25	26	28	♎	29	25 17	25	26	28	♎	29	24 56	24	25
10 4 32	29	1	1	26 29	26	27	29	1	♏	26 8	26	26	29	1	♏	25 47	25	26
10 8 22	♍	2	1	27 20	27	28	♍	2	1	26 59	26	27	♍	2	1	26 37	26	27
10 12 11	1	3	2	28 11	28	28	1	3	2	27 50	27	28	1	3	2	27 28	27	28
10 15 59	2	4	3	29 2	28	29	2	4	3	28 40	28	29	2	4	3	28 18	28	29
10 19 47	3	5	4	29 53	29	♒	3	5	4	29 31	29	♒	3	5	4	29 9	29	♒
10 23 34	4	6	5	0♐ 43	♑	1	4	6	5	0♐ 21	♑	1	4	6	5	29 59	♑	1
10 27 21	5	7	6	1 34	1	2	5	7	6	1 11	1	2	5	7	6	0♐ 49	0	2
10 31 8	6	8	7	2 24	2	3	6	8	7	2 1	2	3	6	8	7	1 39	1	3
10 34 53	7	9	8	3 14	3	4	7	9	8	2 51	2	4	7	9	7	2 28	2	4
10 38 39	8	10	9	4 4	4	5	8	10	8	3 41	3	5	8	10	8	3 18	3	5
10 42 24	9	11	10	4 54	4	6	9	11	9	4 31	4	6	9	11	9	4 8	4	6
10 46 8	10	12	10	5 44	5	7	10	12	10	5 21	5	7	10	12	10	4 57	5	7
10 49 52	11	13	11	6 34	6	8	11	13	11	6 10	6	8	11	13	11	5 46	6	8
10 53 36	12	14	12	7 23	7	9	12	14	12	7 0	7	9	12	14	12	6 36	6	9
10 57 20	13	15	13	8 13	8	10	13	15	13	7 49	8	10	13	15	13	7 25	7	10
11 1 3	14	16	14	9 3	9	11	14	16	14	8 38	9	11	14	16	14	8 14	8	10
11 4 45	15	17	15	9 52	10	12	15	17	15	9 28	9	12	15	17	14	9 3	9	11
11 8 28	16	18	16	10 41	11	13	16	18	15	10 17	10	13	16	18	15	9 52	10	12
11 12 10	17	19	17	11 31	11	14	17	19	16	11 6	11	13	17	19	16	10 41	11	13
11 15 52	18	20	17	12 20	12	15	18	20	17	11 55	12	14	18	19	17	11 30	12	14
11 19 33	19	21	18	13 9	13	16	19	20	18	12 44	13	15	19	20	18	12 19	13	15
11 23 15	20	21	19	13 59	14	16	20	21	19	13 33	14	16	20	21	19	13 8	13	16
11 26 56	21	22	20	14 48	15	17	21	22	20	14 23	15	17	21	22	20	13 57	14	17
11 30 37	22	23	21	15 37	16	18	22	23	21	15 12	16	18	22	23	20	14 46	15	18
11 34 17	23	24	22	16 26	17	19	23	24	21	16 1	16	19	23	24	21	15 35	16	19
11 37 58	24	25	23	17 16	18	20	24	25	22	16 50	17	20	24	25	22	16 24	17	20
11 41 39	25	26	23	18 5	18	21	25	26	23	17 39	18	21	25	26	23	17 13	18	21
11 45 19	26	27	24	18 54	19	22	26	27	24	18 28	19	22	26	27	24	18 2	19	22
11 48 59	27	28	25	19 44	20	23	27	28	25	19 18	20	23	27	28	25	18 51	20	23
11 52 40	28	29	26	20 33	21	24	28	29	26	20 7	21	24	28	29	25	19 40	21	24
11 56 20	29	♏	27	21 22	22	25	29	♏	26	20 56	22	25	29	♏	26	20 30	21	25
HOUSES	4	5	6	7	8	9	4	5	6	7	8	9	4	5	6	7	8	9

LATITUDE 19° S.   LATITUDE 20° S.   LATITUDE 21° S.

LATITUDE 19° N. LATITUDE 20° N. LATITUDE 21° N.

SIDEREAL TIME H M S	10 ♑	11 ♑	12 ♒	ASC ♈ °	ASC ♈ '	2 ♉	3 ♊	10 ♑	11 ♑	12 ♒	ASC ♈ °	ASC ♈ '	2 ♉	3 ♊	10 ♑	11 ♑	12 ♒	ASC ♈ °	ASC ♈ '	2 ♉	3 ♊
18 0 0	0	25	25	0	0	5	5	0	25	24	0	0	6	5	0	25	24	0	0	6	5
18 4 22	1	27	26	1	24	7	6	1	26	26	1	25	7	6	1	26	25	1	26	7	6
18 8 43	2	28	27	2	48	8	7	2	27	27	2	49	8	7	2	27	27	2	51	8	7
18 13 5	3	29	28	4	11	9	8	3	29	28	4	14	9	8	3	28	28	4	16	10	8
18 17 26	4	♒	♓	5	35	10	9	4	♒	29	5	38	11	9	4	29	29	5	42	11	9
18 21 47	5	1	1	6	58	11	10	5	1	♓	7	3	12	10	5	♒	♓	7	7	12	10
18 26 9	6	2	2	8	22	13	11	6	2	2	8	27	13	11	6	2	2	8	32	13	11
18 30 29	7	3	3	9	45	14	12	7	3	3	9	51	14	12	7	3	3	9	57	14	12
18 34 50	8	4	5	11	8	15	13	8	4	4	11	14	15	13	8	4	4	11	21	16	13
18 39 11	9	5	6	12	30	16	14	9	5	6	12	38	16	14	9	5	6	12	45	17	14
18 43 31	10	6	7	13	53	17	15	10	6	7	14	1	18	15	10	6	7	14	9	18	15
18 47 51	11	7	8	15	15	19	16	11	7	8	15	24	19	16	11	7	8	15	33	19	16
18 52 11	12	8	10	16	36	20	17	12	8	10	16	46	20	17	12	8	9	16	56	20	17
18 56 30	13	10	11	17	58	21	18	13	9	11	18	8	21	18	13	9	11	18	19	21	18
19 0 49	14	11	12	19	19	22	19	14	11	12	19	30	22	19	14	10	12	19	42	23	19
19 5 7	15	12	13	20	39	23	20	15	12	13	20	51	23	20	15	12	13	21	4	24	20
19 9 26	16	13	15	22	0	24	21	16	13	15	22	12	24	21	16	13	15	22	25	25	21
19 13 43	17	14	16	23	19	25	22	17	14	16	23	33	26	22	17	14	16	23	47	26	22
19 18 0	18	15	17	24	38	26	23	18	15	17	24	53	27	23	18	15	17	25	7	27	23
19 22 17	19	16	19	25	57	28	24	19	16	19	26	12	28	24	19	16	18	26	27	28	24
19 26 33	20	17	20	27	15	29	25	20	17	20	27	31	29	25	20	17	20	27	47	29	25
19 30 49	21	18	21	28	33	♊	26	21	18	21	28	49	♊	26	21	18	21	29	6	♊	26
19 35 4	22	20	22	29	50	1	27	22	19	22	0♉	7	1	27	22	19	22	0♉	24	1	27
19 39 19	23	21	24	1♉	7	2	28	23	21	24	1	24	2	28	23	21	24	1	42	2	28
19 43 33	24	22	25	2	23	3	29	24	22	25	2	41	3	29	24	22	25	2	59	4	29
19 47 46	25	23	26	3	39	4	♋	25	23	26	3	57	4	♋	25	23	26	4	16	5	♋
19 51 59	26	24	28	4	54	5	1	26	24	28	5	12	5	1	26	24	28	5	32	6	1
19 56 11	27	25	29	6	8	6	2	27	25	29	6	27	6	2	27	25	29	6	47	7	2
20 0 23	28	26	♈	7	22	7	3	28	26	♈	7	42	7	3	28	26	♈	8	2	8	3
20 4 34	29	28	1	8	35	8	4	29	27	1	8	55	8	4	29	27	1	9	16	9	4
20 8 44	♒	29	3	9	47	9	5	♒	29	3	10	8	9	5	♒	28	3	10	30	10	5
20 12 53	1	♓	4	10	59	10	6	1	♓	4	11	21	10	6	1	♓	4	11	43	11	6
20 17 2	2	1	5	12	11	11	7	2	1	5	12	32	11	7	2	1	5	12	55	12	7
20 21 10	3	2	6	13	22	12	7	3	2	6	13	44	12	8	3	2	6	14	6	13	8
20 25 18	4	3	8	14	32	13	8	4	3	8	14	54	13	9	4	3	8	15	17	14	9
20 29 24	5	4	9	15	41	14	9	5	4	9	16	4	14	9	5	4	9	16	28	15	10
20 33 30	6	5	10	16	50	15	10	6	5	10	17	13	15	10	6	5	10	17	37	16	11
20 37 36	7	7	11	17	59	16	11	7	7	11	18	22	16	11	7	6	11	18	46	17	12
20 41 40	8	8	13	19	6	17	12	8	8	13	19	30	17	12	8	8	13	19	55	18	12
20 45 44	9	9	14	20	14	18	13	9	9	14	20	38	18	13	9	9	14	21	2	19	13
20 49 47	10	10	15	21	20	19	14	10	10	15	21	45	19	14	10	10	15	22	10	20	14
20 53 50	11	11	16	22	26	20	15	11	11	16	22	51	20	15	11	11	16	23	16	21	15
20 57 51	12	12	17	23	32	21	16	12	12	18	23	57	21	16	12	12	18	24	22	22	16
21 1 52	13	13	19	24	37	22	17	13	13	19	25	2	22	17	13	13	19	25	28	22	17
21 5 52	14	15	20	25	41	23	18	14	14	20	26	6	23	18	14	14	20	26	32	23	18
HOUSES	4	5	6	7		8	9	4	5	6	7		8	9	4	5	6	7		8	9

LATITUDE 19° S. LATITUDE 20° S. LATITUDE 21° S.

LATITUDE 19° N.   LATITUDE 20° N.   LATITUDE 21° N.

SIDEREAL TIME	10 ♒	11 ♓	12 ♈	ASC ♉	2 ♊	3 ♋	10 ♒	11 ♓	12 ♈	ASC ♉	2 ♊	3 ♋	10 ♒	11 ♓	12 ♈	ASC ♉	2 ♊	3 ♋
H M S	°	°	°	° '	°	°	°	°	°	° '	°	°	°	°	°	° '	°	°
21 9 52	15	16	21	26 45	24	19	15	16	21	27 10	24	19	15	16	21	27 36	24	19
21 13 50	16	17	22	27 48	25	20	16	17	22	28 14	25	20	16	17	22	28 40	25	20
21 17 49	17	18	23	28 51	26	20	17	18	23	29 17	26	21	17	18	24	29 43	26	21
21 21 46	18	19	24	29 53	26	21	18	19	25	0♊ 19	27	21	18	19	25	0♊ 46	27	22
21 25 42	19	20	26	0♊ 54	27	22	19	20	26	1 21	28	22	19	20	26	1 48	28	23
21 29 38	20	21	27	1 56	28	23	20	21	27	2 22	29	23	20	21	27	2 49	29	23
21 33 34	21	22	28	2 56	29	24	21	22	28	3 23	29	24	21	22	28	3 50	♋	24
21 37 28	22	24	29	3 56	♋	25	22	24	29	4 23	♋	25	22	24	29	4 50	1	25
21 41 22	23	25	♉	4 56	1	26	23	25	♉	5 23	1	26	23	25	♉	5 50	2	26
21 45 15	24	26	1	5 55	2	27	24	26	1	6 22	2	27	24	26	2	6 50	2	27
21 49 8	25	27	2	6 54	3	28	25	27	3	7 21	3	28	25	27	3	7 49	3	28
21 53 0	26	28	3	7 52	4	29	26	28	4	8 20	4	29	26	28	4	8 47	4	29
21 56 51	27	29	5	8 50	5	29	27	29	5	9 18	5	♌	27	29	5	9 45	5	♌
22 0 42	28	♈	6	9 48	5	♌	28	♈	6	10 15	6	1	28	♈	6	10 43	6	1
22 4 32	29	1	7	10 45	6	1	29	1	7	11 12	7	1	29	1	7	11 40	7	2
22 8 22	♓	2	8	11 41	7	2	♓	2	8	12 9	7	2	♓	2	8	12 37	8	2
22 12 11	1	3	9	12 38	8	3	1	4	9	13 5	8	3	1	4	9	13 33	9	3
22 15 59	2	5	10	13 34	9	4	2	5	10	14 1	9	4	2	5	10	14 29	9	4
22 19 47	3	6	11	14 29	10	5	3	6	11	14 57	10	5	3	6	11	15 25	10	5
22 23 34	4	7	12	15 24	11	6	4	7	12	15 52	11	6	4	7	12	16 20	11	6
22 27 21	5	8	13	16 19	11	7	5	8	13	16 47	12	7	5	8	13	17 15	12	7
22 31 8	6	9	14	17 13	12	8	6	9	14	17 41	13	8	6	9	15	18 9	13	8
22 34 53	7	10	15	18 8	13	8	7	10	15	18 35	13	9	7	10	16	19 3	14	9
22 38 39	8	11	16	19 1	14	9	8	11	16	19 29	14	9	8	11	17	19 57	15	10
22 42 24	9	12	17	19 55	15	10	9	12	17	20 23	15	10	9	12	18	20 51	15	10
22 46 8	10	13	18	20 48	16	11	10	13	18	21 16	16	11	10	13	19	21 44	16	11
22 49 52	11	14	19	21 41	17	12	11	14	19	22 9	17	12	11	14	20	22 37	17	12
22 53 36	12	15	20	22 34	17	13	12	15	20	23 1	18	13	12	15	21	23 29	18	13
22 57 20	13	16	21	23 26	18	14	13	16	21	23 54	18	14	13	16	22	24 22	19	14
23 1 3	14	17	22	24 18	19	15	14	17	22	24 46	19	15	14	18	23	25 14	20	15
23 4 45	15	18	23	25 10	20	16	15	19	23	25 38	20	16	15	19	24	26 6	20	16
23 8 28	16	19	24	26 2	21	17	16	20	24	26 30	21	17	16	20	25	26 57	21	17
23 12 10	17	21	25	26 54	22	17	17	21	25	27 21	22	18	17	21	25	27 49	22	18
23 15 52	18	22	26	27 45	22	18	18	22	26	28 12	23	18	18	22	26	28 40	23	19
23 19 33	19	23	27	28 36	23	19	19	23	27	29 3	23	19	19	23	27	29 31	24	19
23 23 15	20	24	28	29 27	24	20	20	24	28	29 54	24	20	20	24	28	0♋ 22	25	20
23 26 56	21	25	29	0♋ 18	25	21	21	25	29	0♋ 45	25	21	21	25	29	1 12	25	21
23 30 37	22	26	♊	1 8	26	22	22	26	♊	1 35	26	22	22	26	♊	2 3	26	22
23 34 17	23	27	1	1 59	27	23	23	27	1	2 26	27	23	23	27	1	2 53	27	23
23 37 58	24	28	2	2 49	27	24	24	28	2	3 16	28	24	24	28	2	3 43	28	24
23 41 39	25	29	2	3 39	28	25	25	29	3	4 6	28	25	25	29	3	4 33	29	25
23 45 19	26	♉	3	4 29	29	26	26	♉	4	4 56	29	26	26	♉	4	5 23	♌	26
23 48 59	27	1	4	5 19	♌	26	27	1	5	5 46	♌	27	27	1	5	6 13	0	27
23 52 40	28	2	5	6 9	1	27	28	2	5	6 35	1	27	28	2	6	7 2	1	28
23 56 20	29	3	6	6 58	2	28	29	3	6	7 25	2	28	29	3	7	7 52	2	28
HOUSES	4	5	6	7	8	9	4	5	6	7	8	9	4	5	6	7	8	9

LATITUDE 19° S.   LATITUDE 20° S.   LATITUDE 21° S.

LATITUDE 22° N. LATITUDE 23° N. LATITUDE 24° N.

SIDEREAL TIME			10 ♋	11 ♌	12 ♍	ASC ♎		2 ♎	3 ♏	10 ♋	11 ♌	12 ♍	ASC ♎		2 ♎	3 ♏	10 ♋	11 ♌	12 ♍	ASC ♎		2 ♎	3 ♏
H	M	S	°	°	°	°	'	°	°	°	°	°	°	'	°	°	°	°	°	°	'	°	°
6	0	0	0	1	1	0	0	29	29	0	1	1	0	0	29	29	0	1	1	0	0	29	29
6	4	22	1	2	2	1	1	♏	♐	1	2	2	1	0	♏	♐	1	2	2	1	0	♏	♐
6	8	43	2	3	3	2	1	1	1	2	3	3	2	0	1	1	2	3	3	1	59	1	1
6	13	5	3	4	4	3	2	2	2	3	4	4	3	1	2	2	3	4	4	2	59	2	2
6	17	26	4	5	5	4	3	3	3	4	5	5	4	1	3	3	4	5	5	3	59	3	3
6	21	47	5	6	6	5	3	4	4	5	6	6	5	1	4	4	5	6	6	4	59	4	4
6	26	9	6	7	7	6	4	5	5	6	7	7	6	1	5	5	6	7	7	5	58	5	5
6	30	29	7	8	8	7	4	6	6	7	8	8	7	1	6	6	7	8	9	6	58	6	6
6	34	50	8	9	9	8	4	7	7	8	9	9	8	1	7	7	8	9	10	7	57	7	7
6	39	11	9	10	10	9	5	8	8	9	10	10	9	1	8	8	9	10	11	8	57	8	8
6	43	31	10	11	11	10	5	9	9	10	11	12	10	0	9	9	10	11	12	9	56	9	9
6	47	51	11	12	12	11	5	10	10	11	12	13	11	0	10	10	11	12	13	10	55	10	10
6	52	11	12	13	14	12	5	11	11	12	13	14	11	59	11	11	12	13	14	11	54	11	11
6	56	30	13	14	15	13	5	12	12	13	14	15	12	59	12	12	13	14	15	12	53	12	12
7	0	49	14	15	16	14	4	13	13	14	15	16	13	58	13	13	14	15	16	13	52	13	13
7	5	7	15	16	17	15	4	14	14	15	16	17	14	57	14	14	15	16	17	14	51	14	14
7	9	26	16	17	18	16	3	15	15	16	17	18	15	56	15	15	16	17	18	15	49	15	15
7	13	43	17	18	19	17	3	16	16	17	18	19	16	55	16	16	17	18	19	16	48	16	16
7	18	0	18	19	20	18	2	17	17	18	19	20	17	54	17	17	18	19	20	17	46	17	17
7	22	17	19	20	21	19	1	18	18	19	20	21	18	52	18	18	19	20	21	18	44	18	18
7	26	33	20	21	22	20	0	19	19	20	21	22	19	51	19	19	20	21	22	19	42	19	19
7	30	49	21	22	23	20	58	20	20	21	22	23	20	49	20	20	21	22	23	20	40	20	20
7	35	4	22	23	24	21	57	21	21	22	23	24	21	47	21	21	22	24	24	21	37	21	21
7	39	19	23	24	25	22	55	22	22	23	24	25	22	45	22	22	23	25	25	22	35	22	22
7	43	33	24	25	26	23	53	23	23	24	25	26	23	42	23	23	24	26	26	23	32	23	23
7	47	46	25	26	27	24	51	24	24	25	27	27	24	40	24	24	25	27	27	24	29	24	24
7	51	59	26	27	28	25	48	25	25	26	28	28	25	37	25	25	26	28	28	25	26	25	25
7	56	11	27	29	29	26	46	26	26	27	29	29	26	34	26	26	27	29	29	26	22	26	26
8	0	23	28	♏	♎	27	43	27	27	28	♏	♎	27	31	27	27	28	♏	♎	27	19	26	27
8	4	34	29	1	1	28	40	28	28	29	1	1	28	27	28	28	29	1	1	28	15	27	28
8	8	44	♌	2	2	29	37	29	29	♌	2	2	29	24	29	29	♌	2	2	29	11	28	29
8	12	53	1	3	3	0♏	33	♐	♑	1	3	3	0♏	20	29	♑	1	3	3	0♏	7	29	♑
8	17	2	2	4	4	1	29	1	1	2	4	4	1	16	♐	1	2	4	4	1	2	♐	1
8	21	10	3	5	5	2	25	2	2	3	5	5	2	12	1	2	3	5	5	1	58	1	2
8	25	18	4	6	6	3	21	3	3	4	6	6	3	7	2	3	4	6	6	2	53	2	2
8	29	24	5	7	7	4	17	3	4	5	7	7	4	2	3	4	5	7	7	3	48	3	3
8	33	30	6	8	8	5	12	4	5	6	8	8	4	57	4	4	6	8	8	4	42	4	4
8	37	36	7	9	9	6	7	5	6	7	9	9	5	52	5	5	7	9	9	5	37	5	5
8	41	40	8	10	10	7	2	6	7	8	10	10	6	47	6	6	8	10	10	6	31	6	6
8	45	44	9	11	11	7	57	7	7	9	11	11	7	41	7	7	9	11	11	7	25	7	7
8	49	47	10	12	12	8	51	8	8	10	12	12	8	35	8	8	10	12	12	8	19	7	8
8	53	50	11	13	13	9	46	9	9	11	13	13	9	29	9	9	11	13	13	9	12	8	9
8	57	51	12	14	14	10	40	10	10	12	14	14	10	23	10	10	12	14	14	10	6	9	10
9	1	52	13	15	15	11	33	11	11	13	15	15	11	16	10	11	13	15	15	10	59	10	11
9	5	52	14	16	16	12	27	12	12	14	16	16	12	9	11	12	14	16	16	11	52	11	12
HOUSES			4	5	6	7		8	9	4	5	6	7		8	9	4	5	6	7		8	9

LATITUDE 22° S. LATITUDE 23° S. LATITUDE 24° S.

LATITUDE 22° N.   LATITUDE 23° N.   LATITUDE 24° N.

SIDEREAL TIME	10 Ω	11 ♍	12 ♎	ASC ♏		2 ♐	3 ♑	10 Ω	11 ♍	12 ♎	ASC ♏		2 ♐	3 ♑	10 Ω	11 ♍	12 ♎	ASC ♏		2 ♐	3 ♑
H M S	°	°	°	°	′	°	°	°	°	°	°	′	°	°	°	°	°	°	′	°	°
9 9 52	15	17	17	13	20	13	13	15	17	17	13	2	12	13	15	17	17	12	45	12	13
9 13 50	16	18	18	14	13	13	14	16	18	18	13	55	13	14	16	18	18	13	37	13	14
9 17 49	17	19	19	15	6	14	15	17	19	19	14	48	14	15	17	19	19	14	29	14	15
9 21 46	18	20	20	15	59	15	16	18	20	20	15	40	15	16	18	20	20	15	21	15	16
9 25 42	19	21	21	16	51	16	17	19	21	21	16	32	16	17	19	21	21	16	13	16	17
9 29 38	20	22	22	17	43	17	18	20	22	22	17	24	17	18	20	22	22	17	5	16	17
9 33 34	21	23	23	18	36	18	19	21	23	23	18	16	18	19	21	23	22	17	56	17	18
9 37 28	22	24	24	19	27	19	20	22	24	24	19	8	18	19	22	24	23	18	48	18	19
9 41 22	23	25	25	20	19	20	21	23	25	24	19	59	19	20	23	25	24	19	39	19	20
9 45 15	24	26	25	21	11	21	21	24	26	25	20	50	20	21	24	26	25	20	30	20	21
9 49 8	25	27	26	22	2	21	22	25	27	26	21	41	21	22	25	27	26	21	21	21	22
9 53 0	26	28	27	22	53	22	23	26	28	27	22	32	22	23	26	28	27	22	11	22	23
9 56 51	27	29	28	23	44	23	24	27	29	28	23	23	23	24	27	29	28	23	2	23	24
10 0 42	28	♎	29	24	35	24	25	28	♎	29	24	13	24	25	28	♎	29	23	52	23	25
10 4 32	29	1	♏	25	25	25	26	29	1	♏	25	4	25	26	29	1	♏	24	42	24	26
10 8 22	♍	2	1	26	16	26	27	♍	2	1	25	54	25	27	♍	2	1	25	32	25	27
10 12 11	1	3	2	27	6	27	28	1	3	2	26	44	26	28	1	3	2	26	22	26	28
10 15 59	2	4	3	27	56	28	29	2	4	3	27	34	27	29	2	4	2	27	12	27	29
10 19 47	3	5	4	28	46	28	♒	3	5	4	28	24	28	♒	3	5	3	28	1	28	♒
10 23 34	4	6	5	29	36	29	1	4	6	4	29	13	29	1	4	6	4	28	51	29	1
10 27 21	5	7	5	0♐	26	♑	2	5	7	5	0♐	3	♑	2	5	7	5	29	40	29	2
10 31 8	6	8	6	1	16	1	3	6	8	6	0	52	1	3	6	8	6	0♐	29	♑	2
10 34 53	7	9	7	2	5	2	4	7	9	7	1	42	2	4	7	9	7	1	18	1	3
10 38 39	8	10	8	2	55	3	5	8	10	8	2	31	2	4	8	10	8	2	7	2	4
10 42 24	9	11	9	3	44	4	6	9	11	9	3	20	3	5	9	11	9	2	56	3	5
10 46 8	10	12	10	4	33	4	7	10	12	10	4	9	4	6	10	12	9	3	45	4	6
10 49 52	11	13	11	5	22	5	7	11	13	11	4	58	5	7	11	13	10	4	34	5	7
10 53 36	12	14	12	6	11	6	8	12	14	11	5	47	6	8	12	14	11	5	23	6	8
10 57 20	13	15	12	7	1	7	9	13	15	12	6	36	7	9	13	15	12	6	11	6	9
11 1 3	14	16	13	7	50	8	10	14	16	13	7	25	8	10	14	16	13	7	0	7	10
11 4 45	15	17	14	8	38	9	11	15	17	14	8	14	8	11	15	17	14	7	48	8	11
11 8 28	16	18	15	9	27	10	12	16	18	15	9	2	9	12	16	17	15	8	37	9	12
11 12 10	17	18	16	10	16	11	13	17	18	16	9	51	10	13	17	18	15	9	25	10	13
11 15 52	18	19	17	11	5	11	14	18	19	17	10	40	11	14	18	19	16	10	14	11	14
11 19 33	19	20	18	11	54	12	15	19	20	17	11	28	12	15	19	20	17	11	2	12	15
11 23 15	20	21	18	12	43	13	16	20	21	18	12	17	13	16	20	21	18	11	51	13	16
11 26 56	21	22	19	13	31	14	17	21	22	19	13	6	14	17	21	22	19	12	39	13	17
11 30 37	22	23	20	14	20	15	18	22	23	20	13	54	15	18	22	23	20	13	28	14	18
11 34 17	23	24	21	15	9	16	19	23	24	21	14	43	15	19	23	24	21	14	16	15	19
11 37 58	24	25	22	15	58	17	20	24	25	22	15	32	16	20	24	25	21	15	5	16	20
11 41 39	25	26	23	16	47	18	21	25	26	22	16	20	17	21	25	26	22	15	53	17	21
11 45 19	26	27	23	17	36	18	22	26	27	23	17	9	18	22	26	27	23	16	42	18	22
11 48 59	27	28	24	18	25	19	23	27	28	24	17	58	19	23	27	28	24	17	31	19	23
11 52 40	28	29	25	19	14	20	24	28	29	25	18	47	20	24	28	29	25	18	20	20	24
11 56 20	29	♏	26	20	3	21	25	29	♏	26	19	36	21	25	29	29	25	19	8	21	25
HOUSES	4	5	6	7		8	9	4	5	6	7		8	9	4	5	6	7		8	9

LATITUDE 22° S.   LATITUDE 23° S.   LATITUDE 24° S.

LATITUDE 22° N.   LATITUDE 23° N.   LATITUDE 24° N.

SIDEREAL TIME	10 ♑	11 ♑	12 ♒	ASC ♈	2 ♉	3 ♊	10 ♑	11 ♑	12 ♒	ASC ♈	2 ♉	3 ♊	10 ♑	11 ♑	12 ♒	ASC ♈	2 ♉	3 ♊
H M S	°	°	°	° ′	°	°	°	°	°	° ′	°	°	°	°	°	° ′	°	°
18 0 0	0	25	24	0 0	6	5	0	25	24	0 0	6	5	0	25	24	0 0	6	5
18 4 22	1	26	25	1 26	7	6	1	26	25	1 27	8	6	1	26	25	1 28	8	6
18 8 43	2	27	26	2 53	9	7	2	27	26	2 55	9	7	2	27	26	2 57	9	7
18 13 5	3	28	28	4 19	10	8	3	28	28	4 22	10	8	3	28	27	4 25	10	8
18 17 26	4	29	29	5 45	11	9	4	29	29	5 49	11	9	4	29	29	5 53	11	9
18 21 47	5	♒	♓	7 11	12	10	5	♒	♓	7 16	12	10	5	♒	♓	7 21	13	11
18 26 9	6	2	2	8 37	13	11	6	1	1	8 43	14	11	6	1	1	8 49	14	12
18 30 29	7	3	3	10 3	15	12	7	2	3	10 9	15	12	7	2	2	10 16	15	13
18 34 50	8	4	4	11 28	16	13	8	4	4	11 36	16	13	8	3	4	11 43	16	14
18 39 11	9	5	5	12 53	17	14	9	5	5	13 2	17	14	9	4	5	13 10	17	15
18 43 31	10	6	7	14 18	18	15	10	6	7	14 27	18	16	10	6	6	14 37	19	16
18 47 51	11	7	8	15 43	19	16	11	7	8	15 53	20	17	11	7	8	16 3	20	17
18 52 11	12	8	9	17 7	20	17	12	8	9	17 18	21	18	12	8	9	17 29	21	18
18 56 30	13	9	11	18 31	22	18	13	9	10	18 42	22	19	13	9	10	18 54	22	19
19 0 49	14	10	12	19 54	23	19	14	10	12	20 6	23	20	14	10	12	20 19	23	20
19 5 7	15	11	13	21 17	24	20	15	11	13	21 30	24	21	15	11	13	21 44	24	21
19 9 26	16	13	14	22 39	25	21	16	12	14	22 53	25	22	16	12	14	23 8	26	22
19 13 43	17	14	16	24 1	26	22	17	14	16	24 16	26	23	17	13	16	24 31	27	23
19 18 0	18	15	17	25 22	27	23	18	15	17	25 38	28	24	18	15	17	25 54	28	24
19 22 17	19	16	18	26 43	28	24	19	16	18	26 59	29	25	19	16	18	27 16	29	25
19 26 33	20	17	20	28 3	29	25	20	17	20	28 20	♊	26	20	17	20	28 38	♊	26
19 30 49	21	18	21	29 23	♊	26	21	18	21	29 40	1	27	21	18	21	29 59	1	27
19 35 4	22	19	22	0♉ 42	2	27	22	19	22	1♉ 0	2	28	22	19	22	1♉ 19	2	28
19 39 19	23	20	24	2 0	3	28	23	20	24	2 19	3	28	23	20	24	2 39	3	29
19 43 33	24	22	25	3 18	4	29	24	21	25	3 38	4	29	24	21	25	3 58	4	♋
19 47 46	25	23	26	4 35	5	♋	25	23	26	4 55	5	♋	25	22	26	5 16	5	1
19 51 59	26	24	28	5 52	6	1	26	24	28	6 12	6	1	26	24	27	6 34	7	2
19 56 11	27	25	29	7 8	7	2	27	25	29	7 29	7	2	27	25	29	7 51	8	3
20 0 23	28	26	♈	8 23	8	3	28	26	♈	8 45	8	3	28	26	♈	9 7	9	3
20 4 34	29	27	1	9 38	9	4	29	27	1	10 0	9	4	29	27	1	10 23	10	4
20 8 44	♒	28	3	10 52	10	5	♒	28	3	11 14	10	5	♒	28	3	11 38	11	5
20 12 53	1	♓	4	12 5	11	6	1	29	4	12 28	11	6	1	29	4	12 52	12	6
20 17 2	2	1	5	13 18	12	7	2	♓	5	13 41	12	7	2	♓	5	14 5	13	7
20 21 10	3	2	7	14 30	13	8	3	2	7	14 54	13	8	3	2	7	15 18	14	8
20 25 18	4	3	8	15 41	14	9	4	3	8	16 5	14	9	4	3	8	16 30	15	9
20 29 24	5	4	9	16 52	15	10	5	4	9	17 16	15	10	5	4	9	17 42	16	10
20 33 30	6	5	10	18 2	16	11	6	5	10	18 27	16	11	6	5	10	18 52	17	11
20 37 36	7	6	12	19 11	17	12	7	6	12	19 36	17	12	7	6	12	20 3	18	12
20 41 40	8	8	13	20 20	18	13	8	7	13	20 45	18	13	8	7	13	21 12	19	13
20 45 44	9	9	14	21 28	19	14	9	9	14	21 54	19	14	9	9	14	22 21	20	14
20 49 47	10	10	15	22 35	20	14	10	10	15	23 2	20	15	10	10	15	23 29	21	15
20 53 50	11	11	17	23 42	21	15	11	11	17	24 9	21	16	11	11	17	24 36	22	16
20 57 51	12	12	18	24 48	22	16	12	12	18	25 15	22	16	12	12	18	25 43	22	17
21 1 52	13	13	19	25 54	23	17	13	13	19	26 21	23	17	13	13	19	26 49	23	18
21 5 52	14	14	20	26 59	24	18	14	14	20	27 26	24	18	14	14	20	27 54	24	18
HOUSES	4	5	6	7	8	9	4	5	6	7	8	9	4	5	6	7	8	9

LATITUDE 22° S.   LATITUDE 23° S.   LATITUDE 24° S.

181

LATITUDE 22° N. LATITUDE 23° N. LATITUDE 24° N.

SIDEREAL TIME (H M S)	10 ♒	11 ♓	12 ♈	ASC ♉	2 ♊	3 ♋	10 ♒	11 ♓	12 ♈	ASC ♉	2 ♊	3 ♋	10 ♒	11 ♓	12 ♈	ASC ♉	2 ♊	3 ♋
21 9 52	15	16	21	28 3	25	19	15	16	21	28 31	25	19	15	15	22	28 59	25	19
21 13 50	16	17	23	29 7	26	20	16	17	23	29 35	26	20	16	17	23	0♊ 3	26	20
21 17 49	17	18	24	0♊ 10	26	21	17	18	24	0♊ 38	27	21	17	18	24	1 7	27	21
21 21 46	18	19	25	1 13	27	22	18	19	25	1 41	28	22	18	19	25	2 10	28	22
21 25 42	19	20	26	2 15	28	23	19	20	26	2 43	29	23	19	20	26	3 12	29	23
21 29 38	20	21	27	3 17	29	24	20	21	27	3 45	♋	24	20	21	28	4 14	♋	24
21 33 34	21	22	28	4 18	♋	24	21	22	29	4 46	0	25	21	22	29	5 15	1	25
21 37 28	22	23	♉	5 18	1	25	22	23	♉	5 47	1	26	22	23	♉	6 16	2	26
21 41 22	23	25	1	6 18	2	26	23	25	1	6 47	2	26	23	25	1	7 16	3	27
21 45 15	24	26	2	7 18	3	27	24	26	2	7 47	3	27	24	26	2	8 16	3	27
21 49 8	25	27	3	8 17	4	28	25	27	3	8 46	4	28	25	27	3	9 15	4	28
21 53 0	26	28	4	9 16	5	29	26	28	4	9 44	5	29	26	28	4	10 14	5	29
21 56 51	27	29	5	10 14	5	♌	27	29	5	10 43	6	♌	27	29	6	11 12	6	♌
22 0 42	28	♈	6	11 11	6	1	28	♈	6	11 40	7	1	28	♈	7	12 10	7	1
22 4 32	29	1	7	12 9	7	2	29	1	8	12 38	7	2	29	1	8	13 7	8	2
22 8 22	♓	2	8	13 5	8	3	♓	2	9	13 34	8	3	♓	2	9	14 4	9	3
22 12 11	1	4	9	14 2	9	3	1	4	10	14 31	9	4	1	4	10	15 0	10	4
22 15 59	2	5	11	14 58	10	4	2	5	11	15 27	10	4	2	5	11	15 56	10	5
22 19 47	3	6	12	15 53	11	5	3	6	12	16 22	11	5	3	6	12	16 52	11	6
22 23 34	4	7	13	16 48	11	6	4	7	13	17 18	12	6	4	7	13	17 47	12	6
22 27 21	5	8	14	17 43	12	7	5	8	14	18 12	13	7	5	8	14	18 42	13	7
22 31 8	6	9	15	18 38	13	8	6	9	15	19 7	13	8	6	9	15	19 36	14	8
22 34 53	7	10	16	19 32	14	9	7	10	16	20 1	14	9	7	10	16	20 31	15	9
22 38 39	8	11	17	20 26	15	10	8	11	17	20 55	15	10	8	11	17	21 24	15	10
22 42 24	9	12	18	21 19	16	11	9	12	18	21 48	16	11	9	12	18	22 18	16	11
22 46 8	10	13	19	22 12	17	11	10	13	19	22 41	17	12	10	13	19	23 11	17	12
22 49 52	11	14	20	23 5	17	12	11	14	20	23 34	18	12	11	14	20	24 4	18	13
22 53 36	12	15	21	23 58	18	13	12	15	21	24 27	19	13	12	16	21	24 56	19	14
22 57 20	13	17	22	24 50	19	14	13	17	22	25 19	19	14	13	17	22	25 48	20	14
23 1 3	14	18	23	25 42	20	15	14	18	23	26 11	20	15	14	18	23	26 40	20	15
23 4 45	15	19	24	26 34	21	16	15	19	24	27 3	21	16	15	19	24	27 32	21	16
23 8 28	16	20	25	27 26	22	17	16	20	25	27 54	22	17	16	20	25	28 23	22	17
23 12 10	17	21	26	28 17	22	18	17	21	26	28 45	23	18	17	21	26	29 14	23	18
23 15 52	18	22	27	29 8	23	19	18	22	27	29 37	23	19	18	22	27	0♋ 5	24	19
23 19 33	19	23	28	29 59	24	20	19	23	28	0♋ 27	24	20	19	23	28	0 56	25	20
23 23 15	20	24	29	0♋ 50	25	20	20	24	29	1 18	25	21	20	24	29	1 47	25	21
23 26 56	21	25	♊	1 40	26	21	21	25	♊	2 8	26	21	21	25	♊	2 37	26	22
23 30 37	22	26	1	2 30	27	22	22	26	1	2 59	27	22	22	26	1	3 27	27	22
23 34 17	23	27	1	3 21	27	23	23	27	2	3 49	28	23	23	27	2	4 17	28	23
23 37 58	24	28	2	4 11	28	24	24	28	3	4 39	28	24	24	28	3	5 7	29	24
23 41 39	25	29	3	5 0	29	25	25	29	4	5 28	29	25	25	29	4	5 57	♌	25
23 45 19	26	♉	4	5 50	♌	26	26	♉	5	6 18	♌	26	26	♉	5	6 46	0	26
23 48 59	27	1	5	6 40	1	27	27	1	5	7 7	1	27	27	1	6	7 35	1	27
23 52 40	28	2	6	7 29	2	28	28	2	6	7 57	2	28	28	2	7	8 25	2	28
23 56 20	29	3	7	8 19	2	29	29	3	7	8 46	3	29	29	3	8	9 14	3	29
HOUSES	4	5	6	7	8	9	4	5	6	7	8	9	4	5	6	7	8	9

LATITUDE 22° S. LATITUDE 23° S. LATITUDE 24° S.

LATITUDE 25° N.   LATITUDE 26° N.   LATITUDE 27° N.

SIDEREAL TIME (H M S)	10 ♋	11 ♌	12 ♍	ASC ♎ °	'	2 ♎	3 ♏	10 ♋	11 ♌	12 ♍	ASC ♎ °	'	2 ♎	3 ♏	10 ♋	11 ♌	12 ♍	ASC ♎ °	'	2 ♎	3 ♏
6 0 0	0	1	1	0	0	29	29	0	1	2	0	0	28	29	0	1	2	0	0	28	29
6 4 22	1	2	2	0	59	♏	♐	1	2	3	0	59	29	♐	1	2	3	0	58	29	♐
6 8 43	2	3	3	1	59	1	1	2	3	4	1	58	♏	1	2	3	4	1	57	♏	1
6 13 5	3	4	5	2	58	2	2	3	4	5	2	56	1	2	3	4	5	2	55	1	2
6 17 26	4	5	6	3	57	3	3	4	5	6	3	55	2	3	4	5	6	3	53	2	3
6 21 47	5	6	7	4	56	4	4	5	6	7	4	54	3	4	5	6	7	4	52	3	4
6 26 9	6	7	8	5	55	5	5	6	7	8	5	53	4	5	6	7	8	5	50	4	5
6 30 29	7	8	9	6	54	6	6	7	8	9	6	51	5	6	7	8	9	6	48	5	6
6 34 50	8	9	10	7	54	7	7	8	9	10	7	50	6	7	8	9	10	7	46	6	7
6 39 11	9	10	11	8	52	8	8	9	10	11	8	48	7	8	9	10	11	8	44	7	8
6 43 31	10	11	12	9	51	9	9	10	11	12	9	47	8	9	10	11	12	9	42	8	9
6 47 51	11	12	13	10	50	10	10	11	12	13	10	45	9	10	11	12	13	10	40	9	10
6 52 11	12	13	14	11	49	11	11	12	13	14	11	43	10	11	12	14	14	11	38	10	11
6 56 30	13	14	15	12	47	12	12	13	14	15	12	41	11	12	13	15	15	12	36	11	12
7 0 49	14	15	16	13	46	13	13	14	15	16	13	39	12	13	14	16	16	13	33	12	13
7 5 7	15	16	17	14	44	14	14	15	16	17	14	37	13	14	15	17	17	14	31	13	14
7 9 26	16	17	18	15	42	15	15	16	18	18	15	35	14	15	16	18	18	15	28	14	15
7 13 43	17	18	19	16	40	16	16	17	19	19	16	33	15	16	17	19	19	16	25	15	16
7 18 0	18	19	20	17	38	17	17	18	20	20	17	30	16	17	18	20	20	17	22	16	17
7 22 17	19	21	21	18	36	18	18	19	21	21	18	27	17	18	19	21	21	18	19	17	18
7 26 33	20	22	22	19	33	19	19	20	22	22	19	24	18	19	20	22	22	19	15	18	18
7 30 49	21	23	23	20	31	19	20	21	23	23	20	21	19	20	21	23	23	20	12	19	19
7 35 4	22	24	24	21	28	20	21	22	24	24	21	18	20	21	22	24	24	21	8	20	20
7 39 19	23	25	25	22	25	21	22	23	25	25	22	15	21	22	23	25	25	22	5	21	21
7 43 33	24	26	26	23	22	22	23	24	26	26	23	11	22	23	24	26	26	23	1	22	22
7 47 46	25	27	27	24	18	23	24	25	27	27	24	7	23	23	25	27	27	23	56	23	23
7 51 59	26	28	28	25	15	24	25	26	28	28	25	3	24	24	26	28	28	24	52	24	24
7 56 11	27	29	29	26	11	25	26	27	29	29	25	59	25	25	27	29	29	25	47	25	25
8 0 23	28	♍	♎	27	7	26	27	28	♍	♎	26	55	26	26	28	♍	♎	26	43	26	26
8 4 34	29	1	1	28	3	27	27	29	1	1	27	50	27	27	29	1	1	27	38	27	27
8 8 44	♌	2	2	28	58	28	28	♌	2	2	28	45	28	28	♌	2	2	28	33	27	28
8 12 53	1	3	3	29	54	29	29	1	3	3	29	40	29	29	1	3	3	29	27	28	29
8 17 2	2	4	4	0♏	49	♐	♑	2	4	4	0♏	35	♐	♑	2	4	4	0♏	22	29	♑
8 21 10	3	5	5	1	44	1	1	3	5	5	1	30	1	1	3	5	5	1	16	♐	1
8 25 18	4	6	6	2	39	2	2	4	6	6	2	24	1	2	4	6	6	2	10	1	2
8 29 24	5	7	7	3	33	3	3	5	7	7	3	18	2	3	5	7	7	3	4	2	3
8 33 30	6	8	8	4	27	4	4	6	8	8	4	12	3	4	6	8	8	3	57	3	4
8 37 36	7	9	9	5	22	4	5	7	9	9	5	6	4	5	7	9	9	4	51	4	5
8 41 40	8	10	10	6	15	5	6	8	10	10	6	0	5	6	8	10	10	5	44	5	6
8 45 44	9	11	11	7	9	6	7	9	11	11	6	53	6	7	9	11	11	6	37	6	7
8 49 47	10	12	12	8	3	7	8	10	12	12	7	46	7	8	10	12	12	7	30	7	8
8 53 50	11	13	13	8	56	8	9	11	13	13	8	39	8	9	11	13	13	8	22	8	9
8 57 51	12	14	14	9	49	9	10	12	14	14	9	32	9	10	12	14	14	9	15	8	9
9 1 52	13	15	15	10	42	10	11	13	15	15	10	24	10	11	13	15	15	10	7	9	10
9 5 52	14	16	16	11	34	11	12	14	16	16	11	17	10	11	14	16	16	10	59	10	11
HOUSES	4	5	6	7		8	9	4	5	6	7		8	9	4	5	6	7		8	9

LATITUDE 25° S.   LATITUDE 26° S.   LATITUDE 27° S.

185

LATITUDE 25° N.   LATITUDE 26° N.   LATITUDE 27° N.

SIDEREAL TIME	10 Ω	11 m	12 ≏	ASC m		2 ♐	3 ♑	10 Ω	11 m	12 ≏	ASC m		2 ♐	3 ♑	10 Ω	11 m	12 ≏	ASC m		2 ♐	3 ♑
H M S	°	°	°	°	'	°	°	°	°	°	°	'	°	°	°	°	°	°	'	°	°
9 9 52	15	17	17	12	27	12	13	15	17	17	12	9	11	12	15	17	17	11	50	11	12
9 13 50	16	18	18	13	19	13	14	16	18	18	13	0	12	13	16	18	17	12	42	12	13
9 17 49	17	19	19	14	11	13	14	17	19	19	13	52	13	14	17	19	18	13	33	13	14
9 21 46	18	20	20	15	3	14	15	18	20	19	14	44	14	15	18	20	19	14	25	14	15
9 25 42	19	21	20	15	54	15	16	19	21	20	15	35	15	16	19	21	20	15	16	15	16
9 29 38	20	22	21	16	46	16	17	20	22	21	16	26	16	17	20	22	21	16	6	15	17
9 33 34	21	23	22	17	37	17	18	21	23	22	17	17	17	18	21	23	22	16	57	16	18
9 37 28	22	24	23	18	28	18	19	22	24	23	18	8	18	19	22	24	23	17	47	17	19
9 41 22	23	25	24	19	19	19	20	23	25	24	18	58	18	20	23	25	24	18	38	18	20
9 45 15	24	26	25	20	9	20	21	24	26	25	19	49	19	21	24	26	25	19	28	19	21
9 49 8	25	27	26	21	0	20	22	25	27	26	20	39	20	22	25	27	26	20	18	20	22
9 53 0	26	28	27	21	50	21	23	26	28	27	21	29	21	23	26	28	27	21	8	21	23
9 56 51	27	29	28	22	40	22	24	27	29	28	22	19	22	24	27	29	28	21	57	22	24
10 0 42	28	≏	29	23	30	23	25	28	≏	29	23	9	23	25	28	≏	28	22	47	22	24
10 4 32	29	1	m	24	20	24	26	29	1	29	23	58	24	26	29	1	29	23	36	23	25
10 8 22	m	2	1	25	10	25	27	m	2	m	24	48	24	26	m	2	m	24	25	24	26
10 12 11	1	3	1	26	0	26	28	1	3	1	25	37	25	27	1	3	1	25	14	25	27
10 15 59	2	4	2	26	49	27	29	2	4	2	26	26	26	28	2	4	2	26	3	26	28
10 19 47	3	5	3	27	38	27	29	3	5	3	27	15	27	29	3	5	3	26	52	27	29
10 23 34	4	6	4	28	28	28	♒	4	6	4	28	4	28	♒	4	6	4	27	41	28	♒
10 27 21	5	7	5	29	17	29	1	5	7	5	28	53	29	1	5	7	5	28	30	28	1
10 31 8	6	8	6	0♐	6	♑	2	6	8	6	29	42	♑	2	6	8	5	29	18	29	2
10 34 53	7	9	7	0	55	1	3	7	9	7	0♐	31	1	3	7	9	6	0♐	6	♑	3
10 38 39	8	10	8	1	43	2	4	8	10	7	1	19	1	4	8	10	7	0	55	1	4
10 42 24	9	11	8	2	32	3	5	9	11	8	2	8	2	5	9	11	8	1	43	2	5
10 46 8	10	12	9	3	21	3	6	10	12	9	2	56	3	6	10	12	9	2	31	3	6
10 49 52	11	13	10	4	9	4	7	11	13	10	3	44	4	7	11	13	10	3	19	4	7
10 53 36	12	14	11	4	58	5	8	12	14	11	4	33	5	8	12	14	11	4	8	5	8
10 57 20	13	15	12	5	46	6	9	13	15	12	5	21	6	9	13	15	11	4	56	5	9
11 1 3	14	16	13	6	35	7	10	14	15	12	6	9	7	10	14	15	12	5	44	6	10
11 4 45	15	16	14	7	23	8	11	15	16	13	6	57	7	11	15	16	13	6	31	7	11
11 8 28	16	17	14	8	11	9	12	16	17	14	7	46	8	12	16	17	14	7	19	8	12
11 12 10	17	18	15	9	0	10	13	17	18	15	8	34	9	13	17	18	15	8	7	9	13
11 15 52	18	19	16	9	48	10	14	18	19	16	9	22	10	14	18	19	16	8	55	10	14
11 19 33	19	20	17	10	36	11	15	19	20	17	10	10	11	15	19	20	16	9	43	11	15
11 23 15	20	21	18	11	25	12	16	20	21	18	10	58	12	16	20	21	17	10	31	12	16
11 26 56	21	22	19	12	13	13	17	21	22	18	11	46	13	17	21	22	18	11	19	12	16
11 30 37	22	23	19	13	1	14	18	22	23	19	12	34	14	18	22	23	19	12	7	13	17
11 34 17	23	24	20	13	49	15	19	23	24	20	13	22	14	19	23	24	20	12	55	14	18
11 37 58	24	25	21	14	38	16	20	24	25	21	14	11	15	20	24	25	21	13	43	15	19
11 41 39	25	26	22	15	26	17	21	25	26	22	14	59	16	21	25	26	21	14	31	16	20
11 45 19	26	27	23	16	15	18	22	26	27	23	15	47	17	22	26	26	22	15	19	17	21
11 48 59	27	28	24	17	3	18	23	27	27	23	16	35	18	23	27	27	23	16	7	18	22
11 52 40	28	28	24	17	52	19	24	28	28	24	17	24	19	24	28	28	24	16	56	19	23
11 56 20	29	29	25	18	41	20	25	29	29	25	18	12	20	25	29	29	25	17	44	20	24
HOUSES	4	5	6	7		8	9	4	5	6	7		8	9	4	5	6	7		8	9

LATITUDE 25° S.   LATITUDE 26° S.   LATITUDE 27° S.

LATITUDE 25° N. LATITUDE 26° N. LATITUDE 27° N.

LATITUDE 25° N.

SIDEREAL TIME	10 ♑	11 ♑	12 ♒	ASC ♈		2 ♉	3 ♊
H M S	°	°	°	°	'	°	°
18 0 0	0	25	23	0	0	7	5
18 4 22	1	26	25	1	29	8	6
18 8 43	2	27	26	2	59	9	8
18 13 5	3	28	27	4	28	10	9
18 17 26	4	29	28	5	57	12	10
18 21 47	5	♒	♓	7	26	13	11
18 26 9	6	1	1	8	55	14	12
18 30 29	7	2	2	10	23	15	13
18 34 50	8	3	4	11	51	17	14
18 39 11	9	4	5	13	19	18	15
18 43 31	10	5	6	14	47	19	16
18 47 51	11	7	8	16	14	20	17
18 52 11	12	8	9	17	41	21	18
18 56 30	13	9	10	19	7	22	19
19 0 49	14	10	12	20	33	24	20
19 5 7	15	11	13	21	58	25	21
19 9 26	16	12	14	23	23	26	22
19 13 43	17	13	15	24	47	27	23
19 18 0	18	14	17	26	10	28	24
19 22 17	19	16	18	27	33	29	25
19 26 33	20	17	19	28	56	♊	26
19 30 49	21	18	21	0♉	17	2	27
19 35 4	22	19	22	1	38	3	28
19 39 19	23	20	23	2	59	4	29
19 43 33	24	21	25	4	18	5	♋
19 47 46	25	22	26	5	37	6	1
19 51 59	26	23	27	6	56	7	2
19 56 11	27	25	29	8	13	8	3
20 0 23	28	26	♈	9	30	9	4
20 4 34	29	27	1	10	46	10	5
20 8 44	♒	28	3	12	2	11	6
20 12 53	1	29	4	13	16	12	7
20 17 2	2	♓	5	14	30	13	7
20 21 10	3	2	7	15	44	14	8
20 25 18	4	3	8	16	56	15	9
20 29 24	5	4	9	18	8	16	10
20 33 30	6	5	11	19	19	17	11
20 37 36	7	6	12	20	29	18	12
20 41 40	8	7	13	21	39	19	13
20 45 44	9	8	14	22	48	20	14
20 49 47	10	10	16	23	56	21	15
20 53 50	11	11	17	25	4	22	16
20 57 51	12	12	18	26	11	23	17
21 1 52	13	13	19	27	17	24	18
21 5 52	14	14	21	28	23	25	19
HOUSES	4	5	6	7		8	9

LATITUDE 26° N.

SIDEREAL TIME	10 ♑	11 ♑	12 ♒	ASC ♈		2 ♉	3 ♊
H M S	°	°	°	°	'	°	°
18 0 0	0	24	23	0	0	7	6
18 4 22	1	26	24	1	30	8	7
18 8 43	2	27	26	3	1	9	8
18 13 5	3	28	27	4	31	11	9
18 17 26	4	29	28	6	1	12	10
18 21 47	5	♒	29	7	31	13	11
18 26 9	6	1	♓	9	1	14	12
18 30 29	7	2	2	10	30	16	13
18 34 50	8	3	3	12	0	17	14
18 39 11	9	4	5	13	28	18	15
18 43 31	10	5	6	14	57	19	16
18 47 51	11	6	7	16	25	20	17
18 52 11	12	8	9	17	53	22	18
18 56 30	13	9	10	19	20	23	19
19 0 49	14	10	11	20	47	24	20
19 5 7	15	11	13	22	13	25	21
19 9 26	16	12	14	23	38	26	22
19 13 43	17	13	15	25	3	27	23
19 18 0	18	14	17	26	28	28	24
19 22 17	19	15	18	27	51	♊	25
19 26 33	20	17	19	29	14	1	26
19 30 49	21	18	21	0♉	37	2	27
19 35 4	22	19	22	1	59	3	28
19 39 19	23	20	23	3	20	4	29
19 43 33	24	21	25	4	40	5	♋
19 47 46	25	22	26	6	0	6	1
19 51 59	26	23	27	7	18	7	2
19 56 11	27	25	29	8	37	8	3
20 0 23	28	26	♈	9	54	9	4
20 4 34	29	27	1	11	11	10	5
20 8 44	♒	28	3	12	27	11	6
20 12 53	1	29	4	13	42	12	7
20 17 2	2	♓	5	14	56	13	8
20 21 10	3	1	7	16	10	14	9
20 25 18	4	3	8	17	23	15	9
20 29 24	5	4	9	18	35	16	10
20 33 30	6	5	11	19	46	17	11
20 37 36	7	6	12	20	57	18	12
20 41 40	8	7	13	22	7	19	13
20 45 44	9	8	14	23	16	20	14
20 49 47	10	10	16	24	25	21	15
20 53 50	11	11	17	25	33	22	16
20 57 51	12	12	18	26	40	23	17
21 1 52	13	13	19	27	46	24	18
21 5 52	14	14	21	28	52	25	19
HOUSES	4	5	6	7		8	9

LATITUDE 27° N.

SIDEREAL TIME	10 ♑	11 ♑	12 ♒	ASC ♈		2 ♉	3 ♊
H M S	°	°	°	°	'	°	°
18 0 0	0	24	23	0	0	7	6
18 4 22	1	25	24	1	31	8	7
18 8 43	2	26	25	3	3	10	8
18 13 5	3	28	27	4	34	11	9
18 17 26	4	29	28	6	6	12	10
18 21 47	5	♒	29	7	37	13	11
18 26 9	6	1	♓	9	7	15	12
18 30 29	7	2	2	10	38	16	13
18 34 50	8	3	3	12	8	17	14
18 39 11	9	4	5	13	38	18	15
18 43 31	10	5	6	15	8	20	16
18 47 51	11	6	7	16	37	21	17
18 52 11	12	7	9	18	5	22	18
18 56 30	13	8	10	19	33	23	19
19 0 49	14	10	11	21	1	24	20
19 5 7	15	11	13	22	28	25	21
19 9 26	16	12	14	23	54	27	22
19 13 43	17	13	15	25	20	28	23
19 18 0	18	14	17	26	46	29	24
19 22 17	19	15	18	28	10	♊	25
19 26 33	20	16	19	29	34	1	26
19 30 49	21	18	21	0♉	57	2	27
19 35 4	22	19	22	2	20	3	28
19 39 19	23	20	23	3	41	4	29
19 43 33	24	21	25	5	2	5	♋
19 47 46	25	22	26	6	23	6	1
19 51 59	26	23	27	7	42	8	2
19 56 11	27	24	29	9	1	9	3
20 0 23	28	26	♈	10	19	10	4
20 4 34	29	27	1	11	36	11	5
20 8 44	♒	28	3	12	52	12	6
20 12 53	1	29	4	14	8	13	7
20 17 2	2	♓	5	15	23	14	8
20 21 10	3	1	7	16	37	15	9
20 25 18	4	3	8	17	50	16	10
20 29 24	5	4	9	19	3	17	11
20 33 30	6	5	11	20	14	18	12
20 37 36	7	6	12	21	26	19	12
20 41 40	8	7	13	22	36	20	13
20 45 44	9	8	15	23	45	21	14
20 49 47	10	10	16	24	54	22	15
20 53 50	11	11	17	26	2	23	16
20 57 51	12	12	18	27	10	23	17
21 1 52	13	13	20	28	17	24	18
21 5 52	14	14	21	29	23	25	19
HOUSES	4	5	6	7		8	9

LATITUDE 25° S. LATITUDE 26° S. LATITUDE 27° S.

	LATITUDE 25° N.						LATITUDE 26° N.						LATITUDE 27° N.					
SIDEREAL TIME	10 ≈	11 ♓	12 ♈	ASC ♉	2 ♊	3 ♋	10 ≈	11 ♓	12 ♈	ASC ♉	2 ♊	3 ♋	10 ≈	11 ♓	12 ♈	ASC ♊	2 ♊	3 ♋
H M S	°	°	°	° '	°	°	°	°	°	° '	°	°	°	°	°	° '	°	°
21 9 52	15	15	22	29 28	26	19	15	15	22	29 57	26	20	15	15	22	0 28	26	20
21 13 50	16	17	23	0♊ 32	27	20	16	17	23	1♊ 2	27	21	16	16	23	1 33	27	21
21 17 49	17	18	24	1 36	27	21	17	18	24	2 6	28	21	17	18	25	2 37	28	22
21 21 46	18	19	25	2 39	28	22	18	19	26	3 9	29	22	18	19	26	3 40	29	23
21 25 42	19	20	27	3 42	29	23	19	20	27	4 12	♋	23	19	20	27	4 43	♋	23
21 29 38	20	21	28	4 44	♋	24	20	21	28	5 14	1	24	20	21	28	5 45	1	24
21 33 34	21	22	29	5 45	1	25	21	22	29	6 16	1	25	21	22	29	6 47	2	25
21 37 28	22	23	♉	6 46	2	26	22	23	♉	7 16	2	26	22	23	♉	7 48	3	26
21 41 22	23	25	1	7 46	3	27	23	25	1	8 17	3	27	23	25	2	8 48	4	27
21 45 15	24	26	2	8 46	4	28	24	26	3	9 17	4	28	24	26	3	9 48	4	28
21 49 8	25	27	4	9 45	5	29	25	27	4	10 16	5	29	25	27	4	10 47	5	29
21 53 0	26	28	5	10 44	5	29	26	28	5	11 15	6	♌	26	28	5	11 46	6	♌
21 56 51	27	29	6	11 42	6	♌	27	29	6	12 13	7	0	27	29	6	12 45	7	1
22 0 42	28	♈	7	12 40	7	1	28	♈	7	13 11	8	1	28	♈	7	13 42	8	1
22 4 32	29	1	8	13 37	8	2	29	1	8	14 8	8	2	29	1	9	14 40	9	2
22 8 22	♓	2	9	14 34	9	3	♓	2	9	15 5	9	3	♓	2	10	15 37	10	3
22 12 11	1	4	10	15 31	10	4	1	4	10	16 2	10	4	1	4	11	16 33	10	4
22 15 59	2	5	11	16 27	11	5	2	5	12	16 58	11	5	2	5	12	17 29	11	5
22 19 47	3	6	12	17 22	12	6	3	6	13	17 53	12	6	3	6	13	18 25	12	6
22 23 34	4	7	13	18 17	12	7	4	7	14	18 48	13	7	4	7	14	19 20	13	7
22 27 21	5	8	14	19 12	13	7	5	8	15	19 43	14	8	5	8	15	20 14	14	8
22 31 8	6	9	16	20 7	14	8	6	9	16	20 37	14	8	6	9	16	21 9	15	9
22 34 53	7	10	17	21 1	15	9	7	10	17	21 31	15	9	7	10	17	22 3	16	9
22 38 39	8	11	18	21 54	16	10	8	11	18	22 25	16	10	8	11	18	22 56	16	10
22 42 24	9	12	19	22 48	17	11	9	12	19	23 18	17	11	9	12	19	23 50	17	11
22 46 8	10	13	20	23 41	17	12	10	13	20	24 11	18	12	10	14	20	24 43	18	12
22 49 52	11	15	21	24 34	18	13	11	15	21	25 4	19	13	11	15	21	25 35	19	13
22 53 36	12	16	22	25 26	19	14	12	16	22	25 56	19	14	12	16	22	26 27	20	14
22 57 20	13	17	23	26 18	20	15	13	17	23	26 48	20	15	13	17	23	27 19	21	15
23 1 3	14	18	24	27 10	21	15	14	18	24	27 40	21	16	14	18	24	28 11	21	16
23 4 45	15	19	25	28 2	22	16	15	19	25	28 32	22	16	15	19	25	29 2	22	17
23 8 28	16	20	26	28 53	22	17	16	20	26	29 23	23	17	16	20	26	29 54	23	17
23 12 10	17	21	27	29 44	23	18	17	21	27	0♋14	24	18	17	21	27	0♋44	24	18
23 15 52	18	22	28	0♋35	24	19	18	22	28	1 5	24	19	18	22	28	1 35	25	19
23 19 33	19	23	29	1 25	25	20	19	23	29	1 55	25	20	19	23	29	2 25	25	20
23 23 15	20	24	♊	2 16	26	21	20	24	♊	2 45	26	21	20	24	♊	3 16	26	21
23 26 56	21	25	1	3 6	27	22	21	25	1	3 36	27	22	21	25	1	4 6	27	22
23 30 37	22	26	1	3 56	27	23	22	26	2	4 25	28	23	22	26	2	4 55	28	23
23 34 17	23	27	2	4 46	28	23	23	27	3	5 15	28	24	23	27	3	5 45	29	24
23 37 58	24	28	3	5 36	29	24	24	28	4	6 5	29	24	24	28	4	6 34	♌	25
23 41 39	25	29	4	6 25	♌	25	25	29	5	6 54	♌	25	25	29	5	7 24	0	25
23 45 19	26	♉	5	7 14	1	26	26	♉	6	7 43	1	26	26	♉	6	8 13	1	26
23 48 59	27	1	6	8 4	1	27	27	1	6	8 32	2	27	27	1	7	9 2	2	27
23 52 40	28	2	7	8 53	2	28	28	2	7	9 21	3	28	28	2	8	9 50	3	28
23 56 20	29	3	8	9 42	3	29	29	3	8	10 10	3	29	29	4	9	10 39	4	29
HOUSES	4	5	6	7	8	9	4	5	6	7	8	9	4	5	6	7	8	9

LATITUDE 25° S.   LATITUDE 26° S.   LATITUDE 27° S.

LATITUDE 28° N. LATITUDE 29° N. LATITUDE 30° N.

SIDEREAL TIME	10 S	11 Ω	12 ♍	ASC ♎		2 ♎	3 ♏	10 S	11 Ω	12 ♍	ASC ♎		2 ♎	3 ♏	10 S	11 Ω	12 ♍	ASC ♎		2 ♎	3 ♏
H M S	°	°	°	°	'	°	°	°	°	°	°	'	°	°	°	°	°	°	'	°	°
6 0 0	0	1	2	0	0	28	29	0	2	2	0	0	28	28	0	2	2	0	0	28	28
6 4 22	1	2	3	0	58	29	♐	1	3	3	0	57	29	29	1	3	3	0	57	29	29
6 8 43	2	3	4	1	56	♏	1	2	4	4	1	55	♏	♐	2	4	4	1	54	♏	♐
6 13 5	3	4	5	2	54	1	2	3	5	5	2	52	1	1	3	5	5	2	51	1	1
6 17 26	4	5	6	3	52	2	3	4	6	6	3	50	2	2	4	6	6	3	48	2	2
6 21 47	5	7	7	4	49	3	4	5	7	7	4	47	3	3	5	7	7	4	45	3	3
6 26 9	6	8	8	5	47	4	5	6	8	8	5	44	4	4	6	8	8	5	42	4	4
6 30 29	7	9	9	6	45	5	6	7	9	9	6	42	5	5	7	9	9	6	39	5	5
6 34 50	8	10	10	7	43	6	7	8	10	10	7	39	6	6	8	10	10	7	35	6	6
6 39 11	9	11	11	8	40	7	8	9	11	11	8	36	7	7	9	11	11	8	32	7	7
6 43 31	10	12	12	9	38	8	9	10	12	12	9	33	8	8	10	12	12	9	29	8	8
6 47 51	11	13	13	10	35	9	10	11	13	13	10	30	9	9	11	13	13	10	25	9	9
6 52 11	12	14	14	11	32	10	11	12	14	14	11	27	10	10	12	14	14	11	22	10	10
6 56 30	13	15	15	12	30	11	11	13	15	15	12	24	11	11	13	15	15	12	18	11	11
7 0 49	14	16	16	13	27	12	12	14	16	16	13	20	12	12	14	16	16	13	14	12	12
7 5 7	15	17	17	14	24	13	13	15	17	17	14	17	13	13	15	17	17	14	10	13	13
7 9 26	16	18	18	15	21	14	14	16	18	18	15	13	14	14	16	18	18	15	6	14	14
7 13 43	17	19	19	16	17	15	15	17	19	19	16	10	15	15	17	19	19	16	2	14	15
7 18 0	18	20	20	17	14	16	16	18	20	20	17	6	16	16	18	20	20	16	58	15	16
7 22 17	19	21	21	18	10	17	17	19	21	21	18	2	17	17	19	21	21	17	53	16	17
7 26 33	20	22	22	19	7	18	18	20	22	22	18	58	18	18	20	22	22	18	49	17	18
7 30 49	21	23	23	20	3	19	19	21	23	23	19	53	19	19	21	23	23	19	44	18	19
7 35 4	22	24	24	20	59	20	20	22	24	24	20	49	19	20	22	24	24	20	39	19	20
7 39 19	23	25	25	21	54	21	21	23	25	25	21	44	20	21	23	25	25	21	34	20	21
7 43 33	24	26	26	22	50	22	22	24	26	26	22	39	21	22	24	26	26	22	29	21	22
7 47 46	25	27	27	23	45	23	23	25	27	27	23	34	22	23	25	27	27	23	23	22	23
7 51 59	26	28	28	24	41	23	24	26	28	28	24	29	23	24	26	28	28	24	18	23	24
7 56 11	27	29	29	25	36	24	25	27	29	29	25	24	24	25	27	29	29	25	12	24	25
8 0 23	28	♍	≏	26	31	25	26	28	♍	≏	26	18	25	26	28	♍	≏	26	6	25	26
8 4 34	29	1	1	27	25	26	27	29	1	1	27	13	26	27	29	1	1	27	0	26	27
8 8 44	Ω	2	2	28	20	27	28	Ω	2	2	28	7	27	28	Ω	2	2	27	54	27	28
8 12 53	1	3	3	29	14	28	29	1	3	3	29	1	28	29	1	3	3	28	47	28	29
8 17 2	2	4	4	0♏	8	29	♑	2	4	4	29	54	29	♑	2	4	4	29	40	28	29
8 21 10	3	5	5	1	2	♐	1	3	5	5	0♏	48	♐	1	3	5	5	0♏	34	29	♑
8 25 18	4	6	6	1	55	1	2	4	6	6	1	41	1	2	4	6	6	1	26	♐	1
8 29 24	5	7	7	2	49	2	3	5	7	7	2	34	2	2	5	7	7	2	19	1	2
8 33 30	6	8	8	3	42	3	4	6	8	8	3	27	2	3	6	8	8	3	12	2	3
8 37 36	7	9	9	4	35	4	5	7	9	9	4	20	3	4	7	9	9	4	4	3	4
8 41 40	8	10	10	5	28	5	6	8	10	10	5	12	4	5	8	10	10	4	56	4	5
8 45 44	9	11	11	6	21	5	6	9	11	11	6	4	5	6	9	11	11	5	48	5	6
8 49 47	10	12	12	7	13	6	7	10	12	12	6	56	6	7	10	12	12	6	40	6	7
8 53 50	11	13	13	8	5	7	8	11	13	13	7	48	7	8	11	13	13	7	31	7	8
8 57 51	12	14	14	8	57	8	9	12	14	14	8	40	8	9	12	14	13	8	23	7	9
9 1 52	13	15	15	9	49	9	10	13	15	14	9	32	9	10	13	15	14	9	14	8	10
9 5 52	14	16	16	10	41	10	11	14	16	15	10	23	10	11	14	16	15	10	5	9	11
HOUSES	4	5	6	7		8	9	4	5	6	7		8	9	4	5	6	7		8	9

LATITUDE 28° S. LATITUDE 29° S. LATITUDE 30° S.

LATITUDE 28° N. LATITUDE 29° N. LATITUDE 30° N.

SIDEREAL TIME	10 Ω	11 ♍	12 ♎	ASC ♏	2 ♐	3 ♑	10 Ω	11 ♍	12 ♎	ASC ♏	2 ♐	3 ♑	10 Ω	11 ♍	12 ♎	ASC ♏	2 ♐	3 ♑
H M S	°	°	°	° '	°	°	°	°	°	° '	°	°	°	°	°	° '	°	°
9 9 52	15	17	16	11 32	11	12	15	17	16	11 14	10	12	15	17	16	10 55	10	12
9 13 50	16	18	17	12 24	12	13	16	18	17	12 5	11	13	16	18	17	11 46	11	13
9 17 49	17	19	18	13 15	13	14	17	19	18	12 56	12	14	17	19	18	12 36	12	14
9 21 46	18	20	19	14 5	13	15	18	20	19	13 46	13	15	18	20	19	13 27	13	15
9 25 42	19	21	20	14 56	14	16	19	21	20	14 36	14	16	19	21	20	14 17	14	15
9 29 38	20	22	21	15 47	15	17	20	22	21	15 27	15	17	20	22	21	15 7	14	16
9 33 34	21	23	22	16 37	16	18	21	23	22	16 17	16	18	21	23	22	15 56	15	17
9 37 28	22	24	23	17 27	17	19	22	24	23	17 7	17	18	22	24	23	16 46	16	18
9 41 22	23	25	24	18 17	18	20	23	25	24	17 56	17	19	23	25	24	17 35	17	19
9 45 15	24	26	25	19 7	19	21	24	26	25	18 46	18	20	24	26	24	18 24	18	20
9 49 8	25	27	26	19 57	19	21	25	27	25	19 35	19	21	25	27	25	19 14	19	21
9 53 0	26	28	27	20 46	20	22	26	28	26	20 24	20	22	26	28	26	20 2	20	22
9 56 51	27	29	27	21 35	21	23	27	29	27	21 13	21	23	27	29	27	20 51	21	23
10 0 42	28	♎	28	22 25	22	24	28	♎	28	22 2	22	24	28	♎	28	21 40	21	24
10 4 32	29	1	29	23 14	23	25	29	1	29	22 51	23	25	29	1	29	22 28	22	25
10 8 22	♍	2	♏	24 3	24	26	♍	2	♏	23 40	23	26	♍	2	♏	23 17	23	26
10 12 11	1	3	1	24 52	25	27	1	3	1	24 28	24	27	1	3	1	24 5	24	27
10 15 59	2	4	2	25 40	26	28	2	4	2	25 17	25	28	2	4	1	24 53	25	28
10 19 47	3	5	3	26 29	26	29	3	5	2	26 5	26	29	3	5	2	25 41	26	29
10 23 34	4	6	4	27 17	27	♒	4	6	3	26 53	27	♒	4	6	3	26 29	27	♒
10 27 21	5	7	4	28 6	28	1	5	7	4	27 42	28	1	5	7	4	27 17	27	1
10 31 8	6	8	5	28 54	29	2	6	8	5	28 30	29	2	6	8	5	28 5	28	2
10 34 53	7	9	6	29 42	♑	3	7	9	6	29 17	29	3	7	9	6	28 53	29	2
10 38 39	8	10	7	0♐ 30	1	4	8	10	7	0♐ 5	♑	4	8	10	7	29 40	♑	3
10 42 24	9	11	8	1 18	2	5	9	11	8	0 53	1	5	9	11	7	0♐ 28	1	4
10 46 8	10	12	9	2 6	2	6	10	12	8	1 41	2	6	10	12	8	1 15	2	5
10 49 52	11	13	10	2 54	3	7	11	13	9	2 29	3	6	11	13	9	2 3	3	6
10 53 36	12	14	10	3 42	4	8	12	13	10	3 16	4	7	12	13	10	2 50	3	7
10 57 20	13	14	11	4 30	5	9	13	14	11	4 4	5	8	13	14	11	3 37	4	8
11 1 3	14	15	12	5 18	6	10	14	15	12	4 51	6	9	14	15	12	4 25	5	9
11 4 45	15	16	13	6 5	7	10	15	16	13	5 39	6	10	15	16	12	5 12	6	10
11 8 28	16	17	14	6 53	8	11	16	17	14	6 26	7	11	16	17	13	5 59	7	11
11 12 10	17	18	15	7 41	9	12	17	18	14	7 14	8	12	17	18	14	6 46	8	12
11 15 52	18	19	15	8 28	9	13	18	19	15	8 1	9	13	18	19	15	7 34	9	13
11 19 33	19	20	16	9 16	10	14	19	20	16	8 49	10	14	19	20	16	8 21	10	14
11 23 15	20	21	17	10 4	11	15	20	21	17	9 36	11	15	20	21	17	9 8	10	15
11 26 56	21	22	18	10 52	12	16	21	22	18	10 24	12	16	21	22	17	9 56	11	16
11 30 37	22	23	19	11 39	13	17	22	23	18	11 11	13	17	22	23	18	10 43	12	17
11 34 17	23	24	20	12 27	14	18	23	24	19	11 59	13	18	23	24	19	11 30	13	18
11 37 58	24	25	20	13 15	15	19	24	25	20	12 46	14	19	24	24	20	12 18	14	19
11 41 39	25	26	21	14 3	16	20	25	25	21	13 34	15	20	25	25	21	13 5	15	20
11 45 19	26	26	22	14 51	16	21	26	26	22	14 22	16	21	26	26	21	13 53	16	21
11 48 59	27	27	23	15 39	17	22	27	27	23	15 10	17	22	27	27	22	14 40	17	22
11 52 40	28	28	24	16 27	18	23	28	28	23	15 58	18	23	28	28	23	15 28	18	23
11 56 20	29	29	24	17 15	19	24	29	29	24	16 46	19	24	29	29	24	16 16	18	24
HOUSES	4	5	6	7	8	9	4	5	6	7	8	9	4	5	6	7	8	9

LATITUDE 28° S. LATITUDE 29° S. LATITUDE 30° S.

LATITUDE 28° N. LATITUDE 29° N. LATITUDE 30° N.

SIDEREAL TIME	10 ♎	11 ♏	12 ♏	ASC ♐		2 ♑	3 ♒	10 ♎	11 ♏	12 ♏	ASC ♐		2 ♑	3 ♒	10 ♎	11 ♏	12 ♏	ASC ♐		2 ♑	3 ♒
H M S	°	°	°	°	'	°	°	°	°	°	°	'	°	°	°	°	°	°	'	°	°
12 0 0	0	0	25	18	3	20	25	0	0	25	17	34	20	25	0	0	25	17	4	19	25
12 3 40	1	1	26	18	52	21	26	1	1	26	18	22	21	26	1	1	26	17	52	20	26
12 7 20	2	2	27	19	40	22	27	2	2	27	19	10	22	27	2	2	26	18	40	21	27
12 11 1	3	3	28	20	29	23	28	3	3	27	19	59	23	28	3	3	27	19	28	22	28
12 14 41	4	4	29	21	18	24	29	4	4	28	20	47	23	29	4	3	28	20	17	23	29
12 18 21	5	5	29	22	7	25	♓	5	4	29	21	36	24	♓	5	4	29	21	5	24	♓
12 22 2	6	5	♐	22	56	26	2	6	5	♐	22	25	25	1	6	5	♐	21	54	25	1
12 25 42	7	6	1	23	45	27	3	7	6	1	23	14	26	2	7	6	0	22	43	26	2
12 29 23	8	7	2	24	34	28	4	8	7	2	24	3	27	4	8	7	1	23	32	27	3
12 33 4	9	8	3	25	24	29	5	9	8	2	24	53	28	5	9	8	2	24	21	28	4
12 36 45	10	9	3	26	14	29	6	10	9	3	25	43	29	6	10	9	3	25	11	29	6
12 40 27	11	10	4	27	4	♒	7	11	10	4	26	33	♒	7	11	10	4	26	1	♒	7
12 44 8	12	11	5	27	54	1	8	12	11	5	27	23	1	8	12	10	4	26	51	1	8
12 47 50	13	12	6	28	45	2	9	13	11	6	28	13	2	9	13	11	5	27	41	2	9
12 51 32	14	12	7	29	35	3	10	14	12	6	29	4	3	10	14	12	6	28	31	3	10
12 55 15	15	13	8	0♑	26	4	11	15	13	7	29	55	4	11	15	13	7	29	22	4	11
12 58 57	16	14	8	1	18	5	12	16	14	8	0♑	46	5	12	16	14	8	0♑	13	5	12
13 2 40	17	15	9	2	9	6	13	17	15	9	1	37	6	13	17	15	9	1	4	6	13
13 6 24	18	16	10	3	1	7	14	18	16	10	2	29	7	14	18	16	9	1	56	7	14
13 10 8	19	17	11	3	53	8	15	19	17	10	3	21	8	15	19	17	10	2	48	8	15
13 13 52	20	18	12	4	46	9	16	20	18	11	4	13	9	16	20	18	11	3	40	9	16
13 17 36	21	19	12	5	39	10	18	21	19	12	5	6	10	17	21	18	12	4	33	10	17
13 21 21	22	20	13	6	32	12	19	22	19	13	5	59	11	19	22	19	13	5	26	11	19
13 25 7	23	20	14	7	25	13	20	23	20	14	6	53	12	20	23	20	13	6	19	12	20
13 28 52	24	21	15	8	19	14	21	24	21	15	7	46	13	21	24	21	14	7	13	13	21
13 32 39	25	22	16	9	13	15	22	25	22	15	8	41	14	22	25	22	15	8	7	14	22
13 36 26	26	23	17	10	8	16	23	26	23	16	9	35	15	23	26	23	16	9	2	15	23
13 40 13	27	24	18	11	3	17	24	27	24	17	10	30	17	24	27	24	17	9	57	16	24
13 44 1	28	25	18	11	59	18	25	28	25	18	11	26	18	25	28	25	18	10	52	17	25
13 47 49	29	26	19	12	55	19	26	29	26	19	12	22	19	26	29	25	19	11	48	18	26
13 51 38	♏	27	20	13	51	20	28	♏	26	20	13	18	20	28	♏	26	19	12	44	20	28
13 55 28	1	28	21	14	48	21	29	1	27	21	14	15	21	29	1	27	20	13	41	21	29
13 59 18	2	28	22	15	45	22	♈	2	28	21	15	12	22	♈	2	28	21	14	38	22	♈
14 3 9	3	29	23	16	43	23	1	3	29	22	16	10	23	1	3	29	22	15	36	23	1
14 7 0	4	♐	24	17	41	25	2	4	♐	23	17	8	24	2	4	♐	23	16	34	24	2
14 10 52	5	1	24	18	40	26	3	5	1	24	18	7	26	3	5	1	24	17	33	25	3
14 14 45	6	2	25	19	40	27	4	6	2	25	19	7	27	4	6	2	25	18	33	26	4
14 18 38	7	3	26	20	40	28	5	7	3	26	20	7	28	6	7	3	25	19	33	28	6
14 22 32	8	4	27	21	40	29	7	8	4	27	21	7	29	7	8	3	26	20	33	29	7
14 26 26	9	5	28	22	41	♓	8	9	4	28	22	8	♓	8	9	4	27	21	34	♓	8
14 30 22	10	6	29	23	43	2	9	10	5	28	23	10	1	9	10	5	28	22	36	1	9
14 34 17	11	6	♑	24	45	3	10	11	6	29	24	12	3	10	11	6	29	23	39	2	10
14 38 14	12	7	1	25	48	4	11	12	7	♑	25	15	4	11	12	7	♑	24	42	4	11
14 42 11	13	8	2	26	52	5	12	13	8	1	26	19	5	12	13	8	1	25	46	5	13
14 46 10	14	9	2	27	56	7	14	14	9	2	27	23	6	14	14	9	2	26	50	6	14
HOUSES	4	5	6	7		8	9	4	5	6	7		8	9	4	5	6	7		8	9

LATITUDE 28° S. LATITUDE 29° S. LATITUDE 30° S.

LATITUDE 28° N. LATITUDE 29° N. LATITUDE 30° N.

SIDEREAL TIME H M S	10 ♏	11 ♐	12 ♑	ASC ♑ °	'	2 ♓	3 ♈	10 ♏	11 ♐	12 ♑	ASC ♑ °	'	2 ♓	3 ♈	10 ♏	11 ♐	12 ♑	ASC ♑ °	'	2 ♓	3 ♈
14 50 8	15	10	3	29	1	8	15	15	10	3	28	28	8	15	15	10	3	27	55	7	15
14 54 8	16	11	4	0♒	6	9	16	16	11	4	29	34	9	16	16	11	4	29	1	9	16
14 58 8	17	12	5	1	13	10	17	17	12	5	0♒	41	10	17	17	12	4	0♒	8	10	17
15 2 9	18	13	6	2	19	12	18	18	13	6	1	48	11	18	18	12	5	1	15	11	18
15 6 10	19	14	7	3	27	13	19	19	14	7	2	56	13	19	19	13	6	2	23	13	20
15 10 13	20	15	8	4	35	14	21	20	14	8	4	4	14	21	20	14	7	3	32	14	21
15 14 16	21	16	9	5	45	15	22	21	15	9	5	14	15	22	21	15	8	4	42	15	22
15 18 20	22	16	10	6	54	17	23	22	16	10	6	24	17	23	22	16	9	5	52	16	23
15 22 24	23	17	11	8	5	18	24	23	17	11	7	35	18	24	23	17	10	7	3	18	24
15 26 30	24	18	12	9	16	19	25	24	18	12	8	46	19	25	24	18	11	8	15	19	25
15 30 36	25	19	13	10	29	21	26	25	19	13	9	59	20	26	25	19	12	9	28	20	27
15 34 42	26	20	14	11	41	22	28	26	20	14	11	12	22	28	26	20	13	10	42	22	28
15 38 50	27	21	15	12	55	23	29	27	21	15	12	26	23	29	27	21	14	11	56	23	29
15 42 58	28	22	16	14	10	25	♉	28	22	16	13	41	24	♉	28	22	15	13	12	24	♉
15 47 7	29	23	17	15	25	26	1	29	23	17	14	57	26	1	29	23	16	14	28	26	1
15 51 16	♐	24	18	16	41	27	2	♐	24	18	16	14	27	2	♐	24	17	15	45	27	2
15 55 26	1	25	19	17	58	29	3	1	25	19	17	31	29	3	1	25	18	17	3	29	4
15 59 37	2	26	20	19	16	♈	5	2	26	20	18	49	♈	5	2	25	19	18	22	♈	5
16 3 49	3	27	21	20	34	1	6	3	27	21	20	8	1	6	3	26	20	19	41	1	6
16 8 1	4	28	22	21	54	3	7	4	28	22	21	28	3	7	4	27	21	21	2	3	7
16 12 14	5	29	23	23	14	4	8	5	29	23	22	49	4	8	5	28	22	22	23	4	8
16 16 27	6	♑	24	24	35	5	9	6	♑	24	24	11	5	9	6	29	24	23	46	5	9
16 20 41	7	1	25	25	56	7	10	7	0	25	25	33	7	10	7	♑	25	25	9	7	11
16 24 56	8	2	26	27	19	8	11	8	1	26	26	56	8	12	8	1	26	26	33	8	12
16 29 11	9	3	28	28	42	9	13	9	2	27	28	20	9	13	9	2	27	27	57	10	13
16 33 27	10	4	29	0♓	6	11	14	10	3	28	29	45	11	14	10	3	28	29	23	11	14
16 37 43	11	5	♒	1	30	12	15	11	4	29	1♓	10	12	15	11	4	29	0♓	49	12	15
16 41 59	12	6	1	2	56	13	16	12	5	♒	2	36	14	16	12	5	♒	2	16	14	16
16 46 17	13	7	2	4	22	15	17	13	6	2	4	3	15	17	13	6	1	3	44	15	17
16 50 34	14	8	3	5	49	16	18	14	7	3	5	31	16	18	14	7	2	5	13	16	19
16 54 53	15	9	4	7	16	18	19	15	8	4	6	59	18	20	15	8	4	6	42	18	20
16 59 11	16	10	5	8	44	19	21	16	9	5	8	28	19	21	16	9	5	8	12	19	21
17 3 30	17	11	7	10	12	20	22	17	10	6	9	58	20	22	17	10	6	9	42	21	22
17 7 49	18	12	8	11	42	22	23	18	11	7	11	28	22	23	18	11	7	11	14	22	23
17 12 9	19	13	9	13	11	23	24	19	12	9	12	59	23	24	19	12	8	12	45	23	24
17 16 29	20	14	10	14	41	24	25	20	13	10	14	30	24	25	20	13	10	14	18	25	25
17 20 49	21	15	11	16	12	26	26	21	15	11	16	1	26	26	21	14	11	15	50	26	26
17 25 10	22	16	13	17	43	27	27	22	16	12	17	33	27	27	22	15	12	17	24	27	28
17 29 31	23	17	14	19	14	28	28	23	17	13	19	6	29	28	23	16	13	18	57	29	29
17 33 51	24	18	15	20	46	♉	29	24	18	15	20	39	♉	♊	24	17	14	20	31	♉	♊
17 38 13	25	19	16	22	18	1	♊	25	19	16	22	12	1	1	25	18	16	22	6	1	1
17 42 34	26	20	18	23	50	2	2	26	20	17	23	45	2	2	26	20	17	23	40	3	2
17 46 55	27	21	19	25	22	4	3	27	21	18	25	19	4	3	27	21	18	25	15	4	3
17 51 17	28	22	20	26	55	5	4	28	22	20	26	52	5	4	28	22	19	26	50	5	4
17 55 38	29	23	21	28	27	6	5	29	23	21	28	26	6	5	29	23	21	28	25	7	5
HOUSES	4	5	6	7		8	9	4	5	6	7		8	9	4	5	6	7		8	9

LATITUDE 28° S. LATITUDE 29° S. LATITUDE 30° S.

LATITUDE 28° N. LATITUDE 29° N. LATITUDE 30° N.

SIDEREAL TIME H M S	10 ♑	11 ♑	12 ♒	ASC ♈ °	ASC '	2 ♉	3 ♊	10 ♑	11 ♑	12 ♒	ASC ♈ °	ASC '	2 ♉	3 ♊	10 ♑	11 ♑	12 ♒	ASC ♈ °	ASC '	2 ♉	3 ♊
18 0 0	0	24	23	0	0	7	6	0	24	22	0	0	8	6	0	24	22	0	0	8	6
18 4 22	1	25	24	1	33	9	7	1	25	24	1	34	9	7	1	25	23	1	35	9	7
18 8 43	2	26	25	3	5	10	8	2	26	25	3	8	10	8	2	26	25	3	10	11	8
18 13 5	3	27	26	4	38	11	9	3	27	26	4	41	12	9	3	27	26	4	45	12	9
18 17 26	4	28	28	6	10	12	10	4	28	28	6	15	13	10	4	28	27	6	20	13	10
18 21 47	5	♒	29	7	42	14	11	5	29	29	7	48	14	11	5	29	29	7	54	14	12
18 26 9	6	1	♓	9	14	15	12	6	♒	♓	9	21	15	12	6	♒	♓	9	29	16	13
18 30 29	7	2	2	10	46	16	13	7	2	1	10	54	17	13	7	1	1	11	3	17	14
18 34 50	8	3	3	12	17	17	14	8	3	3	12	27	18	14	8	2	3	12	36	18	15
18 39 11	9	4	4	13	48	19	15	9	4	4	13	59	19	15	9	4	4	14	10	19	16
18 43 31	10	5	6	15	19	20	16	10	5	6	15	30	20	17	10	5	5	15	42	20	17
18 47 51	11	6	7	16	49	21	17	11	6	7	17	1	21	18	11	6	7	17	15	22	18
18 52 11	12	7	8	18	18	22	18	12	7	8	18	32	23	19	12	7	8	18	46	23	19
18 56 30	13	8	10	19	48	23	19	13	8	10	20	2	24	20	13	8	9	20	18	24	20
19 0 49	14	9	11	21	16	25	20	14	9	11	21	32	25	21	14	9	11	21	48	25	21
19 5 7	15	11	12	22	44	26	21	15	10	12	23	1	26	22	15	10	12	23	18	26	22
19 9 26	16	12	14	24	11	27	22	16	12	14	24	29	27	23	16	11	14	24	47	28	23
19 13 43	17	13	15	25	38	28	23	17	13	15	25	57	28	24	17	13	15	26	16	29	24
19 18 0	18	14	17	27	4	29	24	18	14	16	27	24	29	25	18	14	16	27	44	♊	25
19 22 17	19	15	18	28	30	♊	25	19	15	18	28	50	♊	26	19	15	18	29	11	1	26
19 26 33	20	16	19	29	54	1	26	20	16	19	0♉	15	2	27	20	16	19	0♉	37	2	27
19 30 49	21	17	21	1♉	18	2	27	21	17	21	1	40	3	28	21	17	20	2	3	3	28
19 35 4	22	19	22	2	41	4	28	22	18	22	3	4	4	29	22	18	22	3	27	4	29
19 39 19	23	20	23	4	4	5	29	23	20	23	4	27	5	♋	23	19	23	4	51	5	♋
19 43 33	24	21	25	5	25	6	♋	24	21	25	5	49	6	0	24	21	25	6	14	6	1
19 47 46	25	22	26	6	46	7	1	25	22	26	7	11	7	1	25	22	26	7	37	8	2
19 51 59	26	23	27	8	6	8	2	26	23	27	8	32	8	2	26	23	27	8	58	9	3
19 56 11	27	24	29	9	26	9	3	27	24	29	9	52	9	3	27	24	29	10	19	10	4
20 0 23	28	25	♈	10	44	10	4	28	25	♈	11	11	10	4	28	25	♈	11	38	11	5
20 4 34	29	27	1	12	2	11	5	29	27	1	12	29	11	5	29	26	1	12	57	12	5
20 8 44	♒	28	3	13	19	12	6	♒	28	3	13	46	12	6	♒	28	3	14	15	13	6
20 12 53	1	29	4	14	35	13	7	1	29	4	15	3	13	7	1	29	4	15	32	14	7
20 17 2	2	♓	5	15	50	14	8	2	♓	6	16	19	14	8	2	♓	6	16	48	15	8
20 21 10	3	1	7	17	5	15	9	3	1	7	17	34	15	9	3	1	7	18	4	16	9
20 25 18	4	2	8	18	19	16	10	4	2	8	18	48	16	10	4	2	8	19	18	17	10
20 29 24	5	4	9	19	31	17	11	5	4	10	20	1	17	11	5	3	10	20	32	18	11
20 33 30	6	5	11	20	44	18	12	6	5	11	21	14	18	12	6	5	11	21	45	19	12
20 37 36	7	6	12	21	55	19	13	7	6	12	22	25	19	13	7	6	12	22	57	20	13
20 41 40	8	7	13	23	6	20	14	8	7	13	23	36	20	14	8	7	14	24	8	21	14
20 45 44	9	8	15	24	15	21	14	9	8	15	24	46	21	15	9	8	15	25	18	22	15
20 49 47	10	9	16	25	25	22	15	10	9	16	25	56	22	16	10	9	16	26	28	23	16
20 53 50	11	11	17	26	33	23	16	11	11	17	27	4	23	16	11	10	17	27	37	24	17
20 57 51	12	12	18	27	41	24	17	12	12	19	28	12	24	17	12	12	19	28	45	25	18
21 1 52	13	13	20	28	47	25	18	13	13	20	29	19	25	18	13	13	20	29	52	26	18
21 5 52	14	14	21	29	54	26	19	14	14	21	0♊	26	26	19	14	14	21	0♊	59	26	19
HOUSES	4	5	6	7		8	9	4	5	6	7		8	9	4	5	6	7		8	9

LATITUDE 28° S. LATITUDE 29° S. LATITUDE 30° S.

LATITUDE 28° N. LATITUDE 29° N. LATITUDE 30° N.

SIDEREAL TIME H M S	10 ≈	11 ♓	12 ♈	ASC ♊	2 ♊	3 ♋	10 ≈	11 ♓	12 ♈	ASC ♊	2 ♊	3 ♋	10 ≈	11 ♓	12 ♈	ASC ♊	2 ♊	3 ♋
21 9 52	15	15	22	0 59	27	20	15	15	22	1 32	27	20	15	15	23	2 5	27	20
21 13 50	16	16	23	2 4	28	21	16	16	24	2 37	28	21	16	16	24	3 10	28	21
21 17 49	17	18	25	3 8	28	22	17	18	25	3 41	29	22	17	17	25	4 14	29	22
21 21 46	18	19	26	4 12	29	23	18	19	26	4 45	♋	23	18	19	26	5 18	♋	23
21 25 42	19	20	27	5 15	♋	24	19	20	27	5 48	1	24	19	20	28	6 21	1	24
21 29 38	20	21	28	6 17	1	24	20	21	29	6 50	2	25	20	21	29	7 24	2	25
21 33 34	21	22	♉	7 19	2	25	21	22	♉	7 52	2	26	21	22	♉	8 26	3	26
21 37 28	22	23	1	8 20	3	26	22	23	1	8 53	3	26	22	23	1	9 27	4	27
21 41 22	23	25	2	9 20	4	27	23	24	2	9 53	4	27	23	24	2	10 27	5	27
21 45 15	24	26	3	10 20	5	28	24	26	3	10 53	5	28	24	26	4	11 27	5	28
21 49 8	25	27	4	11 20	6	29	25	27	4	11 53	6	29	25	27	5	12 27	6	29
21 53 0	26	28	5	12 19	6	♌	26	28	6	12 52	7	♌	26	28	6	13 26	7	♌
21 56 51	27	29	7	13 17	7	1	27	29	7	13 50	8	1	27	29	7	14 24	8	1
22 0 42	28	♈	8	14 15	8	2	28	♈	8	14 48	9	2	28	♈	8	15 22	9	2
22 4 32	29	1	9	15 12	9	2	29	1	9	15 45	9	3	29	1	9	16 19	10	3
22 8 22	♓	2	10	16 9	10	3	♓	2	10	16 42	10	4	♓	2	10	17 16	11	4
22 12 11	1	4	11	17 5	11	4	1	4	11	17 38	11	4	1	4	12	18 12	11	5
22 15 59	2	5	12	18 1	12	5	2	5	12	18 34	12	5	2	5	13	19 8	12	5
22 19 47	3	6	13	18 57	12	6	3	6	13	19 30	13	6	3	6	14	20 3	13	6
22 23 34	4	7	14	19 52	13	7	4	7	15	20 25	14	7	4	7	15	20 58	14	7
22 27 21	5	8	15	20 47	14	8	5	8	16	21 19	15	8	5	8	16	21 53	15	8
22 31 8	6	9	16	21 41	15	9	6	9	17	22 14	15	9	6	9	17	22 47	16	9
22 34 53	7	10	17	22 35	16	10	7	10	18	23 7	16	10	7	10	18	23 41	17	10
22 38 39	8	11	18	23 28	17	10	8	11	19	24 1	17	11	8	11	19	24 34	17	11
22 42 24	9	12	20	24 21	18	11	9	13	20	24 54	18	11	9	13	20	25 27	18	12
22 46 8	10	14	21	25 14	18	12	10	14	21	25 47	19	12	10	14	21	26 20	19	12
22 49 52	11	15	22	26 7	19	13	11	15	22	26 39	20	13	11	15	22	27 12	20	13
22 53 36	12	16	23	26 59	20	14	12	16	23	27 31	20	14	12	16	23	28 4	21	14
22 57 20	13	17	24	27 51	21	15	13	17	24	28 23	21	15	13	17	24	28 56	21	15
23 1 3	14	18	25	28 42	22	16	14	18	25	29 14	22	16	14	18	25	29 47	22	16
23 4 45	15	19	26	29 34	22	17	15	19	26	0♋ 5	23	17	15	19	26	0♋ 38	23	17
23 8 28	16	20	27	0♋ 25	23	18	16	20	27	0 56	24	18	16	20	27	1 29	24	18
23 12 10	17	21	28	1 15	24	18	17	21	28	1 47	24	19	17	21	28	2 19	25	19
23 15 52	18	22	29	2 6	25	19	18	22	29	2 37	25	19	18	22	29	3 9	26	20
23 19 33	19	23	♊	2 56	26	20	19	23	♊	3 27	26	20	19	23	♊	3 59	26	20
23 23 15	20	24	1	3 46	27	21	20	24	1	4 17	27	21	20	24	1	4 49	27	21
23 26 56	21	25	1	4 36	27	22	21	25	2	5 7	28	22	21	26	2	5 39	28	22
23 30 37	22	26	2	5 26	28	23	22	26	3	5 57	28	23	22	27	3	6 28	29	23
23 34 17	23	27	3	6 15	29	24	23	28	4	6 46	29	24	23	28	4	7 17	♌	24
23 37 58	24	28	4	7 4	♌	25	24	29	5	7 35	♌	25	24	29	5	8 6	0	25
23 41 39	25	♉	5	7 53	1	25	25	♉	6	8 24	1	26	25	♉	6	8 55	1	26
23 45 19	26	1	6	8 42	1	26	26	1	7	9 13	2	26	26	1	7	9 43	2	27
23 48 59	27	2	7	9 31	2	27	27	2	7	10 1	3	27	27	2	8	10 32	3	27
23 52 40	28	3	8	10 20	3	28	28	3	8	10 50	3	28	28	3	9	11 20	4	28
23 56 20	29	4	9	11 8	4	29	29	4	9	11 38	4	29	29	4	10	12 8	4	29
HOUSES	4	5	6	7	8	9	4	5	6	7	8	9	4	5	6	7	8	9

LATITUDE 28° S. LATITUDE 29° S. LATITUDE 30° S.

LATITUDE 31° N. LATITUDE 32° N. LATITUDE 33° N.

SIDEREAL TIME (H M S)	10 ♈	11 ♉	12 ♊	ASC ♋		2 ♌	3 ♍	10 ♈	11 ♉	12 ♊	ASC ♋		2 ♌	3 ♍	10 ♈	11 ♉	12 ♊	ASC ♋		2 ♌	3 ♍
0 0 0	0	5	11	13	27	6	0	0	5	11	13	58	6	0	0	5	12	14	29	6	0
0 3 40	1	6	12	14	14	6	1	1	6	12	14	45	7	1	1	6	13	15	17	7	1
0 7 20	2	7	13	15	2	7	2	2	7	13	15	33	7	2	2	7	14	16	4	8	2
0 11 1	3	8	14	15	50	8	3	3	8	14	16	20	8	3	3	8	14	16	51	9	3
0 14 41	4	9	15	16	37	9	4	4	9	15	17	7	9	4	4	9	15	17	38	9	4
0 18 21	5	10	16	17	24	10	5	5	10	16	17	54	10	5	5	10	16	18	25	10	5
0 22 2	6	11	16	18	12	10	6	6	11	17	18	41	11	6	6	11	17	19	11	11	6
0 25 43	7	12	17	18	59	11	7	7	12	18	19	28	11	7	7	12	18	19	58	12	7
0 29 23	8	13	18	19	46	12	7	8	13	19	20	15	12	7	8	13	19	20	45	13	8
0 33 4	9	14	19	20	33	13	8	9	14	19	21	2	13	8	9	14	20	21	31	13	8
0 36 45	10	15	20	21	20	14	9	10	15	20	21	49	14	9	10	15	21	22	18	14	9
0 40 27	11	16	21	22	7	14	10	11	16	21	22	36	15	10	11	16	22	23	5	15	10
0 44 8	12	17	22	22	54	15	11	12	17	22	23	22	16	11	12	17	22	23	51	16	11
0 47 50	13	18	23	23	41	16	12	13	18	23	24	9	16	12	13	18	23	24	38	17	12
0 51 32	14	19	23	24	28	17	13	14	19	24	24	56	17	13	14	19	24	25	24	17	13
0 55 15	15	20	24	25	15	18	14	15	20	25	25	43	18	14	15	20	25	26	11	18	14
0 58 57	16	21	25	26	2	19	15	16	21	26	26	30	19	15	16	21	26	26	57	19	15
1 2 40	17	22	26	26	49	19	16	17	22	26	27	16	20	16	17	22	27	27	44	20	16
1 6 24	18	23	27	27	36	20	17	18	23	27	28	3	20	17	18	23	28	28	30	21	17
1 10 8	19	24	28	28	24	21	18	19	24	28	28	50	21	18	19	24	29	29	17	22	18
1 13 52	20	25	29	29	11	22	18	20	25	29	29	37	22	18	20	25	29	0♌	4	22	19
1 17 36	21	26	♋	29	58	23	19	21	26	♋	0♌	24	23	19	21	26	♋	0	50	23	19
1 21 21	22	27	0	0♌	45	24	20	22	27	1	1	11	24	20	22	27	1	1	37	24	20
1 25 7	23	28	1	1	33	24	21	23	28	2	1	58	25	21	23	28	2	2	24	25	21
1 28 52	24	29	2	2	20	25	22	24	29	2	2	45	25	22	24	29	3	3	11	26	22
1 32 39	25	♊	3	3	8	26	23	25	♊	3	3	32	26	23	25	♊	4	3	58	27	23
1 36 26	26	1	4	3	55	27	24	26	1	4	4	20	27	24	26	1	5	4	45	27	24
1 40 13	27	1	5	4	43	28	25	27	2	5	5	7	28	25	27	2	5	5	32	28	25
1 44 1	28	2	6	5	31	29	26	28	3	6	5	55	29	26	28	3	6	6	19	29	26
1 47 49	29	3	6	6	18	♍	27	29	4	7	6	42	♍	27	29	4	7	7	6	♍	27
1 51 38	♉	4	7	7	6	0	28	♉	5	8	7	30	1	28	♉	5	8	7	54	1	28
1 55 28	1	5	8	7	55	1	29	1	5	8	8	18	1	29	1	6	9	8	41	2	29
1 59 18	2	6	9	8	43	2	♎	2	6	9	9	6	2	♎	2	7	10	9	29	3	♎
2 3 9	3	7	10	9	31	3	1	3	7	10	9	54	3	1	3	8	11	10	17	3	1
2 7 0	4	8	11	10	20	4	2	4	8	11	10	42	4	2	4	8	11	11	4	4	2
2 10 52	5	9	12	11	8	5	3	5	9	12	11	30	5	3	5	9	12	11	53	5	3
2 14 45	6	10	12	11	57	6	4	6	10	13	12	19	6	4	6	10	13	12	41	6	4
2 18 38	7	11	13	12	46	7	5	7	11	14	13	7	7	5	7	11	14	13	29	7	5
2 22 32	8	12	14	13	35	7	6	8	12	14	13	56	8	6	8	12	15	14	17	8	6
2 26 26	9	13	15	14	24	8	7	9	13	15	14	45	9	7	9	13	16	15	6	9	7
2 30 22	10	14	16	15	14	9	8	10	14	16	15	34	9	8	10	14	17	15	55	10	8
2 34 17	11	15	17	16	3	10	9	11	15	17	16	23	10	9	11	15	17	16	44	10	9
2 38 14	12	16	18	16	53	11	10	12	16	18	17	13	11	10	12	16	18	17	33	11	10
2 42 11	13	17	18	17	43	12	11	13	17	19	18	2	12	11	13	17	19	18	22	12	10
2 46 10	14	18	19	18	33	13	12	14	18	20	18	52	13	12	14	18	20	19	11	13	11
HOUSES	4	5	6	7		8	9	4	5	6	7		8	9	4	5	6	7		8	9

LATITUDE 31° S. LATITUDE 32° S. LATITUDE 33° S.

LATITUDE 31° N. LATITUDE 32° N. LATITUDE 33° N.

SIDEREAL TIME	10 ♉	11 ♊	12 ♋	ASC ♌		2 ♍	3 ♎	10 ♉	11 ♊	12 ♋	ASC ♌		2 ♍	3 ♎	10 ♉	11 ♊	12 ♋	ASC ♌		2 ♍	3 ♎
H M S	°	°	°	°	'	°	°	°	°	°	°	'	°	°	°	°	°	°	'	°	°
2 50 8	15	18	20	19	23	14	13	15	19	21	19	42	14	13	15	19	21	20	1	14	12
2 54 8	16	19	21	20	14	15	14	16	20	21	20	32	15	13	16	20	22	20	51	15	13
2 58 8	17	20	22	21	4	16	15	17	21	22	21	22	16	14	17	21	23	21	40	16	14
3 2 9	18	21	23	21	55	17	16	18	21	23	22	13	17	15	18	22	24	22	31	17	15
3 6 10	19	22	24	22	46	18	17	19	22	24	23	3	18	16	19	23	24	23	21	18	16
3 10 13	20	23	25	23	37	18	18	20	23	25	23	54	19	17	20	24	25	24	11	19	17
3 14 16	21	24	26	24	29	19	19	21	24	26	24	45	19	18	21	24	26	25	2	20	18
3 18 20	22	25	26	25	20	20	20	22	25	27	25	36	20	19	22	25	27	25	53	20	19
3 22 24	23	26	27	26	12	21	21	23	26	28	26	28	21	20	23	26	28	26	44	21	20
3 26 30	24	27	28	27	4	22	22	24	27	28	27	19	22	21	24	27	29	27	35	22	21
3 30 36	25	28	29	27	56	23	23	25	28	29	28	11	23	22	25	28	♌	28	26	23	22
3 34 42	26	29	♌	28	48	24	24	26	29	♌	29	3	24	24	26	29	1	29	18	24	23
3 38 50	27	♋	1	29	41	25	25	27	♋	1	29	55	25	25	27	♋	1	0♍	10	25	24
3 42 58	28	1	2	0♍	33	26	26	28	1	2	0♍	47	26	26	28	1	2	1	2	26	25
3 47 7	29	2	3	1	26	27	27	29	2	3	1	40	27	27	29	2	3	1	54	27	26
3 51 16	♊	3	4	2	19	28	28	♊	3	4	2	33	28	28	♊	3	4	2	46	28	27
3 55 26	1	4	5	3	13	29	29	1	4	5	3	26	29	29	1	4	5	3	38	29	28
3 59 37	2	5	5	4	6	♎	♏	2	5	6	4	19	♎	♏	2	5	6	4	31	♎	29
4 3 49	3	5	6	5	0	1	1	3	6	7	5	12	1	1	3	6	7	5	24	1	♏
4 8 1	4	6	7	5	54	2	2	4	7	8	6	5	2	2	4	7	8	6	17	2	2
4 12 14	5	7	8	6	48	3	3	5	8	9	6	59	3	3	5	8	9	7	10	3	3
4 16 27	6	8	9	7	42	4	4	6	9	9	7	53	4	4	6	9	10	8	3	4	4
4 20 41	7	9	10	8	36	5	5	7	9	10	8	47	5	5	7	10	11	8	57	5	5
4 24 56	8	10	11	9	31	6	6	8	10	11	9	41	6	6	8	11	12	9	51	6	6
4 29 11	9	11	12	10	25	7	7	9	11	12	10	35	7	7	9	12	12	10	44	7	7
4 33 27	10	12	13	11	20	8	8	10	12	13	11	29	8	8	10	13	13	11	38	8	8
4 37 43	11	13	14	12	15	9	9	11	13	14	12	24	9	9	11	14	14	12	33	9	9
4 41 59	12	14	15	13	10	10	10	12	14	15	13	19	10	10	12	14	15	13	27	10	10
4 46 17	13	15	16	14	6	11	11	13	15	16	14	13	11	11	13	15	16	14	21	11	11
4 50 34	14	16	17	15	1	12	12	14	16	17	15	8	12	12	14	16	17	15	16	12	12
4 54 53	15	17	18	15	57	13	13	15	17	18	16	3	13	13	15	17	18	16	10	13	13
4 59 11	16	18	19	16	52	14	14	16	18	19	16	59	14	14	16	18	19	17	5	14	14
5 3 30	17	19	20	17	48	15	15	17	19	20	17	54	15	15	17	19	20	18	0	15	15
5 7 49	18	20	21	18	44	16	16	18	20	21	18	49	16	16	18	20	21	18	55	16	16
5 12 9	19	21	22	19	40	17	17	19	21	22	19	45	17	17	19	21	22	19	50	17	17
5 16 29	20	22	23	20	36	18	18	20	22	23	20	41	18	18	20	22	23	20	45	17	18
5 20 49	21	23	23	21	32	19	19	21	23	24	21	36	19	19	21	23	24	21	40	18	19
5 25 10	22	24	24	22	28	20	20	22	24	25	22	32	20	20	22	24	25	22	36	19	20
5 29 31	23	25	25	23	25	21	21	23	25	26	23	28	21	21	23	25	26	23	31	20	21
5 33 51	24	26	26	24	21	22	22	24	26	27	24	24	22	22	24	26	27	24	27	21	22
5 38 13	25	27	27	25	17	23	23	25	27	28	25	20	23	23	25	27	28	25	22	22	23
5 42 34	26	28	28	26	14	24	24	26	28	29	26	16	24	24	26	28	29	26	18	23	24
5 46 55	27	29	29	27	10	25	25	27	29	♏	27	12	25	25	27	29	♏	27	13	24	25
5 51 17	28	♌	♍	28	7	26	26	28	♌	1	28	8	26	26	28	♌	1	28	9	25	26
5 55 38	29	1	1	29	3	27	27	29	1	2	29	4	27	27	29	1	2	29	4	26	27
HOUSES	4	5	6	7		8	9	4	5	6	7		8	9	4	5	6	7		8	9

LATITUDE 31° S. LATITUDE 32° S. LATITUDE 33° S.

LATITUDE 31° N. LATITUDE 32° N. LATITUDE 33° N.

SIDEREAL TIME H M S	10 S	11 ♌	12 ♍	ASC ♎ ° '	2 ♎	3 ♏	10 S	11 ♌	12 ♍	ASC ♎ ° '	2 ♎	3 ♏	10 S	11 ♌	12 ♍	ASC ♎ ° '	2 ♎	3 ♏
6 0 0	0	2	2	0 0	28	28	0	2	2	0 0	28	28	0	2	3	0 0	27	28
6 4 22	1	3	3	0 57	29	29	1	3	3	0 56	28	29	1	3	4	0 56	28	29
6 8 43	2	4	4	1 53	♏	♐	2	4	4	1 52	29	♐	2	4	5	1 51	29	♐
6 13 5	3	5	5	2 50	1	1	3	5	5	2 48	♏	1	3	5	6	2 47	♏	1
6 17 26	4	6	6	3 46	2	2	4	6	6	3 44	1	2	4	6	7	3 42	1	2
6 21 47	5	7	7	4 43	3	3	5	7	7	4 40	2	3	5	7	8	4 38	2	3
6 26 9	6	8	8	5 39	4	4	6	8	8	5 36	3	4	6	8	9	5 33	3	4
6 30 29	7	9	9	6 35	5	5	7	9	9	6 32	4	5	7	9	10	6 29	4	5
6 34 50	8	10	10	7 32	6	6	8	10	10	7 28	5	6	8	10	11	7 24	5	6
6 39 11	9	11	11	8 28	7	7	9	11	11	8 24	6	7	9	11	12	8 20	6	7
6 43 31	10	12	12	9 24	7	8	10	12	12	9 19	7	8	10	12	12	9 15	7	8
6 47 51	11	13	13	10 20	8	9	11	13	13	10 15	8	9	11	13	13	10 10	8	9
6 52 11	12	14	14	11 16	9	10	12	14	14	11 11	9	10	12	14	14	11 5	9	10
6 56 30	13	15	15	12 12	10	11	13	15	15	12 6	10	11	13	15	15	12 0	10	11
7 0 49	14	16	16	13 8	11	12	14	16	16	13 1	11	12	14	16	16	12 55	11	12
7 5 7	15	17	17	14 3	12	13	15	17	17	13 57	12	13	15	17	17	13 50	12	13
7 9 26	16	18	18	14 59	13	14	16	18	18	14 52	13	14	16	18	18	14 44	13	14
7 13 43	17	19	19	15 54	14	15	17	19	19	15 47	14	15	17	19	19	15 39	14	15
7 18 0	18	20	20	16 50	15	16	18	20	20	16 41	15	16	18	20	20	16 33	15	16
7 22 17	19	21	21	17 45	16	17	19	21	21	17 36	16	17	19	21	21	17 27	16	16
7 26 33	20	22	22	18 40	17	18	20	22	22	18 31	17	18	20	22	22	18 22	17	17
7 30 49	21	23	23	19 35	18	19	21	23	23	19 25	18	19	21	23	23	19 16	18	18
7 35 4	22	24	24	20 29	19	20	22	24	24	20 19	19	20	22	24	24	20 9	18	19
7 39 19	23	25	25	21 24	20	21	23	25	25	21 13	20	21	23	25	25	21 3	19	20
7 43 33	24	26	26	22 18	21	22	24	26	26	22 7	21	21	24	26	26	21 57	20	21
7 47 46	25	27	27	23 12	22	23	25	27	27	23 1	21	22	25	27	27	22 50	21	22
7 51 59	26	28	28	24 6	23	24	26	28	28	23 55	22	23	26	28	28	23 43	22	23
7 56 11	27	29	29	25 0	24	25	27	29	29	24 48	23	24	27	29	29	24 36	23	24
8 0 23	28	♏	♎	25 54	25	25	28	♏	♎	25 41	24	25	28	♏	♎	25 29	24	25
8 4 34	29	1	1	26 47	25	26	29	1	1	26 34	25	26	29	1	1	26 22	25	26
8 8 44	♌	2	2	27 41	26	27	♌	2	2	27 27	26	27	♌	3	2	27 14	26	27
8 12 53	1	3	3	28 34	27	28	1	3	3	28 20	27	28	1	4	3	28 6	27	28
8 17 2	2	4	4	29 27	28	29	2	4	4	29 13	28	29	2	5	4	28 58	28	29
8 21 10	3	5	5	0♏ 19	29	♑	3	5	5	0♏ 5	29	♑	3	6	5	29 50	29	♑
8 25 18	4	6	6	1 12	♐	1	4	6	6	0 57	♐	1	4	7	6	0♏ 42	29	1
8 29 24	5	7	7	2 4	1	2	5	8	7	1 49	1	2	5	8	7	1 34	♐	2
8 33 30	6	8	8	2 56	2	3	6	9	8	2 41	2	3	6	9	8	2 25	1	3
8 37 36	7	9	9	3 48	3	4	7	10	9	3 32	2	4	7	10	9	3 16	2	4
8 41 40	8	10	10	4 40	4	5	8	11	10	4 24	3	5	8	11	10	4 7	3	5
8 45 44	9	11	11	5 31	5	6	9	12	11	5 15	4	6	9	12	10	4 58	4	6
8 49 47	10	12	12	6 23	5	7	10	13	11	6 6	5	7	10	13	11	5 49	5	6
8 53 50	11	13	12	7 14	6	8	11	14	12	6 57	6	8	11	14	12	6 39	6	7
8 57 51	12	14	13	8 5	7	9	12	15	13	7 47	7	9	12	15	13	7 29	6	8
9 1 52	13	15	14	8 56	8	10	13	16	14	8 38	8	9	13	16	14	8 20	7	9
9 5 52	14	16	15	9 46	9	11	14	17	15	9 28	9	10	14	17	15	9 9	8	10
HOUSES	4	5	6	7	8	9	4	5	6	7	8	9	4	5	6	7	8	9

LATITUDE 31° S. LATITUDE 32° S. LATITUDE 33° S.

LATITUDE 31° N.   LATITUDE 32° N.   LATITUDE 33° N.

SIDEREAL TIME	10 ♌	11 ♍	12 ♎	ASC ♏		2 ♐	3 ♑	10 ♌	11 ♍	12 ♎	ASC ♏		2 ♐	3 ♑	10 ♌	11 ♍	12 ♎	ASC ♏		2 ♐	3 ♑
H M S	°	°	°	°	'	°	°	°	°	°	°	'	°	°	°	°	°	°	'	°	°
9 9 52	15	17	16	10	37	10	12	15	17	16	10	18	9	11	15	18	16	9	59	9	11
9 13 50	16	18	17	11	27	11	12	16	18	17	11	8	10	12	16	19	17	10	49	10	12
9 17 49	17	19	18	12	17	12	13	17	19	18	11	58	11	13	17	20	18	11	38	11	13
9 21 46	18	20	19	13	7	12	14	18	20	19	12	47	12	14	18	20	19	12	27	12	14
9 25 42	19	21	20	13	57	13	15	19	21	20	13	37	13	15	19	21	20	13	16	13	15
9 29 38	20	22	21	14	46	14	16	20	22	21	14	26	14	16	20	22	20	14	5	13	16
9 33 34	21	23	22	15	36	15	17	21	23	21	15	15	15	17	21	23	21	14	54	14	17
9 37 28	22	24	23	16	25	16	18	22	24	22	16	4	16	18	22	24	22	15	43	15	18
9 41 22	23	25	23	17	14	17	19	23	25	23	16	53	16	19	23	25	23	16	31	16	19
9 45 15	24	26	24	18	3	18	20	24	26	24	17	41	17	20	24	26	24	17	19	17	20
9 49 8	25	27	25	18	52	18	21	25	27	25	18	30	18	21	25	27	25	18	7	18	21
9 53 0	26	28	26	19	40	19	22	26	28	26	19	18	19	22	26	28	26	18	56	19	22
9 56 51	27	29	27	20	29	20	23	27	29	27	20	6	20	23	27	29	27	19	43	19	22
10 0 42	28	♎	28	21	17	21	24	28	♎	28	20	54	21	24	28	♎	27	20	31	20	23
10 4 32	29	1	29	22	5	22	25	29	1	29	21	42	22	25	29	1	28	21	19	21	24
10 8 22	♍	2	♏	22	54	23	26	♍	2	29	22	30	22	25	♍	2	29	22	6	22	25
10 12 11	1	3	0	23	42	24	27	1	3	♏	23	18	23	26	1	3	♏	22	54	23	26
10 15 59	2	4	1	24	29	24	28	2	4	1	24	5	24	27	2	4	1	23	41	24	27
10 19 47	3	5	2	25	17	25	29	3	5	2	24	53	25	28	3	5	2	24	28	25	28
10 23 34	4	6	3	26	5	26	29	4	6	3	25	40	26	29	4	6	3	25	15	25	29
10 27 21	5	7	4	26	52	27	♒	5	7	4	26	28	27	♒	5	7	3	26	2	26	♒
10 31 8	6	8	5	27	40	28	1	6	8	5	27	15	28	1	6	8	4	26	49	27	1
10 34 53	7	9	6	28	27	29	2	7	9	5	28	2	28	2	7	9	5	27	36	28	2
10 38 39	8	10	6	29	15	♑	3	8	10	6	28	49	29	3	8	10	6	28	23	29	3
10 42 24	9	11	7	0 ♐	2	0	4	9	11	7	29	36	♑	4	9	11	7	29	10	♑	4
10 46 8	10	12	8	0	49	1	5	10	12	8	0 ♐	23	1	5	10	11	8	29	56	1	5
10 49 52	11	12	9	1	36	2	6	11	12	9	1	10	2	6	11	12	8	0 ♐	43	1	6
10 53 36	12	13	10	2	24	3	7	12	13	10	1	57	3	7	12	13	9	1	30	2	7
10 57 20	13	14	11	3	11	4	8	13	14	10	2	44	4	8	13	14	10	2	16	3	8
11 1 3	14	15	11	3	58	5	9	14	15	11	3	30	4	9	14	15	11	3	3	4	9
11 4 45	15	16	12	4	45	6	10	15	16	12	4	17	5	10	15	16	12	3	49	5	10
11 8 28	16	17	13	5	32	7	11	16	17	13	5	4	6	11	16	17	13	4	36	6	11
11 12 10	17	18	14	6	19	7	12	17	18	14	5	51	7	12	17	18	13	5	22	7	12
11 15 52	18	19	15	7	6	8	13	18	19	14	6	38	8	13	18	19	14	6	9	8	13
11 19 33	19	20	16	7	53	9	14	19	20	15	7	24	9	14	19	20	15	6	55	8	14
11 23 15	20	21	16	8	40	10	15	20	21	16	8	11	10	15	20	21	16	7	42	9	15
11 26 56	21	22	17	9	27	11	16	21	22	17	8	58	11	16	21	22	17	8	29	10	16
11 30 37	22	23	18	10	14	12	17	22	23	18	9	45	11	17	22	22	17	9	15	11	17
11 34 17	23	23	19	11	1	13	18	23	23	19	10	32	12	18	23	23	18	10	2	12	18
11 37 58	24	24	20	11	48	14	19	24	24	19	11	19	13	19	24	24	19	10	49	13	19
11 41 39	25	25	20	12	36	14	20	25	25	20	12	6	14	20	25	25	20	11	35	14	20
11 45 19	26	26	21	13	23	15	21	26	26	21	12	53	15	21	26	26	21	12	22	15	21
11 48 59	27	27	22	14	10	16	22	27	27	22	13	40	16	22	27	27	21	13	9	16	22
11 52 40	28	28	23	14	58	17	23	28	28	23	14	27	17	23	28	28	22	13	56	16	23
11 56 20	29	29	24	15	46	18	24	29	29	23	15	15	18	24	29	29	23	14	43	17	24
HOUSES	4	5	6	7		8	9	4	5	6	7		8	9	4	5	6	7		8	9

LATITUDE 31° S.   LATITUDE 32° S.   LATITUDE 33° S.

	LATITUDE 31° N.						LATITUDE 32° N.						LATITUDE 33° N.					
SIDEREAL TIME	10 ♎	11 ♏	12 ♏	ASC ♐	2 ♑	3 ♒	10 ♎	11 ♏	12 ♏	ASC ♐	2 ♑	3 ♒	10 ♎	11 ♏	12 ♏	ASC ♐	2 ♑	3 ♒
H M S	°	°	°	° '	°	°	°	°	°	° '	°	°	°	°	°	° '	°	°
12 0 0	0	0	24	16 33	19	25	0	0	24	16 2	19	25	0	0	24	15 31	18	25
12 3 40	1	1	25	17 21	20	26	1	1	25	16 50	20	26	1	0	25	16 18	19	26
12 7 20	2	2	26	18 9	21	27	2	1	26	17 38	20	27	2	1	25	17 6	20	27
12 11 1	3	2	27	18 57	22	28	3	2	27	18 26	21	28	3	2	26	17 53	21	28
12 14 41	4	3	28	19 45	23	29	4	3	27	19 14	22	29	4	3	27	18 41	22	29
12 18 21	5	4	28	20 34	24	♓	5	4	28	20 2	23	♓	5	4	28	19 29	23	♓
12 22 2	6	5	29	21 22	25	1	6	5	29	20 50	24	1	6	5	29	20 17	24	1
12 25 42	7	6	♐	22 11	26	2	7	6	♐	21 39	25	2	7	6	29	21 6	25	2
12 29 23	8	7	1	23 0	27	3	8	7	1	22 28	26	3	8	7	♐	21 54	26	3
12 33 4	9	8	2	23 49	27	4	9	8	1	23 16	27	4	9	8	1	22 43	27	4
12 36 45	10	9	3	24 39	28	5	10	9	2	24 6	28	5	10	8	2	23 32	28	5
12 40 27	11	9	3	25 28	29	7	11	9	3	24 55	29	6	11	9	3	24 21	29	6
12 44 8	12	10	4	26 18	♒	8	12	10	4	25 45	♒	8	12	10	4	25 11	♒	7
12 47 50	13	11	5	27 8	1	9	13	11	5	26 35	1	9	13	11	4	26 0	1	8
12 51 32	14	12	6	27 58	2	10	14	12	5	27 25	2	10	14	12	5	26 50	2	10
12 55 15	15	13	7	28 49	3	11	15	13	6	28 15	3	11	15	13	6	27 41	3	11
12 58 57	16	14	7	29 40	4	12	16	14	7	29 6	4	12	16	14	7	28 31	4	12
13 2 40	17	15	8	0♑ 31	5	13	17	15	8	29 57	5	13	17	15	8	29 22	5	13
13 6 24	18	16	9	1 23	6	14	18	16	9	0♑ 48	6	14	18	15	8	0♑ 13	6	14
13 10 8	19	17	10	2 14	7	15	19	16	10	1 40	7	15	19	16	9	1 5	7	15
13 13 52	20	17	11	3 6	8	16	20	17	10	2 32	8	16	20	17	10	1 57	8	16
13 17 36	21	18	11	3 59	10	17	21	18	11	3 24	9	17	21	18	11	2 49	9	17
13 21 21	22	19	12	4 52	11	18	22	19	12	4 17	10	18	22	19	12	3 41	10	18
13 25 7	23	20	13	5 45	12	20	23	20	13	5 10	11	20	23	20	12	4 34	11	20
13 28 52	24	21	14	6 39	13	21	24	21	14	6 4	12	21	24	21	13	5 28	12	21
13 32 39	25	22	15	7 33	14	22	25	22	14	6 58	13	22	25	21	14	6 22	13	22
13 36 26	26	23	16	8 27	15	23	26	23	15	7 52	15	23	26	22	15	7 16	14	23
13 40 13	27	24	16	9 22	16	24	27	23	16	8 47	16	24	27	23	16	8 10	15	24
13 44 1	28	24	17	10 17	17	25	28	24	17	9 42	17	25	28	24	17	9 6	16	25
13 47 49	29	25	18	11 13	18	26	29	25	18	10 38	18	26	29	25	17	10 1	18	26
13 51 38	♏	26	19	12 9	19	28	♏	26	19	11 34	19	27	♏	26	18	10 57	19	27
13 55 28	1	27	20	13 6	20	29	1	27	20	12 30	20	29	1	27	19	11 54	20	29
13 59 18	2	28	21	14 3	22	♈	2	28	20	13 28	21	♈	2	28	20	12 51	21	♈
14 3 9	3	29	22	15 1	23	1	3	29	21	14 25	22	1	3	29	21	13 49	22	1
14 7 0	4	♐	22	15 59	24	2	4	♐	22	15 24	24	2	4	♐	22	14 47	23	2
14 10 52	5	1	23	16 58	25	3	5	0	23	16 23	25	3	5	♐	23	15 46	25	3
14 14 45	6	1	24	17 58	26	4	6	1	24	17 22	26	4	6	1	23	16 45	26	4
14 18 38	7	2	25	18 58	27	6	7	2	25	18 22	27	6	7	2	24	17 45	27	6
14 22 32	8	3	26	19 58	29	7	8	3	26	19 23	28	7	8	3	25	18 46	28	7
14 26 26	9	4	27	21 0	♓	8	9	4	26	20 24	♓	8	9	4	26	19 47	29	8
14 30 22	10	5	28	22 2	1	9	10	5	27	21 26	1	9	10	5	27	20 49	♓	9
14 34 17	11	6	29	23 4	2	10	11	6	28	22 28	2	10	11	6	28	21 52	2	10
14 38 14	12	7	♑	24 7	3	11	12	7	29	23 32	3	11	12	7	29	22 55	3	11
14 42 11	13	8	0	25 11	5	13	13	8	♑	24 36	5	13	13	7	♑	23 59	4	13
14 46 10	14	9	1	26 16	6	14	14	8	1	25 40	6	14	14	8	1	25 4	6	14
HOUSES	4	5	6	7	8	9	4	5	6	7	8	9	4	5	6	7	8	9

LATITUDE 31° S.　　　LATITUDE 32° S.　　　LATITUDE 33° S.

LATITUDE 31° N. LATITUDE 32° N. LATITUDE 33° N.

LATITUDE 31° N.

SIDEREAL TIME	10 ♏	11 ♐	12 ♑	ASC ♑ °	'	2 ♓	3 ♈
14 50 8	15	10	2	27	21	7	15
14 54 8	16	10	3	28	27	9	16
14 58 8	17	11	4	29	34	10	17
15 2 9	18	12	5	0♒	41	11	18
15 6 10	19	13	6	1	50	12	20
15 10 13	20	14	7	2	59	14	21
15 14 16	21	15	8	4	9	15	22
15 18 20	22	16	9	5	19	16	23
15 22 24	23	17	10	6	31	18	24
15 26 30	24	18	11	7	43	19	25
15 30 36	25	19	12	8	56	20	27
15 34 42	26	20	13	10	10	22	28
15 38 50	27	21	14	11	25	23	29
15 42 58	28	22	15	12	41	24	♉
15 47 7	29	22	16	13	58	26	1
15 51 16	♐	23	17	15	15	27	3
15 55 26	1	24	18	16	34	28	4
15 59 37	2	25	19	17	53	♈	5
16 3 49	3	26	20	19	13	1	6
16 8 1	4	27	21	20	35	3	7
16 12 14	5	28	22	21	57	4	8
16 16 27	6	29	23	23	20	5	10
16 20 41	7	♑	24	24	43	7	11
16 24 56	8	1	25	26	8	8	12
16 29 11	9	2	26	27	34	10	13
16 33 27	10	3	28	29	0	11	14
16 37 43	11	4	29	0♓	27	12	15
16 41 59	12	5	♒	1	55	14	16
16 46 17	13	6	1	3	24	15	18
16 50 34	14	7	2	4	53	17	19
16 54 53	15	8	3	6	24	18	20
16 59 11	16	9	4	7	55	19	21
17 3 30	17	10	6	9	26	21	22
17 7 49	18	11	7	10	59	22	23
17 12 9	19	12	8	12	32	23	24
17 16 29	20	13	9	14	5	25	25
17 20 49	21	14	10	15	39	26	27
17 25 10	22	15	12	17	13	28	28
17 29 31	23	16	13	18	48	29	29
17 33 51	24	17	14	20	24	♉	♊
17 38 13	25	18	15	21	59	2	1
17 42 34	26	19	17	23	35	3	2
17 46 55	27	20	18	25	11	4	3
17 51 17	28	21	19	26	47	6	4
17 55 38	29	23	20	28	24	7	5
HOUSES	4	5	6	7		8	9

LATITUDE 32° N.

SIDEREAL TIME	10 ♏	11 ♐	12 ♑	ASC ♑ °	'	2 ♓	3 ♈
14 50 8	15	9	2	26	46	7	15
14 54 8	16	10	3	27	52	8	16
14 58 8	17	11	4	28	59	10	17
15 2 9	18	12	5	0♒	6	11	18
15 6 10	19	13	6	1	15	12	20
15 10 13	20	14	7	2	24	14	21
15 14 16	21	15	8	3	34	15	22
15 18 20	22	16	8	4	45	16	23
15 22 24	23	17	9	5	57	18	24
15 26 30	24	18	10	7	10	19	26
15 30 36	25	19	11	8	23	20	27
15 34 42	26	19	12	9	38	22	28
15 38 50	27	20	13	10	53	23	29
15 42 58	28	21	14	12	9	24	♉
15 47 7	29	22	15	13	26	26	1
15 51 16	♐	23	16	14	45	27	3
15 55 26	1	24	17	16	4	28	4
15 59 37	2	25	19	17	23	♈	5
16 3 49	3	26	20	18	44	1	6
16 8 1	4	27	21	20	6	3	7
16 12 14	5	28	22	21	29	4	9
16 16 27	6	29	23	22	52	5	10
16 20 41	7	♑	24	24	17	7	11
16 24 56	8	1	25	25	42	8	12
16 29 11	9	2	26	27	9	10	13
16 33 27	10	3	27	28	36	11	14
16 37 43	11	4	28	0♓	4	12	15
16 41 59	12	5	29	1	33	14	17
16 46 17	13	6	♒	3	3	15	18
16 50 34	14	7	2	4	33	17	19
16 54 53	15	8	3	6	5	18	20
16 59 11	16	9	4	7	37	20	21
17 3 30	17	10	5	9	10	21	22
17 7 49	18	11	6	10	43	22	23
17 12 9	19	12	8	12	17	24	25
17 16 29	20	13	9	13	52	25	26
17 20 49	21	14	10	15	27	26	27
17 25 10	22	15	11	17	3	28	28
17 29 31	23	16	13	18	39	29	29
17 33 51	24	17	14	20	15	♉	♊
17 38 13	25	18	15	21	52	2	1
17 42 34	26	19	16	23	29	3	2
17 46 55	27	20	18	25	7	5	3
17 51 17	28	21	19	26	45	6	4
17 55 38	29	22	20	28	22	7	6
HOUSES	4	5	6	7		8	9

LATITUDE 33° N.

SIDEREAL TIME	10 ♏	11 ♐	12 ♑	ASC ♑ °	'	2 ♓	3 ♈
14 50 8	15	9	1	26	9	7	15
14 54 8	16	10	2	27	15	8	16
14 58 8	17	11	3	28	22	9	17
15 2 9	18	12	4	29	30	11	19
15 6 10	19	13	5	0♒	39	12	20
15 10 13	20	14	6	1	49	13	21
15 14 16	21	15	7	2	59	15	22
15 18 20	22	16	8	4	10	16	23
15 22 24	23	16	9	5	22	17	24
15 26 30	24	17	10	6	35	19	26
15 30 36	25	18	11	7	49	20	27
15 34 42	26	19	12	9	4	22	28
15 38 50	27	20	13	10	20	23	29
15 42 58	28	21	14	11	36	24	♉
15 47 7	29	22	15	12	54	26	2
15 51 16	♐	23	16	14	12	27	3
15 55 26	1	24	17	15	32	28	4
15 59 37	2	25	18	16	53	♈	5
16 3 49	3	26	19	18	14	1	6
16 8 1	4	27	20	19	36	3	7
16 12 14	5	28	21	21	0	4	9
16 16 27	6	29	22	22	24	6	10
16 20 41	7	♑	23	23	49	7	11
16 24 56	8	1	25	25	16	8	12
16 29 11	9	2	26	26	43	10	13
16 33 27	10	3	27	28	11	11	14
16 37 43	11	4	28	29	40	13	16
16 41 59	12	5	29	1♓	10	14	17
16 46 17	13	6	♒	2	41	15	18
16 50 34	14	7	1	4	12	17	19
16 54 53	15	8	3	5	45	18	20
16 59 11	16	9	4	7	18	20	21
17 3 30	17	10	5	8	52	21	22
17 7 49	18	11	6	10	27	22	24
17 12 9	19	12	7	12	2	24	25
17 16 29	20	13	9	13	38	25	26
17 20 49	21	14	10	15	14	27	27
17 25 10	22	15	11	16	51	28	28
17 29 31	23	16	12	18	29	29	29
17 33 51	24	17	13	20	7	♉	♊
17 38 13	25	18	15	21	45	2	1
17 42 34	26	19	16	23	24	3	2
17 46 55	27	20	17	25	3	5	4
17 51 17	28	21	19	26	42	6	5
17 55 38	29	22	20	28	21	7	6
HOUSES	4	5	6	7		8	9

LATITUDE 31° S. LATITUDE 32° S. LATITUDE 33° S.

LATITUDE 31° N.   LATITUDE 32° N.   LATITUDE 33° N.

SIDEREAL TIME	10 ♑	11 ♑	12 ♒	ASC ♈	2 ♉	3 ♊	10 ♑	11 ♑	12 ♒	ASC ♈	2 ♉	3 ♊	10 ♑	11 ♑	12 ♒	ASC ♈	2 ♉	3 ♊
H M S	°	°	°	° '	°	°	°	°	°	° '	°	°	°	°	°	° '	°	°
18 0 0	0	24	22	0 0	8	6	0	23	21	0 0	9	7	0	23	21	0 0	9	7
18 4 22	1	25	23	1 36	10	7	1	24	23	1 38	10	8	1	24	23	1 39	10	8
18 8 43	2	26	24	3 13	11	9	2	26	24	3 15	11	9	2	25	24	3 18	11	9
18 13 5	3	27	26	4 49	12	10	3	27	25	4 53	12	10	3	26	25	4 57	13	10
18 17 26	4	28	27	6 25	13	11	4	28	27	6 31	14	11	4	28	27	6 36	14	11
18 21 47	5	29	28	8 1	15	12	5	29	28	8 8	15	12	5	29	28	8 15	15	12
18 26 9	6	♒	♓	9 36	16	13	6	♒	29	9 45	16	13	6	♒	29	9 53	17	13
18 30 29	7	1	1	11 12	17	14	7	1	♓	11 21	17	14	7	1	♓	11 31	18	14
18 34 50	8	2	2	12 47	18	15	8	2	2	12 57	19	15	8	2	2	13 9	19	15
18 39 11	9	3	4	14 21	20	16	9	3	4	14 33	20	16	9	3	3	14 46	20	16
18 43 31	10	5	5	15 55	21	17	10	4	5	16 8	21	17	10	4	5	16 22	21	17
18 47 51	11	6	7	17 28	22	18	11	5	6	17 43	22	18	11	5	6	17 58	23	18
18 52 11	12	7	8	19 1	23	19	12	7	8	19 17	24	19	12	6	8	19 33	24	19
18 56 30	13	8	9	20 34	24	20	13	8	9	20 50	25	20	13	8	9	21 8	25	20
19 0 49	14	9	11	22 5	26	21	14	9	10	22 23	26	21	14	9	10	22 42	26	21
19 5 7	15	10	12	23 36	27	22	15	10	12	23 55	27	22	15	10	12	24 15	27	22
19 9 26	16	11	13	25 7	28	23	16	11	13	25 27	28	23	16	11	13	25 48	29	23
19 13 43	17	12	15	26 36	29	24	17	12	15	26 57	29	24	17	12	15	27 19	♊	24
19 18 0	18	14	16	28 5	♊	25	18	13	16	28 27	♊	25	18	13	16	28 50	1	25
19 22 17	19	15	18	29 33	1	26	19	15	18	29 56	2	26	19	14	17	0♉ 20	2	26
19 26 33	20	16	19	1♉ 0	2	27	20	16	19	1♉ 24	3	27	20	16	19	1 49	3	27
19 30 49	21	17	20	2 26	4	28	21	17	20	2 51	4	28	21	17	20	3 17	4	28
19 35 4	22	18	22	3 52	5	29	22	18	22	4 18	5	29	22	18	22	4 44	5	29
19 39 19	23	19	23	5 17	6	♋	23	19	23	5 43	6	♋	23	19	23	6 11	7	♋
19 43 33	24	20	25	6 40	7	1	24	20	25	7 8	7	1	24	20	24	7 36	8	1
19 47 46	25	22	26	8 3	8	2	25	21	26	8 31	8	2	25	21	26	9 0	9	2
19 51 59	26	23	27	9 25	9	3	26	23	27	9 54	9	3	26	23	27	10 24	10	3
19 56 11	27	24	29	10 47	10	4	27	24	29	11 16	10	4	27	24	29	11 46	11	4
20 0 23	28	25	♈	12 7	11	5	28	25	♈	12 37	11	5	28	25	♈	13 7	12	5
20 4 34	29	26	2	13 26	12	6	29	26	2	13 56	13	6	29	26	2	14 28	13	6
20 8 44	♒	27	3	14 45	13	7	♒	27	3	15 15	14	7	♒	27	3	15 48	14	7
20 12 53	1	29	4	16 2	14	8	1	29	4	16 34	15	8	1	28	4	17 6	15	8
20 17 2	2	♓	6	17 19	15	8	2	♓	6	17 51	16	9	2	♓	6	18 24	16	9
20 21 10	3	1	7	18 35	16	9	3	1	7	19 7	17	10	3	1	7	19 40	17	10
20 25 18	4	2	8	19 50	17	10	4	2	8	20 22	18	11	4	2	8	20 56	18	11
20 29 24	5	3	10	21 4	18	11	5	3	10	21 37	19	11	5	3	10	22 11	19	12
20 33 30	6	5	11	22 17	19	12	6	4	11	22 50	20	12	6	4	11	23 25	20	13
20 37 36	7	6	12	23 29	20	13	7	6	12	24 3	21	13	7	6	13	24 38	21	14
20 41 40	8	7	14	24 41	21	14	8	7	14	25 15	22	14	8	7	14	25 50	22	14
20 45 44	9	8	15	25 51	22	15	9	8	15	26 26	22	15	9	8	15	27 1	23	15
20 49 47	10	9	16	27 1	23	16	10	9	16	27 36	23	16	10	9	17	28 11	24	16
20 53 50	11	10	18	28 10	24	17	11	10	18	28 45	24	17	11	10	18	29 21	25	17
20 57 51	12	12	19	29 19	25	18	12	12	19	29 54	25	18	12	11	19	0♊ 30	26	18
21 1 52	13	13	20	0♊ 26	26	19	13	13	20	1♊ 1	26	19	13	13	21	1 38	27	19
21 5 52	14	14	21	1 33	27	20	14	14	22	2 8	27	20	14	14	22	2 45	28	20
HOUSES	4	5	6	7	8	9	4	5	6	7	8	9	4	5	6	7	8	9

LATITUDE 31° S.   LATITUDE 32° S.   LATITUDE 33° S.

LATITUDE 31° N.   LATITUDE 32° N.   LATITUDE 33° N.

SIDEREAL TIME H M S	10 ♒	11 ♓	12 ♈	ASC ♊	(′)	2 ♊	3 ♋	10 ♒	11 ♓	12 ♈	ASC ♊	(′)	2 ♊	3 ♋	10 ♒	11 ♓	12 ♈	ASC ♊	(′)	2 ♊	3 ♋
21 9 52	15	15	23	2	39	28	20	15	15	23	3	14	28	21	15	15	23	3	51	29	21
21 13 50	16	16	24	3	44	29	21	16	16	24	4	20	29	22	16	16	24	4	56	29	22
21 17 49	17	17	25	4	49	♋	22	17	17	25	5	24	♋	22	17	17	26	6	1	♋	23
21 21 46	18	19	27	5	53	0	23	18	19	27	6	28	1	23	18	19	27	7	5	1	23
21 25 42	19	20	28	6	56	1	24	19	20	28	7	32	2	24	19	20	28	8	8	2	24
21 29 38	20	21	29	7	58	2	25	20	21	29	8	34	3	25	20	21	29	9	11	3	25
21 33 34	21	22	♉	9	0	3	26	21	22	♉	9	36	4	26	21	22	♉	10	13	4	26
21 37 28	22	23	1	10	2	4	27	22	23	2	10	37	4	27	22	23	2	11	14	5	27
21 41 22	23	24	3	11	2	5	28	23	24	3	11	38	5	28	23	24	3	12	15	6	28
21 45 15	24	26	4	12	2	6	29	24	26	4	12	38	6	29	24	26	4	13	15	7	29
21 49 8	25	27	5	13	2	7	29	25	27	5	13	37	7	♌	25	27	5	14	14	7	♌
21 53 0	26	28	6	14	1	8	♌	26	28	6	14	36	8	0	26	28	7	15	13	8	1
21 56 51	27	29	7	14	59	8	1	27	29	8	15	35	9	1	27	29	8	16	11	9	1
22 0 42	28	♈	8	15	57	9	2	28	♈	9	16	32	10	2	28	♈	9	17	9	10	2
22 4 32	29	1	10	16	54	10	3	29	1	10	17	30	10	3	29	1	10	18	6	11	3
22 8 22	♓	2	11	17	51	11	4	♓	3	11	18	26	11	4	♓	3	11	19	3	12	4
22 12 11	1	4	12	18	47	12	5	1	4	12	19	22	12	5	1	4	12	19	59	13	5
22 15 59	2	5	13	19	43	13	6	2	5	13	20	18	13	6	2	5	14	20	54	13	6
22 19 47	3	6	14	20	38	14	6	3	6	14	21	13	14	7	3	6	15	21	50	14	7
22 23 34	4	7	15	21	33	14	7	4	7	15	22	8	15	7	4	7	16	22	44	15	8
22 27 21	5	8	16	22	27	15	8	5	8	17	23	2	16	8	5	8	17	23	38	16	9
22 31 8	6	9	17	23	21	16	9	6	9	18	23	56	16	9	6	9	18	24	32	17	9
22 34 53	7	10	18	24	15	17	10	7	10	19	24	50	17	10	7	10	19	25	26	18	10
22 38 39	8	12	19	25	8	18	11	8	12	20	25	43	18	11	8	12	20	26	19	18	11
22 42 24	9	13	20	26	1	19	12	9	13	21	26	36	19	12	9	13	21	27	11	19	12
22 46 8	10	14	22	26	54	19	13	10	14	22	27	28	20	13	10	14	22	28	3	20	13
22 49 52	11	15	23	27	46	20	13	11	15	23	28	20	20	14	11	15	23	28	55	21	14
22 53 36	12	16	24	28	37	21	14	12	16	24	29	12	21	14	12	16	24	29	47	22	15
22 57 20	13	17	25	29	29	22	15	13	17	25	0♋	3	22	15	13	17	25	0♋	38	22	15
23 1 3	14	18	26	0♋	20	23	16	14	18	26	0	54	23	16	14	18	26	1	29	23	16
23 4 45	15	19	27	1	11	23	17	15	19	27	1	45	24	17	15	19	27	2	19	24	17
23 8 28	16	20	28	2	2	24	18	16	20	28	2	35	25	18	16	20	28	3	10	25	18
23 12 10	17	21	29	2	52	25	19	17	21	29	3	25	25	19	17	22	29	4	0	26	19
23 15 52	18	22	♊	3	42	26	20	18	22	♊	4	15	26	20	18	23	♊	4	49	26	20
23 19 33	19	23	1	4	32	27	21	19	24	1	5	5	27	21	19	24	1	5	39	27	21
23 23 15	20	25	2	5	21	27	21	20	25	2	5	54	28	21	20	25	2	6	28	28	22
23 26 56	21	26	3	6	11	28	22	21	26	3	6	44	29	22	21	26	3	7	17	29	22
23 30 37	22	27	3	7	0	29	23	22	27	4	7	32	29	23	22	27	4	8	6	♌	23
23 34 17	23	28	4	7	49	♌	24	23	28	5	8	21	♌	24	23	28	5	8	54	1	24
23 37 58	24	29	5	8	38	1	25	24	29	6	9	10	1	25	24	29	6	9	43	1	25
23 41 39	25	♉	6	9	26	2	26	25	♉	7	9	58	2	26	25	♉	7	10	31	2	26
23 45 19	26	1	7	10	15	2	27	26	1	8	10	46	3	27	26	1	8	11	19	3	27
23 48 59	27	2	8	11	3	3	28	27	2	9	11	34	3	28	27	2	9	12	7	4	28
23 52 40	28	3	9	11	51	4	28	28	3	10	12	22	4	29	28	3	10	12	54	5	29
23 56 20	29	4	10	12	39	5	29	29	4	10	13	10	5	29	29	4	11	13	42	5	♍
HOUSES	4	5	6	7		8	9	4	5	6	7		8	9	4	5	6	7		8	9

LATITUDE 31° S.   LATITUDE 32° S.   LATITUDE 33° S.

LATITUDE 34° N. LATITUDE 35° N. LATITUDE 36° N.

SIDEREAL TIME (H M S)	10 ♈	11 ♉	12 ♊	ASC ♋ °	'	2 ♌	3 ♍	10 ♈	11 ♉	12 ♊	ASC ♋ °	'	2 ♌	3 ♍	10 ♈	11 ♉	12 ♊	ASC ♋ °	'	2 ♌	3 ♍
0 0 0	0	5	12	15	1	6	1	0	5	13	15	34	7	1	0	6	13	16	7	7	1
0 3 40	1	6	13	15	48	7	1	1	7	14	16	21	7	1	1	7	14	16	54	8	2
0 7 20	2	7	14	16	35	8	2	2	8	14	17	8	8	2	2	8	15	17	40	9	2
0 11 1	3	8	15	17	22	9	3	3	9	15	17	54	9	3	3	9	16	18	27	9	3
0 14 41	4	9	16	18	9	10	4	4	10	16	18	41	10	4	4	10	17	19	13	10	4
0 18 21	5	10	17	18	56	10	5	5	11	17	19	27	11	5	5	11	18	19	59	11	5
0 22 2	6	11	18	19	42	11	6	6	12	18	20	13	11	6	6	12	18	20	45	12	6
0 25 43	7	12	18	20	29	12	7	7	13	19	21	0	12	7	7	13	19	21	31	13	7
0 29 23	8	13	19	21	15	13	8	8	14	20	21	46	13	8	8	14	20	22	17	13	8
0 33 4	9	14	20	22	1	14	9	9	15	21	22	32	14	9	9	15	21	23	3	14	9
0 36 45	10	15	21	22	48	14	9	10	16	22	23	18	15	10	10	16	22	23	49	15	10
0 40 27	11	16	22	23	34	15	10	11	17	22	24	4	15	10	11	17	23	24	34	16	10
0 44 8	12	17	23	24	20	16	11	12	18	23	24	50	16	11	12	18	24	25	20	17	11
0 47 50	13	18	24	25	7	17	12	13	19	24	25	36	17	12	13	19	25	26	6	17	12
0 51 32	14	19	25	25	53	18	13	14	20	25	26	22	18	13	14	20	25	26	51	18	13
0 55 15	15	20	26	26	39	18	14	15	21	26	27	8	19	14	15	21	26	27	37	19	14
0 58 57	16	21	26	27	25	19	15	16	22	27	27	54	20	15	16	22	27	28	23	20	15
1 2 40	17	22	27	28	12	20	16	17	23	28	28	40	20	16	17	23	28	29	9	21	16
1 6 24	18	23	28	28	58	21	17	18	24	29	29	26	21	17	18	24	29	29	54	21	17
1 10 8	19	24	29	29	44	22	18	19	25	29	0♌	12	22	18	19	25	♋	0♌	40	22	18
1 13 52	20	25	♋	0♌	31	23	19	20	25	♋	0	58	23	19	20	26	1	1	26	23	19
1 17 36	21	26	1	1	17	23	19	21	26	1	1	44	24	20	21	27	2	2	12	24	20
1 21 21	22	27	2	2	3	24	20	22	27	2	2	30	24	20	22	28	2	2	57	25	20
1 25 7	23	28	2	2	50	25	21	23	28	3	3	17	25	21	23	29	3	3	43	25	21
1 28 52	24	29	3	3	37	26	22	24	29	4	4	3	26	22	24	♊	4	4	29	26	22
1 32 39	25	♊	4	4	23	27	23	25	♊	4	4	49	27	23	25	1	5	5	15	27	23
1 36 26	26	1	5	5	10	28	24	26	1	5	5	36	28	24	26	1	6	6	2	28	24
1 40 13	27	2	6	5	57	28	25	27	2	6	6	22	29	25	27	2	7	6	48	29	25
1 44 1	28	3	7	6	44	29	26	28	3	7	7	9	29	26	28	3	7	7	34	♍	26
1 47 49	29	4	8	7	31	♍	27	29	4	8	7	55	♍	27	29	4	8	8	20	0	27
1 51 38	♉	5	8	8	18	1	28	♉	5	9	8	42	1	28	♉	5	9	9	7	1	28
1 55 28	1	6	9	9	5	2	29	1	6	10	9	29	2	29	1	6	10	9	53	2	29
1 59 18	2	7	10	9	52	3	♎	2	7	10	10	16	3	♎	2	7	11	10	40	3	♎
2 3 9	3	8	11	10	40	4	1	3	8	11	11	3	4	1	3	8	12	11	27	4	1
2 7 0	4	9	12	11	27	4	2	4	9	12	11	50	5	2	4	9	13	12	14	5	2
2 10 52	5	10	13	12	15	5	3	5	10	13	12	38	5	3	5	10	13	13	1	6	3
2 14 45	6	11	13	13	3	6	4	6	11	14	13	25	6	4	6	11	14	13	48	6	4
2 18 38	7	12	14	13	51	7	5	7	12	15	14	13	7	5	7	12	15	14	35	7	5
2 22 32	8	12	15	14	39	8	6	8	13	16	15	1	8	6	8	13	16	15	23	8	6
2 26 26	9	13	16	15	27	9	7	9	14	16	15	49	9	7	9	14	17	16	10	9	7
2 30 22	10	14	17	16	16	10	8	10	15	17	16	37	10	8	10	15	18	16	58	10	7
2 34 17	11	15	18	17	4	11	9	11	15	18	17	25	11	8	11	16	19	17	46	11	8
2 38 14	12	16	19	17	53	11	9	12	16	19	18	13	12	9	12	17	19	18	34	12	9
2 42 11	13	17	19	18	42	12	10	13	17	20	19	2	12	10	13	18	20	19	22	13	10
2 46 10	14	18	20	19	31	13	11	14	18	21	19	50	13	11	14	19	21	20	10	13	11
HOUSES	4	5	6	7		8	9	4	5	6	7		8	9	4	5	6	7		8	9

LATITUDE 34° S. LATITUDE 35° S. LATITUDE 36° S.

LATITUDE 34° N. LATITUDE 35° N. LATITUDE 36° N.

SIDEREAL TIME	10 ♉	11 ♊	12 ♋	ASC ♌		2 ♍	3 ♎	10 ♉	11 ♊	12 ♋	ASC ♌		2 ♍	3 ♎	10 ♉	11 ♊	12 ♋	ASC ♌		2 ♍	3 ♎
H M S	°	°	°	°	'	°	°	°	°	°	°	'	°	°	°	°	°	°	'	°	°
2 50 8	15	19	21	20	20	14	12	15	19	22	20	39	14	12	15	19	22	20	59	14	12
2 54 8	16	20	22	21	9	15	13	16	20	22	21	28	15	13	16	20	23	21	47	15	13
2 58 8	17	21	23	21	59	16	14	17	21	23	22	17	16	14	17	21	24	22	36	16	14
3 2 9	18	22	24	22	49	17	15	18	22	24	23	7	17	15	18	22	25	23	25	17	15
3 6 10	19	23	25	23	39	18	16	19	23	25	23	56	18	16	19	23	25	24	14	18	16
3 10 13	20	24	26	24	29	19	17	20	24	26	24	46	19	17	20	24	26	25	4	19	17
3 14 16	21	25	26	25	19	20	18	21	25	27	25	36	20	18	21	25	27	25	53	20	18
3 18 20	22	26	27	26	9	21	19	22	26	28	26	26	21	19	22	26	28	26	43	21	19
3 22 24	23	27	28	27	0	21	20	23	27	29	27	16	21	20	23	27	29	27	33	22	20
3 26 30	24	28	29	27	51	22	21	24	28	29	28	7	22	21	24	28	♋	28	23	22	21
3 30 36	25	28	♋	28	42	23	22	25	29	♋	28	57	23	22	25	29	1	29	13	23	22
3 34 42	26	29	1	29	33	24	23	26	♋	1	29	48	24	23	26	♋	2	0♍	3	24	23
3 38 50	27	♋	2	0♍	24	25	24	27	1	2	0♍	39	25	24	27	1	2	0	54	25	24
3 42 58	28	1	3	1	16	26	25	28	1	3	1	30	26	25	28	2	3	1	45	26	25
3 47 7	29	2	4	2	7	27	26	29	2	4	2	21	27	26	29	3	4	2	35	27	26
3 51 16	♊	3	5	2	59	28	27	♊	3	5	3	13	28	27	♊	4	5	3	27	28	27
3 55 26	1	4	5	3	51	29	28	1	4	6	4	5	29	28	1	5	6	4	18	29	28
3 59 37	2	5	6	4	44	♎	29	2	5	7	4	56	♎	29	2	6	7	5	9	♎	29
4 3 49	3	6	7	5	36	1	♏	3	6	8	5	48	1	♏	3	6	8	6	1	1	♏
4 8 1	4	7	8	6	29	2	1	4	7	8	6	41	2	1	4	7	9	6	52	2	1
4 12 14	5	8	9	7	21	3	2	5	8	9	7	33	3	2	5	8	10	7	44	3	2
4 16 27	6	9	10	8	14	4	3	6	9	10	8	25	4	3	6	9	11	8	36	4	3
4 20 41	7	10	11	9	7	5	4	7	10	11	9	18	5	4	7	10	11	9	29	5	4
4 24 56	8	11	12	10	1	6	5	8	11	12	10	11	6	5	8	11	12	10	21	6	5
4 29 11	9	12	13	10	54	7	6	9	12	13	11	4	7	6	9	12	13	11	13	7	6
4 33 27	10	13	14	11	48	8	7	10	13	14	11	57	8	7	10	13	14	12	6	8	7
4 37 43	11	14	15	12	41	9	8	11	14	15	12	50	9	8	11	14	15	12	59	8	8
4 41 59	12	15	16	13	35	10	10	12	15	16	13	43	10	9	12	15	16	13	52	9	9
4 46 17	13	16	16	14	29	11	11	13	16	17	14	37	10	10	13	16	17	14	45	10	10
4 50 34	14	17	17	15	23	12	12	14	17	18	15	31	11	11	14	17	18	15	38	11	11
4 54 53	15	18	18	16	17	12	13	15	18	19	16	24	12	12	15	18	19	16	31	12	12
4 59 11	16	19	19	17	12	13	14	16	19	20	17	18	13	13	16	19	20	17	25	13	13
5 3 30	17	20	20	18	6	14	15	17	20	21	18	12	14	14	17	20	21	18	18	14	14
5 7 49	18	21	21	19	1	15	16	18	21	21	19	6	15	15	18	21	22	19	12	15	15
5 12 9	19	21	22	19	55	16	17	19	22	22	20	0	16	16	19	22	23	20	5	16	16
5 16 29	20	22	23	20	50	17	18	20	23	23	20	55	17	17	20	23	24	20	59	17	17
5 20 49	21	23	24	21	45	18	19	21	24	24	21	49	18	18	21	24	25	21	53	18	18
5 25 10	22	24	25	22	39	19	20	22	25	25	22	43	19	19	22	25	25	22	47	19	19
5 29 31	23	25	26	23	34	20	21	23	26	26	23	38	20	20	23	26	26	23	41	20	20
5 33 51	24	26	27	24	29	21	22	24	27	27	24	32	21	21	24	27	27	24	35	21	21
5 38 13	25	27	28	25	24	22	23	25	28	28	25	27	22	22	25	28	28	25	29	22	22
5 42 34	26	28	29	26	19	23	24	26	29	29	26	21	23	23	26	29	29	26	23	23	23
5 46 55	27	29	♍	27	15	24	25	27	♌	♍	27	16	24	24	27	♌	♍	27	17	24	24
5 51 17	28	♌	1	28	10	25	26	28	1	1	28	11	25	25	28	1	1	28	12	25	25
5 55 38	29	1	2	29	6	26	27	29	2	2	29	5	26	26	29	2	2	29	6	26	26
HOUSES	4	5	6	7		8	9	4	5	6	7		8	9	4	5	6	7		8	9

LATITUDE 34° S. LATITUDE 35° S. LATITUDE 36° S.

LATITUDE 34° N. LATITUDE 35° N. LATITUDE 36° N.

SIDEREAL TIME	10 ♋	11 ♌	12 ♍	ASC ♎ °	'	2 ♎	3 ♏	10 ♋	11 ♌	12 ♍	ASC ♎ °	'	2 ♎	3 ♏	10 ♋	11 ♌	12 ♍	ASC ♎ °	'	2 ♎	3 ♏
H M S	°	°	°	°	'	°	°	°	°	°	°	'	°	°	°	°	°	°	'	°	°
6 0 0	0	2	3	0	0	27	28	0	3	3	0	0	27	27	0	3	3	0	0	27	27
6 4 22	1	3	4	0	55	28	29	1	4	4	0	55	28	28	1	4	4	0	54	28	28
6 8 43	2	4	5	1	50	29	♐	2	5	5	1	49	29	29	2	5	5	1	48	29	29
6 13 5	3	5	6	2	45	♏	1	3	6	6	2	44	♏	♐	3	6	6	2	43	♏	♐
6 17 26	4	6	7	3	41	1	2	4	7	7	3	39	1	1	4	7	7	3	37	1	1
6 21 47	5	7	8	4	36	2	3	5	8	8	4	33	2	2	5	8	8	4	31	2	2
6 26 9	6	8	9	5	31	3	4	6	9	9	5	28	3	3	6	9	9	5	25	3	3
6 30 29	7	9	10	6	26	4	5	7	10	10	6	22	4	4	7	10	10	6	19	4	4
6 34 50	8	10	11	7	21	5	6	8	11	11	7	17	5	5	8	11	11	7	13	5	5
6 39 11	9	11	12	8	15	6	7	9	12	12	8	11	6	6	9	12	12	8	7	5	6
6 43 31	10	12	13	9	10	7	8	10	13	13	9	5	7	7	10	13	13	9	1	6	7
6 47 51	11	13	14	10	5	8	9	11	14	14	10	0	8	8	11	14	14	9	55	7	8
6 52 11	12	14	15	10	59	9	9	12	15	15	10	54	9	9	12	15	15	10	48	8	9
6 56 30	13	15	16	11	54	10	10	13	16	16	11	48	9	10	13	16	16	11	42	9	10
7 0 49	14	16	17	12	48	11	11	14	17	17	12	42	10	11	14	17	17	12	35	10	11
7 5 7	15	17	18	13	43	12	12	15	18	18	13	36	11	12	15	18	18	13	29	11	12
7 9 26	16	18	18	14	37	13	13	16	19	19	14	29	12	13	16	19	19	14	22	12	13
7 13 43	17	19	19	15	31	14	14	17	20	20	15	23	13	14	17	20	20	15	15	13	14
7 18 0	18	20	20	16	25	14	15	18	21	20	16	17	14	15	18	21	21	16	8	14	15
7 22 17	19	22	21	17	19	15	16	19	22	21	17	10	15	16	19	22	22	17	1	15	16
7 26 33	20	23	22	18	12	16	17	20	23	22	18	3	16	17	20	23	22	17	54	16	17
7 30 49	21	24	23	19	6	17	18	21	24	23	18	56	17	18	21	24	23	18	47	17	18
7 35 4	22	25	24	19	59	18	19	22	25	24	19	49	18	19	22	25	24	19	39	18	19
7 39 19	23	26	25	20	53	19	20	23	26	25	20	42	19	20	23	26	25	20	31	19	20
7 43 33	24	27	26	21	46	20	21	24	27	26	21	35	20	21	24	27	26	21	24	19	21
7 47 46	25	28	27	22	39	21	22	25	28	27	22	27	21	22	25	28	27	22	16	20	22
7 51 59	26	29	28	23	31	22	23	26	29	28	23	19	22	23	26	29	28	23	8	21	23
7 56 11	27	♏	29	24	24	23	24	27	♏	29	24	12	22	24	27	♏	29	23	59	22	24
8 0 23	28	1	♎	25	16	24	25	28	1	♎	25	4	23	25	28	1	♎	24	51	23	24
8 4 34	29	2	1	26	9	25	26	29	2	1	25	55	24	26	29	2	1	25	42	24	25
8 8 44	♌	3	2	27	1	25	27	♌	3	2	26	47	25	27	♌	3	2	26	33	25	26
8 12 53	1	4	3	27	53	26	28	1	4	3	27	39	26	28	1	4	3	27	25	26	27
8 17 2	2	5	4	28	44	27	29	2	5	4	28	30	27	29	2	5	4	28	15	27	28
8 21 10	3	6	5	29	36	28	♑	3	6	5	29	21	28	29	3	6	5	29	6	28	29
8 25 18	4	7	6	0♏	27	29	1	4	7	6	0♏	12	29	♑	4	7	6	29	57	28	♑
8 29 24	5	8	7	1	18	♐	2	5	8	7	1	3	♐	1	5	8	7	0♏	47	29	1
8 33 30	6	9	8	2	9	1	2	6	9	8	1	53	1	2	6	9	8	1	37	♐	2
8 37 36	7	10	9	3	0	2	3	7	10	9	2	44	1	3	7	10	9	2	27	1	3
8 41 40	8	11	9	3	51	3	4	8	11	9	3	34	2	4	8	11	9	3	17	2	4
8 45 44	9	12	10	4	41	4	5	9	12	10	4	24	3	5	9	12	10	4	7	3	5
8 49 47	10	13	11	5	31	4	6	10	13	11	5	14	4	6	10	13	11	4	56	4	6
8 53 50	11	14	12	6	21	5	7	11	14	12	6	4	5	7	11	14	12	5	46	5	7
8 57 51	12	15	13	7	11	6	8	12	15	13	6	53	6	8	12	15	13	6	35	5	8
9 1 52	13	16	14	8	1	7	9	13	16	14	7	43	7	9	13	16	14	7	24	6	9
9 5 52	14	17	15	8	51	8	10	14	17	15	8	32	8	10	14	17	15	8	13	7	10
HOUSES	4	5	6	7		8	9	4	5	6	7		8	9	4	5	6	7		8	9

LATITUDE 34° S. LATITUDE 35° S. LATITUDE 36° S.

LATITUDE 34° N. LATITUDE 35° N. LATITUDE 36° N.

SIDEREAL TIME	10 ♌	11 ♍	12 ♎	ASC ♏		2 ♐	3 ♑	10 ♌	11 ♍	12 ♎	ASC ♏		2 ♐	3 ♑	10 ♌	11 ♍	12 ♎	ASC ♏		2 ♐	3 ♑
H M S	°	°	°	°	′	°	°	°	°	°	°	′	°	°	°	°	°	°	′	°	°
9 9 52	15	18	16	9	40	9	11	15	18	16	9	21	8	11	15	18	16	9	1	8	11
9 13 50	16	19	17	10	29	10	12	16	19	17	10	10	9	12	16	19	17	9	50	9	11
9 17 49	17	20	18	11	18	11	13	17	20	18	10	58	10	13	17	20	17	10	38	10	12
9 21 46	18	21	19	12	7	11	14	18	21	18	11	47	11	14	18	21	18	11	26	11	13
9 25 42	19	21	19	12	56	12	15	19	22	19	12	35	12	15	19	22	19	12	14	11	14
9 29 38	20	22	20	13	44	13	16	20	22	20	13	23	13	15	20	23	20	13	2	12	15
9 33 34	21	23	21	14	33	14	17	21	23	21	14	11	14	16	21	23	21	13	50	13	16
9 37 28	22	24	22	15	21	15	18	22	24	22	14	59	14	17	22	24	22	14	37	14	17
9 41 22	23	25	23	16	9	16	18	23	25	23	15	47	15	18	23	25	23	15	25	15	18
9 45 15	24	26	24	16	57	17	19	24	26	24	16	35	16	19	24	26	24	16	12	16	19
9 49 8	25	27	25	17	45	17	20	25	27	25	17	22	17	20	25	27	24	16	59	17	20
9 53 0	26	28	26	18	33	18	21	26	28	25	18	10	18	21	26	28	25	17	46	17	21
9 56 51	27	29	26	19	20	19	22	27	29	26	18	57	19	22	27	29	26	18	33	18	22
10 0 42	28	♎	27	20	8	20	23	28	♎	27	19	44	20	23	28	♎	27	19	20	19	23
10 4 32	29	1	28	20	55	21	24	29	1	28	20	31	20	24	29	1	28	20	7	20	24
10 8 22	♍	2	29	21	42	22	25	♍	2	29	21	18	21	25	♍	2	29	20	53	21	25
10 12 11	1	3	♏	22	29	22	26	1	3	♏	22	5	22	26	1	3	♏	21	40	22	26
10 15 59	2	4	1	23	16	23	27	2	4	1	22	51	23	27	2	4	0	22	26	23	27
10 19 47	3	5	2	24	3	24	28	3	5	1	23	38	24	28	3	5	1	23	12	23	28
10 23 34	4	6	2	24	50	25	29	4	6	2	24	24	25	29	4	6	2	23	58	24	29
10 27 21	5	7	3	25	37	26	♒	5	7	3	25	11	26	♒	5	7	3	24	45	25	29
10 31 8	6	8	4	26	23	27	1	6	8	4	25	57	26	1	6	8	4	25	31	26	♒
10 34 53	7	9	5	27	10	28	2	7	9	5	26	43	27	2	7	9	5	26	17	27	1
10 38 39	8	10	6	27	57	28	3	8	10	6	27	30	28	3	8	10	5	27	3	28	2
10 42 24	9	11	7	28	43	29	4	9	10	6	28	16	29	4	9	10	6	27	48	28	3
10 46 8	10	11	7	29	29	♑	5	10	11	7	29	2	♑	5	10	11	7	28	34	29	4
10 49 52	11	12	8	0♐	16	1	6	11	12	8	29	48	1	5	11	12	8	29	20	♑	5
10 53 36	12	13	9	1	2	2	7	12	13	9	0♐	34	1	6	12	13	9	0♐	6	1	6
10 57 20	13	14	10	1	48	3	8	13	14	10	1	20	2	7	13	14	9	0	51	2	7
11 1 3	14	15	11	2	35	4	9	14	15	10	2	6	3	8	14	15	10	1	37	3	8
11 4 45	15	16	12	3	21	4	10	15	16	11	2	52	4	9	15	16	11	2	23	4	9
11 8 28	16	17	12	4	7	5	11	16	17	12	3	38	5	10	16	17	12	3	9	5	10
11 12 10	17	18	13	4	53	6	12	17	18	13	4	24	6	11	17	18	13	3	54	5	11
11 15 52	18	19	14	5	40	7	13	18	19	14	5	10	7	12	18	19	13	4	40	6	12
11 19 33	19	20	15	6	26	8	14	19	20	15	5	56	8	13	19	20	14	5	26	7	13
11 23 15	20	21	16	7	12	9	15	20	20	15	6	42	8	14	20	20	15	6	11	8	14
11 26 56	21	21	16	7	59	10	16	21	21	16	7	28	9	15	21	21	16	6	57	9	15
11 30 37	22	22	17	8	45	11	17	22	22	17	8	14	10	16	22	22	17	7	43	10	16
11 34 17	23	23	18	9	31	12	18	23	23	18	9	0	11	17	23	23	17	8	29	11	17
11 37 58	24	24	19	10	18	12	19	24	24	19	9	47	12	18	24	24	18	9	15	12	18
11 41 39	25	25	20	11	4	13	20	25	25	19	10	33	13	19	25	25	19	10	1	12	19
11 45 19	26	26	20	11	51	14	21	26	26	20	11	19	14	20	26	26	20	10	47	13	20
11 48 59	27	27	21	12	38	15	22	27	27	21	12	6	15	21	27	27	21	11	33	14	21
11 52 40	28	28	22	13	25	16	23	28	28	22	12	52	16	22	28	28	21	12	20	15	22
11 56 20	29	29	23	14	12	17	24	29	29	23	13	39	16	23	29	28	22	13	6	16	23
HOUSES	4	5	6	7		8	9	4	5	6	7		8	9	4	5	6	7		8	9

LATITUDE 34° S. LATITUDE 35° S. LATITUDE 36° S.

LATITUDE 34° N. LATITUDE 35° N. LATITUDE 36° N.

SIDEREAL TIME	10 ♎	11 ♎	12 ♏	ASC ♐	2 ♑	3 ♒	10 ♎	11 ♎	12 ♏	ASC ♐	2 ♑	3 ♒	10 ♎	11 ♎	12 ♏	ASC ♐	2 ♑	3 ♒
H M S	°	°	°	° '	°	°	°	°	°	° '	°	°	°	°	°	° '	°	°
12 0 0	0	29	24	14 59	18	25	0	29	23	14 26	17	25	0	29	23	13 53	17	24
12 3 40	1	♏	24	15 46	19	26	1	♏	24	15 13	18	26	1	♏	24	14 39	18	25
12 7 20	2	1	25	16 33	20	27	2	1	25	16 0	19	27	2	1	25	15 26	19	26
12 11 1	3	2	26	17 21	21	28	3	2	26	16 47	20	28	3	2	25	16 13	20	28
12 14 41	4	3	27	18 8	22	29	4	3	26	17 35	21	29	4	3	26	17 0	21	29
12 18 21	5	4	28	18 56	22	♓	5	4	27	18 22	22	♓	5	4	27	17 47	22	♓
12 22 2	6	5	28	19 44	23	1	6	5	28	19 10	23	1	6	5	28	18 35	23	1
12 25 42	7	6	29	20 32	24	2	7	6	29	19 58	24	2	7	5	29	19 23	24	2
12 29 23	8	7	♐	21 20	25	3	8	6	♐	20 46	25	3	8	6	29	20 11	25	3
12 33 4	9	7	1	22 9	26	4	9	7	0	21 34	26	4	9	7	♐	20 59	25	4
12 36 45	10	8	2	22 58	27	5	10	8	1	22 23	27	5	10	8	1	21 47	26	5
12 40 27	11	9	2	23 47	28	6	11	9	2	23 12	28	6	11	9	2	22 35	27	6
12 44 8	12	10	3	24 36	29	7	12	10	3	24 1	29	7	12	10	3	23 24	28	7
12 47 50	13	11	4	25 26	♒	8	13	11	4	24 50	♒	8	13	11	3	24 13	29	8
12 51 32	14	12	5	26 15	1	10	14	12	4	25 39	1	9	14	12	4	25 3	♒	9
12 55 15	15	13	6	27 5	2	11	15	13	5	26 29	2	11	15	12	5	25 52	1	10
12 58 57	16	14	6	27 56	3	12	16	13	6	27 19	3	12	16	13	6	26 42	2	12
13 2 40	17	14	7	28 46	4	13	17	14	7	28 10	4	13	17	14	6	27 33	3	13
13 6 24	18	15	8	29 37	5	14	18	15	8	29 1	5	14	18	15	7	28 23	5	14
13 10 8	19	16	9	0♑ 29	6	15	19	16	8	29 52	6	15	19	16	8	29 14	6	15
13 13 52	20	17	10	1 20	7	16	20	17	9	0♑ 43	7	16	20	17	9	0♑ 5	7	16
13 17 36	21	18	10	2 13	8	17	21	18	10	1 35	8	17	21	18	10	0 57	8	17
13 21 21	22	19	11	3 5	10	18	22	19	11	2 28	9	18	22	18	11	1 49	9	18
13 25 7	23	20	12	3 58	11	19	23	19	12	3 20	10	19	23	19	11	2 42	10	19
13 28 52	24	20	13	4 51	12	21	24	20	13	4 13	11	21	24	20	12	3 35	11	21
13 32 39	25	21	14	5 45	13	22	25	21	13	5 7	12	22	25	21	13	4 28	12	22
13 36 26	26	22	15	6 39	14	23	26	22	14	6 1	14	23	26	22	14	5 22	13	23
13 40 13	27	23	15	7 33	15	24	27	23	15	6 55	15	24	27	23	15	6 16	14	24
13 44 1	28	24	16	8 28	16	25	28	24	16	7 50	16	25	28	24	15	7 11	15	25
13 47 49	29	25	17	9 24	17	26	29	25	17	8 45	17	26	29	25	16	8 6	17	26
13 51 38	♏	26	18	10 20	18	27	♏	26	18	9 41	18	27	♏	25	17	9 1	18	27
13 55 28	1	27	19	11 16	20	29	1	26	18	10 38	19	29	1	26	18	9 58	19	29
13 59 18	2	27	20	12 13	21	♈	2	27	19	11 34	20	♈	2	27	19	10 55	20	♈
14 3 9	3	28	20	13 11	22	1	3	28	20	12 32	22	1	3	28	20	11 52	21	1
14 7 0	4	29	21	14 9	23	2	4	29	21	13 30	23	2	4	29	21	12 50	22	2
14 10 52	5	♐	22	15 8	24	3	5	♐	22	14 29	24	3	5	♐	21	13 48	24	3
14 14 45	6	1	23	16 7	25	4	6	1	23	15 28	25	4	6	1	22	14 48	25	4
14 18 38	7	2	24	17 7	27	6	7	2	24	16 28	26	6	7	2	23	15 48	26	6
14 22 32	8	3	25	18 8	28	7	8	3	24	17 29	28	7	8	2	24	16 48	27	7
14 26 26	9	4	26	19 9	29	8	9	3	25	18 30	29	8	9	3	25	17 49	29	8
14 30 22	10	5	27	20 11	♓	9	10	4	26	19 32	♓	9	10	4	26	18 51	♓	9
14 34 17	11	5	27	21 14	2	10	11	5	27	20 34	1	10	11	5	27	19 54	1	10
14 38 14	12	6	28	22 17	3	12	12	6	28	21 38	3	12	12	6	28	20 57	2	12
14 42 11	13	7	29	23 21	4	13	13	7	29	22 42	4	13	13	7	28	22 1	4	13
14 46 10	14	8	♑	24 26	5	14	14	8	♑	23 47	5	14	14	8	29	23 6	5	14
HOUSES	4	5	6	7	8	9	4	5	6	7	8	9	4	5	6	7	8	9

LATITUDE 34° S. LATITUDE 35° S. LATITUDE 36° S.

LATITUDE 34° N.   LATITUDE 35° N.   LATITUDE 36° N.

SIDEREAL TIME (H M S)	10 ♏	11 ♐	12 ♑	ASC ♑	2 ♓	3 ♈	10 ♏	11 ♐	12 ♑	ASC ♑	2 ♓	3 ♈	10 ♏	11 ♐	12 ♑	ASC ♑	2 ♓	3 ♈
14 50 8	15	9	1	25 31	7	15	15	9	1	24 52	6	15	15	9	0	24 12	6	15
14 54 8	16	10	2	26 38	8	16	16	10	2	25 59	8	16	16	10	1	25 18	8	16
14 58 8	17	11	3	27 45	9	17	17	11	3	27 6	9	18	17	10	2	26 26	9	18
15 2 9	18	12	4	28 53	11	19	18	12	3	28 14	10	19	18	11	3	27 34	10	19
15 6 10	19	13	5	0♒ 2	12	20	19	12	4	29 23	12	20	19	12	4	28 43	12	20
15 10 13	20	14	6	1 12	13	21	20	13	5	0♒ 33	13	21	20	13	5	29 53	13	21
15 14 16	21	14	7	2 22	15	22	21	14	6	1 44	14	22	21	14	6	1♒ 4	14	22
15 18 20	22	15	8	3 34	16	23	22	15	7	2 56	16	23	22	15	7	2 16	16	24
15 22 24	23	16	9	4 46	17	25	23	16	8	4 8	17	25	23	16	8	3 29	17	25
15 26 30	24	17	10	5 59	19	26	24	17	9	5 22	19	26	24	17	9	4 43	18	26
15 30 36	25	18	11	7 13	20	27	25	18	10	6 36	20	27	25	18	10	5 58	20	27
15 34 42	26	19	12	8 29	21	28	26	19	11	7 52	21	28	26	19	11	7 14	21	28
15 38 50	27	20	13	9 45	23	29	27	20	12	9 8	23	29	27	20	12	8 31	23	♉
15 42 58	28	21	14	11 2	24	♉	28	21	13	10 26	24	♉	28	21	13	9 49	24	1
15 47 7	29	22	15	12 20	26	2	29	22	14	11 45	26	2	29	21	14	11 8	26	2
15 51 16	♐	23	16	13 39	27	3	♐	23	15	13 4	27	3	♐	22	15	12 28	27	3
15 55 26	1	24	17	14 59	28	4	1	24	16	14 25	28	4	1	23	16	13 49	28	4
15 59 37	2	25	18	16 20	♈	5	2	25	17	15 46	♈	5	2	24	17	15 11	♈	6
16 3 49	3	26	19	17 42	1	6	3	25	18	17 9	1	7	3	25	18	16 34	1	7
16 8 1	4	27	20	19 5	3	8	4	26	19	18 33	3	8	4	26	19	17 59	3	8
16 12 14	5	28	21	20 29	4	9	5	27	20	19 58	4	9	5	27	20	19 24	4	9
16 16 27	6	29	22	21 55	6	10	6	28	22	21 24	6	10	6	28	21	20 51	6	10
16 20 41	7	♑	23	23 21	7	11	7	29	23	22 50	7	11	7	29	22	22 19	7	11
16 24 56	8	1	24	24 48	8	12	8	♑	24	24 18	9	12	8	♑	23	23 48	9	13
16 29 11	9	1	25	26 16	10	13	9	1	25	25 47	10	14	9	1	24	25 18	10	14
16 33 27	10	2	26	27 45	11	15	10	2	26	27 17	11	15	10	2	26	26 48	11	15
16 37 43	11	3	28	29 15	13	16	11	3	27	28 48	13	16	11	3	27	28 20	13	16
16 41 59	12	4	29	0♓ 46	14	17	12	4	28	0♓ 20	14	17	12	4	28	29 54	14	17
16 46 17	13	5	♒	2 18	16	18	13	5	29	1 53	16	18	13	5	29	1♓ 28	16	18
16 50 34	14	6	1	3 50	17	19	14	6	♒	3 27	17	19	14	6	♒	3 3	17	20
16 54 53	15	7	2	5 24	18	20	15	7	2	5 2	19	21	15	7	1	4 39	19	21
16 59 11	16	8	3	6 58	20	21	16	8	3	6 37	20	22	16	8	3	6 15	20	22
17 3 30	17	9	5	8 33	21	23	17	9	4	8 14	21	23	17	9	4	7 53	22	23
17 7 49	18	10	6	10 9	23	24	18	10	5	9 51	23	24	18	10	5	9 32	23	24
17 12 9	19	12	7	11 46	24	25	19	11	7	11 29	24	25	19	11	6	11 11	25	25
17 16 29	20	13	8	13 23	25	26	20	12	8	13 8	26	26	20	12	7	12 51	26	26
17 20 49	21	14	9	15 1	27	27	21	13	9	14 47	27	27	21	13	9	14 32	27	27
17 25 10	22	15	11	16 39	28	28	22	14	10	16 27	28	28	22	14	10	16 14	29	29
17 29 31	23	16	12	18 18	♉	29	23	15	11	18 7	♉	♊	23	15	11	17 56	♉	♊
17 33 51	24	17	13	19 58	1	♊	24	16	13	19 48	1	1	24	16	12	19 38	2	1
17 38 13	25	18	14	21 38	2	2	25	18	14	21 30	3	2	25	17	14	21 21	3	2
17 42 34	26	19	16	23 18	4	3	26	19	15	23 11	4	3	26	18	15	23 4	4	3
17 46 55	27	20	17	24 58	5	4	27	20	17	24 53	5	4	27	19	16	24 48	6	4
17 51 17	28	21	18	26 39	6	5	28	21	18	26 35	7	5	28	20	18	26 32	7	5
17 55 38	29	22	20	28 19	8	6	29	22	19	28 18	8	6	29	22	19	28 16	8	6
HOUSES	4	5	6	7	8	9	4	5	6	7	8	9	4	5	6	7	8	9

LATITUDE 34° S.   LATITUDE 35° S.   LATITUDE 36° S.

LATITUDE 34° N. LATITUDE 35° N. LATITUDE 36° N.

SIDEREAL TIME (H M S)	10 ♑	11 ♑	12 ♒	ASC ♈	2 ♉	3 ♊	10 ♑	11 ♑	12 ♒	ASC ♈	2 ♉	3 ♊	10 ♑	11 ♑	12 ♒	ASC ♈	2 ♉	3 ♊
18 0 0	0	23	21	0 0	9	7	0	23	21	0 0	9	7	0	23	20	0 0	10	7
18 4 22	1	24	22	1 41	10	8	1	24	22	1 42	11	8	1	24	22	1 44	11	8
18 8 43	2	25	24	3 21	12	9	2	25	23	3 25	12	9	2	25	23	3 28	12	10
18 13 5	3	26	25	5 2	13	10	3	26	25	5 7	13	10	3	26	24	5 12	14	11
18 17 26	4	27	26	6 42	14	11	4	27	26	6 49	15	11	4	27	26	6 56	15	12
18 21 47	5	28	28	8 22	16	12	5	28	27	8 30	16	12	5	28	27	8 39	16	13
18 26 9	6	♒	29	10 2	17	13	6	29	29	10 12	17	14	6	29	28	10 22	18	14
18 30 29	7	1	♓	11 42	18	14	7	♒	♓	11 53	19	15	7	♒	♓	12 4	19	15
18 34 50	8	2	2	13 21	19	15	8	2	2	13 33	20	16	8	1	1	13 46	20	16
18 39 11	9	3	3	14 59	21	16	9	3	3	15 13	21	17	9	3	3	15 28	21	17
18 43 31	10	4	5	16 37	22	17	10	4	4	16 52	22	18	10	4	4	17 9	23	18
18 47 51	11	5	6	18 14	23	18	11	5	6	18 31	23	19	11	5	5	18 49	24	19
18 52 11	12	6	7	19 51	24	20	12	6	7	20 9	25	20	12	6	7	20 28	25	20
18 56 30	13	7	9	21 27	25	21	13	7	9	21 46	26	21	13	7	8	22 7	26	21
19 0 49	14	9	10	23 2	27	22	14	8	10	23 23	27	22	14	8	10	23 45	27	22
19 5 7	15	10	12	24 36	28	23	15	9	11	24 58	28	23	15	9	11	25 21	29	23
19 9 26	16	11	13	26 10	29	24	16	11	13	26 33	29	24	16	10	13	26 57	♊	24
19 13 43	17	12	14	27 42	♊	25	17	12	14	28 7	♊	25	17	12	14	28 32	1	25
19 18 0	18	13	16	29 14	1	26	18	13	16	29 40	2	26	18	13	16	0♉ 6	2	26
19 22 17	19	14	17	0♉ 45	2	27	19	14	17	1♉ 12	3	27	19	14	17	1 40	3	27
19 26 33	20	15	19	2 15	4	28	20	15	19	2 43	4	28	20	15	19	3 12	4	28
19 30 49	21	17	20	3 44	5	29	21	16	20	4 13	5	29	21	16	20	4 42	6	29
19 35 4	22	18	22	5 12	6	29	22	18	21	5 42	6	♋	22	17	21	6 12	7	♋
19 39 19	23	19	23	6 39	7	♋	23	19	23	7 10	7	1	23	19	23	7 41	8	1
19 43 33	24	20	24	8 5	8	1	24	20	24	8 36	8	2	24	20	24	9 9	9	2
19 47 46	25	21	26	9 31	9	2	25	21	26	10 2	10	3	25	21	26	10 36	10	3
19 51 59	26	22	27	10 55	10	3	26	22	27	11 27	11	4	26	22	27	12 1	11	4
19 56 11	27	24	29	12 18	11	4	27	23	29	12 51	12	5	27	23	29	13 26	12	5
20 0 23	28	25	♈	13 40	12	5	28	25	♈	14 14	13	5	28	24	♈	14 49	13	6
20 4 34	29	26	2	15 1	13	6	29	26	2	15 35	14	6	29	26	2	16 11	14	7
20 8 44	♒	27	3	16 21	14	7	♒	27	3	16 56	15	7	♒	27	3	17 32	15	8
20 12 53	1	28	4	17 40	15	8	1	28	4	18 15	16	8	1	28	4	18 52	16	9
20 17 2	2	29	6	18 58	16	9	2	29	6	19 34	17	9	2	29	6	20 11	17	9
20 21 10	3	♓	7	20 15	17	10	3	♓	7	20 52	18	10	3	♓	7	21 29	18	10
20 25 18	4	2	9	21 31	18	11	4	2	9	22 8	19	11	4	2	9	22 46	19	11
20 29 24	5	3	10	22 47	19	12	5	3	10	23 24	20	12	5	3	10	24 2	20	12
20 33 30	6	4	11	24 1	20	13	6	4	11	24 38	21	13	6	4	12	25 17	21	13
20 37 36	7	5	13	25 14	21	14	7	5	13	25 52	22	14	7	5	13	26 31	22	14
20 41 40	8	7	14	26 26	22	15	8	7	14	27 4	23	15	8	6	14	27 44	23	15
20 45 44	9	8	15	27 38	23	16	9	8	16	28 16	24	16	9	8	16	28 56	24	16
20 49 47	10	9	17	28 48	24	16	10	9	17	29 27	25	17	10	9	17	0♊ 7	25	17
20 53 50	11	10	18	29 58	25	17	11	10	18	0♊ 37	26	18	11	10	18	1 17	26	18
20 57 51	12	11	19	1♊ 7	26	18	12	11	20	1 46	27	18	12	11	20	2 26	27	19
21 1 52	13	13	21	2 15	27	19	13	12	21	2 54	27	19	13	12	21	3 34	28	20
21 5 52	14	14	22	3 22	28	20	14	14	22	4 1	28	20	14	14	22	4 42	29	20
HOUSES	4	5	6	7	8	9	4	5	6	7	8	9	4	5	6	7	8	9

LATITUDE 34° S. LATITUDE 35° S. LATITUDE 36° S.

LATITUDE 34° N.   LATITUDE 35° N.   LATITUDE 36° N.

SIDEREAL TIME	10 ♒	11 ♓	12 ♈	ASC ♊	2 ♊	3 ♋	10 ♒	11 ♓	12 ♈	ASC ♊	2 ♊	3 ♋	10 ♒	11 ♓	12 ♈	ASC ♊	2 ♋	3 ♋
H M S	°	°	°	° ′	°	°	°	°	°	° ′	°	°	°	°	°	° ′	°	°
21 9 52	15	15	23	4 29	29	21	15	15	24	5 8	29	21	15	15	24	5 48	0	21
21 13 50	16	16	25	5 34	♋	22	16	16	25	6 13	♋	22	16	16	25	6 54	1	22
21 17 49	17	17	26	6 39	1	23	17	17	26	7 18	1	23	17	17	26	7 59	2	23
21 21 46	18	18	27	7 43	2	24	18	18	27	8 22	2	24	18	18	28	9 3	2	24
21 25 42	19	20	28	8 46	3	25	19	20	29	9 26	3	25	19	20	29	10 6	3	25
21 29 38	20	21	♉	9 49	3	25	20	21	♉	10 28	4	26	20	21	♉	11 9	4	26
21 33 34	21	22	1	10 51	4	26	21	22	1	11 30	5	27	21	22	1	12 11	5	27
21 37 28	22	23	2	11 52	5	27	22	23	2	12 31	6	27	22	23	3	13 12	6	28
21 41 22	23	24	3	12 53	6	28	23	24	4	13 32	6	28	23	24	4	14 12	7	28
21 45 15	24	26	5	13 53	7	29	24	26	5	14 32	7	29	24	26	5	15 12	8	29
21 49 8	25	27	6	14 52	8	♌	25	27	6	15 31	8	♌	25	27	6	16 12	9	♌
21 53 0	26	28	7	15 51	9	1	26	28	7	16 30	9	1	26	28	8	17 10	9	1
21 56 51	27	29	8	16 49	10	2	27	29	8	17 28	10	2	27	29	9	18 8	10	2
22 0 42	28	♈	9	17 47	10	3	28	♈	10	18 26	11	3	28	♈	10	19 5	11	3
22 4 32	29	1	10	18 44	11	3	29	1	11	19 22	12	4	29	1	11	20 2	12	4
22 8 22	♓	3	12	19 40	12	4	♓	3	12	20 19	12	4	♓	3	12	20 59	13	5
22 12 11	1	4	13	20 36	13	5	1	4	13	21 15	13	5	1	4	13	21 54	14	5
22 15 59	2	5	14	21 32	14	6	2	5	14	22 10	14	6	2	5	15	22 49	15	6
22 19 47	3	6	15	22 27	15	7	3	6	15	23 5	15	7	3	6	16	23 44	15	7
22 23 34	4	7	16	23 21	15	8	4	7	16	23 59	16	8	4	7	17	24 38	16	8
22 27 21	5	8	17	24 15	16	9	5	8	18	24 53	17	9	5	8	18	25 32	17	9
22 31 8	6	9	18	25 9	17	10	6	9	19	25 47	17	10	6	9	19	26 25	18	10
22 34 53	7	11	19	26 2	18	10	7	11	20	26 40	18	11	7	11	20	27 18	19	11
22 38 39	8	12	20	26 55	19	11	8	12	21	27 32	19	11	8	12	21	28 11	19	12
22 42 24	9	13	22	27 47	20	12	9	13	22	28 25	20	12	9	13	22	29 3	20	12
22 46 8	10	14	23	28 40	20	13	10	14	23	29 17	21	13	10	14	23	29 55	21	13
22 49 52	11	15	24	29 31	21	14	11	15	24	0♋ 8	22	14	11	15	24	0♋ 46	22	14
22 53 36	12	16	25	0♋ 23	22	15	12	16	25	0 59	22	15	12	16	25	1 37	23	15
22 57 20	13	17	26	1 14	23	16	13	17	26	1 50	23	16	13	17	27	2 27	24	16
23 1 3	14	18	27	2 4	24	16	14	18	27	2 41	24	17	14	18	28	3 18	24	17
23 4 45	15	19	28	2 55	24	17	15	19	28	3 31	25	17	15	20	29	4 8	25	18
23 8 28	16	20	29	3 45	25	18	16	21	29	4 21	26	18	16	21	♊	4 57	26	18
23 12 10	17	22	♊	4 34	26	19	17	22	♊	5 10	26	19	17	22	1	5 47	27	19
23 15 52	18	23	1	5 24	27	20	18	23	1	5 59	27	20	18	23	2	6 36	27	20
23 19 33	19	24	2	6 13	28	21	19	24	2	6 48	28	21	19	24	3	7 25	28	21
23 23 15	20	25	3	7 2	28	22	20	25	3	7 37	29	22	20	25	4	8 13	29	22
23 26 56	21	26	4	7 51	29	23	21	26	4	8 26	♌	23	21	26	5	9 1	♌	23
23 30 37	22	27	5	8 40	♌	24	22	27	5	9 14	0	24	22	27	5	9 49	1	24
23 34 17	23	28	6	9 28	1	24	23	28	6	10 2	1	24	23	28	6	10 37	1	25
23 37 58	24	29	7	10 16	2	25	24	29	7	10 50	2	25	24	29	7	11 25	2	25
23 41 39	25	♉	8	11 4	2	26	25	♉	8	11 38	3	26	25	♉	8	12 13	3	26
23 45 19	26	1	8	11 52	3	27	26	1	9	12 25	4	27	26	1	9	13 0	4	27
23 48 59	27	2	9	12 39	4	28	27	2	10	13 13	4	28	27	2	10	13 47	5	28
23 52 40	28	3	10	13 27	5	29	28	3	11	14 0	5	29	28	4	11	14 34	5	29
23 56 20	29	4	11	14 14	6	♍	29	4	12	14 47	6	♍	29	5	12	15 21	6	♍
HOUSES	4	5	6	7	8	9	4	5	6	7	8	9	4	5	6	7	8	9

LATITUDE 34° S.   LATITUDE 35° S.   LATITUDE 36° S.

LATITUDE 37° N.							LATITUDE 38° N.						LATITUDE 39° N.					

SIDEREAL TIME	10 ♈	11 ♉	12 ♊	ASC ♋	2 ♌	3 ♍	10 ♈	11 ♉	12 ♊	ASC ♋	2 ♌	3 ♍	10 ♈	11 ♉	12 ♊	ASC ♋	2 ♌	3 ♍
H M S	°	°	°	° '	°	°	°	°	°	° '	°	°	°	°	°	° '	°	°
0 0 0	0	6	13	16 41	7	1	0	6	14	17 16	8	1	0	6	14	17 52	8	1
0 3 40	1	7	14	17 28	8	2	1	7	15	18 2	8	2	1	7	15	18 37	9	2
0 7 20	2	8	15	18 14	9	3	2	8	16	18 48	9	3	2	8	16	19 23	9	3
0 11 1	3	9	16	19 0	10	3	3	9	17	19 34	10	4	3	9	17	20 8	10	4
0 14 41	4	10	17	19 46	10	4	4	10	18	20 19	11	4	4	10	18	20 54	11	5
0 18 21	5	11	18	20 32	11	5	5	11	18	21 5	12	5	5	11	19	21 39	12	5
0 22 2	6	12	19	21 17	12	6	6	12	19	21 50	12	6	6	12	20	22 24	13	6
0 25 43	7	13	20	22 3	13	7	7	13	20	22 36	13	7	7	13	21	23 9	13	7
0 29 23	8	14	21	22 49	14	8	8	14	21	23 21	14	8	8	14	22	23 54	14	8
0 33 4	9	15	22	23 34	14	9	9	15	22	24 6	15	9	9	15	22	24 39	15	9
0 36 45	10	16	22	24 20	15	10	10	16	23	24 52	15	10	10	16	23	25 24	16	10
0 40 27	11	17	23	25 5	16	11	11	17	24	25 37	16	11	11	17	24	26 9	17	11
0 44 8	12	18	24	25 51	17	11	12	18	25	26 22	17	12	12	18	25	26 54	17	12
0 47 50	13	19	25	26 36	18	12	13	19	26	27 7	18	12	13	19	26	27 38	18	12
0 51 32	14	20	26	27 21	18	13	14	20	26	27 52	19	13	14	20	27	28 23	19	13
0 55 15	15	21	27	28 7	19	14	15	21	27	28 37	19	14	15	21	28	29 8	20	14
0 58 57	16	22	28	28 52	20	15	16	22	28	29 22	20	15	16	22	29	29 53	20	15
1 2 40	17	23	29	29 38	21	16	17	23	29	0♌ 7	21	16	17	23	29	0♌ 37	21	16
1 6 24	18	24	29	0♌ 23	22	17	18	24	♋	0 52	22	17	18	24	♋	1 22	22	17
1 10 8	19	25	♋	1 9	22	18	19	25	1	1 38	23	18	19	25	1	2 7	23	18
1 13 52	20	26	1	1 54	23	19	20	26	2	2 23	23	19	20	26	2	2 52	24	19
1 17 36	21	27	2	2 40	24	20	21	27	2	3 8	24	20	21	27	3	3 37	24	20
1 21 21	22	28	3	3 25	25	21	22	28	3	3 53	25	21	22	28	4	4 22	25	21
1 25 7	23	29	4	4 11	26	21	23	29	4	4 38	26	21	23	29	5	5 7	26	21
1 28 52	24	♊	4	4 56	26	22	24	♊	5	5 24	27	22	24	♊	5	5 52	27	22
1 32 39	25	1	5	5 42	27	23	25	1	6	6 9	28	23	25	1	6	6 37	28	23
1 36 26	26	2	6	6 28	28	24	26	2	7	6 55	28	24	26	2	7	7 22	29	24
1 40 13	27	3	7	7 14	29	25	27	3	7	7 40	29	25	27	3	8	8 7	29	25
1 44 1	28	4	8	8 0	♍	26	28	4	8	8 26	♍	26	28	4	9	8 52	♍	26
1 47 49	29	5	9	8 46	1	27	29	5	9	9 11	1	27	29	5	10	9 38	1	27
1 51 38	♉	5	10	9 32	1	28	♉	6	10	9 57	2	28	♉	6	10	10 23	2	28
1 55 28	1	6	10	10 18	2	29	1	7	11	10 43	2	29	1	7	11	11 9	3	29
1 59 18	2	7	11	11 4	3	♎	2	8	12	11 29	3	♎	2	8	12	11 54	4	♎
2 3 9	3	8	12	11 51	4	1	3	9	13	12 15	4	1	3	9	13	12 40	4	1
2 7 0	4	9	13	12 37	5	2	4	10	13	13 1	5	2	4	10	14	13 26	5	2
2 10 52	5	10	14	13 24	6	3	5	10	14	13 48	6	3	5	11	15	14 12	6	3
2 14 45	6	11	15	14 11	7	4	6	11	15	14 34	7	4	6	12	15	14 58	7	4
2 18 38	7	12	15	14 58	7	5	7	12	16	15 21	8	5	7	13	16	15 44	8	5
2 22 32	8	13	16	15 45	8	6	8	13	17	16 8	8	6	8	14	17	16 30	9	5
2 26 26	9	14	17	16 32	9	6	9	14	18	16 54	9	6	9	14	18	17 17	9	6
2 30 22	10	15	18	17 19	10	7	10	15	18	17 41	10	7	10	15	19	18 3	10	7
2 34 17	11	16	19	18 7	11	8	11	16	19	18 28	11	8	11	16	20	18 50	11	8
2 38 14	12	17	20	18 55	12	9	12	17	20	19 16	12	9	12	17	21	19 37	12	9
2 42 11	13	18	21	19 42	13	10	13	18	21	20 3	13	10	13	18	21	20 24	13	10
2 46 10	14	19	21	20 30	14	11	14	19	22	20 51	14	11	14	19	22	21 11	14	11
HOUSES	4	5	6	7	8	9	4	5	6	7	8	9	4	5	6	7	8	9

LATITUDE 37° S.　　　LATITUDE 38° S.　　　LATITUDE 39° S.

LATITUDE 37° N. LATITUDE 38° N. LATITUDE 39° N.

SIDEREAL TIME	10 ♉	11 ♊	12 ♋	ASC ♌	2 ♍	3 ♎	10 ♉	11 ♊	12 ♋	ASC ♌	2 ♍	3 ♎	10 ♉	11 ♊	12 ♋	ASC ♌	2 ♍	3 ♎
H M S	°	°	°	° '	°	°	°	°	°	° '	°	°	°	°	°	° '	°	°
2 50 8	15	20	22	21 19	14	12	15	20	23	21 38	15	12	15	20	23	21 59	15	12
2 54 8	16	21	23	22 7	15	13	16	21	24	22 26	15	13	16	21	24	22 46	15	13
2 58 8	17	22	24	22 55	16	14	17	22	24	23 14	16	14	17	22	25	23 34	16	14
3 2 9	18	22	25	23 44	17	15	18	23	25	24 3	17	15	18	23	26	24 22	17	15
3 6 10	19	23	26	24 33	18	16	19	24	26	24 51	18	16	19	24	27	25 10	18	16
3 10 13	20	24	27	25 22	19	17	20	25	27	25 40	19	17	20	25	27	25 58	19	17
3 14 16	21	25	28	26 11	20	18	21	26	28	26 28	20	18	21	26	28	26 46	20	18
3 18 20	22	26	28	27 0	21	19	22	26	29	27 17	21	19	22	27	29	27 35	21	19
3 22 24	23	27	29	27 49	22	20	23	27	♌	28 6	22	20	23	28	♌	28 23	22	20
3 26 30	24	28	♌	28 39	23	21	24	28	0	28 55	23	21	24	29	1	29 12	23	21
3 30 36	25	29	1	29 29	23	22	25	29	1	29 45	23	22	25	♋	2	0♍ 1	24	22
3 34 42	26	♋	2	0♍ 19	24	23	26	♋	2	0♍ 34	24	23	26	0	3	0 50	24	23
3 38 50	27	1	3	1 9	25	24	27	1	3	1 24	25	24	27	1	3	1 39	25	24
3 42 58	28	2	4	1 59	26	25	28	2	4	2 14	26	25	28	2	4	2 29	26	25
3 47 7	29	3	5	2 50	27	26	29	3	5	3 4	27	26	29	3	5	3 18	27	26
3 51 16	♊	4	5	3 40	28	27	♊	4	6	3 54	28	27	♊	4	6	4 8	28	27
3 55 26	1	5	6	4 31	29	28	1	5	7	4 45	29	28	1	5	7	4 58	29	28
3 59 37	2	6	7	5 22	♎	29	2	6	8	5 35	♎	29	2	6	8	5 48	♎	29
4 3 49	3	7	8	6 13	1	♏	3	7	8	6 26	1	♏	3	7	9	6 39	1	♏
4 8 1	4	8	9	7 4	2	1	4	8	9	7 17	2	1	4	8	10	7 29	2	1
4 12 14	5	9	10	7 56	3	2	5	9	10	8 8	3	2	5	9	11	8 20	3	2
4 16 27	6	10	11	8 48	4	3	6	10	11	8 59	4	3	6	10	11	9 10	4	3
4 20 41	7	10	12	9 39	5	4	7	11	12	9 50	5	4	7	11	12	10 1	5	4
4 24 56	8	11	13	10 31	6	5	8	12	13	10 42	6	5	8	12	13	10 52	6	5
4 29 11	9	12	14	11 23	7	6	9	13	14	11 33	7	6	9	13	14	11 43	6	6
4 33 27	10	13	14	12 16	7	7	10	14	15	12 25	7	7	10	14	15	12 35	7	7
4 37 43	11	14	15	13 8	8	8	11	15	16	13 17	8	8	11	15	16	13 26	8	8
4 41 59	12	15	16	14 0	9	9	12	15	17	14 9	9	9	12	16	17	14 17	9	9
4 46 17	13	16	17	14 53	10	10	13	16	17	15 1	10	10	13	17	18	15 9	10	10
4 50 34	14	17	18	15 46	11	11	14	17	18	15 53	11	11	14	18	19	16 1	11	11
4 54 53	15	18	19	16 38	12	12	15	18	19	16 46	12	12	15	19	20	16 53	12	12
4 59 11	16	19	20	17 31	13	13	16	19	20	17 38	13	13	16	20	21	17 45	13	13
5 3 30	17	20	21	18 24	14	14	17	20	21	18 31	14	14	17	21	21	18 37	14	14
5 7 49	18	21	22	19 18	15	15	18	21	22	19 23	15	15	18	21	22	19 29	15	15
5 12 9	19	22	23	20 11	16	16	19	22	23	20 16	16	16	19	22	23	20 21	16	16
5 16 29	20	23	24	21 4	17	17	20	23	24	21 9	17	17	20	23	24	21 14	17	17
5 20 49	21	24	25	21 57	18	18	21	24	25	22 2	18	18	21	24	25	22 6	18	18
5 25 10	22	25	26	22 51	19	19	22	25	26	22 55	19	19	22	25	26	22 59	19	19
5 29 31	23	26	27	23 44	20	20	23	26	27	23 48	20	20	23	26	27	23 51	20	20
5 33 51	24	27	28	24 38	21	21	24	27	28	24 41	21	21	24	27	28	24 44	21	21
5 38 13	25	28	29	25 32	22	22	25	28	29	25 34	22	22	25	28	29	25 36	22	22
5 42 34	26	29	29	26 25	23	23	26	29	♍	26 27	23	23	26	29	♍	26 29	23	23
5 46 55	27	♌	♍	27 19	24	24	27	♌	1	27 20	24	24	27	♌	1	27 22	23	24
5 51 17	28	1	1	28 13	25	25	28	1	2	28 14	25	25	28	1	2	28 14	24	25
5 55 38	29	2	2	29 6	26	26	29	2	3	29 7	26	26	29	2	3	29 7	25	26
HOUSES	4	5	6	7	8	9	4	5	6	7	8	9	4	5	6	7	8	9

LATITUDE 37° S. LATITUDE 38° S. LATITUDE 39° S.

LATITUDE 37° N.   LATITUDE 38° N.   LATITUDE 39° N.

SIDEREAL TIME	10 ♋	11 ♌	12 ♍	ASC ♎	2 ♎	3 ♏	10 ♋	11 ♌	12 ♍	ASC ♎	2 ♎	3 ♏	10 ♋	11 ♌	12 ♍	ASC ♎	2 ♎	3 ♏
H M S	°	°	°	° '	°	°	°	°	°	° '	°	°	°	°	°	° '	°	°
6 0 0	0	3	3	0 0	27	27	0	3	3	0 0	27	27	0	3	4	0 0	26	27
6 4 22	1	4	4	0 54	28	28	1	4	4	0 53	27	28	1	4	5	0 53	27	28
6 8 43	2	5	5	1 47	29	29	2	5	5	1 46	28	29	2	5	6	1 46	28	29
6 13 5	3	6	6	2 41	♏	✗	3	6	6	2 40	29	✗	3	6	7	2 38	29	✗
6 17 26	4	7	7	3 35	1	1	4	7	7	3 33	♏	1	4	7	7	3 31	♏	1
6 21 47	5	8	8	4 28	1	2	5	8	8	4 26	1	2	5	8	8	4 24	1	2
6 26 9	6	9	9	5 22	2	3	6	9	9	5 19	2	3	6	9	9	5 16	2	3
6 30 29	7	10	10	6 16	3	4	7	10	10	6 12	3	4	7	10	10	6 9	3	4
6 34 50	8	11	11	7 9	4	5	8	11	11	7 5	4	5	8	11	11	7 1	4	5
6 39 11	9	12	12	8 3	5	6	9	12	12	7 58	5	6	9	12	12	7 54	5	6
6 43 31	10	13	13	8 56	6	7	10	13	13	8 51	6	7	10	13	13	8 46	6	7
6 47 51	11	14	14	9 49	7	8	11	14	14	9 44	7	8	11	14	14	9 39	7	8
6 52 11	12	15	15	10 42	8	9	12	15	15	10 37	8	9	12	15	15	10 31	8	9
6 56 30	13	16	16	11 36	9	10	13	16	16	11 29	9	10	13	16	16	11 23	9	9
7 0 49	14	17	17	12 29	10	11	14	17	17	12 22	10	11	14	17	17	12 15	9	10
7 5 7	15	18	18	13 22	11	12	15	18	18	13 14	11	12	15	18	18	13 7	10	11
7 9 26	16	19	19	14 14	12	13	16	19	19	14 7	12	13	16	19	19	13 59	11	12
7 13 43	17	20	20	15 7	13	14	17	20	20	14 59	12	14	17	20	20	14 51	12	13
7 18 0	18	21	21	16 0	14	15	18	21	21	15 51	13	15	18	21	21	15 43	13	14
7 22 17	19	22	22	16 52	15	16	19	22	22	16 43	14	15	19	22	22	16 34	14	15
7 26 33	20	23	23	17 44	16	17	20	23	23	17 35	15	16	20	23	23	17 25	15	16
7 30 49	21	24	23	18 37	16	18	21	24	24	18 27	16	17	21	24	24	18 17	16	17
7 35 4	22	25	24	19 29	17	19	22	25	24	19 18	17	18	22	25	24	19 8	17	18
7 39 19	23	26	25	20 21	18	20	23	26	25	20 10	18	19	23	26	25	19 59	18	19
7 43 33	24	27	26	21 12	19	20	24	27	26	21 1	19	20	24	27	26	20 50	19	20
7 47 46	25	28	27	22 4	20	21	25	28	27	21 52	20	21	25	28	27	21 40	19	21
7 51 59	26	29	28	22 56	21	22	26	29	28	22 43	21	22	26	29	28	22 31	20	22
7 56 11	27	♍	29	23 47	22	23	27	♍	29	23 34	22	23	27	♍	29	23 21	21	23
8 0 23	28	1	♎	24 38	23	24	28	1	♎	24 25	22	24	28	1	♎	24 12	22	24
8 4 34	29	2	1	25 29	24	25	29	2	1	25 15	23	25	29	2	1	25 2	23	25
8 8 44	♌	3	2	26 20	25	26	♌	3	2	26 6	24	26	♌	3	2	25 52	24	26
8 12 53	1	4	3	27 10	25	27	1	4	3	26 56	25	27	1	4	3	26 42	25	27
8 17 2	2	5	4	28 1	26	28	2	5	4	27 46	26	28	2	5	4	27 31	26	28
8 21 10	3	6	5	28 51	27	29	3	6	5	28 36	27	29	3	6	5	28 21	27	29
8 25 18	4	7	6	29 41	28	♑	4	7	6	29 26	28	♑	4	7	6	29 10	27	♑
8 29 24	5	8	7	0♏ 31	29	1	5	8	7	0♏ 15	29	1	5	8	6	29 59	28	0
8 33 30	6	9	7	1 21	✗	2	6	9	7	1 5	✗	2	6	9	7	0♏ 48	29	1
8 37 36	7	10	8	2 11	1	3	7	10	8	1 54	0	3	7	10	8	1 37	✗	2
8 41 40	8	11	9	3 0	2	4	8	11	9	2 43	1	4	8	11	9	2 25	1	3
8 45 44	9	12	10	3 49	2	5	9	12	10	3 32	2	4	9	12	10	3 14	2	4
8 49 47	10	13	11	4 38	3	6	10	13	11	4 20	3	5	10	13	11	4 2	3	5
8 53 50	11	14	12	5 27	4	7	11	14	12	5 9	4	6	11	14	12	4 50	3	6
8 57 51	12	15	13	6 16	5	8	12	15	13	5 57	5	7	12	15	13	5 38	4	7
9 1 52	13	16	14	7 5	6	8	13	16	14	6 46	6	8	13	16	14	6 26	5	8
9 5 52	14	17	15	7 53	7	9	14	17	15	7 34	6	8	14	17	15	7 14	6	9
HOUSES	4	5	6	7	8	9	4	5	6	7	8	9	4	5	6	7	8	9

LATITUDE 37° S.   LATITUDE 38° S.   LATITUDE 39° S.

LATITUDE 37° N.　　　　LATITUDE 38° N.　　　　LATITUDE 39° N.

SIDEREAL TIME	10 Ω	11 ♍	12 ≏	ASC ♏	2 ♐	3 ♑	10 Ω	11 ♍	12 ≏	ASC ♏	2 ♐	3 ♑	10 Ω	11 ♍	12 ≏	ASC ♏	2 ♐	3 ♑
H M S	°	°	°	° '	°	°	°	°	°	° '	°	°	°	°	°	° '	°	°
9 9 52	15	18	16	8 41	8	10	15	18	15	8 22	7	10	15	18	15	8 1	7	10
9 13 50	16	19	16	9 30	9	11	16	19	16	9 9	8	11	16	19	16	8 49	8	11
9 17 49	17	20	17	10 18	9	12	17	20	17	9 57	9	12	17	20	17	9 36	9	12
9 21 46	18	21	18	11 5	10	13	18	21	18	10 44	10	13	18	21	18	10 23	9	13
9 25 42	19	22	19	11 53	11	14	19	22	19	11 32	11	14	19	22	19	11 10	10	14
9 29 38	20	23	20	12 40	12	15	20	23	20	12 19	12	15	20	23	20	11 57	11	15
9 33 34	21	24	21	13 28	13	16	21	24	21	13 6	12	16	21	24	21	12 43	12	16
9 37 28	22	24	22	14 15	14	17	22	24	22	13 52	13	17	22	24	21	13 30	13	16
9 41 22	23	25	23	15 2	15	18	23	25	22	14 39	14	18	23	25	22	14 16	14	17
9 45 15	24	26	23	15 49	15	19	24	26	23	15 26	15	19	24	26	23	15 2	15	18
9 49 8	25	27	24	16 36	16	20	25	27	24	16 12	16	20	25	27	24	15 48	15	19
9 53 0	26	28	25	17 23	17	21	26	28	25	16 59	17	20	26	28	25	16 34	16	20
9 56 51	27	29	26	18 9	18	22	27	29	26	17 45	17	21	27	29	26	17 20	17	21
10 0 42	28	≏	27	18 56	19	23	28	≏	27	18 31	18	22	28	≏	26	18 6	18	22
10 4 32	29	1	28	19 42	20	24	29	1	28	19 17	19	23	29	1	27	18 51	19	23
10 8 22	♏	2	29	20 28	20	25	♏	2	28	20 3	20	24	♏	2	28	19 37	20	24
10 12 11	1	3	29	21 14	21	25	1	3	29	20 49	21	25	1	3	29	20 22	20	25
10 15 59	2	4	♏	22 0	22	26	2	4	♏	21 34	22	26	2	4	♏	21 8	21	26
10 19 47	3	5	1	22 46	23	27	3	5	1	22 20	23	27	3	5	1	21 53	22	27
10 23 34	4	6	2	23 32	24	28	4	6	2	23 5	23	28	4	6	1	22 38	23	28
10 27 21	5	7	3	24 18	25	29	5	7	2	23 51	24	29	5	7	2	23 23	24	29
10 31 8	6	8	4	25 4	26	♒	6	8	3	24 36	25	♒	6	8	3	24 8	25	♒
10 34 53	7	9	4	25 49	26	1	7	9	4	25 22	26	1	7	9	4	24 53	25	1
10 38 39	8	9	5	26 35	27	2	8	9	5	26 7	27	2	8	9	5	25 38	26	2
10 42 24	9	10	6	27 20	28	3	9	10	6	26 52	28	3	9	10	6	26 23	27	3
10 46 8	10	11	7	28 6	29	4	10	11	7	27 37	28	4	10	11	6	27 8	28	4
10 49 52	11	12	8	28 51	♑	5	11	12	7	28 22	29	5	11	12	7	27 53	29	5
10 53 36	12	13	8	29 37	1	6	12	13	8	29 8	♑	6	12	13	8	28 38	♑	6
10 57 20	13	14	9	0♐ 22	1	7	13	14	9	29 53	1	7	13	14	9	29 23	1	7
11 1 3	14	15	10	1 8	2	8	14	15	10	0♐ 38	2	8	14	15	10	0♐ 7	1	8
11 4 45	15	16	11	1 53	3	9	15	16	11	1 23	3	9	15	16	10	0 52	2	9
11 8 28	16	17	12	2 39	4	10	16	17	11	2 8	4	10	16	17	11	1 37	3	10
11 12 10	17	18	12	3 24	5	11	17	18	12	2 53	4	11	17	18	12	2 22	4	11
11 15 52	18	19	13	4 9	6	12	18	18	13	3 38	5	12	18	18	13	3 6	5	12
11 19 33	19	19	14	4 55	7	13	19	19	14	4 23	6	13	19	19	13	3 51	6	13
11 23 15	20	20	15	5 40	8	14	20	20	15	5 8	7	14	20	20	14	4 36	7	14
11 26 56	21	21	16	6 26	8	15	21	21	15	5 54	8	15	21	21	15	5 21	8	15
11 30 37	22	22	16	7 11	9	16	22	22	16	6 39	9	16	22	22	16	6 6	8	16
11 34 17	23	23	17	7 57	10	17	23	23	17	7 24	10	17	23	23	17	6 51	9	17
11 37 58	24	24	18	8 43	11	18	24	24	18	8 10	11	18	24	24	17	7 36	10	18
11 41 39	25	25	19	9 28	12	19	25	25	18	8 55	12	19	25	25	18	8 21	11	19
11 45 19	26	26	20	10 14	13	20	26	26	19	9 41	12	20	26	25	19	9 6	12	20
11 48 59	27	27	20	11 0	14	21	27	26	20	10 26	13	21	27	26	20	9 52	13	21
11 52 40	28	27	21	11 46	15	22	28	27	21	11 12	14	22	28	27	21	10 37	14	22
11 56 20	29	28	22	12 32	16	23	29	28	22	11 58	15	23	29	28	21	11 23	15	23
HOUSES	4	5	6	7	8	9	4	5	6	7	8	9	4	5	6	7	8	9

LATITUDE 37° S.　　　　LATITUDE 38° S.　　　　LATITUDE 39° S.

	LATITUDE 37° N.						LATITUDE 38° N.						LATITUDE 39° N.					
SIDEREAL TIME	10 ♎	11 ♎	12 ♏	ASC ♐	2 ♑	3 ♒	10 ♎	11 ♎	12 ♏	ASC ♐	2 ♑	3 ♒	10 ♎	11 ♎	12 ♏	ASC ♐	2 ♑	3 ♒
H M S	°	°	°	° '	°	°	°	°	°	° '	°	°	°	°	°	° '	°	°
12 0 0	0	29	23	13 19	17	24	0	29	22	12 44	16	24	0	29	22	12 8	16	24
12 3 40	1	♏	23	14 5	17	25	1	♏	23	13 30	17	25	1	♏	23	12 54	17	25
12 7 20	2	1	24	14 52	18	26	2	1	24	14 16	18	26	2	1	24	13 40	17	26
12 11 1	3	2	25	15 38	19	27	3	2	25	15 3	19	27	3	2	24	14 26	18	27
12 14 41	4	3	26	16 25	20	28	4	3	26	15 49	20	28	4	2	25	15 13	19	28
12 18 21	5	4	27	17 12	21	29	5	3	26	16 36	21	29	5	3	26	15 59	20	29
12 22 2	6	4	27	17 59	22	♓	6	4	27	17 23	22	♓	6	4	27	16 46	21	♓
12 25 42	7	5	28	18 47	23	2	7	5	28	18 10	23	2	7	5	28	17 33	22	1
12 29 23	8	6	29	19 34	24	3	8	6	29	18 57	24	3	8	6	28	18 20	23	2
12 33 4	9	7	♐	20 22	25	4	9	7	29	19 45	25	4	9	7	29	19 7	24	4
12 36 45	10	8	1	21 10	26	5	10	8	♐	20 33	26	5	10	8	♐	19 55	25	5
12 40 27	11	9	1	21 59	27	6	11	9	1	21 21	27	6	11	9	1	20 42	26	6
12 44 8	12	10	2	22 47	28	7	12	10	2	22 9	28	7	12	9	1	21 30	27	7
12 47 50	13	11	3	23 36	29	8	13	10	3	22 58	29	8	13	10	2	22 19	28	8
12 51 32	14	11	4	24 25	♒	9	14	11	3	23 47	♒	9	14	11	3	23 7	29	9
12 55 15	15	12	5	25 15	1	10	15	12	4	24 36	1	10	15	12	4	23 56	♒	10
12 58 57	16	13	5	26 4	2	11	16	13	5	25 25	2	11	16	13	5	24 45	1	11
13 2 40	17	14	6	26 54	3	13	17	14	6	26 15	3	13	17	14	5	25 35	2	12
13 6 24	18	15	7	27 45	4	14	18	15	7	27 5	4	14	18	15	6	26 25	3	14
13 10 8	19	16	8	28 35	5	15	19	16	7	27 56	5	15	19	15	7	27 15	4	15
13 13 52	20	17	9	29 26	6	16	20	16	8	28 47	6	16	20	16	8	28 5	5	16
13 17 36	21	17	9	0♑ 18	7	17	21	17	9	29 38	7	17	21	17	9	28 56	6	17
13 21 21	22	18	10	1 10	8	18	22	18	10	0♑ 29	8	18	22	18	9	29 48	8	18
13 25 7	23	19	11	2 2	9	19	23	19	11	1 21	9	19	23	19	10	0♑ 40	9	19
13 28 52	24	20	12	2 55	11	20	24	20	11	2 14	10	20	24	20	11	1 32	10	20
13 32 39	25	21	13	3 48	12	22	25	21	12	3 7	11	22	25	21	12	2 24	11	22
13 36 26	26	22	13	4 41	13	23	26	22	13	4 0	12	23	26	21	13	3 18	12	23
13 40 13	27	23	14	5 35	14	24	27	22	14	4 54	14	24	27	22	13	4 11	13	24
13 44 1	28	23	15	6 30	15	25	28	23	15	5 48	15	25	28	23	14	5 5	14	25
13 47 49	29	24	16	7 25	16	26	29	24	16	6 43	16	26	29	24	15	6 0	15	26
13 51 38	♏	25	17	8 21	17	27	♏	25	16	7 39	17	27	♏	25	16	6 55	17	27
13 55 28	1	26	18	9 17	19	29	1	26	17	8 34	18	29	1	26	17	7 51	18	29
13 59 18	2	27	18	10 13	20	♈	2	27	18	9 31	19	♈	2	27	18	8 47	19	♈
14 3 9	3	28	19	11 11	21	1	3	28	19	10 28	21	1	3	27	18	9 44	20	1
14 7 0	4	29	20	12 8	22	2	4	29	20	11 26	22	2	4	28	19	10 42	21	2
14 10 52	5	♐	21	13 7	23	3	5	29	21	12 24	23	3	5	29	20	11 40	23	3
14 14 45	6	0	22	14 6	25	5	6	♐	21	13 23	24	5	6	♐	21	12 39	24	5
14 18 38	7	1	23	15 6	26	6	7	1	22	14 23	25	6	7	1	22	13 38	25	6
14 22 32	8	2	24	16 6	27	7	8	2	23	15 23	27	7	8	2	23	14 38	26	7
14 26 26	9	3	24	17 7	28	8	9	3	24	16 24	28	8	9	3	24	15 39	28	8
14 30 22	10	4	25	18 9	♓	9	10	4	25	17 26	29	9	10	4	24	16 41	29	9
14 34 17	11	5	26	19 12	1	10	11	5	26	18 28	♓	11	11	4	25	17 43	♓	11
14 38 14	12	6	27	20 15	2	12	12	6	27	19 32	2	12	12	5	26	18 47	2	12
14 42 11	13	7	28	21 19	3	13	13	6	28	20 36	3	13	13	6	27	19 51	3	13
14 46 10	14	8	29	22 24	5	14	14	7	28	21 41	4	14	14	7	28	20 55	4	14
HOUSES	4	5	6	7	8	9	4	5	6	7	8	9	4	5	6	7	8	9

LATITUDE 37° N. LATITUDE 38° N. LATITUDE 39° N.

SIDEREAL TIME (H M S)	10 ♏	11 ♐	12 ♑	ASC ♑	2 ♓	3 ♈	10 ♏	11 ♐	12 ♐	ASC ♑	2 ♓	3 ♈	10 ♏	11 ♐	12 ♐	ASC ♑	2 ♓	3 ♈
14 50 8	15	8	0	23 30	6	15	15	8	29	22 46	6	15	15	8	29	22 1	6	15
14 54 8	16	9	1	24 37	7	16	16	9	♑23	53	7	17	16	9	♑23	8	7	17
14 58 8	17	10	2	25 44	9	18	17	10	1	25 1	8	18	17	10	1	24 15	8	18
15 2 9	18	11	3	26 52	10	19	18	11	2	26 9	10	19	18	11	2	25 24	10	19
15 6 10	19	12	4	28 2	11	20	19	12	3	27 18	11	20	19	12	3	26 33	11	20
15 10 13	20	13	4	29 12	13	21	20	13	4	28 29	13	21	20	13	4	27 44	12	21
15 14 16	21	14	5	0♒23	14	22	21	14	5	29 40	14	23	21	13	5	28 55	14	23
15 18 20	22	15	6	1 35	16	24	22	15	6	0♒52	15	24	22	14	5	0♒8	15	24
15 22 24	23	16	7	2 48	17	25	23	15	7	2 6	17	25	23	15	6	1 21	17	25
15 26 30	24	17	8	4 2	18	26	24	16	8	3 20	18	26	24	16	7	2 36	18	26
15 30 36	25	18	9	5 18	20	27	25	17	9	4 36	20	27	25	17	8	3 52	20	28
15 34 42	26	18	10	6 34	21	28	26	18	10	5 52	21	29	26	18	9	5 9	21	29
15 38 50	27	19	11	7 51	23	♉	27	19	11	7 10	23	♉	27	19	10	6 27	22	♉
15 42 58	28	20	12	9 10	24	1	28	20	12	8 29	24	1	28	20	11	7 46	24	1
15 47 7	29	21	13	10 29	26	2	29	21	13	9 49	25	2	29	21	12	9 6	25	2
15 51 16	♐	22	14	11 50	27	3	♐	22	14	11 10	27	3	♐	22	13	10 28	27	4
15 55 26	1	23	15	13 11	28	4	1	23	15	12 32	28	5	1	23	14	11 50	28	5
15 59 37	2	24	16	14 34	♈	6	2	24	16	13 55	♈	6	2	24	15	13 15	♈	6
16 3 49	3	25	17	15 58	1	7	3	25	17	15 20	1	7	3	25	17	14 40	1	7
16 8 1	4	26	19	17 23	3	8	4	26	18	16 46	3	8	4	26	18	16 6	3	8
16 12 14	5	27	20	18 50	4	9	5	27	19	18 13	4	9	5	27	19	17 34	4	10
16 16 27	6	28	21	20 17	6	10	6	28	20	19 41	6	11	6	27	20	19 3	6	11
16 20 41	7	29	22	21 46	7	12	7	29	21	21 10	7	12	7	28	21	20 33	7	12
16 24 56	8	♑	23	23 15	9	13	8	♑	22	22 41	9	13	8	29	22	22 5	9	13
16 29 11	9	1	24	24 46	10	14	9	1	24	24 13	10	14	9	♑	23	23 38	10	14
16 33 27	10	2	25	26 18	12	15	10	2	25	25 46	12	15	10	1	24	25 12	12	15
16 37 43	11	3	26	27 51	13	16	11	3	26	27 20	13	16	11	2	25	26 47	13	17
16 41 59	12	4	27	29 25	15	17	12	4	27	28 55	15	18	12	3	26	28 24	15	18
16 46 17	13	5	29	1♓1	16	19	13	5	28	0♓32	16	19	13	4	28	0♓2	16	19
16 50 34	14	6	♒	2 37	17	20	14	6	29	2 9	18	20	14	5	29	1 41	18	20
16 54 53	15	7	1	4 14	19	21	15	7	♒	3 48	19	21	15	6	♒	3 21	19	21
16 59 11	16	8	2	5 52	20	22	16	8	2	5 28	21	22	16	7	1	5 2	21	22
17 3 30	17	9	3	7 31	22	23	17	9	3	7 8	22	23	17	8	2	6 44	22	24
17 7 49	18	10	5	9 12	23	24	18	10	4	8 50	24	24	18	9	4	8 27	24	25
17 12 9	19	11	6	10 52	25	25	19	11	5	10 32	25	26	19	10	5	10 11	25	26
17 16 29	20	12	7	12 34	26	27	20	12	7	12 16	26	27	20	11	6	11 56	27	27
17 20 49	21	13	8	14 17	28	28	21	13	8	14 0	28	28	21	12	7	13 42	28	28
17 25 10	22	14	9	16 0	29	29	22	14	9	15 45	29	29	22	14	9	15 29	♉	29
17 29 31	23	15	11	17 43	♉	♊	23	15	10	17 30	♉	♊	23	15	10	17 16	1	♊
17 33 51	24	16	12	19 28	2	1	24	16	12	19 16	2	1	24	16	11	19 4	2	1
17 38 13	25	17	13	21 12	3	2	25	17	13	21 3	4	2	25	17	12	20 53	4	3
17 42 34	26	18	15	22 57	5	3	26	18	14	22 50	5	3	26	18	14	22 42	5	4
17 46 55	27	19	16	24 43	6	4	27	19	16	24 37	6	5	27	19	15	24 31	7	5
17 51 17	28	20	17	26 28	7	5	28	20	17	26 24	8	6	28	20	16	26 20	8	6
17 55 38	29	21	19	28 14	9	6	29	21	18	28 12	9	7	29	21	18	28 10	9	7
HOUSES	4	5	6	7	8	9	4	5	6	7	8	9	4	5	6	7	8	9

LATITUDE 37° S. LATITUDE 38° S. LATITUDE 39° S.

LATITUDE 37° N.   LATITUDE 38° N.   LATITUDE 39° N.

SIDEREAL TIME (H M S)			10 ♑	11 ♑	12 ♒	ASC ♈	2 ♉	3 ♊	10 ♑	11 ♑	12 ♒	ASC ♈	2 ♉	3 ♊	10 ♑	11 ♑	12 ♒	ASC ♈	2 ♉	3 ♊
18	0	0	0	22	20	0 0	10	8	0	22	20	0 0	10	8	0	22	19	0 0	11	8
18	4	22	1	24	21	1 46	11	9	1	23	21	1 48	12	9	1	23	21	1 50	12	9
18	8	43	2	25	23	3 32	13	10	2	24	22	3 36	13	10	2	24	22	3 40	14	10
18	13	5	3	26	24	5 17	14	11	3	25	24	5 23	14	11	3	25	23	5 29	15	11
18	17	26	4	27	25	7 3	15	12	4	27	25	7 10	16	12	4	26	25	7 18	16	12
18	21	47	5	28	27	8 48	17	13	5	28	26	8 57	17	13	5	27	26	9 7	18	13
18	26	9	6	29	28	10 32	18	14	6	29	28	10 44	18	14	6	29	28	10 56	19	14
18	30	29	7	♒	♓	12 17	19	15	7	♒	29	12 30	20	15	7	♒	29	12 44	20	15
18	34	50	8	1	1	14 0	21	16	8	1	♓	14 15	21	16	8	1	♓	14 31	21	16
18	39	11	9	2	2	15 43	22	17	9	2	2	16 0	22	17	9	2	2	16 18	23	18
18	43	31	10	3	4	17 26	23	18	10	3	4	17 44	23	18	10	3	3	18 4	24	19
18	47	51	11	5	5	19 8	24	19	11	4	5	19 28	25	19	11	4	5	19 49	25	20
18	52	11	12	6	7	20 48	25	20	12	6	6	21 10	26	20	12	5	6	21 33	26	21
18	56	30	13	7	8	22 29	27	21	13	7	8	22 52	27	21	13	6	8	23 16	28	22
19	0	49	14	8	10	24 8	28	22	14	8	9	24 32	28	22	14	8	9	24 58	29	23
19	5	7	15	9	11	25 46	29	23	15	9	11	26 12	♊	23	15	9	11	26 39	♊	24
19	9	26	16	10	13	27 23	♊	24	16	10	12	27 51	1	24	16	10	12	28 19	1	25
19	13	43	17	11	14	28 59	1	25	17	11	14	29 28	2	25	17	11	14	29 58	2	26
19	18	0	18	13	15	♉ 0 35	3	26	18	12	15	♉ 1 5	3	26	18	12	15	♉ 0 36	4	27
19	22	17	19	14	17	2 9	4	27	19	14	17	2 40	4	27	19	13	17	3 13	5	28
19	26	33	20	15	18	3 42	5	28	20	15	18	4 14	5	28	20	15	18	4 48	6	29
19	30	49	21	16	20	5 14	6	29	21	16	20	5 47	6	29	21	16	20	6 22	7	♋
19	35	4	22	17	21	6 45	7	♋	22	17	21	7 19	8	♋	22	17	21	7 55	8	1
19	39	19	23	18	23	8 14	8	1	23	18	23	8 50	9	1	23	18	23	9 27	9	2
19	43	33	24	20	24	9 43	9	2	24	19	24	10 19	10	2	24	19	24	10 57	10	3
19	47	46	25	21	26	11 10	10	3	25	21	26	11 47	11	3	25	20	26	12 26	11	3
19	51	59	26	22	27	12 37	11	4	26	22	27	13 14	12	4	26	22	27	13 54	12	4
19	56	11	27	23	29	14 2	13	5	27	23	29	14 40	13	5	27	23	29	15 20	13	5
20	0	23	28	24	♈	15 26	14	6	28	24	♈	16 5	14	6	28	24	♈	16 45	15	6
20	4	34	29	26	2	16 49	15	7	29	25	2	17 28	15	7	29	25	2	18 10	16	7
20	8	44	♒	27	3	18 10	16	8	♒	27	3	18 50	16	8	♒	26	3	19 32	17	8
20	12	53	1	28	4	19 31	17	9	1	28	5	20 11	17	9	1	28	5	20 54	18	9
20	17	2	2	29	6	20 50	18	10	2	29	6	21 31	18	10	2	29	6	22 14	19	10
20	21	10	3	♓	7	22 9	19	11	3	♓	7	22 50	19	11	3	♓	8	23 33	20	11
20	25	18	4	2	9	23 26	20	12	4	1	9	24 8	20	12	4	1	9	24 51	21	12
20	29	24	5	3	10	24 42	21	12	5	3	10	25 24	21	13	5	2	10	26 8	22	13
20	33	30	6	4	12	25 58	22	13	6	4	12	26 40	22	14	6	4	12	27 24	23	14
20	37	36	7	5	13	27 12	23	14	7	5	13	27 54	23	15	7	5	13	28 39	24	15
20	41	40	8	6	14	28 25	24	15	8	6	15	29 8	24	15	8	6	15	29 52	25	16
20	45	44	9	8	16	29 37	25	16	9	7	16	♊ 0 20	25	16	9	7	16	♊ 1 5	25	17
20	49	47	10	9	17	♊ 0 48	26	17	10	9	17	1 31	26	17	10	9	18	2 16	26	17
20	53	50	11	10	19	1 58	26	18	11	10	19	2 42	27	18	11	10	19	3 27	27	18
20	57	51	12	11	20	3 8	27	19	12	11	20	3 51	28	19	12	11	20	4 36	28	19
21	1	52	13	12	21	4 16	28	20	13	12	22	4 59	29	20	13	12	22	5 45	29	20
21	5	52	14	14	23	5 23	29	21	14	13	23	6 7	♋	21	14	13	23	6 52	♋	21
HOUSES			4	5	6	7	8	9	4	5	6	7	8	9	4	5	6	7	8	9

LATITUDE 37° S.   LATITUDE 38° S.   LATITUDE 39° S.

LATITUDE 37° N.   LATITUDE 38° N.   LATITUDE 39° N.

SIDEREAL TIME	10 ♒	11 ♓	12 ♈	ASC ♊	2 ♋	3 ♋	10 ♒	11 ♓	12 ♈	ASC ♊	2 ♋	3 ♋	10 ♒	11 ♓	12 ♈	ASC ♊	2 ♋	3 ♋
H M S	°	°	°	° '	°	°	°	°	°	° '	°	°	°	°	°	° '	°	°
21 9 52	15	15	24	6 30	0	22	15	15	24	7 14	1	22	15	15	24	7 59	1	22
21 13 50	16	16	25	7 36	1	22	16	16	26	8 19	2	23	16	16	26	9 5	2	23
21 17 49	17	17	27	8 41	2	23	17	17	27	9 24	2	24	17	17	27	10 9	3	24
21 21 46	18	18	28	9 45	3	24	18	18	28	10 28	3	24	18	18	28	11 13	4	25
21 25 42	19	20	29	10 48	4	25	19	19	29	11 32	4	25	19	19	♉	12 17	5	26
21 29 38	20	21	♉	11 51	5	26	20	21	♉	12 34	5	26	20	21	1	13 19	6	26
21 33 34	21	22	2	12 53	6	27	21	22	2	13 36	6	27	21	22	2	14 21	6	27
21 37 28	22	23	3	13 54	6	28	22	23	3	14 37	7	28	22	23	4	15 22	7	28
21 41 22	23	24	4	14 54	7	29	23	24	5	15 37	8	29	23	24	5	16 22	8	29
21 45 15	24	25	5	15 54	8	Ω	24	25	6	16 37	9	Ω	24	25	6	17 21	9	Ω
21 49 8	25	27	7	16 53	9	0	25	27	7	17 36	9	1	25	27	7	18 20	10	1
21 53 0	26	28	8	17 52	10	1	26	28	8	18 34	10	1	26	28	9	19 18	11	2
21 56 51	27	29	9	18 49	11	2	27	29	9	19 32	11	2	27	29	10	20 16	12	3
22 0 42	28	♈	10	19 47	12	3	28	♈	11	20 29	12	3	28	♈	11	21 13	12	3
22 4 32	29	1	11	20 43	12	4	29	1	12	21 26	13	4	29	1	12	22 9	13	4
22 8 22	♓	3	13	21 39	13	5	♓	3	13	22 21	14	5	♓	3	13	23 5	14	5
22 12 11	1	4	14	22 35	14	6	1	4	14	23 17	14	6	1	4	15	24 0	15	6
22 15 59	2	5	15	23 30	15	7	2	5	15	24 12	15	7	2	5	16	24 55	16	7
22 19 47	3	6	16	24 25	16	7	3	6	16	25 0	16	8	3	6	17	25 49	17	8
22 23 34	4	7	17	25 19	17	8	4	7	18	26 0	17	8	4	7	18	26 42	17	9
22 27 21	5	8	18	26 12	17	9	5	8	19	26 53	18	9	5	8	19	27 36	18	9
22 31 8	6	10	19	27 5	18	10	6	10	20	27 46	19	10	6	10	20	28 28	19	10
22 34 53	7	11	21	27 58	19	11	7	11	21	28 39	19	11	7	11	21	29 20	20	11
22 38 39	8	12	22	28 50	20	12	8	12	22	29 31	20	12	8	12	22	0♋ 12	21	12
22 42 24	9	13	23	29 42	21	13	9	13	23	0♋ 22	21	13	9	13	24	1 4	21	13
22 46 8	10	14	24	0♋ 34	21	13	10	14	24	1 13	22	14	10	14	25	1 55	22	14
22 49 52	11	15	25	1 25	22	14	11	15	25	2 4	23	14	11	15	26	2 45	23	15
22 53 36	12	16	26	2 15	23	15	12	16	26	2 55	23	15	12	16	27	3 35	24	15
22 57 20	13	17	27	3 6	24	16	13	17	27	3 45	24	16	13	18	28	4 25	25	16
23 1 3	14	19	28	3 56	25	17	14	19	28	4 35	25	17	14	19	29	5 15	25	17
23 4 45	15	20	29	4 45	25	18	15	20	29	5 24	26	18	15	20	♊	6 4	26	18
23 8 28	16	21	♊	5 35	26	19	16	21	♊	6 13	27	19	16	21	1	6 53	27	19
23 12 10	17	22	1	6 24	27	19	17	22	1	7 2	27	20	17	22	2	7 41	28	20
23 15 52	18	23	2	7 13	28	20	18	23	2	7 51	28	20	18	23	3	8 30	29	21
23 19 33	19	24	3	8 1	29	21	19	24	3	8 39	29	21	19	24	4	9 18	29	21
23 23 15	20	25	4	8 50	29	22	20	25	4	9 27	Ω	22	20	25	5	10 5	Ω	22
23 26 56	21	26	5	9 38	Ω	23	21	26	5	10 15	1	23	21	26	6	10 53	1	23
23 30 37	22	27	6	10 26	1	24	22	27	6	11 3	1	24	22	28	7	11 40	2	24
23 34 17	23	28	7	11 13	2	25	23	28	7	11 50	2	25	23	29	8	12 27	2	25
23 37 58	24	29	8	12 1	3	26	24	♉	8	12 37	3	26	24	♉	9	13 14	3	26
23 41 39	25	♉	9	12 48	3	26	25	1	9	13 24	4	27	25	1	10	14 1	4	27
23 45 19	26	2	10	13 35	4	27	26	2	10	14 11	4	27	26	2	11	14 47	5	28
23 48 59	27	3	11	14 22	5	28	27	3	11	14 57	5	28	27	3	12	15 34	6	28
23 52 40	28	4	12	15 8	6	29	28	4	12	15 44	6	29	28	4	13	16 20	6	29
23 56 20	29	5	13	15 55	7	♍	29	5	13	16 30	7	♍	29	5	13	17 6	7	♍
HOUSES	4	5	6	7	8	9	4	5	6	7	8	9	4	5	6	7	8	9

LATITUDE 37° S.   LATITUDE 38° S.   LATITUDE 39° S.

LATITUDE 40° N.   LATITUDE 41° N.   LATITUDE 42° N.

SIDEREAL TIME	10 ♈	11 ♉	12 ♊	ASC ♋	2 ♌	3 ♍	10 ♈	11 ♉	12 ♊	ASC ♋	2 ♌	3 ♍	10 ♈	11 ♉	12 ♊	ASC ♋	2 ♌	3 ♍
H M S	°	°	°	° '	°	°	°	°	°	° '	°	°	°	°	°	° '	°	°
0 0 0	0	6	15	18 28	8	1	0	6	15	19 5	9	1	0	7	16	19 43	9	1
0 3 40	1	7	16	19 13	9	2	1	7	16	19 50	9	2	1	8	17	20 27	10	2
0 7 20	2	8	17	19 58	10	3	2	8	17	20 35	10	3	2	9	18	21 12	10	3
0 11 1	3	9	18	20 43	11	4	3	10	18	21 19	11	4	3	10	19	21 56	11	4
0 14 41	4	10	19	21 28	11	5	4	11	19	22 4	12	5	4	11	20	22 41	12	5
0 18 21	5	11	19	22 13	12	5	5	12	20	22 49	12	6	5	12	20	23 25	13	6
0 22 2	6	12	20	22 58	13	6	6	13	21	23 33	13	6	6	13	21	24 9	14	7
0 25 43	7	13	21	23 43	14	7	7	14	22	24 18	14	7	7	14	22	24 53	14	7
0 29 23	8	15	22	24 28	14	8	8	15	23	25 2	15	8	8	15	23	25 37	15	8
0 33 4	9	16	23	25 12	15	9	9	16	23	25 46	16	9	9	16	24	26 21	16	9
0 36 45	10	17	24	25 57	16	10	10	17	24	26 31	16	10	10	17	25	27 5	17	10
0 40 27	11	18	25	26 41	17	11	11	18	25	27 15	17	11	11	18	26	27 49	17	11
0 44 8	12	19	26	27 26	18	12	12	19	26	27 59	18	12	12	19	27	28 33	18	12
0 47 50	13	20	26	28 10	18	13	13	20	27	28 43	19	13	13	20	27	29 16	19	13
0 51 32	14	21	27	28 55	19	13	14	21	28	29 27	19	13	14	21	28	0♌ 0	20	14
0 55 15	15	22	28	29 39	20	14	15	22	29	0♌ 11	20	14	15	22	29	0 44	20	14
0 58 57	16	23	29	0♌ 24	21	15	16	23	♋	0 55	21	15	16	23	♋	1 27	21	15
1 2 40	17	24	♋	1 8	22	16	17	24	0	1 39	22	16	17	24	1	2 11	22	16
1 6 24	18	25	1	1 53	22	17	18	25	1	2 23	23	17	18	25	2	2 55	23	17
1 10 8	19	26	2	2 37	23	18	19	26	2	3 8	23	18	19	26	3	3 39	24	18
1 13 52	20	26	2	3 21	24	19	20	27	3	3 52	24	19	20	27	3	4 22	24	19
1 17 36	21	27	3	4 6	25	20	21	28	4	4 36	25	20	21	28	4	5 6	25	20
1 21 21	22	28	4	4 51	26	21	22	29	5	5 20	26	21	22	29	5	5 50	26	21
1 25 7	23	29	5	5 35	26	22	23	♊	6	6 4	27	22	23	♊	6	6 34	27	22
1 28 52	24	♊	6	6 20	27	22	24	1	6	6 49	27	22	24	1	7	7 18	28	23
1 32 39	25	1	7	7 5	28	23	25	2	7	7 33	28	23	25	2	8	8 2	28	23
1 36 26	26	2	8	7 49	29	24	26	3	8	8 17	29	24	26	3	8	8 46	29	24
1 40 13	27	3	8	8 34	♍	25	27	4	9	9 2	♍	25	27	4	9	9 30	♍	25
1 44 1	28	4	9	9 19	0	26	28	4	10	9 46	1	26	28	5	10	10 14	1	26
1 47 49	29	5	10	10 4	1	27	29	5	10	10 31	1	27	29	6	11	10 58	2	27
1 51 38	♉	6	11	10 49	2	28	♉	6	11	11 16	2	28	♉	7	12	11 43	2	28
1 55 28	1	7	12	11 34	3	29	1	7	12	12 1	3	29	1	8	13	12 27	3	29
1 59 18	2	8	13	12 20	4	♎	2	8	13	12 45	4	♎	2	9	13	13 12	4	♎
2 3 9	3	9	13	13 5	5	1	3	9	14	13 30	5	1	3	10	14	13 56	5	1
2 7 0	4	10	14	13 50	5	2	4	10	15	14 16	6	2	4	10	15	14 41	6	2
2 10 52	5	11	15	14 36	6	3	5	11	15	15 1	6	3	5	11	16	15 26	7	3
2 14 45	6	12	16	15 22	7	4	6	12	16	15 46	7	4	6	12	17	16 11	7	4
2 18 38	7	13	17	16 8	8	5	7	13	17	16 32	8	5	7	13	18	16 56	8	4
2 22 32	8	14	18	16 54	9	5	8	14	18	17 17	9	5	8	14	18	17 41	9	5
2 26 26	9	15	18	17 40	10	6	9	15	19	18 3	10	6	9	15	19	18 26	10	6
2 30 22	10	16	19	18 26	10	7	10	16	20	18 49	11	7	10	16	20	19 12	11	7
2 34 17	11	17	20	19 12	11	8	11	17	21	19 35	11	8	11	17	21	19 57	12	8
2 38 14	12	18	21	19 59	12	9	12	18	21	20 21	12	9	12	18	22	20 43	12	9
2 42 11	13	18	22	20 45	13	10	13	19	22	21 7	13	10	13	19	23	21 29	13	10
2 46 10	14	19	23	21 32	14	11	14	20	23	21 53	14	11	14	20	23	22 15	14	11
HOUSES	4	5	6	7	8	9	4	5	6	7	8	9	4	5	6	7	8	9

LATITUDE 40° S.   LATITUDE 41° S.   LATITUDE 42° S.

LATITUDE 40° N. LATITUDE 41° N. LATITUDE 42° N.

SIDEREAL TIME	10 ♉	11 ♊	12 ♋	ASC ♌	2 ♍	3 ♎	10 ♉	11 ♊	12 ♋	ASC ♌	2 ♍	3 ♎	10 ♉	11 ♊	12 ♋	ASC ♌	2 ♍	3 ♎
H M S	°	°	°	° '	°	°	°	°	°	° '	°	°	°	°	°	° '	°	°
2 50 8	15	20	23	22 19	15	12	15	21	24	22 40	15	12	15	21	24	23 1	15	12
2 54 8	16	21	24	23 6	16	13	16	22	25	23 27	16	13	16	22	25	23 47	16	13
2 58 8	17	22	25	23 54	16	14	17	23	26	24 13	17	14	17	23	26	24 34	17	14
3 2 9	18	23	26	24 41	17	15	18	23	26	25 0	17	15	18	24	27	25 20	18	15
3 6 10	19	24	27	25 29	18	16	19	24	27	25 48	18	16	19	25	28	26 7	18	16
3 10 13	20	25	28	26 16	19	17	20	25	28	26 35	19	17	20	26	29	26 54	19	17
3 14 16	21	26	29	27 4	20	18	21	26	29	27 22	20	18	21	27	29	27 41	20	18
3 18 20	22	27	29	27 52	21	19	22	27	♌	28 10	21	19	22	27	♌	28 28	21	19
3 22 24	23	28	♌	28 40	22	20	23	28	1	28 58	22	20	23	28	1	29 15	22	20
3 26 30	24	29	1	29 29	23	21	24	29	2	29 46	23	21	24	29	2	0♍ 3	23	21
3 30 36	25	♋	2	0♍ 17	24	22	25	♋	2	0♍ 34	24	22	25	♋	3	0 51	24	22
3 34 42	26	1	3	1 6	24	23	26	1	3	1 22	24	23	26	1	4	1 38	25	23
3 38 50	27	2	4	1 55	25	24	27	2	4	2 11	25	24	27	2	5	2 26	25	24
3 42 58	28	3	5	2 44	26	25	28	3	5	2 59	26	25	28	3	5	3 15	26	25
3 47 7	29	4	6	3 33	27	26	29	4	6	3 48	27	26	29	4	6	4 3	27	26
3 51 16	♊	5	6	4 22	28	27	♊	5	7	4 37	28	27	♊	5	7	4 51	28	27
3 55 26	1	5	7	5 12	29	28	1	6	8	5 26	29	28	1	6	8	5 40	29	28
3 59 37	2	6	8	6 2	♎	29	2	7	9	6 15	♎	29	2	7	9	6 29	♎	29
4 3 49	3	7	9	6 51	1	♏	3	8	9	7 4	1	♏	3	8	10	7 18	1	♏
4 8 1	4	8	10	7 41	2	1	4	9	10	7 54	2	1	4	9	11	8 7	2	1
4 12 14	5	9	11	8 31	3	2	5	9	11	8 44	3	2	5	10	11	8 56	3	2
4 16 27	6	10	12	9 22	4	3	6	10	12	9 33	4	3	6	11	12	9 45	4	3
4 20 41	7	11	13	10 12	5	4	7	11	13	10 23	5	4	7	12	13	10 35	4	4
4 24 56	8	12	14	11 3	5	5	8	12	14	11 13	5	5	8	13	14	11 24	5	4
4 29 11	9	13	14	11 53	6	6	9	13	15	12 4	6	6	9	14	15	12 14	6	5
4 33 27	10	14	15	12 44	7	7	10	14	16	12 54	7	7	10	14	16	13 4	7	6
4 37 43	11	15	16	13 35	8	8	11	15	17	13 44	8	8	11	15	17	13 54	8	7
4 41 59	12	16	17	14 26	9	9	12	16	17	14 35	9	9	12	16	18	14 44	9	8
4 46 17	13	17	18	15 17	10	10	13	17	18	15 26	10	10	13	17	19	15 34	10	9
4 50 34	14	18	19	16 9	11	11	14	18	19	16 17	11	11	14	18	20	16 25	11	10
4 54 53	15	19	20	17 0	12	12	15	19	20	17 7	12	12	15	19	20	17 15	12	11
4 59 11	16	20	21	17 52	13	13	16	20	21	17 59	13	13	16	20	21	18 5	13	12
5 3 30	17	21	22	18 43	14	14	17	21	22	18 50	14	14	17	21	22	18 56	14	13
5 7 49	18	22	23	19 35	15	15	18	22	23	19 41	15	15	18	22	23	19 47	15	14
5 12 9	19	23	24	20 27	16	16	19	23	24	20 32	16	16	19	23	24	20 38	16	15
5 16 29	20	24	24	21 19	17	17	20	24	25	21 24	17	17	20	24	25	21 29	16	16
5 20 49	21	25	25	22 11	18	18	21	25	26	22 15	18	18	21	25	26	22 19	17	17
5 25 10	22	26	26	23 3	19	19	22	26	27	23 6	18	19	22	26	27	23 10	18	18
5 29 31	23	27	27	23 55	20	20	23	27	27	23 58	19	19	23	27	28	24 2	19	19
5 33 51	24	28	28	24 47	21	21	24	28	28	24 50	20	20	24	28	29	24 53	20	20
5 38 13	25	29	29	25 39	21	22	25	29	29	25 41	21	21	25	29	♍	25 44	21	21
5 42 34	26	29	♍	26 31	22	23	26	♌	♍	26 33	22	22	26	♌	0	26 35	22	22
5 46 55	27	♌	1	27 23	23	24	27	1	1	27 25	23	23	27	1	1	27 26	23	23
5 51 17	28	1	2	28 15	24	25	28	2	2	28 16	24	24	28	2	2	28 17	24	24
5 55 38	29	2	3	29 8	25	26	29	3	3	29 8	25	25	29	3	3	29 9	25	25
HOUSES	4	5	6	7	8	9	4	5	6	7	8	9	4	5	6	7	8	9

LATITUDE 40° S. LATITUDE 41° S. LATITUDE 42° S.

LATITUDE 40° N. LATITUDE 41° N. LATITUDE 42° N.

SIDEREAL TIME	10 ♐	11 ♌	12 ♍	ASC ♎		2 ♎	3 ♏	10 ♐	11 ♌	12 ♍	ASC ♎		2 ♎	3 ♏	10 ♐	11 ♌	12 ♍	ASC ♎		2 ♎	3 ♏
H M S	°	°	°	°	'	°	°	°	°	°	°	'	°	°	°	°	°	°	'	°	°
6 0 0	0	3	4	0	0	26	27	0	4	4	0	0	26	26	0	4	4	0	0	26	26
6 4 22	1	4	5	0	52	27	28	1	5	5	0	52	27	27	1	5	5	0	51	27	27
6 8 43	2	5	6	1	45	28	29	2	6	6	1	44	28	28	2	6	6	1	43	28	28
6 13 5	3	6	7	2	37	29	♐	3	7	7	2	35	29	♐	3	7	7	2	34	29	♐
6 17 26	4	7	8	3	29	♏	1	4	8	8	3	27	♏	♐	4	8	8	3	25	♏	♐
6 21 47	5	8	9	4	21	1	1	5	9	9	4	19	1	1	5	9	9	4	16	0	1
6 26 9	6	9	9	5	13	2	2	6	10	10	5	10	2	2	6	10	10	5	7	1	2
6 30 29	7	10	10	6	5	3	3	7	11	11	6	2	3	3	7	11	11	5	58	2	3
6 34 50	8	11	11	6	57	4	4	8	11	12	6	54	3	4	8	12	12	6	50	3	4
6 39 11	9	12	12	7	49	5	5	9	12	12	7	45	4	5	9	13	13	7	41	4	5
6 43 31	10	13	13	8	41	6	6	10	13	13	8	36	5	6	10	14	14	8	31	5	6
6 47 51	11	14	14	9	33	6	7	11	14	14	9	28	6	7	11	15	14	9	22	6	7
6 52 11	12	15	15	10	25	7	8	12	15	15	10	19	7	8	12	16	15	10	13	7	8
6 56 30	13	16	16	11	17	8	9	13	16	16	11	10	8	9	13	17	16	11	4	8	9
7 0 49	14	17	17	12	8	9	10	14	17	17	12	1	9	10	14	18	17	11	55	9	10
7 5 7	15	18	18	13	0	10	11	15	18	18	12	53	10	11	15	19	18	12	45	10	11
7 9 26	16	19	19	13	51	11	12	16	19	19	13	43	11	12	16	20	19	13	35	10	12
7 13 43	17	20	20	14	43	12	13	17	20	20	14	34	12	13	17	21	20	14	26	11	13
7 18 0	18	21	21	15	34	13	14	18	21	21	15	25	13	14	18	22	21	15	16	12	14
7 22 17	19	22	22	16	25	14	15	19	22	22	16	16	13	15	19	23	22	16	6	13	15
7 26 33	20	23	23	17	16	15	16	20	23	23	17	6	14	16	20	24	23	16	56	14	16
7 30 49	21	24	24	18	7	16	17	21	24	24	17	56	15	17	21	25	24	17	46	15	16
7 35 4	22	25	25	18	57	16	18	22	25	25	18	47	16	18	22	26	25	18	36	16	17
7 39 19	23	26	25	19	48	17	19	23	26	25	19	37	17	19	23	26	26	19	25	17	18
7 43 33	24	27	26	20	38	18	20	24	27	26	20	27	18	20	24	27	26	20	15	18	19
7 47 46	25	28	27	21	29	19	21	25	28	27	21	16	19	21	25	28	27	21	4	19	20
7 51 59	26	29	28	22	19	20	22	26	29	28	22	6	20	21	26	29	28	21	53	19	21
7 56 11	27	♍	29	23	9	21	23	27	♍	29	22	56	21	22	27	♍	29	22	42	20	22
8 0 23	28	1	♎	23	58	22	24	28	1	♎	23	45	21	23	28	1	♎	23	31	21	23
8 4 34	29	2	1	24	48	23	25	29	2	1	24	34	22	24	29	2	1	24	20	22	24
8 8 44	♌	3	2	25	38	24	25	♌	3	2	25	23	23	25	♌	3	2	25	9	23	25
8 12 53	1	4	3	26	27	24	26	1	4	3	26	12	24	26	1	4	3	25	57	24	26
8 17 2	2	5	4	27	16	25	27	2	5	4	27	1	25	27	2	5	4	26	45	25	27
8 21 10	3	6	5	28	5	26	28	3	6	5	27	49	26	28	3	6	5	27	34	25	28
8 25 18	4	7	6	28	54	27	29	4	7	6	28	38	27	29	4	7	5	28	22	26	29
8 29 24	5	8	6	29	43	28	♑	5	8	6	29	26	28	♑	5	8	6	29	9	27	♑
8 33 30	6	9	7	0♏	31	29	1	6	9	7	0♏	14	28	1	6	9	7	29	57	28	1
8 37 36	7	10	8	1	20	♐	2	7	10	8	1	2	29	2	7	10	8	0♏	45	29	2
8 41 40	8	11	9	2	8	1	3	8	11	9	1	50	♐	3	8	11	9	1	32	♐	3
8 45 44	9	12	10	2	56	1	4	9	12	10	2	38	1	4	9	12	10	2	19	1	3
8 49 47	10	13	11	3	44	2	5	10	13	11	3	25	2	5	10	13	11	3	6	1	4
8 53 50	11	14	12	4	31	3	6	11	14	12	4	12	3	6	11	14	12	3	53	2	5
8 57 51	12	15	13	5	19	4	7	12	15	13	5	0	4	7	12	15	12	4	40	3	6
9 1 52	13	16	14	6	6	5	8	13	16	13	5	47	4	7	13	16	13	5	26	4	7
9 5 52	14	17	14	6	54	6	9	14	17	14	6	33	5	8	14	17	14	6	13	5	8
HOUSES	4	5	6	7		8	9	4	5	6	7		8	9	4	5	6	7		8	9

LATITUDE 40° S. LATITUDE 41° S. LATITUDE 42° S.

LATITUDE 40° N. LATITUDE 41° N. LATITUDE 42° N.

SIDEREAL TIME	10 Ω	11 ♍	12 ♎	ASC ♏	2 ♐	3 ♑	10 Ω	11 ♍	12 ♎	ASC ♏	2 ♐	3 ♑	10 Ω	11 ♍	12 ♎	ASC ♏	2 ♐	3 ♑
H M S	°	°	°	° ′	°	°	°	°	°	° ′	°	°	°	°	°	° ′	°	°
9 9 52	15	18	15	7 41	7	10	15	18	15	7 20	6	9	15	18	15	6 59	6	9
9 13 50	16	19	16	8 28	7	11	16	19	16	8 7	7	10	16	19	16	7 45	7	10
9 17 49	17	20	17	9 15	8	12	17	20	17	8 53	8	11	17	20	17	8 31	7	11
9 21 46	18	21	18	10 1	9	12	18	21	18	9 39	9	12	18	21	18	9 17	8	12
9 25 42	19	22	19	10 48	10	13	19	22	19	10 25	9	13	19	22	18	10 3	9	13
9 29 38	20	23	20	11 34	11	14	20	23	19	11 11	10	14	20	23	19	10 48	10	14
9 33 34	21	24	20	12 20	12	15	21	24	20	11 57	11	15	21	24	20	11 34	11	15
9 37 28	22	25	21	13 6	12	16	22	25	21	12 43	12	16	22	25	21	12 19	12	16
9 41 22	23	25	22	13 52	13	17	23	25	22	13 28	13	17	23	26	22	13 4	12	17
9 45 15	24	26	23	14 38	14	18	24	26	23	14 14	14	18	24	26	23	13 49	13	18
9 49 8	25	27	24	15 24	15	19	25	27	24	14 59	15	19	25	27	23	14 34	14	19
9 53 0	26	28	25	16 10	16	20	26	28	24	15 44	15	20	26	28	24	15 19	15	20
9 56 51	27	29	25	16 55	17	21	27	29	25	16 30	16	21	27	29	25	16 4	16	20
10 0 42	28	♎	26	17 40	17	22	28	♎	26	17 15	17	22	28	♎	26	16 48	17	21
10 4 32	29	1	27	18 26	18	23	29	1	27	17 59	18	23	29	1	27	17 33	17	22
10 8 22	♍	2	28	19 11	19	24	♍	2	28	18 44	19	24	♍	2	28	18 17	18	23
10 12 11	1	3	29	19 56	20	25	1	3	29	19 29	20	25	1	3	28	19 2	19	24
10 15 59	2	4	♏	20 41	21	26	2	4	29	20 14	20	26	2	4	29	19 46	20	25
10 19 47	3	5	0	21 26	22	27	3	5	♏	20 58	21	26	3	5	♏	20 30	21	26
10 23 34	4	6	1	22 11	22	28	4	6	1	21 43	22	27	4	6	1	21 14	22	27
10 27 21	5	7	2	22 55	23	29	5	7	2	22 27	23	28	5	7	2	21 58	22	28
10 31 8	6	8	3	23 40	24	♒	6	8	3	23 11	24	29	6	7	2	22 42	23	29
10 34 53	7	8	4	24 25	25	1	7	8	3	23 56	25	♒	7	8	3	23 26	24	♒
10 38 39	8	9	4	25 9	26	2	8	9	4	24 40	25	1	8	9	4	24 10	25	1
10 42 24	9	10	5	25 54	27	3	9	10	5	25 24	26	2	9	10	5	24 54	26	2
10 46 8	10	11	6	26 39	28	4	10	11	6	26 8	27	3	10	11	6	25 38	27	3
10 49 52	11	12	7	27 23	28	4	11	12	7	26 52	28	4	11	12	6	26 21	27	4
10 53 36	12	13	8	28 7	29	5	12	13	7	27 37	29	5	12	13	7	27 5	28	5
10 57 20	13	14	8	28 52	♑	6	13	14	8	28 21	♑	6	13	14	8	27 49	29	6
11 1 3	14	15	9	29 36	1	7	14	15	9	29 5	0	7	14	15	9	28 33	♑	7
11 4 45	15	16	10	0♐21	2	8	15	16	10	29 49	1	8	15	16	10	29 16	1	8
11 8 28	16	17	11	1 5	3	9	16	17	11	0♐33	2	9	16	16	10	0♐0	2	9
11 12 10	17	17	12	1 50	4	10	17	17	11	1 17	3	10	17	17	11	0♐44	3	10
11 15 52	18	18	12	2 34	4	11	18	18	12	2 1	4	11	18	18	12	1 27	3	11
11 19 33	19	19	13	3 19	5	12	19	19	13	2 45	5	12	19	19	13	2 11	4	12
11 23 15	20	20	14	4 3	6	13	20	20	14	3 29	6	13	20	20	13	2 55	5	13
11 26 56	21	21	15	4 48	7	14	21	21	14	4 14	7	14	21	21	14	3 39	6	14
11 30 37	22	22	16	5 32	8	15	22	22	15	4 58	7	15	22	22	15	4 23	7	15
11 34 17	23	23	16	6 17	9	17	23	23	16	5 42	8	16	23	23	16	5 7	8	16
11 37 58	24	24	17	7 2	10	18	24	24	17	6 27	9	17	24	23	16	5 51	9	17
11 41 39	25	25	18	7 47	11	19	25	24	18	7 11	10	18	25	24	17	6 35	10	18
11 45 19	26	25	19	8 32	11	20	26	25	18	7 56	11	19	26	25	18	7 19	10	19
11 48 59	27	26	19	9 17	12	21	27	26	19	8 41	12	20	27	26	19	8 4	11	20
11 52 40	28	27	20	10 2	13	22	28	27	20	9 25	13	22	28	27	20	8 48	12	21
11 56 20	29	28	21	10 47	14	23	29	28	21	10 10	14	23	29	28	20	9 33	13	22
HOUSES	4	5	6	7	8	9	4	5	6	7	8	9	4	5	6	7	8	9

LATITUDE 40° S. LATITUDE 41° S. LATITUDE 42° S.

	LATITUDE 40° N.						LATITUDE 41° N.						LATITUDE 42° N.					
SIDEREAL TIME	10 ♎	11 ♎	12 ♏	ASC ♐	2 ♑	3 ♒	10 ♎	11 ♎	12 ♏	ASC ♐	2 ♑	3 ♒	10 ♎	11 ♎	12 ♏	ASC ♐	2 ♑	3 ♒
H M S	°	°	°	° '	°	°	°	°	°	° '	°	°	°	°	°	° '	°	°
12 0 0	0	29	22	11 32	15	24	0	29	21	10 55	15	24	0	29	21	10 17	14	23
12 3 40	1	♏	23	12 18	16	25	1	♏	22	11 40	15	25	1	♏	22	11 2	15	25
12 7 20	2	1	23	13 3	17	26	2	1	23	12 26	16	26	2	0	23	11 47	16	26
12 11 1	3	1	24	13 49	18	27	3	1	24	13 11	17	27	3	1	23	12 32	17	27
12 14 41	4	2	25	14 35	19	28	4	2	24	13 57	18	28	4	2	24	13 18	18	28
12 18 21	5	3	26	15 21	20	29	5	3	25	14 43	19	29	5	3	25	14 3	19	29
12 22 2	6	4	26	16 8	21	♓	6	4	26	15 29	20	♓	6	4	26	14 49	20	♓
12 25 42	7	5	27	16 54	22	1	7	5	27	16 15	21	1	7	5	26	15 35	21	1
12 29 23	8	6	28	17 41	23	2	8	6	28	17 1	22	2	8	6	27	16 21	22	2
12 33 4	9	7	29	18 28	24	3	9	7	28	17 48	23	3	9	6	28	17 7	23	3
12 36 45	10	8	♐	19 15	25	5	10	7	29	18 35	24	4	10	7	29	17 54	24	4
12 40 27	11	8	0	20 3	26	6	11	8	♐	19 22	25	6	11	8	♐	18 40	25	5
12 44 8	12	9	1	20 50	27	7	12	9	1	20 9	26	7	12	9	0	19 27	26	7
12 47 50	13	10	2	21 38	28	8	13	10	1	20 57	27	8	13	10	1	20 15	27	8
12 51 32	14	11	3	22 27	29	9	14	11	2	21 45	28	9	14	11	2	21 2	28	9
12 55 15	15	12	3	23 15	♒	10	15	12	3	22 33	29	10	15	11	3	21 50	29	10
12 58 57	16	13	4	24 4	1	11	16	13	4	23 22	♒	11	16	12	3	22 39	♒	11
13 2 40	17	14	5	24 53	2	12	17	13	5	24 11	1	12	17	13	4	23 27	1	12
13 6 24	18	14	6	25 43	3	13	18	14	5	25 0	2	13	18	14	5	24 16	2	13
13 10 8	19	15	7	26 33	4	15	19	15	6	25 50	3	15	19	15	6	25 5	3	14
13 13 52	20	16	7	27 23	5	16	20	16	7	26 40	4	16	20	16	7	25 55	4	16
13 17 36	21	17	8	28 14	6	17	21	17	8	27 30	5	17	21	17	7	26 45	5	17
13 21 21	22	18	9	29 5	7	18	22	18	9	28 21	7	18	22	18	8	27 36	6	18
13 25 7	23	19	10	29 57	8	19	23	18	9	29 12	8	19	23	18	9	28 27	7	19
13 28 52	24	20	11	0♑ 48	9	20	24	19	10	0♑ 4	9	20	24	19	10	29 18	8	20
13 32 39	25	20	11	1 41	10	22	25	20	11	0 56	10	21	25	20	11	0♑ 10	9	21
13 36 26	26	21	12	2 34	12	23	26	21	12	1 49	11	23	26	21	11	1 2	11	23
13 40 13	27	22	13	3 27	13	24	27	22	13	2 42	12	24	27	22	12	1 55	12	24
13 44 1	28	23	14	4 21	14	25	28	23	13	3 35	13	25	28	23	13	2 48	13	25
13 47 49	29	24	15	5 15	15	26	29	24	14	4 29	15	26	29	23	14	3 42	14	26
13 51 38	♏	25	15	6 10	16	27	♏	25	15	5 24	16	27	♏	24	15	4 36	15	27
13 55 28	1	26	16	7 6	17	29	1	25	16	6 19	17	29	1	25	15	5 31	17	29
13 59 18	2	26	17	8 2	19	♈	2	26	17	7 15	18	♈	2	26	16	6 27	18	♈
14 3 9	3	27	18	8 59	20	1	3	27	18	8 12	19	1	3	27	17	7 23	19	1
14 7 0	4	28	19	9 56	21	2	4	28	18	9 9	21	2	4	28	18	8 20	20	2
14 10 52	5	29	20	10 54	22	3	5	29	19	10 6	22	3	5	29	19	9 17	21	3
14 14 45	6	♐	21	11 53	23	5	6	♐	20	11 5	23	5	6	29	20	10 15	23	5
14 18 38	7	1	21	12 52	25	6	7	1	21	12 4	24	6	7	♐	20	11 14	24	6
14 22 32	8	2	22	13 52	26	7	8	1	22	13 4	26	7	8	1	21	12 14	25	7
14 26 26	9	3	23	14 53	27	8	9	2	23	14 4	27	8	9	2	22	13 14	27	8
14 30 22	10	3	24	15 54	29	9	10	3	24	15 6	28	9	10	3	23	14 16	28	9
14 34 17	11	4	25	16 57	♓	11	11	4	24	16 8	♓	11	11	4	24	15 18	29	11
14 38 14	12	5	26	18 0	1	12	12	5	25	17 11	1	12	12	5	25	16 20	♓	12
14 42 11	13	6	27	19 4	3	13	13	6	26	18 15	2	13	13	6	26	17 24	2	13
14 46 10	14	7	28	20 8	4	14	14	7	27	19 20	4	14	14	7	27	18 29	3	14
HOUSES	4	5	6	7	8	9	4	5	6	7	8	9	4	5	6	7	8	9

LATITUDE 40° S.   LATITUDE 41° S.   LATITUDE 42° S.

	LATITUDE 40° N.						LATITUDE 41° N.						LATITUDE 42° N.					
SIDEREAL TIME	10 ♏	11 ♐	12 ♐	ASC ♑	2 ♓	3 ♈	10 ♏	11 ♐	12 ♐	ASC ♑	2 ♓	3 ♈	10 ♏	11 ♐	12 ♐	ASC ♑	2 ♓	3 ♈
H M S	°	°	°	° ′	°	°	°	°	°	° ′	°	°	°	°	°	° ′	°	°
14 50 8	15	8	28	21 14	5	15	15	8	28	20 25	5	16	15	7	27	19 34	5	16
14 54 8	16	9	29	22 21	7	17	16	9	29	21 32	6	17	16	8	28	20 41	6	17
14 58 8	17	10	♑	23 28	8	18	17	9	♑	22 39	8	18	17	9	29	21 48	8	18
15 2 9	18	11	1	24 37	9	19	18	10	1	23 48	9	19	18	10	♑	22 57	9	19
15 6 10	19	11	2	25 46	11	20	19	11	2	24 57	11	20	19	11	1	24 6	10	21
15 10 13	20	12	3	26 57	12	22	20	12	3	26 8	12	22	20	12	2	25 17	12	22
15 14 16	21	13	4	28 9	14	23	21	13	4	27 20	13	23	21	13	3	26 28	13	23
15 18 20	22	14	5	29 21	15	24	22	14	4	28 32	15	24	22	14	4	27 41	15	24
15 22 24	23	15	6	0♒ 35	17	25	23	15	5	29 46	16	25	23	15	5	28 55	16	25
15 26 30	24	16	7	1 50	18	26	24	16	6	1♒ 1	18	27	24	16	6	0♒ 10	18	27
15 30 36	25	17	8	3 6	19	28	25	17	7	2 18	19	28	25	16	7	1 27	19	28
15 34 42	26	18	9	4 23	21	29	26	18	8	3 35	21	29	26	17	8	2 45	21	29
15 38 50	27	19	10	5 41	22	♉	27	19	9	4 54	22	♉	27	18	9	4 4	22	♉
15 42 58	28	20	11	7 1	24	1	28	19	10	6 14	24	1	28	19	10	5 24	24	2
15 47 7	29	21	12	8 22	25	2	29	20	11	7 35	25	3	29	20	11	6 45	25	3
15 51 16	♐	22	13	9 44	27	4	♐	21	12	8 57	27	4	♐	21	12	8 8	27	4
15 55 26	1	22	14	11 7	28	5	1	22	13	10 21	28	5	1	22	13	9 33	28	5
15 59 37	2	23	15	12 32	♈	6	2	23	14	11 46	♈	6	2	23	14	10 59	♈	6
16 3 49	3	24	16	13 57	1	7	3	24	16	13 13	1	7	3	24	15	12 26	1	8
16 8 1	4	25	17	15 25	3	9	4	25	17	14 41	3	9	4	25	16	13 54	3	9
16 12 14	5	26	18	16 53	4	10	5	26	18	16 10	4	10	5	26	17	15 24	5	10
16 16 27	6	27	19	18 23	6	11	6	27	19	17 41	6	11	6	27	18	16 56	6	11
16 20 41	7	28	20	19 54	7	12	7	28	20	19 13	8	12	7	28	19	18 29	8	12
16 24 56	8	29	21	21 27	9	13	8	29	21	20 47	9	13	8	29	20	20 4	9	14
16 29 11	9	♑	23	23 1	10	14	9	♑	22	22 22	11	15	9	♑	22	21 40	11	15
16 33 27	10	1	24	24 36	12	16	10	1	23	23 58	12	16	10	1	23	23 17	12	16
16 37 43	11	2	25	26 13	13	17	11	2	24	25 36	14	17	11	2	24	24 56	14	17
16 41 59	12	3	26	27 50	15	18	12	3	26	27 15	15	18	12	3	25	26 37	15	18
16 46 17	13	4	27	29 29	17	19	13	4	27	28 55	17	19	13	4	26	28 19	17	20
16 50 34	14	5	28	1♓ 10	18	20	14	5	28	0♓ 37	18	21	14	5	27	0♓ 2	18	21
16 54 53	15	6	♒	2 51	20	21	15	6	29	2 20	20	22	15	6	29	1 47	20	22
16 59 11	16	7	1	4 34	21	23	16	7	♒	4 4	21	23	16	7	♒	3 33	22	23
17 3 30	17	8	2	6 18	23	24	17	8	1	5 50	23	24	17	8	1	5 20	23	24
17 7 49	18	9	3	8 3	24	25	18	9	3	7 37	24	25	18	9	2	7 9	25	25
17 12 9	19	10	4	9 49	25	26	19	10	4	9 24	26	26	19	10	3	8 59	26	27
17 16 29	20	11	6	11 35	27	27	20	11	5	11 13	27	27	20	11	5	10 49	28	28
17 20 49	21	12	7	13 23	28	28	21	12	6	13 3	29	29	21	12	6	12 41	29	29
17 25 10	22	13	8	15 12	♉	29	22	13	8	14 54	♉	♊	22	13	7	14 34	♉	♊
17 29 31	23	14	9	17 1	1	♊	23	14	9	16 45	2	1	23	14	9	16 28	2	1
17 33 51	24	15	11	18 51	3	2	24	15	10	18 37	3	2	24	15	10	18 22	3	2
17 38 13	25	16	12	20 42	4	3	25	16	12	20 30	5	3	25	16	11	20 18	5	3
17 42 34	26	17	13	22 33	6	4	26	17	13	22 23	6	4	26	17	12	22 13	6	4
17 46 55	27	19	15	24 24	7	5	27	18	14	24 17	7	5	27	18	14	24 10	8	5
17 51 17	28	20	16	26 16	8	6	28	19	16	26 11	9	6	28	19	15	26 6	9	7
17 55 38	29	21	17	28 8	10	7	29	20	17	28 6	10	7	29	20	17	28 3	11	8
HOUSES	4	5	6	7	8	9	4	5	6	7	8	9	4	5	6	7	8	9

LATITUDE 40° S.   LATITUDE 41° S.   LATITUDE 42° S.

	LATITUDE 40° N.						LATITUDE 41° N.						LATITUDE 42° N.					
SIDEREAL TIME	10 ♑	11 ♑	12 ♒	ASC ♈		2 ♉	3 ♊	10 ♑	11 ♑	12 ♒	ASC ♈		2 ♉	3 ♊	10 ♑	11 ♑	12 ♒	ASC ♈
H M S	°	°	°	°	'	°	°	°	°	°	°	'	°	°	°	°	°	° '	°	°

SIDEREAL TIME (H M S)	10 ♑	11 ♑	12 ♒	ASC ♈ (° ')	2 ♉	3 ♊	10 ♑	11 ♑	12 ♒	ASC ♈ (° ')	2 ♉	3 ♊	10 ♑	11 ♑	12 ♒	ASC ♈ (° ')	2 ♉	3 ♊
18 0 0	0	22	19	0 0	11	8	0	22	18	0 0	12	8	0	21	18	0 0	12	9
18 4 22	1	23	20	1 52	13	9	1	23	20	1 54	13	10	1	22	19	1 57	13	10
18 8 43	2	24	22	3 44	14	10	2	24	21	3 49	14	11	2	23	21	3 54	15	11
18 13 5	3	25	23	5 36	15	11	3	25	23	5 43	16	12	3	25	22	5 50	16	12
18 17 26	4	26	24	7 27	17	13	4	26	24	7 37	17	13	4	26	24	7 47	18	13
18 21 47	5	27	26	9 18	18	14	5	27	25	9 30	18	14	5	27	25	9 42	19	14
18 26 9	6	28	27	11 9	19	15	6	28	27	11 23	20	15	6	28	27	11 38	20	15
18 30 29	7	29	29	12 59	21	16	7	29	28	13 15	21	16	7	29	28	13 32	21	16
18 34 50	8	♒	♓	14 48	22	17	8	♒	♓	15 6	22	17	8	♒	29	15 26	23	17
18 39 11	9	2	2	16 37	23	18	9	1	1	16 57	24	18	9	1	♓	17 19	24	18
18 43 31	10	3	3	18 25	24	19	10	3	3	18 47	25	19	10	2	2	19 11	25	19
18 47 51	11	4	5	20 11	26	20	11	4	4	20 36	26	20	11	3	4	21 1	27	20
18 52 11	12	5	6	21 57	27	21	12	5	6	22 23	27	21	12	5	5	22 51	28	21
18 56 30	13	6	7	23 42	28	22	13	6	7	24 10	29	22	13	6	7	24 40	29	22
19 0 49	14	7	9	25 26	29	23	14	7	9	25 56	♊	23	14	7	8	26 27	♊	23
19 5 7	15	9	10	27 9	♊	24	15	8	10	27 40	1	24	15	8	10	28 13	1	24
19 9 26	16	10	12	28 50	2	25	16	9	12	29 23	2	25	16	9	12	29 58	3	25
19 13 43	17	11	13	0♉ 31	3	26	17	11	13	1♉ 5	3	26	17	10	13	1♉ 41	4	26
19 18 0	18	12	15	2 10	4	27	18	12	15	2 45	4	27	18	12	15	3 23	5	27
19 22 17	19	13	17	3 47	5	28	19	13	16	4 24	6	28	19	13	16	5 4	6	28
19 26 33	20	14	18	5 24	6	29	20	14	18	6 2	7	29	20	14	18	6 43	7	29
19 30 49	21	16	20	6 59	7	♋	21	15	19	7 38	8	♋	21	15	19	8 20	8	♋
19 35 4	22	17	21	8 33	9	1	22	17	21	9 13	9	1	22	16	21	9 56	10	1
19 39 19	23	18	23	10 6	10	2	23	18	22	10 47	10	2	23	18	22	11 31	11	2
19 43 33	24	19	24	11 37	11	3	24	19	24	12 19	11	3	24	19	24	13 4	12	3
19 47 46	25	20	26	13 7	12	4	25	20	26	13 50	12	4	25	20	25	14 36	13	4
19 51 59	26	21	27	14 35	13	5	26	21	27	15 19	13	5	26	21	27	16 6	14	5
19 56 11	27	23	29	16 3	14	6	27	23	29	16 47	14	6	27	22	29	17 34	15	6
20 0 23	28	24	♈	17 28	15	7	28	24	♈	18 14	16	7	28	24	♈	19 1	16	7
20 4 34	29	25	2	18 53	16	8	29	25	2	19 39	17	8	29	25	2	20 27	17	8
20 8 44	♒	26	3	20 16	17	8	♒	26	3	21 3	18	9	♒	26	3	21 52	18	9
20 12 53	1	28	5	21 38	18	9	1	27	5	22 25	19	10	1	27	5	23 15	19	10
20 17 2	2	29	6	22 59	19	10	2	29	6	23 46	20	11	2	28	6	24 36	20	11
20 21 10	3	♓	8	24 19	20	11	3	♓	8	25 6	21	11	3	♓	8	25 56	21	12
20 25 18	4	1	9	25 37	21	12	4	1	9	26 25	22	12	4	1	9	27 15	22	13
20 29 24	5	2	11	26 54	22	13	5	2	11	27 42	23	13	5	2	11	28 33	23	14
20 33 30	6	4	12	28 10	23	14	6	3	12	28 59	24	14	6	3	12	29 50	24	14
20 37 36	7	5	13	29 25	24	15	7	5	14	0♊ 14	25	15	7	5	14	1♊ 5	25	15
20 41 40	8	6	15	0♊ 39	25	16	8	6	15	1 28	26	16	8	6	15	2 19	26	16
20 45 44	9	7	16	1 51	26	17	9	7	17	2 40	26	17	9	7	17	3 32	27	17
20 49 47	10	8	18	3 3	27	18	10	8	18	3 52	27	18	10	8	18	4 43	28	18
20 53 50	11	10	19	4 14	28	19	11	10	19	5 3	28	19	11	9	20	5 54	29	19
20 57 51	12	11	21	5 23	29	19	12	11	21	6 12	29	20	12	11	21	7 3	♋	20
21 1 52	13	12	22	6 32	♋	20	13	12	22	7 21	♋	21	13	12	22	8 12	1	21
21 5 52	14	13	23	7 39	1	21	14	13	24	8 28	1	21	14	13	24	9 19	2	22
HOUSES	4	5	6	7		8	9	4	5	6	7		8	9	4	5	6	7	8	9

LATITUDE 40° S.   LATITUDE 41° S.   LATITUDE 42° S.

LATITUDE 40° N. LATITUDE 41° N. LATITUDE 42° N.

SIDEREAL TIME	10 ♒	11 ♓	12 ♈	ASC ♊		2 ♋	3 ♋	10 ♒	11 ♓	12 ♈	ASC ♊		2 ♋	3 ♋	10 ♒	11 ♓	12 ♈	ASC ♊		2 ♋	3 ♋
H M S	°	°	°	°	'	°	°	°	°	°	°	'	°	°	°	°	°	°	'	°	°
21 9 52	15	15	25	8	46	2	22	15	14	25	9	35	2	22	15	14	25	10	26	3	23
21 13 50	16	16	26	9	52	2	23	16	16	26	10	40	3	23	16	16	27	11	31	3	23
21 17 49	17	17	27	10	56	3	24	17	17	28	11	45	4	24	17	17	28	12	36	4	24
21 21 46	18	18	29	12	0	4	25	18	18	29	12	49	5	25	18	18	29	13	40	5	25
21 25 42	19	19	♉	13	3	5	26	19	19	♉	13	52	6	26	19	19	♉	14	42	6	26
21 29 38	20	21	1	14	6	6	27	20	21	2	14	54	6	27	20	21	2	15	44	7	27
21 33 34	21	22	3	15	7	7	27	21	22	3	15	56	7	28	21	22	3	16	46	8	28
21 37 28	22	23	4	16	8	8	28	22	23	4	16	56	8	29	22	23	5	17	46	9	29
21 41 22	23	24	5	17	8	9	29	23	24	6	17	56	9	29	23	24	6	18	46	10	♌
21 45 15	24	25	7	18	7	9	♌	24	25	7	18	55	10	♌	24	25	7	19	45	10	1
21 49 8	25	27	8	19	6	10	1	25	27	8	19	54	11	1	25	27	9	20	43	11	1
21 53 0	26	28	9	20	4	11	2	26	28	9	20	51	12	2	26	28	10	21	40	12	2
21 56 51	27	29	10	21	1	12	3	27	29	11	21	48	12	3	27	29	11	22	37	13	3
22 0 42	28	♈	11	21	58	13	4	28	♈	12	22	45	13	4	28	♈	12	23	33	14	4
22 4 32	29	1	13	22	54	14	4	29	1	13	23	41	14	5	29	1	13	24	29	15	5
22 8 22	♓	3	14	23	50	15	5	♓	3	14	24	36	15	5	♓	3	15	25	24	15	6
22 12 11	1	4	15	24	45	15	6	1	4	15	25	31	16	6	1	4	16	26	18	16	7
22 15 59	2	5	16	25	39	16	7	2	5	17	26	25	17	7	2	5	17	27	12	17	7
22 19 47	3	6	17	26	33	17	8	3	6	18	27	18	17	8	3	6	18	28	5	18	8
22 23 34	4	7	18	27	26	18	9	4	7	19	28	11	18	9	4	7	19	28	58	19	9
22 27 21	5	8	20	28	19	19	10	5	9	20	29	4	19	10	5	9	21	29	50	19	10
22 31 8	6	10	21	29	12	19	10	6	10	21	29	56	20	11	6	10	22	0♋	42	20	11
22 34 53	7	11	22	0♋	3	20	11	7	11	22	0♋	48	21	12	7	11	23	1	33	21	12
22 38 39	8	12	23	0	55	21	12	8	12	23	1	39	21	12	8	12	24	2	24	22	13
22 42 24	9	13	24	1	46	22	13	9	13	25	2	30	22	13	9	13	25	3	15	23	13
22 46 8	10	14	25	2	37	23	14	10	14	26	3	20	23	14	10	14	26	4	5	23	14
22 49 52	11	15	26	3	27	23	15	11	15	27	4	10	24	15	11	16	27	4	55	24	15
22 53 36	12	17	27	4	17	24	16	12	17	28	5	0	25	16	12	17	28	5	44	25	16
22 57 20	13	18	28	5	7	25	16	13	18	29	5	49	25	17	13	18	29	6	33	26	17
23 1 3	14	19	29	5	56	26	17	14	19	♊	6	38	26	17	14	19	♊	7	21	27	18
23 4 45	15	20	♊	6	45	27	18	15	20	1	7	27	27	18	15	20	1	8	10	27	19
23 8 28	16	21	1	7	33	27	19	16	21	2	8	15	28	19	16	21	2	8	58	28	19
23 12 10	17	22	2	8	22	28	20	17	22	3	9	3	29	20	17	22	3	9	45	29	20
23 15 52	18	23	3	9	10	29	21	18	23	4	9	51	29	21	18	23	4	10	33	♌	21
23 19 33	19	24	4	9	57	♌	22	19	24	5	10	38	♌	22	19	25	5	11	20	0	22
23 23 15	20	25	5	10	45	0	22	20	26	6	11	25	1	23	20	26	6	12	6	1	23
23 26 56	21	27	6	11	32	1	23	21	27	7	12	12	2	23	21	27	7	12	53	2	24
23 30 37	22	28	7	12	19	2	24	22	28	8	12	59	2	24	22	28	8	13	39	3	24
23 34 17	23	29	8	13	6	3	25	23	29	9	13	45	3	25	23	29	9	14	25	4	25
23 37 58	24	♉	9	13	52	4	26	24	♉	10	14	31	4	26	24	♉	10	15	11	4	26
23 41 39	25	1	10	14	39	4	27	25	1	11	15	17	5	27	25	1	11	15	57	5	27
23 45 19	26	2	11	15	25	5	28	26	2	12	16	3	6	28	26	2	12	16	42	6	28
23 48 59	27	3	12	16	11	6	29	27	3	13	16	49	6	29	27	3	13	17	28	7	29
23 52 40	28	4	13	16	57	7	29	28	4	14	17	34	7	29	28	4	14	18	13	7	♍
23 56 20	29	5	14	17	42	7	♍	29	5	15	18	20	8	♍	29	5	15	18	58	8	0
HOUSES	4	5	6	7		8	9	4	5	6	7		8	9	4	5	6	7		8	9

LATITUDE 40° S. LATITUDE 41° S. LATITUDE 42° S.

LATITUDE 43° N.   LATITUDE 44° N.   LATITUDE 45° N.

SIDEREAL TIME (H M S)	10 ♈	11 ♉	12 ♊	ASC ♋		2 ♌	3 ♍	10 ♈	11 ♉	12 ♊	ASC ♋		2 ♌	3 ♍	10 ♈	11 ♉	12 ♊	ASC ♋		2 ♌	3 ♍
0 0 0	0	7	17	20	21	9	1	0	7	17	21	1	10	2	0	7	18	21	42	10	2
0 3 40	1	8	17	21	6	10	2	1	8	18	21	45	10	2	1	8	19	22	25	11	3
0 7 20	2	9	18	21	50	11	3	2	9	19	22	29	11	3	2	9	20	23	9	12	3
0 11 1	3	10	19	22	34	12	4	3	10	20	23	13	12	4	3	10	20	23	52	12	4
0 14 41	4	11	20	23	18	12	5	4	11	21	23	56	13	5	4	11	21	24	35	13	5
0 18 21	5	12	21	24	2	13	6	5	12	22	24	40	13	6	5	12	22	25	18	14	6
0 22 2	6	13	22	24	46	14	7	6	13	23	25	23	14	7	6	13	23	26	1	15	7
0 25 43	7	14	23	25	29	15	7	7	14	23	26	6	15	8	7	15	24	26	44	15	8
0 29 23	8	15	24	26	13	15	8	8	15	24	26	50	16	8	8	16	25	27	27	16	9
0 33 4	9	16	25	26	56	16	9	9	16	25	27	33	16	9	9	17	26	28	10	17	9
0 36 45	10	17	25	27	40	17	10	10	17	26	28	16	17	10	10	18	27	28	53	18	10
0 40 27	11	18	26	28	23	18	11	11	18	27	28	59	18	11	11	19	27	29	35	18	11
0 44 8	12	19	27	29	7	18	12	12	19	28	29	42	19	12	12	20	28	0♌	18	19	12
0 47 50	13	20	28	29	50	19	13	13	20	29	0♌	25	20	13	13	21	29	1	0	20	13
0 51 32	14	21	29	0♌	34	20	14	14	21	29	1	8	20	14	14	22	♋	1	43	21	14
0 55 15	15	22	♋	1	17	21	14	15	22	♋	1	51	21	15	15	23	1	2	26	21	15
0 58 57	16	23	1	2	0	22	15	16	23	1	2	34	22	15	16	24	2	3	8	22	16
1 2 40	17	24	1	2	44	22	16	17	24	2	3	17	23	16	17	25	3	3	51	23	16
1 6 24	18	25	2	3	27	23	17	18	25	3	4	0	23	17	18	26	3	4	33	24	17
1 10 8	19	26	3	4	10	24	18	19	26	4	4	43	24	18	19	27	4	5	16	24	18
1 13 52	20	27	4	4	54	25	19	20	27	5	5	26	25	19	20	28	5	5	58	25	19
1 17 36	21	28	5	5	37	25	20	21	28	5	6	9	26	20	21	29	6	6	41	26	20
1 21 21	22	29	6	6	21	26	21	22	29	6	6	52	26	21	22	♊	7	7	24	27	21
1 25 7	23	♊	6	7	4	27	22	23	♊	7	7	35	27	22	23	1	8	8	6	28	22
1 28 52	24	1	7	7	48	28	23	24	1	8	8	18	28	23	24	2	8	8	49	28	23
1 32 39	25	2	8	8	31	29	23	25	2	9	9	1	29	23	25	3	9	9	32	29	23
1 36 26	26	3	9	9	15	29	24	26	3	9	9	45	♍	24	26	4	10	10	15	♍	24
1 40 13	27	4	10	9	59	♍	25	27	4	10	10	28	0	25	27	5	11	10	58	1	25
1 44 1	28	5	11	10	42	1	26	28	5	11	11	11	1	26	28	6	12	11	41	1	26
1 47 49	29	6	11	11	26	2	27	29	6	12	11	55	2	27	29	7	12	12	24	2	27
1 51 38	♉	7	12	12	10	3	28	♉	7	13	12	38	3	28	♉	7	13	13	7	3	28
1 55 28	1	8	13	12	54	3	29	1	8	14	13	22	4	29	1	8	14	13	50	4	29
1 59 18	2	9	14	13	38	4	♎	2	9	14	14	6	4	♎	2	9	15	14	33	5	♎
2 3 9	3	10	15	14	23	5	1	3	10	15	14	49	5	1	3	10	16	15	17	5	1
2 7 0	4	11	16	15	7	6	2	4	11	16	15	33	6	2	4	11	17	16	0	6	2
2 10 52	5	12	16	15	51	7	3	5	12	17	16	17	7	3	5	12	17	16	44	7	3
2 14 45	6	13	17	16	36	7	4	6	13	18	17	1	8	4	6	13	18	17	27	8	4
2 18 38	7	14	18	17	21	8	4	7	14	19	17	46	8	4	7	14	19	18	11	9	4
2 22 32	8	15	19	18	5	9	5	8	15	19	18	30	9	5	8	15	20	18	55	9	5
2 26 26	9	15	20	18	50	10	6	9	16	20	19	15	10	6	9	16	21	19	39	10	6
2 30 22	10	16	21	19	35	11	7	10	17	21	19	59	11	7	10	17	22	20	23	11	7
2 34 17	11	17	21	20	20	12	8	11	18	22	20	44	12	8	11	18	22	21	8	12	8
2 38 14	12	18	22	21	6	12	9	12	19	23	21	29	13	9	12	19	23	21	52	13	9
2 42 11	13	19	23	21	51	13	10	13	20	24	22	14	13	10	13	20	24	22	37	14	10
2 46 10	14	20	24	22	37	14	11	14	20	24	22	59	14	11	14	21	25	23	21	14	11
HOUSES	4	5	6	7		8	9	4	5	6	7		8	9	4	5	6	7		8	9

LATITUDE 43° S.   LATITUDE 44° S.   LATITUDE 45° S.

LATITUDE 43° N.   LATITUDE 44° N.   LATITUDE 45° N.

SIDEREAL TIME	10 ♉	11 ♊	12 ♋	ASC ♌		2 ♍	3 ♎	10 ♉	11 ♊	12 ♋	ASC ♌		2 ♍	3 ♎	10 ♉	11 ♊	12 ♋	ASC ♌		2 ♍	3 ♎
H M S	°	°	°	°	′	°	°	°	°	°	°	′	°	°	°	°	°	°	′	°	°
2 50 8	15	21	25	23	22	15	12	15	21	25	23	44	15	12	15	22	26	24	6	15	12
2 54 8	16	22	26	24	8	16	13	16	22	26	24	30	16	13	16	23	26	24	51	16	13
2 58 8	17	23	26	24	54	17	14	17	23	27	25	15	17	14	17	24	27	25	36	17	14
3 2 9	18	24	27	25	40	18	15	18	24	28	26	1	18	15	18	25	28	26	22	18	15
3 6 10	19	25	28	26	27	18	16	19	25	29	26	47	19	16	19	25	29	27	7	19	16
3 10 13	20	26	29	27	13	19	17	20	26	29	27	33	19	17	20	26	Ω	27	53	19	17
3 14 16	21	27	Ω	28	0	20	18	21	27	Ω	28	19	20	18	21	27	1	28	38	20	18
3 18 20	22	28	1	28	47	21	19	22	28	1	29	5	21	19	22	28	1	29	24	21	19
3 22 24	23	29	1	29	33	22	20	23	29	2	29	52	22	20	23	29	2	0♍	10	22	20
3 26 30	24	♋	2	0♍	20	23	21	24	♋	3	0♍	38	23	21	24	♋	3	0	56	23	20
3 30 36	25	1	3	1	8	24	22	25	1	4	1	25	24	22	25	1	4	1	43	24	21
3 34 42	26	1	4	1	55	25	23	26	2	4	2	12	25	23	26	2	5	2	29	25	22
3 38 50	27	2	5	2	43	25	24	27	3	5	2	59	25	23	27	3	6	3	16	26	23
3 42 58	28	3	6	3	30	26	25	28	4	6	3	46	26	24	28	4	7	4	2	26	24
3 47 7	29	4	7	4	18	27	26	29	5	7	4	34	27	25	29	5	7	4	49	27	25
3 51 16	♊	5	7	5	6	28	27	♊	6	8	5	21	28	26	♊	6	8	5	36	28	26
3 55 26	1	6	8	5	54	29	27	1	6	9	6	9	29	27	1	7	9	6	23	29	27
3 59 37	2	7	9	6	43	♎	28	2	7	10	6	57	♎	28	2	8	10	7	11	♎	28
4 3 49	3	8	10	7	31	1	29	3	8	10	7	44	1	29	3	9	11	7	58	1	29
4 8 1	4	9	11	8	20	2	♏	4	9	11	8	33	2	♏	4	10	12	8	46	2	♏
4 12 14	5	10	12	9	8	3	1	5	10	12	9	21	3	1	5	11	13	9	34	3	1
4 16 27	6	11	13	9	57	4	2	6	11	13	10	9	4	2	6	11	13	10	21	3	2
4 20 41	7	12	14	10	46	4	3	7	12	14	10	58	4	3	7	12	14	11	9	4	3
4 24 56	8	13	14	11	35	5	4	8	13	15	11	46	5	4	8	13	15	11	58	5	4
4 29 11	9	14	15	12	24	6	5	9	14	16	12	35	6	5	9	14	16	12	46	6	5
4 33 27	10	15	16	13	14	7	6	10	15	17	13	24	7	6	10	15	17	13	34	7	6
4 37 43	11	16	17	14	3	8	7	11	16	17	14	13	8	7	11	16	18	14	23	8	7
4 41 59	12	17	18	14	53	9	8	12	17	18	15	2	9	8	12	17	19	15	11	9	8
4 46 17	13	18	19	15	43	10	9	13	18	19	15	51	10	9	13	18	19	16	0	10	9
4 50 34	14	19	20	16	33	11	10	14	19	20	16	41	11	10	14	19	20	16	49	11	10
4 54 53	15	20	21	17	23	12	11	15	20	21	17	30	12	11	15	20	21	17	38	12	11
4 59 11	16	21	22	18	13	13	12	16	21	22	18	20	13	12	16	21	22	18	27	12	12
5 3 30	17	21	22	19	3	14	13	17	22	23	19	9	14	13	17	22	23	19	16	13	13
5 7 49	18	22	23	19	53	15	14	18	23	24	19	59	14	14	18	23	24	20	5	14	14
5 12 9	19	23	24	20	43	15	15	19	24	25	20	49	15	15	19	24	25	20	55	15	15
5 16 29	20	24	25	21	34	16	16	20	25	25	21	39	16	16	20	25	26	21	44	16	16
5 20 49	21	25	26	22	24	17	17	21	26	26	22	29	17	17	21	26	27	22	33	17	17
5 25 10	22	26	27	23	15	18	18	22	26	27	23	19	18	18	22	27	28	23	23	18	18
5 29 31	23	27	28	24	5	19	19	23	27	28	24	9	19	19	23	28	28	24	12	19	19
5 33 51	24	28	29	24	56	20	20	24	28	29	24	59	20	20	24	29	29	25	2	20	20
5 38 13	25	29	♍	25	46	21	21	25	29	♍	25	49	21	21	25	Ω	♍	25	52	21	21
5 42 34	26	Ω	1	26	37	22	22	26	Ω	1	26	39	22	22	26	1	1	26	41	22	22
5 46 55	27	1	2	27	28	23	23	27	1	2	27	29	23	23	27	2	2	27	31	23	23
5 51 17	28	2	3	28	18	24	24	28	2	3	28	20	24	24	28	3	3	28	21	23	24
5 55 38	29	3	3	29	9	25	25	29	3	4	29	10	25	25	29	3	4	29	10	24	25
HOUSES	4	5	6	7		8	9	4	5	6	7		8	9	4	5	6	7		8	9

LATITUDE 43° S.   LATITUDE 44° S.   LATITUDE 45° S.

LATITUDE 43° N.   LATITUDE 44° N.   LATITUDE 45° N.

SIDEREAL TIME	10 ♋	11 ♌	12 ♍	ASC ♎	2 ♎	3 ♏	10 ♋	11 ♌	12 ♍	ASC ♎	2 ♎	3 ♏	10 ♋	11 ♌	12 ♍	ASC ♎	2 ♎	3 ♏
H M S	°	°	°	° '	°	°	°	°	°	° '	°	°	°	°	°	° '	°	°
6 0 0	0	4	4	0 0	26	26	0	4	5	0 0	25	26	0	4	5	0 0	25	26
6 4 22	1	5	5	0 51	27	27	1	5	5	0 50	26	27	1	5	6	0 50	26	27
6 8 43	2	6	6	1 42	27	28	2	6	6	1 40	27	28	2	6	7	1 39	27	27
6 13 5	3	7	7	2 32	28	29	3	7	7	2 31	28	29	3	7	7	2 29	28	28
6 17 26	4	8	8	3 23	29	♐	4	8	8	3 21	29	♐	4	8	8	3 19	29	29
6 21 47	5	9	9	4 14	♏	1	5	9	9	4 11	♏	1	5	9	9	4 8	♏	♐
6 26 9	6	10	10	5 4	1	2	6	10	10	5 1	1	2	6	10	10	4 58	1	1
6 30 29	7	11	11	5 55	2	3	7	11	11	5 51	2	3	7	11	11	5 48	2	2
6 34 50	8	12	12	6 45	3	4	8	12	12	6 41	3	4	8	12	12	6 37	2	3
6 39 11	9	13	13	7 36	4	5	9	13	13	7 31	4	4	9	13	13	7 27	3	4
6 43 31	10	14	14	8 26	5	6	10	14	14	8 21	5	5	10	14	14	8 16	4	5
6 47 51	11	15	15	9 17	6	7	11	15	15	9 11	5	6	11	15	15	9 5	5	6
6 52 11	12	16	15	10 7	7	8	12	16	16	10 1	6	7	12	16	16	9 55	6	7
6 56 30	13	17	16	10 57	8	9	13	17	16	10 51	7	8	13	17	17	10 44	7	8
7 0 49	14	18	17	11 47	8	10	14	18	17	11 40	8	9	14	18	18	11 33	8	9
7 5 7	15	19	18	12 37	9	10	15	19	18	12 30	9	10	15	19	18	12 22	9	10
7 9 26	16	20	19	13 27	10	11	16	20	19	13 19	10	11	16	20	19	13 11	10	11
7 13 43	17	21	20	14 17	11	12	17	21	20	14 9	11	12	17	21	20	14 0	11	12
7 18 0	18	22	21	15 7	12	13	18	22	21	14 58	12	13	18	22	21	14 49	11	13
7 22 17	19	23	22	15 57	13	14	19	23	22	15 47	13	14	19	23	22	15 37	12	14
7 26 33	20	24	23	16 46	14	15	20	24	23	16 36	13	15	20	24	23	16 26	13	15
7 30 49	21	25	24	17 36	15	16	21	25	24	17 25	14	16	21	25	24	17 14	14	16
7 35 4	22	26	25	18 25	16	17	22	26	25	18 14	15	17	22	26	25	18 2	15	17
7 39 19	23	27	26	19 14	16	18	23	27	26	19 2	16	18	23	27	26	18 51	16	18
7 43 33	24	28	26	20 3	17	19	24	28	27	19 51	17	19	24	28	27	19 39	17	19
7 47 46	25	29	27	20 52	18	20	25	29	27	20 39	18	20	25	29	27	20 26	17	19
7 51 59	26	♍	28	21 40	19	21	26	♍	28	21 27	19	21	26	♍	28	21 14	18	20
7 56 11	27	1	29	22 29	20	22	27	1	29	22 16	20	22	27	1	29	22 2	19	21
8 0 23	28	2	♎	23 17	21	23	28	2	♎	23 3	20	23	28	2	♎	22 49	20	22
8 4 34	29	3	1	24 6	22	24	29	3	1	23 51	21	24	29	3	1	23 37	21	23
8 8 44	♌	3	2	24 54	23	25	♌	4	2	24 39	22	24	♌	4	2	24 24	22	24
8 12 53	1	4	3	25 42	23	26	1	5	3	25 26	23	25	1	5	3	25 11	23	25
8 17 2	2	5	4	26 30	24	27	2	6	4	26 14	24	26	2	6	4	25 58	23	26
8 21 10	3	6	5	27 17	25	28	3	7	5	27 1	25	27	3	7	4	26 44	24	27
8 25 18	4	7	5	28 5	26	29	4	7	5	27 48	26	28	4	8	5	27 31	25	28
8 29 24	5	8	6	28 52	27	29	5	8	6	28 35	26	29	5	9	6	28 17	26	29
8 33 30	6	9	7	29 40	28	♑	6	9	7	29 22	27	♑	6	10	7	29 4	27	♑
8 37 36	7	10	8	0♏ 27	29	1	7	10	8	0♏ 8	28	1	7	10	8	29 50	28	1
8 41 40	8	11	9	1 13	29	2	8	11	9	0 55	29	2	8	11	9	0♏ 36	29	2
8 45 44	9	12	10	2 0	♐	3	9	12	10	1 41	♐	3	9	12	10	1 22	29	3
8 49 47	10	13	11	2 47	1	4	10	13	11	2 27	1	4	10	13	11	2 7	♐	4
8 53 50	11	14	12	3 33	2	5	11	14	11	3 13	1	5	11	14	11	2 53	1	5
8 57 51	12	15	12	4 20	3	6	12	15	12	3 59	2	6	12	15	12	3 38	2	5
9 1 52	13	16	13	5 6	4	7	13	16	13	4 45	3	7	13	16	13	4 24	3	6
9 5 52	14	17	14	5 52	4	8	14	17	14	5 30	4	8	14	17	14	5 9	4	7
HOUSES	4	5	6	7	8	9	4	5	6	7	8	9	4	5	6	7	8	9

LATITUDE 43° S.   LATITUDE 44° S.   LATITUDE 45° S.

LATITUDE 43° N. LATITUDE 44° N. LATITUDE 45° N.

SIDEREAL TIME	10 Ω	11 ♍	12 ♎	ASC ♏		2 ♐	3 ♑	10 Ω	11 ♍	12 ♎	ASC ♏		2 ♐	3 ♑	10 Ω	11 ♍	12 ♎	ASC ♏		2 ♐	3 ♑
H M S	°	°	°	°	'	°	°	°	°	°	°	'	°	°	°	°	°	°	'	°	°
9 9 52	15	18	15	6	38	5	9	15	18	15	6	16	5	9	15	18	15	5	54	4	8
9 13 50	16	19	16	7	23	6	10	16	19	16	7	1	6	10	16	19	16	6	39	5	9
9 17 49	17	20	17	8	9	7	11	17	20	17	7	46	6	10	17	20	16	7	23	6	10
9 21 46	18	21	18	8	54	8	12	18	21	17	8	31	7	11	18	21	17	8	8	7	11
9 25 42	19	22	18	9	40	9	13	19	22	18	9	16	8	12	19	22	18	8	52	8	12
9 29 38	20	23	19	10	25	9	14	20	23	19	10	1	9	13	20	23	19	9	37	8	13
9 33 34	21	24	20	11	10	10	15	21	24	20	10	45	10	14	21	24	20	10	21	9	14
9 37 28	22	25	21	11	55	11	15	22	25	21	11	30	11	15	22	25	21	11	5	10	15
9 41 22	23	26	22	12	39	12	16	23	26	22	12	14	11	16	23	26	21	11	49	11	16
9 45 15	24	26	23	13	24	13	17	24	26	22	12	59	12	17	24	26	22	12	33	12	17
9 49 8	25	27	23	14	9	14	18	25	27	23	13	43	13	18	25	27	23	13	16	13	18
9 53 0	26	28	24	14	53	14	19	26	28	24	14	27	14	19	26	28	24	14	0	13	19
9 56 51	27	29	25	15	37	15	20	27	29	25	15	11	15	20	27	29	25	14	43	14	20
10 0 42	28	♎	26	16	22	16	21	28	♎	26	15	54	16	21	28	♎	25	15	27	15	21
10 4 32	29	1	27	17	6	17	22	29	1	26	16	38	16	22	29	1	26	16	10	16	22
10 8 22	♍	2	27	17	50	18	23	♍	2	27	17	22	17	23	♍	2	27	16	53	17	23
10 12 11	1	3	28	18	34	19	24	1	3	28	18	5	18	24	1	3	28	17	36	18	23
10 15 59	2	4	29	19	18	19	25	2	4	29	18	49	19	25	2	4	29	18	19	18	24
10 19 47	3	5	♏	20	1	20	26	3	5	♏	19	32	20	26	3	5	29	19	2	19	25
10 23 34	4	6	1	20	45	21	27	4	6	0	20	15	21	27	4	6	♏	19	45	20	26
10 27 21	5	7	1	21	29	22	28	5	7	1	20	59	21	28	5	7	1	20	28	21	27
10 31 8	6	7	2	22	12	23	29	6	7	2	21	42	22	29	6	7	2	21	11	22	28
10 34 53	7	8	3	22	56	24	♒	7	8	3	22	25	23	♒	7	8	2	21	54	22	29
10 38 39	8	9	4	23	39	24	1	8	9	4	23	8	24	1	8	9	3	22	36	23	♒
10 42 24	9	10	5	24	23	25	2	9	10	4	23	51	25	2	9	10	4	23	19	24	1
10 46 8	10	11	5	25	6	26	3	10	11	5	24	34	25	3	10	11	5	24	2	25	2
10 49 52	11	12	6	25	50	27	4	11	12	6	25	17	26	4	11	12	6	24	44	26	3
10 53 36	12	13	7	26	33	28	5	12	13	7	26	0	27	5	12	13	6	25	27	27	4
10 57 20	13	14	8	27	16	29	6	13	14	7	26	43	28	6	13	14	7	26	9	27	5
11 1 3	14	15	8	28	0	29	7	14	15	8	27	26	29	7	14	14	8	26	52	28	6
11 4 45	15	16	9	28	43	♑	8	15	15	9	28	9	♑	8	15	15	9	27	34	29	7
11 8 28	16	16	10	29	26	1	9	16	16	10	28	52	1	9	16	16	9	28	17	♑	8
11 12 10	17	17	11	0♐	10	2	10	17	17	10	29	35	1	10	17	17	10	29	0	1	9
11 15 52	18	18	12	0	53	3	11	18	18	11	0♐	18	2	11	18	18	11	29	42	2	10
11 19 33	19	19	12	1	37	4	12	19	19	12	1	1	3	12	19	19	12	0♐	25	3	11
11 23 15	20	20	13	2	20	5	13	20	20	13	1	44	4	13	20	20	12	1	7	3	12
11 26 56	21	21	14	3	4	5	14	21	21	14	2	27	5	14	21	21	13	1	50	4	13
11 30 37	22	22	15	3	47	6	15	22	22	14	3	10	6	15	22	22	14	2	33	5	14
11 34 17	23	23	15	4	31	7	16	23	22	15	3	54	7	16	23	22	15	3	16	6	15
11 37 58	24	23	16	5	14	8	17	24	23	16	4	37	7	17	24	23	15	3	59	7	16
11 41 39	25	24	17	5	58	9	18	25	24	17	5	20	8	18	25	24	16	4	42	8	18
11 45 19	26	25	18	6	42	10	19	26	25	17	6	4	9	19	26	25	17	5	25	9	19
11 48 59	27	26	18	7	26	11	20	27	26	18	6	47	10	20	27	26	18	6	8	10	20
11 52 40	28	27	19	8	10	12	21	28	27	19	7	31	11	21	28	27	18	6	51	10	21
11 56 20	29	28	20	8	54	13	22	29	28	20	8	15	12	22	29	27	19	7	35	11	22
HOUSES	4	5	6	7		8	9	4	5	6	7		8	9	4	5	6	7		8	9

LATITUDE 43° S. LATITUDE 44° S. LATITUDE 45° S.

LATITUDE 43° N. LATITUDE 44° N. LATITUDE 45° N.

SIDEREAL TIME	10 ♎	11 ♎	12 ♏	ASC ♐	2 ♑	3 ♒	10 ♎	11 ♎	12 ♏	ASC ♐	2 ♑	3 ♒	10 ♎	11 ♎	12 ♏	ASC ♐	2 ♑	3 ♒
H M S	°	°	°	° '	°	°	°	°	°	° '	°	°	°	°	°	° '	°	°
12 0 0	0	29	21	9 39	13	23	0	28	20	8 59	13	23	0	28	20	8 18	12	23
12 3 40	1	29	21	10 23	14	24	1	29	21	9 43	14	24	1	29	21	9 2	13	24
12 7 20	2	♏	22	11 8	15	25	2	♏	22	10 27	15	25	2	♏	22	9 46	14	25
12 11 1	3	1	23	11 52	16	26	3	1	23	11 12	16	26	3	1	22	10 30	15	26
12 14 41	4	2	24	12 37	17	28	4	2	23	11 56	17	27	4	2	23	11 14	16	27
12 18 21	5	3	25	13 23	18	29	5	3	24	12 41	18	28	5	3	24	11 58	17	28
12 22 2	6	4	25	14 8	19	♓	6	4	25	13 26	19	♓	6	3	25	12 43	18	29
12 25 42	7	5	26	14 53	20	1	7	4	26	14 11	19	1	7	4	25	13 27	19	♓
12 29 23	8	5	27	15 39	21	2	8	5	26	14 56	20	2	8	5	26	14 12	20	2
12 33 4	9	6	28	16 25	22	3	9	6	27	15 42	21	3	9	6	27	14 57	21	3
12 36 45	10	7	28	17 11	23	4	10	7	28	16 28	22	4	10	7	28	15 43	22	4
12 40 27	11	8	29	17 58	24	5	11	8	29	17 14	23	5	11	8	28	16 28	23	5
12 44 8	12	9	♐	18 44	25	6	12	9	29	18 0	24	6	12	8	29	17 14	24	6
12 47 50	13	10	1	19 31	26	8	13	9	♐	18 47	25	7	13	9	♐	18 1	25	7
12 51 32	14	10	1	20 19	27	9	14	10	1	19 33	26	9	14	10	1	18 47	26	8
12 55 15	15	11	2	21 6	28	10	15	11	2	20 21	27	10	15	11	1	19 34	27	10
12 58 57	16	12	3	21 54	29	11	16	12	3	21 8	29	11	16	12	2	20 21	28	11
13 2 40	17	13	4	22 42	♒	12	17	13	3	21 56	♒	12	17	13	3	21 8	29	12
13 6 24	18	14	5	23 31	1	13	18	14	4	22 44	1	13	18	14	4	21 56	♒	13
13 10 8	19	15	5	24 20	2	14	19	15	5	23 33	2	14	19	14	4	22 44	1	14
13 13 52	20	16	6	25 9	3	16	20	15	6	24 22	3	15	20	15	5	23 33	2	15
13 17 36	21	16	7	25 59	4	17	21	16	6	25 11	4	17	21	16	6	24 22	3	17
13 21 21	22	17	8	26 49	6	18	22	17	7	26 1	5	18	22	17	7	25 11	4	18
13 25 7	23	18	8	27 39	7	19	23	18	8	26 51	6	19	23	18	8	26 1	6	19
13 28 52	24	19	9	28 30	8	20	24	19	9	27 42	7	20	24	19	8	26 51	7	20
13 32 39	25	20	10	29 22	9	21	25	20	10	28 33	8	21	25	19	9	27 42	8	21
13 36 26	26	21	11	0♑ 14	10	23	26	20	10	29 24	10	23	26	20	10	28 33	9	23
13 40 13	27	22	12	1 6	11	24	27	21	11	0♑ 16	11	24	27	21	11	29 24	10	24
13 44 1	28	22	12	1 59	12	25	28	22	12	1 9	12	25	28	22	12	0♑ 17	11	25
13 47 49	29	23	13	2 53	14	26	29	23	13	2 2	13	26	29	23	12	1 9	13	26
13 51 38	♏	24	14	3 47	15	27	♏	24	14	2 56	14	27	♏	24	13	2 3	14	27
13 55 28	1	25	15	4 42	16	29	1	25	14	3 50	16	29	1	25	14	2 57	15	29
13 59 18	2	26	16	5 37	17	♈	2	26	15	4 45	17	♈	2	25	15	3 51	16	♈
14 3 9	3	27	17	6 33	19	1	3	26	16	5 40	18	1	3	26	16	4 46	18	1
14 7 0	4	28	17	7 29	20	2	4	27	17	6 37	19	2	4	27	16	5 42	19	2
14 10 52	5	28	18	8 26	21	3	5	28	18	7 33	21	3	5	28	17	6 39	20	3
14 14 45	6	29	19	9 24	22	5	6	29	19	8 31	22	5	6	29	18	7 36	21	5
14 18 38	7	♐	20	10 23	24	6	7	♐	19	9 29	23	6	7	♐	19	8 34	23	6
14 22 32	8	1	21	11 22	25	7	8	1	20	10 28	24	7	8	1	20	9 32	24	7
14 26 26	9	2	22	12 22	26	8	9	2	21	11 28	26	8	9	1	21	10 32	25	8
14 30 22	10	3	23	13 23	28	10	10	3	22	12 29	27	10	10	2	21	11 32	27	10
14 34 17	11	4	23	14 25	29	11	11	3	23	13 30	29	11	11	3	22	12 33	28	11
14 38 14	12	5	24	15 28	♓	12	12	4	24	14 33	♓	12	12	4	23	13 36	♓	12
14 42 11	13	5	25	16 31	2	13	13	5	25	15 36	1	13	13	5	24	14 39	1	13
14 46 10	14	6	26	17 36	3	14	14	6	26	16 40	3	15	14	6	25	15 42	2	15
HOUSES	4	5	6	7	8	9	4	5	6	7	8	9	4	5	6	7	8	9

LATITUDE 43° S. LATITUDE 44° S. LATITUDE 45° S.

LATITUDE 43° N. LATITUDE 44° N. LATITUDE 45° N.

SIDEREAL TIME	10 ♏	11 ♐	12 ♐	ASC ♑		2 ♓	3 ♈	10 ♏	11 ♐	12 ♐	ASC ♑		2 ♓	3 ♈	10 ♏	11 ♐	12 ♐	ASC ♑		2 ♓	3 ♈
H M S	°	°	°	°	'	°	°	°	°	°	°	'	°	°	°	°	°	°	'	°	°
14 50 8	15	7	27	18	41	4	16	15	7	26	17	45	4	16	15	7	26	16	47	4	16
14 54 8	16	8	28	19	47	6	17	16	8	27	18	52	6	17	16	8	27	17	53	5	17
14 58 8	17	9	29	20	55	7	18	17	9	28	19	59	7	18	17	8	28	19	0	7	18
15 2 9	18	10	♑	22	3	9	19	18	10	29	21	7	8	20	18	9	29	20	8	8	20
15 6 10	19	11	1	23	13	10	21	19	10	♑	22	16	10	21	19	10	29	21	18	10	21
15 10 13	20	12	2	24	23	12	22	20	11	1	23	27	11	22	20	11	♑	22	28	11	22
15 14 16	21	13	2	25	35	13	23	21	12	2	24	39	13	23	21	12	1	23	40	13	23
15 18 20	22	13	3	26	48	15	24	22	13	3	25	52	14	24	22	13	2	24	52	14	25
15 22 24	23	14	4	28	2	16	26	23	14	4	27	6	16	26	23	14	3	26	7	16	26
15 26 30	24	15	5	29	17	18	27	24	15	5	28	21	17	27	24	15	4	27	22	17	27
15 30 36	25	16	6	0♒	34	19	28	25	16	6	29	38	19	28	25	16	5	28	39	19	28
15 34 42	26	17	7	1	52	21	29	26	17	7	0♒	56	20	29	26	17	6	29	57	20	♉
15 38 50	27	18	8	3	11	22	♉	27	18	8	2	15	22	♉	27	17	7	1♒	17	22	1
15 42 58	28	19	9	4	31	24	2	28	19	9	3	36	24	2	28	18	8	2	38	23	2
15 47 7	29	20	10	5	53	25	3	29	20	10	4	58	25	3	29	19	9	4	0	25	3
15 51 16	♐21	11	7	17		27	4	♐21	11	6	22		27	4	♐20	10	5	24		27	5
15 55 26	1	22	12	8	42	28	5	1	21	12	7	48	28	6	1	21	11	6	50	28	6
15 59 37	2	23	13	10	8	♈	7	2	22	13	9	14	♈	7	2	22	12	8	17	♈	7
16 3 49	3	24	14	11	36	1	8	3	23	14	10	43	1	8	3	23	13	9	46	1	8
16 8 1	4	25	16	13	5	3	9	4	24	15	12	13	3	9	4	24	14	11	17	3	9
16 12 14	5	26	17	14	36	5	10	5	25	16	13	45	5	10	5	25	15	12	50	5	11
16 16 27	6	26	18	16	8	6	11	6	26	17	15	18	6	12	6	26	16	14	24	6	12
16 20 41	7	27	19	17	42	8	13	7	27	18	16	53	8	13	7	27	18	16	0	8	13
16 24 56	8	28	20	19	18	9	14	8	28	19	18	29	9	14	8	28	19	17	37	10	14
16 29 11	9	29	21	20	55	11	15	9	29	20	20	8	11	15	9	29	20	19	17	11	16
16 33 27	10	♑	22	22	34	12	16	10	♑	22	21	48	13	16	10	♑	21	20	58	13	17
16 37 43	11	1	23	24	14	14	17	11	1	23	23	29	14	18	11	1	22	22	41	14	18
16 41 59	12	2	24	25	56	16	19	12	2	24	25	13	16	19	12	2	23	24	26	16	19
16 46 17	13	3	26	27	40	17	20	13	3	25	26	58	17	20	13	3	24	26	13	18	20
16 50 34	14	4	27	29	25	19	21	14	4	26	28	44	19	21	14	4	26	28	1	19	21
16 54 53	15	5	28	1♓	11	20	22	15	5	27	0♓	33	20	22	15	5	27	29	51	21	23
16 59 11	16	6	29	2	59	22	23	16	6	29	2	22	22	24	16	6	28	1♓	43	22	24
17 3 30	17	7	♒	4	48	23	24	17	7	♒	4	14	24	25	17	7	29	3	37	24	25
17 7 49	18	8	2	6	39	25	26	18	8	1	6	6	25	26	18	8	♒	5	32	25	26
17 12 9	19	9	3	8	31	26	27	19	9	2	8	1	27	27	19	9	2	7	28	27	27
17 16 29	20	10	4	10	24	28	28	20	10	4	9	56	28	28	20	10	3	9	26	29	28
17 20 49	21	11	5	12	18	29	29	21	11	5	11	53	♉	29	21	11	4	11	25	♉	♊
17 25 10	22	12	7	14	13	♉	♊	22	12	6	13	51	1	♊	22	12	6	13	26	2	1
17 29 31	23	14	8	16	9	2	1	23	13	7	15	49	3	2	23	13	7	15	28	3	2
17 33 51	24	15	9	18	6	4	2	24	14	9	17	49	4	3	24	14	8	17	30	5	3
17 38 13	25	16	11	20	4	5	4	25	15	10	19	50	6	4	25	15	10	19	34	6	4
17 42 34	26	17	12	22	3	7	5	26	16	11	21	51	7	5	26	16	11	21	38	8	5
17 46 55	27	18	13	24	2	8	6	27	17	13	23	53	9	6	27	17	12	23	43	9	6
17 51 17	28	19	15	26	1	10	7	28	19	14	25	55	10	7	28	18	14	25	48	11	7
17 55 38	29	20	16	28	0	11	8	29	20	16	27	57	12	8	29	19	15	27	54	12	8
HOUSES	4	5	6	7		8	9	4	5	6	7		8	9	4	5	6	7		8	9

LATITUDE 43° S. LATITUDE 44° S. LATITUDE 45° S.

LATITUDE 43° N. LATITUDE 44° N. LATITUDE 45° N.

SIDEREAL TIME	10 ♑	11 ♑	12 ♒	ASC ♈	2 ♉	3 ♊	10 ♑	11 ♑	12 ♒	ASC ♈	2 ♉	3 ♊	10 ♑	11 ♑	12 ♒	ASC ♈	2 ♉	3 ♊
H M S	°	°	°	° '	°	°	°	°	°	° '	°	°	°	°	°	° '	°	°
18 0 0	0	21	17	0 0	13	9	0	21	17	0 0	13	9	0	20	17	0 0	13	10
18 4 22	1	22	19	2 0	14	10	1	22	18	2 3	14	10	1	22	18	2 6	15	11
18 8 43	2	23	20	3 59	15	11	2	23	20	4 5	16	11	2	23	19	4 12	16	12
18 13 5	3	24	22	5 58	17	12	3	24	21	6 7	17	13	3	24	21	6 17	18	13
18 17 26	4	25	23	7 57	18	13	4	25	23	8 9	19	14	4	25	22	8 22	19	14
18 21 47	5	26	25	9 56	19	14	5	26	24	10 10	20	15	5	26	24	10 26	20	15
18 26 9	6	28	26	11 54	21	15	6	27	26	12 11	21	16	6	27	25	12 30	22	16
18 30 29	7	29	28	13 51	22	16	7	28	27	14 11	23	17	7	28	27	14 32	23	17
18 34 50	8	♒	29	15 47	23	18	8	♒	29	16 9	24	18	8	29	28	16 34	24	18
18 39 11	9	1	♓	17 42	25	19	9	1	♓	18 7	25	19	9	♒	♓	18 35	26	19
18 43 31	10	2	2	19 36	26	20	10	2	2	20 4	26	20	10	2	1	20 34	27	20
18 47 51	11	3	4	21 29	27	21	11	3	3	21 59	28	21	11	3	3	22 32	28	21
18 52 11	12	4	5	23 21	28	22	12	4	5	23 54	29	22	12	4	5	24 28	♊	22
18 56 30	13	6	7	25 12	♊	23	13	5	6	25 46	♊	23	13	5	6	26 23	1	23
19 0 49	14	7	8	27 1	1	24	14	6	8	27 38	1	24	14	6	8	28 17	2	24
19 5 7	15	8	10	28 49	2	25	15	8	10	29 27	3	25	15	7	9	0♉ 9	3	25
19 9 26	16	9	11	0♉ 35	3	26	16	9	11	1♉ 16	4	26	16	9	11	1 59	4	26
19 13 43	17	10	13	2 20	4	27	17	10	13	3 2	5	27	17	10	12	3 47	6	27
19 18 0	18	11	14	4 4	6	28	18	11	14	4 47	6	28	18	11	14	5 34	7	28
19 22 17	19	13	16	5 46	7	29	19	12	16	6 31	7	29	19	12	16	7 19	8	29
19 26 33	20	14	18	7 26	8	♋	20	14	17	8 12	8	♋	20	13	17	9 2	9	♋
19 30 49	21	15	19	9 5	9	1	21	15	19	9 52	10	1	21	14	19	10 43	10	1
19 35 4	22	16	21	10 42	10	2	22	16	21	11 31	11	2	22	16	20	12 23	11	2
19 39 19	23	17	22	12 18	11	3	23	17	22	13 7	12	3	23	17	22	14 0	12	3
19 43 33	24	19	24	13 52	12	4	24	18	24	14 46	13	4	24	18	24	15 36	14	4
19 47 46	25	20	25	15 24	13	4	25	20	25	16 15	14	5	25	19	25	17 10	15	5
19 51 59	26	21	27	16 55	14	5	26	21	27	17 47	15	6	26	21	27	18 43	16	6
19 56 11	27	22	29	18 24	16	6	27	22	29	19 17	16	7	27	22	29	20 14	17	7
20 0 23	28	23	♈	19 52	17	7	28	23	♈	20 46	17	8	28	23	♈	21 43	18	8
20 4 34	29	25	2	21 18	18	8	29	24	2	22 12	18	9	29	24	2	23 10	19	9
20 8 44	♒	26	3	22 43	19	9	♒	26	3	23 38	19	9	♒	25	3	24 36	20	10
20 12 53	1	27	5	24 7	20	10	1	27	5	25 2	20	10	1	27	5	26 0	21	11
20 17 2	2	28	6	25 29	21	11	2	28	6	26 24	21	11	2	28	7	27 22	22	12
20 21 10	3	29	8	26 49	22	12	3	29	8	27 45	22	12	3	29	8	28 43	23	13
20 25 18	4	♓	9	28 8	23	13	4	♓	10	29 4	23	13	4	♓	10	0♊ 3	24	13
20 29 24	5	2	11	29 26	24	14	5	2	11	0♊ 22	24	14	5	2	11	1 21	25	14
20 33 30	6	3	12	0♊ 43	25	15	6	3	13	1 39	25	15	6	3	13	2 38	26	15
20 37 36	7	4	14	1 58	26	16	7	4	14	2 54	26	16	7	4	14	3 53	27	16
20 41 40	8	6	15	3 12	27	17	8	6	16	4 8	27	17	8	5	16	5 8	28	17
20 45 44	9	7	17	4 25	28	17	9	7	17	5 21	28	18	9	7	17	6 20	29	18
20 49 47	10	8	18	5 37	28	18	10	8	19	6 33	29	19	10	8	19	7 32	♋	19
20 53 50	11	9	20	6 47	29	19	11	9	20	7 44	♋	20	11	9	20	8 42	1	20
20 57 51	12	11	21	7 57	♋	20	12	10	22	8 53	1	20	12	10	22	9 52	1	21
21 1 52	13	12	23	9 5	1	21	13	12	23	10 1	2	21	13	12	23	11 0	2	22
21 5 52	14	13	24	10 13	2	22	14	13	24	11 8	3	22	14	13	25	12 7	3	22
HOUSES	4	5	6	7	8	9	4	5	6	7	8	9	4	5	6	7	8	9

LATITUDE 43° S. LATITUDE 44° S. LATITUDE 45° S.

LATITUDE 43° N.   LATITUDE 44° N.   LATITUDE 45° N.

SIDEREAL TIME	10 ≈	11 ♓	12 ♈	ASC ♊		2 ♋	3 ♋	10 ≈	11 ♓	12 ♈	ASC ♊		2 ♋	3 ♋	10 ≈	11 ♓	12 ♈	ASC ♊		2 ♋	3 ♋
H M S	°	°	°	°	'	°	°	°	°	°	°	'	°	°	°	°	°	°	'	°	°
21 9 52	15	14	26	11	19	3	23	15	14	26	12	15	4	23	15	14	26	13	13	4	23
21 13 50	16	16	27	12	24	4	24	16	15	27	13	20	4	24	16	15	28	14	18	5	24
21 17 49	17	17	28	13	29	5	25	17	17	29	14	24	5	25	17	17	29	15	21	6	25
21 21 46	18	18	♉	14	32	6	25	18	18	♉	15	27	6	26	18	18	♉	16	24	7	26
21 25 42	19	19	1	15	35	7	26	19	19	1	16	30	7	27	19	19	2	17	27	8	27
21 29 38	20	20	2	16	37	7	27	20	20	3	17	31	8	27	20	20	3	18	28	9	28
21 33 34	21	22	4	17	38	8	28	21	22	4	18	32	9	28	21	22	5	19	28	9	29
21 37 28	22	23	5	18	38	9	29	22	23	6	19	32	10	29	22	23	6	20	28	10	29
21 41 22	23	24	6	19	37	10	♌	23	24	7	20	31	11	♌	23	24	7	21	26	11	♌
21 45 15	24	25	8	20	36	11	1	24	25	8	21	29	11	1	24	25	9	22	24	12	1
21 49 8	25	27	9	21	34	12	2	25	27	9	22	27	12	2	25	27	10	23	21	13	2
21 53 0	26	28	10	22	31	13	2	26	28	11	23	23	13	3	26	28	11	24	18	14	3
21 56 51	27	29	11	23	27	13	3	27	29	12	24	20	14	4	27	29	12	25	14	14	4
22 0 42	28	♈	13	24	23	14	4	28	♈	13	25	15	15	4	28	♈	14	26	9	15	5
22 4 32	29	1	14	25	18	15	5	29	1	14	26	10	16	5	29	1	15	27	3	16	5
22 8 22	♓	3	15	26	13	16	6	♓	3	16	27	4	16	6	♓	3	16	27	57	17	6
22 12 11	1	4	16	27	7	17	7	1	4	17	27	58	17	7	1	4	17	28	51	18	7
22 15 59	2	5	18	28	1	18	8	2	5	18	28	51	18	8	2	5	19	29	43	18	8
22 19 47	3	6	19	28	54	18	8	3	6	19	29	44	19	9	3	6	20	0♋	36	19	9
22 23 34	4	7	20	29	46	19	9	4	7	20	0♋	36	20	10	4	7	21	1	27	20	10
22 27 21	5	9	21	0♋	38	20	10	5	9	22	1	27	20	10	5	9	22	2	18	21	11
22 31 8	6	10	22	1	30	21	11	6	10	23	2	18	21	11	6	10	23	3	9	22	11
22 34 53	7	11	23	2	21	22	12	7	11	24	3	9	22	12	7	11	24	3	59	22	12
22 38 39	8	12	24	3	11	22	13	8	12	25	3	59	23	13	8	12	26	4	49	23	13
22 42 24	9	13	26	4	1	23	14	9	13	26	4	49	24	14	9	13	27	5	38	24	14
22 46 8	10	14	27	4	51	24	14	10	15	27	5	38	24	15	10	15	28	6	27	25	15
22 49 52	11	16	28	5	40	25	15	11	16	28	6	27	25	15	11	16	29	7	16	26	16
22 53 36	12	17	29	6	29	25	16	12	17	29	7	16	26	16	12	17	♊	8	4	26	16
22 57 20	13	18	♊	7	18	26	17	13	18	♊	8	4	27	17	13	18	1	8	52	27	17
23 1 3	14	19	1	8	6	27	18	14	19	1	8	52	27	18	14	19	2	9	39	28	18
23 4 45	15	20	2	8	54	28	19	15	20	3	9	39	28	19	15	20	3	10	26	29	19
23 8 28	16	21	3	9	41	29	20	16	21	4	10	27	29	20	16	22	4	11	13	29	20
23 12 10	17	22	4	10	29	29	20	17	23	5	11	13	♌	21	17	23	5	11	59	♌	21
23 15 52	18	24	5	11	16	♌	21	18	24	6	12	0	1	21	18	24	6	12	46	1	22
23 19 33	19	25	6	12	2	1	22	19	25	7	12	46	1	22	19	25	7	13	32	2	22
23 23 15	20	26	7	12	49	2	23	20	26	8	13	32	2	23	20	26	8	14	17	2	23
23 26 56	21	27	8	13	35	2	24	21	27	9	14	18	3	24	21	27	9	15	3	3	24
23 30 37	22	28	9	14	21	3	25	22	28	10	15	4	4	25	22	28	10	15	48	4	25
23 34 17	23	29	10	15	7	4	25	23	29	11	15	49	4	26	23	29	11	16	33	5	26
23 37 58	24	♉	11	15	52	5	26	24	♉	11	16	34	5	26	24	♉	12	17	17	5	26
23 41 39	25	1	12	16	37	5	27	25	2	12	17	19	6	27	25	2	13	18	2	6	27
23 45 19	26	2	13	17	23	6	28	26	3	13	18	4	7	28	26	3	14	18	46	7	28
23 48 59	27	4	14	18	8	7	29	27	4	14	18	48	7	29	27	4	15	19	30	8	29
23 52 40	28	5	15	18	52	8	♍	28	5	15	19	33	8	♍	28	5	16	20	14	8	♍
23 56 20	29	6	16	19	37	9	1	29	6	16	20	17	9	1	29	6	17	20	58	9	1
HOUSES	4	5	6	7		8	9	4	5	6	7		8	9	4	5	6	7		8	9

LATITUDE 43° S.   LATITUDE 44° S.   LATITUDE 45° S.

LATITUDE 46° N.   LATITUDE 47° N.   LATITUDE 48° N.

SIDEREAL TIME (H M S)	10 ♈	11 ♉	12 ♊	ASC ♋	2 ♌	3 ♍	10 ♈	11 ♉	12 ♊	ASC ♋	2 ♌	3 ♍	10 ♈	11 ♉	12 ♊	ASC ♋	2 ♌	3 ♍
0 0 0	0	7	18	22 24	10	2	0	8	19	23 6	11	2	0	8	20	23 50	11	2
0 3 40	1	8	19	23 7	11	3	1	9	20	23 49	11	3	1	9	21	24 33	12	3
0 7 20	2	9	20	23 50	12	4	2	10	21	24 32	12	4	2	10	22	25 15	13	4
0 11 1	3	11	21	24 33	13	4	3	11	22	25 14	13	4	3	11	22	25 57	13	5
0 14 41	4	12	22	25 15	13	5	4	12	23	25 56	14	5	4	12	23	26 38	14	5
0 18 21	5	13	23	25 58	14	6	5	13	23	26 39	14	6	5	13	24	27 20	15	6
0 22 2	6	14	24	26 40	15	7	6	14	24	27 21	15	7	6	14	25	28 2	16	7
0 25 43	7	15	25	27 23	16	8	7	15	25	28 3	16	8	7	15	26	28 43	16	8
0 29 23	8	16	25	28 5	16	9	8	16	26	28 45	17	9	8	16	27	29 25	17	9
0 33 4	9	17	26	28 48	17	9	9	17	27	29 27	17	10	9	17	28	0♌ 6	18	10
0 36 45	10	18	27	29 30	18	10	10	18	28	0♌ 8	18	10	10	18	29	0 48	19	11
0 40 27	11	19	28	0♌ 12	19	11	11	19	29	0 50	19	11	11	19	29	1 29	19	11
0 44 8	12	20	29	0 55	19	12	12	20	♋	1 32	20	12	12	20	♋	2 10	20	12
0 47 50	13	21	♋	1 37	20	13	13	21	0	2 14	20	13	13	21	1	2 52	21	13
0 51 32	14	22	1	2 19	21	14	14	22	1	2 56	21	14	14	23	2	3 33	22	14
0 55 15	15	23	1	3 1	22	15	15	23	2	3 37	22	15	15	24	3	4 14	22	15
0 58 57	16	24	2	3 43	22	16	16	24	3	4 19	23	16	16	25	4	4 56	23	16
1 2 40	17	25	3	4 25	23	16	17	25	4	5 1	23	17	17	26	4	5 37	24	17
1 6 24	18	26	4	5 7	24	17	18	26	5	5 42	24	17	18	27	5	6 18	24	17
1 10 8	19	27	5	5 50	25	18	19	27	5	6 24	25	18	19	28	6	6 59	25	18
1 13 52	20	28	6	6 32	25	19	20	28	6	7 6	26	19	20	29	7	7 41	26	19
1 17 36	21	29	6	7 14	26	20	21	29	7	7 48	26	20	21	♊	8	8 22	27	20
1 21 21	22	♊	7	7 56	27	21	22	♊	8	8 29	27	21	22	1	9	9 3	28	21
1 25 7	23	1	8	8 38	28	22	23	1	9	9 11	28	22	23	2	9	9 45	28	22
1 28 52	24	2	9	9 21	29	23	24	2	10	9 53	29	23	24	3	10	10 26	29	23
1 32 39	25	3	10	10 3	29	24	25	3	10	10 35	♍	24	25	4	11	11 7	♍	24
1 36 26	26	4	11	10 45	♍	24	26	4	11	11 17	0	24	26	5	12	11 49	1	24
1 40 13	27	5	11	11 28	1	25	27	5	12	11 59	1	25	27	5	13	12 31	1	25
1 44 1	28	6	12	12 11	2	26	28	6	13	12 41	2	26	28	6	13	13 12	2	26
1 47 49	29	7	13	12 53	2	27	29	7	14	13 23	3	27	29	7	14	13 54	3	27
1 51 38	♉	8	14	13 36	3	28	♉	8	14	14 5	3	28	♉	8	15	14 36	4	28
1 55 28	1	9	15	14 19	4	29	1	9	15	14 48	4	29	1	9	16	15 18	4	29
1 59 18	2	10	15	15 1	5	♎	2	10	16	15 30	5	♎	2	10	17	16 0	5	♎
2 3 9	3	11	16	15 44	6	1	3	11	17	16 13	6	1	3	11	17	16 42	6	1
2 7 0	4	12	17	16 28	6	2	4	12	18	16 55	7	2	4	12	18	17 24	7	2
2 10 52	5	13	18	17 11	7	3	5	13	18	17 38	7	3	5	13	19	18 6	8	3
2 14 45	6	14	19	17 54	8	3	6	14	19	18 21	8	3	6	14	20	18 48	8	3
2 18 38	7	14	20	18 37	9	4	7	15	20	19 4	9	4	7	15	21	19 31	9	4
2 22 32	8	15	20	19 21	10	5	8	16	21	19 47	10	5	8	16	21	20 13	10	5
2 26 26	9	16	21	20 4	10	6	9	17	22	20 30	11	6	9	17	22	20 56	11	6
2 30 22	10	17	22	20 48	11	7	10	18	23	21 13	11	7	10	18	23	21 39	12	7
2 34 17	11	18	23	21 32	12	8	11	19	23	21 57	12	8	11	19	24	22 22	12	8
2 38 14	12	19	24	22 16	13	9	12	20	24	22 40	13	9	12	20	25	23 5	13	9
2 42 11	13	20	24	23 0	14	10	13	20	25	23 24	14	10	13	21	25	23 48	14	10
2 46 10	14	21	25	23 44	15	11	14	21	26	24 8	15	11	14	22	26	24 31	15	11
HOUSES	4	5	6	7	8	9	4	5	6	7	8	9	4	5	6	7	8	9

LATITUDE 46° N.   LATITUDE 47° N.   LATITUDE 48° N.

SIDEREAL TIME	10 ♉	11 ♊	12 ♋	ASC ♌ °	'	2 ♍	3 ♎	10 ♉	11 ♊	12 ♋	ASC ♌ °	'	2 ♍	3 ♎	10 ♉	11 ♊	12 ♋	ASC ♌ °	'	2 ♍	3 ♎
H M S																					
2 50 8	15	22	26	24	29	15	12	15	22	27	24	52	15	12	15	23	27	25	15	16	12
2 54 8	16	23	27	25	13	16	13	16	23	27	25	36	16	13	16	24	28	25	58	16	13
2 58 8	17	24	28	25	58	17	14	17	24	28	26	20	17	14	17	25	29	26	42	17	14
3 2 9	18	25	29	26	43	18	15	18	25	29	27	4	18	15	18	25	♌	27	26	18	15
3 6 10	19	26	29	27	28	19	16	19	26	♌	27	49	19	16	19	26	0	28	10	19	15
3 10 13	20	27	♌	28	13	20	17	20	27	1	28	33	20	17	20	27	1	28	54	20	16
3 14 16	21	28	1	28	58	20	18	21	28	1	29	18	20	17	21	28	2	29	38	21	17
3 18 20	22	29	2	29	43	21	18	22	29	2	0♍	3	21	18	22	29	3	0♍	23	21	18
3 22 24	23	♋	3	0♍	29	22	19	23	♋	3	0	48	22	19	23	♋	4	1	7	22	19
3 26 30	24	0	4	1	15	23	20	24	1	4	1	33	23	20	24	1	4	1	52	23	20
3 30 36	25	1	4	2	0	24	21	25	2	5	2	18	24	21	25	2	5	2	37	24	21
3 34 42	26	2	5	2	46	25	22	26	3	6	3	4	25	22	26	3	6	3	22	25	22
3 38 50	27	3	6	3	32	26	23	27	4	6	3	50	26	23	27	4	7	4	7	26	23
3 42 58	28	4	7	4	19	26	24	28	5	7	4	35	26	24	28	5	8	4	52	26	24
3 47 7	29	5	8	5	5	27	25	29	5	8	5	21	27	25	29	6	9	5	38	27	25
3 51 16	♊	6	9	5	52	28	26	♊	6	9	6	7	28	26	♊	7	9	6	23	28	26
3 55 26	1	7	9	6	38	29	27	1	7	10	6	54	29	27	1	8	10	7	9	29	27
3 59 37	2	8	10	7	25	♎	28	2	8	11	7	40	♎	28	2	9	11	7	55	♎	28
4 3 49	3	9	11	8	12	1	29	3	9	12	8	26	1	29	3	10	12	8	41	1	29
4 8 1	4	10	12	8	59	2	♏	4	10	12	9	13	2	♏	4	10	13	9	27	2	♏
4 12 14	5	11	13	9	47	3	1	5	11	13	10	0	3	1	5	11	14	10	13	3	1
4 16 27	6	12	14	10	34	3	2	6	12	14	10	47	3	2	6	12	14	10	59	3	2
4 20 41	7	13	15	11	21	4	3	7	13	15	11	34	4	3	7	13	15	11	46	4	3
4 24 56	8	14	15	12	9	5	4	8	14	16	12	21	5	4	8	14	16	12	33	5	4
4 29 11	9	15	16	12	57	6	5	9	15	17	13	8	6	5	9	15	17	13	19	6	5
4 33 27	10	16	17	13	45	7	6	10	16	18	13	55	7	6	10	16	18	14	6	7	6
4 37 43	11	16	18	14	33	8	7	11	17	18	14	43	8	7	11	17	19	14	53	8	7
4 41 59	12	17	19	15	21	9	8	12	18	19	15	30	9	8	12	18	20	15	40	9	7
4 46 17	13	18	20	16	9	10	9	13	19	20	16	18	10	9	13	19	20	16	27	10	8
4 50 34	14	19	21	16	57	11	10	14	20	21	17	6	11	10	14	20	21	17	15	10	9
4 54 53	15	20	22	17	46	11	11	15	21	22	17	54	11	11	15	21	22	18	2	11	10
4 59 11	16	21	22	18	34	12	12	16	21	23	18	42	12	12	16	22	23	18	49	12	11
5 3 30	17	22	23	19	23	13	13	17	22	24	19	30	13	13	17	23	24	19	37	13	12
5 7 49	18	23	24	20	12	14	14	18	23	24	20	18	14	13	18	24	25	20	25	14	13
5 12 9	19	24	25	21	0	15	15	19	24	25	21	6	15	14	19	25	26	21	12	15	14
5 16 29	20	25	26	21	49	16	16	20	25	26	21	55	16	15	20	26	27	22	0	16	15
5 20 49	21	26	27	22	38	17	17	21	26	27	22	43	17	16	21	27	27	22	48	17	16
5 25 10	22	27	28	23	27	18	18	22	27	28	23	31	18	17	22	27	28	23	36	18	17
5 29 31	23	28	29	24	16	19	19	23	28	29	24	20	19	18	23	28	29	24	24	18	18
5 33 51	24	29	♍	25	5	20	20	24	29	♍	25	8	19	19	24	29	♍	25	12	19	19
5 38 13	25	♌	0	25	54	21	20	25	♌	1	25	57	20	20	25	♌	1	26	0	20	20
5 42 34	26	1	1	26	43	21	21	26	1	2	26	45	21	21	26	1	2	26	48	21	21
5 46 55	27	2	2	27	32	22	22	27	2	2	27	34	22	22	27	2	3	27	36	22	22
5 51 17	28	3	3	28	22	23	23	28	3	3	28	23	23	23	28	3	4	28	24	23	23
5 55 38	29	4	4	29	11	24	24	29	4	4	29	11	24	24	29	4	4	29	12	24	24
HOUSES	4	5	6	7		8	9	4	5	6	7		8	9	4	5	6	7		8	9

LATITUDE 46° S.   LATITUDE 47° S.   LATITUDE 48° S.

LATITUDE 46° N. LATITUDE 47° N. LATITUDE 48° N.

SIDEREAL TIME	10 ♋	11 ♌	12 ♍	ASC ♎		2 ♎	3 ♏	10 ♋	11 ♌	12 ♍	ASC ♎		2 ♎	3 ♏	10 ♋	11 ♌	12 ♍	ASC ♎		2 ♎	3 ♏
H M S	°	°	°	°	'	°	°	°	°	°	°	'	°	°	°	°	°	°	'	°	°
6 0 0	0	5	5	0	0	25	25	0	5	5	0	0	25	25	0	5	5	0	0	25	25
6 4 22	1	6	6	0	49	26	26	1	6	6	0	49	26	26	1	6	6	0	48	26	26
6 8 43	2	7	7	1	38	27	27	2	7	7	1	37	27	27	2	7	7	1	36	26	27
6 13 5	3	8	8	2	28	28	28	3	8	8	2	26	28	28	3	8	8	2	24	27	28
6 17 26	4	9	9	3	17	29	29	4	9	9	3	15	28	29	4	9	9	3	12	28	29
6 21 47	5	10	9	4	6	♏	♐	5	10	10	4	3	29	♐	5	10	10	4	0	29	♐
6 26 9	6	10	10	4	55	0	1	6	11	11	4	52	♏	1	6	11	11	4	48	♏	1
6 30 29	7	11	11	5	44	1	2	7	12	11	5	40	1	2	7	12	12	5	36	1	2
6 34 50	8	12	12	6	33	2	3	8	13	12	6	29	2	3	8	13	12	6	24	2	3
6 39 11	9	13	13	7	22	3	4	9	14	13	7	17	3	4	9	14	13	7	12	3	3
6 43 31	10	14	14	8	11	4	5	10	15	14	8	5	4	5	10	15	14	8	0	3	4
6 47 51	11	15	15	9	0	5	6	11	16	15	8	54	5	6	11	16	15	8	48	4	5
6 52 11	12	16	16	9	48	6	7	12	17	16	9	42	6	7	12	17	16	9	35	5	6
6 56 30	13	17	17	10	37	7	8	13	17	17	10	30	6	8	13	18	17	10	23	6	7
7 0 49	14	18	18	11	26	8	9	14	18	18	11	18	7	9	14	19	18	11	11	7	8
7 5 7	15	19	19	12	14	8	10	15	19	19	12	6	8	9	15	20	19	11	58	8	9
7 9 26	16	20	19	13	3	9	11	16	20	19	12	54	9	10	16	21	20	12	45	9	10
7 13 43	17	21	20	13	51	10	12	17	21	20	13	42	10	11	17	22	20	13	33	10	11
7 18 0	18	22	21	14	39	11	13	18	22	21	14	30	11	12	18	23	21	14	20	10	12
7 22 17	19	23	22	15	27	12	14	19	23	22	15	17	12	13	19	23	22	15	7	11	13
7 26 33	20	24	23	16	15	13	14	20	24	23	16	5	12	14	20	24	23	15	54	12	14
7 30 49	21	25	24	17	3	14	15	21	25	24	16	52	13	15	21	25	24	16	41	13	15
7 35 4	22	26	25	17	51	15	16	22	26	25	17	39	14	16	22	26	25	17	27	14	16
7 39 19	23	27	26	18	39	15	17	23	27	26	18	26	15	17	23	27	26	18	14	15	17
7 43 33	24	28	27	19	26	16	18	24	28	27	19	13	16	18	24	28	27	19	1	16	18
7 47 46	25	29	27	20	13	17	19	25	29	27	20	0	17	19	25	29	27	19	47	16	19
7 51 59	26	♍	28	21	1	18	20	26	♍	28	20	47	18	20	26	♍	28	20	33	17	20
7 56 11	27	1	29	21	48	19	21	27	1	29	21	34	18	21	27	1	29	21	19	18	20
8 0 23	28	2	♎	22	35	20	22	28	2	♎	22	20	19	22	28	2	♎	22	5	19	21
8 4 34	29	3	1	23	22	21	23	29	3	1	23	6	20	23	29	3	1	22	51	20	22
8 8 44	♌	4	2	24	8	21	24	♌	4	2	23	53	21	24	♌	4	2	23	37	21	23
8 12 53	1	5	3	24	55	22	25	1	5	3	24	39	22	25	1	5	3	24	22	21	24
8 17 2	2	6	4	25	41	23	26	2	6	4	25	25	23	25	2	6	4	25	8	22	25
8 21 10	3	7	4	26	28	24	27	3	7	4	26	10	24	26	3	7	4	25	53	23	26
8 25 18	4	8	5	27	14	25	28	4	8	5	26	56	24	27	4	8	5	26	38	24	27
8 29 24	5	9	6	28	0	26	29	5	9	6	27	42	25	28	5	9	6	27	23	25	28
8 33 30	6	10	7	28	45	26	♑	6	10	7	28	27	26	29	6	10	7	28	8	26	29
8 37 36	7	11	8	29	31	27	0	7	11	8	29	12	27	♑	7	11	8	28	53	26	♑
8 41 40	8	12	9	0♏	17	28	1	8	12	9	29	57	28	1	8	12	9	29	37	27	1
8 45 44	9	12	10	1	2	29	2	9	13	10	0♏	42	29	2	9	13	9	0♏	22	28	2
8 49 47	10	13	10	1	47	♐	3	10	13	10	1	27	29	3	10	14	10	1	6	29	3
8 53 50	11	14	11	2	32	1	4	11	14	11	2	11	♐	4	11	15	11	1	50	♐	4
8 57 51	12	15	12	3	17	1	5	12	15	12	2	56	1	5	12	15	12	2	34	0	5
9 1 52	13	16	13	4	2	2	6	13	16	13	3	40	2	6	13	16	13	3	18	1	5
9 5 52	14	17	14	4	47	3	7	14	17	14	4	24	3	7	14	17	14	4	2	2	6
HOUSES	4	5	6	7		8	9	4	5	6	7		8	9	4	5	6	7		8	9

LATITUDE 46° S. LATITUDE 47° S. LATITUDE 48° S.

	LATITUDE 46° N.						LATITUDE 47° N.						LATITUDE 48° N.					
SIDEREAL TIME	10 Ω	11 ♍	12 ♎	ASC ♏	2 ♐	3 ♑	10 Ω	11 ♍	12 ♎	ASC ♏	2 ♐	3 ♑	10 Ω	11 ♍	12 ♎	ASC ♏	2 ♐	3 ♑
H M S	°	°	°	° '	°	°	°	°	°	° '	°	°	°	°	°	° '	°	°
9 9 52	15	18	15	5 31	4	8	15	18	15	5 8	3	8	15	18	14	4 45	3	7
9 13 50	16	19	15	6 16	5	9	16	19	15	5 52	4	9	16	19	15	5 29	4	8
9 17 49	17	20	16	7 0	6	10	17	20	16	6 36	5	10	17	20	16	6 12	5	9
9 21 46	18	21	17	7 44	6	11	18	21	17	7 20	6	10	18	21	17	6 55	5	10
9 25 42	19	22	18	8 28	7	12	19	22	18	8 3	7	11	19	22	18	7 38	6	11
9 29 38	20	23	19	9 12	8	13	20	23	19	8 47	7	12	20	23	18	8 21	7	12
9 33 34	21	24	20	9 56	9	14	21	24	19	9 30	8	13	21	24	19	9 4	8	13
9 37 28	22	25	20	10 39	10	15	22	25	20	10 13	9	14	22	25	20	9 47	9	14
9 41 22	23	26	21	11 23	10	16	23	26	21	10 56	10	15	23	26	21	10 29	9	15
9 45 15	24	27	22	12 6	11	16	24	27	22	11 39	11	16	24	27	22	11 12	10	16
9 49 8	25	27	23	12 49	12	17	25	27	23	12 22	12	17	25	27	22	11 54	11	17
9 53 0	26	28	24	13 32	13	18	26	28	23	13 5	12	18	26	28	23	12 36	12	18
9 56 51	27	29	24	14 16	14	19	27	29	24	13 47	13	19	27	29	24	13 18	13	19
10 0 42	28	♎	25	14 59	15	20	28	♎	25	14 30	14	20	28	♎	25	14 0	13	20
10 4 32	29	1	26	15 41	15	21	29	1	26	15 12	15	21	29	1	26	14 42	14	21
10 8 22	♍	2	27	16 24	16	22	♍	2	27	15 55	16	22	♍	2	26	15 24	15	22
10 12 11	1	3	28	17 7	17	23	1	3	27	16 37	16	23	1	3	27	16 6	16	23
10 15 59	2	4	28	17 49	18	24	2	4	28	17 19	17	24	2	4	28	16 48	17	24
10 19 47	3	5	29	18 32	19	25	3	5	29	18 1	18	25	3	5	29	17 29	17	25
10 23 34	4	6	♏	19 15	19	26	4	6	♏	18 43	19	26	4	6	29	18 11	18	25
10 27 21	5	6	1	19 57	20	27	5	6	0	19 25	20	27	5	6	♏	18 53	19	26
10 31 8	6	7	1	20 39	21	28	6	7	1	20 7	20	28	6	7	1	19 34	20	27
10 34 53	7	8	2	21 22	22	29	7	8	2	20 49	21	29	7	8	2	20 15	21	28
10 38 39	8	9	3	22 4	23	♒	8	9	3	21 31	22	♒	8	9	2	20 57	21	29
10 42 24	9	10	4	22 46	24	1	9	10	4	22 12	23	1	9	10	3	21 38	22	♒
10 46 8	10	11	5	23 28	24	2	10	11	4	22 54	24	2	10	11	4	22 19	23	1
10 49 52	11	12	5	24 10	25	3	11	12	5	23 36	25	3	11	12	5	23 1	24	2
10 53 36	12	13	6	24 53	26	4	12	13	6	24 18	25	4	12	13	6	23 42	25	3
10 57 20	13	14	7	25 35	27	5	13	13	7	24 59	26	5	13	13	6	24 23	26	4
11 1 3	14	14	8	26 17	28	6	14	14	7	25 41	27	6	14	14	7	25 4	26	5
11 4 45	15	15	8	26 59	29	7	15	15	8	26 23	28	7	15	15	8	25 46	27	6
11 8 28	16	16	9	27 41	29	8	16	16	9	27 4	29	8	16	16	8	26 27	28	7
11 12 10	17	17	10	28 23	♑	9	17	17	10	27 46	♑	9	17	17	9	27 8	29	9
11 15 52	18	18	11	29 5	1	10	18	18	10	28 28	0	10	18	18	10	27 50	♑	10
11 19 33	19	19	11	29 48	2	11	19	19	11	29 10	1	11	19	19	11	28 31	1	11
11 23 15	20	20	12	0♐ 30	3	12	20	20	12	29 52	2	12	20	19	11	29 12	1	12
11 26 56	21	21	13	1 12	4	13	21	20	13	0♐ 33	3	13	21	20	12	29 54	2	13
11 30 37	22	21	14	1 55	5	14	22	21	13	1 15	4	14	22	21	13	0♐ 35	3	14
11 34 17	23	22	14	2 37	5	15	23	22	14	1 57	5	15	23	22	14	1 17	4	15
11 37 58	24	23	15	3 20	6	16	24	23	15	2 39	6	16	24	23	14	1 58	5	16
11 41 39	25	24	16	4 2	7	17	25	24	16	3 21	7	17	25	24	15	2 40	6	17
11 45 19	26	25	17	4 45	8	18	26	25	16	4 4	7	18	26	25	16	3 22	7	18
11 48 59	27	26	17	5 27	9	19	27	26	17	4 46	8	19	27	25	17	4 3	8	19
11 52 40	28	26	18	6 10	10	21	28	26	18	5 28	9	20	28	26	17	4 45	8	20
11 56 20	29	27	19	6 53	11	22	29	27	19	6 11	10	21	29	27	18	5 27	9	21
HOUSES	4	5	6	7	8	9	4	5	6	7	8	9	4	5	6	7	8	9

LATITUDE 46° N. LATITUDE 47° N. LATITUDE 48° N.

SIDEREAL TIME	10 ♎	11 ♎	12 ♏	ASC ♐	2 ♑	3 ♒	10 ♎	11 ♎	12 ♏	ASC ♐	2 ♑	3 ♒	10 ♎	11 ♎	12 ♏	ASC ♐	2 ♑	3 ♒
H M S	°	°	°	° '	°	°	°	°	°	° '	°	°	°	°	°	° '	°	°
12 0 0	0	28	20	7 36	12	23	0	28	19	6 54	11	22	0	28	19	6 10	10	22
12 3 40	1	29	20	8 20	13	24	1	29	20	7 36	12	24	1	29	20	6 52	11	23
12 7 20	2	♏	21	9 3	14	25	2	♏	21	8 19	13	25	2	♏	20	7 34	12	24
12 11 1	3	1	22	9 47	14	26	3	1	21	9 2	14	26	3	0	21	8 17	13	26
12 14 41	4	2	23	10 30	15	27	4	1	22	9 46	15	27	4	1	22	9 0	14	27
12 18 21	5	2	23	11 14	16	28	5	2	23	10 29	16	28	5	2	23	9 43	15	28
12 22 2	6	3	24	11 58	17	29	6	3	24	11 13	17	29	6	3	23	10 26	16	29
12 25 42	7	4	25	12 43	18	♓	7	4	24	11 57	18	♓	7	4	24	11 9	17	♓
12 29 23	8	5	26	13 27	19	1	8	5	25	12 41	19	1	8	5	25	11 53	18	1
12 33 4	9	6	26	14 12	20	3	9	6	26	13 25	20	2	9	5	25	12 36	19	2
12 36 45	10	7	27	14 57	21	4	10	6	27	14 9	21	4	10	6	26	13 20	20	3
12 40 27	11	7	28	15 42	22	5	11	7	27	14 54	22	5	11	7	27	14 5	21	5
12 44 8	12	8	29	16 27	23	6	12	8	28	15 39	23	6	12	8	28	14 49	22	6
12 47 50	13	9	29	17 13	24	7	13	9	29	16 24	24	7	13	9	28	15 34	23	7
12 51 32	14	10	♐	17 59	25	8	14	10	♐	17 10	25	8	14	10	29	16 19	24	8
12 55 15	15	11	1	18 46	26	9	15	11	0	17 56	26	9	15	10	♐	17 4	25	9
12 58 57	16	12	2	19 32	27	11	16	11	1	18 42	27	10	16	11	1	17 50	26	10
13 2 40	17	13	2	20 19	28	12	17	12	2	19 28	28	12	17	12	1	18 36	27	12
13 6 24	18	13	3	21 6	29	13	18	13	3	20 15	29	13	18	13	2	19 22	28	13
13 10 8	19	14	4	21 54	♒	14	19	14	3	21 2	♒	14	19	14	3	20 9	29	14
13 13 52	20	15	5	22 42	2	15	20	15	4	21 50	1	15	20	15	4	20 56	♒	15
13 17 36	21	16	6	23 31	3	16	21	16	5	22 38	2	16	21	15	5	21 44	1	16
13 21 21	22	17	6	24 20	4	18	22	17	6	23 26	3	18	22	16	5	22 32	3	17
13 25 7	23	18	7	25 9	5	19	23	17	7	24 15	4	19	23	17	6	23 20	4	19
13 28 52	24	18	8	25 59	6	20	24	18	7	25 5	5	20	24	18	7	24 9	5	20
13 32 39	25	19	9	26 49	7	21	25	19	8	25 54	7	21	25	19	8	24 58	6	21
13 36 26	26	20	9	27 40	8	22	26	20	9	26 45	8	22	26	20	8	25 47	7	22
13 40 13	27	21	10	28 31	10	24	27	21	10	27 35	9	24	27	20	9	26 38	8	24
13 44 1	28	22	11	29 23	11	25	28	22	10	28 27	10	25	28	21	10	27 28	10	25
13 47 49	29	23	12	0♑ 15	12	26	29	22	11	29 18	11	26	29	22	11	28 20	11	26
13 51 38	♏	23	13	1 8	13	27	♏	23	12	0♑ 11	13	27	♏	23	12	29 12	12	27
13 55 28	1	24	13	2 1	15	29	1	24	13	1 4	14	29	1	24	12	0♑ 4	13	29
13 59 18	2	25	14	2 55	16	♈	2	25	14	1 57	15	♈	2	25	13	0 57	15	♈
14 3 9	3	26	15	3 50	17	1	3	26	14	2 52	16	1	3	26	14	1 51	16	1
14 7 0	4	27	16	4 45	18	2	4	27	15	3 46	18	2	4	26	15	2 45	17	2
14 10 52	5	28	17	5 41	20	3	5	28	16	4 42	19	4	5	27	16	3 40	19	4
14 14 45	6	29	18	6 38	21	5	6	28	17	5 38	20	5	6	28	16	4 36	20	5
14 18 38	7	29	18	7 36	22	6	7	29	18	6 35	22	6	7	29	17	5 33	21	6
14 22 32	8	♐	19	8 34	24	7	8	♐	19	7 33	23	7	8	♐	18	6 30	23	7
14 26 26	9	1	20	9 33	25	8	9	1	19	8 32	24	9	9	1	19	7 28	24	9
14 30 22	10	2	21	10 33	26	10	10	2	20	9 32	26	10	10	2	20	8 27	25	10
14 34 17	11	3	22	11 34	28	11	11	3	21	10 32	27	11	11	2	21	9 27	27	11
14 38 14	12	4	23	12 36	29	12	12	4	22	11 33	29	12	12	3	21	10 28	28	12
14 42 11	13	5	23	13 38	♓	13	13	4	23	12 36	♓	14	13	4	22	11 30	♓	14
14 46 10	14	6	24	14 42	2	15	14	5	24	13 39	2	15	14	5	23	12 32	1	15
HOUSES	4	5	6	7	8	9	4	5	6	7	8	9	4	5	6	7	8	9

LATITUDE 46° S. LATITUDE 47° S. LATITUDE 48° S.

LATITUDE 46° N. LATITUDE 47° N. LATITUDE 48° N.

SIDEREAL TIME	10 ♏	11 ♐	12 ♐	ASC ♑	2 ♓	3 ♈	10 ♏	11 ♐	12 ♐	ASC ♑	2 ♓	3 ♈	10 ♏	11 ♐	12 ♐	ASC ♑	2 ♓	3 ♈
H M S	°	°	°	° '	°	°	°	°	°	° '	°	°	°	°	°	° '	°	°
14 50 8	15	6	25	15 47	3	16	15	6	25	14 43	3	16	15	6	24	13 36	3	16
14 54 8	16	7	26	16 52	5	17	16	7	26	15 48	5	17	16	7	25	14 41	4	17
14 58 8	17	8	27	17 59	6	18	17	8	26	16 55	6	19	17	8	26	15 47	6	19
15 2 9	18	9	28	19 7	8	20	18	9	27	18 2	8	20	18	9	27	16 54	7	20
15 6 10	19	10	29	20 16	9	21	19	10	28	19 11	9	21	19	9	28	18 3	9	21
15 10 13	20	11	♑	21 26	11	22	20	11	29	20 21	11	22	20	10	29	19 12	10	23
15 14 16	21	12	1	22 38	12	24	21	11	♑	21 32	12	24	21	11	29	20 23	12	24
15 18 20	22	13	2	23 50	14	25	22	12	1	22 45	14	25	22	12	♑	21 35	13	25
15 22 24	23	14	3	25 4	15	26	23	13	2	23 59	15	26	23	13	1	22 49	15	26
15 26 30	24	14	4	26 20	17	27	24	14	3	25 14	17	27	24	14	2	24 4	17	28
15 30 36	25	15	5	27 36	19	29	25	15	4	26 31	18	29	25	15	3	25 21	18	29
15 34 42	26	16	5	28 55	20	♉	26	16	5	27 49	20	♉	26	16	4	26 39	20	♉
15 38 50	27	17	6	0♒ 14	22	1	27	17	6	29 9	22	1	27	17	5	27 59	22	1
15 42 58	28	18	7	1 36	23	2	28	18	7	0♒ 30	23	2	28	18	6	29 20	23	3
15 47 7	29	19	8	2 59	25	4	29	19	8	1 53	25	4	29	18	7	0♒ 43	25	4
15 51 16	♐	20	10	4 23	27	5	♐	20	9	3 18	27	5	♐	19	8	2 8	26	5
15 55 26	1	21	11	5 49	28	6	1	21	10	4 44	28	6	1	20	9	3 35	28	6
15 59 37	2	22	12	7 17	♈	7	2	22	11	6 12	♈	7	2	21	10	5 4	♈	8
16 3 49	3	23	13	8 47	1	8	3	22	12	7 42	2	9	3	22	11	6 34	2	9
16 8 1	4	24	14	10 18	3	10	4	23	13	9 14	3	10	4	23	12	8 7	3	10
16 12 14	5	25	15	11 51	5	11	5	24	14	10 48	5	11	5	24	13	9 41	5	11
16 16 27	6	26	16	13 26	6	12	6	25	15	12 24	6	12	6	25	14	11 18	7	13
16 20 41	7	27	17	15 3	8	13	7	26	16	14 2	8	14	7	26	16	12 56	8	14
16 24 56	8	28	18	16 42	10	15	8	27	17	15 42	10	15	8	27	17	14 37	10	15
16 29 11	9	29	19	18 22	11	16	9	28	18	17 24	11	16	9	28	18	16 20	12	16
16 33 27	10	♑	20	20 5	13	17	10	29	20	19 8	13	17	10	29	19	18 6	13	17
16 37 43	11	0	21	21 49	15	18	11	♑	21	20 54	15	18	11	♑	20	19 53	15	19
16 41 59	12	1	23	23 36	16	19	12	1	22	22 42	16	20	12	1	21	21 43	17	20
16 46 17	13	2	24	25 24	18	21	13	2	23	24 32	18	21	13	2	22	23 35	18	21
16 50 34	14	3	25	27 15	19	22	14	3	24	26 24	20	22	14	3	24	25 29	20	22
16 54 53	15	4	26	29 7	21	23	15	4	26	28 18	21	23	15	4	25	27 25	22	23
16 59 11	16	5	27	1♓ 1	23	24	16	5	27	0♓ 14	23	24	16	5	26	29 24	23	25
17 3 30	17	6	29	2 56	24	25	17	6	28	2 13	25	25	17	6	27	1♓ 25	25	26
17 7 49	18	7	♒	4 54	26	26	18	7	29	4 13	26	27	18	7	29	3 27	27	27
17 12 9	19	9	1	6 53	27	28	19	8	♒	6 14	28	28	19	8	♒	5 32	28	28
17 16 29	20	10	2	8 54	29	29	20	9	2	8 18	29	29	20	9	1	7 39	♉	29
17 20 49	21	11	4	10 56	♉	♊	21	10	3	10 23	♉	♊	21	10	2	9 48	1	♊
17 25 10	22	12	5	12 59	2	1	22	11	4	12 30	3	1	22	11	4	11 58	3	2
17 29 31	23	13	6	15 4	4	2	23	12	6	14 38	4	2	23	12	5	14 9	5	3
17 33 51	24	14	8	17 10	5	3	24	13	7	16 47	6	4	24	13	6	16 23	6	4
17 38 13	25	15	9	19 17	7	4	25	14	8	18 58	7	5	25	14	8	18 37	8	5
17 42 34	26	16	10	21 24	8	5	26	16	10	21 9	9	6	26	15	9	20 52	9	6
17 46 55	27	17	12	23 33	10	7	27	17	11	23 21	10	7	27	16	11	23 8	11	7
17 51 17	28	18	13	25 41	11	8	28	18	13	25 34	12	8	28	17	12	25 25	12	8
17 55 38	29	19	15	27 51	13	9	29	19	14	27 47	13	9	29	18	13	27 43	14	9
HOUSES	4	5	6	7	8	9	4	5	6	7	8	9	4	5	6	7	8	9

LATITUDE 46° S. LATITUDE 47° S. LATITUDE 48° S.

LATITUDE 46° N.   LATITUDE 47° N.   LATITUDE 48° N.

SIDEREAL TIME	10 ♑	11 ♑	12 ♒	ASC ♈	2 ♉	3 ♊	10 ♑	11 ♑	12 ♒	ASC ♈	2 ♉	3 ♊	10 ♑	11 ♑	12 ♒	ASC ♈	2 ♉	3 ♊
H M S	°	°	°	° ′	°	°	°	°	°	° ′	°	°	°	°	°	° ′	°	°
18 0 0	0	20	16	0 0	14	10	0	20	15	0 0	15	10	0	19	15	0 0	15	11
18 4 22	1	21	17	2 9	15	11	1	21	17	2 13	16	11	1	21	16	2 17	17	12
18 8 43	2	22	19	4 19	17	12	2	22	18	4 26	17	12	2	22	18	4 35	18	13
18 13 5	3	23	20	6 27	18	13	3	23	20	6 39	19	13	3	23	19	6 52	19	14
18 17 26	4	25	22	8 36	20	14	4	24	21	8 51	20	14	4	24	21	9 8	21	15
18 21 47	5	26	23	10 43	21	15	5	25	23	11 2	22	16	5	25	22	11 23	22	16
18 26 9	6	27	25	12 50	22	16	6	26	24	13 13	23	17	6	26	24	13 37	24	17
18 30 29	7	28	26	14 56	24	17	7	28	26	15 22	24	18	7	27	25	15 51	25	18
18 34 50	8	29	28	17 1	25	18	8	29	27	17 30	26	19	8	28	27	18 2	26	19
18 39 11	9	♒	29	19 4	26	19	9	♒	29	19 37	27	20	9	♒	29	20 12	28	20
18 43 31	10	1	♓	21 6	28	20	10	1	♓	21 42	28	21	10	1	♓	22 21	29	21
18 47 51	11	2	3	23 7	29	21	11	2	2	23 46	♊	22	11	2	2	24 28	♊	22
18 52 11	12	4	4	25 6	♊	23	12	3	4	25 47	1	23	12	3	3	26 33	1	23
18 56 30	13	5	6	27 4	1	24	13	5	5	27 47	2	24	13	4	5	28 35	3	24
19 0 49	14	6	7	28 59	3	25	14	6	7	29 46	3	25	14	5	7	0♉36	4	25
19 5 7	15	7	9	0♉53	4	26	15	7	9	1♉42	4	26	15	7	8	2 35	5	26
19 9 26	16	8	11	2 45	5	27	16	8	10	3 36	6	27	16	8	10	4 31	6	27
19 13 43	17	9	12	4 36	6	28	17	9	12	5 28	7	28	17	9	12	6 25	8	28
19 18 0	18	11	14	6 24	7	29	18	10	14	7 18	8	29	18	10	13	8 17	9	29
19 22 17	19	12	15	8 11	9	♋	19	12	15	9 6	9	♋	19	11	15	10 7	10	♋
19 26 33	20	13	17	9 55	10	0	20	13	17	10 52	10	1	20	13	17	11 54	11	1
19 30 49	21	14	19	11 38	11	1	21	14	19	12 36	12	2	21	14	18	13 40	12	2
19 35 4	22	15	20	13 18	12	2	22	15	20	14 18	13	3	22	15	20	15 23	13	3
19 39 19	23	17	22	14 57	13	3	23	16	22	15 58	14	4	23	16	22	17 4	14	4
19 43 33	24	18	24	16 34	14	4	24	18	24	17 36	15	5	24	17	23	18 42	16	5
19 47 46	25	19	25	18 9	15	5	25	19	25	19 12	16	6	25	19	25	20 19	17	6
19 51 59	26	20	27	19 42	16	6	26	20	27	20 46	17	7	26	20	27	21 53	18	7
19 56 11	27	22	29	21 13	17	7	27	21	28	22 18	18	8	27	21	28	23 26	19	8
20 0 23	28	23	♈	22 43	18	8	28	23	♈	23 48	19	8	28	22	♈	24 56	20	9
20 4 34	29	24	2	24 11	19	9	29	24	2	25 16	20	9	29	24	2	26 25	21	10
20 8 44	♒	25	3	25 37	20	10	♒	25	3	26 42	21	10	♒	25	4	27 52	22	11
20 12 53	1	26	5	27 1	22	11	1	26	5	28 7	22	11	1	26	5	29 17	23	12
20 17 2	2	28	7	28 24	23	12	2	28	7	29 30	23	12	2	27	7	0♊40	24	12
20 21 10	3	29	8	29 46	24	13	3	29	8	0♊51	24	13	3	29	8	2 1	25	13
20 25 18	4	♓	10	1♊5	25	14	4	♓	10	2 11	25	14	4	♓	10	3 21	26	14
20 29 24	5	1	11	2 24	25	15	5	1	12	3 29	26	15	5	1	12	4 39	27	15
20 33 30	6	3	13	3 40	26	16	6	3	13	4 46	27	16	6	2	13	5 56	28	16
20 37 36	7	4	15	4 56	27	16	7	4	15	6 1	28	17	7	4	15	7 11	29	17
20 41 40	8	5	16	6 10	28	17	8	5	16	7 15	29	18	8	5	17	8 25	♋	18
20 45 44	9	6	18	7 22	29	18	9	6	18	8 28	♋	19	9	6	18	9 37	1	19
20 49 47	10	8	19	8 34	♋	19	10	8	19	9 39	1	19	10	7	20	10 48	1	20
20 53 50	11	9	21	9 44	1	20	11	9	21	10 49	2	20	11	9	21	11 57	2	21
20 57 51	12	10	22	10 53	2	21	12	10	22	11 58	3	21	12	10	23	13 6	3	21
21 1 52	13	12	24	12 1	3	22	13	11	24	13 5	4	22	13	11	24	14 13	4	22
21 5 52	14	13	25	13 8	4	23	14	13	25	14 12	4	23	14	13	26	15 19	5	23
HOUSES	4	5	6	7	8	9	4	5	6	7	8	9	4	5	6	7	8	9

	LATITUDE 46° N.						LATITUDE 47° N.						LATITUDE 48° N.					
SIDEREAL TIME	10 ≈	11 ✕	12 ♈	ASC ♊	2 ♋	3 ♋	10 ≈	11 ✕	12 ♈	ASC ♊	2 ♋	3 ♋	10 ≈	11 ✕	12 ♈	ASC ♊	2 ♋	3 ♋
H M S	°	°	°	° ′	°	°	°	°	°	° ′	°	°	°	°	°	° ′	°	°
21 9 52	15	14	27	14 13	5	24	15	14	27	15 17	5	24	15	14	27	16 24	6	24
21 13 50	16	15	28	15 18	6	24	16	15	28	16 21	6	25	16	15	29	17 28	7	25
21 17 49	17	17	29	16 22	7	25	17	16	♉	17 24	7	26	17	16	♉	18 30	8	26
21 21 46	18	18	♉	17 24	7	26	18	18	1	18 27	8	26	18	18	2	19 32	9	27
21 25 42	19	19	2	18 26	8	27	19	19	3	19 28	9	27	19	19	3	20 33	9	28
21 29 38	20	20	4	19 27	9	28	20	20	4	20 28	10	28	20	20	5	21 33	10	28
21 33 34	21	22	5	20 27	10	29	21	21	6	21 28	11	29	21	21	6	22 32	11	29
21 37 28	22	23	6	21 26	11	♌	22	23	7	22 27	11	♌	22	23	7	23 30	12	♌
21 41 22	23	24	8	22 24	12	1	23	24	8	23 25	12	1	23	24	9	24 27	13	1
21 45 15	24	25	9	23 22	12	1	24	25	10	24 22	13	2	24	25	10	25 24	14	2
21 49 8	25	27	10	24 19	13	2	25	26	11	25 18	14	2	25	26	11	26 20	14	3
21 53 0	26	28	12	25 15	14	3	26	28	12	26 14	15	3	26	28	13	27 15	15	4
21 56 51	27	29	13	26 10	15	4	27	29	14	27 8	16	4	27	29	14	28 9	16	4
22 0 42	28	♈	14	27 5	16	5	28	♈	15	28 3	16	5	28	♈	15	29 3	17	5
22 4 32	29	1	15	27 59	17	6	29	1	16	28 56	17	6	29	1	17	29 56	18	6
22 8 22	✕	3	17	28 52	17	7	✕	3	17	29 49	18	7	✕	3	18	0♋ 48	18	7
22 12 11	1	4	18	29 45	18	7	1	4	19	0♋ 42	19	8	1	4	19	1 40	19	8
22 15 59	2	5	19	0♋ 37	19	8	2	5	20	1 33	20	8	2	5	20	2 32	20	9
22 19 47	3	6	20	1 29	20	9	3	6	21	2 25	20	9	3	6	22	3 22	21	10
22 23 34	4	8	22	2 20	21	10	4	8	22	3 15	21	10	4	8	23	4 13	22	10
22 27 21	5	9	23	3 11	21	11	5	9	23	4 6	22	11	5	9	24	5 2	22	11
22 31 8	6	10	24	4 1	22	12	6	10	25	4 55	23	12	6	10	25	5 51	23	12
22 34 53	7	11	25	4 51	23	12	7	11	26	5 45	23	13	7	11	26	6 40	24	13
22 38 39	8	12	26	5 40	24	13	8	12	27	6 34	24	13	8	13	27	7 28	25	14
22 42 24	9	14	27	6 29	24	14	9	14	28	7 22	25	14	9	14	29	8 16	25	15
22 46 8	10	15	28	7 18	25	15	10	15	29	8 10	26	15	10	15	♊	9 4	26	15
22 49 52	11	16	29	8 6	26	16	11	16	♊	8 58	27	16	11	16	1	9 51	27	16
22 53 36	12	17	♊	8 54	27	17	12	17	1	9 45	27	17	12	17	2	10 38	28	17
22 57 20	13	18	2	9 41	28	17	13	18	2	10 32	28	18	13	18	3	11 24	29	18
23 1 3	14	19	3	10 28	28	18	14	20	3	11 18	29	19	14	20	4	12 10	29	19
23 4 45	15	21	4	11 14	29	19	15	21	4	12 4	♌	19	15	21	5	12 56	♌	20
23 8 28	16	22	5	12 1	♌	20	16	22	5	12 50	0	20	16	22	6	13 41	1	20
23 12 10	17	23	6	12 47	1	21	17	23	6	13 36	1	21	17	23	7	14 26	2	21
23 15 52	18	24	7	13 33	1	22	18	24	7	14 21	2	22	18	24	8	15 11	2	22
23 19 33	19	25	8	14 18	2	23	19	25	8	15 6	3	23	19	25	9	15 55	3	23
23 23 15	20	26	9	15 3	3	23	20	26	9	15 51	3	24	20	27	10	16 40	4	24
23 26 56	21	27	10	15 48	4	24	21	28	10	16 35	4	24	21	28	11	17 24	5	25
23 30 37	22	29	11	16 33	4	25	22	29	11	17 19	5	25	22	29	12	18 7	5	25
23 34 17	23	♉	12	17 17	5	26	23	♉	12	18 3	6	26	23	♉	13	18 51	6	26
23 37 58	24	1	13	18 2	6	27	24	1	13	18 47	6	27	24	1	14	19 34	7	27
23 41 39	25	2	14	18 46	7	28	25	2	14	19 31	7	28	25	2	15	20 17	7	28
23 45 19	26	3	15	19 30	7	28	26	3	15	20 14	8	29	26	3	16	21 0	8	29
23 48 59	27	4	16	20 13	8	29	27	4	16	20 58	9	29	27	4	17	21 43	9	♍
23 52 40	28	5	16	20 57	9	♍	28	5	17	21 41	9	♍	28	6	18	22 26	10	0
23 56 20	29	6	17	21 40	10	1	29	6	18	22 24	10	1	29	7	19	23 8	10	1
HOUSES	4	5	6	7	8	9	4	5	6	7	8	9	4	5	6	7	8	9

LATITUDE 46° S.   LATITUDE 47° S.   LATITUDE 48° S.

LATITUDE 49° N. LATITUDE 50° N. LATITUDE 51° N.

SIDEREAL TIME H M S	10 ♈	11 ♉	12 ♊	ASC ♋	2 ♌	3 ♍	10 ♈	11 ♉	12 ♊	ASC ♋	2 ♌	3 ♍	10 ♈	11 ♉	12 ♊	ASC ♋	2 ♌	3 ♍
0 0 0	0	8	20	24 36	12	2	0	8	21	25 22	12	2	0	9	22	26 10	12	2
0 3 40	1	9	21	25 17	12	3	1	9	22	26 3	13	3	1	10	23	26 51	13	3
0 7 20	2	10	22	25 59	13	4	2	10	23	26 44	13	4	2	11	24	27 31	14	4
0 11 1	3	11	23	26 40	14	5	3	12	24	27 25	14	5	3	12	25	28 12	15	5
0 14 41	4	12	24	27 22	14	6	4	13	25	28 6	15	6	4	13	26	28 52	15	6
0 18 21	5	13	25	28 3	15	6	5	14	26	28 47	16	7	5	14	26	29 32	16	7
0 22 2	6	14	26	28 44	16	7	6	15	27	29 28	16	7	6	15	27	0♌ 12	17	7
0 25 43	7	16	27	29 25	17	8	7	16	27	0♌ 8	17	8	7	16	28	0 52	17	8
0 29 23	8	17	27	0♌ 6	17	9	8	17	28	0 49	18	9	8	17	29	1 32	18	9
0 33 4	9	18	28	0 47	18	10	9	18	29	1 29	19	10	9	18	♋	2 12	19	10
0 36 45	10	19	29	1 28	19	11	10	19	♋	2 10	19	11	10	19	1	2 52	20	11
0 40 27	11	20	♋	2 9	20	11	11	20	1	2 50	20	12	11	20	2	3 32	20	12
0 44 8	12	21	1	2 50	20	12	12	21	2	3 30	21	12	12	21	2	4 12	21	13
0 47 50	13	22	2	3 31	21	13	13	22	2	4 11	21	13	13	22	3	4 52	22	13
0 51 32	14	23	3	4 12	22	14	14	23	3	4 51	22	14	14	23	4	5 31	22	14
0 55 15	15	24	3	4 52	23	15	15	24	4	5 31	23	15	15	25	5	6 11	23	15
0 58 57	16	25	4	5 33	23	16	16	25	5	6 11	24	16	16	26	6	6 51	24	16
1 2 40	17	26	5	6 14	24	17	17	26	6	6 52	24	17	17	27	6	7 31	25	17
1 6 24	18	27	6	6 55	25	17	18	27	7	7 32	25	18	18	28	7	8 10	25	18
1 10 8	19	28	7	7 35	26	18	19	28	7	8 12	26	18	19	29	8	8 50	26	18
1 13 52	20	29	8	8 16	26	19	20	29	8	8 53	27	19	20	♊	9	9 30	27	19
1 17 36	21	♊	8	8 57	27	20	21	♊	9	9 33	27	20	21	1	10	10 10	28	20
1 21 21	22	1	9	9 38	28	21	22	1	10	10 13	28	21	22	2	11	10 50	28	21
1 25 7	23	2	10	10 19	29	22	23	2	11	10 54	29	22	23	3	11	11 30	29	22
1 28 52	24	3	11	11 0	29	23	24	3	11	11 34	♍	23	24	4	12	12 10	♍	23
1 32 39	25	4	12	11 41	♍	24	25	4	12	12 15	0	24	25	5	13	12 50	1	24
1 36 26	26	5	12	12 22	1	24	26	5	13	12 55	1	25	26	6	14	13 30	1	25
1 40 13	27	6	13	13 3	2	25	27	6	14	13 36	2	25	27	7	14	14 10	2	25
1 44 1	28	7	14	13 44	2	26	28	7	15	14 17	3	26	28	8	15	14 50	3	26
1 47 49	29	8	15	14 25	3	27	29	8	15	14 57	3	27	29	9	16	15 30	4	27
1 51 38	♉	9	16	15 7	4	28	♉	9	16	15 38	4	28	♉	9	17	16 11	4	28
1 55 28	1	10	16	15 48	5	29	1	10	17	16 19	5	29	1	10	18	16 51	5	29
1 59 18	2	11	17	16 30	5	♎	2	11	18	17 0	6	♎	2	11	18	17 32	6	♎
2 3 9	3	12	18	17 11	6	1	3	12	19	17 41	6	1	3	12	19	18 12	7	1
2 7 0	4	13	19	17 53	7	2	4	13	19	18 23	7	2	4	13	20	18 53	7	2
2 10 52	5	14	20	18 35	8	3	5	14	20	19 4	8	3	5	14	21	19 34	8	3
2 14 45	6	15	20	19 17	9	3	6	15	21	19 45	9	3	6	15	22	20 14	9	3
2 18 38	7	15	21	19 59	9	4	7	16	22	20 27	10	4	7	16	22	20 55	10	4
2 22 32	8	16	22	20 41	10	5	8	17	23	21 8	10	5	8	17	23	21 37	10	5
2 26 26	9	17	23	21 23	11	6	9	18	23	21 50	11	6	9	18	24	22 18	11	6
2 30 22	10	18	24	22 5	12	7	10	19	24	22 32	12	7	10	19	25	22 59	12	7
2 34 17	11	19	24	22 48	13	8	11	20	25	23 14	13	8	11	20	26	23 41	13	8
2 38 14	12	20	25	23 30	13	9	12	21	26	23 56	13	9	12	21	26	24 22	14	9
2 42 11	13	21	26	24 13	14	10	13	22	27	24 38	14	10	13	22	27	25 4	14	10
2 46 10	14	22	27	24 56	15	11	14	22	27	25 20	15	11	14	23	28	25 46	15	11
HOUSES	4	5	6	7	8	9	4	5	6	7	8	9	4	5	6	7	8	9

LATITUDE 49° S. LATITUDE 50° S. LATITUDE 51° S.

			LATITUDE 49° N.								LATITUDE 50° N.								LATITUDE 51° N.						

SIDEREAL TIME			10 ♉	11 ♊	12 ♋	ASC ♌	2 ♍	3 ♎	10 ♉	11 ♊	12 ♋	ASC ♌	2 ♍	3 ♎	10 ♉	11 ♊	12 ♋	ASC ♌	2 ♍	3 ♎
H	M	S	°	°	°	° '	°	°	°	°	°	° '	°	°	°	°	°	° '	°	°
2	50	8	15	23	28	25 39	16	12	15	23	28	26 3	16	12	15	24	29	26 28	16	12
2	54	8	16	24	28	26 22	17	13	16	24	29	26 45	17	13	16	25	29	27 10	17	12
2	58	8	17	25	29	27 5	17	14	17	25	♌	27 28	17	13	17	26	♌	27 52	18	13
3	2	9	18	26	♌	27 48	18	14	18	26	1	28 11	18	14	18	27	1	28 34	18	14
3	6	10	19	27	1	28 32	19	15	19	27	1	28 54	19	15	19	28	2	29 17	19	15
3	10	13	20	28	2	29 15	20	16	20	28	2	29 37	20	16	20	28	3	29 59	20	16
3	14	16	21	29	2	29 59	21	17	21	29	3	0♍ 20	21	17	21	29	3	0♍ 42	21	17
3	18	20	22	♋	3	0♍ 43	21	18	22	♋	4	1 4	22	18	22	♋	4	1 25	22	18
3	22	24	23	1	4	1 27	22	19	23	1	5	1 47	22	19	23	1	5	2 8	22	19
3	26	30	24	1	5	2 11	23	20	24	2	5	2 31	23	20	24	2	6	2 51	23	20
3	30	36	25	2	6	2 56	24	21	25	3	6	3 15	24	21	25	3	7	3 34	24	21
3	34	42	26	3	7	3 40	25	22	26	4	7	3 59	25	22	26	4	7	4 18	25	22
3	38	50	27	4	7	4 25	26	23	27	5	8	4 43	26	23	27	5	8	5 1	26	23
3	42	58	28	5	8	5 9	27	24	28	6	9	5 27	27	24	28	6	9	5 45	27	24
3	47	7	29	6	9	5 54	27	25	29	6	9	6 11	27	25	29	7	10	6 29	27	25
3	51	16	♊	7	10	6 39	28	26	♊	7	10	6 56	28	26	♊	8	11	7 13	28	26
3	55	26	1	8	11	7 25	29	27	1	8	11	7 41	29	27	1	9	12	7 57	29	26
3	59	37	2	9	11	8 10	♎	28	2	9	12	8 25	♎	28	2	10	12	8 41	♎	27
4	3	49	3	10	12	8 55	1	29	3	10	13	9 10	1	29	3	11	13	9 25	1	28
4	8	1	4	11	13	9 41	2	♏	4	11	14	9 55	2	29	4	12	14	10 10	2	29
4	12	14	5	12	14	10 27	3	1	5	12	14	10 40	2	♏	5	12	15	10 55	2	♏
4	16	27	6	13	15	11 12	3	2	6	13	15	11 26	3	1	6	13	16	11 39	3	1
4	20	41	7	14	16	11 58	4	3	7	14	16	12 11	4	2	7	14	16	12 24	4	2
4	24	56	8	15	17	12 45	5	3	8	15	17	12 57	5	3	8	15	17	13 9	5	3
4	29	11	9	15	17	13 31	6	4	9	16	18	13 42	6	4	9	16	18	13 54	6	4
4	33	27	10	16	18	14 17	7	5	10	17	19	14 28	7	5	10	17	19	14 39	7	5
4	37	43	11	17	19	15 3	8	6	11	18	19	15 14	8	6	11	18	20	15 25	8	6
4	41	59	12	18	20	15 50	9	7	12	19	20	16 0	9	7	12	19	21	16 10	8	7
4	46	17	13	19	21	16 37	9	8	13	20	21	16 46	9	8	13	20	21	16 56	9	8
4	50	34	14	20	22	17 23	10	9	14	21	22	17 32	10	9	14	21	22	17 41	10	9
4	54	53	15	21	22	18 10	11	10	15	21	23	18 19	11	10	15	22	23	18 27	11	10
4	59	11	16	22	23	18 57	12	11	16	22	24	19 5	12	11	16	23	24	19 13	12	11
5	3	30	17	23	24	19 44	13	12	17	23	25	19 51	13	12	17	24	25	19 59	13	12
5	7	49	18	24	25	20 31	14	13	18	24	25	20 38	14	13	18	25	26	20 45	14	13
5	12	9	19	25	26	21 18	15	14	19	25	26	21 24	15	14	19	26	27	21 31	14	14
5	16	29	20	26	27	22 5	16	15	20	26	27	22 11	15	15	20	26	27	22 17	15	15
5	20	49	21	27	28	22 53	16	16	21	27	28	22 58	16	16	21	27	28	23 3	16	16
5	25	10	22	28	29	23 40	17	17	22	28	29	23 45	17	17	22	28	29	23 49	17	16
5	29	31	23	29	29	24 27	18	18	23	29	♍	24 31	18	18	23	29	♍	24 35	18	17
5	33	51	24	♌	♍	25 15	19	19	24	♌	1	25 18	19	19	24	♌	1	25 22	19	18
5	38	13	25	1	1	26 2	20	20	25	1	1	26 5	20	20	25	1	2	26 8	20	19
5	42	34	26	2	2	26 50	21	21	26	2	2	26 52	21	21	26	2	3	26 54	21	20
5	46	55	27	3	3	27 37	22	22	27	3	3	27 39	22	21	27	3	3	27 41	21	21
5	51	17	28	3	4	28 25	23	23	28	4	4	28 26	22	22	28	4	4	28 27	22	22
5	55	38	29	4	5	29 12	24	24	29	5	5	29 13	23	23	29	5	5	29 14	23	23
HOUSES			4	5	6	7	8	9	4	5	6	7	8	9	4	5	6	7	8	9

LATITUDE 49° S. LATITUDE 50° S. LATITUDE 51° S.

LATITUDE 49° N. LATITUDE 50° N. LATITUDE 51° N.

SIDEREAL TIME	10 ♋	11 ♌	12 ♍	ASC ♎	2 ♎	3 ♏	10 ♋	11 ♌	12 ♍	ASC ♎	2 ♎	3 ♏	10 ♋	11 ♌	12 ♍	ASC ♎	2 ♎	3 ♏
H M S	°	°	°	° '	°	°	°	°	°	° '	°	°	°	°	°	° '	°	°
6 0 0	0	5	6	0 0	24	25	0	6	6	0 0	24	24	0	6	6	0 0	24	24
6 4 22	1	6	6	0 48	25	26	1	7	7	0 47	25	25	1	7	7	0 46	25	25
6 8 43	2	7	7	1 35	26	27	2	8	8	1 34	26	26	2	8	8	1 33	26	26
6 13 5	3	8	8	2 23	27	27	3	9	8	2 21	27	27	3	9	9	2 19	27	27
6 17 26	4	9	9	3 10	28	28	4	9	9	3 8	28	28	4	10	9	3 6	27	28
6 21 47	5	10	10	3 58	29	29	5	10	10	3 55	29	29	5	11	10	3 52	28	29
6 26 9	6	11	11	4 45	♏	♐	6	11	11	4 42	29	♐	6	12	11	4 38	29	♐
6 30 29	7	12	12	5 33	1	1	7	12	12	5 29	♏	1	7	13	12	5 25	♏	1
6 34 50	8	13	13	6 20	1	2	8	13	13	6 15	1	2	8	14	13	6 11	1	2
6 39 11	9	14	14	7 7	2	3	9	14	14	7 2	2	3	9	14	14	6 57	2	3
6 43 31	10	15	14	7 55	3	4	10	15	15	7 49	3	4	10	15	15	7 43	3	4
6 47 51	11	16	15	8 42	4	5	11	16	15	8 36	4	5	11	16	16	8 29	3	4
6 52 11	12	17	16	9 29	5	6	12	17	16	9 22	5	6	12	17	16	9 15	4	5
6 56 30	13	18	17	10 16	6	7	13	18	17	10 9	5	7	13	18	17	10 1	5	6
7 0 49	14	19	18	11 3	7	8	14	19	18	10 55	6	8	14	19	18	10 47	6	7
7 5 7	15	20	19	11 50	8	9	15	20	19	11 41	7	9	15	20	19	11 33	7	8
7 9 26	16	21	20	12 37	8	10	16	21	20	12 28	8	9	16	21	20	12 19	8	9
7 13 43	17	22	21	13 23	9	11	17	22	21	13 14	9	10	17	22	21	13 4	9	10
7 18 0	18	23	21	14 10	10	12	18	23	21	14 0	10	11	18	23	22	13 50	9	11
7 22 17	19	24	22	14 57	11	13	19	24	22	14 46	11	12	19	24	22	14 35	10	12
7 26 33	20	25	23	15 43	12	14	20	25	23	15 32	11	13	20	25	23	15 21	11	13
7 30 49	21	26	24	16 29	13	15	21	26	24	16 18	12	14	21	26	24	16 6	12	14
7 35 4	22	27	25	17 15	13	15	22	27	25	17 3	13	15	22	27	25	16 51	13	15
7 39 19	23	27	26	18 2	14	16	23	28	26	17 49	14	16	23	28	26	17 36	14	16
7 43 33	24	28	27	18 48	15	17	24	29	27	18 34	15	17	24	29	27	18 21	14	16
7 47 46	25	29	27	19 33	16	18	25	♏	28	19 20	16	18	25	♏	28	19 5	15	18
7 51 59	26	♏	28	20 19	17	19	26	1	28	20 5	16	19	26	1	28	19 50	16	18
7 56 11	27	1	29	21 5	18	20	27	1	29	20 50	17	20	27	2	29	20 35	17	19
8 0 23	28	2	♎	21 50	19	21	28	2	♎	21 35	18	21	28	3	♎	21 19	18	20
8 4 34	29	3	1	22 35	19	22	29	3	1	22 19	19	22	29	4	1	22 3	18	21
8 8 44	♌	4	2	23 21	20	23	♌	4	2	23 4	20	23	♌	4	2	22 47	19	22
8 12 53	1	5	3	24 6	21	24	1	5	3	23 49	21	24	1	5	3	23 31	20	23
8 17 2	2	6	3	24 51	22	25	2	6	3	24 33	21	24	2	6	3	24 15	21	24
8 21 10	3	7	4	25 35	23	26	3	7	4	25 17	22	25	3	7	4	24 59	22	25
8 25 18	4	8	5	26 20	23	27	4	8	5	26 1	23	26	4	8	5	25 42	23	26
8 29 24	5	9	6	27 4	24	28	5	9	6	26 45	24	27	5	9	6	26 26	23	27
8 33 30	6	10	7	27 49	25	29	6	10	7	27 29	25	28	6	10	7	27 9	24	28
8 37 36	7	11	8	28 33	26	29	7	11	8	28 13	25	29	7	11	8	27 52	25	29
8 41 40	8	12	9	29 17	27	♑	8	12	8	28 56	26	♑	8	12	8	28 35	26	♑
8 45 44	9	13	9	0♏ 1	28	1	9	13	9	29 40	27	1	9	13	9	29 18	27	1
8 49 47	10	14	10	0 45	28	2	10	14	10	0♏ 23	28	2	10	14	10	0♏ 1	27	2
8 53 50	11	15	11	1 28	29	3	11	15	11	1 6	29	3	11	15	11	0 43	28	2
8 57 51	12	16	12	2 12	♐	4	12	16	12	1 49	29	4	12	16	12	1 26	29	2
9 1 52	13	16	13	2 55	1	5	13	17	13	2 32	♐	5	13	17	12	2 8	♐	4
9 5 52	14	17	13	3 38	2	6	14	17	13	3 15	1	6	14	18	13	2 50	1	5
HOUSES	4	5	6	7	8	9	4	5	6	7	8	9	4	5	6	7	8	9

LATITUDE 49° S. LATITUDE 50° S. LATITUDE 51° S.

| | LATITUDE 49° N. | | | | | LATITUDE 50° N. | | | | | LATITUDE 51° N. | | | | |

SIDEREAL TIME	10 ♌	11 ♍	12 ♎	ASC ♏	2 ♐	3 ♑	10 ♌	11 ♍	12 ♎	ASC ♏	2 ♐	3 ♑	10 ♌	11 ♍	12 ♎	ASC ♏	2 ♐	3 ♑
H M S	°	°	°	° '	°	°	°	°	°	° '	°	°	°	°	°	° '	°	°
9 9 52	15	18	14	4 21	2	7	15	18	14	3 57	2	7	15	18	14	3 32	1	6
9 13 50	16	19	15	5 4	3	8	16	19	15	4 40	3	8	16	19	15	4 14	2	7
9 17 49	17	20	16	5 47	4	9	17	20	16	5 22	3	8	17	20	16	4 56	3	8
9 21 46	18	21	17	6 30	5	10	18	21	17	6 4	4	9	18	21	16	5 38	4	9
9 25 42	19	22	17	7 12	6	11	19	22	17	6 46	5	10	19	22	17	6 19	4	10
9 29 38	20	23	18	7 55	6	12	20	23	18	7 28	6	11	20	23	18	7 1	5	11
9 33 34	21	24	19	8 37	7	13	21	24	19	8 10	7	12	21	24	19	7 42	6	12
9 37 28	22	25	20	9 19	8	14	22	25	20	8 52	7	13	22	25	20	8 23	7	13
9 41 22	23	26	21	10 1	9	15	23	26	20	9 33	8	14	23	26	20	9 5	8	14
9 45 15	24	27	21	10 43	10	15	24	27	21	10 15	9	15	24	27	21	9 46	8	15
9 49 8	25	27	22	11 25	10	16	25	27	22	10 56	10	16	25	27	22	10 26	9	16
9 53 0	26	28	23	12 7	11	17	26	28	23	11 37	11	17	26	28	23	11 7	10	17
9 56 51	27	29	24	12 49	12	18	27	29	24	12 19	11	18	27	29	23	11 48	11	18
10 0 42	28	♎	25	13 30	13	19	28	♎	24	13 0	12	19	28	♎	24	12 28	12	19
10 4 32	29	1	25	14 12	14	20	29	1	25	13 41	13	20	29	1	25	13 9	12	20
10 8 22	♍	2	26	14 53	14	21	♍	2	26	14 22	14	21	♍	2	26	13 49	13	21
10 12 11	1	3	27	15 35	15	22	1	3	27	15 3	15	22	1	3	26	14 30	14	21
10 15 59	2	4	28	16 16	16	23	2	4	27	15 43	15	23	2	4	27	15 10	15	22
10 19 47	3	5	28	16 57	17	24	3	5	28	16 24	16	24	3	5	28	15 50	16	23
10 23 34	4	6	29	17 38	18	25	4	5	29	17 5	17	25	4	5	29	16 30	16	24
10 27 21	5	6	♏	18 19	18	26	5	6	♏	17 45	18	26	5	6	29	17 10	17	25
10 31 8	6	7	1	19 0	19	27	6	7	0	18 26	19	27	6	7	♏	17 50	18	26
10 34 53	7	8	1	19 41	20	28	7	8	1	19 6	19	28	7	8	1	18 30	19	27
10 38 39	8	9	2	20 22	21	29	8	9	2	19 47	20	29	8	9	2	19 10	19	28
10 42 24	9	10	3	21 3	22	♒	9	10	3	20 27	21	♒	9	10	2	19 50	20	29
10 46 8	10	11	4	21 44	22	1	10	11	3	21 7	22	1	10	11	3	20 30	21	♒
10 49 52	11	12	4	22 25	23	2	11	12	4	21 48	23	2	11	12	4	21 10	22	1
10 53 36	12	13	5	23 5	24	3	12	12	5	22 28	23	3	12	12	5	21 50	23	2
10 57 20	13	13	6	23 46	25	4	13	13	6	23 8	24	4	13	13	5	22 29	24	3
11 1 3	14	14	7	24 27	26	5	14	14	6	23 49	25	5	14	14	6	23 9	24	4
11 4 45	15	15	7	25 8	27	6	15	15	7	24 29	26	6	15	15	7	23 49	25	5
11 8 28	16	16	8	25 48	27	7	16	16	8	25 9	27	7	16	16	8	24 29	26	7
11 12 10	17	17	9	26 29	28	8	17	17	9	25 49	28	8	17	17	8	25 8	27	8
11 15 52	18	18	10	27 10	29	9	18	18	9	26 30	28	9	18	17	9	25 48	28	9
11 19 33	19	19	10	27 51	♑	10	19	18	10	27 10	29	10	19	18	10	26 28	28	10
11 23 15	20	19	11	28 32	1	11	20	19	11	27 50	♑	11	20	19	10	27 8	29	11
11 26 56	21	20	12	29 13	2	12	21	20	11	28 31	1	12	21	20	11	27 48	♑	12
11 30 37	22	21	13	29 54	3	13	22	21	12	29 11	2	13	22	21	12	28 28	1	13
11 34 17	23	22	13	0♐ 35	3	14	23	22	13	29 52	3	14	23	22	13	29 8	2	14
11 37 58	24	23	14	1 16	4	16	24	23	14	0♐ 32	3	15	24	23	13	29 48	3	15
11 41 39	25	24	15	1 57	5	17	25	23	14	1 13	4	16	25	23	14	0♐ 28	4	16
11 45 19	26	24	16	2 38	6	18	26	24	15	1 54	5	17	26	24	15	1 8	4	17
11 48 59	27	25	16	3 20	7	19	27	25	16	2 35	6	18	27	25	15	1 48	5	18
11 52 40	28	26	17	4 1	8	20	28	26	17	3 16	7	20	28	26	16	2 29	6	19
11 56 20	29	27	18	4 43	9	21	29	27	17	3 57	8	21	29	27	17	3 9	7	20
HOUSES	4	5	6	7	8	9	4	5	6	7	8	9	4	5	6	7	8	9

| LATITUDE 49° S. | LATITUDE 50° S. | LATITUDE 51° S. |

	LATITUDE 49° N.						LATITUDE 50° N.						LATITUDE 51° N.					
SIDEREAL TIME	10 ♎	11 ♎	12 ♏	ASC ♐	2 ♑	3 ♒	10 ♎	11 ♎	12 ♏	ASC ♐	2 ♑	3 ♒	10 ♎	11 ♎	12 ♏	ASC ♐	2 ♑	3 ♒
H M S	°	°	°	° '	°	°	°	°	°	° '	°	°	°	°	°	° '	°	°
12 0 0	0	28	18	5 24	10	22	0	28	18	4 38	9	22	0	28	18	3 50	8	21
12 3 40	1	29	19	6 6	10	23	1	28	19	5 19	10	23	1	28	18	4 31	9	23
12 7 20	2	29	20	6 48	11	24	2	29	19	6 1	11	24	2	29	19	5 12	10	24
12 11 1	3	♏	21	7 30	12	25	3	♏	20	6 42	12	25	3	♏	20	5 53	11	25
12 14 41	4	1	21	8 13	13	26	4	1	21	7 24	12	26	4	1	20	6 34	12	26
12 18 21	5	2	22	8 55	14	28	5	2	22	8 6	13	27	5	2	21	7 15	13	27
12 22 2	6	3	23	9 38	15	29	6	3	22	8 48	14	28	6	2	22	7 57	14	28
12 25 42	7	4	24	10 20	16	♓	7	3	23	9 30	15	♓	7	3	23	8 38	14	29
12 29 23	8	4	24	11 3	17	1	8	4	24	10 13	16	1	8	4	23	9 20	15	♓
12 33 4	9	5	25	11 47	18	2	9	5	25	10 55	17	2	9	5	24	10 2	16	2
12 36 45	10	6	26	12 30	19	3	10	6	25	11 38	18	3	10	6	25	10 45	17	3
12 40 27	11	7	27	13 14	20	4	11	7	26	12 21	19	4	11	7	26	11 27	18	4
12 44 8	12	8	27	13 58	21	6	12	8	27	13 5	20	5	12	7	26	12 10	19	5
12 47 50	13	9	28	14 42	22	7	13	8	27	13 48	21	7	13	8	27	12 53	20	6
12 51 32	14	9	29	15 27	23	8	14	9	28	14 32	22	8	14	9	28	13 36	21	8
12 55 15	15	10	29	16 11	24	9	15	10	29	15 17	23	9	15	10	28	14 20	23	9
12 58 57	16	11	♐	16 57	25	10	16	11	♐	16 1	24	10	16	11	29	15 4	24	10
13 2 40	17	12	1	17 42	26	11	17	12	0	16 46	26	11	17	12	♐	15 48	25	11
13 6 24	18	13	2	18 28	27	13	18	13	1	17 31	27	12	18	12	1	16 33	26	12
13 10 8	19	14	2	19 14	28	14	19	13	2	18 17	28	14	19	13	1	17 18	27	14
13 13 52	20	14	3	20 0	♒	15	20	14	3	19 3	29	15	20	14	2	18 3	28	15
13 17 36	21	15	4	20 47	1	16	21	15	3	19 49	♒	16	21	15	3	18 49	29	16
13 21 21	22	16	5	21 35	2	17	22	16	4	20 36	1	17	22	16	4	19 35	♒	17
13 25 7	23	17	5	22 22	3	19	23	17	5	21 23	2	19	23	16	4	20 21	1	18
13 28 52	24	18	6	23 11	4	20	24	18	6	22 10	3	20	24	17	5	21 8	3	20
13 32 39	25	19	7	23 59	5	21	25	18	6	22 58	5	21	25	18	6	21 55	4	21
13 36 26	26	19	8	24 48	6	22	26	19	7	23 47	6	22	26	19	7	22 43	5	22
13 40 13	27	20	9	25 38	8	24	27	20	8	24 36	7	23	27	20	7	23 31	6	23
13 44 1	28	21	9	26 28	9	25	28	21	9	25 25	8	25	28	21	8	24 20	7	25
13 47 49	29	22	10	27 19	10	26	29	22	10	26 15	9	26	29	21	9	25 10	9	26
13 51 38	♏	23	11	28 10	11	27	♏	23	10	27 6	11	27	♏	22	10	26 0	10	27
13 55 28	1	24	12	29 2	13	29	1	23	11	27 57	12	29	1	23	10	26 50	11	28
13 59 18	2	24	13	29 54	14	♈	2	24	12	28 49	13	♈	2	24	11	27 41	13	♈
14 3 9	3	25	13	0♑ 47	15	1	3	25	13	29 42	15	1	3	25	12	28 33	14	1
14 7 0	4	26	14	1 41	17	2	4	26	14	0♑ 35	16	2	4	26	13	29 25	15	2
14 10 52	5	27	15	2 36	18	4	5	27	14	1 29	17	4	5	26	14	0♑ 18	17	4
14 14 45	6	28	16	3 31	19	5	6	28	15	2 23	19	5	6	27	14	1 12	18	5
14 18 38	7	29	17	4 27	21	6	7	28	16	3 18	20	6	7	28	15	2 7	19	6
14 22 32	8	♐	17	5 24	22	7	8	29	17	4 15	21	7	8	29	16	3 2	21	7
14 26 26	9	0	18	6 21	23	9	9	♐	18	5 12	23	9	9	♐	17	3 59	22	9
14 30 22	10	1	19	7 20	25	10	10	1	18	6 9	24	10	10	1	18	4 56	24	10
14 34 17	11	2	20	8 19	26	11	11	2	19	7 8	26	11	11	2	19	5 54	25	11
14 38 14	12	3	21	9 19	28	12	12	3	20	8 8	27	13	12	2	19	6 52	27	13
14 42 11	13	4	22	10 21	29	14	13	4	21	9 8	29	14	13	3	20	7 52	28	14
14 46 10	14	5	22	11 23	♓	15	14	4	22	10 10	♓	15	14	4	21	8 53	♓	15
HOUSES	4	5	6	7	8	9	4	5	6	7	8	9	4	5	6	7	8	9

LATITUDE 49° N.   LATITUDE 50° N.   LATITUDE 51° N.

SIDEREAL TIME	10 ♏	11 ♐	12 ♐	ASC ♑	2 ♓	3 ♈	10 ♏	11 ♐	12 ♐	ASC ♑	2 ♓	3 ♈	10 ♏	11 ♐	12 ♐	ASC ♑	2 ♓	3 ♈
H M S	°	°	°	° '	°	°	°	°	°	° '	°	°	°	°	°	° '	°	°
14 50 8	15	6	23	12 26	2	16	15	5	23	11 13	2	16	15	5	22	9 55	1	17
14 54 8	16	6	24	13 31	4	18	16	6	24	12 16	3	18	16	6	23	10 58	3	18
14 58 8	17	7	25	14 36	5	19	17	7	24	13 21	5	19	17	7	24	12 3	4	19
15 2 9	18	8	26	15 43	7	20	18	8	25	14 27	6	20	18	8	25	13 8	6	20
15 6 10	19	9	27	16 51	8	21	19	9	26	15 35	8	22	19	8	25	14 15	8	22
15 10 13	20	10	28	18 0	10	23	20	10	27	16 44	10	23	20	9	26	15 23	9	23
15 14 16	21	11	29	19 10	12	24	21	11	28	17 54	11	24	21	10	27	16 32	11	24
15 18 20	22	12	♑	20 22	13	25	22	11	29	19 5	13	25	22	11	28	17 43	13	26
15 22 24	23	13	1	21 36	15	27	23	12	♑	20 18	14	27	23	12	29	18 55	14	27
15 26 30	24	14	2	22 51	16	28	24	13	1	21 32	16	28	24	13	♑	20 9	16	28
15 30 36	25	14	2	24 7	18	29	25	14	2	22 48	18	29	25	14	1	21 25	18	29
15 34 42	26	15	3	25 25	20	♉	26	15	3	24 6	20	♉	26	15	2	22 42	19	♉
15 38 50	27	16	4	26 45	21	2	27	16	4	25 25	21	2	27	16	3	24 1	21	2
15 42 58	28	17	5	28 6	23	3	28	17	5	26 47	23	3	28	17	4	25 22	23	3
15 47 7	29	18	6	29 29	25	4	29	18	6	28 10	25	4	29	17	5	26 45	25	5
15 51 16	♐	19	7	0♒ 54	26	5	♐	19	7	29 35	26	6	♐	18	6	28 10	26	6
15 55 26	1	20	8	2 21	28	7	1	20	8	1♒ 2	28	7	1	19	7	29 37	28	7
15 59 37	2	21	9	3 50	♈	8	2	21	9	2 31	♈	8	2	20	8	1♒ 6	♈	8
16 3 49	3	22	11	5 21	2	9	3	21	10	4 2	2	9	3	21	9	2 37	2	10
16 8 1	4	23	12	6 54	3	10	4	22	11	5 35	3	11	4	22	10	4 11	3	11
16 12 14	5	24	13	8 29	5	12	5	23	12	7 11	5	12	5	23	11	5 47	5	12
16 16 27	6	25	14	10 6	7	13	6	24	13	8 49	7	13	6	24	12	7 25	7	13
16 20 41	7	26	15	11 46	8	14	7	25	14	10 29	9	14	7	25	13	9 6	9	15
16 24 56	8	27	16	13 28	10	15	8	26	15	12 10	10	16	8	26	14	10 50	11	16
16 29 11	9	28	17	15 12	12	17	9	27	16	13 57	12	17	9	27	15	12 36	12	17
16 33 27	10	29	18	16 58	14	18	10	28	17	15 45	14	18	10	28	17	14 25	14	18
16 37 43	11	29	19	18 47	15	19	11	29	19	17 36	16	19	11	29	18	16 17	16	20
16 41 59	12	♑	20	20 39	17	20	12	♑	19	19 29	17	20	12	♑	19	18 12	18	21
16 46 17	13	1	22	22 33	19	21	13	1	21	21 25	19	22	13	1	20	20 10	19	22
16 50 34	14	2	23	24 29	20	23	14	2	22	23 23	21	23	14	2	21	22 11	21	23
16 54 53	15	3	24	26 28	22	24	15	3	23	25 24	22	24	15	3	22	24 14	23	24
16 59 11	16	4	25	28 29	24	25	16	4	24	27 28	24	25	16	4	24	26 21	25	26
17 3 30	17	5	27	0♓ 32	25	26	17	5	26	29 34	26	26	17	5	25	28 30	26	27
17 7 49	18	6	28	2 38	27	27	18	6	27	1♓ 43	28	28	18	6	26	0♓ 43	28	28
17 12 9	19	8	29	4 46	29	28	19	7	28	3 55	29	29	19	7	27	2 58	♉	29
17 16 29	20	9	♒	6 56	♉	♊	20	8	♒	6 9	♉	♊	20	8	29	5 16	1	♊
17 20 49	21	10	2	9 8	2	1	21	9	1	8 25	2	1	21	9	♒	7 36	3	1
17 25 10	22	11	3	11 22	4	2	22	10	2	10 43	4	2	22	10	1	9 59	5	3
17 29 31	23	12	4	13 38	5	3	23	11	4	13 3	6	3	23	11	3	12 24	6	4
17 33 51	24	13	6	15 55	7	4	24	12	5	15 25	7	5	24	12	4	14 51	8	5
17 38 13	25	14	7	18 14	8	5	25	13	6	17 48	9	6	25	13	6	17 19	10	6
17 42 34	26	15	8	20 34	10	6	26	14	8	20 13	10	7	26	14	7	19 49	11	7
17 46 55	27	16	10	22 54	11	8	27	16	9	22 39	12	8	27	15	8	22 21	13	8
17 51 17	28	17	11	25 16	13	9	28	17	11	25 5	14	9	28	16	10	24 53	14	9
17 55 38	29	18	13	27 38	14	10	29	18	12	27 33	15	10	29	17	11	27 27	16	11
HOUSES	4	5	6	7	8	9	4	5	6	7	8	9	4	5	6	7	8	9

LATITUDE 49° S.   LATITUDE 50° S.   LATITUDE 51° S.

LATITUDE 49° N.   LATITUDE 50° N.   LATITUDE 51° N.

SIDEREAL TIME	10 ♑	11 ♑	12 ♒	ASC ♈	2 ♉	3 ♊	10 ♑	11 ♑	12 ♒	ASC ♈	2 ♉	3 ♊	10 ♑	11 ♑	12 ♒	ASC ♈	2 ♉	3 ♊
H M S	°	°	°	° '	°	°	°	°	°	° '	°	°	°	°	°	° '	°	°
18 0 0	0	19	14	0 0	16	11	0	19	13	0 0	17	11	0	18	13	0 0	17	12
18 4 22	1	20	16	2 22	17	12	1	20	15	2 27	18	12	1	19	14	2 33	19	13
18 8 43	2	21	17	4 44	19	13	2	21	16	4 55	19	13	2	21	16	5 7	20	14
18 13 5	3	22	19	7 6	20	14	3	22	18	7 21	21	14	3	22	17	7 39	22	15
18 17 26	4	24	20	9 26	22	15	4	23	20	9 47	22	16	4	23	19	10 11	23	16
18 21 47	5	25	22	11 46	23	16	5	24	21	12 12	24	17	5	24	20	12 41	24	17
18 26 9	6	26	23	14 5	24	17	6	25	23	14 35	25	18	6	25	22	15 9	26	18
18 30 29	7	27	25	16 22	26	18	7	27	24	16 57	26	19	7	26	24	17 36	27	19
18 34 50	8	28	26	18 38	27	19	8	28	26	19 17	28	20	8	27	25	20 1	29	20
18 39 11	9	29	28	20 52	28	20	9	29	28	21 35	29	21	9	29	27	22 24	♊	21
18 43 31	10	♒	♓	23 4	♊	21	10	♒	29	23 51	♊	22	10	♒	29	24 44	1	22
18 47 51	11	2	1	25 14	1	22	11	1	♓	26 5	2	23	11	1	♓	27 2	3	23
18 52 11	12	3	3	27 22	2	24	12	2	2	28 17	3	24	12	2	2	29 17	4	24
18 56 30	13	4	5	29 28	3	25	13	4	4	0♉ 26	4	25	13	3	4	1♉ 30	5	25
19 0 49	14	5	6	1♉ 31	5	26	14	5	6	2 32	6	26	14	4	5	3 39	6	26
19 5 7	15	6	8	3 32	6	27	15	6	8	4 36	7	27	15	6	7	5 46	8	27
19 9 26	16	7	10	5 31	7	28	16	7	9	6 37	8	28	16	7	9	7 49	9	28
19 13 43	17	9	11	7 27	8	29	17	8	11	8 35	9	29	17	8	11	9 50	10	29
19 18 0	18	10	13	9 21	10	♋	18	10	13	10 31	10	♋	18	9	12	11 48	11	♋
19 22 17	19	11	15	11 13	11	1	19	11	14	12 24	11	1	19	10	14	13 43	12	1
19 26 33	20	12	16	13 2	12	1	20	12	16	14 15	13	2	20	12	16	15 35	13	2
19 30 49	21	13	18	14 48	13	2	21	13	18	16 3	14	3	21	13	18	17 24	15	3
19 35 4	22	15	20	16 32	14	3	22	14	20	17 48	15	4	22	14	19	19 10	16	4
19 39 19	23	16	22	18 14	15	4	23	16	21	19 31	16	5	23	15	21	20 54	17	5
19 43 33	24	17	23	19 54	16	5	24	17	23	21 11	17	6	24	17	23	22 35	18	6
19 47 46	25	18	25	21 31	17	6	25	18	25	22 49	18	7	25	18	25	24 13	19	7
19 51 59	26	20	27	23 6	18	7	26	19	27	24 25	19	8	26	19	27	25 49	20	8
19 56 11	27	21	28	24 39	19	8	27	21	28	25 58	20	9	27	20	28	27 23	21	9
20 0 23	28	22	♈	26 10	21	9	28	22	♈	27 29	21	9	28	22	♈	28 54	22	10
20 4 34	29	23	2	27 39	22	10	29	23	2	28 58	22	10	29	23	2	0♊ 23	23	11
20 8 44	♒	25	4	29 6	23	11	♒	24	4	0♊ 25	23	11	♒	24	4	1 50	24	12
20 12 53	1	26	5	0♊ 31	24	12	1	26	5	1 50	24	12	1	25	5	3 15	25	13
20 17 2	2	27	7	1 54	25	13	2	27	7	3 13	25	13	2	27	7	4 38	26	13
20 21 10	3	28	9	3 15	26	14	3	28	9	4 35	26	14	3	28	9	5 59	27	14
20 25 18	4	♓	10	4 35	27	15	4	29	10	5 54	27	15	4	29	11	7 18	28	15
20 29 24	5	1	12	5 53	28	16	5	♓	12	7 12	28	16	5	♓	12	8 35	29	16
20 33 30	6	2	14	7 9	28	16	6	2	14	8 28	29	17	6	2	14	9 51	♋	17
20 37 36	7	3	15	8 24	29	17	7	3	16	9 42	♋	18	7	3	16	11 5	1	18
20 41 40	8	5	17	9 38	♋	18	8	5	17	10 55	1	19	8	4	17	12 17	2	19
20 45 44	9	6	18	10 50	1	19	9	6	19	12 6	2	19	9	6	19	13 28	3	20
20 49 47	10	7	20	12 0	2	20	10	7	20	13 16	3	20	10	7	21	14 37	4	21
20 53 50	11	9	22	13 9	3	21	11	8	22	14 25	4	21	11	8	22	15 45	5	22
20 57 51	12	10	23	14 17	4	22	12	10	24	15 33	5	22	12	10	24	16 52	5	22
21 1 52	13	11	25	15 24	5	23	13	11	25	16 39	6	23	13	11	26	17 57	6	23
21 5 52	14	12	26	16 29	6	24	14	12	27	17 44	6	24	14	12	27	19 2	7	24
HOUSES	4	5	6	7	8	9	4	5	6	7	8	9	4	5	6	7	8	9

LATITUDE 49° S.   LATITUDE 50° S.   LATITUDE 51° S.

LATITUDE 49° N. LATITUDE 50° N. LATITUDE 51° N.

SIDEREAL TIME H M S	10 ♒	11 ♓	12 ♈	ASC ♊	2 ♋	3 ♋	10 ♒	11 ♓	12 ♈	ASC ♊	2 ♋	3 ♋	10 ♒	11 ♓	12 ♈	ASC ♊	2 ♋	3 ♋
21 9 52	15	14	28	17 34	7	24	15	14	28	18 47	7	25	15	13	29	20 5	8	25
21 13 50	16	15	29	18 37	8	25	16	15	♉	19 50	8	26	16	15	♉	21 7	9	26
21 17 49	17	16	♉	19 39	8	26	17	16	1	20 52	9	26	17	16	2	22 8	10	27
21 21 46	18	18	2	20 41	9	27	18	17	3	21 52	10	27	18	17	3	23 8	11	28
21 25 42	19	19	4	21 41	10	28	19	19	4	22 52	11	28	19	19	5	24 6	11	28
21 29 38	20	20	5	22 40	11	29	20	20	6	23 51	12	29	20	20	6	25 4	12	29
21 33 34	21	21	7	23 39	12	♌	21	21	7	24 48	12	♌	21	21	8	26 1	13	♌
21 37 28	22	23	8	24 36	13	0	22	23	9	25 45	13	1	22	23	9	26 58	14	1
21 41 22	23	24	9	25 33	13	1	23	24	10	26 42	14	2	23	24	11	27 53	15	2
21 45 15	24	25	11	26 29	14	2	24	25	11	27 37	15	2	24	25	12	28 48	16	3
21 49 8	25	26	12	27 24	15	3	25	26	13	28 31	16	3	25	26	13	29 42	16	4
21 53 0	26	28	13	28 19	16	4	26	28	14	29 25	16	4	26	28	15	0♋ 35	17	4
21 56 51	27	29	15	29 13	17	5	27	29	15	0♋ 18	17	5	27	29	16	1 27	18	5
22 0 42	28	♈	16	0♋ 6	17	6	28	♈	17	1 11	18	6	28	♈	17	2 19	19	6
22 4 32	29	1	17	0 58	18	6	29	1	18	2 3	19	7	29	2	19	3 10	20	7
22 8 22	♓	3	19	1 50	19	7	♓	3	19	2 54	20	7	♓	3	20	4 0	20	8
22 12 11	1	4	20	2 41	20	8	1	4	21	3 45	20	8	1	4	21	4 50	21	9
22 15 59	2	5	21	3 32	21	9	2	5	22	4 35	21	9	2	5	23	5 40	22	9
22 19 47	3	6	22	4 22	21	10	3	7	23	5 24	22	10	3	7	24	6 29	23	10
22 23 34	4	8	24	5 12	22	11	4	8	24	6 13	23	11	4	8	25	7 17	23	11
22 27 21	5	9	25	6 1	23	11	5	9	25	7 2	24	12	5	9	26	8 5	24	12
22 31 8	6	10	26	6 49	24	12	6	10	27	7 50	24	12	6	10	27	8 52	25	13
22 34 53	7	11	27	7 38	25	13	7	11	28	8 37	25	13	7	12	29	9 39	26	14
22 38 39	8	13	28	8 25	25	14	8	13	29	9 24	26	14	8	13	♊	10 25	26	14
22 42 24	9	14	29	9 13	26	15	9	14	♊	10 11	27	15	9	14	1	11 11	27	15
22 46 8	10	15	♊	10 0	27	16	10	15	1	10 57	27	16	10	15	2	11 57	28	16
22 49 52	11	16	2	10 46	28	16	11	16	2	11 43	28	17	11	16	3	12 42	29	17
22 53 36	12	17	3	11 32	28	17	12	18	3	12 29	29	17	12	18	4	13 27	29	18
22 57 20	13	19	4	12 18	29	18	13	19	4	13 14	♌	18	13	19	5	14 12	♌	18
23 1 3	14	20	5	13 3	♌	19	14	20	6	13 59	0	19	14	20	6	14 56	1	19
23 4 45	15	21	6	13 49	1	20	15	21	7	14 43	1	20	15	21	7	15 40	2	20
23 8 28	16	22	7	14 33	1	21	16	22	8	15 28	2	21	16	22	9	16 24	2	21
23 12 10	17	23	8	15 18	2	21	17	23	9	16 12	3	22	17	24	10	17 7	3	22
23 15 52	18	24	9	16 2	3	22	18	25	10	16 55	3	22	18	25	11	17 50	4	23
23 19 33	19	26	10	16 46	3	23	19	26	11	17 39	4	23	19	26	12	18 33	4	23
23 23 15	20	27	11	17 30	4	24	20	27	12	18 22	5	24	20	27	13	19 15	5	24
23 26 56	21	28	12	18 13	5	25	21	28	13	19 5	5	25	21	28	14	19 58	6	25
23 30 37	22	29	13	18 57	6	26	22	29	14	19 47	6	26	22	29	15	20 40	7	26
23 34 17	23	♉	14	19 40	6	26	23	♉	15	20 30	7	27	23	♉	16	21 22	7	27
23 37 58	24	1	15	20 22	7	27	24	2	16	21 12	8	27	24	2	16	22 3	8	28
23 41 39	25	2	16	21 5	8	28	25	3	17	21 54	8	28	25	3	17	22 45	9	28
23 45 19	26	4	17	21 47	9	29	26	4	18	22 36	9	29	26	4	18	23 26	10	29
23 48 59	27	5	18	22 30	9	♍	27	5	18	23 18	10	♍	27	5	19	24 7	10	♍
23 52 40	28	6	19	23 12	10	1	28	6	19	23 59	11	1	28	6	20	24 48	11	1
23 56 20	29	7	20	23 54	11	1	29	7	20	24 41	11	2	29	7	21	25 29	12	2
HOUSES	4	5	6	7	8	9	4	5	6	7	8	9	4	5	6	7	8	9

LATITUDE 49° S. LATITUDE 50° S. LATITUDE 51° S.

LATITUDE 52° N.   LATITUDE 53° N.   LATITUDE 54° N.

SIDEREAL TIME	10 ♈	11 ♉	12 ♊	ASC ♋		2 ♌	3 ♍	10 ♈	11 ♉	12 ♊	ASC ♋		2 ♌	3 ♍	10 ♈	11 ♉	12 ♊	ASC ♋		2 ♌	3 ♍
H M S	°	°	°	°	′	°	°	°	°	°	°	′	°	°	°	°	°	°	′	°	°
0 0 0	0	9	23	26	59	13	3	0	9	24	27	50	13	3	0	9	25	28	42	14	3
0 3 40	1	10	24	27	39	14	3	1	10	25	28	29	14	4	1	11	26	29	21	14	4
0 7 20	2	11	25	28	19	14	4	2	11	26	29	9	15	4	2	12	27	0♌	0	15	5
0 11 1	3	12	26	28	59	15	5	3	12	26	29	48	15	5	3	13	27	0♌	38	16	5
0 14 41	4	13	26	29	39	16	6	4	14	27	0♌	27	16	6	4	14	28	1	17	17	6
0 18 21	5	14	27	0♌	18	16	7	5	15	28	1	6	17	7	5	15	29	1	55	17	7
0 22 2	6	15	28	0	58	17	8	6	16	29	1	45	18	8	6	16	♋	2	34	18	8
0 25 43	7	16	29	1	38	18	8	7	17	♋	2	24	18	9	7	17	1	3	12	19	9
0 29 23	8	18	♋	2	17	19	9	8	18	1	3	3	19	9	8	18	2	3	50	19	10
0 33 4	9	19	1	2	56	19	10	9	19	2	3	42	20	10	9	19	2	4	29	20	10
0 36 45	10	20	2	3	36	20	11	10	20	2	4	21	20	11	10	20	3	5	7	21	11
0 40 27	11	21	2	4	15	21	12	11	21	3	4	59	21	12	11	21	4	5	45	21	12
0 44 8	12	22	3	4	54	21	13	12	22	4	5	38	22	13	12	23	5	6	23	22	13
0 47 50	13	23	4	5	34	22	13	13	23	5	6	17	23	14	13	24	6	7	1	23	14
0 51 32	14	24	5	6	13	23	14	14	24	6	6	55	23	14	14	25	7	7	39	24	14
0 55 15	15	25	6	6	52	24	15	15	25	6	7	34	24	15	15	26	7	8	17	24	15
0 58 57	16	26	6	7	31	24	16	16	26	7	8	13	25	16	16	27	8	8	56	25	16
1 2 40	17	27	7	8	11	25	17	17	27	8	8	52	25	17	17	28	9	9	34	26	17
1 6 24	18	28	8	8	50	26	18	18	28	9	9	30	26	18	18	29	10	10	12	26	18
1 10 8	19	29	9	9	29	26	19	19	29	10	10	9	27	19	19	♊	10	10	50	27	19
1 13 52	20	♊	10	10	8	27	19	20	♊	10	10	48	28	19	20	1	11	11	28	28	20
1 17 36	21	1	10	10	48	28	20	21	1	11	11	26	28	20	21	2	12	12	6	29	20
1 21 21	22	2	11	11	27	29	21	22	2	12	12	5	29	21	22	3	13	12	44	29	21
1 25 7	23	3	12	12	6	29	22	23	3	13	12	44	♍	22	23	4	14	13	23	♍	22
1 28 52	24	4	13	12	46	♍	23	24	4	14	13	23	0	23	24	5	14	14	1	1	23
1 32 39	25	5	14	13	25	1	24	25	5	14	14	2	1	24	25	6	15	14	39	1	24
1 36 26	26	6	14	14	5	2	25	26	6	15	14	41	2	25	26	7	16	15	18	2	25
1 40 13	27	7	15	14	44	2	25	27	7	16	15	20	3	25	27	8	17	15	56	3	26
1 44 1	28	8	16	15	24	3	26	28	8	17	15	59	3	26	28	9	17	16	35	4	26
1 47 49	29	9	17	16	4	4	27	29	9	17	16	38	4	27	29	10	18	17	14	4	27
1 51 38	♉	10	18	16	44	5	28	♉	10	18	17	18	5	28	♉	11	19	17	52	5	28
1 55 28	1	11	18	17	24	5	29	1	11	19	17	57	6	29	1	12	20	18	31	6	29
1 59 18	2	12	19	18	4	6	♎	2	12	20	18	36	6	♎	2	13	21	19	10	7	♎
2 3 9	3	13	20	18	44	7	1	3	13	21	19	16	7	1	3	14	21	19	49	7	1
2 7 0	4	14	21	19	24	8	2	4	14	21	19	56	8	2	4	15	22	20	28	8	2
2 10 52	5	15	21	20	4	8	2	5	15	22	20	35	9	2	5	16	23	21	7	9	2
2 14 45	6	16	22	20	44	9	3	6	16	23	21	15	9	3	6	17	24	21	47	10	3
2 18 38	7	17	23	21	25	10	4	7	17	24	21	55	10	4	7	18	24	22	26	10	4
2 22 32	8	18	24	22	6	11	5	8	18	24	22	35	11	5	8	19	25	23	5	11	5
2 26 26	9	19	25	22	46	11	6	9	19	25	23	15	12	6	9	19	26	23	45	12	6
2 30 22	10	19	25	23	27	12	7	10	20	26	23	56	12	7	10	20	27	24	25	13	7
2 34 17	11	20	26	24	8	13	8	11	21	27	24	36	13	8	11	21	27	25	5	13	8
2 38 14	12	21	27	24	49	14	9	12	22	28	25	16	14	9	12	22	28	25	44	14	9
2 42 11	13	22	28	25	30	15	10	13	23	28	25	57	15	10	13	23	29	26	24	15	10
2 46 10	14	23	28	26	11	15	11	14	24	29	26	38	15	11	14	24	♌	27	5	16	10
HOUSES	4	5	6	7		8	9	4	5	6	7		8	9	4	5	6	7		8	9

LATITUDE 52° N. LATITUDE 53° N. LATITUDE 54° N.

SIDEREAL TIME	10 ♉	11 ♊	12 ♋	ASC ♌	2 ♍	3 ♎	10 ♉	11 ♊	12 ♌	ASC ♌	2 ♍	3 ♎	10 ♉	11 ♊	12 ♌	ASC ♌	2 ♍	3 ♎
H M S	°	°	°	° '	°	°	°	°	°	° '	°	°	°	°	°	° '	°	°
2 50 8	15	24	29	26 53	16	12	15	25	0	27 19	16	11	15	25	0	27 45	16	11
2 54 8	16	25	Ω	27 34	17	12	16	26	1	28 0	17	12	16	26	1	28 25	17	12
2 58 8	17	26	1	28 16	18	13	17	27	1	28 41	18	13	17	27	2	29 6	18	13
3 2 9	18	27	2	28 58	19	14	18	27	2	29 22	19	14	18	28	3	29 47	19	14
3 6 10	19	28	2	29 40	19	15	19	28	3	0♏ 3	19	15	19	29	4	0♏ 27	20	15
3 10 13	20	29	3	0♏ 22	20	16	20	29	4	0 45	20	16	20	♋	4	1 8	20	16
3 14 16	21	♋	4	1 4	21	17	21	♋	5	1 26	21	17	21	1	5	1 50	21	17
3 18 20	22	1	5	1 46	22	18	22	1	5	2 8	22	18	22	2	6	2 31	22	18
3 22 24	23	2	6	2 29	23	19	23	2	6	2 50	23	19	23	3	7	3 12	23	19
3 26 30	24	3	6	3 11	23	20	24	3	7	3 32	23	20	24	3	7	3 54	23	20
3 30 36	25	4	7	3 54	24	21	25	4	8	4 14	24	21	25	4	8	4 35	24	20
3 34 42	26	4	8	4 37	25	22	26	5	8	4 57	25	22	26	5	9	5 17	25	21
3 38 50	27	5	9	5 20	26	23	27	6	9	5 39	26	22	27	6	10	5 59	26	22
3 42 58	28	6	10	6 3	27	24	28	7	10	6 22	27	23	28	7	11	6 41	27	23
3 47 7	29	7	10	6 46	27	24	29	8	11	7 5	27	24	29	8	11	7 23	27	24
3 51 16	♊	8	11	7 30	28	25	♊	9	12	7 47	28	25	♊	9	12	8 5	28	25
3 55 26	1	9	12	8 13	29	26	1	10	12	8 30	29	26	1	10	13	8 48	29	26
3 59 37	2	10	13	8 57	≏	27	2	10	13	9 14	≏	27	2	11	14	9 30	≏	27
4 3 49	3	11	14	9 41	1	28	3	11	14	9 57	1	28	3	12	15	10 13	1	28
4 8 1	4	12	14	10 25	2	29	4	12	15	10 40	2	29	4	13	15	10 56	2	29
4 12 14	5	13	15	11 9	2	♏	5	13	16	11 24	2	♏	5	14	16	11 39	2	♏
4 16 27	6	14	16	11 53	3	1	6	14	16	12 7	3	1	6	15	17	12 22	3	1
4 20 41	7	15	17	12 37	4	2	7	15	17	12 51	4	2	7	15	18	13 5	4	2
4 24 56	8	16	18	13 22	5	3	8	16	18	13 35	5	3	8	16	19	13 48	5	3
4 29 11	9	17	19	14 6	6	4	9	17	19	14 19	6	4	9	17	19	14 31	6	4
4 33 27	10	17	19	14 51	7	5	10	18	20	15 3	7	5	10	18	20	15 15	7	4
4 37 43	11	18	20	15 36	7	6	11	19	21	15 47	7	6	11	19	21	15 58	7	5
4 41 59	12	19	21	16 21	8	7	12	20	21	16 31	8	7	12	20	22	16 42	8	7
4 46 17	13	20	22	17 6	9	8	13	21	22	17 16	9	7	13	21	23	17 26	9	7
4 50 34	14	21	23	17 51	10	9	14	22	23	18 0	10	8	14	22	23	18 10	10	8
4 54 53	15	22	24	18 36	11	10	15	22	24	18 45	11	9	15	23	24	18 54	11	9
4 59 10	16	23	24	19 21	12	11	16	23	25	19 29	12	10	16	24	25	19 38	12	10
5 3 30	17	24	25	20 6	13	11	17	24	26	20 14	12	11	17	25	26	20 22	12	11
5 7 49	18	25	26	20 52	13	12	18	25	26	20 59	13	12	18	26	27	21 6	13	12
5 12 9	19	26	27	21 37	14	13	19	26	27	21 44	14	13	19	27	28	21 50	14	13
5 16 29	20	27	28	22 23	15	14	20	27	28	22 29	15	14	20	27	28	22 35	15	14
5 20 49	21	28	29	23 8	16	15	21	28	29	23 14	16	15	21	28	29	23 19	16	15
5 25 10	22	29	29	23 54	17	16	22	29	♏	23 59	17	16	22	29	♏	24 3	17	16
5 29 31	23	Ω	♏	24 39	18	17	23	Ω	1	24 44	18	17	23	Ω	1	24 48	17	17
5 33 51	24	1	1	25 25	19	18	24	1	1	25 29	18	18	24	1	2	25 32	18	18
5 38 13	25	1	2	26 11	19	19	25	2	2	26 14	19	19	25	2	3	26 17	19	19
5 42 34	26	2	3	26 57	20	20	26	3	3	26 59	20	20	26	3	3	27 2	20	19
5 46 55	27	3	4	27 43	21	21	27	4	4	27 44	21	21	27	4	4	27 46	21	20
5 51 17	28	4	5	28 28	22	22	28	5	5	28 30	22	22	28	5	5	28 31	22	21
5 55 38	29	5	5	29 14	23	23	29	6		29 15	23	23	29	6	6	29 15	22	22
HOUSES	4	5	6	7	8	9	4	5	6	7	8	9	4	5	6	7	8	9

LATITUDE 52° S. LATITUDE 53° S. LATITUDE 54° S.

LATITUDE 52° N.   LATITUDE 53° N.   LATITUDE 54° N.

SIDEREAL TIME	10 ♋	11 ♌	12 ♍	ASC ♎	2 ♎	3 ♏	10 ♋	11 ♌	12 ♍	ASC ♎	2 ♎	3 ♏	10 ♋	11 ♌	12 ♍	ASC ♎	2 ♎	3 ♏
H M S	°	°	°	° '	°	°	°	°	°	° '	°	°	°	°	°	° '	°	°
6 0 0	0	6	6	0 0	24	24	0	6	6	0 0	24	24	0	7	7	0 0	23	23
6 4 22	1	7	7	0 46	25	25	1	7	7	0 45	24	24	1	8	8	0 45	24	24
6 8 43	2	8	8	1 32	25	26	2	8	8	1 30	25	25	2	9	8	1 29	25	25
6 13 5	3	9	9	2 17	26	27	3	9	9	2 16	26	26	3	10	9	2 14	26	26
6 17 26	4	10	10	3 3	27	28	4	10	10	3 1	27	27	4	11	10	2 58	27	27
6 21 47	5	11	11	3 49	28	29	5	11	11	3 46	28	28	5	11	11	3 43	27	28
6 26 9	6	12	11	4 35	29	29	6	12	12	4 31	29	29	6	12	12	4 28	28	29
6 30 29	7	13	12	5 21	♏	♐	7	13	12	5 16	29	♐	7	13	13	5 12	29	♐
6 34 50	8	14	13	6 6	1	1	8	14	13	6 1	♏	1	8	14	13	5 57	♏	1
6 39 11	9	15	14	6 52	1	2	9	15	14	6 46	1	2	9	15	14	6 41	1	2
6 43 31	10	16	15	7 37	2	3	10	16	15	7 31	2	3	10	16	15	7 25	2	3
6 47 51	11	17	16	8 23	3	4	11	17	16	8 16	3	4	11	17	16	8 10	2	3
6 52 11	12	18	17	9 8	4	5	12	18	17	9 1	4	5	12	18	17	8 54	3	4
6 56 30	13	19	17	9 54	5	6	13	19	18	9 46	4	6	13	19	18	9 38	4	5
7 0 49	14	19	18	10 39	6	7	14	20	18	10 31	5	7	14	20	18	10 22	5	6
7 5 7	15	20	19	11 24	6	8	15	21	19	11 15	6	8	15	21	19	11 6	6	7
7 9 26	16	21	20	12 9	7	9	16	22	20	12 0	7	8	16	22	20	11 50	7	8
7 13 43	17	22	21	12 54	8	10	17	23	21	12 44	8	9	17	23	21	12 34	7	9
7 18 0	18	23	22	13 39	9	11	18	23	22	13 29	9	10	18	24	22	13 18	8	10
7 22 17	19	24	23	14 24	10	12	19	24	23	14 13	9	11	19	25	23	14 2	9	11
7 26 33	20	25	23	15 9	11	13	20	25	23	14 57	10	12	20	26	23	14 45	10	12
7 30 49	21	26	24	15 54	11	13	21	26	24	15 41	11	13	21	26	24	15 29	11	13
7 35 4	22	27	25	16 38	12	14	22	27	25	16 25	12	14	22	27	25	16 12	11	14
7 39 19	23	28	26	17 23	13	15	23	28	26	17 9	13	15	23	28	26	16 55	12	15
7 43 33	24	29	27	18 7	14	16	24	29	27	17 53	14	16	24	29	27	17 38	13	15
7 47 46	25	♏	28	18 51	15	17	25	♏	28	18 36	14	17	25	♏	28	18 21	14	16
7 51 59	26	1	28	19 35	16	18	26	1	28	19 20	15	18	26	1	28	19 4	15	17
7 56 11	27	2	29	20 19	16	19	27	2	29	20 3	16	19	27	2	29	19 47	15	18
8 0 23	28	3	♎	21 3	17	20	28	3	♎	20 46	17	20	28	3	♎	20 30	16	19
8 4 34	29	4	1	21 47	18	21	29	4	1	21 30	18	20	29	4	1	21 12	17	20
8 8 44	♌	5	2	22 30	19	22	♌	5	2	22 13	18	21	♌	5	2	21 55	18	21
8 12 53	1	6	3	23 14	20	23	1	6	3	22 55	19	22	1	6	3	22 37	19	22
8 17 2	2	6	3	23 57	20	24	2	7	3	23 38	20	23	2	7	3	23 19	19	23
8 21 10	3	7	4	24 40	21	25	3	8	4	24 21	21	24	3	8	4	24 1	20	24
8 25 18	4	8	5	25 23	22	26	4	8	5	25 3	22	25	4	9	5	24 43	21	25
8 29 24	5	9	6	26 6	23	26	5	9	6	25 46	22	26	5	10	6	25 25	22	26
8 33 30	6	10	7	26 49	24	27	6	10	7	26 28	23	27	6	10	7	26 6	23	27
8 37 36	7	11	7	27 31	24	28	7	11	7	27 10	24	28	7	11	7	26 48	23	27
8 41 40	8	12	8	28 14	25	29	8	12	8	27 52	25	29	8	12	8	27 29	24	28
8 45 44	9	13	9	28 56	26	♑	9	13	9	28 34	25	♑	9	13	9	28 10	25	29
8 49 47	10	14	10	29 38	27	1	10	14	10	29 15	26	1	10	14	10	28 52	26	♑
8 53 50	11	15	11	0♏ 20	28	2	11	15	11	29 57	27	2	11	15	10	29 33	26	1
8 57 51	12	16	11	1 2	28	3	12	16	11	0♏ 38	28	3	12	16	11	0♏ 13	27	2
9 1 52	13	17	12	1 44	29	4	13	17	12	1 19	29	3	13	17	12	0 54	28	3
9 5 52	14	18	13	2 26	♐	5	14	18	13	2 0	29	4	14	18	13	1 35	29	4
HOUSES	4	5	6	7	8	9	4	5	6	7	8	9	4	5	6	7	8	9

LATITUDE 52° S.   LATITUDE 53° S.   LATITUDE 54° S.

LATITUDE 52° N. LATITUDE 53° N. LATITUDE 54° N.

SIDEREAL TIME	10 ♌	11 ♍	12 ♎	ASC ♏ °	'	2 ♐	3 ♑	10 ♌	11 ♍	12 ♎	ASC ♏ °	'	2 ♐	3 ♑	10 ♌	11 ♍	12 ♎	ASC ♏ °	'	2 ♐	3 ♑
H M S	°	°	°	°	'	°	°	°	°	°	°	'	°	°	°	°	°	°	'	°	°
9 9 52	15	18	14	3	7	1	6	15	19	14	2	41	0	5	15	19	14	2	15	0	5
9 13 50	16	19	15	3	49	2	7	16	19	15	3	22	1	6	16	20	14	2	55	0	6
9 17 49	17	20	15	4	30	2	8	17	20	15	4	3	2	7	17	20	15	3	36	1	7
9 21 46	18	21	16	5	11	3	9	18	21	16	4	44	2	8	18	21	16	4	16	2	8
9 25 42	19	22	17	5	52	4	10	19	22	17	5	24	3	9	19	22	17	4	55	3	9
9 29 38	20	23	18	6	33	5	11	20	23	18	6	4	4	10	20	23	17	5	35	3	10
9 33 34	21	24	19	7	14	5	11	21	24	18	6	45	5	11	21	24	18	6	15	4	11
9 37 28	22	25	19	7	54	6	12	22	25	19	7	25	6	12	22	25	19	6	55	5	11
9 41 22	23	26	20	8	35	7	13	23	26	20	8	5	6	13	23	26	20	7	34	6	12
9 45 15	24	27	21	9	16	8	14	24	27	21	8	45	7	14	24	27	20	8	13	6	13
9 49 8	25	28	22	9	56	9	15	25	28	21	9	25	8	15	25	28	21	8	53	7	14
9 53 0	26	28	22	10	36	9	16	26	28	22	10	4	9	16	26	28	22	9	32	8	15
9 56 51	27	29	23	11	16	10	17	27	29	23	10	44	9	17	27	29	23	10	11	9	16
10 0 42	28	≏	24	11	56	11	18	28	≏	24	11	24	10	18	28	≏	23	10	50	9	17
10 4 32	29	1	25	12	36	12	19	29	1	24	12	3	11	19	29	1	24	11	29	10	18
10 8 22	♍	2	25	13	16	12	20	♍	2	25	12	42	12	20	♍	2	25	12	8	11	19
10 12 11	1	3	26	13	56	13	21	1	3	26	13	22	13	21	1	3	26	12	46	12	20
10 15 59	2	4	27	14	36	14	22	2	4	27	14	1	13	22	2	4	26	13	25	13	21
10 19 47	3	5	28	15	16	15	23	3	5	27	14	40	14	23	3	4	27	14	4	13	22
10 23 34	4	5	28	15	55	16	24	4	5	28	15	19	15	24	4	5	28	14	42	14	23
10 27 21	5	6	29	16	35	16	25	5	6	29	15	58	16	25	5	6	29	15	21	15	24
10 31 8	6	7	♏	17	14	17	26	6	7	♏	16	37	16	26	6	7	29	15	59	16	25
10 34 53	7	8	1	17	54	18	27	7	8	0	17	16	17	27	7	8	♏	16	37	16	26
10 38 39	8	9	1	18	33	19	28	8	9	1	17	55	18	28	8	9	1	17	16	17	27
10 42 24	9	10	2	19	12	20	29	9	10	2	18	34	19	29	9	10	1	17	54	18	28
10 46 8	10	11	3	19	52	20	♒	10	11	2	19	12	20	♒	10	10	2	18	32	19	29
10 49 52	11	11	4	20	31	21	1	11	11	3	19	51	20	1	11	11	3	19	10	20	♒
10 53 36	12	12	4	21	10	22	2	12	12	4	20	30	21	2	12	12	4	19	48	20	1
10 57 20	13	13	5	21	49	23	3	13	13	5	21	8	22	3	13	13	4	20	26	21	2
11 1 3	14	14	6	22	29	24	4	14	14	5	21	47	23	4	14	14	5	21	4	22	3
11 4 45	15	15	6	23	8	24	5	15	15	6	22	26	24	5	15	15	6	21	43	23	4
11 8 28	16	16	7	23	47	25	6	16	16	7	23	5	24	6	16	16	6	22	21	23	5
11 12 10	17	17	8	24	26	26	7	17	16	7	23	43	25	7	17	17	7	22	59	24	6
11 15 52	18	17	9	25	6	27	8	18	17	8	24	22	26	8	18	17	8	23	37	25	7
11 19 33	19	18	9	25	45	28	9	19	18	9	25	1	27	9	19	18	9	24	15	26	9
11 23 15	20	19	10	26	24	28	10	20	19	10	25	39	28	10	20	19	9	24	53	27	10
11 26 56	21	20	11	27	4	29	11	21	20	10	26	18	28	11	21	20	10	25	31	28	11
11 30 37	22	21	11	27	43	♑	12	22	21	11	26	57	29	12	22	20	11	26	10	28	12
11 34 17	23	22	12	28	22	1	14	23	21	12	27	36	♑	13	23	21	11	26	48	29	13
11 37 58	24	22	13	29	2	2	15	24	22	12	28	15	1	14	24	22	12	27	26	♑	14
11 41 39	25	23	14	29	42	3	16	25	23	13	28	54	2	15	25	23	13	28	5	1	15
11 45 19	26	24	14	0♐	21	4	17	26	24	14	29	33	3	16	26	24	13	28	43	2	16
11 48 59	27	25	15	1	1	4	18	27	25	15	0♐	12	4	18	27	25	14	29	22	3	17
11 52 40	28	26	16	1	41	5	19	28	26	15	0	51	4	19	28	25	15	0♐	0	3	18
11 56 20	29	27	16	2	21	6	20	29	26	16	1	31	5	20	29	26	16	0	39	4	19
HOUSES	4	5	6	7		8	9	4	5	6	7		8	9	4	5	6	7		8	9

LATITUDE 52° S. LATITUDE 53° S. LATITUDE 54° S.

LATITUDE 52° N. LATITUDE 53° N. LATITUDE 54° N.

SIDEREAL TIME	10 ♎	11 ♎	12 ♏	ASC ♐	2 ♑	3 ♒	10 ♎	11 ♎	12 ♏	ASC ♐	2 ♑	3 ♒	10 ♎	11 ♎	12 ♏	ASC ♐	2 ♑	3 ♒
H M S	°	°	°	° '	°	°	°	°	°	° '	°	°	°	°	°	° '	°	°
12 0 0	0	27	17	3 1	7	21	0	27	17	2 10	6	21	0	27	16	1 18	5	21
12 3 40	1	28	18	3 41	8	22	1	28	17	2 49	7	22	1	28	17	1 57	6	22
12 7 20	2	29	19	4 21	9	23	2	29	18	3 29	8	23	2	29	18	2 36	7	23
12 11 1	3	♏	19	5 2	10	25	3	♏	19	4 9	9	24	3	♏	18	3 15	8	24
12 14 41	4	1	20	5 42	11	26	4	0	20	4 49	10	25	4	0	19	3 54	9	25
12 18 21	5	1	21	6 23	12	27	5	1	20	5 29	11	27	5	1	20	4 33	10	26
12 22 2	6	2	21	7 4	13	28	6	2	21	6 9	12	28	6	2	20	5 13	11	27
12 25 42	7	3	22	7 45	14	29	7	3	22	6 50	13	29	7	3	21	5 53	12	29
12 29 23	8	4	23	8 26	15	♓	8	4	22	7 30	14	♓	8	4	22	6 33	13	♓
12 33 4	9	5	24	9 8	16	1	9	5	23	8 11	15	1	9	4	23	7 13	14	1
12 36 45	10	6	24	9 49	17	3	10	5	24	8 52	16	2	10	5	23	7 53	15	2
12 40 27	11	6	25	10 31	18	4	11	6	24	9 33	17	4	11	6	24	8 34	16	3
12 44 8	12	7	26	11 13	19	5	12	7	25	10 15	18	5	12	7	25	9 14	17	5
12 47 50	13	8	26	11 56	20	6	13	8	26	10 57	19	6	13	8	25	9 55	18	6
12 51 32	14	9	27	12 39	21	7	14	9	27	11 39	20	7	14	8	26	10 37	19	7
12 55 15	15	10	28	13 22	22	9	15	9	27	12 21	21	8	15	9	27	11 18	20	8
12 58 57	16	10	29	14 5	23	10	16	10	28	13 3	22	10	16	10	27	12 0	21	9
13 2 40	17	11	29	14 48	24	11	17	11	29	13 46	23	11	17	11	28	12 42	22	11
13 6 24	18	12	♐	15 32	25	12	18	12	29	14 29	24	12	18	12	29	13 24	23	12
13 10 8	19	13	1	16 16	26	13	19	13	♐	15 13	25	13	19	12	♐	14 7	24	13
13 13 52	20	14	2	17 1	27	15	20	14	1	15 57	26	15	20	13	0	14 50	25	14
13 17 36	21	15	2	17 46	28	16	21	14	2	16 41	27	16	21	14	1	15 34	26	16
13 21 21	22	15	3	18 31	29	17	22	15	2	17 26	28	17	22	15	2	16 17	27	17
13 25 7	23	16	4	19 17	♒	18	23	16	3	18 11	♒	18	23	16	2	17 1	29	18
13 28 52	24	17	5	20 3	2	20	24	17	4	18 56	1	20	24	17	3	17 46	♒	19
13 32 39	25	18	5	20 50	3	21	25	18	5	19 42	2	21	25	17	4	18 31	1	21
13 36 26	26	19	6	21 37	4	22	26	18	5	20 28	3	22	26	18	5	19 16	2	22
13 40 13	27	20	7	22 24	5	23	27	19	6	21 15	4	23	27	19	5	20 2	3	23
13 44 1	28	20	8	23 13	7	25	28	20	7	22 2	6	25	28	20	6	20 49	5	25
13 47 49	29	21	8	24 1	8	26	29	21	8	22 50	7	26	29	21	7	21 35	6	26
13 51 38	♏	22	9	24 50	9	27	♏	22	8	23 38	8	27	♏	21	8	22 23	7	27
13 55 28	1	23	10	25 40	10	28	1	23	9	24 27	10	28	1	22	8	23 11	9	28
13 59 18	2	24	11	26 30	12	♈	2	23	10	25 16	11	♈	2	23	9	23 59	10	♈
14 3 9	3	24	11	27 21	13	1	3	24	11	26 7	12	1	3	24	10	24 48	11	1
14 7 0	4	25	12	28 13	14	2	4	25	11	26 57	14	2	4	25	11	25 38	13	2
14 10 52	5	26	13	29 5	16	4	5	26	12	27 49	15	4	5	26	12	26 29	14	4
14 14 45	6	27	14	29 58	17	5	6	27	13	28 41	16	5	6	26	12	27 20	16	5
14 18 38	7	28	15	0♑ 52	19	6	7	28	14	29 34	18	6	7	27	13	28 12	17	6
14 22 32	8	29	15	1 47	20	8	8	28	15	0♑ 27	19	8	8	28	14	29 4	18	8
14 26 26	9	♐	16	2 42	21	9	9	29	15	1 22	21	9	9	29	15	29 58	20	9
14 30 22	10	0	17	3 38	23	10	10	♐	16	2 17	22	10	10	♐	15	0♑ 52	21	10
14 34 17	11	1	18	4 35	24	11	11	1	17	3 13	24	12	11	1	16	1 47	23	12
14 38 14	12	2	19	5 33	26	13	12	2	18	4 11	25	13	12	1	17	2 43	25	13
14 42 11	13	3	19	6 33	28	14	13	3	19	5 9	27	14	13	2	18	3 40	26	14
14 46 10	14	4	20	7 33	29	15	14	3	20	6 8	28	15	14	3	19	4 38	28	16
HOUSES	4	5	6	7	8	9	4	5	6	7	8	9	4	5	6	7	8	9

LATITUDE 52° S. LATITUDE 53° S. LATITUDE 54° S.

LATITUDE 52° N.   LATITUDE 53° N.   LATITUDE 54° N.

SIDEREAL TIME	10 ♏	11 ♐	12 ♐	ASC ♑	2 ♓	3 ♈	10 ♏	11 ♐	12 ♐	ASC ♑	2 ♓	3 ♈	10 ♏	11 ♐	12 ♐	ASC ♑	2 ♒	3 ♈
H M S	°	°	°	° '	°	°	°	°	°	° '	°	°	°	°	°	° '	°	°
14 50 8	15	5	21	8 34	1	17	15	4	20	7 8	0	17	15	4	20	5 38	29	17
14 54 8	16	6	22	9 36	2	18	16	5	21	8 9	2	18	16	5	20	6 38	♓	18
14 58 8	17	6	23	10 39	4	19	17	6	22	9 12	3	19	17	6	21	7 39	3	20
15 2 9	18	7	24	11 44	5	21	18	7	23	10 16	5	21	18	7	22	8 42	4	21
15 6 10	19	8	25	12 50	7	22	19	8	24	11 21	7	22	19	7	23	9 46	6	22
15 10 13	20	9	26	13 57	9	23	20	9	25	12 27	8	23	20	8	24	10 51	8	24
15 14 16	21	10	26	15 6	10	24	21	10	26	13 35	10	25	21	9	25	11 58	10	25
15 18 20	22	11	27	16 16	12	26	22	10	26	14 44	12	26	22	10	26	13 6	11	26
15 22 24	23	12	28	17 28	14	27	23	11	27	15 55	14	27	23	11	27	14 16	13	28
15 26 30	24	13	29	18 41	16	28	24	12	28	17 7	15	29	24	12	27	15 27	15	29
15 30 36	25	13	♑	19 56	17	♉	25	13	29	18 21	17	♉	25	13	28	16 40	17	♉
15 34 42	26	14	1	21 13	19	1	26	14	♑	19 37	19	1	26	14	29	17 55	19	2
15 38 50	27	15	2	22 31	21	2	27	15	1	20 55	21	3	27	14	♑	19 12	20	3
15 42 58	28	16	3	23 52	23	4	28	16	2	22 15	22	4	28	15	1	20 31	22	4
15 47 7	29	17	4	25 14	24	5	29	17	3	23 37	24	5	29	16	2	21 52	24	5
15 51 16	♐	18	5	26 39	26	6	♐	18	4	25 1	26	6	♐	17	3	23 15	26	7
15 55 26	1	19	6	28 5	28	7	1	18	5	26 27	28	8	1	18	4	24 41	28	8
15 59 37	2	20	7	29 34	♈	9	2	19	6	27 55	♈	9	2	19	5	26 9	♈	9
16 3 49	3	21	8	♒ 5	2	10	3	20	7	29 26	2	10	3	20	6	27 39	2	11
16 8 1	4	22	9	2 39	3	11	4	21	8	1♒ 0	4	12	4	21	7	29 13	4	12
16 12 14	5	23	10	4 15	5	12	5	22	9	2 36	5	13	5	22	8	0♒49	6	13
16 16 27	6	24	11	5 54	7	14	6	23	10	4 16	7	14	6	23	9	2 28	7	14
16 20 41	7	24	12	7 36	9	15	7	24	11	5 58	9	15	7	24	10	4 10	9	16
16 24 56	8	25	13	9 20	11	16	8	25	12	7 43	11	17	8	25	11	5 55	11	17
16 29 11	9	26	15	11 8	13	17	9	26	14	9 31	13	18	9	26	13	7 44	13	18
16 33 27	10	27	16	12 58	14	19	10	27	15	11 22	15	19	10	26	14	9 36	15	19
16 37 43	11	28	17	14 52	16	20	11	28	16	13 17	17	20	11	27	15	11 32	17	21
16 41 59	12	29	18	16 48	18	21	12	29	17	15 15	18	22	12	28	16	13 32	19	22
16 46 17	13	♑	19	18 48	20	22	13	♑	18	17 17	20	23	13	29	17	15 35	21	23
16 50 34	14	1	20	20 51	22	24	14	1	19	19 22	22	24	14	♑	18	17 43	22	24
16 54 53	15	2	22	22 57	23	25	15	2	21	21 31	24	25	15	1	20	19 54	24	26
16 59 11	16	3	23	25 7	25	26	16	3	22	23 43	26	26	16	2	21	22 10	26	27
17 3 30	17	4	24	27 19	27	27	17	4	23	26 0	27	28	17	3	22	24 30	28	28
17 7 49	18	5	25	29 35	29	28	18	5	24	28 19	29	29	18	4	23	26 54	♉	29
17 12 9	19	6	27	1♓54	♉	II	19	6	26	0♓43	♉	II	19	5	25	29 21	2	II
17 16 29	20	7	28	4 16	2	1	20	7	27	3 9	3	1	20	6	26	1♓53	3	2
17 20 49	21	8	29	6 41	4	2	21	8	28	5 40	4	2	21	7	27	4 29	5	3
17 25 10	22	9	♒	9 9	5	3	22	9	♒	8 13	6	3	22	9	29	7 9	7	4
17 29 31	23	10	2	11 39	7	4	23	10	1	10 49	8	5	23	10	♒	9 52	8	5
17 33 51	24	12	3	14 12	9	5	24	11	2	13 28	9	6	24	11	1	12 38	10	6
17 38 13	25	13	5	16 47	10	6	25	12	4	16 10	11	7	25	12	3	15 27	12	7
17 42 34	26	14	6	19 23	12	8	26	13	5	18 53	13	8	26	13	4	18 18	13	8
17 46 55	27	15	8	22 1	13	9	27	14	7	21 38	14	9	27	14	6	21 12	15	10
17 51 17	28	16	9	24 40	15	10	28	15	8	24 25	16	10	28	15	7	24 7	17	11
17 55 38	29	17	10	27 20	17	11	29	16	10	27 12	17	11	29	16	9	27 3	18	12
HOUSES	4	5	6	7	8	9	4	5	6	7	8	9	4	5	6	7	8	9

LATITUDE 52° S.   LATITUDE 53° S.   LATITUDE 54° S.

LATITUDE 52° N.   LATITUDE 53° N.   LATITUDE 54° N.

SIDEREAL TIME	10 ♑	11 ♑	12 ♒	ASC ♈	2 ♉	3 ♊	10 ♑	11 ♑	12 ♒	ASC ♈	2 ♉	3 ♊	10 ♑	11 ♑	12 ♒	ASC ♈	2 ♉	3 ♊
H M S	°	°	°	° '	°	°	°	°	°	° '	°	°	°	°	°	° '	°	°
18 0 0	0	18	12	0 0	18	12	0	18	11	0 0	19	12	0	17	10	0 0	20	13
18 4 22	1	19	13	2 40	20	13	1	19	13	2 48	20	14	1	18	12	2 57	21	14
18 8 43	2	20	15	5 20	21	14	2	20	14	5 35	22	15	2	19	13	5 53	23	15
18 13 5	3	21	17	7 59	22	15	3	21	16	8 22	23	16	3	20	15	8 48	24	16
18 17 26	4	22	18	10 37	24	16	4	22	17	11 7	25	17	4	22	17	11 42	26	17
18 21 47	5	24	20	13 13	25	17	5	23	19	13 50	26	18	5	23	18	14 33	27	18
18 26 9	6	25	21	15 48	27	18	6	24	21	16 32	28	19	6	24	20	17 22	29	19
18 30 29	7	26	23	18 21	28	20	7	25	22	19 11	29	20	7	25	22	20 8	♊	20
18 34 50	8	27	25	20 51	29	21	8	27	24	21 47	♊	21	8	26	23	22 51	1	21
18 39 11	9	28	26	23 19	♊	22	9	28	26	24 20	2	22	9	27	25	25 31	3	23
18 43 31	10	29	28	25 44	2	23	10	29	27	26 51	3	23	10	28	27	28 7	4	24
18 47 51	11	♒	♓	28 6	3	24	11	♒	29	29 17	4	24	11	♒	28	0♉ 39	5	25
18 52 11	12	2	1	0♉ 25	5	25	12	1	♓	1♉ 41	6	25	12	1	♓	3 6	7	26
18 56 30	13	3	3	2 41	6	26	13	2	3	4 0	7	26	13	2	2	5 30	8	27
19 0 49	14	4	5	4 53	7	27	14	4	4	6 17	8	27	14	3	4	7 50	9	28
19 5 7	15	5	7	7 3	8	28	15	5	6	8 29	9	28	15	4	6	10 6	10	29
19 9 26	16	6	8	9 9	10	29	16	6	8	10 38	11	29	16	6	8	12 17	12	♋
19 13 43	17	8	10	11 12	11	♋	17	7	10	12 43	12	♋	17	7	9	14 25	13	1
19 18 0	18	9	12	13 12	12	1	18	8	12	14 45	13	1	18	8	11	16 28	14	2
19 22 17	19	10	14	15 8	13	2	19	10	13	16 43	14	2	19	9	13	18 28	15	3
19 26 33	20	11	16	17 2	14	3	20	11	15	18 38	15	3	20	11	15	20 24	16	4
19 30 49	21	13	17	18 52	15	4	21	12	17	20 29	16	4	21	12	17	22 16	17	4
19 35 4	22	14	19	20 40	17	5	22	13	19	22 17	18	5	22	13	19	24 5	19	5
19 39 19	23	15	21	22 24	18	6	23	15	21	24 2	19	6	23	14	21	25 50	20	6
19 43 33	24	16	23	24 6	19	6	24	16	23	25 44	20	7	24	16	23	27 32	21	7
19 47 46	25	18	25	25 45	20	7	25	17	25	27 24	21	8	25	17	24	29 11	22	8
19 51 59	26	19	27	27 21	21	8	26	18	26	29 0	22	9	26	18	26	0♊ 47	23	9
19 56 11	27	20	28	28 55	22	9	27	20	28	0♊ 34	23	10	27	19	28	2 21	24	10
20 0 23	28	21	♈	0♊ 26	23	10	28	21	♈	2 5	24	11	28	21	♈	3 51	25	11
20 4 34	29	23	2	1 55	24	11	29	22	2	3 33	25	12	29	22	2	5 19	26	12
20 8 44	♒	24	4	3 21	25	12	♒	24	4	4 59	26	12	♒	23	4	6 45	27	13
20 12 53	1	25	6	4 46	26	13	1	25	6	6 23	27	13	1	25	6	8 8	28	14
20 17 2	2	26	7	6 8	27	14	2	26	8	7 45	28	14	2	26	8	9 29	29	15
20 21 10	3	28	9	7 29	28	15	3	27	9	9 5	29	15	3	27	10	10 48	♋	16
20 25 18	4	29	11	8 47	29	16	4	29	11	10 23	♋	16	4	28	11	12 5	1	16
20 29 24	5	♓	13	10 4	♋	17	5	♓	13	11 39	1	17	5	♓	13	13 20	2	17
20 33 30	6	2	14	11 19	1	17	6	1	15	12 53	2	18	6	1	15	14 33	3	18
20 37 36	7	3	16	12 32	2	18	7	3	16	14 5	3	19	7	2	17	15 44	3	19
20 41 40	8	4	18	13 44	3	19	8	4	18	15 16	3	20	8	4	19	16 54	4	20
20 45 44	9	6	20	14 54	4	20	9	5	20	16 25	4	20	9	5	20	18 2	5	21
20 49 47	10	7	21	16 3	4	21	10	7	22	17 33	5	21	10	6	22	19 9	6	22
20 53 50	11	8	23	17 10	5	22	11	8	23	18 39	6	22	11	8	24	20 14	7	23
20 57 51	12	9	25	18 16	6	23	12	9	25	19 44	7	23	12	9	26	21 18	8	23
21 1 52	13	11	26	19 21	7	24	13	11	27	20 48	8	24	13	10	27	22 21	9	24
21 5 52	14	12	28	20 24	8	24	14	12	28	21 51	9	25	14	12	29	23 22	10	25
HOUSES	4	5	6	7	8	9	4	5	6	7	8	9	4	5	6	7	8	9

	LATITUDE 52° N.						LATITUDE 53° N.						LATITUDE 54° N.					
SIDEREAL TIME	10 ♒	11 ♓	12 ♈	ASC ♊	2 ♋	3 ♋	10 ♒	11 ♓	12 ♉	ASC ♊	2 ♋	3 ♋	10 ♒	11 ♓	12 ♉	ASC ♊	2 ♋	3 ♋
H M S	°	°	°	° '	°	°	°	°	°	° '	°	°	°	°	°	° '	°	°
21 9 52	15	13	29	21 26	9	25	15	13	0	22 52	10	26	15	13	1	24 22	10	26
21 13 50	16	15	♉	22 27	10	26	16	15	2	23 52	10	27	16	14	2	25 22	11	27
21 17 49	17	16	2	23 27	11	27	17	16	3	24 51	11	27	17	16	4	26 20	12	28
21 21 46	18	17	4	24 27	11	28	18	17	5	25 49	12	28	18	17	5	27 17	13	29
21 25 42	19	19	6	25 25	12	29	19	18	6	26 47	13	29	19	18	7	28 13	14	29
21 29 38	20	20	7	26 22	13	♌	20	20	8	27 43	14	♌	20	20	9	29 8	15	♌
21 33 34	21	21	9	27 18	14	0	21	21	9	28 38	15	1	21	21	10	0♋ 2	15	1
21 37 28	22	22	10	28 13	15	1	22	22	11	29 33	15	2	22	22	12	0 56	16	2
21 41 22	23	24	11	29 8	15	2	23	24	12	0♋ 26	16	3	23	24	13	1 48	17	3
21 45 15	24	25	13	0♋ 2	16	3	24	25	14	1 19	17	3	24	25	14	2 40	18	4
21 49 8	25	26	14	0 55	17	4	25	26	15	2 11	18	4	25	26	16	3 31	18	4
21 53 0	26	28	16	1 47	18	5	26	28	16	3 3	19	5	26	28	17	4 22	19	5
21 56 51	27	29	17	2 39	19	6	27	29	18	3 53	19	6	27	29	19	5 12	20	6
22 0 42	28	♈	18	3 30	19	6	28	♈	19	4 44	20	7	28	♈	20	6 1	21	7
22 4 32	29	2	20	4 20	20	7	29	2	20	5 33	21	7	29	2	21	6 49	22	8
22 8 22	♓	3	21	5 10	21	8	♓	3	22	6 22	22	8	♓	3	23	7 37	22	9
22 12 11	1	4	22	5 59	22	9	1	4	23	7 10	22	9	1	4	24	8 25	23	9
22 15 59	2	5	23	6 47	22	10	2	5	24	7 58	23	10	2	5	25	9 11	24	10
22 19 47	3	7	25	7 36	23	10	3	7	26	8 45	24	11	3	7	27	9 58	25	11
22 23 34	4	8	26	8 23	24	11	4	8	27	9 32	25	12	4	8	28	10 44	25	12
22 27 21	5	9	27	9 10	25	12	5	9	28	10 18	25	12	5	9	29	11 29	26	13
22 31 8	6	10	28	9 57	25	13	6	10	29	11 4	26	13	6	11	♊	12 14	27	13
22 34 53	7	12	29	10 43	26	14	7	12	♊	11 49	27	14	7	12	1	12 59	28	14
22 38 39	8	13	♊	11 29	27	15	8	13	2	12 34	28	15	8	13	3	13 43	28	15
22 42 24	9	14	2	12 14	28	15	9	14	3	13 19	28	16	9	14	4	14 26	29	16
22 46 8	10	15	3	12 59	28	16	10	15	4	14 3	29	16	10	16	5	15 10	♌	17
22 49 52	11	17	4	13 44	29	17	11	17	5	14 47	♌	17	11	17	6	15 53	0	18
22 53 36	12	18	5	14 28	♌	18	12	18	6	15 31	1	18	12	18	7	16 36	1	18
22 57 20	13	19	6	15 12	1	19	13	19	7	16 14	1	19	13	19	8	17 18	2	19
23 1 3	14	20	7	15 55	1	20	14	20	8	16 57	2	20	14	21	9	18 0	3	20
23 4 45	15	21	8	16 38	2	20	15	22	9	17 39	3	21	15	22	10	18 42	3	21
23 8 28	16	23	9	17 21	3	21	16	23	10	18 21	3	21	16	23	11	19 23	4	22
23 12 10	17	24	10	18 4	4	22	17	24	11	19 3	4	22	17	24	12	20 5	5	22
23 15 52	18	25	11	18 47	4	23	18	25	12	19 45	5	23	18	25	13	20 46	5	23
23 19 33	19	26	12	19 29	5	24	19	26	13	20 27	6	24	19	27	14	21 26	6	24
23 23 15	20	27	13	20 11	6	24	20	28	14	21 8	6	25	20	28	15	22 7	7	25
23 26 56	21	29	14	20 52	6	25	21	29	15	21 49	7	25	21	29	16	22 47	7	25
23 30 37	22	♉	15	21 34	7	26	22	♉	16	22 30	8	26	22	♉	17	23 27	8	26
23 34 17	23	1	16	22 15	8	27	23	1	17	23 10	8	27	23	1	18	24 7	9	27
23 37 58	24	2	17	22 56	9	28	24	2	18	23 51	9	28	24	3	19	24 47	10	28
23 41 39	25	3	18	23 37	9	29	25	3	19	24 31	10	29	25	4	20	25 27	10	29
23 45 19	26	4	19	24 18	10	29	26	5	20	25 11	10	♍	26	5	21	26 6	11	♍
23 48 59	27	5	20	24 58	11	♍	27	6	21	25 51	11	0	27	6	22	26 45	12	0
23 52 40	28	7	21	25 39	11	1	28	7	22	26 31	12	1	28	7	23	27 24	12	1
23 56 20	29	8	22	26 19	12	2	29	8	23	27 11	13	2	29	8	24	28 3	13	2
HOUSES	4	5	6	7	8	9	4	5	6	7	8	9	4	5	6	7	8	9

LATITUDE 52° S.   LATITUDE 53° S.   LATITUDE 54° S.

LATITUDE 55° N.   LATITUDE 56° N.   LATITUDE 57° N.

SIDEREAL TIME	10 ♈	11 ♉	12 ♊	ASC ♋		2 ♌	3 ♍	10 ♈	11 ♉	12 ♊	ASC ♌		2 ♌	3 ♍	10 ♈	11 ♉	12 ♊	ASC ♌		2 ♌	3 ♍
H M S	°	°	°	°	'	°	°	°	°	°	°	'	°	°	°	°	°	°	'	°	°
0 0 0	0	10	26	29	36	14	3	0	10	27	0	32	15	3	0	11	28	1	30	15	3
0 3 40	1	11	27	0♌	15	15	4	1	11	28	1	10	15	4	1	12	29	2	6	16	4
0 7 20	2	12	28	0	53	16	5	2	12	29	1	47	16	5	2	13	♋	2	43	17	5
0 11 1	3	13	28	1	31	16	6	3	14	29	2	24	17	6	3	14	1	3	19	17	6
0 14 41	4	14	29	2	8	17	6	4	15	♋	3	1	18	7	4	15	1	3	56	18	7
0 18 21	5	15	♋	2	46	18	7	5	16	1	3	38	18	7	5	16	2	4	32	19	7
0 22 2	6	16	1	3	24	18	8	6	17	2	4	15	19	8	6	17	3	5	9	19	8
0 25 43	7	18	2	4	2	19	9	7	18	3	4	52	20	9	7	18	4	5	45	20	9
0 29 23	8	19	3	4	39	20	10	8	19	4	5	29	20	10	8	20	5	6	21	21	10
0 33 4	9	20	3	5	17	20	10	9	20	4	6	6	21	11	9	21	6	6	58	21	11
0 36 45	10	21	4	5	54	21	11	10	21	5	6	43	22	11	10	22	6	7	34	22	12
0 40 27	11	22	5	6	32	22	12	11	22	6	7	20	22	12	11	23	7	8	10	23	12
0 44 8	12	23	6	7	9	23	13	12	23	7	7	57	23	13	12	24	8	8	46	23	13
0 47 50	13	24	7	7	47	23	14	13	24	8	8	34	24	14	13	25	9	9	22	24	14
0 51 32	14	25	7	8	24	24	15	14	26	8	9	11	24	15	14	26	9	9	59	25	15
0 55 15	15	26	8	9	2	25	15	15	27	9	9	48	25	16	15	27	10	10	35	25	16
0 58 57	16	27	9	9	39	25	16	16	28	10	10	24	26	16	16	28	11	11	11	26	16
1 2 40	17	28	10	10	17	26	17	17	29	11	11	1	26	17	17	29	12	11	47	27	17
1 6 24	18	29	11	10	54	27	18	18	♊	12	11	38	27	18	18	♊	12	12	23	28	18
1 10 8	19	♊	11	11	32	27	19	19	1	12	12	15	28	19	19	1	13	13	0	28	19
1 13 52	20	1	12	12	10	28	20	20	2	13	12	52	29	20	20	2	14	13	36	29	20
1 17 36	21	2	13	12	47	29	20	21	3	14	13	29	29	20	21	3	15	14	12	♍	21
1 21 21	22	3	14	13	25	♍	21	22	4	15	14	6	♍	21	22	4	16	14	49	0	21
1 25 7	23	4	14	14	2	0	22	23	5	15	14	43	1	22	23	5	16	15	25	1	22
1 28 52	24	5	15	14	40	1	23	24	6	16	15	20	1	23	24	6	17	16	2	2	23
1 32 39	25	6	16	15	18	2	24	25	7	17	15	58	2	24	25	7	18	16	38	2	24
1 36 26	26	7	17	15	56	2	25	26	8	18	16	35	3	25	26	8	18	17	15	3	25
1 40 13	27	8	17	16	34	3	26	27	9	18	17	12	3	26	27	9	19	17	52	4	26
1 44 1	28	9	18	17	12	4	26	28	10	19	17	50	4	26	28	10	20	18	28	4	26
1 47 49	29	10	19	17	50	5	27	29	11	20	18	27	5	27	29	11	21	19	5	5	27
1 51 38	♉	11	20	18	28	5	28	♉	12	21	19	5	6	28	♉	12	21	19	42	6	28
1 55 28	1	12	21	19	6	6	29	1	13	21	19	42	6	29	1	13	22	20	19	7	29
1 59 18	2	13	21	19	45	7	♎	2	14	22	20	20	7	♎	2	14	23	20	56	7	♎
2 3 9	3	14	22	20	23	8	1	3	15	23	20	58	8	1	3	15	24	21	33	8	1
2 7 0	4	15	23	21	1	8	2	4	16	24	21	36	9	2	4	16	24	22	11	9	2
2 10 52	5	16	24	21	40	9	2	5	17	24	22	14	9	2	5	17	25	22	48	9	2
2 14 45	6	17	24	22	19	10	3	6	18	25	22	52	10	3	6	18	26	23	26	10	3
2 18 38	7	18	25	22	58	11	4	7	19	26	23	30	11	4	7	19	27	24	3	11	4
2 22 32	8	19	26	23	36	11	5	8	20	27	24	8	11	5	8	20	27	24	41	12	5
2 26 26	9	20	27	24	15	12	6	9	21	27	24	47	12	6	9	21	28	25	19	12	6
2 30 22	10	21	27	24	55	13	7	10	21	28	25	25	13	7	10	22	29	25	57	13	7
2 34 17	11	22	28	25	34	14	8	11	22	29	26	4	14	8	11	23	♌	26	35	14	8
2 38 14	12	23	29	26	13	14	9	12	23	♌	26	43	14	9	12	24	0	27	13	15	9
2 42 11	13	24	♌	26	53	15	10	13	24	0	27	22	15	9	13	25	1	27	51	15	9
2 46 10	14	25	0	27	32	16	10	14	25	1	28	1	16	10	14	26	2	28	30	16	10
HOUSES	4	5	6	7		8	9	4	5	6	7		8	9	4	5	6	7		8	9

LATITUDE 55° S.   LATITUDE 56° S.   LATITUDE 57° S.

LATITUDE 55° N. LATITUDE 56° N. LATITUDE 57° N.

SIDEREAL TIME	10 ♉	11 ♊	12 ♌	ASC ♌		2 ♍	3 ♎	10 ♉	11 ♊	12 ♌	ASC ♌		2 ♍	3 ♎	10 ♉	11 ♊	12 ♌	ASC ♌		2 ♍	3 ♎
H M S	°	°	°	°	'	°	°	°	°	°	°	'	°	°	°	°	°	°	'	°	°
2 50 8	15	26	1	28	12	17	11	15	26	2	28	40	17	11	15	27	2	29	8	17	11
2 54 8	16	27	2	28	52	17	12	16	27	3	29	19	17	12	16	28	3	29	47	18	12
2 58 8	17	27	3	29	32	18	13	17	28	3	29	58	18	13	17	29	4	0♍	25	18	13
3 2 9	18	28	3	0♍	12	19	14	18	29	4	0♍	38	19	14	18	♋	5	1	4	19	14
3 6 10	19	29	4	0	52	20	15	19	♋	5	1	17	20	15	19	0	5	1	43	20	15
3 10 13	20	♋	5	1	33	20	16	20	1	6	1	57	21	16	20	1	6	2	23	21	16
3 14 16	21	1	6	2	13	21	17	21	2	6	2	37	21	17	21	2	7	3	2	21	17
3 18 20	22	2	6	2	54	22	18	22	3	7	3	17	22	18	22	3	8	3	41	22	17
3 22 24	23	3	7	3	34	23	19	23	4	8	3	57	23	18	23	4	8	4	21	23	18
3 26 30	24	4	8	4	15	24	19	24	4	9	4	38	24	19	24	5	9	5	1	24	19
3 30 36	25	5	9	4	56	24	20	25	5	9	5	18	24	20	25	6	10	5	40	24	20
3 34 42	26	6	10	5	38	25	21	26	6	10	5	59	25	21	26	7	11	6	20	25	21
3 38 50	27	7	10	6	19	26	22	27	7	11	6	39	26	22	27	8	11	7	0	26	22
3 42 58	28	8	11	7	0	27	23	28	8	12	7	20	27	23	28	9	12	7	41	27	23
3 47 7	29	9	12	7	42	28	24	29	9	12	8	1	28	24	29	10	13	8	21	28	24
3 51 16	♊	9	13	8	24	28	25	♊	10	13	8	42	28	25	♊	11	14	9	1	28	25
3 55 26	1	10	13	9	5	29	26	1	11	14	9	23	29	26	1	11	14	9	42	29	26
3 59 37	2	11	14	9	47	♎	27	2	12	15	10	5	♎	27	2	12	15	10	23	♎	26
4 3 49	3	12	15	10	29	1	28	3	13	15	10	46	1	28	3	13	16	11	3	1	27
4 8 1	4	13	16	11	12	2	29	4	14	16	11	28	2	28	4	14	17	11	44	2	28
4 12 14	5	14	17	11	54	2	♏	5	15	17	12	10	2	29	5	15	18	12	26	2	29
4 16 27	6	15	17	12	36	3	1	6	15	18	12	51	3	♏	6	16	18	13	7	3	♏
4 20 41	7	16	18	13	19	4	1	7	16	19	13	33	4	1	7	17	19	13	48	4	1
4 24 56	8	17	19	14	1	5	2	8	17	19	14	15	5	2	8	18	20	14	29	5	2
4 29 11	9	18	20	14	44	6	3	9	18	20	14	57	6	3	9	19	21	15	11	6	3
4 33 27	10	19	21	15	27	6	4	10	19	21	15	40	6	4	10	20	21	15	53	6	4
4 37 43	11	20	21	16	10	7	5	11	20	22	16	22	7	5	11	20	22	16	34	7	5
4 41 59	12	20	22	16	53	8	6	12	21	23	17	4	8	6	12	21	23	17	16	8	6
4 46 17	13	21	23	17	36	9	7	13	22	23	17	47	9	7	13	22	24	17	58	9	7
4 50 34	14	22	24	18	20	10	8	14	23	24	18	30	10	8	14	23	25	18	40	10	7
4 54 53	15	23	25	19	3	11	9	15	24	25	19	12	10	9	15	24	25	19	22	10	8
4 59 11	16	24	25	19	46	11	10	16	25	26	19	55	11	10	16	25	26	20	4	11	9
5 3 30	17	25	26	20	30	12	11	17	25	27	20	38	12	11	17	26	27	20	46	12	10
5 7 49	18	26	27	21	13	13	12	18	26	27	21	21	13	11	18	27	28	21	29	13	11
5 12 9	19	27	28	21	57	14	13	19	27	28	22	4	14	12	19	28	29	22	11	14	12
5 16 29	20	28	29	22	41	15	14	20	28	29	22	47	15	13	20	29	29	22	54	14	13
5 20 49	21	29	♏	23	25	16	15	21	29	♏	23	30	15	14	21	♌	♏	23	36	15	14
5 25 10	22	♌	0	24	8	16	15	22	♌	1	24	13	16	15	22	0	1	24	19	16	15
5 29 31	23	1	1	24	52	17	16	23	1	1	24	57	17	16	23	1	2	25	1	17	16
5 33 51	24	2	2	25	36	18	17	24	2	2	25	40	18	17	24	2	3	25	44	18	17
5 38 13	25	2	3	26	20	19	18	25	3	3	26	23	19	18	25	3	3	26	26	18	18
5 42 34	26	3	4	27	4	20	19	26	4	4	27	7	20	19	26	4	4	27	9	19	19
5 46 55	27	4	4	27	48	21	20	27	5	5	27	50	20	20	27	5	5	27	52	20	19
5 51 17	28	5	5	28	32	21	21	28	6	6	28	33	21	21	28	6	6	28	35	21	20
5 55 38	29	6	6	29	16	22	22	29	7	6	29	17	22	22	29	7	7	29	17	22	21
HOUSES	4	5	6	7		8	9	4	5	6	7		8	9	4	5	6	7		8	9

LATITUDE 55° S. LATITUDE 56° S. LATITUDE 57° S.

LATITUDE 55° N. LATITUDE 56° N. LATITUDE 57° N.

SIDEREAL TIME	10 ♋	11 ♌	12 ♍	ASC ♎	2 ♎	3 ♏	10 ♋	11 ♌	12 ♍	ASC ♎	2 ♎	3 ♏	10 ♋	11 ♌	12 ♍	ASC ♎	2 ♎	3 ♏
H M S	°	°	°	° '	°	°	°	°	°	° '	°	°	°	°	°	° '	°	°
6 0 0	0	7	7	0 0	23	23	0	7	7	0 0	23	23	0	8	7	0 0	23	22
6 4 22	1	8	8	0 44	24	24	1	8	8	0 43	24	23	1	9	8	0 43	23	23
6 8 43	2	9	9	1 28	25	25	2	9	9	1 27	24	24	2	10	9	1 25	24	24
6 13 5	3	10	9	2 12	26	26	3	10	10	2 10	25	25	3	11	10	2 8	25	25
6 17 26	4	11	10	2 56	26	27	4	11	10	2 53	26	26	4	11	11	2 51	26	26
6 21 47	5	12	11	3 40	27	28	5	12	11	3 37	27	27	5	12	12	3 34	27	27
6 26 9	6	13	12	4 24	28	28	6	13	12	4 20	28	28	6	13	12	4 16	27	28
6 30 29	7	14	13	5 8	29	29	7	14	13	5 3	29	29	7	14	13	4 59	28	29
6 34 50	8	15	14	5 52	♏	♐	8	15	14	5 47	29	♐	8	15	14	5 41	29	♐
6 39 11	9	15	14	6 35	0	1	9	16	15	6 30	♏	1	9	16	15	6 24	♏	0
6 43 31	10	16	15	7 19	1	2	10	17	15	7 13	1	2	10	17	16	7 6	1	1
6 47 51	11	17	16	8 3	2	3	11	18	16	7 56	2	3	11	18	16	7 49	1	2
6 52 11	12	18	17	8 47	3	4	12	19	17	8 39	3	4	12	19	17	8 31	2	3
6 56 30	13	19	18	9 30	4	5	13	19	18	9 22	3	5	13	20	18	9 14	3	4
7 0 49	14	20	19	10 14	5	6	14	20	19	10 5	4	5	14	21	19	9 56	4	5
7 5 7	15	21	19	10 57	5	7	15	21	20	10 48	5	6	15	22	20	10 38	5	6
7 9 26	16	22	20	11 40	6	8	16	22	20	11 30	6	7	16	23	20	11 20	5	7
7 13 43	17	23	21	12 24	7	9	17	23	21	12 13	7	8	17	23	21	12 2	6	8
7 18 0	18	24	22	13 7	8	10	18	24	22	12 56	7	9	18	24	22	12 44	7	9
7 22 17	19	25	23	13 50	9	10	19	25	23	13 38	8	10	19	25	23	13 26	8	10
7 26 33	20	26	24	14 33	9	11	20	26	24	14 20	9	11	20	26	24	14 7	9	10
7 30 49	21	27	24	15 16	10	12	21	27	24	15 3	10	12	21	27	24	14 49	9	11
7 35 4	22	28	25	15 59	11	13	22	28	25	15 45	11	13	22	28	25	15 31	10	12
7 39 19	23	29	26	16 41	12	14	23	29	26	16 27	11	14	23	29	26	16 12	11	13
7 43 33	24	29	27	17 24	13	15	24	♍	27	17 9	12	15	24	♍	27	16 53	12	14
7 47 46	25	♍	28	18 6	13	16	25	1	28	17 50	13	15	25	1	28	17 34	12	15
7 51 59	26	1	28	18 48	14	17	26	2	28	18 32	14	16	26	2	28	18 16	13	16
7 56 11	27	2	29	19 31	15	18	27	2	29	19 14	15	17	27	3	29	18 57	14	17
8 0 23	28	3	♎	20 13	16	19	28	3	♎	19 55	15	18	28	4	♎	19 37	15	18
8 4 34	29	4	1	20 55	17	20	29	4	1	20 37	16	19	29	4	1	20 18	16	19
8 8 44	♌	5	2	21 36	17	21	♌	5	2	21 18	17	20	♌	5	2	20 59	16	19
8 12 53	1	6	2	22 18	18	21	1	6	2	21 59	18	21	1	6	2	21 39	17	20
8 17 2	2	7	3	23 0	19	22	2	7	3	22 40	18	22	2	7	3	22 19	18	21
8 21 10	3	8	4	23 41	20	23	3	8	4	23 21	19	23	3	8	4	23 0	19	22
8 25 18	4	9	5	24 22	20	24	4	9	5	24 1	20	24	4	9	5	23 40	19	23
8 29 24	5	10	6	25 4	21	25	5	10	6	24 42	21	25	5	10	6	24 20	20	24
8 33 30	6	11	6	25 45	22	26	6	11	6	25 22	21	26	6	11	6	24 59	21	25
8 37 36	7	11	7	26 26	23	27	7	12	7	26 3	22	26	7	12	7	25 39	22	26
8 41 40	8	12	8	27 6	24	28	8	12	8	26 43	23	27	8	13	8	26 19	22	27
8 45 44	9	13	9	27 47	24	29	9	13	9	27 23	24	28	9	13	9	26 58	23	28
8 49 47	10	14	10	28 27	25	♑	10	14	9	28 3	24	29	10	14	9	27 37	24	29
8 53 50	11	15	10	29 8	26	1	11	15	10	28 43	25	♑	11	15	10	28 17	25	♑
8 57 51	12	16	11	29 48	27	2	12	16	11	29 22	26	1	12	16	11	28 56	25	0
9 1 52	13	17	12	0♏ 28	27	3	13	17	12	0♏ 2	27	2	13	17	12	29 35	26	1
9 5 52	14	18	13	1 8	28	3	14	18	13	0 41	27	3	14	18	12	0♏ 13	27	2
HOUSES	4	5	6	7	8	9	4	5	6	7	8	9	4	5	6	7	8	9

LATITUDE 55° S. LATITUDE 56° S. LATITUDE 57° S.

LATITUDE 55° N.   LATITUDE 56° N.   LATITUDE 57° N.

SIDEREAL TIME (H M S)	10 Ω	11 ♍	12 ≏	ASC ♏	2 ♏	3 ♐	10 Ω	11 ♍	12 ≏	ASC ♏	2 ♏	3 ♐	10 Ω	11 ♍	12 ≏	ASC ♏	2 ♏	3 ♐
9 9 52	15	19	13	1 48	29	4	15	19	13	1 20	28	4	15	19	13	0 52	28	3
9 13 50	16	20	14	2 28	♐	5	16	20	14	1 59	29	5	16	20	14	1 30	28	4
9 17 49	17	20	15	3 7	0	6	17	21	15	2 38	♐	6	17	21	15	2 9	29	5
9 21 46	18	21	16	3 47	1	7	18	21	16	3 17	0	7	18	21	15	2 47	♐	6
9 25 42	19	22	16	4 26	2	8	19	22	16	3 56	1	8	19	22	16	3 25	0	7
9 29 38	20	23	17	5 5	3	9	20	23	17	4 35	2	9	20	23	17	4 3	1	8
9 33 34	21	24	18	5 45	3	10	21	24	18	5 13	3	9	21	24	18	4 41	2	9
9 37 28	22	25	19	6 24	4	11	22	25	19	5 52	3	10	22	25	18	5 19	3	10
9 41 22	23	26	19	7 2	5	12	23	26	19	6 30	4	11	23	26	19	5 57	3	11
9 45 15	24	27	20	7 41	6	13	24	27	20	7 8	5	12	24	27	20	6 34	4	12
9 49 8	25	28	21	8 20	6	14	25	28	21	7 46	6	13	25	28	21	7 12	5	13
9 53 0	26	28	22	8 59	7	15	26	28	21	8 24	6	14	26	28	21	7 49	6	14
9 56 51	27	29	22	9 37	8	16	27	29	22	9 2	7	15	27	29	22	8 27	6	15
10 0 42	28	≏	23	10 15	9	17	28	≏	23	9 40	8	16	28	≏	23	9 4	7	16
10 4 32	29	1	24	10 54	9	18	29	1	24	10 18	9	17	29	1	23	9 41	8	17
10 8 22	♍	2	25	11 32	10	19	♍	2	24	10 55	9	18	♍	2	24	10 18	9	18
10 12 11	1	3	25	12 10	11	20	1	3	25	11 33	10	19	1	3	25	10 55	9	19
10 15 59	2	4	26	12 48	12	21	2	4	26	12 10	11	20	2	4	26	11 32	10	20
10 19 47	3	4	27	13 26	13	22	3	4	27	12 48	12	21	3	4	26	12 8	11	21
10 23 34	4	5	28	14 4	13	23	4	5	27	13 25	12	22	4	5	27	12 45	12	22
10 27 21	5	6	28	14 42	14	24	5	6	28	14 2	13	23	5	6	28	13 22	12	23
10 31 8	6	7	29	15 20	15	25	6	7	29	14 40	14	24	6	7	28	13 58	13	24
10 34 53	7	8	♏	15 58	16	26	7	8	29	15 17	15	25	7	8	29	14 35	14	25
10 38 39	8	9	0	16 35	16	27	8	9	♏	15 54	15	26	8	9	♏	15 11	14	26
10 42 24	9	10	1	17 13	17	28	9	10	1	16 31	16	27	9	9	0	15 48	15	27
10 46 8	10	10	2	17 50	18	29	10	10	1	17 8	17	28	10	10	1	16 24	16	28
10 49 52	11	11	3	18 28	19	♒	11	11	2	17 45	18	29	11	11	2	17 0	17	29
10 53 36	12	12	3	19 6	19	1	12	12	3	18 22	18	♒	12	12	2	17 37	18	♒
10 57 20	13	13	4	19 43	20	2	13	13	4	18 59	19	1	13	13	3	18 13	18	1
11 1 3	14	14	5	20 21	21	3	14	14	4	19 36	20	2	14	14	4	18 49	19	2
11 4 45	15	15	5	20 58	22	4	15	14	5	20 12	21	3	15	14	5	19 25	20	3
11 8 28	16	15	6	21 36	23	5	16	15	6	20 49	22	4	16	15	5	20 1	21	4
11 12 10	17	16	7	22 13	23	6	17	16	6	21 26	22	6	17	16	6	20 38	21	5
11 15 52	18	17	7	22 51	24	7	18	17	7	22 3	23	7	18	17	7	21 14	22	6
11 19 33	19	18	8	23 28	25	8	19	18	8	22 40	24	8	19	18	7	21 50	23	7
11 23 15	20	19	9	24 6	26	9	20	19	8	23 17	25	9	20	18	8	22 26	24	8
11 26 56	21	20	10	24 43	27	10	21	19	9	23 54	26	10	21	19	9	23 2	24	9
11 30 37	22	20	10	25 21	27	11	22	20	10	24 31	26	11	22	20	9	23 39	25	10
11 34 17	23	21	11	25 58	28	12	23	21	10	25 8	27	12	23	21	10	24 15	26	12
11 37 58	24	22	12	26 36	29	14	24	22	11	25 45	28	13	24	22	11	24 51	27	13
11 41 39	25	23	12	27 14	♑	15	25	23	12	26 22	29	14	25	23	11	25 28	28	14
11 45 19	26	24	13	27 52	1	16	26	23	12	26 59	♑	15	26	23	12	26 4	29	15
11 48 59	27	24	14	28 29	2	17	27	24	13	27 36	1	16	27	24	13	26 41	29	16
11 52 40	28	25	14	29 7	2	18	28	25	14	28 13	1	18	28	25	13	27 17	♑	17
11 56 20	29	26	15	29 45	3	19	29	26	15	28 50	2	19	29	26	14	27 54	1	18
HOUSES	4	5	6	7	8	9	4	5	6	7	8	9	4	5	6	7	8	9

LATITUDE 55° S.   LATITUDE 56° S.   LATITUDE 57° S.

LATITUDE 55° N. LATITUDE 56° N. LATITUDE 57° N.

SIDEREAL TIME	10 ♎	11 ♎	12 ♏	ASC ♐	2 ♑	3 ♒	10 ♎	11 ♎	12 ♏	ASC ♏	2 ♑	3 ♒	10 ♎	11 ♎	12 ♏	ASC ♏	2 ♑	3 ♒
H M S	°	°	°	° '	°	°	°	°	°	° '	°	°	°	°	°	° '	°	°
12 0 0	0	27	16	0 24	4	20	0	27	15	29 28	3	20	0	27	15	28 30	2	19
12 3 40	1	28	16	1 2	5	21	1	28	16	0♐ 5	4	21	1	27	15	29 7	3	21
12 7 20	2	29	17	1 40	6	23	2	28	17	0 43	5	22	2	28	16	29 44	4	22
12 11 1	3	29	18	2 19	7	24	3	29	17	1 21	6	23	3	29	17	0♐ 21	5	23
12 14 41	4	♏	18	2 57	8	25	4	♏	18	1 59	7	25	4	♏	17	0 58	5	24
12 18 21	5	1	19	3 36	9	26	5	1	19	2 37	8	26	5	1	18	1 35	6	25
12 22 2	6	2	20	4 15	10	27	6	2	19	3 15	8	27	6	1	19	2 12	7	27
12 25 42	7	3	21	4 54	11	28	7	2	20	3 53	9	28	7	2	19	2 50	8	28
12 29 23	8	3	21	5 33	12	♓	8	3	21	4 31	10	29	8	3	20	3 28	9	29
12 33 4	9	4	22	6 12	13	1	9	4	21	5 10	11	♓	9	4	21	4 5	10	♓
12 36 45	10	5	23	6 52	13	2	10	5	22	5 49	12	2	10	5	21	4 43	11	1
12 40 27	11	6	23	7 32	14	3	11	6	23	6 28	13	3	11	5	22	5 21	12	3
12 44 8	12	7	24	8 12	15	4	12	6	23	7 7	14	4	12	6	23	6 0	13	4
12 47 50	13	7	25	8 52	16	6	13	7	24	7 46	15	5	13	7	23	6 38	14	5
12 51 32	14	8	25	9 33	18	7	14	8	25	8 26	16	7	14	8	24	7 17	15	6
12 55 15	15	9	26	10 13	19	8	15	9	26	9 6	17	8	15	8	25	7 56	16	8
12 58 57	16	10	27	10 54	20	9	16	10	26	9 46	18	9	16	9	26	8 35	17	9
13 2 40	17	11	28	11 35	21	10	17	10	27	10 26	19	10	17	10	26	9 15	18	10
13 6 24	18	11	28	12 17	22	12	18	11	28	11 7	21	12	18	11	27	9 54	19	11
13 10 8	19	12	29	12 59	23	13	19	12	28	11 48	22	13	19	12	28	10 34	20	13
13 13 52	20	13	♐	13 41	24	14	20	13	29	12 29	23	14	20	12	28	11 15	21	14
13 17 36	21	14	0	14 24	25	16	21	14	♐	13 11	24	15	21	13	29	11 55	23	15
13 21 21	22	15	1	15 6	26	17	22	14	0	13 53	25	17	22	14	♐	12 36	24	17
13 25 7	23	15	2	15 50	27	18	23	15	1	14 35	26	18	23	15	0	13 17	25	18
13 28 52	24	16	3	16 33	29	19	24	16	2	15 18	27	19	24	16	1	13 59	26	19
13 32 39	25	17	3	17 17	♒	21	25	17	3	16 1	29	21	25	16	2	14 41	27	20
13 36 26	26	18	4	18 2	1	22	26	18	3	16 44	♒	22	26	17	3	15 23	29	22
13 40 13	27	19	5	18 47	2	23	27	18	4	17 28	1	23	27	18	3	16 6	♒	23
13 44 1	28	19	5	19 32	4	25	28	19	5	18 12	2	24	28	19	4	16 49	1	24
13 47 49	29	20	6	20 18	5	26	29	20	5	18 57	4	26	29	20	5	17 33	3	26
13 51 38	♏	21	7	21 4	6	27	♏	21	6	19 43	5	27	♏	20	5	18 17	4	27
13 55 28	1	22	8	21 51	8	28	1	22	7	20 28	6	28	1	21	6	19 2	5	28
13 59 18	2	23	8	22 39	9	♈	2	22	8	21 15	8	♈	2	22	7	19 47	7	♈
14 3 9	3	24	9	23 27	10	1	3	23	8	22 2	9	1	3	23	8	20 33	8	1
14 7 0	4	24	10	24 16	12	2	4	24	9	22 49	11	2	4	24	8	21 19	9	2
14 10 52	5	25	11	25 5	13	4	5	25	10	23 37	12	4	5	24	9	22 6	11	4
14 14 45	6	26	12	25 55	15	5	6	26	11	24 26	14	5	6	25	10	22 53	12	5
14 18 38	7	27	12	26 46	16	6	7	26	11	25 16	15	6	7	26	11	23 41	14	7
14 22 32	8	28	13	27 37	18	8	8	27	12	26 6	17	8	8	27	11	24 30	15	8
14 26 26	9	29	14	28 30	19	9	9	28	13	26 57	18	9	9	28	12	25 20	17	9
14 30 22	10	29	15	29 23	21	10	10	29	14	27 49	20	11	10	29	13	26 10	19	11
14 34 17	11	♐	15	0♑ 17	22	12	11	♐	15	28 42	21	12	11	29	14	27 1	20	12
14 38 14	12	1	16	1 12	24	13	12	1	15	29 35	23	13	12	♐	14	27 53	22	13
14 42 11	13	2	17	2 7	25	14	13	1	16	0♑ 30	25	15	13	1	15	28 46	24	15
14 46 10	14	3	18	3 4	27	16	14	2	17	1 25	26	16	14	2	16	29 40	25	16
HOUSES	4	5	6	7	8	9	4	5	6	7	8	9	4	5	6	7	8	9

LATITUDE 55° S. LATITUDE 56° S. LATITUDE 57° S.

LATITUDE 55° N. LATITUDE 56° N. LATITUDE 57° N.

SIDEREAL TIME (H M S)	10 ♏	11 ↗	12 ↗	ASC ♑ °	ASC '	2 ♒	3 ♈	10 ♏	11 ↗	12 ↗	ASC ♑ °	ASC '	2 ♒	3 ♈	10 ♏	11 ↗	12 ↗	ASC ♑ °	ASC '	2 ♒	3 ♈
14 50 8	15	4	19	4	2	29	17	15	3	18	2	21	28	17	15	3	17	0	35	27	17
14 54 8	16	4	20	5	1	♓	18	16	4	19	3	19	♓	19	16	4	18	1	31	29	19
14 58 8	17	5	20	6	1	2	20	17	5	19	4	18	1	20	17	4	18	2	28	♓	20
15 2 9	18	6	21	7	3	4	21	18	6	20	5	18	3	21	18	5	19	3	26	2	22
15 6 10	19	7	22	8	5	6	22	19	7	21	6	19	5	23	19	6	20	4	26	4	23
15 10 13	20	8	23	9	9	7	24	20	7	22	7	21	7	24	20	7	21	5	27	6	24
15 14 16	21	9	24	10	15	9	25	21	8	23	8	25	9	25	21	8	22	6	29	8	26
15 18 20	22	10	25	11	22	11	26	22	9	24	9	31	10	27	22	9	23	7	32	10	27
15 22 24	23	10	26	12	30	13	28	23	10	25	10	37	12	28	23	10	24	8	37	12	28
15 26 30	24	11	26	13	40	15	29	24	11	25	11	46	14	29	24	10	24	9	44	14	♉
15 30 36	25	12	27	14	52	16	♉	25	12	26	12	56	16	♉	25	11	25	10	53	16	1
15 34 42	26	13	28	16	6	18	2	26	13	27	14	9	18	2	26	12	26	12	3	18	2
15 38 50	27	14	29	17	21	20	3	27	14	28	15	23	20	3	27	13	27	13	16	20	4
15 42 58	28	15	♑	18	39	22	4	28	14	29	16	39	22	5	28	14	28	14	30	22	5
15 47 7	29	16	1	19	59	24	6	29	15	♑	17	58	24	6	29	15	29	15	47	24	6
15 51 16	↗	17	2	21	21	26	7	↗	16	1	19	18	26	7	↗	16	♑	17	6	26	8
15 55 26	1	18	3	22	46	28	8	1	17	2	20	42	28	9	1	17	1	18	27	28	9
15 59 37	2	19	4	24	13	♈	10	2	18	3	22	8	♈	10	2	17	2	19	51	♈	10
16 3 49	3	19	5	25	43	2	11	3	19	4	23	36	2	11	3	18	3	21	18	2	12
16 8 1	4	20	6	27	15	4	12	4	20	5	25	8	4	13	4	19	4	22	48	4	13
16 12 14	5	21	7	28	51	6	14	5	21	6	26	43	6	14	5	20	5	24	22	6	14
16 16 27	6	22	8	0♒	30	8	15	6	22	7	28	21	8	15	6	21	6	25	58	8	16
16 20 41	7	23	9	2	12	10	16	7	23	8	0♒	2	10	16	7	22	7	27	39	10	17
16 24 56	8	24	10	3	57	12	17	8	24	9	1	47	12	18	8	23	8	29	23	12	18
16 29 11	9	25	11	5	46	13	19	9	25	10	3	36	14	19	9	24	9	1♒	11	14	20
16 33 27	10	26	13	7	39	15	20	10	25	11	5	29	16	20	10	25	10	3	4	16	21
16 37 43	11	27	14	9	36	17	21	11	26	13	7	26	18	22	11	26	11	5	1	18	22
16 41 59	12	28	15	11	37	19	22	12	27	14	9	28	20	23	12	27	12	7	4	20	23
16 46 17	13	29	16	13	42	21	24	13	28	15	11	35	22	24	13	28	14	9	11	22	25
16 50 34	14	♑	17	15	52	23	25	14	29	16	13	46	24	25	14	29	15	11	24	24	26
16 54 53	15	1	18	18	6	25	26	15	♑	17	16	3	26	27	15	♑	16	13	42	26	27
16 59 11	16	2	20	20	24	27	27	16	1	18	18	24	27	28	16	1	17	16	7	28	28
17 3 30	17	3	21	22	48	29	28	17	2	20	20	51	29	29	17	2	18	18	37	♉	29
17 7 49	18	4	22	25	16	♉	♊	18	3	21	23	24	♉	♊	18	3	20	21	14	2	♊
17 12 9	19	5	23	27	49	2	1	19	4	22	26	2	3	1	19	4	21	23	57	4	2
17 16 29	20	6	25	0♓	26	4	2	20	5	24	28	45	5	3	20	5	22	26	47	6	3
17 20 49	21	7	26	3	8	6	3	21	6	25	1♓	34	7	4	21	6	24	29	43	8	4
17 25 10	22	8	27	5	54	8	4	22	7	26	4	28	9	5	22	7	25	2♓	46	10	5
17 29 31	23	9	29	8	45	9	6	23	8	28	7	27	10	6	23	8	26	5	54	11	7
17 33 51	24	10	♒	11	39	11	7	24	10	29	10	31	12	7	24	9	28	9	9	13	8
17 38 13	25	11	2	14	37	13	8	25	11	♒	13	38	14	8	25	10	29	12	28	15	9
17 42 34	26	12	3	17	38	14	9	26	12	2	16	50	15	9	26	11	♒	15	53	17	10
17 46 55	27	13	5	20	41	16	10	27	13	3	20	5	17	11	27	12	2	19	21	18	11
17 51 17	28	14	6	23	46	18	11	28	14	5	23	22	19	12	28	13	4	22	52	20	12
17 55 38	29	15	8	26	53	19	12	29	15	7	26	40	20	13	29	14	5	26	26	22	13
HOUSES	4	5	6	7		8	9	4	5	6	7		8	9	4	5	6	7		8	9

LATITUDE 55° S. LATITUDE 56° S. LATITUDE 57° S.

	LATITUDE 55° N.						LATITUDE 56° N.						LATITUDE 57° N.					

SIDEREAL TIME	10 ♑	11 ♑	12 ♒	ASC ♈	2 ♉	3 ♊	10 ♑	11 ♑	12 ♒	ASC ♈	2 ♉	3 ♊	10 ♑	11 ♑	12 ♒	ASC ♈	2 ♉	3 ♊
H M S	°	°	°	° '	°	°	°	°	°	° '	°	°	°	°	°	° '	°	°
18 0 0	0	17	9	0 0	21	13	0	16	8	0 0	22	14	0	15	7	0 0	23	15
18 4 22	1	18	11	3 7	22	15	1	17	10	3 20	23	15	1	17	8	3 34	25	16
18 8 43	2	19	12	6 14	24	16	2	18	11	6 38	25	16	2	18	10	7 8	26	17
18 13 5	3	20	14	9 19	25	17	3	19	13	9 55	27	17	3	19	12	10 39	28	18
18 17 26	4	21	16	12 22	27	18	4	21	15	13 10	28	18	4	20	13	14 7	29	19
18 21 47	5	22	17	15 23	28	19	5	22	16	16 22	29	19	5	21	15	17 32	♊	20
18 26 9	6	23	19	18 21	♊	20	6	23	18	19 29	♊	20	6	22	17	20 51	2	21
18 30 29	7	24	21	21 15	1	21	7	24	20	22 33	2	22	7	23	19	24 6	4	22
18 34 50	8	26	22	24 6	3	22	8	25	21	25 32	4	23	8	25	20	27 14	5	23
18 39 11	9	27	24	26 52	4	23	9	26	23	28 26	5	24	9	26	22	0ŏ 17	6	24
18 43 31	10	28	26	29 34	5	24	10	27	25	1ŏ 15	6	25	10	27	24	3 13	8	25
18 47 51	11	29	28	2ŏ 11	7	25	11	29	27	3 58	8	26	11	28	26	6 3	9	26
18 52 11	12	♒	♓	4 44	8	26	12	♒	29	6 36	9	27	12	29	28	8 46	10	27
18 56 30	13	2	1	7 12	9	27	13	1	♓	9 9	10	28	13	♒	♓	11 23	12	28
19 0 49	14	3	3	9 36	10	28	14	2	3	11 36	12	29	14	2	2	13 53	13	29
19 5 7	15	4	5	11 54	12	29	15	3	4	13 57	13	♋	15	3	4	16 18	14	♋
19 9 26	16	5	7	14 8	13	♋	16	5	6	16 14	14	1	16	4	6	18 36	15	1
19 13 43	17	6	9	16 18	14	1	17	6	8	18 25	15	2	17	5	8	20 49	16	2
19 18 0	18	8	11	18 23	15	2	18	7	10	20 32	16	3	18	7	10	22 56	18	3
19 22 17	19	9	13	20 24	16	3	19	8	12	22 34	17	4	19	8	12	24 59	19	4
19 26 33	20	10	15	22 21	17	4	20	10	14	24 31	19	5	20	9	14	26 56	20	5
19 30 49	21	11	17	24 14	19	5	21	11	16	26 24	20	5	21	10	16	28 49	21	6
19 35 4	22	13	18	26 3	20	6	22	12	18	28 13	21	6	22	12	18	0♊ 37	22	7
19 39 19	23	14	20	27 48	21	7	23	14	20	29 58	22	7	23	13	20	2 21	23	8
19 43 33	24	15	22	29 30	22	8	24	15	22	1♊ 39	23	8	24	14	22	4 2	24	9
19 47 46	25	16	24	1♊ 9	23	9	25	16	24	3 17	24	9	25	16	24	5 38	25	10
19 51 59	26	18	26	2 45	24	10	26	17	26	4 52	25	10	26	17	26	7 12	26	11
19 56 11	27	19	28	4 17	25	11	27	19	28	6 24	26	11	27	18	28	8 42	27	12
20 0 23	28	20	♈	5 47	26	11	28	20	♈	7 52	27	12	28	20	♈	10 9	28	13
20 4 34	29	22	2	7 14	27	12	29	21	2	9 18	28	13	29	21	2	11 33	29	13
20 8 44	♒	23	4	8 39	28	13	♒	23	4	10 42	29	14	♒	22	4	12 54	♋	14
20 12 53	1	24	6	10 1	29	14	1	24	6	12 2	♋	15	1	24	6	14 13	1	15
20 17 2	2	26	8	11 21	♋	15	2	25	8	13 21	1	16	2	25	8	15 30	2	16
20 21 10	3	27	10	12 39	1	16	3	27	10	14 37	2	16	3	26	10	16 44	3	17
20 25 18	4	28	12	13 54	2	17	4	28	12	15 51	3	17	4	28	12	17 57	4	18
20 29 24	5	♓	14	15 8	3	18	5	29	14	17 4	4	18	5	29	14	19 7	5	19
20 33 30	6	1	15	16 20	4	19	6	♓	16	18 14	5	19	6	♓	16	20 16	6	20
20 37 36	7	2	17	17 30	4	20	7	2	18	19 23	5	20	7	2	18	21 23	6	20
20 41 40	8	4	19	18 38	5	20	8	3	20	20 29	6	21	8	3	20	22 28	7	21
20 45 44	9	5	21	19 45	6	21	9	5	21	21 35	7	22	9	4	22	23 31	8	22
20 49 47	10	6	23	20 51	7	22	10	6	23	22 39	8	23	10	6	24	24 33	9	23
20 53 50	11	8	24	21 55	8	23	11	7	25	23 41	9	23	11	7	26	25 34	10	24
20 57 51	12	9	26	22 57	9	24	12	9	27	24 42	10	24	12	8	28	26 34	11	25
21 1 52	13	10	28	23 59	10	25	13	10	29	25 42	11	25	13	10	29	27 32	12	26
21 5 52	14	12	ŏ	24 59	10	26	14	11	ŏ	26 41	11	26	14	11	ŏ	28 29	12	26
HOUSES	4	5	6	7	8	9	4	5	6	7	8	9	4	5	6	7	8	9

LATITUDE 55° S.	LATITUDE 56° S.	LATITUDE 57° S.

	LATITUDE 55° N.						LATITUDE 56° N.						LATITUDE 57° N.					
SIDEREAL TIME	10 ♒	11 ♓	12 ♉	ASC ♊	2 ♋	3 ♋	10 ♒	11 ♓	12 ♉	ASC ♊	2 ♋	3 ♋	10 ♒	11 ♓	12 ♉	ASC ♊	2 ♋	3 ♋
H M S	°	°	°	° '	°	°	°	°	°	° '	°	°	°	°	°	° '	°	°
21 9 52	15	13	1	25 58	11	26	15	13	2	27 39	12	27	15	13	3	29 25	13	27
21 13 50	16	14	3	26 56	12	27	16	14	4	28 35	13	28	16	14	5	0♋20	14	28
21 17 49	17	16	5	27 53	13	28	17	15	5	29 30	14	29	17	15	6	1 14	15	29
21 21 46	18	17	6	28 48	14	29	18	17	7	0♋25	15	29	18	17	8	2 7	16	♌
21 25 42	19	18	8	29 43	15	♌	19	18	9	1 18	15	♌	19	18	10	2 59	16	1
21 29 38	20	20	9	0♋37	15	1	20	19	10	2 11	16	1	20	19	11	3 50	17	1
21 33 34	21	21	11	1 30	16	1	21	21	12	3 3	17	2	21	21	13	4 40	18	2
21 37 28	22	22	12	2 23	17	2	22	22	13	3 54	18	3	22	22	15	5 30	19	3
21 41 22	23	24	14	3 14	18	3	23	24	15	4 44	19	4	23	23	16	6 19	19	4
21 45 15	24	25	15	4 5	18	4	24	25	16	5 34	19	4	24	25	18	7 7	20	5
21 49 8	25	26	17	4 55	19	5	25	26	18	6 23	20	5	25	26	19	7 54	21	6
21 53 0	26	28	18	5 44	20	6	26	28	19	7 11	21	6	26	28	21	8 41	22	6
21 56 51	27	29	20	6 33	21	6	27	29	21	7 58	22	7	27	29	22	9 27	22	7
22 0 42	28	♈	21	7 21	22	7	28	♈	22	8 45	22	8	28	♈	23	10 13	23	8
22 4 32	29	2	22	8 9	22	8	29	2	24	9 32	23	8	29	2	25	10 58	24	9
22 8 22	♓	3	24	8 56	23	9	♓	3	25	10 17	24	9	♓	3	26	11 43	25	10
22 12 11	1	4	25	9 42	24	10	1	4	26	11 3	25	10	1	4	27	12 27	25	10
22 15 59	2	5	26	10 28	25	11	2	6	28	11 48	25	11	2	6	29	13 11	26	11
22 19 47	3	7	28	11 13	25	11	3	7	29	12 32	26	12	3	7	♊	13 54	27	12
22 23 34	4	8	29	11 58	26	12	4	8	♊	13 16	27	12	4	8	1	14 37	27	13
22 27 21	5	9	♊	12 43	27	13	5	9	1	13 59	27	13	5	10	3	15 19	28	14
22 31 8	6	11	1	13 27	27	14	6	11	3	14 42	28	14	6	11	4	16 1	29	14
22 34 53	7	12	3	14 10	28	15	7	12	4	15 25	29	15	7	12	5	16 43	♌	15
22 38 39	8	13	4	14 54	29	15	8	13	5	16 7	♌	16	8	13	6	17 24	0	16
22 42 24	9	14	5	15 36	♌	16	9	15	6	16 49	0	16	9	15	7	18 5	1	17
22 46 8	10	16	6	16 19	0	17	10	16	7	17 31	1	17	10	16	9	18 45	2	18
22 49 52	11	17	7	17 1	1	18	11	17	8	18 12	2	18	11	17	10	19 26	2	18
22 53 36	12	18	8	17 43	2	19	12	18	9	18 53	2	19	12	19	11	20 6	3	19
22 57 20	13	20	9	18 25	2	19	13	20	11	19 34	3	20	13	20	12	20 45	4	20
23 1 3	14	21	10	19 6	3	20	14	21	12	20 14	4	20	14	21	13	21 25	4	21
23 4 45	15	22	11	19 47	4	21	15	22	13	20 54	4	21	15	22	14	22 4	5	22
23 8 28	16	23	12	20 27	5	22	16	23	14	21 34	5	22	16	24	15	22 43	6	22
23 12 10	17	24	14	21 8	5	23	17	25	15	22 14	6	23	17	25	16	23 22	7	23
23 15 52	18	26	15	21 48	6	23	18	26	16	22 53	7	24	18	26	17	24 0	7	24
23 19 33	19	27	16	22 28	7	24	19	27	17	23 32	7	24	19	27	18	24 39	8	25
23 23 15	20	28	17	23 8	7	25	20	28	18	24 11	8	25	20	29	19	25 17	9	25
23 26 56	21	29	17	23 48	8	26	21	♉	19	24 50	9	26	21	♉	20	25 55	9	26
23 30 37	22	♉	18	24 27	9	27	22	1	20	25 29	9	27	22	1	21	26 32	10	27
23 34 17	23	2	19	25 6	9	27	23	2	21	26 7	10	28	23	2	22	27 10	11	28
23 37 58	24	3	20	25 45	10	28	24	3	22	26 45	11	28	24	3	23	27 48	11	29
23 41 39	25	4	21	26 24	11	29	25	4	22	27 23	11	29	25	5	24	28 25	12	29
23 45 19	26	5	22	27 3	12	♍	26	5	23	28 1	12	♍	26	6	25	29 2	13	♍
23 48 59	27	6	23	27 41	12	1	27	7	24	28 39	13	1	27	7	25	29 39	13	1
23 52 40	28	7	24	28 20	13	1	28	8	25	29 17	13	2	28	8	26	0♌16	14	2
23 56 20	29	9	25	28 58	14	2	29	9	26	29 55	14	2	29	9	27	0 53	15	3
HOUSES	4	5	6	7	8	9	4	5	6	7	8	9	4	5	6	7	8	9

LATITUDE 58° N. LATITUDE 59° N. LATITUDE 60° N.

SIDEREAL TIME	10 ♈	11 ♉	12 ♊	ASC ♋	2 ♌	3 ♍	10 ♈	11 ♉	12 ♋	ASC ♌	2 ♌	3 ♍	10 ♈	11 ♉	12 ♋	ASC ♌	2 ♌	3 ♍
H M S	°	°	°	° '	°	°	°	°	°	° '	°	°	°	°	°	° '	°	°
0 0 0	0	11	29	2 29	16	4	0	11	1	3 31	16	4	0	12	2	4 34	17	4
0 3 40	1	12	♋	3 5	17	4	1	13	2	4 6	17	5	1	13	3	5 9	18	5
0 7 20	2	13	1	3 41	17	5	2	14	2	4 41	18	5	2	14	4	5 43	18	6
0 11 1	3	14	2	4 17	18	6	3	15	3	5 16	18	6	3	15	5	6 17	19	6
0 14 41	4	16	3	4 52	19	7	4	16	4	5 51	19	7	4	17	5	6 51	20	7
0 18 21	5	17	3	5 28	19	8	5	17	5	6 26	20	8	5	18	6	7 25	20	8
0 22 2	6	18	4	6 4	20	8	6	18	6	7 0	20	9	6	19	7	7 59	21	9
0 25 43	7	19	5	6 39	21	9	7	20	6	7 35	21	9	7	20	8	8 33	22	10
0 29 23	8	20	6	7 15	21	10	8	21	7	8 10	22	10	8	21	8	9 7	22	10
0 33 4	9	21	7	7 50	22	11	9	22	8	8 45	22	11	9	22	9	9 41	23	11
0 36 45	10	22	7	8 26	23	12	10	23	9	9 19	23	12	10	24	10	10 15	23	12
0 40 27	11	23	8	9 1	23	12	11	24	9	9 54	24	13	11	25	11	10 49	24	13
0 44 8	12	24	9	9 37	24	13	12	25	10	10 29	24	13	12	26	11	11 23	25	14
0 47 50	13	26	10	10 12	25	14	13	26	11	11 4	25	14	13	27	12	11 57	25	14
0 51 32	14	27	11	10 48	25	15	14	27	12	11 39	26	15	14	28	13	12 31	26	15
0 55 15	15	28	11	11 23	26	16	15	28	12	12 13	26	16	15	29	14	13 5	27	16
0 58 57	16	29	12	11 59	27	17	16	29	13	12 48	27	17	16	♊	14	13 39	27	17
1 2 40	17	♊	13	12 34	27	17	17	♊	14	13 23	28	17	17	1	15	14 13	28	18
1 6 24	18	1	14	13 10	28	18	18	2	15	13 58	28	18	18	2	16	14 47	29	18
1 10 8	19	2	14	13 46	29	19	19	3	15	14 33	29	19	19	3	17	15 21	29	19
1 13 52	20	3	15	14 21	29	20	20	4	16	15 8	♍	20	20	4	17	15 56	♍	20
1 17 36	21	4	16	14 57	♍	21	21	5	17	15 43	0	21	21	5	18	16 30	1	21
1 21 21	22	5	17	15 33	1	21	22	6	18	16 18	1	22	22	6	19	17 4	1	22
1 25 7	23	6	17	16 8	1	22	23	7	18	16 53	2	22	23	7	19	17 39	2	22
1 28 52	24	7	18	16 44	2	23	24	8	19	17 28	2	23	24	9	20	18 13	3	23
1 32 39	25	8	19	17 20	3	24	25	9	20	18 3	3	24	25	10	21	18 48	3	24
1 36 26	26	9	19	17 56	3	25	26	10	20	18 39	4	25	26	11	21	19 22	4	25
1 40 13	27	10	20	18 32	4	26	27	11	21	19 14	4	26	27	12	22	19 57	5	26
1 44 1	28	11	21	19 8	5	26	28	12	22	19 49	5	26	28	13	23	20 32	5	27
1 47 49	29	12	22	19 45	5	27	29	13	23	20 25	6	27	29	14	24	21 7	6	27
1 51 38	♉	13	22	20 21	6	28	♉	14	23	21 1	6	28	♉	15	24	21 41	7	28
1 55 28	1	14	23	20 57	7	29	1	15	24	21 36	7	29	1	16	25	22 16	7	29
1 59 18	2	15	24	21 34	8	♎	2	16	25	22 12	8	♎	2	17	26	22 52	8	♎
2 3 9	3	16	24	22 10	8	1	3	17	25	22 48	9	1	3	18	26	23 27	9	1
2 7 0	4	17	25	22 47	9	2	4	18	26	23 24	9	2	4	18	27	24 2	10	2
2 10 52	5	18	26	23 24	10	2	5	19	27	24 0	10	2	5	19	28	24 38	10	2
2 14 45	6	19	27	24 0	10	3	6	20	28	24 36	11	3	6	20	28	25 13	11	3
2 18 38	7	20	27	24 37	11	4	7	21	28	25 13	11	4	7	21	29	25 49	12	4
2 22 32	8	21	28	25 14	12	5	8	22	29	25 49	12	5	8	22	♌	26 24	12	5
2 26 26	9	22	29	25 52	13	6	9	22	♌	26 25	13	6	9	23	1	27 0	13	6
2 30 22	10	23	♌	26 29	13	7	10	23	0	27 2	14	7	10	24	1	27 36	14	7
2 34 17	11	24	0	27 6	14	8	11	24	1	27 39	14	8	11	25	2	28 12	14	7
2 38 14	12	25	1	27 44	15	8	12	25	2	28 16	15	8	12	26	3	28 48	15	8
2 42 11	13	26	2	28 22	16	9	13	26	3	28 53	16	9	13	27	3	29 25	16	9
2 46 10	14	26	2	28 59	16	10	14	27	3	29 30	16	10	14	28	4	0♍ 1	17	10
HOUSES	4	5	6	7	8	9	4	5	6	7	8	9	4	5	6	7	8	9

LATITUDE 58° S. LATITUDE 59° S. LATITUDE 60° S.

LATITUDE 58° N.   LATITUDE 59° N.   LATITUDE 60° N.

SIDEREAL TIME	10 ♉	11 ♊	12 ♌	ASC ♌	2 ♍	3 ♎	10 ♉	11 ♊	12 ♌	ASC ♍	2 ♍	3 ♎	10 ♉	11 ♊	12 ♌	ASC ♍	2 ♍	3 ♎
H M S	°	°	°	° '	°	°	°	°	°	° '	°	°	°	°	°	° '	°	°
2 50 8	15	27	3	29 37	17	11	15	28	4	0 7	17	11	15	29	5	0 38	17	11
2 54 8	16	28	4	0♍15	18	12	16	29	5	0 44	18	12	16	♋	5	1 15	18	12
2 58 8	17	29	5	0 53	18	13	17	♋	5	1 22	19	13	17	1	6	1 51	19	13
3 2 9	18	♋	5	1 32	19	14	18	1	6	2 0	19	14	18	2	7	2 28	20	14
3 6 10	19	1	6	2 10	20	15	19	2	7	2 37	20	14	19	3	8	3 5	20	14
3 10 13	20	2	7	2 49	21	15	20	3	8	3 15	21	15	20	3	8	3 43	21	15
3 14 16	21	3	8	3 27	21	16	21	4	8	3 53	22	16	21	4	9	4 20	22	16
3 18 20	22	4	8	4 6	22	17	22	5	9	4 31	22	17	22	5	10	4 57	22	17
3 22 24	23	5	9	4 45	23	18	23	5	10	5 10	23	18	23	6	10	5 35	23	18
3 26 30	24	6	10	5 24	24	19	24	6	10	5 48	24	19	24	7	11	6 13	24	19
3 30 36	25	7	11	6 3	25	20	25	7	11	6 27	25	20	25	8	12	6 51	25	20
3 34 42	26	7	11	6 42	25	21	26	8	12	7 5	25	21	26	9	13	7 29	25	21
3 38 50	27	8	12	7 22	26	22	27	9	13	7 44	26	22	27	10	13	8 7	26	21
3 42 58	28	9	13	8 1	27	23	28	10	13	8 23	27	22	28	11	14	8 45	27	22
3 47 7	29	10	14	8 41	28	24	29	11	14	9 2	28	23	29	11	15	9 23	28	23
3 51 16	♊	11	14	9 21	28	24	♊	12	15	9 41	28	24	♊	12	15	10 2	28	24
3 55 26	1	12	15	10 1	29	25	1	13	16	10 20	29	25	1	13	16	10 40	29	25
3 59 37	2	13	16	10 41	♎	26	2	14	16	11 0	♎	26	2	14	17	11 19	♎	26
4 3 49	3	14	17	11 21	1	27	3	14	17	11 39	1	27	3	15	18	11 58	1	27
4 8 1	4	15	17	12 1	1	28	4	15	18	12 19	1	28	4	16	18	12 37	1	28
4 12 14	5	16	18	12 42	2	29	5	16	19	12 59	2	29	5	17	19	13 16	2	29
4 16 27	6	16	19	13 22	3	♏	6	17	19	13 39	3	♏	6	18	20	13 55	3	29
4 20 41	7	17	20	14 3	4	1	7	18	20	14 19	4	1	7	19	21	14 34	4	♏
4 24 56	8	18	20	14 44	5	2	8	19	21	14 59	5	1	8	19	21	15 14	5	1
4 29 11	9	19	21	15 25	5	3	9	20	22	15 39	5	2	9	20	22	15 53	5	2
4 33 27	10	20	22	16 6	6	4	10	21	22	16 19	6	3	10	21	23	16 33	6	3
4 37 43	11	21	23	16 47	7	4	11	22	23	17 0	7	4	11	22	24	17 13	7	4
4 41 59	12	22	23	17 28	8	5	12	22	24	17 40	8	5	12	23	24	17 53	8	5
4 46 17	13	23	24	18 9	9	6	13	23	25	18 21	9	6	13	24	25	18 32	8	6
4 50 34	14	24	25	18 51	9	7	14	24	25	19 1	9	7	14	25	26	19 12	9	7
4 54 53	15	25	26	19 32	10	8	15	25	26	19 42	10	8	15	26	27	19 52	10	8
4 59 11	16	25	27	20 13	11	9	16	26	27	20 23	11	9	16	27	27	20 33	11	8
5 3 30	17	26	27	20 55	12	10	17	27	28	21 4	12	10	17	27	28	21 13	12	9
5 7 49	18	27	28	21 37	13	11	18	28	29	21 45	12	11	18	28	29	21 53	12	10
5 12 9	19	28	29	22 18	13	12	19	29	29	22 26	13	11	19	29	♏22	22 33	13	11
5 16 29	20	29	♏	23 0	14	13	20	♌	♏	23 7	14	12	20	♌	1	23 14	14	12
5 20 49	21	♌	1	23 42	15	14	21	0	1	23 48	15	13	21	1	1	23 54	15	13
5 25 10	22	1	1	24 24	16	15	22	1	2	24 29	16	14	22	2	2	24 35	15	14
5 29 31	23	2	2	25 6	17	15	23	2	2	25 11	16	15	23	3	3	25 15	16	15
5 33 51	24	3	3	25 48	17	16	24	3	3	25 52	17	16	24	4	4	25 56	17	16
5 38 13	25	4	4	26 30	18	17	25	4	4	26 33	18	17	25	5	4	26 37	18	17
5 42 34	26	5	5	27 12	19	18	26	5	5	27 14	19	18	26	5	5	27 17	19	17
5 46 55	27	5	5	27 54	20	19	27	6	6	27 56	20	19	27	6	6	27 58	19	18
5 51 17	28	6	6	28 36	21	20	28	7	6	28 37	20	20	28	7	7	28 39	20	19
5 55 38	29	7	7	29 18	21	21	29	8	7	29 19	21	21	29	8	8	29 19	21	20
HOUSES	4	5	6	7	8	9	4	5	6	7	8	9	4	5	6	7	8	9

LATITUDE 58° S.   LATITUDE 59° S.   LATITUDE 60° S.

LATITUDE 58° N. LATITUDE 59° N. LATITUDE 60° N.

LATITUDE 58° N.

SIDEREAL TIME (H M S)	10 ♐	11 Ω	12 ♍	ASC ≏	2 ≏	3 ♏
6 0 0	0	8	8	0 0	22	22
6 4 22	1	9	9	0 42	23	23
6 8 43	2	10	9	1 24	24	24
6 13 5	3	11	10	2 6	25	25
6 17 26	4	12	11	2 48	25	25
6 21 47	5	13	12	3 30	26	26
6 26 9	6	14	13	4 12	27	27
6 30 29	7	15	13	4 54	28	28
6 34 50	8	15	14	5 36	29	29
6 39 11	9	16	15	6 18	29	♐
6 43 31	10	17	16	7 0	♏	1
6 47 51	11	18	17	7 42	1	2
6 52 11	12	19	17	8 23	2	3
6 56 30	13	20	18	9 5	3	4
7 0 49	14	21	19	9 47	3	5
7 5 7	15	22	20	10 28	4	5
7 9 26	16	23	21	11 9	5	6
7 13 43	17	24	21	11 51	6	7
7 18 0	18	25	22	12 32	7	8
7 22 17	19	26	23	13 13	7	9
7 26 33	20	26	24	13 54	8	10
7 30 49	21	27	25	14 35	9	11
7 35 4	22	28	25	15 16	10	12
7 39 19	23	29	26	15 57	10	13
7 43 33	24	♏	27	16 38	11	14
7 47 46	25	1	28	17 18	12	14
7 51 59	26	2	29	17 59	13	15
7 56 11	27	3	29	18 39	13	16
8 0 23	28	4	≏	19 19	14	17
8 4 34	29	5	1	19 59	15	18
8 8 44	Ω	6	2	20 39	16	19
8 12 53	1	6	2	21 19	16	20
8 17 2	2	7	3	21 59	17	21
8 21 10	3	8	4	22 38	18	22
8 25 18	4	9	5	23 18	19	23
8 29 24	5	10	5	23 57	19	23
8 33 30	6	11	6	24 36	20	24
8 37 36	7	12	7	25 15	21	25
8 41 40	8	13	8	25 54	22	26
8 45 44	9	14	9	26 33	22	27
8 49 47	10	15	9	27 11	23	28
8 53 50	11	15	10	27 50	24	29
8 57 51	12	16	11	28 28	25	♑
9 1 52	13	17	12	29 7	25	1
9 5 52	14	18	12	29 45	26	2

LATITUDE 59° N.

SIDEREAL TIME (H M S)	10 ♐	11 Ω	12 ♍	ASC ≏	2 ≏	3 ♏
6 0 0	0	9	8	0 0	22	21
6 4 22	1	9	9	0 41	23	22
6 8 43	2	10	10	1 23	24	23
6 13 5	3	11	10	2 4	24	24
6 17 26	4	12	11	2 46	25	25
6 21 47	5	13	12	3 27	26	26
6 26 9	6	14	13	4 8	27	27
6 30 29	7	15	13	4 49	28	28
6 34 50	8	16	14	5 31	28	29
6 39 11	9	17	15	6 12	29	♐
6 43 31	10	18	16	6 53	♏	0
6 47 51	11	19	17	7 34	1	1
6 52 11	12	19	18	8 15	1	2
6 56 30	13	20	18	8 56	2	3
7 0 49	14	21	19	9 37	3	4
7 5 7	15	22	20	10 18	4	5
7 9 26	16	23	21	10 59	5	6
7 13 43	17	24	21	11 39	5	7
7 18 0	18	25	22	12 20	6	8
7 22 17	19	26	23	13 0	7	8
7 26 33	20	27	24	13 41	8	9
7 30 49	21	28	25	14 21	8	10
7 35 4	22	29	25	15 1	9	11
7 39 19	23	29	26	15 41	10	12
7 43 33	24	♏	27	16 21	11	13
7 47 46	25	1	28	17 1	11	14
7 51 59	26	2	29	17 41	12	15
7 56 11	27	3	29	18 21	13	16
8 0 23	28	4	≏	19 0	14	16
8 4 34	29	5	1	19 40	14	17
8 8 44	Ω	6	2	20 19	15	18
8 12 53	1	7	2	20 58	16	19
8 17 2	2	8	3	21 37	17	20
8 21 10	3	8	4	22 16	17	21
8 25 18	4	9	5	22 55	18	22
8 29 24	5	10	5	23 33	19	23
8 33 30	6	11	6	24 12	20	24
8 37 36	7	12	7	24 50	20	25
8 41 40	8	13	8	25 29	21	25
8 45 44	9	14	8	26 7	22	26
8 49 47	10	15	9	26 45	22	27
8 53 50	11	16	10	27 23	23	28
8 57 51	12	16	11	28 0	24	29
9 1 52	13	17	11	28 38	25	♑
9 5 52	14	18	12	29 16	25	1

LATITUDE 60° N.

SIDEREAL TIME (H M S)	10 ♐	11 Ω	12 ♍	ASC ≏	2 ≏	3 ♏
6 0 0	0	9	8	0 0	22	21
6 4 22	1	10	9	0 41	22	22
6 8 43	2	11	10	1 21	23	23
6 13 5	3	12	11	2 2	24	24
6 17 26	4	13	11	2 43	25	25
6 21 47	5	13	12	3 23	26	25
6 26 9	6	14	13	4 4	26	26
6 30 29	7	15	14	4 45	27	27
6 34 50	8	16	15	5 25	28	28
6 39 11	9	17	15	6 6	29	29
6 43 31	10	18	16	6 46	29	♐
6 47 51	11	19	17	7 27	♏	1
6 52 11	12	20	18	8 7	1	2
6 56 30	13	21	18	8 47	2	3
7 0 49	14	22	19	9 27	3	3
7 5 7	15	22	20	10 8	3	4
7 9 26	16	23	21	10 48	4	5
7 13 43	17	24	22	11 28	5	6
7 18 0	18	25	22	12 7	6	7
7 22 17	19	26	23	12 47	6	8
7 26 33	20	27	24	13 27	7	9
7 30 49	21	28	25	14 7	8	10
7 35 4	22	29	25	14 46	9	11
7 39 19	23	♏	26	15 26	9	11
7 43 33	24	1	27	16 5	10	12
7 47 46	25	1	28	16 44	11	13
7 51 59	26	2	29	17 23	12	14
7 56 11	27	3	29	18 2	12	15
8 0 23	28	4	≏	18 41	13	16
8 4 34	29	5	1	19 20	14	17
8 8 44	Ω	6	2	19 58	15	18
8 12 53	1	7	2	20 37	15	19
8 17 2	2	8	3	21 15	16	19
8 21 10	3	9	4	21 53	17	20
8 25 18	4	9	5	22 31	17	21
8 29 24	5	10	5	23 9	18	22
8 33 30	6	11	6	23 47	19	23
8 37 36	7	12	7	24 25	20	24
8 41 40	8	13	8	25 3	20	25
8 45 44	9	14	8	25 40	21	26
8 49 47	10	15	9	26 17	22	27
8 53 50	11	16	10	26 55	22	27
8 57 51	12	16	10	27 32	23	28
9 1 52	13	17	11	28 9	24	29
9 5 52	14	18	12	28 45	25	♑

| HOUSES | 4 | 5 | 6 | 7 | 8 | 9 |

LATITUDE 58° N. LATITUDE 59° N. LATITUDE 60° N.

SIDEREAL TIME (H M S)	10 ♌	11 ♍	12 ♎	ASC ♏	2 ♏	3 ♑	10 ♌	11 ♍	12 ♎	ASC ♎	2 ♏	3 ♑	10 ♌	11 ♍	12 ♎	ASC ♎	2 ♏	3 ♑
9 9 52	15	19	13	0 23	27	3	15	19	13	29 53	26	2	15	19	13	29 22	25	1
9 13 50	16	20	14	1 1	28	4	16	20	14	♏ 30	27	3	16	20	13	29 59	26	2
9 17 49	17	21	14	1 38	28	4	17	21	14	1 7	27	4	17	21	14	♏ 35	27	3
9 21 46	18	22	15	2 16	29	5	18	22	15	1 44	28	5	18	22	15	1 12	27	4
9 25 42	19	22	16	2 54	♐	6	19	22	16	2 21	29	6	19	23	16	1 48	28	5
9 29 38	20	23	17	3 31	0	7	20	23	16	2 58	♐	7	20	23	16	2 24	29	6
9 33 34	21	24	17	4 8	1	8	21	24	17	3 35	0	8	21	24	17	3 0	29	7
9 37 28	22	25	18	4 46	2	9	22	25	18	4 11	1	8	22	25	18	3 36	♐	8
9 41 22	23	26	19	5 23	3	10	23	26	19	4 47	2	9	23	26	18	4 11	1	9
9 45 15	24	27	20	6 0	3	11	24	27	19	5 24	2	10	24	27	19	4 47	2	10
9 49 8	25	28	20	6 36	4	12	25	28	20	6 0	3	11	25	28	20	5 22	2	11
9 53 0	26	28	21	7 13	5	13	26	28	21	6 36	4	12	26	28	20	5 58	3	12
9 56 51	27	29	22	7 50	6	14	27	29	21	7 12	5	13	27	29	21	6 33	4	12
10 0 42	28	♎	22	8 26	6	15	28	♎	22	7 48	5	14	28	♎	22	7 8	4	13
10 4 32	29	1	23	9 3	7	16	29	1	23	8 24	6	15	29	1	23	7 44	5	14
10 8 22	♍	2	24	9 39	8	17	♍	2	24	8 59	7	16	♍	2	23	8 19	6	15
10 12 11	1	3	25	10 15	8	18	1	3	24	9 35	7	17	1	3	24	8 53	6	16
10 15 59	2	4	25	10 52	9	19	2	4	25	10 11	8	18	2	3	25	9 28	7	17
10 19 47	3	4	26	11 28	10	20	3	4	26	10 46	9	19	3	4	25	10 3	8	18
10 23 34	4	5	27	12 4	11	21	4	5	26	11 21	10	20	4	5	26	10 38	9	19
10 27 21	5	6	27	12 40	11	22	5	6	27	11 57	10	21	5	6	27	11 12	9	20
10 31 8	6	7	28	13 16	12	23	6	7	28	12 32	11	22	6	7	27	11 47	10	21
10 34 53	7	8	29	13 52	13	24	7	8	28	13 7	12	23	7	8	28	12 21	11	23
10 38 39	8	9	29	14 27	13	25	8	8	29	13 42	12	24	8	8	29	12 56	11	24
10 42 24	9	9	♏	15 3	14	26	9	9	♏	14 17	13	25	9	9	29	13 30	12	25
10 46 8	10	10	1	15 39	15	27	10	10	0	14 52	14	26	10	10	♏	14 4	13	26
10 49 52	11	11	1	16 14	16	28	11	11	1	15 27	15	27	11	11	1	14 39	13	27
10 53 36	12	12	2	16 50	16	29	12	12	2	16 2	15	28	12	12	1	15 13	14	28
10 57 20	13	13	3	17 26	17	♒	13	13	2	16 37	16	♒	13	12	2	15 47	15	29
11 1 3	14	13	3	18 1	18	1	14	13	3	17 12	17	1	14	13	3	16 21	16	♒
11 4 45	15	14	4	18 37	19	2	15	14	4	17 47	18	2	15	14	3	16 55	16	1
11 8 28	16	15	5	19 12	19	3	16	15	4	18 21	18	3	16	15	4	17 29	17	2
11 12 10	17	16	5	19 48	20	4	17	16	5	18 56	19	4	17	16	5	18 3	18	3
11 15 52	18	17	6	20 23	21	6	18	17	6	19 31	20	5	18	16	5	18 37	19	4
11 19 33	19	18	7	20 59	22	7	19	17	6	20 6	21	7	19	17	6	19 11	19	5
11 23 15	20	18	7	21 34	23	8	20	18	7	20 41	21	7	20	18	7	19 45	20	6
11 26 56	21	19	8	22 10	23	9	21	19	8	21 15	22	8	21	19	7	20 19	21	8
11 30 37	22	20	9	22 45	24	10	22	20	8	21 50	23	9	22	20	8	20 53	22	9
11 34 17	23	21	9	23 21	25	11	23	21	9	22 25	24	10	23	20	8	21 27	22	10
11 37 58	24	22	10	23 56	26	12	24	21	10	23 0	24	12	24	21	9	22 1	23	11
11 41 39	25	22	11	24 32	27	13	25	22	10	23 34	25	13	25	22	10	22 35	24	12
11 45 19	26	23	11	25 8	27	14	26	23	11	24 9	26	14	26	23	10	23 9	25	13
11 48 59	27	24	12	25 43	28	16	27	24	12	24 44	27	15	27	24	11	23 43	25	15
11 52 40	28	25	13	26 19	29	17	28	25	12	25 19	28	16	28	24	12	24 17	26	16
11 56 20	29	26	13	26 55	♑	18	29	25	13	25 54	28	17	29	25	12	24 51	27	17
HOUSES	4	5	6	7	8	9	4	5	6	7	8	9	4	5	6	7	8	9

LATITUDE 58° S. LATITUDE 59° S. LATITUDE 60° S.

LATITUDE 58° N. LATITUDE 59° N. LATITUDE 60° N.

SIDEREAL TIME	10 ♎	11 ♎	12 ♏	ASC ♏	2 ♑	3 ♒	10 ♎	11 ♎	12 ♏	ASC ♏	2 ♐	3 ♒	10 ♎	11 ♎	12 ♏	ASC ♏	2 ♐	3 ♒
H M S	°	°	°	° ′	°	°	°	°	°	° ′	°	°	°	°	°	° ′	°	°
12 0 0	0	26	14	27 31	1	19	0	26	14	26 29	29	19	0	26	13	25 26	28	18
12 3 40	1	27	15	28 7	1	20	1	27	14	27 4	♑	20	1	27	14	26 0	29	19
12 7 20	2	28	15	28 43	2	21	2	28	15	27 40	1	21	2	28	14	26 34	29	20
12 11 1	3	29	16	29 19	3	23	3	29	16	28 15	2	22	3	28	15	27 9	♑	22
12 14 41	4	♏	17	29 55	4	24	4	29	16	28 50	3	23	4	29	16	27 43	1	23
12 18 21	5	0	17	0♐ 32	5	25	5	♏	17	29 26	4	25	5	♏	16	28 18	2	24
12 22 2	6	1	18	1 8	6	26	6	1	18	0♐ 1	4	26	6	1	17	28 52	3	25
12 25 42	7	2	19	1 45	7	27	7	2	18	0 37	5	27	7	1	17	29 27	4	27
12 29 23	8	3	19	2 21	8	29	8	2	19	1 13	.6	28	8	2	18	0♐	5	28
12 33 4	9	3	20	2 58	9	♓	9	3	19	1 49	7	29	9	3	19	0 37	6	29
12 36 45	10	4	21	3 35	10	1	10	4	20	2 25	8	♓	10	4	19	1 12	6	♓
12 40 27	11	5	21	4 13	11	2	11	5	21	3 1	9	2	11	5	20	1 47	7	2
12 44 8	12	6	22	4 50	12	4	12	6	21	3 38	10	3	12	5	21	2 23	8	3
12 47 50	13	7	23	5 28	13	5	13	6	22	4 14	11	4	13	6	21	2 58	9	4
12 51 32	14	7	23	6 5	14	6	14	7	23	4 51	12	6	14	7	22	3 34	10	5
12 55 15	15	8	24	6 43	15	7	15	8	23	5 28	13	7	15	8	23	4 10	11	7
12 58 57	16	9	25	7 22	16	9	16	9	24	6 5	14	8	16	8	23	4 46	12	8
13 2 40	17	10	26	8 0	17	10	17	9	25	6 43	15	10	17	9	24	5 22	13	9
13 6 24	18	11	26	8 39	18	11	18	10	25	7 20	16	11	18	10	25	5 59	14	11
13 10 8	19	11	27	9 18	19	12	19	11	26	7 58	17	12	19	11	25	6 36	16	12
13 13 52	20	12	28	9 57	20	14	20	12	27	8 36	18	14	20	11	26	7 12	17	13
13 17 36	21	13	28	10 37	21	15	21	13	27	9 15	20	15	21	12	27	7 50	18	15
13 21 21	22	14	29	11 16	22	16	22	13	28	9 53	21	16	22	13	27	8 27	19	16
13 25 7	23	15	♐	11 56	24	18	23	14	29	10 32	22	18	23	14	28	9 5	20	17
13 28 52	24	15	0	12 37	25	19	24	15	29	11 12	23	19	24	15	29	9 43	21	19
13 32 39	25	16	1	13 18	26	20	25	16	♐	11 51	24	20	25	15	29	10 21	23	20
13 36 26	26	17	2	13 59	27	22	26	17	1	12 31	26	22	26	16	♐	11 0	24	21
13 40 13	27	18	2	14 41	28	23	27	17	2	13 11	27	23	27	17	1	11 38	25	23
13 44 1	28	18	3	15 23	♒	24	28	18	2	13 52	28	24	28	18	1	12 18	26	24
13 47 49	29	19	4	16 5	1	26	29	19	3	14 33	♒	26	29	19	2	12 57	28	26
13 51 38	♏	20	5	16 48	2	27	♏	20	4	15 15	1	27	♏	19	3	13 37	29	27
13 55 28	1	21	5	17 31	4	28	1	20	4	15 57	2	28	1	20	3	14 18	♒	28
13 59 18	2	22	6	18 15	5	♈	2	21	5	16 39	4	♈	2	21	4	14 59	2	♈
14 3 9	3	22	7	18 59	7	1	3	22	6	17 22	5	1	3	22	5	15 40	3	1
14 7 0	4	23	7	19 44	8	2	4	23	6	18 5	7	3	4	22	5	16 21	5	3
14 10 52	5	24	8	20 30	10	4	5	24	7	18 49	8	4	5	23	6	17 4	6	4
14 14 45	6	25	9	21 16	11	5	6	24	8	19 34	10	5	6	24	7	17 46	8	5
14 18 38	7	26	10	22 2	13	7	7	25	9	20 19	11	7	7	25	8	18 30	10	7
14 22 32	8	27	10	22 50	14	8	8	26	9	21 4	13	8	8	26	8	19 14	11	8
14 26 26	9	27	11	23 38	16	9	9	27	10	21 51	14	9	9	26	9	19 58	13	10
14 30 22	10	28	12	24 27	17	11	10	28	11	22 38	16	11	10	27	10	20 43	15	11
14 34 17	11	29	13	25 16	19	12	11	29	12	23 25	18	12	11	28	11	21 29	16	12
14 38 14	12	♐	13	26 6	21	13	12	29	12	24 14	20	14	12	29	11	22 15	18	14
14 42 11	13	1	14	26 58	22	15	13	♐	13	25 3	21	15	13	♐	12	23 2	20	15
14 46 10	14	1	15	27 50	24	16	14	1	14	25 53	23	16	14	0	13	23 50	22	17
HOUSES	4	5	6	7	8	9	4	5	6	7	8	9	4	5	6	7	8	9

LATITUDE 58° S. LATITUDE 59° S. LATITUDE 60° S.

	LATITUDE 58° N.						LATITUDE 59° N.						LATITUDE 60° N.					
SIDEREAL TIME	10 ♏	11 ♐	12 ♐	ASC ♐	2 ♒	3 ♈	10 ♏	11 ♐	12 ♐	ASC ♐	2 ♒	3 ♈	10 ♏	11 ♐	12 ♐	ASC ♐	2 ♒	3 ♈
H M S	°	°	°	° ′	°	°	°	°	°	° ′	°	°	°	°	°	° ′	°	°
14 50 8	15	2	16	28 43	26	18	15	2	15	26 44	25	18	15	1	14	24 39	24	18
14 54 8	16	3	17	29 37	28	19	16	3	15	27 36	27	19	16	2	14	25 29	26	20
14 58 8	17	4	17	0♑ 32	♓	20	17	3	16	28 30	29	21	17	3	15	26 20	27	21
15 2 9	18	5	18	1 28	1	22	18	4	17	29 24	♓	22	18	4	16	27 11	29	22
15 6 10	19	6	19	2 26	3	23	19	5	18	0♑ 19	2	23	19	5	17	28 4	♓	24
15 10 13	20	6	20	3 25	5	25	20	6	19	1 15	4	25	20	5	17	28 58	3	25
15 14 16	21	7	21	4 25	7	26	21	7	19	2 13	6	26	21	6	18	29 53	6	27
15 18 20	22	8	22	5 26	9	27	22	8	20	3 12	8	28	22	7	19	0♑ 49	8	28
15 22 24	23	9	22	6 29	11	29	23	8	21	4 13	11	29	23	8	20	1 47	10	29
15 26 30	24	10	23	7 34	13	♉	24	9	22	5 15	13	♉	24	9	21	2 46	12	♉
15 30 36	25	11	24	8 40	15	1	25	10	23	6 19	15	2	25	10	22	3 47	14	2
15 34 42	26	12	25	9 49	17	3	26	11	24	7 24	17	3	26	10	22	4 50	16	4
15 38 50	27	12	26	10 59	19	4	27	12	25	8 32	19	5	27	11	23	5 54	18	5
15 42 58	28	13	27	12 11	21	5	28	13	25	9 41	21	6	28	12	24	7 0	21	6
15 47 7	29	14	28	13 25	23	7	29	14	26	10 53	23	7	29	13	25	8 8	23	8
15 51 16	♐	15	29	14 42	26	8	♐	15	27	12 7	25	9	♐	14	26	9 19	25	9
15 55 26	1	16	♑	16 1	28	10	1	15	28	13 23	28	10	1	15	27	10 32	28	10
15 59 37	2	17	1	17 23	♈	11	2	16	29	14 42	♈	11	2	16	28	11 47	♈	12
16 3 49	3	18	2	18 48	2	12	3	17	♑	16 4	2	13	3	17	29	13 5	2	13
16 8 1	4	19	3	20 16	4	13	4	18	1	17 29	4	14	4	17	♑	14 27	4	15
16 12 14	5	20	4	21 47	6	15	5	19	2	18 58	6	15	5	18	1	15 51	7	16
16 16 27	6	21	5	23 22	8	16	6	20	3	20 30	9	17	6	19	2	17 20	9	17
16 20 41	7	22	6	25 1	10	17	7	21	4	22 6	11	18	7	20	3	18 52	11	19
16 24 56	8	22	7	26 43	13	19	8	22	5	23 46	13	19	8	21	4	20 28	14	20
16 29 11	9	23	8	28 30	15	20	9	23	6	25 30	15	21	9	22	5	22 10	16	21
16 33 27	10	24	9	0♒ 22	17	21	10	24	7	27 20	17	22	10	23	6	23 56	18	22
16 37 43	11	25	10	2 18	19	23	11	25	8	29 17	20	23	11	24	7	25 47	20	24
16 41 59	12	26	11	4 20	21	24	12	26	10	1♒ 15	22	24	12	25	8	27 45	23	25
16 46 17	13	27	12	6 28	23	25	13	27	11	3 22	24	26	13	26	9	29 49	25	26
16 50 34	14	28	13	8 41	25	26	14	27	12	5 35	26	27	14	27	10	2♒ 1	27	28
16 54 53	15	29	15	11 1	27	28	15	28	13	7 56	28	28	15	28	11	4 20	29	29
16 59 11	16	♑	16	13 28	29	29	16	29	14	10 24	♉	29	16	29	12	6 48	♉	♊
17 3 30	17	1	17	16 2	♉	♊	17	♑	15	13 0	2	♊	17	♑	14	9 25	3	1
17 7 49	18	2	18	18 43	3	1	18	1	17	15 44	4	2	18	1	15	12 12	5	3
17 12 9	19	3	20	21 31	5	2	19	2	18	18 38	6	3	19	2	16	15 9	7	4
17 16 29	20	4	21	24 28	7	4	20	3	19	21 40	8	4	20	3	17	18 18	9	5
17 20 49	21	5	22	27 32	9	5	21	4	21	24 53	10	6	21	4	19	21 38	11	6
17 25 10	22	6	24	0♓ 44	11	6	22	6	22	28 15	12	7	22	5	20	25 11	13	7
17 29 31	23	7	25	4 3	13	7	23	7	23	1♓ 47	14	8	23	6	22	28 56	15	9
17 33 51	24	8	26	7 30	14	8	24	8	25	5 28	16	9	24	7	23	2♓ 53	17	10
17 38 13	25	9	28	11 3	16	10	25	9	26	9 17	17	10	25	8	24	7 3	19	11
17 42 34	26	10	29	14 43	18	11	26	10	28	13 15	19	11	26	9	26	11 23	21	12
17 46 55	27	12	♒	18 27	20	12	27	11	29	17 20	21	13	27	10	27	15 53	23	13
17 51 17	28	13	2	22 16	21	13	28	12	♒	21 30	23	14	28	11	29	20 31	24	14
17 55 38	29	14	4	26 7	23	14	29	13	2	25 44	24	15	29	12	♒	25 14	26	16
HOUSES	4	5	6	7	8	9	4	5	6	7	8	9	4	5	6	7	8	9

LATITUDE 58° S.   LATITUDE 59° S.   LATITUDE 60° S.

LATITUDE 58° N.   LATITUDE 59° N.   LATITUDE 60° N.

SIDEREAL TIME (H M S)	10 ♑	11 ♑	12 ♒	ASC ♈		2 ♉	3 ♊	10 ♑	11 ♑	12 ♒	ASC ♈		2 ♉	3 ♊	10 ♑	11 ♑	12 ♒	ASC ♈		2 ♉	3 ♊
18 0 0	0	15	5	0	0	25	15	0	14	4	0	0	26	16	0	13	2	0	0	28	17
18 4 22	1	16	7	3	53	26	16	1	15	6	4	16	28	17	1	14	4	4	46	29	18
18 8 43	2	17	9	7	44	28	17	2	16	7	8	30	29	18	2	16	6	9	29	♊	19
18 13 5	3	18	10	11	33	29	18	3	17	9	12	40	♊	19	3	17	7	14	7	3	20
18 17 26	4	19	12	15	17	♊	20	4	19	11	16	45	2	20	4	18	9	18	37	4	21
18 21 47	5	20	14	18	57	2	21	5	20	13	20	43	4	21	5	19	11	22	57	6	22
18 26 9	6	22	16	22	30	4	22	6	21	14	24	32	5	22	6	20	13	27	7	7	23
18 30 29	7	23	17	25	57	5	23	7	22	16	28	13	7	23	7	21	15	1♉	4	8	24
18 34 50	8	24	19	29	16	6	24	8	23	18	1♉	45	8	24	8	23	17	4	49	10	25
18 39 11	9	25	21	2♉	28	8	25	9	24	20	5	7	9	26	9	24	19	8	22	11	26
18 43 31	10	26	23	5	32	9	26	10	26	22	8	20	11	27	10	25	21	11	42	13	27
18 47 51	11	28	25	8	29	10	27	11	27	24	11	22	12	28	11	26	23	14	51	14	28
18 52 11	12	29	27	11	17	12	28	12	28	26	14	16	13	29	12	27	25	17	48	15	29
18 56 30	13	♒	29	13	58	13	29	13	29	28	17	0	15	♋	13	29	27	20	35	16	♋
19 0 49	14	1	♓	16	32	14	♋	14	♒	♓	19	36	16	1	14	♒	29	23	12	18	1
19 5 7	15	2	3	18	59	15	1	15	2	2	22	4	17	2	15	1	♓	25	40	19	2
19 9 26	16	4	5	21	19	17	2	16	3	4	24	25	18	3	16	2	3	27	59	20	3
19 13 43	17	5	7	23	32	18	3	17	4	6	26	38	19	3	17	4	5	0♊	11	21	4
19 18 0	18	6	9	25	40	19	4	18	6	8	28	45	20	4	18	5	7	2	15	22	5
19 22 17	19	7	11	27	42	20	5	19	7	10	0♊	45	22	5	19	6	10	4	13	23	6
19 26 33	20	9	13	29	38	21	6	20	8	13	2	40	23	6	20	8	12	6	4	24	7
19 30 49	21	10	15	1♊	30	22	7	21	9	15	4	30	24	7	21	9	14	7	50	25	8
19 35 4	22	11	17	3	17	23	8	22	11	17	6	14	25	8	22	10	16	9	32	26	10
19 39 19	23	13	20	4	59	24	8	23	12	19	7	54	26	9	23	11	19	11	8	27	10
19 43 33	24	14	22	6	38	25	9	24	13	21	9	30	27	10	24	13	21	12	40	28	11
19 47 46	25	15	24	8	13	26	10	25	15	24	11	2	28	11	25	14	23	14	9	29	12
19 51 59	26	17	26	9	44	27	11	26	16	26	12	31	29	12	26	15	26	15	33	♋	13
19 56 11	27	18	28	11	12	28	12	27	17	28	13	56	♋	13	27	17	28	16	55	1	13
20 0 23	28	19	♈	12	37	29	13	28	19	♈	15	18	1	14	28	18	♈	18	13	2	14
20 4 34	29	20	2	13	59	♋	14	29	20	2	16	37	2	15	29	20	2	19	28	3	15
20 8 44	♒	22	4	15	18	1	15	♒	21	5	17	53	3	15	♒	21	5	20	41	4	16
20 12 53	1	23	7	16	35	2	16	1	23	7	19	7	4	16	1	22	7	21	52	5	17
20 17 2	2	25	9	17	49	3	17	2	24	9	20	19	5	17	2	24	9	23	0	6	18
20 21 10	3	26	11	19	1	4	18	3	25	11	21	28	5	18	3	25	12	24	6	7	19
20 25 18	4	27	13	20	11	5	18	4	27	13	22	36	6	19	4	26	14	25	10	8	20
20 29 24	5	29	15	21	20	6	19	5	28	15	23	41	7	20	5	28	16	26	13	8	20
20 33 30	6	♓	17	22	26	7	20	6	♓	17	24	45	8	21	6	29	18	27	14	9	21
20 37 36	7	1	19	23	31	8	21	7	1	19	25	47	9	22	7	♓	20	28	13	10	22
20 41 40	8	3	21	24	34	8	22	8	2	22	26	48	10	22	8	2	22	29	11	11	23
20 45 44	9	4	23	25	35	9	23	9	4	24	27	47	11	23	9	3	24	0♋	7	12	24
20 49 47	10	5	25	26	35	10	24	10	5	26	28	45	11	24	10	5	27	1	2	13	25
20 53 50	11	7	27	27	34	11	24	11	7	28	29	41	12	25	11	6	29	1	56	13	25
20 57 51	12	8	29	28	32	12	25	12	8	29	0♋	36	13	26	12	8	♉	2	49	14	26
21 1 52	13	10	♉	29	28	13	26	13	9	♉	1	30	14	27	13	9	3	3	40	15	27
21 5 52	14	11	2	0♋	23	13	27	14	11	3	2	24	15	27	14	10	4	4	31	16	28
HOUSES	4	5	6	7		8	9	4	5	6	7		8	9	4	5	6	7		8	9

LATITUDE 58° S.   LATITUDE 59° S.   LATITUDE 60° S.

LATITUDE 58° N. LATITUDE 59° N. LATITUDE 60° N.

SIDEREAL TIME	10 ♒	11 ♓	12 ♉	ASC ♋ °	ASC '	2 ♋	3 ♋	10 ♒	11 ♓	12 ♉	ASC ♋ °	ASC '	2 ♋	3 ♋	10 ♒	11 ♓	12 ♉	ASC ♋ °	ASC '	2 ♋	3 ♋
H M S	°	°	°	°	'	°	°	°	°	°	°	'	°	°	°	°	°	°	'	°	°
21 9 52	15	12	4	1	17	14	28	15	12	5	3	16	15	28	15	12	6	5	21	16	29
21 13 50	16	14	6	2	10	15	29	16	14	7	4	7	16	29	16	13	8	6	10	17	♌
21 17 49	17	15	8	3	2	16	29	17	15	9	4	57	17	♌	17	15	10	6	58	18	0
21 21 46	18	17	9	3	54	17	♌	18	16	10	5	46	18	1	18	16	12	7	45	19	1
21 25 42	19	18	11	4	44	17	1	19	18	12	6	35	18	1	19	18	14	8	31	19	2
21 29 38	20	19	13	5	33	18	2	20	19	14	7	22	19	2	20	19	15	9	17	20	3
21 33 34	21	21	14	6	22	19	3	21	21	16	8	9	20	3	21	20	17	10	2	21	4
21 37 28	22	22	16	7	10	20	3	22	22	17	8	56	21	4	22	22	19	10	46	22	4
21 41 22	23	23	17	7	58	20	4	23	23	19	9	41	21	5	23	23	20	11	30	22	5
21 45 15	24	25	19	8	44	21	5	24	25	20	10	26	22	6	24	25	22	12	14	23	6
21 49 8	25	26	20	9	30	22	6	25	26	22	11	11	23	6	25	26	24	12	56	24	7
21 53 0	26	28	22	10	16	23	7	26	27	23	11	55	24	7	26	27	25	13	39	25	8
21 56 51	27	29	23	11	1	23	8	27	29	25	12	38	24	8	27	29	27	14	20	25	8
22 0 42	28	♈	25	11	45	24	8	28	♈	26	13	21	25	9	28	♈	28	15	1	26	9
22 4 32	29	2	26	12	29	25	9	29	2	28	14	3	26	10	29	2	29	15	42	27	10
22 8 22	♓	3	28	13	12	25	10	♓	3	29	14	45	26	10	♓	3	♊	16	23	27	11
22 12 11	1	4	29	13	55	26	11	1	4	♊	15	27	27	11	1	4	2	17	3	28	11
22 15 59	2	6	♊	14	37	27	12	2	6	2	16	8	28	12	2	6	4	17	42	29	12
22 19 47	3	7	2	15	19	28	12	3	7	3	16	49	28	13	3	7	5	18	22	29	13
22 23 34	4	8	3	16	1	28	13	4	8	4	17	29	29	13	4	9	6	19	0	♌	14
22 27 21	5	10	4	16	42	29	14	5	10	6	18	9	♌	14	5	10	7	19	39	1	15
22 31 8	6	11	5	17	23	♌	15	6	11	7	18	48	1	15	6	11	9	20	17	1	15
22 34 53	7	12	6	18	3	0	15	7	12	8	19	28	1	16	7	13	10	20	55	2	16
22 38 39	8	14	8	18	44	1	16	8	14	9	20	7	2	17	8	14	11	21	33	3	17
22 42 24	9	15	9	19	23	2	17	9	15	10	20	45	3	17	9	15	12	22	10	3	18
22 46 8	10	16	10	20	3	2	18	10	16	12	21	24	3	18	10	17	13	22	48	4	19
22 49 52	11	18	11	20	42	3	19	11	18	13	22	2	4	19	11	18	14	23	24	5	19
22 53 36	12	19	12	21	21	4	19	12	19	14	22	40	5	20	12	19	16	24	1	5	20
22 57 20	13	20	13	22	0	4	20	13	20	15	23	17	5	21	13	21	17	24	38	6	21
23 1 3	14	21	14	22	38	5	21	14	22	16	23	55	6	21	14	22	18	25	14	7	22
23 4 45	15	23	15	23	17	6	22	15	23	17	24	32	7	22	15	23	19	25	50	7	22
23 8 28	16	24	16	23	55	7	23	16	24	18	25	9	7	23	16	25	20	26	26	8	23
23 12 10	17	25	17	24	32	7	23	17	26	19	25	46	8	24	17	26	21	27	2	9	24
23 15 52	18	26	18	25	10	8	24	18	27	20	26	22	9	24	18	27	22	27	37	9	25
23 19 33	19	28	19	25	47	9	25	19	28	21	26	59	9	25	19	28	23	28	13	10	25
23 23 15	20	29	20	26	25	9	26	20	29	22	27	35	10	26	20	♉	24	28	48	11	26
23 26 56	21	♉	21	27	2	10	27	21	♉	23	28	11	11	27	21	1	24	29	23	11	27
23 30 37	22	1	22	27	39	11	27	22	2	24	28	47	11	28	22	2	25	29	58	12	28
23 34 17	23	3	23	28	15	11	28	23	3	25	29	23	12	28	23	3	26	0♌	33	13	29
23 37 58	24	4	24	28	52	12	29	24	4	26	29	59	12	29	24	5	27	1	8	13	29
23 41 39	25	5	25	29	28	13	♍	25	5	26	0♌	34	13	♍	25	6	28	1	42	14	♍
23 45 19	26	6	26	0♌	5	13	0	26	7	27	1	10	14	1	26	7	29	2	17	14	1
23 48 59	27	7	27	0	41	14	1	27	8	28	1	45	14	1	27	8	♋	2	51	15	2
23 52 40	28	9	28	1	17	15	2	28	9	29	2	20	15	2	28	10	1	3	26	16	2
23 56 20	29	10	29	1	53	15	3	29	10	♋	2	56	16	3	29	11	1	4	0	16	3
HOUSES	4	5	6	7		8	9	4	5	6	7		8	9	4	5	6	7		8	9

LATITUDE 58° S. LATITUDE 59° S. LATITUDE 60° S.

LATITUDE 61° N.　LATITUDE 62° N.　LATITUDE 63° N.

SIDEREAL TIME	10 ♈	11 ♉	12 ♋	ASC ♌	2 ♌	3 ♍	10 ♈	11 ♉	12 ♋	ASC ♌	2 ♌	3 ♍	10 ♈	11 ♉	12 ♋	ASC ♌	2 ♌	3 ♍
H M S	°	°	°	° '	°	°	°	°	°	° '	°	°	°	°	°	° '	°	°
0 0 0	0	13	4	5 40	18	4	0	13	6	6 48	18	4	0	14	8	7 59	19	5
0 3 40	1	14	5	6 14	18	5	1	14	6	7 21	19	5	1	15	8	8 31	20	5
0 7 20	2	15	5	6 47	19	6	2	16	7	7 53	20	6	2	16	9	9 2	20	6
0 11 1	3	16	6	7 20	20	6	3	17	8	8 25	20	7	3	18	10	9 33	21	7
0 14 41	4	17	7	7 53	20	7	4	18	9	8 58	21	8	4	19	10	10 5	21	8
0 18 21	5	18	8	8 26	21	8	5	19	9	9 30	21	8	5	20	11	10 36	22	9
0 22 2	6	20	8	9 0	21	9	6	20	10	10 2	22	9	6	21	12	11 7	23	9
0 25 43	7	21	9	9 33	22	10	7	22	11	10 35	23	10	7	22	13	11 39	23	10
0 29 23	8	22	10	10 6	23	11	8	23	12	11 7	23	11	8	24	13	12 10	24	11
0 33 4	9	23	11	10 39	23	11	9	24	12	11 39	24	11	9	25	14	12 41	24	12
0 36 45	10	24	11	11 12	24	12	10	25	13	12 11	25	12	10	26	15	13 13	25	12
0 40 27	11	25	12	11 45	25	13	11	26	14	12 44	25	13	11	27	15	13 44	26	13
0 44 8	12	26	13	12 19	25	14	12	27	14	13 16	26	14	12	28	16	14 16	26	14
0 47 50	13	28	14	12 52	26	14	13	28	15	13 48	26	15	13	29	17	14 47	27	15
0 51 32	14	29	14	13 25	27	15	14	♊	16	14 21	27	15	14	♊	17	15 19	28	16
0 55 15	15	♊	15	13 58	27	16	15	1	16	14 53	28	16	15	2	18	15 50	28	16
0 58 57	16	1	16	14 32	28	17	16	2	17	15 26	28	17	16	3	19	16 22	29	17
1 2 40	17	2	16	15 5	29	18	17	3	18	15 58	29	18	17	4	19	16 54	29	18
1 6 24	18	3	17	15 38	29	18	18	4	18	16 31	♍	19	18	5	20	17 25	♍	19
1 10 8	19	4	18	16 12	♍	19	19	5	19	17 4	0	19	19	6	21	17 57	1	19
1 13 52	20	5	18	16 45	0	20	20	6	20	17 36	1	20	20	7	21	18 29	1	20
1 17 36	21	6	19	17 19	1	21	21	7	20	18 9	2	21	21	8	22	19 1	2	21
1 21 21	22	7	20	17 52	2	22	22	8	21	18 42	2	22	22	9	22	19 33	3	22
1 25 7	23	8	21	18 26	2	22	23	9	22	19 15	3	23	23	10	23	20 5	3	23
1 28 52	24	9	21	19 0	3	23	24	10	22	19 48	4	23	24	11	24	20 37	4	23
1 32 39	25	10	22	19 33	4	24	25	11	23	20 21	4	24	25	12	24	21 9	5	24
1 36 26	26	11	23	20 7	4	25	26	12	24	20 54	5	25	26	14	25	21 42	5	25
1 40 13	27	12	23	20 41	5	26	27	13	24	21 27	5	26	27	15	26	22 14	6	26
1 44 1	28	13	24	21 15	6	27	28	14	25	22 0	6	27	28	16	26	22 47	7	27
1 47 49	29	14	25	21 49	6	27	29	15	26	22 34	7	27	29	17	27	23 19	7	27
1 51 38	♉	15	25	22 24	7	28	♉	16	26	23 7	7	28	♉	18	28	23 52	8	28
1 55 28	1	16	26	22 58	8	29	1	17	27	23 41	8	29	1	19	28	24 25	8	29
1 59 18	2	17	27	23 32	8	♎	2	18	28	24 14	9	♎	2	20	29	24 58	9	♎
2 3 9	3	18	27	24 7	9	1	3	19	28	24 48	9	1	3	21	♌	25 31	10	1
2 7 0	4	19	28	24 41	10	2	4	20	29	25 22	10	1	4	22	0	26 4	10	1
2 10 52	5	20	29	25 16	11	2	5	21	♌	25 56	11	2	5	23	1	26 37	11	2
2 14 45	6	21	29	25 51	11	3	6	22	0	26 30	11	3	6	23	1	27 10	12	3
2 18 38	7	22	♌	26 26	12	4	7	23	1	27 4	12	4	7	24	2	27 44	12	4
2 22 32	8	23	1	27 1	13	5	8	24	2	27 38	13	5	8	25	3	28 17	13	5
2 26 26	9	24	1	27 36	13	6	9	25	2	28 13	14	6	9	26	3	28 51	14	6
2 30 22	10	25	2	28 11	14	7	10	26	3	28 47	14	7	10	27	4	29 25	14	6
2 34 17	11	26	3	28 47	15	7	11	27	4	29 22	15	7	11	28	5	29 59	15	7
2 38 14	12	27	4	29 22	15	8	12	28	4	29 57	16	8	12	29	5	0♍ 33	16	8
2 42 11	13	28	4	29 58	16	9	13	29	5	0♍ 32	16	9	13	♋	6	1 7	17	9
2 46 10	14	29	5	0♍ 34	17	10	14	♋	6	1 7	17	10	14	1	7	1 41	17	10
HOUSES	4	5	6	7	8	9	4	5	6	7	8	9	4	5	6	7	8	9

LATITUDE 61° S.　LATITUDE 62° S.　LATITUDE 63° S.

LATITUDE 61° N. LATITUDE 62° N. LATITUDE 63° N.

LATITUDE 61° N.

SIDEREAL TIME (H M S)	10 ♉	11 ♋	12 ♌	ASC ♍	2 ♍	3 ♎
2 50 8	15	0	6	1 9	18	11
2 54 8	16	1	6	1 45	18	12
2 58 8	17	2	7	2 22	19	13
3 2 9	18	2	8	2 58	20	13
3 6 10	19	3	8	3 34	20	14
3 10 13	20	4	9	4 11	21	15
3 14 16	21	5	10	4 47	22	16
3 18 20	22	6	10	5 24	23	17
3 22 24	23	7	11	6 1	23	18
3 26 30	24	8	12	6 38	24	19
3 30 36	25	9	13	7 15	25	19
3 34 42	26	10	13	7 53	25	20
3 38 50	27	10	14	8 30	26	21
3 42 58	28	11	15	9 7	27	22
3 47 7	29	12	15	9 45	28	23
3 51 16	♊	13	16	10 23	28	24
3 55 26	1	14	17	11 1	29	25
3 59 37	2	15	18	11 39	♎	26
4 3 49	3	16	18	12 17	1	27
4 8 1	4	17	19	12 55	1	27
4 12 14	5	17	20	13 34	2	28
4 16 27	6	18	20	14 12	3	29
4 20 41	7	19	21	14 51	4	♏
4 24 56	8	20	22	15 29	4	1
4 29 11	9	21	23	16 8	5	2
4 33 27	10	22	23	16 47	6	3
4 37 43	11	23	24	17 26	7	4
4 41 59	12	24	25	18 5	8	5
4 46 17	13	24	26	18 44	8	5
4 50 34	14	25	26	19 24	9	6
4 54 53	15	26	27	20 3	10	7
4 59 11	16	27	28	20 43	11	8
5 3 30	17	28	29	21 22	11	9
5 7 49	18	29	29	22 2	12	10
5 12 9	19	♌	♍	22 41	13	11
5 16 29	20	1	1	23 21	14	12
5 20 49	21	1	2	24 1	14	13
5 25 10	22	2	2	24 41	15	13
5 29 31	23	3	3	25 20	16	14
5 33 51	24	4	4	26 0	17	15
5 38 13	25	5	5	26 40	18	16
5 42 34	26	6	6	27 20	18	17
5 46 55	27	7	6	28 0	19	18
5 51 17	28	8	7	28 40	20	19
5 55 38	29	9	8	29 20	21	20
HOUSES	4	5	6	7	8	9

LATITUDE 62° N.

SIDEREAL TIME (H M S)	10 ♉	11 ♋	12 ♌	ASC ♍	2 ♍	3 ♎
2 50 8	15	1	6	1 42	18	11
2 54 8	16	2	7	2 17	18	12
2 58 8	17	2	8	2 53	19	12
3 2 9	18	3	8	3 28	20	13
3 6 10	19	4	9	4 4	21	14
3 10 13	20	5	10	4 40	21	15
3 14 16	21	6	11	5 16	22	16
3 18 20	22	7	11	5 52	23	17
3 22 24	23	8	12	6 28	23	18
3 26 30	24	9	13	7 4	24	18
3 30 36	25	10	13	7 41	25	19
3 34 42	26	10	14	8 17	26	20
3 38 50	27	11	15	8 54	26	21
3 42 58	28	12	15	9 31	27	22
3 47 7	29	13	16	10 8	28	23
3 51 16	♊	14	17	10 45	28	24
3 55 26	1	15	18	11 22	29	25
3 59 37	2	16	18	11 59	♎	25
4 3 49	3	17	19	12 37	1	26
4 8 1	4	17	20	13 14	1	27
4 12 14	5	18	20	13 52	2	28
4 16 27	6	19	21	14 30	3	29
4 20 41	7	20	22	15 8	4	♏
4 24 56	8	21	23	15 46	4	1
4 29 11	9	22	23	16 24	5	2
4 33 27	10	23	24	17 2	6	2
4 37 43	11	23	25	17 40	7	3
4 41 59	12	24	25	18 18	7	4
4 46 17	13	25	26	18 57	8	5
4 50 34	14	26	27	19 35	9	6
4 54 53	15	27	28	20 14	10	7
4 59 11	16	28	28	20 53	10	8
5 3 30	17	29	29	21 32	11	9
5 7 49	18	29	♍	22 10	12	10
5 12 9	19	♌	1	22 49	13	10
5 16 29	20	1	1	23 28	13	11
5 20 49	21	2	2	24 7	14	12
5 25 10	22	3	3	24 46	15	13
5 29 31	23	4	4	25 25	16	14
5 33 51	24	5	4	26 5	17	15
5 38 13	25	6	5	26 44	17	16
5 42 34	26	6	6	27 23	18	17
5 46 55	27	7	7	28 2	19	17
5 51 17	28	8	7	28 41	20	18
5 55 38	29	9	8	29 21	20	19
HOUSES	4	5	6	7	8	9

LATITUDE 63° N.

SIDEREAL TIME (H M S)	10 ♉	11 ♋	12 ♌	ASC ♍	2 ♍	3 ♎
2 50 8	15	2	7	2 16	18	11
2 54 8	16	3	8	2 50	19	11
2 58 8	17	4	9	3 25	19	12
3 2 9	18	4	9	4 0	20	13
3 6 10	19	5	10	4 34	21	14
3 10 13	20	6	11	5 10	21	15
3 14 16	21	7	11	5 45	22	16
3 18 20	22	8	12	6 20	23	17
3 22 24	23	9	13	6 55	23	17
3 26 30	24	10	13	7 31	24	18
3 30 36	25	11	14	8 7	25	20
3 34 42	26	11	15	8 43	26	20
3 38 50	27	12	15	9 19	26	21
3 42 58	28	13	16	9 55	27	22
3 47 7	29	14	17	10 31	28	23
3 51 16	♊	15	18	11 7	28	23
3 55 26	1	16	18	11 44	29	24
3 59 37	2	17	19	12 20	♎	25
4 3 49	3	17	20	12 57	1	26
4 8 1	4	18	20	13 34	1	27
4 12 14	5	19	21	14 11	2	28
4 16 27	6	20	22	14 48	3	29
4 20 41	7	21	22	15 25	4	♏
4 24 56	8	22	23	16 2	4	0
4 29 11	9	22	24	16 39	5	1
4 33 27	10	23	25	17 17	6	2
4 37 43	11	24	25	17 54	7	3
4 41 59	12	25	26	18 32	7	4
4 46 17	13	26	27	19 10	8	5
4 50 34	14	27	27	19 47	9	6
4 54 53	15	28	28	20 25	10	7
4 59 11	16	28	29	21 3	10	7
5 3 30	17	29	♍	21 41	11	8
5 7 49	18	♌	0	22 19	12	9
5 12 9	19	1	1	22 58	13	10
5 16 29	20	2	2	23 36	13	11
5 20 49	21	3	3	24 14	14	12
5 25 10	22	4	3	24 52	15	13
5 29 31	23	4	4	25 31	16	14
5 33 51	24	5	5	26 9	16	14
5 38 13	25	6	6	26 48	17	15
5 42 34	26	7	6	27 26	18	16
5 46 55	27	8	7	28 5	19	17
5 51 17	28	9	8	28 43	19	18
5 55 38	29	10	8	29 21	20	19
HOUSES	4	5	6	7	8	9

LATITUDE 61° S. LATITUDE 62° S. LATITUDE 63° S.

LATITUDE 61° N. LATITUDE 62° N. LATITUDE 63° N.

SIDEREAL TIME (H M S)	10 ♋	11 ♌	12 ♍	ASC ♎		2 ♎	3 ♏	10 ♋	11 ♌	12 ♍	ASC ♎		2 ♎	3 ♏	10 ♋	11 ♌	12 ♍	ASC ♎		2 ♎	3 ♏
6 0 0	0	9	9	0	0	21	21	0	10	9	0	0	21	20	0	10	9	0	0	21	20
6 4 22	1	10	9	0	40	22	21	1	11	10	0	39	22	21	1	11	10	0	39	22	20
6 8 43	2	11	10	1	20	23	22	2	12	10	1	19	23	22	2	12	11	1	17	22	21
6 13 5	3	12	11	2	0	24	23	3	13	11	1	58	23	23	3	13	11	1	55	23	22
6 17 26	4	13	12	2	40	24	24	4	13	12	2	37	24	24	4	14	12	2	34	24	23
6 21 47	5	14	12	3	20	25	25	5	14	13	3	16	25	24	5	15	13	3	12	24	24
6 26 9	6	15	13	4	0	26	26	6	15	13	3	55	26	25	6	16	14	3	51	25	25
6 30 29	7	16	14	4	40	27	27	7	16	14	4	35	26	26	7	16	14	4	29	26	26
6 34 50	8	17	15	5	19	28	28	8	17	15	5	14	27	27	8	17	15	5	8	27	26
6 39 11	9	17	16	5	59	28	29	9	18	16	5	53	28	28	9	18	16	5	46	27	27
6 43 31	10	18	16	6	39	29	29	10	19	17	6	32	29	29	10	19	17	6	24	28	28
6 47 51	11	19	17	7	19	♏	♐	11	20	17	7	11	29	♐	11	20	17	7	2	29	29
6 52 11	12	20	18	7	58	1	1	12	20	18	7	50	♏	1	12	21	18	7	41	♏	♐
6 56 30	13	21	19	8	38	1	2	13	21	19	8	28	1	1	13	22	19	8	19	0	1
7 0 49	14	22	19	9	17	2	3	14	22	20	9	7	2	2	14	23	20	8	57	1	2
7 5 7	15	23	20	9	57	3	4	15	23	20	9	46	2	3	15	23	20	9	35	2	2
7 9 26	16	24	21	10	36	4	5	16	24	21	10	25	3	4	16	24	21	10	13	3	3
7 13 43	17	25	22	11	16	4	6	17	25	22	11	3	4	5	17	25	22	10	50	3	4
7 18 0	18	25	22	11	55	5	6	18	26	23	11	42	5	6	18	26	23	11	28	4	5
7 22 17	19	26	23	12	34	6	7	19	27	23	12	20	5	7	19	27	23	12	6	5	6
7 26 33	20	27	24	13	13	7	8	20	28	24	12	58	6	7	20	28	24	12	43	5	7
7 30 49	21	28	25	13	52	7	9	21	28	25	13	36	7	8	21	29	25	13	21	6	8
7 35 4	22	29	26	14	31	8	10	22	29	26	14	14	7	9	22	♏	26	13	58	7	8
7 39 19	23	♏	26	15	9	9	11	23	♏	26	14	52	8	10	23	0	26	14	35	8	9
7 43 33	24	1	27	15	48	10	12	24	1	27	15	30	9	11	24	1	27	15	12	8	10
7 47 46	25	2	28	16	26	10	13	25	2	28	16	8	10	12	25	2	28	15	49	9	11
7 51 59	26	3	29	17	5	11	13	26	3	29	16	46	10	13	26	3	29	16	26	10	12
7 56 11	27	3	29	17	43	12	14	27	4	29	17	23	11	13	27	4	29	17	3	10	13
8 0 23	28	4	♎	18	21	12	15	28	5	♎	18	1	12	14	28	5	♎	17	40	11	13
8 4 34	29	5	1	18	59	13	16	29	5	1	18	38	12	15	29	6	1	18	16	12	14
8 8 44	♌	6	2	19	37	14	17	♌	6	2	19	15	13	16	♌	7	2	18	53	12	15
8 12 53	1	7	2	20	15	15	18	1	7	2	19	52	14	17	1	7	2	19	29	13	16
8 17 2	2	8	3	20	53	15	19	2	8	3	20	29	15	18	2	8	3	20	5	14	17
8 21 10	3	9	4	21	30	16	20	3	9	4	21	6	15	19	3	9	4	20	41	15	18
8 25 18	4	10	5	22	7	17	20	4	10	4	21	43	16	20	4	10	4	21	17	15	19
8 29 24	5	11	5	22	45	17	21	5	11	5	22	19	17	20	5	11	5	21	53	16	19
8 33 30	6	11	6	23	22	18	22	6	12	6	22	56	17	21	6	12	6	22	29	17	20
8 37 36	7	12	7	23	59	19	23	7	12	7	23	32	18	22	7	13	7	23	5	17	21
8 41 40	8	13	7	24	36	20	24	8	13	7	24	8	19	23	8	13	7	23	40	18	22
8 45 44	9	14	8	25	13	20	25	9	14	8	24	44	19	24	9	14	8	24	15	19	23
8 49 47	10	15	9	25	49	21	26	10	15	9	25	20	20	25	10	15	9	24	50	19	24
8 53 50	11	16	10	26	26	22	27	11	16	9	25	56	21	26	11	16	9	25	26	20	25
8 57 51	12	17	10	27	2	22	28	12	17	10	26	32	22	27	12	17	10	26	0	21	26
9 1 52	13	17	11	27	38	23	28	13	18	11	27	7	22	28	13	18	11	26	35	21	26
9 5 52	14	18	12	28	15	24	29	14	18	12	27	43	23	28	14	19	11	27	10	22	27
HOUSES	4	5	6	7		8	9	4	5	6	7		8	9	4	5	6	7		8	9

LATITUDE 61° S. LATITUDE 62° S. LATITUDE 63° S.

	LATITUDE 61° N.						LATITUDE 62° N.						LATITUDE 63° N.					

SIDEREAL TIME	10 Ω	11 ♍	12 ♎	ASC ♎	2 ♏	3 ♐	10 Ω	11 ♍	12 ♎	ASC ♎	2 ♏	3 ♐	10 Ω	11 ♍	12 ♎	ASC ♎	2 ♏	3 ♐
H M S	°	°	°	° '	°	°	°	°	°	° '	°	°	°	°	°	° '	°	°
9 9 52	15	19	12	28 51	24	0	15	19	12	28 18	24	29	15	19	12	27 44	23	28
9 13 50	16	20	13	29 26	25	1	16	20	13	28 53	24	♈	16	20	13	28 19	23	29
9 17 49	17	21	14	0♏ 2	26	2	17	21	14	29 28	25	1	17	21	13	28 53	24	♈
9 21 46	18	22	15	0 38	26	3	18	22	14	0♏ 3	26	2	18	22	14	29 27	25	1
9 25 42	19	23	15	1 13	27	4	19	23	15	0 38	26	3	19	23	15	0♏ 1	25	2
9 29 38	20	23	16	1 49	28	5	20	23	16	1 13	27	4	20	24	16	0 35	26	3
9 33 34	21	24	17	2 24	29	6	21	24	16	1 47	28	5	21	24	16	1 9	27	4
9 37 28	22	25	17	2 59	29	7	22	25	17	2 22	28	6	22	25	17	1 43	27	5
9 41 22	23	26	18	3 34	♐	8	23	26	18	2 56	29	7	23	26	18	2 16	28	6
9 45 15	24	27	19	4 9	1	9	24	27	19	3 30	♐	8	24	27	18	2 50	29	7
9 49 8	25	28	19	4 44	1	10	25	28	19	4 4	0	9	25	28	19	3 23	29	7
9 53 0	26	28	20	5 19	2	11	26	29	20	4 38	1	10	26	29	20	3 56	♐	8
9 56 51	27	29	21	5 53	3	12	27	29	21	5 12	2	11	27	29	20	4 29	0	9
10 0 42	28	♎	22	6 28	3	13	28	♎	21	5 46	2	12	28	♎	21	5 2	1	10
10 4 32	29	1	22	7 2	4	14	29	1	22	6 19	3	13	29	1	22	5 35	2	11
10 8 22	♍	2	23	7 36	5	15	♍	2	23	6 53	4	14	♍	2	22	6 8	2	12
10 12 11	1	3	24	8 11	5	16	1	3	23	7 26	4	15	1	3	23	6 41	3	13
10 15 59	2	3	24	8 45	6	17	2	3	24	8 0	5	16	2	3	23	7 13	4	14
10 19 47	3	4	25	9 19	7	18	3	4	25	8 33	6	17	3	4	24	7 46	4	15
10 23 34	4	5	26	9 53	7	19	4	5	25	9 6	6	18	4	5	25	8 18	5	16
10 27 21	5	6	26	10 27	8	20	5	6	26	9 39	7	19	5	6	25	8 51	6	18
10 31 8	6	7	27	11 0	9	21	6	7	26	10 12	8	20	6	7	26	9 23	6	19
10 34 53	7	8	28	11 34	9	22	7	7	27	10 45	8	21	7	7	27	9 55	7	20
10 38 39	8	8	28	12 8	10	23	8	8	28	11 18	9	22	8	8	27	10 27	8	21
10 42 24	9	9	29	12 41	11	24	9	9	28	11 51	10	23	9	9	28	10 59	8	22
10 46 8	10	10	♏	13 15	12	25	10	10	29	12 24	10	24	10	10	29	11 31	9	23
10 49 52	11	11	0	13 48	12	26	11	11	♏	12 56	11	25	11	11	29	12 3	9	24
10 53 36	12	12	1	14 22	13	27	12	11	0	13 29	12	26	12	11	♏	12 35	10	25
10 57 20	13	12	1	14 55	14	28	13	12	1	14 2	12	27	13	12	1	13 6	11	26
11 1 3	14	13	2	15 28	14	29	14	13	2	14 34	13	28	14	13	1	13 38	11	27
11 4 45	15	14	3	16 2	15	♒	15	14	2	15 7	14	29	15	14	2	14 10	12	28
11 8 28	16	15	3	16 35	16	1	16	15	3	15 39	14	♒	16	14	2	14 41	13	29
11 12 10	17	16	4	17 8	16	2	17	15	4	16 12	15	2	17	15	3	15 13	13	♒
11 15 52	18	16	5	17 41	17	4	18	16	4	16 44	16	3	18	16	4	15 44	14	2
11 19 33	19	17	5	18 15	18	5	19	17	5	17 16	16	4	19	17	4	16 16	15	3
11 23 15	20	18	6	18 48	19	6	20	18	5	17 49	17	5	20	18	5	16 47	15	4
11 26 56	21	19	7	19 21	19	7	21	19	6	18 21	18	6	21	18	6	17 19	16	5
11 30 37	22	19	7	19 54	20	8	22	19	7	18 53	18	7	22	19	6	17 50	17	6
11 34 17	23	20	8	20 27	21	9	23	20	7	19 25	19	8	23	20	7	18 21	17	8
11 37 58	24	21	9	21 0	22	10	24	21	8	19 58	20	10	24	21	7	18 53	18	9
11 41 39	25	22	9	21 34	22	12	25	22	9	20 30	21	11	25	21	8	19 24	19	10
11 45 19	26	23	10	22 7	23	13	26	22	9	21 2	21	12	26	22	9	19 55	20	11
11 48 59	27	23	10	22 40	24	14	27	23	10	21 35	22	13	27	23	9	20 27	20	12
11 52 40	28	24	11	23 13	25	15	28	24	10	22 7	23	14	28	24	10	20 58	21	14
11 56 20	29	25	12	23 46	25	16	29	25	11	22 39	24	16	29	25	10	21 29	22	15
HOUSES	4	5	6	7	8	9	4	5	6	7	8	9	4	5	6	7	8	9

	LATITUDE 61° S.			LATITUDE 62° S.			LATITUDE 63° S.	

	LATITUDE 61° N.						LATITUDE 62° N.						LATITUDE 63° N.					
SIDEREAL TIME	10 ♎	11 ♎	12 ♏	ASC ♏	2 ♐	3 ♒	10 ♎	11 ♎	12 ♏	ASC ♏	2 ♐	3 ♒	10 ♎	11 ♎	12 ♏	ASC ♏	2 ♐	3 ♒
H M S	°	°	°	° ′	°	°	°	°	°	° ′	°	°	°	°	°	° ′	°	°
12 0 0	0	26	12	24 20	26	17	0	26	12	23 12	24	17	0	25	11	22 1	22	16
12 3 40	1	27	13	24 53	27	19	1	26	12	23 44	25	18	1	26	12	22 32	23	17
12 7 20	2	27	14	25 27	28	20	2	27	13	24 16	26	19	2	27	12	23 4	24	19
12 11 1	3	28	14	26 0	29	21	3	28	14	24 49	27	21	3	28	13	23 35	25	20
12 14 41	4	29	15	26 34	29	22	4	29	14	25 21	28	22	4	28	13	24 7	25	21
12 18 21	5	♏	16	27 7	♑	24	5	29	15	25 54	28	23	5	29	14	24 38	26	22
12 22 2	6	0	16	27 41	1	25	6	♏	15	26 27	29	24	6	♏	15	25 10	27	24
12 25 42	7	1	17	28 15	2	26	7	1	16	26 59	♑	26	7	1	15	25 41	28	25
12 29 23	8	2	17	28 48	3	27	8	2	17	27 32	1	27	8	1	16	26 13	29	26
12 33 4	9	3	18	29 22	4	29	9	2	17	28 5	2	28	9	2	17	26 45	29	28
12 36 45	10	3	19	29 56	5	♓	10	3	18	28 38	3	29	10	3	17	27 16	♑	29
12 40 27	11	4	19	0♐ 31	6	1	11	4	19	29 11	3	♓	11	4	18	27 48	1	♓
12 44 8	12	5	20	1 5	6	2	12	5	19	29 44	4	2	12	4	18	28 20	2	2
12 47 50	13	6	21	1 39	7	4	13	5	20	0♐ 17	5	3	13	5	19	28 52	3	3
12 51 32	14	7	21	2 14	8	5	14	6	20	0 51	6	5	14	6	20	29 25	4	4
12 55 15	15	7	22	2 49	9	6	15	7	21	1 24	7	6	15	7	20	29 57	5	6
12 58 57	16	8	23	3 24	10	8	16	8	22	1 58	8	7	16	7	21	0♐ 29	6	7
13 2 40	17	9	23	3 59	11	9	17	8	22	2 32	9	9	17	8	21	1 2	7	8
13 6 24	18	10	24	4 34	13	10	18	9	23	3 6	10	10	18	9	22	1 34	8	10
13 10 8	19	10	24	5 10	14	12	19	10	24	3 40	11	11	19	10	23	2 7	9	11
13 13 52	20	11	25	5 45	15	13	20	11	24	4 14	12	13	20	10	23	2 40	10	13
13 17 36	21	12	26	6 21	16	14	21	12	25	4 49	14	14	21	11	24	3 13	11	14
13 21 21	22	13	26	6 57	17	16	22	12	26	5 24	15	16	22	12	25	3 46	12	15
13 25 7	23	13	27	7 33	18	17	23	13	26	5 58	16	17	23	13	25	4 19	13	17
13 28 52	24	14	28	8 10	19	19	24	14	27	6 34	17	18	24	13	26	4 53	14	18
13 32 39	25	15	28	8 47	21	20	25	15	27	7 9	18	20	25	14	26	5 27	15	20
13 36 26	26	16	29	9 24	22	21	26	15	28	7 44	19	21	26	15	27	6 1	17	21
13 40 13	27	17	♐	10 1	23	23	27	16	29	8 20	21	23	27	16	28	6 35	18	22
13 44 1	28	17	0	10 39	24	24	28	17	29	8 56	22	24	28	16	28	7 9	19	24
13 47 49	29	18	1	11 17	26	26	29	18	♐	9 33	23	25	29	17	29	7 44	21	25
13 51 38	♏	19	2	11 56	27	27	♏	18	1	10 9	25	27	♏	18	♐	8 19	22	27
13 55 28	1	20	2	12 34	29	28	1	19	1	10 46	26	28	1	19	0	8 54	23	28
13 59 18	2	20	3	13 14	♒	♈	2	20	2	11 24	28	♈	2	19	1	9 29	25	♈
14 3 9	3	21	4	13 53	1	1	3	21	3	12 1	29	1	3	20	2	10 5	26	1
14 7 0	4	22	4	14 33	3	3	4	21	3	12 39	♒	3	4	21	2	10 41	28	3
14 10 52	5	23	5	15 13	5	4	5	22	4	13 18	2	4	5	22	3	11 17	♒	4
14 14 45	6	24	6	15 54	6	5	6	23	5	13 57	4	6	6	23	3	11 54	1	6
14 18 38	7	24	7	16 36	8	7	7	24	5	14 36	6	7	7	23	4	12 31	3	7
14 22 32	8	25	7	17 17	9	8	8	25	6	15 16	7	8	8	24	5	13 8	5	9
14 26 26	9	26	8	18 0	11	10	9	25	7	15 56	9	10	9	25	5	13 46	7	10
14 30 22	10	27	9	18 43	13	11	10	26	7	16 36	11	11	10	26	6	14 24	8	12
14 34 17	11	28	9	19 26	15	13	11	27	8	17 18	13	13	11	26	7	15 3	10	13
14 38 14	12	28	10	20 11	16	14	12	28	9	17 59	15	14	12	27	7	15 42	12	14
14 42 11	13	29	11	20 55	18	15	13	29	10	18 42	17	16	13	28	8	16 21	14	16
14 46 10	14	♐	12	21 41	20	17	14	29	10	19 25	18	17	14	29	9	17 1	16	17
HOUSES	4	5	6	7	8	9	4	5	6	7	8	9	4	5	6	7	8	9

LATITUDE 61° N.   LATITUDE 62° N.   LATITUDE 63° N.

SIDEREAL TIME	10 ♏	11 ♐	12 ♐	ASC ♐ °	'	2 ♒	3 ♈	10 ♏	11 ♐	12 ♐	ASC ♐ °	'	2 ♒	3 ♈	10 ♏	11 ♏	12 ♐	ASC ♐ °	'	2 ♒	3 ♈
H M S																					
14 50 8	15	1	12	22	27	22	18	15	0	11	20	8	20	19	15	29	10	17	42	18	19
14 54 8	16	2	13	23	15	24	20	16	1	12	20	53	23	20	16	♐	10	18	23	21	20
14 58 8	17	2	14	24	3	26	21	17	2	12	21	38	25	22	17	1	11	19	5	23	22
15 2 9	18	3	15	24	52	28	23	18	3	13	22	24	27	23	18	2	12	19	48	25	23
15 6 10	19	4	15	25	41	♓	24	19	3	14	23	10	29	24	19	3	12	20	31	27	25
15 10 13	20	5	16	26	32	2	26	20	4	15	23	58	♓	26	20	3	13	21	15	♓	26
15 14 16	21	6	17	27	24	5	27	21	5	15	24	47	3	27	21	4	14	22	0	2	28
15 18 20	22	6	18	28	18	7	28	22	6	16	25	36	6	29	22	5	15	22	45	4	29
15 22 24	23	7	18	29	12	9	♉	23	7	17	26	27	8	♉	23	6	15	23	32	7	♉
15 26 30	24	8	19	0♑	8	11	1	24	7	18	27	19	10	2	24	7	16	24	20	9	2
15 30 36	25	9	20	1	5	13	3	25	8	18	28	12	13	3	25	7	17	25	8	12	4
15 34 42	26	10	21	2	4	16	4	26	9	19	29	7	15	5	26	8	18	25	58	14	5
15 38 50	27	11	22	3	4	18	5	27	10	20	0♑	3	17	6	27	9	18	26	49	17	7
15 42 58	28	12	23	4	7	20	7	28	11	21	1	1	20	7	28	10	19	27	42	19	8
15 47 7	29	12	23	5	11	23	8	29	12	22	2	0	22	9	29	11	20	28	36	22	9
15 51 16	♐	13	24	6	17	25	10	♐	12	23	3	2	25	10	♐	12	21	29	32	25	11
15 55 26	1	14	25	7	26	27	11	1	13	23	4	5	27	12	1	12	22	0♑	29	27	12
15 59 37	2	15	26	8	37	♈	12	2	14	24	5	11	♈	13	2	13	22	1	28	♈	14
16 3 49	3	16	27	9	51	2	14	3	15	25	6	19	2	14	3	14	23	2	30	2	15
16 8 1	4	17	28	11	7	5	15	4	16	26	7	30	5	16	4	15	24	3	34	5	17
16 12 14	5	18	29	12	27	7	17	5	17	27	8	44	7	17	5	16	25	4	40	8	18
16 16 27	6	19	♑	13	51	9	18	6	18	28	10	1	10	19	6	17	26	5	49	10	19
16 20 41	7	19	1	15	18	12	19	7	19	29	11	21	12	20	7	18	27	7	2	13	21
16 24 56	8	20	2	16	49	14	21	8	19	♑	12	46	15	21	8	19	28	8	18	16	22
16 29 11	9	21	3	18	25	16	22	9	20	1	14	15	17	23	9	19	29	9	37	18	24
16 33 27	10	22	4	20	6	19	23	10	21	2	15	49	20	24	10	20	♑	11	2	21	25
16 37 43	11	23	5	21	53	21	25	11	22	3	17	29	22	25	11	21	0	12	31	23	26
16 41 59	12	24	6	23	46	23	26	12	23	4	19	14	25	27	12	22	1	14	7	26	28
16 46 17	13	25	7	25	46	26	27	13	24	5	21	7	27	28	13	23	3	15	48	28	29
16 50 34	14	26	8	27	53	28	28	14	25	6	23	7	29	29	14	24	4	17	38	♉	♊
16 54 53	15	27	9	0♒	9	♉	♊	15	26	7	25	16	♉	♊	15	25	5	19	35	3	2
16 59 11	16	28	10	2	34	2	1	16	27	8	27	35	4	2	16	26	6	21	43	6	3
17 3 30	17	29	12	5	10	5	2	17	28	9	0♒	5	6	3	17	27	7	24	2	8	4
17 7 49	18	♑	13	7	56	7	3	18	29	11	2	48	8	4	18	28	8	26	34	10	5
17 12 9	19	1	14	10	56	9	5	19	♑	12	5	45	11	6	19	29	9	29	22	13	7
17 16 29	20	2	15	14	8	11	6	20	1	13	8	58	13	7	20	♑	11	2♒	28	15	8
17 20 49	21	3	17	17	36	13	7	21	2	14	12	29	15	8	21	1	12	5	54	17	9
17 25 10	22	4	18	21	19	15	8	22	3	16	16	19	17	9	22	2	13	9	45	19	10
17 29 31	23	5	20	25	18	17	10	23	4	17	20	31	19	10	23	3	14	14	5	21	12
17 33 51	24	6	21	29	34	19	11	24	5	19	25	6	21	12	24	4	16	18	56	24	13
17 38 13	25	7	22	4♓	6	21	12	25	6	20	0♓	5	23	13	25	5	17	24	22	26	14
17 42 34	26	8	24	8	54	23	13	26	7	22	5	28	25	14	26	6	19	0♓	25	27	15
17 46 55	27	9	25	13	57	25	14	27	8	23	11	13	27	15	27	7	20	7	6	29	16
17 51 17	28	10	27	19	11	26	15	28	9	25	17	17	29	16	28	8	22	14	22	♊	18
17 55 38	29	11	29	24	33	28	16	29	10	26	23	35	♊	17	29	9	24	22	4	3	19
HOUSES	4	5	6	7		8	9	4	5	6	7		8	9	4	5	6	7		8	9

LATITUDE 61° S.   LATITUDE 62° S.   LATITUDE 63° S.

LATITUDE 61° N.   LATITUDE 62° N.   LATITUDE 63° N.

SIDEREAL TIME	10 ♑	11 ♑	12 ≈	ASC ♈	2 ♊	3 ♊	10 ♑	11 ♑	12 ♑	ASC ♈	2 ♊	3 ♊	10 ♑	11 ♑	12 ♑	ASC ♈	2 ♊	3 ♊
H M S	°	°	°	° ′	°	°	°	°	°	° ′	°	°	°	°	°	° ′	°	°
18 0 0	0	12	0	0 0	0	18	0	11	28	0 0	2	19	0	10	25	0 0	5	20
18 4 22	1	14	2	5 27	1	19	1	13	≈	6 25	4	20	1	11	27	7 56	6	21
18 8 43	2	15	4	10 49	3	20	2	14	1	12 43	5	21	2	12	29	15 38	8	22
18 13 5	3	16	5	16 3	5	21	3	15	3	18 47	7	22	3	14	≈	22 54	10	23
18 17 26	4	17	7	21 6	6	22	4	16	5	24 32	8	23	4	15	3	29 35	11	24
18 21 47	5	18	9	25 54	8	23	5	17	7	29 55	10	24	5	16	4	5♉ 38	13	25
18 26 9	6	19	11	0♉ 26	9	24	6	18	9	4♉ 54	11	25	6	17	6	11 4	14	26
18 30 29	7	20	13	4 42	10	25	7	20	11	9 29	13	26	7	18	9	15 55	15	27
18 34 50	8	22	15	8 41	12	26	8	21	13	13 41	14	27	8	20	11	20 15	17	28
18 39 11	9	23	17	12 24	13	27	9	22	15	17 31	16	28	9	21	13	24 6	18	29
18 43 31	10	24	19	15 52	15	28	10	23	17	21 2	17	29	10	22	15	27 32	19	♋
18 47 51	11	25	21	19 4	16	29	11	24	19	24 15	18	♋	11	23	17	0♊ 38	21	1
18 52 11	12	27	23	22 4	17	♋	12	26	22	27 12	19	1	12	25	20	3 26	22	2
18 56 30	13	28	25	24 50	18	1	13	27	24	29 55	21	2	13	26	22	5 58	23	3
19 0 49	14	29	28	27 26	20	2	14	28	26	2♊ 25	22	3	14	27	24	8 17	24	4
19 5 7	15	≈	♓	29 51	21	3	15	29	28	4 44	23	4	15	28	27	10 25	25	5
19 9 26	16	2	2	2♊ 7	22	4	16	≈	♓	6 53	24	5	16	29	29	12 22	26	6
19 13 43	17	3	4	4 14	23	5	17	2	3	8 53	25	6	17	1	♓	14 12	27	7
19 18 0	18	4	7	6 14	24	6	18	3	5	10 46	26	7	18	2	4	15 53	29	8
19 22 17	19	5	9	8 7	25	7	19	5	8	12 31	27	8	19	4	7	17 29	♋	9
19 26 33	20	7	11	9 54	26	8	20	6	10	14 11	28	9	20	5	9	18 58	0	10
19 30 49	21	8	14	11 35	27	9	21	7	13	15 45	29	10	21	6	12	20 23	1	11
19 35 4	22	9	16	13 11	28	10	22	9	15	17 14	♋	11	22	8	14	21 42	2	11
19 39 19	23	11	18	14 42	29	11	23	10	18	18 39	1	11	23	9	17	22 58	3	12
19 43 33	24	12	21	16 9	♋	11	24	11	20	19 59	2	12	24	11	20	24 11	4	13
19 47 46	25	13	23	17 33	1	12	25	13	23	21 16	3	13	25	12	22	25 20	5	14
19 51 59	26	15	25	18 53	2	13	26	14	25	22 30	4	14	26	13	25	26 26	6	15
19 56 11	27	16	28	20 9	3	14	27	16	28	23 41	5	15	27	15	28	27 30	7	16
20 0 23	28	18	♈	21 23	4	15	28	17	♈	24 49	6	16	28	16	♈	28 32	8	17
20 4 34	29	19	3	22 34	5	16	29	18	3	25 55	7	17	29	18	3	29 31	8	18
20 8 44	≈	20	5	23 43	6	17	≈	20	5	26 58	7	18	≈	19	5	0♋ 28	9	18
20 12 53	1	22	7	24 49	7	18	1	21	8	28 0	8	18	1	21	8	1 24	10	19
20 17 2	2	23	10	25 53	7	18	2	23	10	28 59	9	19	2	22	11	2 18	11	20
20 21 10	3	25	12	26 56	8	19	3	24	13	29 57	10	20	3	23	13	3 11	12	21
20 25 18	4	26	14	27 56	9	20	4	25	15	0♋ 53	11	21	4	25	16	4 2	12	22
20 29 24	5	27	17	28 55	10	21	5	27	17	1 48	12	22	5	26	18	4 52	13	23
20 33 30	6	29	19	29 52	11	22	6	28	20	2 41	12	23	6	28	21	5 40	14	23
20 37 36	7	♓	21	0♋ 48	12	23	7	♓	22	3 33	13	23	7	29	23	6 28	15	24
20 41 40	8	2	23	1 42	12	24	8	1	24	4 24	14	24	8	♓	26	7 15	15	25
20 45 44	9	3	25	2 36	13	24	9	3	27	5 13	15	25	9	2	28	8 0	16	26
20 49 47	10	4	28	3 28	14	25	10	4	29	6 2	15	26	10	4	♉	8 45	17	27
20 53 50	11	6	♉	4 19	15	26	11	6	♉	6 50	16	27	11	5	3	9 29	18	27
20 57 51	12	7	2	5 8	15	27	12	7	3	7 36	17	27	12	7	5	10 12	18	28
21 1 52	13	9	4	5 57	16	28	13	8	5	8 22	18	28	13	8	7	10 55	19	29
21 5 52	14	10	6	6 45	17	28	14	10	7	9 7	18	29	14	10	9	11 37	20	♌
HOUSES	4	5	6	7	8	9	4	5	6	7	8	9	4	5	6	7	8	9

LATITUDE 61° S.   LATITUDE 62° S.   LATITUDE 63° S.

LATITUDE 61° N.   LATITUDE 62° N.   LATITUDE 63° N.

SIDEREAL TIME	10 ♒	11 ♓	12 ♉	ASC ♋ °	'	2 ♋	3 ♋	10 ♒	11 ♓	12 ♉	ASC ♋ °	'	2 ♋	3 ♌	10 ♒	11 ♓	12 ♉	ASC ♋ °	'	2 ♋	3 ♌
H M S	°	°	°	°	'	°	°	°	°	°	°	'	°	°	°	°	°	°	'	°	°
21 9 52	15	12	8	7	33	18	29	15	11	10	9	52	19	0	15	11	12	12	18	20	1
21 13 50	16	13	10	8	19	18	♌	16	13	12	10	35	20	1	16	13	14	12	59	21	1
21 17 49	17	15	12	9	5	19	1	17	14	13	11	18	20	1	17	14	16	13	39	22	2
21 21 46	18	16	14	9	49	20	2	18	16	15	12	1	21	2	18	16	18	14	18	23	3
21 25 42	19	17	15	10	34	21	2	19	17	17	12	42	22	3	19	17	20	14	57	23	4
21 29 38	20	19	17	11	17	21	3	20	19	19	13	24	23	4	20	18	22	15	36	24	4
21 33 34	21	20	19	12	0	22	4	21	20	21	14	4	23	5	21	20	23	16	14	25	5
21 37 28	22	22	21	12	43	23	5	22	22	23	14	44	24	5	22	21	25	16	52	25	6
21 41 22	23	23	22	13	24	23	6	23	23	24	15	24	25	6	23	23	27	17	29	26	7
21 45 15	24	25	24	14	6	24	6	24	24	26	16	3	25	7	24	24	29	18	6	27	7
21 49 8	25	26	25	14	47	25	7	25	26	28	16	42	26	8	25	26	♊	18	43	27	8
21 53 0	26	27	27	15	27	26	8	26	27	29	17	21	27	9	26	27	2	19	19	28	9
21 56 51	27	29	29	16	7	26	9	27	29	♊	17	59	27	9	27	29	4	19	55	28	10
22 0 42	28	♈	♊	16	46	27	10	28	♈	2	18	36	28	10	28	♈	5	20	31	29	11
22 4 32	29	2	1	17	26	28	10	29	2	4	19	14	29	11	29	2	7	21	6	♌	11
22 8 22	♓	3	3	18	4	28	11	♓	3	5	19	51	29	12	♓	3	8	21	41	0	12
22 12 11	1	4	4	18	43	29	12	1	5	7	20	27	♌	12	1	5	9	22	16	1	13
22 15 59	2	6	6	19	21	♌	13	2	6	8	21	4	1	13	2	6	11	22	51	2	14
22 19 47	3	7	7	19	59	0	13	3	7	9	21	40	1	14	3	8	12	23	25	2	14
22 23 34	4	9	8	20	36	1	14	4	9	11	22	16	2	15	4	9	13	23	59	3	15
22 27 21	5	10	9	21	13	2	15	5	10	12	22	51	3	15	5	10	15	24	33	4	16
22 31 8	6	11	11	21	50	2	16	6	12	13	23	26	3	16	6	12	16	25	7	4	17
22 34 53	7	13	12	22	27	3	17	7	13	14	24	2	4	17	7	13	17	25	41	5	17
22 38 39	8	14	13	23	3	4	17	8	14	15	24	36	4	18	8	15	18	26	14	5	18
22 42 24	9	16	14	23	39	4	18	9	16	16	25	11	5	18	9	16	19	26	47	6	19
22 46 8	10	17	15	24	15	5	19	10	17	18	25	46	6	19	10	17	20	27	20	7	20
22 49 52	11	18	16	24	50	6	20	11	19	19	26	20	6	20	11	19	21	27	53	7	20
22 53 36	12	20	17	25	26	6	20	12	20	20	26	54	7	21	12	20	22	28	26	8	21
22 57 20	13	21	19	26	1	7	21	13	21	21	27	28	8	22	13	22	23	28	58	9	22
23 1 3	14	22	20	26	36	7	22	14	23	22	28	2	8	22	14	23	24	29	31	9	23
23 4 45	15	24	21	27	11	8	23	15	24	23	28	36	9	23	15	24	25	0♌	3	10	23
23 8 28	16	25	22	27	46	9	23	16	25	24	29	9	10	24	16	26	26	0	35	10	24
23 12 10	17	26	23	28	21	9	24	17	27	25	29	43	10	25	17	27	27	1	8	11	25
23 15 52	18	28	24	28	55	10	25	18	28	26	0♌	16	11	25	18	28	28	1	40	12	26
23 19 33	19	29	24	29	29	11	26	19	29	27	0	49	11	26	19	♉	29	2	12	12	26
23 23 15	20	♉	25	0♌	4	11	27	20	♉	27	1	22	12	27	20	1	♋	2	44	13	27
23 26 56	21	1	26	0	38	12	27	21	2	28	1	55	13	28	21	2	1	3	15	13	28
23 30 37	22	3	27	1	12	13	28	22	3	29	2	28	13	28	22	4	1	3	47	14	29
23 34 17	23	4	28	1	45	13	29	23	4	♋	3	1	14	29	23	5	2	4	19	15	29
23 37 58	24	5	29	2	19	14	♍	24	6	1	3	33	15	♍	24	6	3	4	50	15	♍
23 41 39	25	6	♋	2	53	14	0	25	7	2	4	6	15	1	25	8	4	5	22	16	1
23 45 19	26	8	1	3	26	15	1	26	8	2	4	39	16	1	26	9	5	5	53	17	2
23 48 59	27	9	1	4	0	16	2	27	9	3	5	11	16	2	27	10	5	6	25	17	2
23 52 40	28	10	2	4	33	16	3	28	11	4	5	44	17	3	28	11	6	6	56	18	3
23 56 20	29	11	3	5	7	17	3	29	12	5	6	16	18	4	29	13	7	7	28	18	4
HOUSES	4	5	6	7		8	9	4	5	6	7		8	9	4	5	6	7		8	9

LATITUDE 61° S.   LATITUDE 62° S.   LATITUDE 63° S.

LATITUDE 64° N.   LATITUDE 65° N.   LATITUDE 66° N.

SIDEREAL TIME	10 ♈	11 ♉	12 ♋	ASC ♌		2 ♌	3 ♍	10 ♈	11 ♉	12 ♋	ASC ♌		2 ♌	3 ♍	10 ♈	11 ♉	12 ♋	ASC ♌		2 ♌	3 ♍
H M S	°	°	°	°	'	°	°	°	°	°	°	'	°	°	°	°	°	°	'	°	°
0 0 0	0	15	10	9	12	20	5	0	16	12	10	28	20	5	0	17	15	11	47	21	6
0 3 40	1	16	10	9	43	20	6	1	17	13	10	58	21	6	1	18	15	12	15	22	6
0 7 20	2	17	11	10	13	21	6	2	18	13	11	27	22	7	2	19	16	12	43	22	7
0 11 1	3	18	12	10	43	21	7	3	20	14	11	56	22	7	3	21	17	13	12	23	8
0 14 41	4	20	12	11	14	22	8	4	21	15	12	25	23	8	4	22	17	13	40	23	8
0 18 21	5	21	13	11	44	23	9	5	22	15	12	55	23	9	5	23	18	14	8	24	9
0 22 2	6	22	14	12	14	23	10	6	23	16	13	24	24	10	6	25	18	14	36	25	10
0 25 43	7	23	14	12	45	24	10	7	25	17	13	53	25	10	7	26	19	15	5	25	11
0 29 23	8	25	15	13	15	24	11	8	26	17	14	23	25	11	8	27	19	15	33	26	11
0 33 4	9	26	16	13	46	25	12	9	27	18	14	52	26	12	9	29	20	16	1	26	12
0 36 45	10	27	16	14	16	26	13	10	28	18	15	22	26	13	10	Ⅱ	20	16	30	27	13
0 40 27	11	28	17	14	47	26	13	11	29	19	15	51	27	14	11	1	21	16	58	28	14
0 44 8	12	29	18	15	17	27	14	12	Ⅱ	20	16	21	27	14	12	2	22	17	27	28	14
0 47 50	13	Ⅱ	18	15	48	28	15	13	2	20	16	51	28	15	13	4	22	17	56	29	15
0 51 32	14	2	19	16	18	28	16	14	3	21	17	20	29	16	14	5	23	18	24	29	16
0 55 15	15	3	20	16	49	29	16	15	4	21	17	50	29	17	15	6	23	18	53	♍	17
0 58 57	16	4	20	17	20	29	17	16	5	22	18	20	♍	17	16	7	24	19	22	0	17
1 2 40	17	5	21	17	51	♍	18	17	7	23	18	50	1	18	17	9	24	19	51	1	18
1 6 24	18	6	21	18	22	1	19	18	8	23	19	20	1	19	18	10	25	20	20	2	19
1 10 8	19	7	22	18	53	1	20	19	9	24	19	50	2	20	19	11	25	20	49	2	20
1 13 52	20	8	23	19	24	2	20	20	10	24	20	20	2	20	20	12	26	21	18	3	21
1 17 36	21	10	23	19	55	2	21	21	11	25	20	50	3	21	21	13	27	21	48	3	21
1 21 21	22	11	24	20	26	3	22	22	12	25	21	20	4	22	22	15	27	22	17	4	22
1 25 7	23	12	25	20	57	4	23	23	13	26	21	51	4	23	23	16	28	22	47	5	23
1 28 52	24	13	25	21	28	4	23	24	15	27	22	21	5	24	24	17	28	23	16	5	24
1 32 39	25	14	26	22	0	5	24	25	16	27	22	52	5	24	25	18	29	23	46	6	24
1 36 26	26	15	26	22	31	6	25	26	17	28	23	23	6	25	26	19	29	24	16	6	25
1 40 13	27	16	27	23	3	6	26	27	18	28	23	53	7	26	27	20	♌	24	45	7	26
1 44 1	28	17	28	23	35	7	27	28	19	29	24	24	7	27	28	21	1	25	15	8	27
1 47 49	29	18	28	24	6	8	27	29	20	♌	24	55	8	27	29	22	1	25	45	8	27
1 51 38	♉	19	29	24	38	8	28	♉	21	0	25	26	9	28	♉	24	2	26	16	9	28
1 55 28	1	20	29	25	10	9	29	1	22	1	25	57	9	29	1	25	2	26	46	10	29
1 59 18	2	21	♌	25	42	9	♎	2	23	1	26	29	10	♎	2	26	3	27	16	10	♎
2 3 9	3	22	1	26	15	10	1	3	24	2	27	0	10	1	3	27	3	27	47	11	1
2 7 0	4	23	1	26	47	11	1	4	25	3	27	31	11	1	4	28	4	28	18	11	1
2 10 52	5	24	2	27	19	11	2	5	26	3	28	3	12	2	5	28	5	28	48	12	2
2 14 45	6	25	3	27	52	12	3	6	27	4	28	35	12	3	6	29	5	29	19	13	3
2 18 38	7	26	3	28	25	13	4	7	28	4	29	7	13	4	7	♋	6	29	50	13	4
2 22 32	8	27	4	28	57	13	5	8	29	5	29	39	14	5	8	1	6	0♍	21	14	5
2 26 26	9	28	5	29	30	14	6	9	29	6	0♍	11	14	5	9	2	7	0	53	15	5
2 30 22	10	29	5	0♍	3	15	6	10	♋	6	0	43	15	6	10	3	7	1	24	15	6
2 34 17	11	♋	6	0	36	15	7	11	1	7	1	15	16	7	11	4	8	1	55	16	7
2 38 14	12	0	6	1	10	16	8	12	2	7	1	48	16	8	12	5	9	2	27	17	8
2 42 11	13	1	7	1	43	17	9	13	3	8	2	20	17	9	13	5	9	2	59	17	9
2 46 10	14	2	8	2	16	17	10	14	4	9	2	53	18	10	14	6	10	3	31	18	9
HOUSES	4	5	6	7		8	9	4	5	6	7		8	9	4	5	6	7		8	9

LATITUDE 64° S.   LATITUDE 65° S.   LATITUDE 66° S.

LATITUDE 64° N. **LATITUDE 65° N.** **LATITUDE 66° N.**

SIDEREAL TIME	10 ♉	11 ♋	12 ♌	ASC ♍		2 ♍	3 ♎	10 ♉	11 ♋	12 ♌	ASC ♍		2 ♍	3 ♎	10 ♉	11 ♋	12 ♌	ASC ♍		2 ♍	3 ♎
H M S	°	°	°	°	'	°	°	°	°	°	°	'	°	°	°	°	°	°	'	°	°
2 50 8	15	3	8	2	50	18	11	15	5	9	3	26	18	10	15	7	10	4	3	18	10
2 54 8	16	4	9	3	24	19	11	16	6	10	3	59	19	11	16	8	11	4	35	19	11
2 58 8	17	5	10	3	58	19	12	17	6	11	4	32	20	12	17	8	12	5	7	20	12
3 2 9	18	6	10	4	32	20	13	18	7	11	5	5	20	13	18	9	12	5	40	20	13
3 6 10	19	7	11	5	6	21	14	19	8	12	5	39	21	14	19	10	13	6	12	21	14
3 10 13	20	7	12	5	40	21	15	20	9	13	6	12	22	15	20	11	13	6	45	22	14
3 14 16	21	8	12	6	15	22	16	21	10	13	6	46	22	15	21	12	14	7	18	22	15
3 18 20	22	9	13	6	49	23	16	22	11	14	7	19	23	16	22	12	15	7	51	23	16
3 22 24	23	10	14	7	24	24	17	23	11	14	7	53	24	17	23	13	15	8	24	24	17
3 26 30	24	11	14	7	59	24	18	24	12	15	8	27	24	18	24	14	16	8	57	24	18
3 30 36	25	12	15	8	34	25	19	25	13	16	9	1	25	19	25	15	17	9	30	25	19
3 34 42	26	13	16	9	9	26	20	26	14	16	9	36	26	20	26	15	17	10	4	26	19
3 38 50	27	13	16	9	44	26	21	27	15	17	10	10	26	20	27	16	18	10	37	27	20
3 42 58	28	14	17	10	19	27	22	28	15	18	10	45	27	21	28	17	19	11	11	27	21
3 47 7	29	15	18	10	55	28	22	29	16	18	11	19	28	22	29	18	19	11	45	28	22
3 51 16	♊16	18	11	30		29	23	♊17	19	11	54		29	23	♊18	20	12	19		29	23
3 55 26	1	17	19	12	6	29	24	1	18	20	12	29	29	24	1	19	20	12	53	29	24
3 59 37	2	18	20	12	42	♎	25	2	19	20	13	4	♎	25	2	20	21	13	27	♎	24
4 3 49	3	18	20	13	18	1	26	3	19	21	13	39	1	26	3	21	22	14	1	1	25
4 8 1	4	19	21	13	54	1	27	4	20	22	14	14	1	26	4	21	22	14	36	1	26
4 12 14	5	20	22	14	30	2	28	5	21	22	14	50	2	27	5	22	23	15	10	2	27
4 16 27	6	21	22	15	6	3	28	6	22	23	15	25	3	28	6	23	24	15	45	3	28
4 20 41	7	22	23	15	43	4	29	7	23	24	16	1	3	29	7	24	24	16	20	3	29
4 24 56	8	22	24	16	19	4	♏	8	23	24	16	37	4	♏	8	25	25	16	55	4	29
4 29 11	9	23	24	16	56	5	1	9	24	25	17	12	5	1	9	25	26	17	30	5	♏
4 33 27	10	24	25	17	32	6	2	10	25	26	17	48	6	1	10	26	26	18	5	6	1
4 37 43	11	25	26	18	9	6	3	11	26	26	18	24	6	2	11	27	27	18	40	6	2
4 41 59	12	26	27	18	46	7	4	12	27	27	19	0	7	3	12	28	28	19	15	7	3
4 46 17	13	27	27	19	23	8	4	13	27	28	19	36	8	4	13	28	28	19	50	8	4
4 50 34	14	27	28	20	0	9	5	14	28	29	20	13	8	5	14	29	29	20	26	8	4
4 54 53	15	28	29	20	37	9	6	15	29	29	20	49	9	6	15	♌	♍21	1		9	5
4 59 11	16	29	29	21	14	10	7	16	♌	♍	21	25	10	7	16	1	1	21	37	10	6
5 3 30	17	♌	♍	21	51	11	8	17	1	1	22	2	11	7	17	2	1	22	12	10	7
5 7 49	18	1	1	22	29	12	9	18	2	1	22	38	11	8	18	2	2	22	48	11	8
5 12 9	19	2	2	23	6	12	10	19	2	2	23	15	12	9	19	3	3	23	24	12	9
5 16 29	20	2	2	23	44	13	10	20	3	3	23	52	13	10	20	4	3	24	0	13	10
5 20 49	21	3	3	24	21	14	11	21	4	3	24	28	14	11	21	5	4	24	36	13	10
5 25 10	22	4	4	24	59	15	12	22	5	4	25	5	14	12	22	6	5	25	12	14	11
5 29 31	23	5	4	25	36	15	13	23	6	5	25	42	15	13	23	6	5	25	48	15	12
5 33 51	24	6	5	26	14	16	14	24	7	6	26	19	16	13	24	7	6	26	24	15	13
5 38 13	25	7	6	26	51	17	15	25	7	6	26	55	16	14	25	8	7	27	0	16	14
5 42 34	26	8	7	27	29	17	16	26	8	7	27	32	17	15	26	9	7	27	36	17	15
5 40 55	27	8	7	28	7	18	16	27	9	8	28	9	18	16	27	10	8	28	12	18	15
5 51 17	28	9	8	28	45	19	17	28	10	8	28	46	19	17	28	11	9	28	48	18	16
5 55 38	29	10	9	29	22	20	18	29	11	9	29	23	19	18	29	11	10	29	24	19	17
HOUSES	4	5	6	7		8	9	4	5	6	7		8	9	4	5	6	7		8	9

LATITUDE 64° S. **LATITUDE 65° S.** **LATITUDE 66° S.**

LATITUDE 64° N.   LATITUDE 65° N.   LATITUDE 66° N.

SIDEREAL TIME	10 ♋	11 ♌	12 ♍	ASC ♎ °	'	2 ♎	3 ♏	10 ♋	11 ♌	12 ♍	ASC ♎ °	'	2 ♎	3 ♏	10 ♋	11 ♌	12 ♍	ASC ♎ °	'	2 ♎	3 ♏
H M S	°	°	°	°	'	°	°	°	°	°	°	'	°	°	°	°	°	°	'	°	°
6 0 0	0	11	10	0	0	20	19	0	12	10	0	0	20	18	0	12	10	0	0	20	18
6 4 22	1	12	10	0	38	21	20	1	12	11	0	37	21	19	1	13	11	0	36	20	19
6 8 43	2	13	11	1	15	22	21	2	13	11	1	14	22	20	2	14	12	1	12	21	19
6 13 5	3	14	12	1	53	23	22	3	14	12	1	51	22	21	3	15	12	1	48	22	20
6 17 26	4	14	13	2	31	23	22	4	15	13	2	28	23	22	4	15	13	2	24	23	21
6 21 47	5	15	13	3	9	24	23	5	16	14	3	5	24	23	5	16	14	3	0	23	22
6 26 9	6	16	14	3	46	25	24	6	17	14	3	41	24	23	6	17	15	3	36	24	23
6 30 29	7	17	15	4	24	26	25	7	17	15	4	18	25	24	7	18	15	4	12	25	24
6 34 50	8	18	15	5	1	26	26	8	18	16	4	55	26	25	8	19	16	4	48	25	24
6 39 11	9	19	16	5	39	27	27	9	19	16	5	32	27	26	9	20	17	5	24	26	25
6 43 31	10	20	17	6	16	28	28	10	20	17	6	8	27	27	10	20	17	6	0	27	26
6 47 51	11	20	18	6	54	28	28	11	21	18	6	45	28	28	11	21	18	6	36	27	27
6 52 11	12	21	18	7	31	29	29	12	22	19	7	22	29	28	12	22	19	7	12	28	28
6 56 30	13	22	19	8	9	♏	♐	13	23	19	7	58	29	29	13	23	20	7	48	29	28
7 0 49	14	23	20	8	46	1	1	14	23	20	8	35	♏	♐	14	24	20	8	23	29	29
7 5 7	15	24	21	9	23	1	2	15	24	21	9	11	1	1	15	25	21	8	59	♏	♐
7 9 26	16	25	21	10	0	2	3	16	25	22	9	47	1	2	16	26	22	9	34	1	1
7 13 43	17	26	22	10	37	3	3	17	26	22	10	24	2	3	17	26	22	10	10	2	2
7 18 0	18	26	23	11	14	3	4	18	27	23	11	0	3	3	18	27	23	10	45	2	2
7 22 17	19	27	24	11	51	4	5	19	28	24	11	36	4	4	19	28	24	11	20	3	3
7 26 33	20	28	24	12	28	5	6	20	29	24	12	12	4	5	20	29	24	11	55	4	4
7 30 49	21	29	25	13	4	6	7	21	29	25	12	48	5	6	21	♍	25	12	30	4	5
7 35 4	22	♍	26	13	41	6	8	22	♍	26	13	23	6	7	22	1	26	13	5	5	5
7 39 19	23	1	26	14	17	7	8	23	1	27	13	59	6	7	23	1	27	13	40	6	6
7 43 33	24	2	27	14	54	8	9	24	2	27	14	35	7	8	24	2	27	14	15	6	7
7 47 46	25	2	28	15	30	8	10	25	3	28	15	10	8	9	25	3	28	14	50	7	8
7 51 59	26	3	29	16	6	9	11	26	4	29	15	46	8	10	26	4	29	15	24	8	9
7 56 11	27	4	29	16	42	10	12	27	4	29	16	21	9	11	27	5	29	15	59	8	9
8 0 23	28	5	♎	17	18	10	12	28	5	♎	16	56	10	11	28	6	♎	16	33	9	10
8 4 34	29	6	1	17	54	11	13	29	6	1	17	31	10	12	29	6	1	17	7	10	11
8 8 44	♌	7	1	18	30	12	14	♌	7	1	18	6	11	13	♌	7	1	17	41	10	12
8 12 53	1	8	2	19	5	12	15	1	8	2	18	41	12	14	1	8	2	18	15	11	12
8 17 2	2	8	3	19	41	13	16	2	9	3	19	15	12	15	2	9	3	18	49	11	13
8 21 10	3	9	4	20	16	14	17	3	10	4	19	50	13	15	3	10	3	19	23	12	14
8 25 18	4	10	4	20	51	14	17	4	10	4	20	24	14	16	4	11	4	19	56	13	15
8 29 24	5	11	5	21	26	15	18	5	11	5	20	59	14	17	5	11	5	20	30	13	15
8 33 30	6	12	6	22	1	16	19	6	12	6	21	33	15	18	6	12	6	21	3	14	16
8 37 36	7	13	6	22	36	16	20	7	13	6	22	7	16	19	7	13	6	21	36	15	17
8 41 40	8	14	7	23	11	17	21	8	14	7	22	41	16	19	8	14	7	22	9	15	18
8 45 44	9	14	8	23	45	18	22	9	15	8	23	14	17	20	9	15	8	22	42	16	18
8 49 47	10	15	9	24	20	18	23	10	15	8	23	48	17	21	10	16	8	23	15	17	19
8 53 50	11	16	9	24	54	19	23	11	16	9	24	21	18	22	11	16	9	23	48	17	20
8 57 51	12	17	10	25	28	20	24	12	17	10	24	55	19	23	12	17	10	24	20	18	21
9 1 52	13	18	11	26	2	20	25	13	18	10	25	28	19	24	13	18	10	24	53	18	22
9 5 52	14	19	11	26	36	21	26	14	19	11	26	1	20	24	14	19	11	25	25	19	22
HOUSES	4	5	6	7		8	9	4	5	6	7		8	9	4	5	6	7		8	9

LATITUDE 64° S.   LATITUDE 65° S.   LATITUDE 66° S.

LATITUDE 64° N. LATITUDE 65° N. LATITUDE 66° N.

SIDEREAL TIME	10 Ω	11 ♏	12 ♎	ASC ♎		2 ♏	3 ♐	10 Ω	11 ♏	12 ♎	ASC ♎		2 ♏	3 ♐	10 Ω	11 ♏	12 ♎	ASC ♎		2 ♏	3 ♐
H M S	°	°	°	°	′	°	°	°	°	°	°	′	°	°	°	°	°	°	′	°	°
9 9 52	15	19	12	27	10	22	27	15	20	12	26	34	21	25	15	20	12	25	57	20	23
9 13 50	16	20	13	27	44	22	28	16	20	12	27	7	21	26	16	21	12	26	29	20	24
9 17 49	17	21	13	28	17	23	29	17	21	13	27	40	22	27	17	21	13	27	1	21	25
9 21 46	18	22	14	28	50	24	♑	18	22	14	28	12	23	28	18	22	13	27	33	21	25
9 25 42	19	23	15	29	24	24	0	19	23	14	28	45	23	29	19	23	14	28	5	22	26
9 29 38	20	24	15	29	57	25	1	20	24	15	29	17	24	♑	20	24	15	28	36	23	27
9 33 34	21	24	16	0♏	30	25	2	21	25	16	29	49	24	1	21	25	15	29	7	23	28
9 37 28	22	25	17	1	3	26	3	22	25	16	0♏	21	25	1	22	25	16	29	39	24	29
9 41 22	23	26	17	1	35	27	4	23	26	17	0	53	26	2	23	26	17	0♏	10	24	♑
9 45 15	24	27	18	2	8	27	5	24	27	18	1	25	26	3	24	27	17	0	41	25	1
9 49 8	25	28	19	2	41	28	6	25	28	18	1	57	27	4	25	28	18	1	12	25	2
9 53 0	26	29	19	3	13	29	7	26	29	19	2	29	27	5	26	29	19	1	42	26	2
9 56 51	27	29	20	3	45	29	8	27	29	20	3	0	28	6	27	29	19	2	13	27	3
10 0 42	28	♎	21	4	18	♐	9	28	♎	20	3	31	29	7	28	♎	20	2	44	27	4
10 4 32	29	1	21	4	50	1	10	29	1	21	4	3	29	8	29	1	20	3	14	28	5
10 8 22	♏	2	22	5	22	1	11	♏	2	21	4	34	♐	9	♏	2	21	3	44	28	6
10 12 11	1	3	22	5	54	2	12	1	3	22	5	5	0	10	1	3	22	4	15	29	8
10 15 59	2	3	23	6	25	2	13	2	3	23	5	36	1	11	2	3	22	4	45	29	9
10 19 47	3	4	24	6	57	3	14	3	4	23	6	7	2	12	3	4	23	5	15	♐	10
10 23 34	4	5	24	7	29	4	15	4	5	24	6	37	2	13	4	5	24	5	44	1	11
10 27 21	5	6	25	8	0	4	16	5	6	25	7	8	3	14	5	6	24	6	14	1	12
10 31 8	6	7	26	8	32	5	17	6	6	25	7	39	3	15	6	6	25	6	44	2	13
10 34 53	7	7	26	9	3	5	18	7	7	26	8	9	4	17	7	7	25	7	13	2	14
10 38 39	8	8	27	9	34	6	19	8	8	26	8	40	5	18	8	8	26	7	43	3	15
10 42 24	9	9	28	10	5	7	20	9	9	27	9	10	5	19	9	9	27	8	12	3	17
10 46 8	10	10	28	10	36	7	22	10	10	28	9	40	6	20	10	9	27	8	42	4	18
10 49 52	11	10	29	11	7	8	23	11	10	28	10	10	6	21	11	10	28	9	11	5	19
10 53 36	12	11	29	11	38	9	24	12	11	29	10	40	7	22	12	11	28	9	40	5	20
10 57 20	13	12	♏	12	9	9	25	13	12	29	11	10	7	23	13	12	29	10	9	6	21
11 1 3	14	13	1	12	40	10	26	14	13	♏	11	40	8	25	14	13	♏	10	38	6	23
11 4 45	15	14	1	13	11	10	27	15	13	1	12	10	9	26	15	13	0	11	7	7	24
11 8 28	16	14	2	13	42	11	28	16	14	1	12	40	9	27	16	14	1	11	36	7	25
11 12 10	17	15	2	14	12	12	29	17	15	2	13	9	10	28	17	15	1	12	4	8	26
11 15 52	18	16	3	14	43	12	♒	18	16	3	13	39	10	29	18	16	2	12	33	8	28
11 19 33	19	17	4	15	13	13	2	19	16	3	14	9	11	♒	19	16	2	13	2	9	29
11 23 15	20	17	4	15	44	14	3	20	17	4	14	38	12	2	20	17	3	13	30	10	♒
11 26 56	21	18	5	16	14	14	4	21	18	4	15	8	12	3	21	18	4	13	59	10	1
11 30 37	22	19	6	16	45	15	5	22	19	5	15	37	13	4	22	19	4	14	27	11	3
11 34 17	23	20	6	17	15	16	7	23	20	5	16	7	13	5	23	19	5	14	55	11	4
11 37 58	24	20	7	17	46	16	8	24	20	6	16	36	14	7	24	20	5	15	24	12	5
11 41 39	25	21	7	18	16	17	9	25	21	7	17	5	15	8	25	21	6	15	52	12	7
11 45 19	26	22	8	18	46	18	10	26	22	7	17	35	15	9	26	22	7	16	20	13	8
11 48 59	27	23	9	19	17	18	12	27	23	8	18	4	16	10	27	22	7	16	48	13	9
11 52 40	28	24	9	19	47	19	13	28	23	8	18	33	17	12	28	23	8	17	17	14	11
11 56 20	29	24	10	20	17	20	14	29	24	9	19	2	17	13	29	24	8	17	45	15	12
HOUSES	4	5	6	7		8	9	4	5	6	7		8	9	4	5	6	7		8	9

LATITUDE 64° S. LATITUDE 65° S. LATITUDE 66° S.

	LATITUDE 64° N.						LATITUDE 65° N.						LATITUDE 66° N.					
SIDEREAL TIME	10 ♎	11 ♎	12 ♏	ASC ♏	2 ♐	3 ♒	10 ♎	11 ♎	12 ♏	ASC ♏	2 ♐	3 ♒	10 ♎	11 ♎	12 ♏	ASC ♏	2 ♐	3 ♒
H M S	°	°	°	° '	°	°	°	°	°	° '	°	°	°	°	°	° '	°	°
12 0 0	0	25	10	20 48	20	15	0	25	10	19 32	18	14	0	24	9	18 13	15	13
12 3 40	1	26	11	21 18	21	17	1	25	10	20 1	18	16	1	25	9	18 41	16	15
12 7 20	2	27	12	21 48	22	18	2	26	11	20 30	19	17	2	26	10	19 9	16	16
12 11 1	3	27	12	22 19	22	19	3	27	11	20 59	20	18	3	27	11	19 37	17	17
12 14 41	4	28	13	22 49	23	20	4	28	12	21 28	20	20	4	27	11	20 5	17	19
12 18 21	5	29	13	23 19	24	22	5	28	13	21 58	21	21	5	28	12	20 33	18	20
12 22 2	6	♏	14	23 50	25	23	6	29	13	22 27	22	22	6	29	12	21 1	19	21
12 25 42	7	0	15	24 20	25	24	7	♏	14	22 56	22	24	7	♏	13	21 29	19	23
12 29 23	8	1	15	24 51	26	26	8	1	14	23 25	23	25	8	0	13	21 57	20	24
12 33 4	9	2	16	25 21	27	27	9	1	15	23 55	24	26	9	1	14	22 25	20	26
12 36 45	10	2	16	25 52	28	28	10	2	15	24 24	25	28	10	2	15	22 53	21	27
12 40 27	11	3	17	26 22	28	♓	11	3	16	24 53	25	29	11	2	15	23 21	22	28
12 44 8	12	4	18	26 53	29	1	12	4	17	25 23	26	♓	12	3	16	23 49	22	♓
12 47 50	13	5	18	27 24	♑	2	13	4	17	25 52	27	2	13	4	16	24 17	23	1
12 51 32	14	5	19	27 55	1	4	14	5	18	26 22	28	3	14	5	17	24 45	23	3
12 55 15	15	6	19	28 26	2	5	15	6	18	26 51	28	5	15	5	17	25 13	24	4
12 58 57	16	7	20	28 57	3	7	16	7	19	27 21	29	6	16	6	18	25 41	25	6
13 2 40	17	8	21	29 28	4	8	17	7	20	27 50	♑	8	17	7	18	26 9	25	7
13 6 24	18	8	21	29 59	5	9	18	8	20	28 20	1	9	18	8	19	26 37	26	9
13 10 8	19	9	22	0♐ 30	6	11	19	9	21	28 50	2	10	19	8	20	27 5	27	10
13 13 52	20	10	22	1 2	7	12	20	9	21	29 19	3	12	20	9	20	27 33	28	11
13 17 36	21	11	23	1 33	8	14	21	10	22	29 49	4	13	21	10	21	28 1	28	13
13 21 21	22	11	24	2 5	9	15	22	11	22	0♐ 19	5	15	22	10	21	28 29	29	14
13 25 7	23	12	24	2 36	10	17	23	12	23	0 49	6	16	23	11	22	28 58	♑	16
13 28 52	24	13	25	3 8	11	18	24	12	24	1 19	7	18	24	12	22	29 26	1	17
13 32 39	25	14	25	3 40	12	19	25	13	24	1 50	8	19	25	13	23	29 54	2	19
13 36 26	26	14	26	4 13	13	21	26	14	25	2 20	9	21	26	13	24	0♐ 23	3	21
13 40 13	27	15	27	4 45	15	22	27	15	25	2 50	10	22	27	14	24	0 51	4	22
13 44 1	28	16	27	5 17	16	24	28	15	26	3 21	12	24	28	15	25	1 20	5	24
13 47 49	29	17	28	5 50	17	25	29	16	27	3 52	13	25	29	16	25	1 48	6	25
13 51 38	♏	17	28	6 23	19	27	♏	17	27	4 23	14	27	♏	16	26	2 17	7	27
13 55 28	1	18	29	6 56	20	28	1	18	28	4 54	16	28	1	17	26	2 46	9	28
13 59 18	2	19	♐	7 30	22	♈	2	18	28	5 25	17	♈	2	18	27	3 15	10	♈
14 3 9	3	20	0	8 3	23	1	3	19	29	5 56	19	1	3	18	28	3 44	12	1
14 7 0	4	20	1	8 37	25	3	4	20	♐	6 27	20	3	4	19	28	4 13	14	3
14 10 52	5	21	2	9 11	26	4	5	21	0	6 59	22	4	5	20	29	4 42	16	4
14 14 45	6	22	2	9 45	28	6	6	21	1	7 31	24	6	6	21	29	5 11	17	6
14 18 38	7	23	3	10 20	♒	7	7	22	1	8 3	26	7	7	21	♐	5 40	19	8
14 22 32	8	23	3	10 55	2	9	8	23	2	8 35	28	9	8	22	0	6 10	22	9
14 26 26	9	24	4	11 30	4	10	9	24	3	9 7	♒	10	9	23	1	6 39	24	11
14 30 22	10	25	5	12 5	6	12	10	24	3	9 40	2	12	10	24	2	7 9	26	12
14 34 17	11	26	5	12 41	7	13	11	25	4	10 13	4	13	11	24	2	7 38	28	14
14 38 14	12	26	6	13 17	10	15	12	26	4	10 46	6	15	12	25	3	8 8	♒	15
14 42 11	13	27	7	13 54	12	16	13	27	5	11 19	8	17	13	26	3	8 38	3	17
14 46 10	14	28	7	14 31	14	18	14	27	6	11 53	10	18	14	26	4	9 8	6	19
HOUSES	4	5	6	7	8	9	4	5	6	7	8	9	4	5	6	7	8	9

LATITUDE 64° S.   LATITUDE 65° S.   LATITUDE 66° S.

LATITUDE 64° N.

SIDEREAL TIME (H M S)	10 ♏	11 ♏	12 ♐	ASC ♐	2 ♒	3 ♈
14 50 8	15	29	8	15 8	16	19
14 54 8	16	♐	9	15 46	18	21
14 58 8	17	0	9	16 24	21	22
15 2 9	18	1	10	17 3	23	24
15 6 10	19	2	11	17 43	25	25
15 10 13	20	3	11	18 23	28	27
15 14 16	21	3	12	19 3	♓	28
15 18 20	22	4	13	19 45	3	♉
15 22 24	23	5	13	20 27	5	1
15 26 30	24	6	14	21 10	8	3
15 30 36	25	7	15	21 53	11	4
15 34 42	26	7	16	22 38	13	6
15 38 50	27	8	16	23 23	16	7
15 42 58	28	9	17	24 10	19	9
15 47 7	29	10	18	24 58	21	10
15 51 16	♐	11	19	25 47	24	12
15 55 26	1	12	19	26 37	27	13
15 59 37	2	12	20	27 29	♈	15
16 3 49	3	13	21	28 23	3	16
16 8 1	4	14	22	29 18	5	17
16 12 14	5	15	23	0♑ 16	8	19
16 16 27	6	16	23	1 16	11	20
16 20 41	7	17	24	2 18	14	22
16 24 56	8	17	25	3 23	17	23
16 29 11	9	18	26	4 32	19	25
16 33 27	10	19	27	5 44	22	26
16 37 43	11	20	28	7 0	25	27
16 41 59	12	21	29	8 21	27	29
16 46 17	13	22	♑	9 48	♉	♊
16 50 34	14	23	1	11 21	3	1
16 54 53	15	24	2	13 2	5	3
16 59 11	16	25	3	14 51	8	4
17 3 30	17	25	4	16 51	10	5
17 7 49	18	26	5	19 4	13	7
17 12 9	19	27	6	21 31	15	8
17 16 29	20	28	7	24 17	18	9
17 20 49	21	29	9	27 26	20	10
17 25 10	22	♑	10	1♒ 2	22	12
17 29 31	23	1	11	5 12	24	13
17 33 51	24	2	13	10 3	27	14
17 38 13	25	3	14	15 46	29	15
17 42 34	26	4	15	22 29	♊	17
17 46 55	27	6	17	0♓ 21	3	18
17 51 17	28	7	19	9 22	5	19
17 55 38	29	8	20	19 23	6	20
HOUSES	4	5	6	7	8	9

LATITUDE 65° N.

SIDEREAL TIME (H M S)	10 ♏	11 ♏	12 ♐	ASC ♐	2 ♒	3 ♈
14 50 8	15	28	6	12 27	13	20
14 54 8	16	29	7	13 1	15	21
14 58 8	17	♐	8	13 36	18	23
15 2 9	18	0	8	14 11	20	24
15 6 10	19	1	9	14 46	23	26
15 10 13	20	2	10	15 22	25	27
15 14 16	21	3	10	15 58	28	29
15 18 20	22	3	11	16 34	♓	♉
15 22 24	23	4	12	17 11	4	2
15 26 30	24	5	12	17 49	6	3
15 30 36	25	6	13	18 27	9	5
15 34 42	26	6	14	19 6	12	7
15 38 50	27	7	14	19 45	15	8
15 42 58	28	8	15	20 25	18	10
15 47 7	29	9	16	21 6	21	11
15 51 16	♐	10	16	21 48	24	13
15 55 26	1	10	17	22 30	27	14
15 59 37	2	11	18	23 14	♈	16
16 3 49	3	12	18	23 59	3	17
16 8 1	4	13	19	24 45	6	18
16 12 14	5	14	20	25 32	9	20
16 16 27	6	14	21	26 21	12	21
16 20 41	7	15	22	27 11	15	23
16 24 56	8	16	22	28 4	18	24
16 29 11	9	17	23	28 58	21	26
16 33 27	10	18	24	29 56	24	27
16 37 43	11	19	25	0♑ 56	27	29
16 41 59	12	20	26	1 59	29	♊
16 46 17	13	20	26	3 6	♉	1
16 50 34	14	21	27	4 18	5	3
16 54 53	15	22	28	5 35	8	4
16 59 11	16	23	29	6 58	11	6
17 3 30	17	24	♑	8 30	13	7
17 7 49	18	25	1	10 10	16	8
17 12 9	19	26	2	12 3	19	10
17 16 29	20	27	3	14 11	21	11
17 20 49	21	28	5	16 38	24	12
17 25 10	22	29	6	19 30	26	13
17 29 31	23	♑	7	22 55	28	15
17 33 51	24	1	8	27 5	♊	16
17 38 13	25	2	10	2♒ 19	3	17
17 42 34	26	3	11	9 0	5	18
17 46 55	27	4	13	17 42	7	20
17 51 17	28	5	14	29 5	9	21
17 55 38	29	6	16	3♓ 27	11	22
HOUSES	4	5	6	7	8	9

LATITUDE 66° N.

SIDEREAL TIME (H M S)	10 ♏	11 ♏	12 ♐	ASC ♐	2 ♒	3 ♈
14 50 8	15	27	5	9 38	9	20
14 54 8	16	28	5	10 9	11	22
14 58 8	17	29	6	10 39	14	23
15 2 9	18	29	6	11 10	17	25
15 6 10	19	♐	7	11 41	20	26
15 10 13	20	1	8	12 12	22	28
15 14 16	21	2	8	12 43	25	♉
15 18 20	22	2	9	13 15	28	1
15 22 24	23	3	9	13 46	♓	3
15 26 30	24	4	10	14 18	4	4
15 30 36	25	5	11	14 51	7	6
15 34 42	26	5	11	15 23	10	7
15 38 50	27	6	12	15 56	14	9
15 42 58	28	7	12	16 29	17	10
15 47 7	29	8	13	17 2	20	12
15 51 16	♐	8	14	17 36	23	14
15 55 26	1	9	14	18 10	26	15
15 59 37	2	10	15	18 44	♈	17
16 3 49	3	11	16	19 19	3	18
16 8 1	4	11	16	19 54	6	20
16 12 14	5	12	17	20 30	9	21
16 16 27	6	13	18	21 7	13	23
16 20 41	7	14	18	21 44	16	24
16 24 56	8	15	19	22 22	19	26
16 29 11	9	15	20	23 1	22	27
16 33 27	10	16	20	23 40	26	29
16 37 43	11	17	21	24 21	29	♊
16 41 59	12	18	22	25 4	♉	2
16 46 17	13	19	22	25 47	5	3
16 50 34	14	19	23	26 33	8	5
16 54 53	15	20	24	27 21	11	6
16 59 11	16	21	25	28 11	14	7
17 3 30	17	22	26	29 4	17	9
17 7 49	18	23	26	0♑ 2	20	10
17 12 9	19	24	27	1 4	23	12
17 16 29	20	24	28	2 13	26	13
17 20 49	21	25	29	3 30	29	14
17 25 10	22	26	♑	4 59	♊	16
17 29 31	23	27	1	6 44	4	17
17 33 51	24	28	2	8 54	6	18
17 38 13	25	29	3	11 41	9	20
17 42 34	26	♑	5	15 32	11	21
17 46 55	27	1	6	21 21	13	22
17 51 17	28	2	7	1♒ 17	15	23
17 55 38	29	3	9	21 9	17	25
HOUSES	4	5	6	7	8	9

LATITUDE 64° S. LATITUDE 65° S. LATITUDE 66° S.

LATITUDE 64° N. LATITUDE 65° N. LATITUDE 66° N.

SIDEREAL TIME	10 ♑	11 ♑	12 ♑	ASC ♈		2 ♊	3 ♊	10 ♑	11 ♑	12 ♑	ASC ♈		2 ♊	3 ♊	10 ♑	11 ♑	12 ♑	ASC ♈		2 ♊	3 ♊
H M S	°	°	°	°	'	°	°	°	°	°	°	'	°	°	°	°	°	°	'	°	°
18 0 0	0	9	22	0	0	8	21	0	7	17	0	0	13	23	0	4	11	0	0	19	26
18 4 22	1	10	24	10	37	10	22	1	8	19	16	33	14	24	1	5	13	8♉	51	21	27
18 8 43	2	11	25	20	38	11	23	2	9	21	0♉	55	16	25	2	7	15	28	43	23	28
18 13 5	3	12	27	29	39	13	24	3	10	23	12	18	17	26	3	8	17	8♊	39	24	29
18 17 26	4	13	29	7♉	31	15	26	4	12	25	21	0	19	27	4	9	19	14	28	25	♋
18 21 47	5	15	♒	14	14	16	27	5	13	27	27	41	20	28	5	10	21	18	19	27	1
18 26 9	6	16	3	19	57	17	28	6	14	29	2♊	55	22	29	6	12	24	21	6	28	2
18 30 29	7	17	6	24	48	19	29	7	15	♒	7	5	23	♋	7	13	26	23	16	29	3
18 34 50	8	18	8	28	58	20	♋	8	17	4	10	30	24	1	8	14	29	25	1	♋	4
18 39 11	9	20	10	2♊	34	21	1	9	18	6	13	22	25	2	9	16	♒	26	30	1	5
18 43 31	10	21	12	5	43	23	2	10	19	9	15	49	27	3	10	17	4	27	47	2	6
18 47 51	11	22	15	8	29	24	3	11	20	11	17	57	28	4	11	18	7	28	56	3	6
18 52 11	12	23	17	10	56	25	4	12	22	14	19	50	29	5	12	20	10	29	58	4	7
18 56 30	13	25	20	13	9	26	5	13	23	17	21	30	♋	6	13	21	13	0♋	56	4	8
19 0 49	14	26	22	15	9	27	5	14	24	19	23	2	1	7	14	23	16	1	49	5	9
19 5 7	15	27	25	16	58	28	6	15	26	22	24	25	2	8	15	24	19	2	39	6	10
19 9 26	16	29	27	18	39	29	7	16	27	25	25	42	3	9	16	25	22	3	27	7	11
19 13 43	17	♒	♓	20	12	♋	8	17	29	28	26	54	4	10	17	27	25	4	13	8	11
19 18 0	18	1	3	21	39	1	9	18	♒	♓	28	1	4	10	18	28	28	4	56	8	12
19 22 17	19	3	5	23	0	2	10	19	1	3	29	4	5	11	19	♒	♓	5	39	9	13
19 26 33	20	4	8	24	16	3	11	20	3	6	0♋	4	6	12	20	1	4	6	20	10	14
19 30 49	21	5	11	25	28	4	12	21	4	9	1	2	7	13	21	3	8	6	59	10	15
19 35 4	22	7	13	26	37	5	13	22	6	12	1	56	8	14	22	4	11	7	38	11	15
19 39 19	23	8	16	27	42	6	13	23	7	15	2	49	8	15	23	6	14	8	16	12	16
19 43 33	24	10	19	28	44	7	14	24	9	18	3	39	9	16	24	7	17	8	53	12	17
19 47 46	25	11	22	29	44	7	15	25	10	21	4	28	10	16	25	9	21	9	30	13	18
19 51 59	26	13	25	0♋	42	8	16	26	12	24	5	15	11	17	26	10	24	10	6	14	19
19 56 11	27	14	27	1	37	9	17	27	13	27	6	1	12	18	27	12	27	10	41	14	19
20 0 23	28	15	♈	2	31	10	18	28	14	♈	6	46	12	19	28	13	♈	11	16	15	20
20 4 34	29	17	3	3	23	11	18	29	16	3	7	30	13	20	29	15	4	11	50	16	21
20 8 44	♒	18	6	4	13	11	19	♒	17	6	8	12	14	20	♒	16	7	12	24	16	22
20 12 53	1	20	9	5	2	12	20	1	19	9	8	54	14	21	1	18	10	12	58	17	22
20 17 2	2	21	11	5	50	13	21	2	20	12	9	35	15	22	2	20	13	13	31	18	23
20 21 10	3	23	14	6	37	14	22	3	22	15	10	15	16	23	3	21	16	14	4	18	24
20 25 18	4	24	17	7	22	14	23	4	23	18	10	54	16	24	4	23	20	14	37	19	25
20 29 24	5	26	19	8	7	15	23	5	25	21	11	33	17	24	5	24	23	15	9	19	25
20 33 30	6	27	22	8	50	16	24	6	27	24	12	11	18	25	6	26	26	15	42	20	26
20 37 36	7	29	25	9	33	17	25	7	28	26	12	49	18	26	7	27	29	16	14	21	27
20 41 40	8	♓	27	10	15	17	26	8	♓	29	13	26	19	27	8	29	♉	16	45	21	28
20 45 44	9	2	♉	10	57	18	27	9	1	♉	14	2	20	27	9	♓	5	17	17	22	28
20 49 47	10	3	2	11	37	19	27	10	3	5	14	38	20	28	10	2	8	17	48	22	29
20 53 50	11	5	5	12	17	19	28	11	4	7	15	14	21	29	11	4	10	18	19	23	♌
20 57 51	12	6	7	12	57	20	29	12	6	10	15	49	22	♌	12	5	13	18	50	24	1
21 1 52	13	8	9	13	36	21	♌	13	7	12	16	24	22	0	13	7	16	19	21	24	1
21 5 52	14	9	12	14	14	21	0	14	9	15	16	59	23	1	14	8	19	19	51	25	2
HOUSES	4	5	6	7		8	9	4	5	6	7		8	9	4	5	6	7		8	9

LATITUDE 64° S. LATITUDE 65° S. LATITUDE 66° S.

LATITUDE 64° N.

SIDEREAL TIME (H M S)	10 ≈	11 ✕	12 ♉	ASC ♋	2 ♋	3 ♌
21 9 52	15	11	14	14 52	22	1
21 13 50	16	12	16	15 29	23	2
21 17 49	17	14	18	16 6	23	3
21 21 46	18	15	20	16 43	24	4
21 25 42	19	17	23	17 19	25	4
21 29 38	20	18	24	17 55	25	5
21 33 34	21	20	26	18 30	26	6
21 37 28	22	21	28	19 5	27	7
21 41 22	23	23	II	19 40	27	7
21 45 15	24	24	2	20 15	28	8
21 49 8	25	26	4	20 49	28	9
21 53 0	26	27	5	21 23	29	10
21 56 51	27	29	7	21 57	Ω	10
22 0 42	28	♈	8	22 30	0	11
22 4 32	29	2	10	23 4	1	12
22 8 22	✕	3	11	23 37	2	13
22 12 11	1	5	13	24 10	2	13
22 15 59	2	6	14	24 43	3	14
22 19 47	3	8	15	25 15	3	15
22 23 34	4	9	17	25 47	4	16
22 27 21	5	11	18	26 20	5	16
22 31 8	6	12	19	26 52	5	17
22 34 53	7	13	20	27 24	6	18
22 38 39	8	15	21	27 55	6	19
22 42 24	9	16	22	28 27	7	19
22 46 8	10	18	23	28 58	8	20
22 49 52	11	19	24	29 30	8	21
22 53 36	12	21	25	0Ω 1	9	22
22 57 20	13	22	26	0 32	9	22
23 1 3	14	23	27	1 3	10	23
23 4 45	15	25	28	1 34	11	24
23 8 28	16	26	29	2 5	11	25
23 12 10	17	28	S	2 36	12	25
23 15 52	18	29	1	3 7	12	26
23 19 33	19	♉	2	3 38	13	27
23 23 15	20	2	2	4 8	14	28
23 26 56	21	3	3	4 39	14	28
23 30 37	22	4	4	5 9	15	29
23 34 17	23	6	5	5 40	15	♍
23 37 58	24	7	5	6 10	16	0
23 41 39	25	8	6	6 41	17	1
23 45 19	26	10	7	7 11	17	2
23 48 59	27	11	8	7 41	18	3
23 52 40	28	12	8	8 12	18	3
23 56 20	29	13	9	8 42	19	4
HOUSES	4	5	6	7	8	9

LATITUDE 65° N.

SIDEREAL TIME (H M S)	10 ≈	11 ✕	12 ♉	ASC ♋	2 ♋	3 ♌
21 9 52	15	10	17	17 33	24	2
21 13 50	16	12	20	18 7	24	3
21 17 49	17	13	22	18 41	25	3
21 21 46	18	15	24	19 14	26	4
21 25 42	19	17	26	19 47	26	5
21 29 38	20	18	28	20 20	27	6
21 33 34	21	20	II	20 53	27	6
21 37 28	22	21	2	21 25	28	7
21 41 22	23	23	4	21 57	29	8
21 45 15	24	24	6	22 29	29	9
21 49 8	25	26	8	23 1	Ω	9
21 53 0	26	27	10	23 33	0	10
21 56 51	27	29	11	24 4	1	11
22 0 42	28	♈	13	24 35	2	12
22 4 32	29	2	14	25 6	2	12
22 8 22	✕	3	16	25 37	3	13
22 12 11	1	5	17	26 8	3	14
22 15 59	2	6	18	26 39	4	15
22 19 47	3	8	20	27 10	5	15
22 23 34	4	9	21	27 40	5	16
22 27 21	5	11	22	28 10	6	17
22 31 8	6	12	23	28 41	6	18
22 34 53	7	14	24	29 11	7	18
22 38 39	8	15	25	29 41	8	19
22 42 24	9	17	26	0Ω 11	8	20
22 46 8	10	18	27	0 41	9	21
22 49 52	11	20	28	1 10	9	21
22 53 36	12	21	29	1 40	10	22
22 57 20	13	22	S	2 10	10	23
23 1 3	14	24	1	2 39	11	23
23 4 45	15	25	2	3 9	12	24
23 8 28	16	27	2	3 38	12	25
23 12 10	17	28	3	4 8	13	26
23 15 52	18	29	4	4 37	13	26
23 19 33	19	♉	5	5 7	14	27
23 23 15	20	2	5	5 36	15	28
23 26 56	21	4	6	6 5	15	29
23 30 37	22	5	7	6 35	16	29
23 34 17	23	6	8	7 4	16	♍
23 37 58	24	8	8	7 33	17	1
23 41 39	25	9	9	8 2	17	2
23 45 19	26	10	10	8 32	18	2
23 48 59	27	12	10	9 1	19	3
23 52 40	28	13	11	9 30	19	4
23 56 20	29	14	12	9 59	20	5
HOUSES	4	5	6	7	8	9

LATITUDE 66° N.

SIDEREAL TIME (H M S)	10 ≈	11 ✕	12 ♉	ASC ♋	2 ♋	3 ♌
21 9 52	15	10	21	20 22	25	3
21 13 50	16	11	24	20 52	26	4
21 17 49	17	13	27	21 22	27	4
21 21 46	18	15	29	21 52	27	5
21 25 42	19	16	II	22 22	28	6
21 29 38	20	18	4	22 51	28	6
21 33 34	21	19	6	23 21	29	7
21 37 28	22	21	8	23 50	Ω	8
21 41 22	23	22	11	24 20	0	9
21 45 15	24	24	13	24 49	1	9
21 49 8	25	26	14	25 18	1	10
21 53 0	26	27	16	25 47	2	11
21 56 51	27	29	18	26 16	2	12
22 0 42	28	♈	20	26 45	3	12
22 4 32	29	2	21	27 14	4	13
22 8 22	✕	3	23	27 43	4	14
22 12 11	1	5	24	28 12	5	14
22 15 59	2	6	25	28 40	5	15
22 19 47	3	8	26	29 9	6	16
22 23 34	4	9	27	29 37	6	17
22 27 21	5	11	28	0Ω 6	7	17
22 31 8	6	13	29	0 34	8	18
22 34 53	7	14	S	1 2	8	19
22 38 39	8	16	1	1 31	9	20
22 42 24	9	17	2	1 59	9	20
22 46 8	10	19	2	2 27	10	21
22 49 52	11	20	3	2 55	10	22
22 53 36	12	21	4	3 23	11	22
22 57 20	13	23	5	3 51	12	23
23 1 3	14	24	5	4 19	12	24
23 4 45	15	26	6	4 47	13	25
23 8 28	16	27	7	5 15	13	25
23 12 10	17	29	7	5 43	14	26
23 15 52	18	♉	8	6 11	14	27
23 19 33	19	2	8	6 39	15	28
23 23 15	20	3	9	7 7	15	28
23 26 56	21	4	10	7 35	16	29
23 30 37	22	6	10	8 3	17	♍
23 34 17	23	7	11	8 31	17	0
23 37 58	24	9	11	8 59	18	1
23 41 39	25	10	12	9 27	18	2
23 45 19	26	11	13	9 55	19	3
23 48 59	27	13	13	10 23	19	3
23 52 40	28	14	14	10 51	20	4
23 56 20	29	15	14	11 19	21	5
HOUSES	4	5	6	7	8	9

LATITUDE 64° S. LATITUDE 65° S. LATITUDE 66° S.

100 YEAR ROSICRUCIAN EPHEMERIDES

1900 - 2000 at Midnight (0 hour TDT)

- One page per month
- Daily declinations
- Complete aspectarian
- Eclipses and lunar phases
- Daily lunar true node
- Sewn binding
- Latest space date

- Calculated by computer

INTERNATIONAL EDITION - 1250 PAGES
ENGLISH - DEUTSCH - ESPAÑOL - FRANÇAIS

The most accurate 100 Year ephemeris available ! It has been calculated and typeset entirely by computer, utilizing the new 1984 standards of the International Astronomical Union and the latest results of space research conducted by NASA and the Jet Propulsion Laboratory. All the information required by beginners and advanced students alike is clearly presented on one page per month.

For astrological use, the extreme accuracy of the astronomical data has been rounded to the nearest second of arc for the luminaries and to the nearest minute of arc for the other planets. The times of aspects were rounded to the nearest minute after being computed to the nearest second. Includes complete aspectarian, daily declinations, eclipses, lunar phases, ingresses, and void-of-course. Easy to read printing, sewn binding, and durable cover. International Edition with introduction in four languages.

THE ROSICRUCIAN FELLOWSHIP, P.O. Box 713 Oceanside, CA 92054, USA

ÉPHÉMÉRIDES ROSICRUCIENNES POUR 100 ANS

1900 - 2000 à Minuit (0 heure TDT)

- Une page par mois
- Déclinaisons données chaque jour
- Tableau complet des aspects planétaires
- Eclipses et phases lunaires
- Nœud lunaire vrai donné chaque jour
- Les plus récentes données spaciales

- Calculées par ordinateur

EDITION INTERNATIONALE - 1250 PAGES
ANGLAIS - FRANÇAIS - ALLEMAND - ESPAGNOL

Ce sont les éphémérides pour 100 ans les plus précises sur le marché ! Elles ont été calculées et mises en page entièrement par ordinateur, basées sur les plus récentes références (1984) de l'Union Astronomique Internationale ainsi que sur les résultats des recherches spatiales conduites par la NASA et le « Jet Propulsion Laboratory ». Toutes les informations nécessaires aux débutants ainsi qu'aux étudiants les plus avancés sont présentées de manière claire en une page par mois.

A des fins astrologiques, l'extrême précision astronomique des données de base a été arrondie à la seconde près pour les luminaires, et à la minute près pour les autres planètes. Le moment exact des aspects a été arrondi à la minute près après avoir été calculé à la seconde près. Vous trouverez, en plus, un tableau complet des aspects, les déclinaisons journalières, les éclipses, les phases lunaires, l'heure d'entrée dans les signes, les périodes lunaires dites « vides d'aspects ». L'impression est facile à lire, la reliure est cousue, et la couverture spéciale très solide. L'introduction à cette Edition Internationale est présentée en quatre langues.

THE ROSICRUCIAN FELLOWSHIP, P.O. Box 713 Oceanside, CA 92054, USA

100 JAHRE ROSICRUCIAN EPHEMERIDEN

1900 - 2000 Mitternacht (0 Uhr)

- Eine Seite pro Monat
- Tägliche Deklinationen
- Komplettes Aspektarium
- Ekliptik und Mond Phasen
- Wahre tägliche Mondknoten
- Neueste Weltraum Daten

- Errechnet durch Computer

INTERNATIONALE AUSGABE - 1250 SEITEN
ENGLISCH - DEUTSCH - SPANISCH - FRANZÖSISCH

Die genaueste 100 Jahr Ephemeride ist erhältlich. Sie wurde errechnet und gedruckt durch Computer, bei Benutzung des neuen Standarts der Internationalen Astronomischen Union von 1984 und den letzten Ergebnisse der Raumfahrt, erarbeitet von der NASA und der Luftfahrt. Alle Informationen, die Anfänger und Fortgeschrittene benötigen sind deutlich auf einer Seite per Monat gegeben.

Zum astrologischen Gebrauch werden die äusserst genauen astronomischen Werte abgerundet zur nächsten Bogen-Sekunde für die Sonne und den Mond und zur nächsten Bogen-Minute für die Planeten. Die aspekte sind abgerundet zur nächsten Minute, nachdem die nächste Sekunde errechnet wurde. Enthält das komplette Aspektarium, tägliche Deklinationen, Eklipsen Mond-Phasen (Eintritt und leere Plätze).

Leicht lesbarer Druck, Faden-gebunden, fester Einband.
Internationale Ausgabe mit Einführung in vier Sprachen.

THE ROSICRUCIAN FELLOWSHIP, P.O. Box 713, Oceanside CA 92054, USA

EFEMERIDES ROSACRUCES DE 100 AÑOS

1900 - 2000 a la Medianoche (0 horas TDT)

- Una pagina por mes
- Declinaciones diarias
- Aspectación completa
- Eclipses y fases lunares
- Nodo lunar verdadero diario
- Pasta cosida
- Datos especiales más recientes

- Calculados por computador

EDICIÓN INTERNACIONAL - 1250 PAGINAS
INGLES - ALEMAN – ESPAÑOL - FRANCES

¡Las efemérides de 100 años más exactas a su disposición! Se han calculado y tipografiado totalmente por computador, usando las nuevas normas establecidas por la Unión Astronómica Internacional en 1984, y las más recientes conclusiones de las investigaciones espaciales conducidas por la NASA, así como del Jet Propulsion Laboratory. Toda la información necesaria tanto para los estudiantes principiantes como los avanzados es claramente presentada en una página cada mes.

Para uso astrológico, la extrema exactitud de la información astrológica ha sido redondeada al más cercano segundo de arco para las luminarias y al más cercano minuto de arco para los otros planetas. Los tiempos de los aspectos fueron redondeados al más cercano minuto, después de haber sido computados al más cercano segundo. Incluyen aspectación completa, declinaciones diarias, eclipses, fases lunares, ingresos y vacía de curso. Fáciles de leer, pasta cosida y cubierta durable. Edición Internacional con introducción en cuatro idiomas.

THE ROSICRUCIAN FELLOWSHIP, P.O. Box 713 Oceanside, CA 92054, USA

ADDITIONAL ASTROLOGICAL MATERIALS

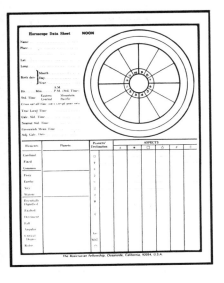

Horoscope Data Sheets
NOON

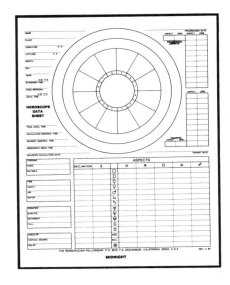

Horoscope Data Sheets
MIDNIGHT

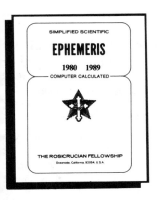

10 Yr NOON

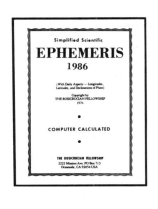

1 Yr NOON

10 YEAR EPHEMERIDES— (NOON) Available for 1880-1999, paperbound. Longitude, declination, and Daily aspectarian.

1 YEAR EPHEMERIDES— (NOON) Available for any year 1857—1999. Same data as 10 year.

The following booklets available in English only

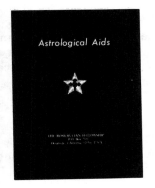

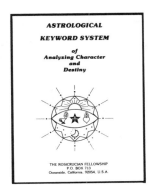

ASTROLOGICAL AIDS—23 page booklet which contains much information on the spiritual aspects of Astrology. Aids to finding rising sign and rectification of birthtime by events.

KEYWORD SYSTEM—16 page booklet giving the keywords of signs/planets.

The Rosicrucian Fellowship, P.O. Box 713, Oceanside, CA 92054

AUTRES FOURNITURES POUR LES CALCULS ASTROLOGIQUES

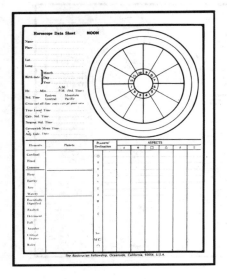

Feuille de calcul du thème astrologique à Midi

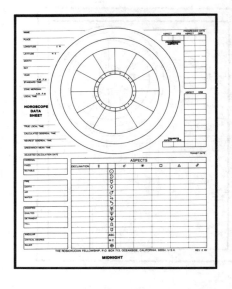

Feuille de calcul du thème astrologique à Minuit

10 ans (midi)   1 an (midi)

. EPHEMERIDES POUR 10 ANS (A MIDI). Disponibles pour les années all de 1880 à 1999, reliées. Longitu déclinaison, et aspects journaliers.

. EPHEMERIDES POUR I AN (A MIDI). Disponibles pour n'importe qu année allant de 1857 à 1999. Même d nées que dans les EPHEMERIDES pour ans.

Les livrets suivants ne sont disponibles qu anglais.

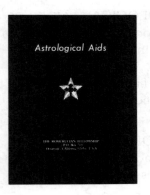

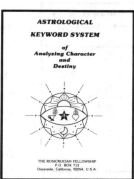

. AIDES ASTROLOGIQUES, livret de pages contenant de nombreuses infor tions sur les aspects spirituels de l'Astrolo Ils permettent de trouver le signe à l'Asc dant et de corriger l'heure de naissance fonction de certains événements de la du sujet.

. SYSTEME DES MOTS-CLES, livret de pages qui donne les mots-clés des signe planètes.

The Rosicrucian Fellowship, P.O. Box 713, Oceanside, CA 92054

ASTROLOGISCHE HILFSMITTEL

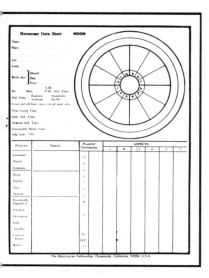

Horoskopwertbogen

12 Uhr

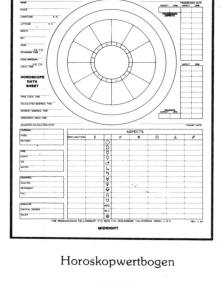

Horoskopwertbogen

24 Uhr

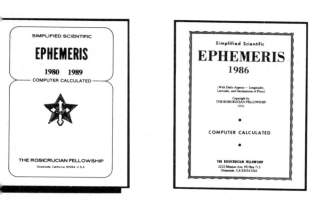

10 Jahr
12 Uhr

1 Jahr
12 Uhr

10-Jahr-Ephemeriden-(mittags). Erhältlich für die Jahre 1880 bis 1999, Taschenbuch. Breite, Abweichung und täglicher Aspeckt.

1-Jahr-Ephemeriden (mittags). Erhältlich für die Jahre 1857 bis 1999. Die gleichen Werte wie bei 10 Jahr.

Die folgenden Hefte sind nur in Englisch erhältlich

ASTROLOGISCHE HILFEN — 23 seitiges Heft, das viel Information über die geistigen Aspekte der Astrologie enthält. Ist behilflich beim Finden von aufsteigenden Zeichen und bei Rektifikation der Geburtszeit nach Ereignissen.

SCHLÜSSELWORTSYSTEM — 16 seitiges Heft, das die Schlüsselworte der Zeichen/Planeten angibt.

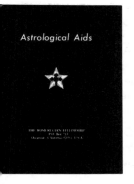

The Rosicrucian Fellowship, P.O. Box 713, Oceanside, CA 92054

MATERIALES
ASTROLOGICOS
ADICIONALES

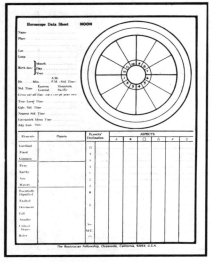

Hojas de horóscopo
MEDIODIA

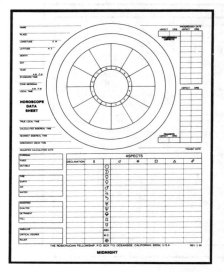

Hojas de horóscopo
MEDIANOCHE

EFEMERIDES DE 10 AÑOS EN INGLES (MEDIODIA). Disponibles desde 1880 hasta 1999, en rústica. Longitud, declinación, y aspectación diaria.

EFEMERIDES DE 1 AÑO EN INGLES (MEDIODIA) Disponibles desde 1857 hasta 1999. Tiene la misma información que las de 10 años.

Los siguientes folletos están disponibles (Inglés)

AYUDAS ASTROLOGICAS—un folleto de 23 páginas que contiene mucha información sobre los aspectos espirituales de la Astrología. Ayudas para encontrar el signo ascendente y rectificación de la hora de nacimiento tomando en cuenta ciertos acontecimientos en la vida de la persona.

SISTEMA DE NOTAS CLAVES—Un folleto de 16 páginas que da las notas claves de los signos y los planetas.

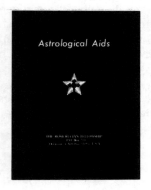

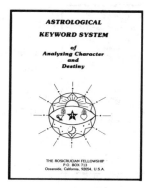

The Rosicrucian Fellowship, P.O. Box 713, Oceanside, CA 92054